MARKETING
REAL PEOPLE, REAL DECISIONS

MyMarketingLab

MyLab and Mastering, Pearson's leading online learning products, deliver customisable content and highly personalised study paths, responsive learning tools, and real-time evaluation and diagnostics. Used by over ten million students and educators across the globe, MyLab and Mastering products give educators the ability to move each student toward the moment that matters most—the moment of true understanding and learning.

FOR STUDENTS

- **Personalised study plan:** MyMarketingLab gives you the opportunity to test yourself on key concepts and skills, and generates a study plan based on topics you have not yet mastered. The study plan links to interactive exercises with guidance, to give you help when you need it most.
- **Pearson eText:** the Pearson eText gives students access to an ebook that can be used on the go, and allows them to highlight, search and take notes as they read online. Access to the ebook depends on the package the student has bought.
- **Mini simulations:** move beyond the basics with interactive simulations that place you in a realistic marketing situation and require you to make decisions based on marketing concepts.
- **Videos:** interviews with top executives and marketing managers from a wide range of companies, including many of the ones you'll read about in this book, provide you with the opportunity to test your knowledge and apply the theory to real-world scenarios.

FOR EDUCATORS

- **Online assignments, tests, quizzes:** you can easily create homework assignments, quizzes or tests and assign these to students.
- **Incentivised reading:** easily assign chapters from the eText and monitor student interaction with resources.
- **Gradebook:** assignments are automatically graded and visible at a glance.
- **Instructor's Manual and PowerPoint slides:** additional instructor material is also available from www.pearsoned.co.uk/solomon

REGISTER NOW TO BENEFIT FROM THESE RESOURCES

A student access code card may have been included with your textbook at a reduced cost. If you do not have an access code, you can you can buy access online.

To buy access or register with your code, visit **www.pe**

For educator access, contact your Pearson account man

Praise for the first European edition of *Marketing: Real People, Real Decisions*

"Seen through the lens of real-life situations and people, it captures the mood, direction and reality of marketing today . . . it is very much a text of the noughties; modern, youthful with a particular emphasis on the technologically-enabled times in which we live. It is a feet-on-the-ground text, which comprehensively covers all the standard marketing theories, updates them to modern living, but, MOST IMPORTANTLY acknowledges that despite all the theory, reality is different and challenging. It reflects the fact that studying marketing is much more than learning theories and rules, that there is a requirement to make decisions, that there are always a number of choices available, and that a key element of implementing marketing is accountability, measurement and learning from the practical outcome, whether or not that was as intended. It is a text which brings marketing to life and brings life to marketing."

Marilyn Hunt, University of Worcester

"A treasure trove of information and insight"

Yvonne McGivern, Market Research Society

"The way the real cases are used in this text is an innovative attempt to engage and inspire students"

Fiona Syson, Edgehill University

"How refreshing to see a text that combines real life views of practitioners with those of academics and students"

Janet Hull, Institute of Practioners of Advertising

"A highly engaging marketing textbook with up-to-date coverage of marketing concepts, a broad range of European marketing applications and lots of opportunities for student discussion and problem-solving."

Sally McKechnie, Nottingham University

"Up-to-date, interesting and relevant cases and scenarios which challenge students to put themselves in the shoes of modern marketing decision makers."

Matthew Wood, University of Brighton

"Engages students with real world business issues and challenges them to come to decisions"

Colin Mason, University of Strathclyde

Second European Edition

Solomon • Marshall • Stuart • Barnes • Mitchell

MARKETING

Real People, Real Decisions

Harlow, England • London • New York • Boston • San Francisco • Toronto • Sydney
Auckland • Singapore • Hong Kong • Tokyo • Seoul • Taipei • New Delhi
Cape Town • São Paulo • Mexico City • Madrid • Amsterdam • Munich • Paris • Milan

Pearson Education Limited

Edinburgh Gate
Harlow
Essex CM20 2JE
England

and Associated Companies throughout the world

Visit us on the World Wide Web at:
www.pearson.com/uk

Authorised adaptation from the United States edition, entitled *Marketing: Real People, Real Choices,* seventh edition, ISBN: 978-0-13-217684-2 by Michael R. Solomon, Greg W. Marshall and Elnora W. Stuart, published by Pearson Education, Inc., publishing as Prentice Hall, copyright © 2012.

First published 2009

Second edition published 2013

© Pearson Education Limited 2013

ISBN 978-0-273-75816-7

British Library Cataloguing-in-Publication Data
A catalogue record for this book is available from the British Library

Library of Congress Cataloging-in-Publication Data
Marketing : real people, real decisions / Solomon . . . [et al.]. — 2nd European ed.
    p. cm.
 ISBN 978-0-273-75816-7
 1. Marketing—Vocational guidance. I. Solomon, Michael R.
 HF5415.35.S65   2013
 658.8—dc23
                                                    2012038513

10 9 8 7 6 5 4 3
17 16

Typeset in 10/12.5 Goudy by 73
Printed and bound by L.E.G.O. S.P.A., Italy

*To Gail, Amanda, Zachary, Alexandra, Orly, Squishy,
and Kelbie Rae – my favourite market segment*

M.S.

To Patti and Justin

G.M.

To Sonny, Patrick, Gabriela, and Marge

E.S.

*This book is dedicated to my mother, Elizabeth Mitchell, who
died 1 July 1988, for her unfailing belief in and support
for me during my academic studies*

V.M.

To my family, friends and colleagues, thanks for the continued support!

B.B.

Brief contents

Contents

1 What is marketing?   2

2 Strategy and environment

48

3 Marketing research

104

4 Consumer behaviour

148

8 Managing the product 298

9 Services marketing 340

10 Pricing the product 374

14 Retail and distribution   524

Preface

Whether you are a student, a managing practitioner or marketing tutor, what is distinctive about this marketing text book is that it presents marketing from the perspective of the people who actually *do* marketing and make real decisions. In the text, you will meet real marketers i.e. those in industry who make marketing decisions every day. We have carefully focused on specific case scenarios to broaden learning and help students consider more real-life situations, in addition to providing the core essentials relating to the themes of each chapter.

This book has been developed for those who aspire to work in marketing roles, as well as those who don't. If you fall into the first category, you'll soon learn the basics, to enable you to understand how marketers contribute to the creation of value. If you fall into the second category, then hopefully by the time you have worked your way through this text, we will have been able to persuade you to move into the first category. Even if you don't the text highlights the ways in which the principles of marketing apply to many fields of business, from sports to accounting. Regardless of your reasons for studying marketing, we have worked hard to develop lively material in an attempt to stimulate your thinking, allow you to consider alternative options and make decisions. You don't just read about it, you are actively involved in decisions.

Meet Real Marketers, Who Make Decisions

The Real People, Real Decisions case scenarios which appear at the beginning of each chapter make this text book unique. Each scenario highlights a marketer from a real company and asks you to consider a dilemma which the marketer had to face, along with three options from which he or she had to choose. You are asked to think about which option you would choose and why. Custom-made films have been produced and are available which include interviews with many of these featured marketers. Each one discusses his or her role at the company and the decision-making process used to solve the dilemma.

In the 'Real People, Other Voices feature' (including 'Across the Hall') students, tutors and industrial practitioners throughout Europe have been consulted and asked to provide commentary, discuss the options and select one to help solve the dilemma.

Finally, at the end of each chapter, you'll discover the marketer's 'real choice' in a 'How it Worked Out' feature. Many of these features include an explanation of how the company uses marketing metrics to measure its success. Essentially, every chapter offers a situation, a variety of options, and then an outcome, along with some explanation of why this course of action was taken. No other marketing text book has this structure or emphasis on real decision-making.

Real Marketing Topics and Events

This European text reflects what's happening right now in the world of marketing. You'll start by learning the most recent definition of just what marketing is. You'll learn that marketing focuses on creating and transferring value from providers to consumers, and ensuring that all parties in any marketing transaction are satisfied (making it more likely they'll continue to do business in the future). These steps include:

*   Making Marketing Value Decisions
*   Understanding Consumers' Value Needs
*   Creating the Value Proposition
*   Communicating the Value Proposition
*   Delivering the Value Proposition

Ethics and Sustainability in Marketing

Because the role of ethics in business and in marketing is so important we focus on ethics not just in a single chapter but throughout the book, providing coverage in two distinct ways:

- We include topical coverage of ethical and sustainability issues in each chapter.
- Students have an opportunity to consider and discuss issues relating to ethical dilemmas and marketing mistakes which have been 'pulled from the headlines', and focus on newsworthy stories about ethical or unethical decisions.

An Easy-to-Follow Marketing Plan Template

Chapter 2 refers to a pullout template of a marketing plan (available as part of the online learning resources) which you may be able to use to complement your course work as you make your way through the book. The template provides a framework which will enable you to organise marketing concepts by chapter and create a solid marketing plan of your own. We encourage you to keep this as a handy reference.

Measuring the Value of Marketing through Marketing Metrics

Just how do marketers add value to a company and can that value be quantified? Increasingly businesses demand accountability, and marketers respond by developing a variety of 'scorecards' which show how specific marketing activities directly affect their company's return on investment (ROI). In real life the decisions that marketers make come increasingly from data and calculations, and less often from instinct. Throughout the book you'll find numerous *Marketing Metrics* boxes which provide real-world examples of the measures marketers use to help them make good decisions.

Marketing in Action: End-of-Chapter Case Investigations

Each chapter concludes with an exciting Marketing in Action mini-case about a real firm, or a real issue facing real marketers. Questions at the end let 'you make the call' to get the company on the right track, or consider the problem in greater depth.

Acknowledgements

We feature many talented marketers and successful companies in this book. In developing it, we also were fortunate to work with a team of exceptionally talented and creative people at Pearson in Harlow. Rachel Gear and Tim Parker were instrumental in helping us stay on track, meet deadlines and provide invaluable support when it was most needed – many thanks as without them this book would not have made it.

A special note of appreciation goes to Sonia Iun and Ting Lu at Sheffield University Management School and Adam Szuts at CASS Business School for their great support in helping assemble chapter material and photographs to ensure this text is as fresh and timely as possible. No book is complete without a solid supplements package. We extend out thanks to our dedicated supplement authors, particularly Professor Bob Shaw for his work on marketing metrics. Finally, our utmost thanks and appreciation go to our friends and families for their continued support and encouragement. Without them this project would not be possible.

Many people have worked to make this text a success. The guidance and recommendations of the following participants have helped us update and improve the chapters and the supplements:

Review Board

These reviewers consistently gave thorough feedback throughout the writing process which proved invaluable in the development of the chapters.

Paul Harbone, City University
Elisabeth Bruggen, Maastricht University, The Netherlands
Anne Sinnott, Dublin City University, Ireland
Mona Moufahim, University of Nottingham

Craig Hirst, Sheffield Hallam University
Ayantunji Gbadamosi, University of East London
Matthew Wood, University of Brighton

Executives Featured in 'Real People, Real Decisions'

Chapter 1: Steve Perry, Commercial Director of Visa Europe.

Chapter 2: Kevin Parkin, A decision Maker at Davy-Markham.

Chapter 3: Ryan Garton, Consumer Insights Director at Discover Financial Services.

Chapter 4: Julia Cordua, Vice President of Marketing at (RED).

Chapter 5: Paul Baxter-Gibson, A Decision Maker at Lucore.

Chapter 6: Jochen Barth, A Decision Maker at &samhoud.

Chapter 7: Fraser Chisholm, Head of Media Propositions and Communications, Royal Mail.

Chapter 8: MadsKjær, CEO and present Chairman of the board of Kjaer Group.

Chapter 9: Karen Wosskow, A Decision Maker at KBW Management.

Chapter 10: Mike Blundell, A Decision Maker and Senior Director at Blundells Estate Agents.

Chapter 11: James Dalton, Managing Director of Fonemedia Ltd.

Chapter 12: Anthony Levy, Chairman of the Fresh Produce Consortium.

Chapter 13: James McCaffrey, A Decision Maker at Towergate.

Chapter 14: Julia Gash, A Decision Maker at Bag It Don't Bin It.

Contributions to the 'Marketing in Action' case studies

Chapter 1: written by Dr Paul Harborne, City University, London.

Chapter 3: written by Leandro Galli, Warwick Business School.

Chapter 4: written by TunjiGbadamosi, University of East London.

Chapter 6: written by Kristy Xu, Madeleine Aaron, NYU and Anastasia Stathopoulou, Cass Business School

Chapter 8: written by Soren Askegaard and Simon Torp, University of Southern Denmark

Chapter 9: written by DrRonikaChakrabarti, Lancaster University Management School and Gustavo Jacomelli

Chapter 10: written by Dr Lien Le Monkhouse, Sheffield University Management School

Chapter 12: written by Adam Szuts, Cass Business School

Chapter 13: written by JayaramManda, Al Torkpour, and Anastasia Stathopoulou, Cass Business School.

Chapter 14: written by Richard Hodgins, University of Sheffield.

Contributions to the 'Across the Hall' boxes

Keith Edelman Olympic Park Legacy Company

Anurag Saxena, Managing Director Linkcoz Ltd.

Professor Cary L. Cooper CBE, Distinguished Professor of Organizational Psychology and Health, Lancaster University Management School.

Shane Redding, Founder of Think Direct Ltd, expert in business-to-business marketing and Chair of the institute of Direct Marketing's B2B Council.

Dr Rob Britton, Principal at AirLearn Inc.

Jim Surguy, Senior Partner, Harvest

Jamie Mitchell, CEO Daylesord Organic Ltd Teaching Fellow, London Business School.

Diane Earles, Chartered Institute of Marketing.

John Flynn, Worshipful Company of Marketors.

Florian Mayer, Senior Brand Manager International Markets Carlsberg Group.

Alan Giles, Chairman of Fat Face.

Nigel Tomlinson

Philippe Gardiner, Vice-President of Hilton Hotels.

Jenny P Cotton, Mortons Marketing

Academics featured in the 'Real People, Other Voices' boxes

David Chalcraft, University of Westminster

Andrew Whalley, School of Management, Royal Holloway, University of London

Katrin Horn, Leeds Metropolitan University

Zubin Sethna, Westminster Business School, University of Westminster

Benny Sweeney, University of West Scotland

Matthew Wood, University of Brighton

Nigel Bradley, Senior Lecturer at the University of Westminster

Peter Ruddock, University of Central Lancashire

Dr Angela Wright, Westminster Business School

Tao Jiang, Senior Teaching Fellow, Leeds University Business School

Marilyn Hunt, University of Worcester

Connie Nolan, Programme Director, MSc Marketing at Canterbury Christ Church University and Chartered Marketer, CiM

Guided tour of the book

Real Voices open each chapter by introducing a real marketer and a genuine dilemma they've faced. In each situation there are three potential options; think about which one you would choose if you were in their shoes.

In **Real People, Other Voices** you'll hear marketing academics and students discuss the options and offer their own advice on which solution to adopt.

In **Across the Hall** practitioners and academics from related disciplines offer a fresh perspective on the dilemma.

At the end of each chapter you'll discover the marketer's **real decision.** They'll reveal why the decision was made, the benefits and problems, and the marketing metrics used to measure the outcome's success.

Marketing Metrics in every chapter provide real-world examples of the calculations marketers use to inform their decisions. As more and more businesses demand accountability, marketers have responded by developing a variety of "scorecards" that show how specific marketing activities directly affect their companies' fortunes.

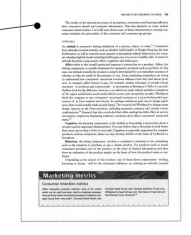

Marketing Ethics and Sustainability boxes explore topical issues from the headlines, encouraging you to debate these complex and increasingly important topics.

Marketers don't always get things right, and **Marketing Misstakes** features give you examples of where companies have made poor decisions or overlooked issues that damaged their business. Think about what you would do differently in their position.

Every chapter ends with a wealth of resources to extend your knowledge. The **Chapter Review**, **Chapter Summary** and list of **Key Terms** will help with revision, while **Real People, Real Surfers** directs you to useful links on the web. The **Marketing Plan** exercise and **Marketing in Action** feature help you put your learning into practice dealing with real marketing problems. Finally, **Delve Deeper** gives more academic grounding in the issues discussed in the chapter, and points you to readings that will further your knowledge of the field.

Guided tour of MyMarketingLab

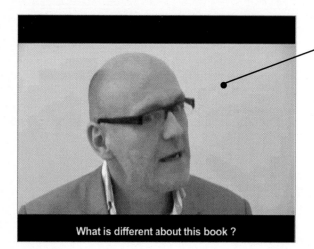

What is different about this book ?

MyMarketingLab offers a wealth of resources that put you in control of your learning by testing your knowledge, identifying the areas you need to study further and creating a personalised Study Plan.

The **interactive marketing plan** breaks down the essential aspects of marketing planning into a series of simple steps. Click on each stage in the marketing plan to see the questions that you should be considering and where in the text you'll find these issues discussed.

Interactive Marketing Plan

This interactive marketing plan breaks down this essential aspect of marketing planning into a series of simple steps and shows you how to use the book to guide you. Click on each step in the marketing plan to see the questions that you should be answering in your plan, and where in the text you'll find these issues discussed. There's also a version of the plan that you can print out and fill in to practice your new skills.

How to use this interactive Marketing Plan template

Here is a useful interactive template which works as a roadmap both for developing a marketing plan and for guiding you through your studies.

There are two sources of advice when filling in your marketing plan. As you move through each step click on "what questions do I need to answer in this part of the plan?" to see what sort of issues you should be considering. Click on "where do I go to find the answer?" to see which chapters in Marketing: Real People, Real Decisions will help you. By the time you've finished, we hope that all these elements will come together and you will be able to understand how real marketers make real decisions.

Click on this link to download a complete word version of this template plan Interactive_Marketing_Plan-dl.doc

Building a Marketing Plan

   I. Situation Analysis

      Where do I go to find the answer?

         Chapter 1: What is marketing?
         Chapter 2: Strategy & Environment
         Chapter 3: Marketing Research
      Answer :

Mini-simulations allow you to apply your knowledge to real-life situations and see the results of making certain decisions.

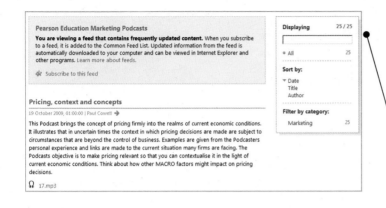

Podcasts present chapter summaries and interviews in an engaging way that's ideal for those who learn by listening or want to revise while working on something else.

Marketing Metrics Interactions help you use calculations to test your skills and make marketing decisions.

Marketing on YouTube

Play the below videos to watch a variety of innovative YouTube videos that explore and exemplify different aspects of marketing. When you need to take a break from studying there are also fun clips available in the section "Take a Break" to help you unwind when deadlines are looming!

What is Viral Marketing? New - September 2010

Mass Effect Viral Marketing explained.

Watch a variety of embedded **YouTube** videos that explore and exemplify different aspects of marketing.

About the Authors

MICHAEL R. SOLOMON

MICHAEL R. SOLOMON, Ph.D., joined the Haub School of Business at Saint Joseph's University in Philadelphia as Professor of Marketing in 2006, where he also serves as Director of the Center for Consumer Research. From 1995 to 2006, he was the Human Sciences Professor of Consumer Behaviour at Auburn University. Prior to joining Auburn in 1995, he was Chairman of the Department of Marketing in School of Business at Rutgers University, New Brunswick, New Jersey. Professor Solomon's primary research interests include consumer behavior and lifestyle issues, branding strategy, the symbolic aspects of products, the psychology of fashion, decoration, and image, services marketing, and the development of visually oriented online research methodologies. He currently sits on the Editorial Boards of the *Journal of Consumer Behaviour*, the *European Business Review*, and the *Journal of Retailing*, and also completed a six-year term on the Board of Governors of the Academy of Marketing Science. In addition to other books, he is also the author of the Pearson text *Consumer Behavior: Buying, Having and Being*, which is widely used in universities throughout the world. Professor Solomon frequently appears on television and radio shows such as *The Today Show*, *Good Morning America*, Channel one, The Wall Street Journal Radio Network, and National Public Radio to comment on consumer behavior and marketing issues.

GREG W. MARSHALL

GREG W. MARSHALL, Ph.D., is the Charles Harwood Professor of Marketing and Strategy in the Crummer Graduate School of Business at Rollins College, Winter Park, Florida. Prior to joining Rollins, he served on the faculties of Oklahoma State University, the University of South Florida and Texas Christian University. He earned a BSBA in Marketing and an MBA from the University of Tulsa, and a Ph.D. in Marketing from Oklahoma State University. Professor Marshall's research interests centre on issues surrounding sales force and sales manager performance, decision-making by marketing managers, and intraorganisational relationships. He currently serves on the Editorial Boards of the *Journal of the Academy of Marketing Science*, *Journal of Business Research*, and *Industrial Marketing Management*, and he is Editor of the *Journal of Marketing Theory and Practice*, and former editor of the *Journal of Personal Selling & Sales Management*. Professor Marshall is President-Elect of the Academy of Marketing Science, Past-President of the American Marketing Association Academic Division, and a Fellow and Past-President of the Society for Marketing Advances. His industry experience prior to entering academe includes product management, field sales management, and retail management positions with firms such as Warner-Lambert, the Mennen Company, and Target Corporation.

ELNORA W. STUART

ELNORA W. STUART, Ph.D., is Professor of Marketing at the University of South Carolina Upstate. Prior to joining USC Upstate in 2008, she was Professor of Marketing and the BP Egypt Oil Professor of Management Studies at The American University in Cairo, Professor of Marketing at Winthrop University in Rock Hill, South Carolina, and on the faculty of the University of South Carolina. She is also a regular visiting professor at Instituto de Empresa in Madrid, Spain. She earned a B.A. degree in Theatre/Speech from the University of North Carolina at Greensboro and both a Master of Arts in Journalism and Mass Communication and Ph.D. in Marketing from the University of South Carolina. Professor Stuart's research has been published in major academic journals including the *Journal of Consumer Research, Journal of Advertising, Journal of Business Research,* and *Journal of Public Policy and Marketing.* For over 25 years she has served as a consultant for numerous business and not-for-profit organizations in the United States and in Egypt.

BRADLEY R. BARNES

BRADLEY R. BARNES, Ph.D., is the Associate Dean for Internationalisation and Professor of International Management & Marketing at Sheffield University Management School. Prior to this appointment he was the Hong Kong Alumni Endowed Chair Professor of International Management at Kent Business School, University of Kent. Before joining academia Professor Barnes worked extensively in export, services and business-to-business marketing. He obtained his BA in Business at Sheffield Business School, his M.Sc. in Marketing from the University of Huddersfield and his Ph.D. from the University of Leeds. Professor Barnes researches in the area of Anglo-Chinese Business, building on much of his practitioner expertise in the area of international marketing in a business-to-business context. He currently serves on the Editorial Boards of *Industrial Marketing Management, International Marketing Review, International Journal of Advertising* and *Journal of Medical Marketing.* His research has appeared in a number of academic as well as practitioner-led journals including *Industrial Marketing Management, Psychology & Marketing, European Journal of Marketing, Journal of Marketing Management, International Journal of Advertising , Journal of Business-to-Business Marketing, International Business Review, Journal of International Marketing* and *Journal of International Business studies* among others.

VINCENT W. MITCHELL

VINCENT-WAYNE MITCHELL is Professor of Marketing Cass Business School, City University London. His Ph.D. is in professional Services Marketing and he has published over 200 academic and practitioner papers in journals such as *Harvard Business Review, Journal of Consumer Psychology, Journal of Economic Psychology, Journal of Business Ethics, British Journal of Management* and has won 8 Best Paper Awards. He sits on the Editorial Boards of six international journals as well as being and Expert Adviser for the Office of Fair Trading, and Head of Marketing at Cass. He has undertaken work for numerous organisations and received research funding and support from the DTI, Cooperative Bank, British Brandowners Group, Coca Cola, Boots, KPMG, Viatel, Hillier Parker May and Rowdon, Tesco, The Solicitor's Journal and Addenbrookes Hospital. His research has been extensively reported in the Financial Times, The Times, The Guardian, The Daily Telegraph, THES, Radios 1 and 4, Granada TV, BBC's Inside Story, Ten O'clock News, Working Lunch, and he has made regular appearances on Watchdog.

Publisher's acknowledgements

We are grateful to the following for permission to reproduce copyright material:

Figures

Figure 8.7 from *Building Customer-Based Brand Equity: A Blueprint for Creating Strong Brands*, Working Paper Series, Report 01–107 (Keller, K. L. 2001) p.7, with permission from Kevin Lane Keller; Figure 9.2 adapted from How to design a service, *European Journal of Marketing*, 16(1), p.52 (Shostack, G. L. 1993). © Emerald Group Publishing Limited all rights reserved; Figure 9.3 from Engineering customer experiences, *Marketing Management*, 8(3), pp.8–19, Exhibit 4 (Carbone, L.P. and Haeckel, S.H. 1994). Use of the image by Pearson Education Ltd. is permitted by Lewis P. Carbone and/or Experience Engineering, Inc; Figure 14.1 reprinted with the permission of Free Press, a Division of Simon & Schuster, Inc., from *Competitive Advantage: Creating and Sustaining Superior Performance* by Michael E. Porter. Copyright © 1985, 1998 by Michael E. Porter. All rights reserved; Figure B.3 from *Marketing Payback*, FT Prentice Hall (Shaw, R. and Merrick, D. 2005). With permission from Pearson Education Ltd; Figure on page 600 from Figure in Case Study written by David Merrick and Bryan Finn, Business Economics Ltd. and Vince Mitchell, reproduced by permission of David Merrick and Bryan Finn, copyright Business Economics Limited.

Tables

Table 2.2 adapted from http://en.wikipedia.org/wiki/European_Community_competition_law, available under Creative Commons Attribution-ShareAlike 3.0 Unported License, to http://creativecommons.org/licenses/by-sa/3.0/ and http://europa.edu/index_en.htm, © European Union, 1995–2012; Table 2.3 adapted from EU Parliament, http://www.europarl.europa.edu/parliament/public/staticdisplay.do?language=ed&id=146, © European Union, 1995–201,Council of the EU, http://www.consillium.europa.eu/showpage.asp?lang=en, © European Union, 1995–2012 and http://europa.eu/abc/panorama/howorganised/index_en.htm#commission, © European Union, 1995–2012; Table 6.1 reprinted by permission of *Harvard Business Review*. From Is your company ready for one-to-one marketing? by Peppers, D., Rogers, M. and Dorf, B., January-February 1999, pp. 151–60. Copyright © 1999 by Harvard Business Publishing; all rights reserved; Table 11.3 from Word of Mouth 101: An Introduction to Word of Mouth Marketing, accessed July 17, 2006, at www.woman.org/wom101.htm, Word of Mouth Marketing Association (WOMMA).

Text

Extracts on pages 9, 165, 317, 474, 477 adapted from Metrics that Matter - to Marketing Managers, *Marketing JRM*, Vol. 1, pp. 18–23 (Farris, P. *et al.* 2010), with permission from the authors; Extract on page 18 adapted from Inside Marketing & PR: Make it green and keep them keen: Consumers are becoming more environmentally aware and demand the same from their brands, which means a new role for marketers, says Caitlin Fitzsimmons, *The Guardian* 21 January 2008 (Fitzsimmons, C.). Copyright Guardian News & Media Ltd.

2008; Extract on page 19 adapted from The ASA sees red about 'green claims in ads', *Marketing Week*, 6 December 2007; Extracts on pages 31, 323 adapted from Farris, Paul W.; Bendle, Neil T.; Pfeifer, Phillip E.; Reibstein, David J., *Marketing Metrics: The Definitive Guide to Measuring Marketing Performance, 2nd*, ©2010. Printed and Electronically reproduced by permission of Pearson Education, Inc., Upper Saddle River, New Jersey; Extracts on pages 38, 112, 483 reprinted with permission from Educator Insights: International Marketing Blunders Revisited, *Journal of International Marketing*, 4(1), published by the American Marketing Association (Dalgic, T., Heijblom, R. 1996), pp.81–91; Extract on page 39 adapted from Vicar's war on 'wicked' Playboy *Daily Mail*, 21/05/2008 (Brooke, C.), *Daily Mail*, reproduced with permission; Extract on page 53 mission statement, http://www.madd.org/about-us/mission/, with permission from Mothers Against Drunk Driving; Extract on page 66 adapted from Seeing the Investor Value in Being Green by Alison Gregor. From The New York Times, 3 March © 2010 The New York Times. All rights reserved. Used by permission and protected by the Copyright Laws in the United States. The printing, copyright, redistribution, or retransmission of this Content without express written permission is prohibited; Extract on page 115 adapted from Loyalty cards used to kill off local stores by Graeme Wilson, *The Telegraph*, 8 June 2007, http://www.telegraph.co.uk/news/uknews/1553956/Loyalty-cards-used-to-kill-off-local-stores.html, copyright © Telegraph Media Group Limited; Extract on page 163 adapted from Cruel consumer cost of the human egg trade by Helena Smith, *The Observer*, 20 April 2006, © Helena Smith; Extract on page 233 from M&S profits soar 13%, *Metro*, 25 May 2011, Metro, reproduced with permission; Extract on page 235 adapted from The onslaught: Half of all children aged four don't know their own name - but two thirds of three-year-olds can recognise the McDonald's golden arches, *The Guardian*, 25 October 2005 (Freedland, J.). Copyright Guardian News & Media Ltd. 2005; Exhibit on page 260 adapted from 10 Product and Campaign Blunders To Learn From by Ritu, http://marketinghackz.com/10-product-and-campaign-blunders-to-learn-from/, with permission from Jason Drohn; Extract on page 286 adapted from *Consumers International - Press Briefing: International Bad Products Awards 2007*, December (Consumers International 2007), Consumers International; Extract on page 322 adapted from Innocent hit by dramatic sales slide by Jemima Bokaie. Reproduced from *Marketing*, 23 September 2008, with permission of the copyright holder Haymarket; Extract on page 356 from Hotels in France embrace the virtue of going green, Agence France-Presse, 6 July 2010; Extract on page 387 adapted from Walker's Crisps go green, http://www.themanufacturer.com/uk/detail.html?contents_id=7024, with permission from SayOne Media; Extract on page 406 from Pricing gas causes sparks, *Utility Week*, 27(16), p.5 reproduced from *Utility Week* 13 July 2007; Extract on page 427 from Word of Mouth 101: An Introduction to Word of Mouth Marketing, accessed July 17, 2006, at www.woman.org/wom101.htm, provided by the Word of Mouth Marketing Association (WOMMA); Extract on page 435 adapted from Resurgent French Connection ditches blunt marketing tools, and thank FCUK, *The Guardian*, 13 March 2011 (Wood, Z.). Copyright Guardian News & Media Ltd. 2011; Extract on page 469 adapted from Secrets and lies of beauty industry laid bare by advertising watchdog by Sam Lister, *The Times*, 11 May 2005. © Sam Lister. News International Trading Ltd. 11 May 2005; Extract on page 505 from Time's up for phone giant's boxes, *Metro*, 15 June 2011, p.55, *Metro*, reproduced with permission; Extract on page 553 from £23m profit birthday gift for Mulberry by Jane Atherton, *Metro*, 17 June 2011, *Metro*, reproduced with permission; Extract on page 554 adapted from Cash-strapped Britons flock to discount stores Aldi and Lidl, *The Guardian*, 1 February 2011 (Wood, Z.). Copyright Guardian News & Media Ltd. 2011; Extract on page 558 adapted from This blockbuster is one you mustn't miss by Mark Ritson, *Marketing Week*, 30 September 2010, http://www.marketingweek.

co.uk/opinion/this-blockbuster-is-one-you-mustnt-miss/3018752.article; Extract on pages 599–600 written by David Merrick and Bryan Finn, Business Ecomonics Ltd. and Vince Mitchell, reproduced by permission of David Merrick and Bryan Finn, copyright Business Economics Limited.

The Financial Times

Extract on page 209 adapted from Many GreenPac products hang on the selves of top retailers by Jonathan Moules, *Financial Times* (London), 12 May 2007, http://www.ft.com/cms/s/0/c728a62e-0026-11dc-8c98-000b5df10621.html#axzz1pIRYaB8E, © The Financial Times Limited 2007. All Rights Reserved.

Photographs

The publisher would like to thank the following for their kind permission to reproduce their photographs:

(Key: b-bottom; c-centre; l-left; r-right; t-top)

3 Visa Europe 2012. 12 Linden Research, Inc.: (t). 18 Reprinted with the permission of The Timberland Company. 29 Getty Images: Apic. 31 Getty Images: EMMANUEL DUNAND / AFP. 34 The Center for Consumer Freedom. 57 Courtesy of Polish National Tourist Office. 59 Corbis: EPA / ANDY RAIN. 66 Getty Images: Bennett Raglin 2011. 77 easyJet. 84 CAP. 109 Getty Images: Lintao Zhang. 122 www.trendwatching.com. 123 Alamy Images: Chris Warham. 129 IPA Touchpoints. 161 The Absolut Company. 166 Alamy Images: Richard Naude. 169 Alamy Images: David TW Gee. 170 IKEA Ltd. 171 Alamy Images: Jeffrey Blackler. 177 Redux: Ruby Washington / The New York Times. 194 DHL. 202 DHL. 208 Courtesy of Volvo Car Corporation. 226 Alamy Images: Sergio Azenha. 227 Honda(UK). 229 Getty Images. 232 Getty Images: Bloomberg. 237 PhotoDisc: Photolink / F. Schussler. 239 Rex Features: Andrew Schofield. 257 Images reproduced with kind permission of Royal Mail Group Ltd. 265 Getty Images. 271 Courtesy of Toyota (GB) Ltd. 284 Getty Images: PETER PARKS / AFP. 287 Alamy Images: P.Cox. 289 Images reproduced with kind permission of Royal Mail Group Ltd. 302 BMW. 303 RKCR/Y&R: Client; Danone / Directors; Mark Denton & Sean De Sparengo @ Coy! Communications. 315 Getty Images: Robert Caplin / Bloomberg. 324 Rex Features: Martin Lee. 327 Alamy Images: Mary Germanou. 341 Alamy Images: Eric Murphy. 343 Greenpeace UK. 346 Getty Images: Mark Thompson. 364 Alamy Images: Jeff Morgan 02 (t), Croatian National Tourist Board (b). 379 Alamy Images: Iain Masterton. 392 Alamy Images: geophoto. 394 Alamy Images: Jeff Morgan 10. 404 Getty Images: George Rose. 419 Alamy Images: doughoughton. 421 Getty Images: Chris Jackson. 425 Alamy Images: Jeff Morgan 05. 426 Alamy Images: Patrick Batchelder. 440 Alamy Images: Jeff Morgan 16. 460 Alamy Images: Christian Ciureanu. 461 Alamy Images: David Gee. 463 Alamy Images: Caro. 467 Getty Images: BuzzFoto / FilmMagic. 472 Getty Images: Matthew Lloyd. 473 Alamy Images: Jinny Goodman. 484 Getty Images: Sports Illustrated / Simon Bruty. 504 DHL. 529 Fotolia.com: iofoto. 535 Alamy Images: Jochen Tack. 541 BMW. 550 Alamy Images: Howard Harrison. 552 Alamy Images: Jochen Tack. 565 Alamy Images: Paris Franz (b). Pearson Education Ltd: (t)

In some instances we have been unable to trace the owners of copyright material, and we would appreciate any information that would enable us to do so.

Chapter 1
What is marketing?

Meet Steve Perry,
Commercial Director of Visa Europe

Q & A with Steve Perry

What I do when I'm not working
Manage a small, organic vineyard in Northern Italy

Career high
Made the world's first euro transaction

Best business book you've read
Funky Business

What drives me:
Personal development

My management style
Direct but inclusive

Don't do this when interviewing with me
Repeat the question

Favourite drink
Dolcetto wine

Best holiday you've ever had
Kayaking in the Swedish Archipelago

r Steve Perry joined Visa in 1990 and is Executive Vice President and Commercial Director for Visa Europe, based in London. He is responsible for delivering Visa's business plans and strategies in 36 markets, with a team present in 20 countries. Prior to joining Visa, Steve was Group Economist for the TSB group. He holds a masters degree in economics from the University of London and a doctorate in the same subject from the University of Keele.

Steve is a Non-Executive Director and Chair of the ARF of E-ACT, a fast-growing foundation established to promote excellence in education and learning in City Academies. He is also a board member of the CBI Financial Services Council, the 2012 Social Legacy Board and TheCityUK. Steve was awarded the title of Cavaliere by the President of Italy in July 2005.

Real people, real decisions
Decision time at Visa Europe

Visa is the world's leading electronic payment system and one of the most trusted global brands since its beginnings in 1958 when the first card was issued in California. Visa Europe is the exclusive licensee of the Visa brand and technology in Europe. It is a membership association which unites some 4000 payment service providers, who issue Visa cards and sign up merchants to accept Visa payments. Its mission is to become 'the world's most trusted currency'. Unusually in today's corporate world, Visa Europe is a not-for-profit organisation and has a somewhat atypical business model, in that it is a consumer brand, but operates entirely on a business-to-business basis. Contrary to many people's preconceptions, its primary business is in debit cards as opposed to credit cards. In fact, around three-quarters of the 500 million Visa cards issued in Europe are now debit cards and across Europe around €1 in every €8 of consumer spending takes place on a Visa card, the most advanced being Iceland, where Visa cards account for around 75 per cent of all consumer spending.

As one of the world's leading consumer brands, it is a long-term partner of the Olympic and Paralympic Games and, more recently, it has also become a sponsor of the FIFA World Cup. For the London 2012 Olympic and Paralympic Games, for example, Visa Europe is supporting all 1400 athletes in the UK's Team 2012 – some of whom are featuring in TV advertising campaigns and making special appearances at Visa-related initiatives.

As the official payments partner of the Olympic and Paralympic Games, Visa is also responsible for managing payments in and around the event and is using London 2012 to accelerate the introduction of 'touch and go' contactless payments by installing them in many of the city's buses and taxis, as well as in all McDonald's restaurants and other stadium outlets. Visa Europe is also leading the way in mobile payments and specially equipped mobile handsets can be used to make payments at the 130,000 locations across Europe that accept Visa payWave.

Visa Europe is playing a leading role in the modernisation of the wider European payments market. In 2004, the European Central Bank outlined its vision for a Single European Payments Area (SEPA), in which it should become

Photo 1.1 Visa, sponsor of the London Olympics 2012
Source: Visa Europe 2012

possible for every European citizen to use the same payment card, in the same way, and under the same conditions wherever they travel in Europe. In response, Visa Europe developed a debit card solution called V PAY, the first truly European payment system designed specifically for SEPA, which is entirely based on chip and PIN technology and can be used in the same secure way everywhere in Europe. Visa Europe therefore offered flexible ways for banks to introduce V PAY as a SEPA-compliant solution, backed up by the lower costs of running a chip and PIN payment card programme, and the scale economies of participating in the Visa Europe system (such as joint marketing initiatives and access to flexible, low-cost transaction processing services). However, for V PAY to become a success, it was not only necessary to create a compelling proposition for consumers and retailers, but also necessary to convince banks that V PAY would bring tangible benefits to their respective businesses. The question facing Dr Steve Perry was, how does Visa Europe try to move European banks over to V PAY as the preferred SEPA-compliant payment card solution?

Steve considers his options . . .

Option 1 Target trans-European banks

This strategy involves trying to convince major banks, which operate across Europe, to adopt V PAY. The advantage of this approach is that such banks tend to be influential market leaders and others will therefore be more willing to follow suit. In addition, it helps Visa Europe to focus its selling efforts. The disadvantage is that there are few obvious candidates. For example, some big banks are present in Italy and Germany, with little visibility elsewhere. Meanwhile, others have their operations focused in countries such as Austria, Hungary and Slovenia. Another disadvantage is that, while the HQs of these banks might be convinced, they do not always have the ability to mandate adoption in each of the national territories in which they operate.

Option 2 Target one country at a time

With this option, Visa Europe would analyse each country separately to see where the conditions for adoption are the most favourable and then, having convinced the majority of the banks to migrate to V PAY, try to build momentum in other countries. The advantage of this approach is that it can be possible to achieve critical mass in a given country very quickly and that there are country-specific issues which need to be taken into account. For example, there may be particular issues with fraud (which V PAY could help to solve) and the banking community may have a traditional allegiance to the Visa Europe system. In other countries, the banking community may have invested considerable resources in its own national debit system, and there may therefore be significant political barriers to the introduction of an entirely new scheme. The disadvantage is that it is an 'all or nothing' strategy and if the country itself is relatively

small, it may not provide enough impetus for banks in other countries to follow suit.

Option 3 Target a combination of country and bank

For this option, Visa Europe would combine some market analysis of where the largest number of cards is located, and where it also has a strong relationship with certain individual banks. This approach is particularly relevant in a country such as Germany, where nearly half of all of Europe's direct debit cards are actually issued, but where the banking community is highly fragmented. The advantage here relates to the sheer size of the potential market, and the opportunity to present a stronger business case to individual banks or banking communities. The disadvantage is the fact that an opportunistic bank-by-bank approach is resource intensive. It takes time to engage with individual banks and, even then, many want to be reassured that other players in their market are also intending to migrate to V PAY (otherwise the network effects which are so necessary in the bank card business will be absent). Conversely, some banks may want to go their own way, introducing something which is different to and differentiating from their competitors. Meanwhile, the level of fragmentation in the German market means that there are few institutions in the country that can wield true market-moving influence.

Objectives

When you finish reading this chapter, you will be able to understand:

1 Who marketers are, where they work, and marketing's role in the firm

2 What marketing is and how it provides value to people involved in the marketing process

3 The evolution of the marketing concept

4 The range of services and goods that are marketed.

5 How value is created from the perspectives of customers, producers and society

6 The basics of marketing planning and the marketing mix tools used in the marketing process

Welcome to a branded world

I'm imagining myself on television, in a commercial for a new product – wine cooler? tanning lotion? sugarless gum? – and I'm moving in jump-cut, walking along a beach, the film is black-and-white, purposefully scratched, eerie vague pop music from the mid-1960s accompanies the footage, it echoes, sounds as if it's coming from a calliope. Now I'm looking into the camera, now I'm holding up the product – a new mousse? tennis shoes? – now my hair is windblown then it's day then night then day again and then it's night.

(from Bret Easton Ellis, *American Psycho* (1991), p. 327)

Alex wakes up with a groan as the latest iTunes blares from the next bedroom. Why does her housemate have to download these loud ringtones onto her mobile and then leave it on so early in the morning? She throws back the IKEA sheets and rolls off her new Sealy mattress. As Alex stumbles across the room in her pyjamas from H&M, her senses are further assaulted as she catches wafts of her housemate's favourite perfume from Gaultier. She pours herself a steaming cup of Illy coffee from the Krups coffeemaker and stirs in a spoonful of Splenda. As she starts to grab a Yoplait from the Electrolux fridge, she checks her Blackberry and suddenly remembers: big job interview with P&G today! Good thing she texted her friends last night to get advice about what to wear so she wouldn't have to think about it this morning. Alex does a quick scan of *The Financial Times* online, checks the forecast on weather.com, and for one last time Googles the executive who will be interviewing her. Hopefully he won't remember to check out her page on Facebook; those photos she posted from her trip to Ibiza don't exactly communicate a professional image! Well, he'll be more impressed by the volunteer work she's doing with Amnesty International to build a buzz about horrific labour conditions in developing countries. Just in case, she glances down at her wrist to be sure she's wearing her turquoise advocacy bracelet (which new cause was that for, anyway?).

Alex slips into her sleek new TM Lewin suit, slides on her Prada shoes, grabs her Louis Vuitton briefcase that was a graduation present from her parents, and climbs into her Peugeot 207. While listening to the Coke ad blaring over her Sony radio, Alex finds herself looking forward to tomorrow. The pressure will be off, and she can put on the new casual outfit she picked up at Zara. Then, it'll be out to that hot new bar to look for Mr Right – or maybe a few Mr Wrongs.

 ## Welcome to Brand You

Marketing is all around us. Indeed, some might say we live in a branded world. Like Alex, you have encounters with many marketers even before you leave for the day. Ads. Products. TV. The web. Charitable causes.

What's more, like Alex: YOU are a **product**. That may sound weird, but companies like P&G couldn't exist if you weren't. After all, you have 'market value' as a person – you have qualities that set you apart from others and abilities other people want and need. After you finish this course, you'll have even more **value** because you'll know about the field of marketing and how this field relates to you both as a future businessperson and as a **consumer**. In addition to learning about how marketing influences each of us, you'll have a better understanding of what it means to be 'Brand You'.

Although it may seem strange to think about the marketing of people, in reality we often talk about ourselves and others in marketing terms. It is common for us to speak of 'positioning' ourselves for job interviews or to tell our friends not to 'sell themselves short'. Some people who are looking to find love even refer to themselves as 'being in the market for love'. In addition, many consumers hire personal image consultants to devise a 'marketing strategy' for them, while others undergo plastic surgery or makeovers to improve their 'product images'. The desire to package and promote ourselves is the reason for personal goods and services markets ranging from cosmetics and exercise equipment to CV specialists and dating agencies.[1] So, the principles of marketing apply to people, just as they apply to coffee, convertibles and computer microprocessors. Of course, there are differences in how we go about marketing each of these, but the general idea remains the same: marketing is a fundamental part of our lives both as consumers and as participants in the business world. We'll tell you why throughout this book. But first, we need to answer the basic questions of marketing: Who? Where? What? When? and Why? Let's start with Who and Where.

Marketing ethics and sustainability

Researching yourself . . .

When is the last time you were on Facebook? In fact so many people check their Facebook profile regularly that by 2012 it was one of the top ten websites in the world according to Alexa.com. Despite Facebook's success in the early stages of its existence, there are still many questions and concerns that could limit its long-term future. Up to 35 per cent of US companies now routinely check out a job applicant's Facebook posting and can reject him or her if they find unacceptable material there: www.msnbc.msn.com/id/20202935.

Debate, discuss, disagree

1 Do you think companies checking up on applicants' personal lives is right?

2 What do you think of the development of websites such as Facebook and Bebo?

  ## The who and where of marketing

www.pearsoned.co.uk/Solomon

Objective

1

Who marketers are, where they work, and marketing's role in the firm

Marketers come from many different backgrounds. Although many have earned marketing degrees, others have backgrounds in areas such as engineering or agriculture. Retailers and fashion marketers may have training in merchandising or design. Advertising copywriters often have degrees in their native language, such as English, French or Spanish. **E-marketers** who do business over the internet might have studied computer science.

Marketers work in a variety of locations. They work in **consumer goods** companies such as Burger King or Black & Decker or at service companies like Universal Studios or British Airways. You'll see them in retail organisations like Zara and at companies that manufacture products for other companies to use like Hewlett-Packard. You'll see them at new media companies like squarefruit.co.uk, mobilemedia.com and at 'buzz-building' public relations organisations like vbma.net.

And, although you may assume that the typical marketing job is in a large, consumer-oriented company such as Gillette or Benetton, marketers work in other types of organisations too, including charities, healthcare, universities and railway companies.

No matter where they work, all marketers are real people who make choices that affect themselves, their companies, and very often thousands or even millions of consumers. That's why at the beginning of each chapter we'll introduce you to marketing professionals like Steve Perry in a feature called 'Real people, real decisions'.

 ## Marketing's role in the firm: working cross-functionally

What role do marketers play in a firm? The importance organisations assign to marketing activities varies a lot. Top management in some firms is very marketing-oriented, like Sir Richard Branson at Virgin or Sir Stelios Haji-Ioannou at easyJet (especially when the chief executive officer comes from the marketing ranks), whereas in other companies marketing is an afterthought. However, analysts estimate that for some countries one-third of chief executives come from marketing backgrounds, so it's worth knowing about marketing.

Sometimes the company uses the term marketing when what it really means is sales or advertising. In some organisations, particularly small not-for-profit ones, there may not be anyone in the company specifically designated as 'the marketing person'. In contrast, some firms such as professional service firms, e.g. legal firms, where people are the product, realise that marketing is a part of virtually everyone's job.

No matter what size the firm, a marketer's decisions affect – and are affected by – the firm's other operations. Marketing managers must work with financial and accounting officers to figure out whether products are profitable, to set marketing budgets, and to determine prices. They must work with people in manufacturing to be sure that products are produced on time and in the right quantities. Marketers also must work with research-and-development specialists to create products that meet consumers' **needs**.

 ## Where do YOU fit in? careers in marketing

Marketing is an incredibly exciting, diverse discipline brimming with opportunities. There are many paths to a marketing career; we've tried to summarise the most typical ones here. Look at Table 1.1 and think about which path might interest you. Now that you've had a glimpse of who marketers are and where they work, it's time to dig into what marketing really is.

Marketing Field	Where Can I Work?	What Entry-Level Position Can I Get?	What Course Work Do I Need?
Advertising	Advertising agency: Media research and creative departments; account work. Large corporation: Advertising department; brand/product management. Media: Magazine, newspaper, radio and television selling; management consulting; marketing research	Account coordinator (traffic department); assistant account executive; assistant media buyer; research assistant; assistant brand manager	Undergraduate business degree
Brand Management	Any size corporation: Coordinate the activities of specialists in production, sales, advertising, promotion, R&D, marketing research, purchasing, distribution, package development and finance	Associate brand manager	MBA preferred but a few companies recruit undergraduates. Expect a sales training programme in the field from one to four months and in-house classes and seminars
Business-to-Business Marketing	Any size corporation: Only a few companies recruit on campus, so be prepared to search out job opportunities on your own, as well as interview on campus	Sales representative; market research administrator; product manager; pricing administrator; product administrator; assistant marketing manager; sales administrator; assistant sales manager; sales service administrator	Undergraduate business degree. A broad background of subjects is generally better than concentrating on just one area. A technical degree may be important or even required in high-technology areas. Courses in industrial marketing and marketing strategy are very helpful
Direct-Response Marketing	Any size corporation: Marketing-oriented firms, including those offering consumer goods, industrial products, financial institutions and other types of service establishments. Entrepreneurs seeking to enter business for themselves	Direct-response marketing is expanding rapidly and includes direct mail, print and broadcast media, telephone marketing, catalogues, in-home presentations, and door-to-door marketing. Seek counsel from officers and directors of the Direct Marketing Association and the Direct Selling Association	Undergraduate business degree. Supplemental work in communications, psychology, and/or computer systems is recommended

Table 1.1 Careers in marketing

Marketing Field	Where Can I Work?	What Entry-Level Position Can I Get?	What Course Work Do I Need?
Distribution Channel Management	Any size corporation, including transportation corporations: The analysis, planning and control of activities concerned with the procurement and distribution of goods. The activities include transportation, warehousing, forecasting, order processing, inventory control, production planning, site selection and customer service	Physical distribution manager; inventory control manager; traffic manager; distribution centre manager; distribution planning analyst; customer service manager; transportation marketing and operations management	Undergraduate business degree and MBA. Broad background in the core functional areas of business, with particular emphasis on distribution-related topics such as logistics, transportation, purchasing and negotiation
International Marketing	Large corporations: Marketing department at corporate headquarters	Domestic sales position with an international firm may be the best first step towards international opportunities	MBA. A broadly based background in marketing is recommended, with some emphasis on sales management and market research
Marketing Models and Systems Analysis	Large corporations: Consult managers who are having difficulty with marketing problems	Undergraduate: few positions available unless you have prior work experience. Graduate: market analyst, market research specialist and management scientist	MBA. Preparation in statistics, mathematics and the behavioural sciences
Marketing Research	Any size corporation: Provide management with information about consumers, the marketing environment and the competition	Assistant market analyst or assistant product analyst level	MBA, although prior experience and training may improve an undergraduate's chances
New Product Planning	Any size corporation: Marketing of consumer products, consumer industries, advertising agencies, consulting firms, public agencies, medical agencies, retailing management	Assistant manager or director of product planning or new product development	MBA
Retail Management	Retail corporations	Assistant buyer positions; department manager positions	Undergraduate business degree
Sales and Sales Management	Profit and non-profit organisations: Financial, insurance, consulting and government	Trade sales representative who sells to a wholesaler or retailer. Missionary sales representative in manufacturing who sells to retailers or decision makers. Pharmaceutical representative is an example. Technical sales representative who sells to specified accounts within a designated geographic area	Undergraduate business degree. MBA. *Helpful courses:* consumer behaviour psychology; sociology; economics; anthropology; cost accounting; computer science; statistical analysis; communications; drama; creative writing. Language courses, if you're interested in international marketing. Engineering or physical science courses if you're interested in technical selling
Services Marketing	Any size corporations: Banking and financial service institutions, healthcare organisations, leisure-oriented businesses, and in various other service settings	Assistant brand manager; assistant sales manager	Undergraduate business degree. MBA. Additional coursework in management policy, research, advertising and promotion, quantitative analysis, consumer behaviour, and the behavioural sciences should prove useful

Table 1.1 Careers in marketing (*continued*)

Source: This information was adapted from an excellent compilation prepared by the Marketing faculty of the Marshall School of Business, University of Southern California: www.marshall.usc.edu/web/marketing.cfm?doc_id=2890. For recent salary figures broken down by job type and region, visit *Marketing Week*/Ball & Hoolahan, Marketing Salary Survey 2008, www.marketingweek.co.uk.

Objective

2

What marketing is and how it provides value to people involved in the marketing process

The value of marketing

Marketing. Lots of people talk about it, but what is it? When you ask people to define marketing, you get many answers. Some people say, 'That's what happens when a pushy salesman tries to sell me something I don't want.' Other people say, 'Oh, that's simple – TV commercials.' Students might answer, 'That's a course I have to take before I can get my business degree.' Each of these responses has a grain of truth in it, but the official definition of marketing, according to the UK's Chartered Institute of Marketing, is 'the management process responsible for identifying, anticipating and satisfying customer requirements profitably'.[2] In September 2007 a new definition of marketing was proposed by the institution to reflect the changes that had occurred during the past 30 years since the old definition was introduced in 1976.

The proposed new definition reads:

> The strategic business function that creates value by stimulating, facilitating and fulfilling customer demand.
> It does this by building brands, nurturing innovation, developing relationships, creating good customer service and communicating benefits.
> By operating customer-centrically, marketing brings positive returns on investment, satisfies shareholders and **stakeholders** from business and the community, and contributes to positive behavioural change and a sustainable business future.[3]

The basic idea of this somewhat complicated definition is that marketing is all about delivering value to everyone who is affected by a transaction. Let's take a closer look at the different parts of this definition.

Marketing is about meeting needs

One aspect is that marketing is about meeting the **needs** of diverse stakeholders including buyers, sellers, investors in a company, community residents, and even citizens of the nations where goods and services are made or sold – in other words, any person or organisation that has a 'stake' in the marketing exchange.

One important stakeholder is the consumer. A consumer is the ultimate user of a good or service. Consumers can be individuals or organisations, whether a company, government, student association or charity. We like to say that the consumer is king (or queen), but it's important not to lose sight of the fact that the seller also has needs – to make a profit, to remain in business, and even to take pride in selling the highest quality products

Marketing metrics

If you can't measure it, you can't manage it

Measurable performance and accountability have become the keys to marketing success. To justify the financial risks and benefits of their decisions, marketers are required to understand their markets quantitatively. For instance, they must be able to quantify the values of products, customers and distribution channels, measure new opportunities and the investments needed to realise them. These tasks necessitate a strong command of measurements and of the systems and formulas that generate them – in short they require metrics. A metric is a measuring system that quantifies a trend, dynamic or characteristic. Metrics are used to explain phenomena, diagnose causes, share findings and project the results of future events. They encourage rigour and objectivity in decision making, while facilitating understanding and collaboration.[4]

possible. This is particularly true for artistic products. Madonna is a good example of someone who constantly tries to create an ever-changing high-quality artistic product.

A need is the difference between a consumer's actual state and some ideal or desired state. When the difference is big enough, the consumer is motivated to take action to satisfy the need. When you're hungry, you buy a snack. If you're not happy with your hair, you get a new hairstyle.

Needs are related to physical functions (such as eating) or to psychological ones (such as wanting to look good). Levi Strauss & Company is one company that tries to meet needs of consumers to look good as well as their basic need to be clothed. The company's research indicates that people wear Levi's jeans to signal things about themselves and their desired image. So much so that sometimes the company even receives a worn-out, handed-down pair in the mail, with a letter from the owner requesting that the jeans be given a proper burial, such was their psychological attachment to their jeans![5]

A **want** is a desire for a particular product to satisfy a need in specific ways that depends on an individual's history, learning experiences and cultural environment. For example, two classmates' stomachs rumble during a lunchtime lecture, and both need food. However, as they are different individuals with different personal histories and experiences, one student may be a health nut who wants a fruit smoothie, while the other wants a greasy cheeseburger and fries.

A product delivers a **benefit** when it satisfies a need or want. For marketers to be successful, they must develop products that provide one or more benefits that are important to consumers while also convincing consumers that their product is better than a competitor's product. As management expert Peter Drucker observed, 'The aim of marketing is to make selling superfluous.'[6]

Everyone can want your product, but that doesn't ensure sales unless they have the means to obtain it. When you couple desire with the buying power or resources to satisfy a want, the result is **demand**. So, the potential customers for a snappy, red BMW convertible are the people who want the car minus those who can't afford to buy or lease one. A **market** consists of all the consumers who share a common need that can be satisfied by a specific product and who have the resources, willingness and authority to make the purchase.

A **marketplace** used to be only a location where buying and selling occurs face to face, such as a street corner or an open-air market where people sell fruits and vegetables much as they have done for thousands of years. However, in today's 'wired' world buyers and sellers might not even see each other. The modern marketplace may take the form of a glitzy shopping centre, a mail-order catalogue, a television shopping network like QVC, an eBay auction, or an **e-commerce** website like Amazon. Indeed, a marketplace may not even exist in the physical world – as players of online games will tell you. Residents of cyberworlds like the Sims, SecondLife.com and Project Entropia buy and sell virtual real estate – with real money. One Project Entropian recently paid over €75,000 (that's in real money) for a space resort he calls Club Neverdie. He plans to develop the station's facilities and sell homes for game dollars, which the project's developer converts into US dollars at a 10:1 exchange rate.[7]

Marketing is about creating utility and value

Marketing activities play a major role in the creation of utility; the term refers to all the benefits we receive from using a product or service. When reading this section, begin to think about how much value might be created for consumers for each of the options

Steve Perry at Visa is considering. By working to ensure that people have the type of product they want, and where and when they want it, marketing develops **utility,** which is what creates value. Value can be seen as the perceived utility minus the perceived sacrifice the consumer has to make in order to obtain the utility the product or service offers. Marketing can provide several different kinds of utility in order to generate value for consumers:

- Form utility is the benefit marketing provides by transforming raw materials into finished products, as when a dress manufacturer combines silk, thread and zips to create a bridesmaid's dress, i.e. doing something you can't or don't want to do for yourself.

- Place utility is the benefit marketing provides by making products available where customers want them. The most sophisticated evening gown sewn in a chic Paris designer's studio is of little use to a bridesmaid in Copenhagen if it isn't shipped to her in time.

- Time utility is the benefit marketing provides by storing products until they are needed. For example, finishing your wedding dress on the day of the wedding is not providing time utility.

- Possession utility is the benefit marketing provides by enabling the consumer to own and use the product or store it for future use. For example, a bride can hire or buy her wedding dress.

Marketers provide utility in many ways; now, let's see how customers 'take delivery' of this added value.

 ## Marketing is about exchange relationships

At the heart of every marketing act – big or small – is something referred to as an 'exchange relationship'. An **exchange** occurs when something is obtained in return for something else. The buyer receives an object, service or idea that satisfies a need and the seller receives something he or she feels is of equivalent value. For example, a politician can agree to work towards certain goals in exchange for your vote, or a minister can offer you salvation in return for your faith. As Christian Gronroos from Sweden puts it: 'Marketing is to establish, maintain and enhance long-term customer relationships at a profit, so that the objectives of the parties involved are met. This is done by mutual exchange and fulfilment of promises.'[8]

For an exchange to occur, at least two people or organisations must be willing to make a trade, and each must have something the other wants. Think about eBay. The two parties must be able to communicate with each other, like on eBay. Both parties must agree on the value of the thing to be exchanged on eBay and how it will be carried out, usually by post. Each party also must be free to accept or reject the other's terms for the exchange. Underlying these conditions are expectations that all aspects of the exchange will be ethical and honest, i.e. the money will arrive and whatever was bought will be sent. In addition, not being able to return faulty goods, for example, does not constitute a valid exchange. Think also about music piracy, where music labels claim they lose millions of euros a year when consumers download songs without paying for them. However, a lot of people who download music don't feel that they are participating in an unfair exchange and say it is the fault of record companies that charge way too much for new songs. What do you think?

The debate over music downloading reminds us that an agreed-on transfer of value must occur for an exchange to take place.

| Photo 1.2 | Some transactions today, like those in the online world of Second Life, are virtual exchanges. *Source:* Linden Research, Inc. |

Real people, other voices

Advice for Steve Perry

David Chalcraft
University of Westminster

I would recommend Option 3. Option 1 offers the benefits of beginning with those clients most likely to willingly work with Visa to adopt this new system but it is a very fragmented approach. This is labour intensive and runs the risk of sparking off rivalries between banks that are considering rival systems. Thus the campaign could fail to reach 'critical mass'.

Option 2 runs the risk of taking a long time to achieve consensus within a single country market. Delay may allow others to enter the European market and become established in other countries, leading to a struggle for market control between several systems. This could be expensive.

Option 3 is likely to be the most complex and, as suggested, will be resource intensive. However, this is a price worth paying to achieve the goal of a transnational introduction and roll-out. Banking is an industry that depends on high levels of trust between different players in the market and also between suppliers such as Visa and their banking clients. In many ways it also is a rather conservative industry and can be slow to adopt new innovations, partly because a great deal is at stake.

Visa starts with some major advantages. Firstly, the European Central Bank has clearly stated that a single European-wide payment system should be introduced. Secondly, Visa is a long-established, major supplier in the market that is trusted by major banking institutions. Thirdly, Visa's clients should be able to see the obvious benefits to their consumers of being able to use such a system. Fourthly, the scale cost benefits to the banks of adopting such a system should be clear. On this basis the argument is not about whether such a system should be introduced, but how and with which supplier.

Visa should leverage its strong relationships and trusted status with leading banks to engage the banking industry as a whole in a given country in a debate about how the ECB's aim can be realised and why the V Pay system is the right solution. In this way the network benefits so valued in the industry should be readily apparent to all involved. This task should be undertaken simultaneously in several of the major European member countries. Winning over a leading economy such as Germany in this manner whilst also having engaged some of the main pan-European banks should give the critical mass needed to progressively roll this out across the European market. Those banks that have agreed to adopt V Pay will have an incentive to help ensure its introduction into other countries and Visa should work with them to market and communicate this development to the banks' many retail consumers.

When did marketing begin?
The evolution of a concept

Objective

3

The evolution of the marketing concept

Although it sounds like good old common sense to us, believe it or not the notion that businesses and other organisations succeed when they satisfy customers' needs actually is a recent idea. Before the 1950s, marketing was basically a means of making production more efficient. Let's take a quick look at how the marketing discipline has developed. Table 1.2 tells us about some of the more recent events in this marketing history.

Table 1.2
Marketing history

Year	Event
1954–55	Three volumes of *The Lord of Rings* is published in Britain
1956	The first self-service Tesco supermarket opens in a converted cinema in Maldon, UK
1958	The British era of Formula 1 begins when Mike Hawthorn becomes a champion in a Ferrari 246
1961	Mattel introduces the Barbie doll in Europe
1962	Ford's first ever rear-wheel-drive car, the Cortina model, goes on sale in Britain. The Beatles record their 'Please Please Me' single which reaches number 2 in the official UK chart
1963	The Pepsi Generation kicks off the cola wars
1965	All TV commercials for cigarettes are banned in the UK
1968	The famous *Hair* musical opens at Shaftesbury Theatre in London, one day after the abolition of theatre censorship
1970	Following the birth of the mass package holiday business, British European Airways (today British Airways) establishes its own charter airline
1971	First European McDonald's outlet opens in Zaandam, Netherlands
1972	The Swedish band ABBA is formed and wins the Eurovision contest two years later with the song 'Waterloo'
1974	DHL opens its first office in London
1978	The band Queen releases the *Jazz* album featuring hit singles such as 'Fat Bottomed Girls' and 'Bicycle Race'
1979	Sony introduces the first Walkman
1980	Ted Turner creates CNN
1983	Microsoft Windows is announced and sells for £100

Table 1.2
Marketing history
(*continued*)

1985	Nike releases the Air Jordan, Michael Jordan's signature shoe. New Coke is launched, Old Coke is brought back 79 days later
1986	Launch of *The Independent* newspaper in Britain
1987	MTV Europe launches First GAP store opens outside the US, in London
1991	Nokia equipment is used to make the world's first GSM call
1992	EuroDisney opens in Paris
1995	eBay is founded by Pierre Omidyar in his California living room
1998	Germany's Daimler-Benz acquires America's Chrysler Corporation for more than $38 billion in stock to create a new global auto-making giant called Daimler-Chrysler
2003	Amazon debuts its 'search Inside the Book' feature that allows users to search the full text of more than 33 million pages from over 120,000 printed books

The production era up until 1930

The classic example of this era is Henry Ford's Model T. Even from the start in 1908, when the 'Tin Lizzie', or 'flivver' as the T was known, sold for $825, Henry Ford continued to make improvements in production. By 1912, Ford got so efficient that the car sold for $575, a price even the Ford employees who made the car could afford.[9] As the price continued to drop, Ford sold even more flivvers. By 1921, the Model T Ford had 60 per cent of the new car market. In 1924, the ten-millionth Model T rolled off the assembly line. This was about getting the price right for customers and the way to achieve that was through streamlining the production process. Henry Ford actually got his production ideas of letting the car move through a factory and each worker doing a selected set of jobs from watching the process in a slaughterhouse!

Ford's focus illustrates a **production orientation**, which works best in a seller's market when demand is greater than supply because it focuses on the most efficient ways to produce products. On top of this, there weren't a lot of other cars competing for drivers in the 1920s so consumers had to take whatever was available. Firms that focus on a production orientation tend to view the market as a homogeneous group that will be satisfied with the basic function of a product. Sometimes this view is too narrow. For example, in a classic article Levitt talks about how Procter & Gamble's Ivory soap had been in decline for some time in the 1960s because the company viewed the brand as plain old soap, not as a cleansing product that could provide other benefits as well. Ivory soap lost business to newer deodorant and 'beauty' soaps containing cold cream that exploited this market.[10]

The selling era, 1920–64

This **selling orientation** is a company-centred, rather than a client-centred approach to conducting business which means that management tends to ignore what customers really want or need; in the case of a goods producer the company tries to move products out of warehouses so that inventories don't pile up. When a product's availability exceeds demand in a buyer's market, businesses may engage in the 'hard sell', where salespeople aggressively push their products. For example, when a salesperson tries to give buyers the impression that the product would be available for only a short period of time, that the deal might be withdrawn at any time and that they would not be offered the opportunity to think the decision over. During the Great Depression in the 1930s, when money was scarce for most people, firms shifted their focus from a product orientation to selling their goods in any way they could.

The selling orientation regained popularity after the Second World War in the UK. This was because the UK had dramatically increased its industrial capacity to manufacture tanks, combat boots, parachutes and countless other wartime goods. After the war, this industrial capacity was converted to producing consumer goods.

However, once consumers had bought all the things they couldn't get during the war years, and their initial needs and wants were satisfied, they became more selective. The race for consumers was on and prevailed well into the 1950s. But consumers as a rule don't like to be forced into buying, and the hard sell gave marketing a bad image. Think about the days of the travelling salesman selling encylopaedia or vacuum cleaners and applying high-pressure doorstep selling techniques. Companies that still follow a selling orientation tend to be more successful at making one-time sales rather than building repeat business. This focus is most likely to be found among companies that sell unsought goods – products that people don't tend to buy without some prodding. For example, most of us aren't keen to shop for life insurance, so some encouragement may be necessary to splurge out on something that will one day pay for your final resting place.

 ## The consumer era, 1957–98

> The marketing world came to terms with the fact that **return on investment** depended upon brand equity, and brand equity depends upon brand loyalty . . . Marketers have come to realise that it is better to first find out what the customer wants and then offer a suitable product rather than make a product first and then try to find a customer. (www.marketingcrossing.com/article/220022/How-the-Customer-Became-king)

As the world's most successful firms began to adopt a **consumer orientation**, marketers had a way to outdo the competition – and marketing's importance was also elevated in the firm. Marketers did research to understand the needs of different consumers, assisted in tailoring products to the needs of these various groups, and did an even better job of designing marketing messages than in the days of the selling orientation. To assist marketing to deliver consistently good quality products to meet consumers' needs and do this repeatedly better than the competition, **Total Quality Management** (TQM) was widely followed in the marketing community, which involves all employees from the assembly line onward in continuous product quality improvement. When Italian fashion giant Diesel opened its new flagship store in Mayfair, London, in spring 2006, the company took an unusual approach to recruiting staff by holding an out-of-the-ordinary themed recruitment day, where applicants were given a welcome pack that included an application form and a questionnaire to test what they would do in certain situations when serving consumers. Diesel head of retail Ruth Dangerfield explains: 'We need social beings who can engage quite comfortably with people. We are also looking for a good cross-section of people to reflect our mix of customers.'[11] Diesel took this approach to recruitment because of the personality of the shop, to express its brand, and because potential staff members were also customers who needed to be treated with respect. Diesel has found that it pays to have a consumer orientation that satisfies customers' needs and wants.

Another example of a company thinking about customers who are also its employees is Google. It offers its engineers a '20 per cent time', which means that they can take a day off each week to work on anything they are passionate about, and it does not have to be related to their daily jobs. Google News, Google Suggest, Orkut and Google Mail are products of the 20 per cent projects, among many other Google services which have been born out of allowing employees to act as customers.[12]

The New Era: make money and act ethically, 1988 to the present

Over time, many forward-thinking organisations began to see their commitment to quality and to 'just' satisfying consumers' needs during a single transaction as being insufficient. Instead, they began to focus on a **New Era orientation** that meant building long-term bonds with customers and acknowledging the role of business within society.

Within this approach, the concept of **customer relationship management** (CRM) was developed which involves systematically tracking consumers' preferences and behaviours over time in order to tailor the **value proposition** as closely as possible to each individual's unique wants and needs. With the advent of the web, a CRM approach became easier to implement as more and more firms started to rely heavily on the web to connect with consumers, using it to personalise its messages and products to better meet the needs of each individual consumer. For example, Marks & Spencer has implemented the CRM approach to make sure the company can respond quickly and effectively to customers. Before an agent answers a call they can check the customer's previous M&S orders in the system.

During the early 2000s, dot-com companies took a beating in the marketplace because of reduced business spending, market correction and outsourcing. Nevertheless many analysts believe that this was just a preliminary shakeout and that the heyday of the internet is yet to come. Indeed, some marketing analysts suggest that the web has created a paradigm shift for business, meaning that companies must adhere to a new model or pattern of how to profit in a wired world. They argue that we are moving towards an

Marketing ethics and sustainability

Eco-friendliness or enlightened self-interest?

Society is becoming more concerned about the impact of consumption on the environment and firms are keen to prove their eco credentials with the big names claiming to have embraced the 'green movement'. BMW, for example, claimed their electric car creates '0% emissions'; however, they failed to mention the environmental impact of the power stations that produce the electricity and the emissions created in the manufacture of the vehicle. One major hotel chain recently asked guests to forgo their daily room clean – and saved themselves £60,000 in the process. Using environmental claims to save money is one thing, but using the environment as an excuse to charge more is another. Kenco's decaffeinated coffee is available in 'eco packs' – lighter, less packaging, so great for the environment. But in ASDA, Tesco, Morrison's and Sainsbury's you'll pay more gram-for-gram for the coffee in the eco packs than for the same product in the standard glass jars.[13]

Debate, discuss, disagree

1   Do you think 'being green' should come with a 'premium'?

attention economy, where a company's success will be measured by its share of mind rather than its share of market. This means that companies must find new and innovative ways to stand out from the crowd and become an integral part of consumers' lives rather than just being a dry distraction from it. For example, in 2007 Apple released the iPhone, which not only can play movies and music but also functions as a mobile phone so that people use it a lot more during their everyday lives than if it could only entertain them. Some of the ways of integrating with consumers' lives are focusing on business ethics, social benefits and accountability.

Focusing on social benefits

Another result of this new way of long-term thinking was the social **marketing concept**, which maintains that marketers must satisfy customers' needs in ways that are not only profitable for the firm but also benefit society.

Many firms practise this philosophy by satisfying society's environmental and social needs for a cleaner, safer environment by developing recyclable packaging, adding extra safety features such as car air bags, voluntarily modifying a manufacturing process to reduce pollution, and sponsoring campaigns to address social problems. By doing these, the company improves its brand image and reputation among customers and potential customers which ultimately results in a larger market share and improved profits for the firm. Today, New Era companies have abandoned this one-shot approach and instead make a long-term commitment to tackle a social problem, such as illiteracy or child abuse. New Era firms believe that cause marketing activities, when done right, yield a double benefit: they address a pressing social need and sales of their products increase as a result. Safeway grocery chain believes customers are more likely to respond to cause marketing activities that help charities in their own backyards. Safeway will donate up to $1 million in its 'Shop and Care' programme that lets US customers designate up to 10 per cent of their purchases to the charity of their choice from a list of local non-profit organisations.

The Avon Breast Cancer Crusade is a well-known example of cause marketing. In 2005, the programme reached $450 million worldwide for access to care and finding a cure. The money has been raised in part by Avon independent sales representatives, who sell a variety of pink-ribbon products, as well as by Avon Foundation events such as the Avon Walk for Breast Cancer series. The Avon Breast Cancer Crusade has supported programmes in 50 countries around the world, each of which undertakes its own fundraising and awareness initiatives.

One of the biggest UK retailing companies, Marks & Spencer, is one of the firms that believes social and cause-related marketing is good for its customers and good for the company, in terms of reputation and profit. In 2006 the company was named for the second time as Company of the Year at Business in the Community's Awards for Excellence. In his laudation, HRH Prince of Wales said: 'M&S had a hugely successful year on the high street and has not only almost reinvented itself but in doing so has never sacrificed its commitment to responsible business practice – indeed it has continued to lead the way.'[14] M&S engages in social issues, such as animal welfare, non-GM foods, improved labour standards, fish sourcing and pesticides.

Within just one year, M&S was the first retailer in the UK to introduce a range of Fairtrade cotton clothing and convert all tea and coffee to Fairtrade; it removed additives and hydrogenated fats from over 700 prepared products; it provided 2500 people – including homeless and disabled – with work experience; it converted sandwich packaging to cardboard sourced from well managed forests; besides its support of Breakthrough Breast Cancer.

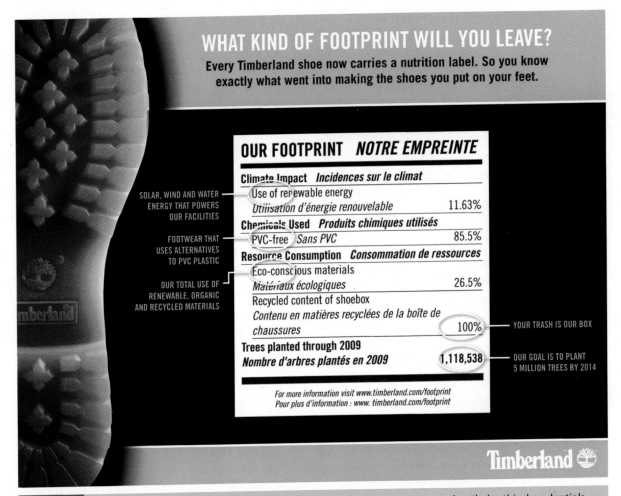

WHAT KIND OF FOOTPRINT WILL YOU LEAVE?

Every Timberland shoe now carries a nutrition label. So you know exactly what went into making the shoes you put on your feet.

SOLAR, WIND AND WATER ENERGY THAT POWERS OUR FACILITIES

FOOTWEAR THAT USES ALTERNATIVES TO PVC PLASTIC

OUR TOTAL USE OF RENEWABLE, ORGANIC AND RECYCLED MATERIALS

OUR FOOTPRINT *NOTRE EMPREINTE*

Climate Impact *Incidences sur le climat*
Use of renewable energy
Utilisation d'énergie renouvelable — 11.63%

Chemicals Used *Produits chimiques utilisés*
PVC-free *Sans PVC* — 85.5%

Resource Consumption *Consommation de ressources*
Eco-conscious materials
Matériaux écologiques — 26.5%
Recycled content of shoebox
Contenu en matières recyclées de la boîte de chaussures — 100% — YOUR TRASH IS OUR BOX

Trees planted through 2009
Nombre d'arbres plantés en 2009 — 1,118,538 — OUR GOAL IS TO PLANT 5 MILLION TREES BY 2014

For more information visit www.timberland.com/footprint
Pour plus d'information : www. timberland.com/footprint

Timberland

| Photo 1.3 | In a new era of making money and acting ethically, companies are promoting their ethical credentials *Source:* Reprinted with the permission of The Timberland Company |

Marketing ethics and sustainability

Make it green and keep them keen . . .

Everyone seems to be embracing the green marketing trend – from fast-moving consumer goods giants such as Procter & Gamble, with a campaign for Ariel detergent encouraging consumers to wash their clothes at 30°C instead of 40°C, to boutique brands such as smoothie maker Innocent Drinks' campaign emphasising the good provenance of its ingredients and the fact that its bottles are now made from 100 per cent recycled plastic. Tesco's Green Clubcard offered users points incentives for buying and using environmentally friendly products. Charlotte Mullen, human resources and marketing director at a recruitment agency, says companies are interested in green marketing not only as a consumer-facing communication, but also as a way of presenting themselves to potential candidates as a desirable place to work.

Source: Adapted from Inside Marketing & PR: Make it green and keep them keen by Caitlin Fitzsimmons, *The Guardian* 21 January 2008. Copyright Guardian News & Media Ltd. 2008

Debate, discuss, disagree

1 How much does a greener product make you keener to buy?

2 How much does a greener company make you keener to work for them?

Marketing ethics and sustainability

The ASA sees red about 'green' claims in ads

However, not everything is as green as it seems. The Advertising Standards Authority (ASA) in the UK has pledged to crack down on the so-called 'greenwash' in advertising in a bid to quell growing public concern. For example, it upheld a complaint concerning Boeing UK after a press ad about the yet-to-launch 746-8 said that it produced 'less than 75 grams of CO_2 per passenger km'. The ad was found to be misleading because Boeing had based its figures on the aircraft being 100 per cent full and not on the UK government standards figure of 79.7 per cent when calculating CO_2 emissions. Joel Makower, co-founder and executive editor of Greener World Media, says that consumers are becoming increasingly wary of so-called greenwash and view it as a sales tactic.

Adapted from *Marketing Week*, 6 December 2007

Debate, discuss, disagree

1 What is your opinion about greenwashing in general?

2 How much do you think consumers are sceptical of companies' green credentials?

Business ethics

A slew of corporate scandals in recent years have rocked the business world. Some of the major ones include:

- In autumn 2001, Enron revealed a massive accounting fraud. The US energy company had hidden hundreds of millions of dollars of debt through unethical and illegal accounting practices with the assistance of the nationally renowned accounting firm Arthur Anderson. Former Enron chief executive Ken Lay was on trial in 2006 for using off-the-books partnerships to manipulate Enron's finances and defraud investors. He maintained his innocence of conspiracy but he was found guilty in June 2006 and sentenced to jail.

- In 2002, when the US telecommunications company WorldCom collapsed into bankruptcy after revealing it had falsified its financial statements by roughly $11 billion, the US General Services Administration banned government contracts with the company, stating that WorldCom 'lacked internal controls and business ethics'. In July 2005, chief executive Bernard Ebbers was sentenced to 25 years in prison.

- In late 2003, Italian dairy-foods giant Parmalat went into bankruptcy and its founder landed in jail when the company failed to account for at least €8 billion.

The fallout from these and other cases raises the issue of how damaging unethical practices can be to society at large. The business press is filled with articles about accountability, corporate accounting practices and government regulation as the public and corporate world reassess what we define as ethical behaviour. When major companies defraud the public, everyone suffers. Thousands of people lose their jobs, and in many cases the pensions they counted on to support them in retirement vanish overnight. Other stakeholders are punished as well, including stockholders who lose their investments and consumers who end up paying for worthless merchandise or services. All taxpayers may wind up paying a penalty as well, if governments decide to 'bail out' an industry or company such as Northern Rock in the UK or the US savings-and-loan industry and Chrysler some years ago.

Marketing ethics and sustainability

Be good, do good and make more money

The practice of corporate social responsibility is not new. In the mid-nineteenth century, English textile manufacturer Sir Titus Salt built a model community for his workers. He had both a selfless and a selfish interest in doing so; he believed that well-housed and cared-for workers would be healthier and more productive. Henry Ford held a similar philosophy; he paid his assembly line workers extremely well to be sure they had enough money to buy his cars! Today, social responsibility activities are likely to go beyond treating one's employees humanely; they are also likely to include promoting environmental stewardship, engaging in cause marketing and promoting cultural diversity.

Firms that believe in social responsibility possess a value system that goes beyond the short-term bottom line. Instead, they consider the short- and long-term effects of decisions on the company, its employees, consumers, the community and the world at large. Which are the current corporate leaders in social responsibility? *Business Ethics* magazine in the US annually rates companies and lists the top 100 corporate citizens. In 2007, the top six companies were Cummins, Green Mountain Coffee Roasters, Advanced Micro Devices, Nike, Motorola and Intel Corporation.

Debate, discuss, disagree

1   Discuss the pros and cons of there being a law on forcing companies to be socially responsible.

We think ethics are so important we've made a feature of them throughout this book in the inserts 'Marketing ethics and sustainability'. Ethics are rules of conduct – how most people in a culture judge what is right and what is wrong. Business ethics are basic values that guide a firm's behaviour. These values govern decisions managers make about what goes into their products, how they are advertised and sold, and how they are disposed of. Developing good business ethics is the first step towards creating social profit, which is the firm's normal profit plus or minus any externalities that occur during the transactions. In other words, when firms want to determine their social profit they have to take into account any benefit or harm they cause to other parties during their business activities. Good business ethics are very important for companies because this ensures that customers will trust them in the short and long term and that they can retain honest staff who won't carry out questionable business practices. The Chartered Institute of Marketing in the UK created its code of ethics (www.cim.co.uk).

Because each culture has its own set of values, beliefs and customs, ethical business behaviour varies in different parts of the world. Take bribery and extortion, for example. Bribery occurs when someone voluntarily offers payment to get an illegal advantage. Extortion occurs when someone in authority extracts payment under duress.[15] Some businesspeople give bribes to speed up required work, secure a contract, or avoid having a contract cancelled. Such payments are a way of life in many countries because many people consider them as natural as giving a waiter a tip for good service. In European countries, however, paying bribes is perceived as both illegal and unethical.

Codes of ethics

With so many rules – written and unwritten – floating around, how do business managers know what upper management and investors expect of them? Many firms develop their own codes of ethics – written standards of behaviour to which everyone in the organisation must subscribe. These documents eliminate confusion about what the firm considers to be ethically acceptable behaviour for employees. For example, the Dow Chemical

Marketing ethics and sustainability

False beauty claims

One place where ethical business practices can be on show is the beauty industry. Only months after a L'Oreal mascara advert was criticised for featuring the actress Penelope Cruz in false eyelashes, Rimmel's promotion starring the Croydon-born model Kate Moss similarly incurred the wrath of the Advertising Standards Authority. The agency behind Rimmel's television and magazine campaigns denied that Moss wore false lashes during the shoot but produced no evidence to prove it, the authority said. Rimmel's 'Magnif eyes mascara' adverts broke the rules by using images that might have exaggerated the product's benefits, it added. The television advert's claim that the mascara gave '70 per cent more lash lift' could have misled viewers because it referred to a change in appearance, not actual lash length.

Debate, discuss, disagree

1   What do you think?

2   Is this reasonable exaggeration which most consumers understand or a misleading way to generate sales?

Company's Code of Business Conduct, available through its website at www.dow.com in 16 languages, is based on Dow's stated corporate values of integrity and respect for people. The code deals with issues of diversity, the environment, financial integrity, accurate company records, conflicts of interest, obligations to customers, competitors and regulators, computer systems and telecommunications security, safeguarding important information, interactions with the public and corporate social responsibility.

 ## People fighting back: consumerism

Organised activities that bring about social and political change are not new to developed nations. Women's right to vote, child labour laws, the minimum wage, equal employment opportunities and the ban on nuclear weapons testing have all resulted from social movements where citizens, public and private organisations, and businesses worked to change society. Consumerism is the social movement directed towards protecting consumers from harmful business practices.

In the US, the modern consumerism movement began in the 1960s, when bestselling books – such as Rachel Carson's *Silent Spring*, which attacked the irresponsible use of pesticides, and Ralph Nader's *Unsafe at any Speed*, which exposed safety defects in General Motors' Corvair cars – put pressure on businesses to mend their ways. Consumers organised to call for safer products and honest information, and they boycotted companies that did not comply with their demands.

In his 1961 inaugural speech, US President John F. Kennedy outlined what became known as the Consumer Bill of Rights, which includes the following:

● The right to be safe: products should not be dangerous when used as intended. Organisations such as the Consumer Products Safety Board and *Consumer Reports* magazine regularly identify products they find to be unsafe.

● The right to be informed: businesses should provide consumers with adequate information to make intelligent product choices. This right means that product information provided by advertising, packaging and salespeople should be honest and complete.

- The right to be heard: consumers should have the means to complain or express their displeasure in order to obtain redress or retribution from companies. Government agencies and industry self-regulatory groups should respond to every customer complaint.

- The right to choose freely: consumers should be able to choose from a variety of products. No one business should be allowed to control the price, quality, or availability of goods and services.

In the EU there are ten principles governing consumer protection (see Table 1.3).

Table 1.3
EU Consumer rights

1. Buy what you want, where you want EU law entitles you to 'shop until you drop' without having to worry about paying customs duty or additional VAT when you return home
2. If it doesn't work, send it back What if you buy a new television set and it immediately breaks down? Under EU law, if a product you buy does not confirm to the agreement you made with the seller at the time of purchase, you can take it back and have it repaired or replaced. Alternatively, you can ask for a price reduction, or a complete refund of your money
3. High safety standards for food and consumer goods Look around your local supermarket – you will see products from across the whole of Europe. Are they all safe? Yes, they have to be. Though no system of regulation can guarantee consumers zero risk, or 100 per cent safety, EU countries have among the highest safety standards in the world
4. Know what you are eating How can you find out what's in your food? EU food labelling enables you to know what you are eating. Full details of the ingredients used to make a food product must be given on the label, along with details of any colouring, preservatives, sweeteners and other chemical additives used
5. Contracts should be fair to customers Have you ever signed a contract without reading all the small print? What if that small print says the deposit you just paid is non-refundable – even if the company fails to deliver its side of the bargain? EU law says these types of unfair contact terms are prohibited
6. Sometimes consumers can change their mind What if a salesman turns up unexpectedly at your home and somehow persuades you to sign a contract to have double glazing installed, or new carpets, costing hundreds of euros? EU law protects you against this sort of doorstep selling. As a general principle, you can cancel such a contract within seven days
7. Making it easier to compare prices How do you compare the price of two different brands of breakfast cereal when one comes in a 375g box and the other in a 500g box? EU law requires supermarkets to give you the 'unit price' of products – for example, how much they cost per kilo or per litre – to help make it easier for you to decide which one is cheaper by weight
8. Consumers should not be misled You receive a letter from a mail order company congratulating you on having won first prize in a lottery they have organised. It turns out, however, to be no more than a scam to get you to contact them so they can try to talk you into placing an order with them. You have not, in fact, won a prize. Is this kind of marketing legal? No. Advertising that misleads or deceives consumers is prohibited under EU law. In addition, when you are dealing with telesales, mail order or online retailers, sellers must be open and honest with you. EU law requires them to give you full details of who they are, what they are selling, how much it costs (including taxes and delivery charges) and how long it will take for them to deliver it
9. Protection while you are on holiday What if you go on a package holiday and the tour operator goes bankrupt? What if the package holiday brochure promised you a luxury hotel and what you get is a building site? In both these cases EU law offers you protection. Package tour operators must have arrangements in place to get you home should they go bankrupt while you are on holiday. They must also offer you compensation if your holiday does not correspond to what they promised in their brochure

Table 1.3
EU Consumer
rights *(continued)*

10. Effective redress for cross-border issues
    The European Consumer Centres Network (EEC-Net) is an EU-wide network to promote consumer confidence by advising citizens on their rights as consumers in the EU and helping them to solve disputes. These centres can advise you about your rights when you shop across borders and help you seek redress if you have a dispute with a trader in another EU country

Focusing on accountability

New Era firms place a much greater emphasis on accountability. This means demonstrating that marketing creates more financial value than it costs, and that marketing resources have been applied with the maximum possible effect. To do this, you must adopt and align three working practices, as illustrated in Figure 1.1, the infinity model (so called because of the figure's resemblance to the symbol for infinity).

How to imagine value   Imagination is fundamental to marketing, creating value by finding better ways of spending marketing money. Old ideas wear out, markets evolve, customers and competitors change, campaigns slow down, so old marketing spending patterns must constantly change to drive value.

Don't misunderstand it. It is not just a matter of artistic sensibility or superior customer empathy, more than anything it's an ability to recognise and respond to failure, particularly rejection of ideas by customers. Every marketer faces this rejection and the good ones respond with ingenuity, with deliberate, even obsessive reflection on customer rejection and a search for new solutions. Prediction holds up a mirror to the marketing imagination, and usually the response is 'try again' because customers don't like the idea.

You need to generate a stream of ideas to create value at three levels:

strategic marketing investment;

value proposition;

marketing mix.

Strategic marketing investment ideas are needed at the top of every organisation. Distribute marketing funding strategically, putting money where it will have the maximum impact and taking it away when its impact is marginal. Don't assume that marketing's

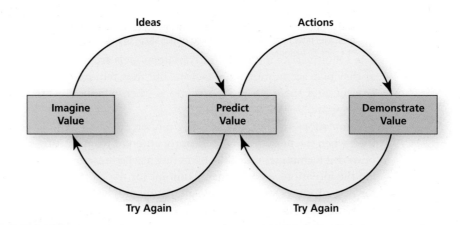

Figure 1.1	The infinity model of accountable marketing
	How to imagine value

funding should necessarily go up or down in proportion to the growth or decline in the sales for the product or market. All strategic marketing investment ideas should be subjected to predictive evaluation and you should manage your marketing resource allocation as a strategic portfolio, with one unifying model guiding the distribution of marketing funds.

Value proposition ideas are at the heart of imaginative marketing spending. The aim here is to deliver value to customers, and to the company, by delivering the right product (or service) at the right price. You do this by inventing a stream of ideas to keep your proposition appealing: re-packaging, re-pricing, new varieties, coordinated price and feature changes, big new product ideas. All value proposition ideas should be subjected to predictive tests, and the totality of ideas should be managed as a balanced portfolio taking into account risks and rewards.

Marketing mix ideas are the most commonplace, and they often dominate marketing spending. The mix is a marketing term for the multitude of activities that encourage customers to buy more products, more often, for more money. The mix includes press advertising, radio, outdoor, TV, direct, database and email marketing, banner advertising, blogs and search engines, new product development, packaging, consumer promotions, trade promotions, sponsorship, public relations, corporate hospitality, gifts, literature and brochures, events, call centres, personal selling and key account management. Every year hundreds, or even thousands, of ideas may be created to make these elementary marketing activities better. You must ensure too many small ideas are not allowed to proliferate without adequate scrutiny, to ensure that they are effectively screened and selected.

How to predict value   You need to predict how marketing ideas will generate value before choosing to implement them. This is different from the forecasts that are done during annual budgeting, as the aim here is to predict the value likely to be contributed by a new marketing idea or campaign (although similar methods may be employed).

You must choose an appropriate method of predictive modelling to suit the idea that is being assessed. Your choice depends on the degree of novelty of the idea, the time horizon and availability and quality of data. There are three main approaches to choose from:

extrapolations from the past;

simulations of the future;

analogies and scenarios.

Extrapolations of the past are a good choice when the new idea is similar to something you have already done and historical data is readily available. There are numerous techniques available for analysing historical data, from simple univariate analysis to sophisticated multivariate models. Multivariate models are more powerful than univariate ones, as they take account of more factors, but they require the employment of a skilled statistician, and there are many situations when simple univariate methods are the most appropriate.

Simulations of the future mostly rely on canvassing the views of customers, and are used when the new idea is significantly different from existing ideas. There are numerous powerful techniques available, from test marketing, simulated test marketing and surveying the intentions of customer. Conjoint (or trade-off) analysis seeks to predict demand for new products or services by simulating purchase intentions in terms of product features, price, level of service, design, etc. When skilfully executed these simulation methods have an excellent potential.

Analogies with existing situations can also provide powerful evidence with which to evaluate a new idea. You need to make a systematic comparison between your new idea and some existing product or campaign. It is sometimes helpful to combine the insights

Marketing metrics

Diageo's activity evaluator

Global drinks company Diageo has introduced a new decision-analysis procedure called the activity evaluator, which is used as a control on all marketing proposals. Managers have to forecast, before they run any new activity, what its effects will be. They must also determine how the effects are to be measured.

Often there is a requirement for research – before/during/after – to measure the incremental effects. Expenditure and resources for the activity evaluator are set aside as a routine component of every marketing activity budget.

from analogies into a range of future scenarios, incorporating a range of forecasting assumptions at the same time: for example, best-case and worst-case scenarios.

Prediction is never perfect, so don't dismiss it for this reason. By using systematic methods to screen and select marketing ideas, you have a level playing field for comparing ideas, you enforce a disciplined selection process, and you provide food for thought when the ideas are getting refined and made workable.

How to demonstrate value   Think of this as detective work, not as accounting; it involves gathering a chain of evidence, as illustrated in Figure 1.2.

First, find out exactly how and why marketing money is being used. Find out how marketing activities are funded, what each one costs, whether it was procured effectively, and what was the thinking process that led to the particular cost deployment. Analyse the patterns of marketing activity too, by region, product or brand. Don't just settle for the total spend figure, dig into the logic behind the numbers.

Second, find out how customers responded to marketing activities. Get into as much detail as possible, compare responses to different marketing activities, compare products, regions, brands, look at customer activity over time and compare it with marketing activity, and discover what causes strong customer responses and what is weak. Don't assume that any old customer data is adequate; insist on getting customer data that can be linked back to marketing activity.

Third, investigate the patterns of revenues and profits. You must look for clues about the factors that shape your revenue and profit patterns. Once again, compare products, regions and brands, look at customer activity and revenue responses, and track them right back to marketing activity. Sometimes evidence is strong, other times you will have to use your judgement, but usually there are enough clues to answer the above questions.

| Figure 1.2 | The marketing value chain |

Marketing metrics

Kraft

Consumer food manufacturer Kraft routinely uses modelling methods to extract insights about the effectiveness of its marketing activities. Tom Lloyd holds the post of Group Market Analytics Manager. His role is to ensure that the response to every element of the marketing mix is understood by decision makers – advertising, consumer promotion, trade promotion, pricing, new product development. He offers the following advice to anyone who is planning to establish their own modelling capabilities:

1 Start with the problem, not the tool (avoid the man with the model, if all you have is a hammer, every problem looks like a nail).

2 Don't get sidetracked by black-box debates (steer clear of anybody who says that you just feed raw data in, press a button and the answers come out).

3 Choose your modeller carefully – buy in the quality of work you need.

4 Model-fits are just the starting point (ask about the forecasting strength of the model).

5 Use your logic and ask stupid questions (if it doesn't feel right, say so).

Finally, gather data from outside your own firm. You are looking for external factors that have influenced your revenue and profit patterns. These will include competitor activity, economic trends and daily and seasonal customer habitual activity patterns.

When you've completed this analysis, don't just look at it as a yes or no answer to the question 'has marketing added value?' Learn from your findings and use them to refine your ideas and calibrate your predictions. Learning to select new ideas more reliably is the biggest benefit of demonstrating marketing's value.

Marketing can drive substantial financial value that far exceeds its costs. The practices that support this are described by the infinity model. These practices can, and should, be adopted by all marketing organisations, whatever their size or sector. There are many

Across the hall

Advice for Steve Pery

Keith Edelman

Olympic Park Legacy Company

In formulating which option to follow one needs to determine the key strategic success factors that will enable Visa meet its objectives. The payments systems will provide the next battlefield for the global financial institutions industry as technology has now opened up a myriad of options for making payments. How many people had ever heard of PayPal a decade ago but now it is a very well known internet payment system. Then there is Visa and MasterCard, well known for both debit and credit cards but not the brand of choice on the internet.

This is therefore a situation where first-mover advantage is imperative and it will need to ensure that penetration is as high as possible and is achieved in the shortest possible time.

With this background let us now consider the options:

Option 1: As indicated there are very few banks that cover all European markets as most European financial institutions are retail based and have strong domestic market shares but have not grown outside these markets. There are a very few examples such as Santander which have exposure to a number of countries but have some significant gaps in Europe. This option alone therefore depends on convincing a small number of entities to join. Failure could therefore yield no results.

Option 2: If one targets individual countries then competitors could just miss out those countries whilst building in a network of other countries. This strategy could lead to isolation and thereby extinction.

Option 3 therefore is the best option. It is clearly the most expansive and costly but the prize for success is also high.

choices of technique to support each practice area, and they can be chosen to suit the needs and resources of each organisation. By adopting these practices, marketing will be more accountable for the value created by the money it spends, and it will have a better reputation and more influence in the boardroom.

Have you ever considered that your employer is your customer and needs to measure return on investment in you and your effectiveness? Employers have needs just like every other consumer.

What can be marketed?

Marketing applies to more than just canned peas or cola drinks. Some of the best marketers come from the ranks of services companies such as Group 4 Securicor (a security firm) or **not-for-profit organisations** such as Greenpeace. In this book, we'll refer to any good, service, idea, place or person that can be marketed as a product, even though what is being sold may not take a physical form. Is there any limit to what marketers can market? The basic answer is no, so long as the rules of exchange apply.

Consumer goods and services

Objective

4

The range of services and goods that are marketed

Consumer goods are the tangible products that individual consumers purchase for personal or family use. **Services** are intangible products that we pay for and use but never own. Service transactions contribute on average more than 70 per cent to the gross national product of the EU and present special challenges to marketers.[16]

In both cases, though, keep in mind that the consumer is looking to obtain some underlying value, such as convenience, security or status, from a marketing exchange which can come from different competing sources. For example, both a new CD and a ticket to a local concert may cost about the same, and each provides the benefit of musical enjoyment, but one is a consumer good and the latter a service.

Business-to-business goods and services

Business-to-business marketing is the marketing of goods and services from one organisation to another for further processing or for use in their business operations. Although we usually relate marketing to consumers, more goods are sold to businesses and other organisations than to consumers. For example, car makers buy tons of steel to use in the manufacturing process, and they buy computer systems to track manufacturing costs and other information essential to operations.

Not-for-profit marketing

As noted earlier, you don't have to be a businessperson to use marketing principles. Many not-for-profit organisations, including museums, zoos, charities and even churches, practise the marketing concept. The WWF has just undergone a major global rebranding with a new strap line 'for a living planet' and Medicins Sans Frontières (Doctors without Borders) has heart-wrenching ads on TV and even sends junior doctors out on the streets to collect donations. Local governments are getting into the act as they adopt marketing techniques to create more effective taxpayer services and to attract new businesses and industries to their counties and cities.

Idea, place and people marketing

Marketing principles also get people to endorse ideas or to improve their behaviour. Many organisations work hard to convince consumers to use seat belts, not to drop litter, to engage in safe sex, or to believe that one political system (democracy, totalitarianism) is preferable to another. Religion (Christianity, Islam) and art (realism, abstract) also compete for acceptance in a 'marketplace'. We are all familiar with tourism marketing that promotes exotic resorts like Monaco or Ibiza. For many developing countries like Thailand, tourism may be the best opportunity available for economic growth. Even cities are getting in on the act: e.g. the UK's capital with the Visit London campaign, using www.londontown.com. Recently, Glasgow has joined the city race and will spend £1.7 million on a new advertising and marketing campaign with the slogan 'Glasgow, Scotland with Style'.[17] Other European cities, such as Amsterdam, Barcelona, Berlin, Copenhagen and Stockholm are following suit. Finally, politicians, athletes, performers use marketing to their advantage (just think about the spin doctors around Gordon Brown or Formula 1 legend Lewis Hamilton as a brand).

You may have heard the expression, 'stars are made, not born'. There's a lot of truth to that. Beyonce Knowles may have a great voice and David Beckham may be a superb shot, but talent alone doesn't make thousands or even millions of people buy CDs or stadium seats. Whether a concert or a football match, they and their managers developed a 'product' that they hoped would appeal to some segment of the population.

Some of the same principles that go into 'creating' a celebrity apply to you. An entertainer – whether a busker or Pavarotti – must 'package' his or her talents, identify a **target market** that is likely to be interested, and work hard to gain exposure to these potential customers by appearing in the right musical venues. In the same way, everyday people like Alex, whom you met at the start of the chapter, 'package' themselves by summing up their accomplishments on a CV and distributing it at venues like Monster.com to attract potential buyers.

Marketing ethics and sustainability

The politics in marketing

'Gordon wants to be like Maggie. But he doesn't want to be like Tony. Tony also wanted to be like Maggie. But Maggie only wanted to be like Ronnie. Now Dave, he wants to be like Tony. But he doesn't want to be like William, or Iain, or Michael. And certainly not like Maggie either.' One thing is clear: most people don't want to be like any of them! Marketing politics, marketing personality, marketing toothpaste, marketing a football club: they're all converging on the same game of market positioning, the trick of finding out where your audience would like you to be, and locating yourself there. The electorate might be unnerved by too much of this. It starts them asking what you're really for, and where the real you is to be found. They do not look to political leadership for a mirror image of themselves alone. So the first dilemma is if politicians just find out what people want and then try and do it, why don't we just have a market research company like MORI-NOP run the country? The second issue is that, as we apply marketing communication techniques to politicians, the party with the biggest budget will have the greatest impact. Think Coca-Cola! Is this right?

Debate, discuss, disagree

1 Should politics be determined by pounds?

2 What do you think of these dilemmas?

'Something of value' to whom?

Objective

5

How value is created from the perspectives of customers, producers and society

So far, we've talked a lot about marketing delivering value to customers and we said that value is the perceived benefits minus the perceived costs in terms of time, money or emotion. But here's the tricky part: value is in the eye of the beholder. Your mother may believe that you are the greatest person on the planet, but a prospective employer may form a different conclusion. A big part of marketing is to communicate these benefits as the value proposition to the customer that fairly and accurately sums up the value that the customer will realise if he or she purchases the product or service. Let's look at value from the different perspectives of the parties that are involved in an exchange: the customers, the sellers and society.

Value from the customer's perspective

Think about buying a new pair of shoes. You have narrowed the choice down to several options. Your purchase decision no doubt will be affected by the ratio of costs versus benefits for each type of shoe. Remember, the value proposition includes the whole bundle of benefits the firm promises to deliver, not just the benefits of the product itself. For example, although most people probably couldn't run faster or jump higher if they were wearing Adidas versus Puma, many die-hard loyalists swear by their favourite brand. These arch-rivals are largely marketed in terms of their images – meanings that have been carefully crafted with the help of legions of athletes, slickly produced commercials and millions of euros. When you buy a pair of Microrides made by Adidas, you may be doing more than choosing shoes to wear – you may also be making a statement about the type of person you are or wish you were. You can probably think of possessions you own with which you've 'bonded' in some way – that is, their value to you goes beyond their function, for example your favourite sweatshirt or piece of jewellery.

evian la pure

Sa pureté,
seule l'eau d'evian va la chercher aussi haut
Sa légèreté,
seul l'immense filtre de la montagne
pouvait la lui donner.

allez vivre à la montagne...   ou buvez beaucoup d'eau d'evian !

Photo 1.4   Evian hopes to build demand for water as an alternative to other stylish beverage options
Source: Getty Images/Apic

Value from the seller's perspective

We've seen that marketing transactions produce value for buyers, but how do sellers experience value, and how do they decide whether a transaction is valuable? One answer is obvious: they determine whether the exchange is profitable to them. Another is prestige among rivals or pride in doing what they do well. Some firms by definition don't even care about making money; non-profit organisations like Greenpeace, or children.org regard value in terms of their ability to motivate and educate the public, or to increase the living standards of impoverished children.

Now more than ever marketers are searching for new and better ways to accurately measure just what kind of value they are delivering, how this stacks up to the competition, and – as we'll see next – in some cases even whether the relationship they have with a customer possesses enough value for them to continue it.

Calculating the value of a customer

Intelligent companies today understand that making money from a single transaction doesn't provide the kind of value they desire. Instead, their goal is to satisfy the customer over and over again so that they can build a long-term relationship rather than just having a 'one-night stand'.

In recent years many firms have transformed the way they do business and have begun to regard consumers as partners in the transaction rather than as passive 'recipients'. That explains why it's becoming more common for companies to develop loyalty schemes such as Tesco's clubcard and Scandinavan Airlines' Eurobonus card which reward customers for using the company.

Tesco's decision to reward its customers means the company has learned an important secret: it often is more expensive to attract new customers than it is to retain current ones. In fact, it doesn't always hold. In recent years, companies have been asking, 'How much is this customer really worth to us?' This way of thinking is similar to how we may decide which friends are 'worth keeping'.

Companies that calculate the **lifetime value of a customer** look at how much profit they expect to make from a particular customer, including each and every purchase he or she will make from them now and in the future.

Providing value to stakeholders by creating a competitive advantage

All things being equal, a firm creates value for stakeholders when it convinces customers that they will acquire greater value by buying its products rather than those of competitors. Companies are able to accomplish this goal because underlying all marketing strategies is the desire to create a **competitive advantage** for the firm. A firm has a competitive advantage when it is able to provide customers with a benefit the competition can't, thus giving consumers a reason to choose one product over another.

How does a firm go about creating a competitive advantage? The first step is to identify what it does really well. A **distinctive competency** is a firm's capability which is superior to that of its competition. For example, Coca-Cola's success in global markets – Coke commands 50 per cent of the world's soft-drink business – is related to its distinctive competencies in distribution and marketing communications.

Coke's distribution system got a jump on the competition during the Second World War. To enable US soldiers fighting overseas to enjoy a five-cent Coke, the US government assisted Coca-Cola in building 64 overseas bottling plants. Coke's skilful marketing communications programme, a second distinctive competency, has contributed to its global success. In addition to its television commercials, Coke has blanketed less developed countries such as Tanzania with its print advertisements so that even people without televisions will think of Coke when they get thirsty.

The second step in developing a competitive advantage is to turn a distinctive competency into a **differential benefit** – one that is important to customers. Differential benefits set products apart from competitors' products by providing either something unique, or more of something that customers want. Unique benefits provide reasons for customers to pay a premium for a firm's products and exhibit a strong brand preference. For many years, loyal Apple computer users benefited from superior graphics compared with their PC-using counterparts. When PC manufacturers caught up with this competitive advantage, Apple relied on its inventive product designers to create another differential benefit – futuristic looking

Photo 1.4	Marketers try to show us how their products will create value *Source:* Getty Images/EMMANUEL DUNAND/AFP

computers in a multitude of colours. This competitive advantage even caused many loyal PC users to take a bite of the Apple.

Note that a differential benefit does not necessarily mean simply offering something different. For example, Apple created a 'Hockey Puck' USB mouse which was differentiated by a revolutionary design, but as far as ergonomics go it was possibly the worst-designed mouse. Many iMac users complained that it was literally painful to use it for extended periods of time. It quickly fell out of favour and generated a market for third-party input devices that functioned with the iMac.[18] The moral: effective product benefits must be both different from the competition and wanted by customers because they have utility.

Adding value through the value chain

One approach to understanding the delivery of value and satisfaction is the **value chain**. This term refers to a series of activities involved in designing, producing, marketing, delivering and supporting any product.[19]

This concept reminds us that every product starts with raw materials that are of relatively limited value to the end customer. Each link in the chain has the potential to either add or remove value from the product the customer eventually buys. The successful firm is the one that can perform one or more of these activities better than other firms – this is its competitive advantage. The main activities of value chain members include the following:

- Bringing in materials to make the product, referred to as inbound logistics.
- Converting the materials into the final product, referred to as operations.
- Shipping out the final product, referred to as outbound logistics.
- Marketing the final product, where marketing and sales come into play.
- Servicing the product/customer, referred to as service.

Marketing metrics

Brand equity

Brand equity is notoriously difficult to measure. It can be thought of as the comparative value of a product with a particular brand name compared with the value of a product without the brand name. If consumers have strong, positive feelings about a brand and are willing to pay extra to choose it over others, you are in marketing heaven. According to David Aaker, there are ten attributes of a brand that can be used to determine its strength which need to be tracked separately; Differentiation, Satisfaction or Loyalty, Perceived Quality, Leadership or Popularity, Perceived Value, Brand Personality, Organisational Associations, Brand Awareness, Market Share, and Market Price and Distribution Coverage. A simple measure that reliably tracks the value of a brand over time is the *revenue premium* metric, which compares the revenue a brand generates with the revenue gener-ated by a similar private-label product (that doesn't have any brand identification). In this case, brand equity is just the difference in revenue (net price times volume) between a branded good and a corresponding private label. Interbrand conducts a study every year to measure the equity of global brands and rank the best 100. In its 2011 rankings the top five brands were: (1) Coca-Cola, (2) IBM, (3) Microsoft, (4) Google and (5) GE. Check out www.interbrand.com for full details.[20]

Source: Farris, Paul W.; Bendle, Neil T.; Pfeifer, Phillip E.; Reibstein, David J., *Marketing Metrics: The Definitive Guide to Measuring Marketing Performance, 2nd*, © 2010. Printed and Electronically reproduced by permission of Pearson Education, Inc., Upper Saddle River, New Jersey

Inbound Logistics	Operations	Outbound Logistics	Marketing and Sales	Service
• Planar lithium battery (Sony) • Hard drive (Toshiba) • MP3 decoder and controller chip (PortalPlayer) • Flash memory chip (Sharp Electronics) • Stereo digital-to-analogue converter (Wolfson Microelectronics) • Firewire interface controller (Texas Instruments)	• Consumer research • New-product-development team • Engineering and production	• Transport companies • Wholesalers • Retailers	• Advertising • Sales force	• Computer technicians

Figure 1.3   A value chain for the Apple iPod

For example, you buy a new Apple iPod at your shop. Have you ever thought about all the people and steps involved in designing, manufacturing and delivering that product to the shop – not to mention other people who create brand advertising, conduct consumer research to figure out what people like or dislike about their mobile music players or even make the box it comes in or those little plastic peanuts that keep the unit from being damaged in shipment?

As Figure 1.3 shows, all these companies (and more) belong to Apple's value chain. This means that Apple must make a lot of decisions. What electronic components will go into its music players? What accessories will be included in the package? What transport companies, wholesalers, and retailers will deliver the iPods to shops? What service will it provide to customers after the sale? And what marketing strategies will it use? In some cases, members of a value chain will work together to coordinate their activities to be more efficient and thus create a competitive advantage.

This book is organised around the sequence of steps necessary to ensure that the appropriate value exchange occurs and that both parties to the transaction are satisfied. Figure 1.4 shows these steps. Basically, this involves learning about what marketers do as a product makes its way through the value chain from manufacturers into your hands. We'll start with a focus on how companies decide what to make, how and where to sell it, and whom to sell it to. Then we'll take a look at how they decide to 'position' the product in the marketplace, including choices about what it should look like, how its value should be communicated to customers, and how much to charge for it. As we reach the end of our marketing journey, we'll talk about how the product actually gets delivered to consumers.

Consumer-generated value: from audience to community

One of the most exciting new developments in the marketing world is the evolution of how consumers interact with marketers. In particular, we're seeing everyday people actually generating value instead of just buying it – consumers are becoming advertising directors, retailers and new product development consultants. They are creating their

| Figure 1.4 | Making and delivering value |

own ads (some flattering, some not) for products and posting them on sites like YouTube.com. They are buying and selling merchandise ranging from Beatles memorabilia to washing machines (to body parts, but that's another story) on eBay. They are sharing ideas for new styles with fashion designers, and customising their own unique versions of products on websites. These changes mean that marketers need to adjust their thinking about customers: they need to stop thinking of buyers as a passive audience and start thinking of them as a brand community that is motivated to participate in both the production and the consumption of what companies sell. In fact we have sampled a few of these videos related to marketing and at the end of each chapter in our 'Real people, real surfers' section will be giving you ones to look at which illustrate various points in the chapter. We'll talk more about this phenomenon later, but for now think about these recent examples of consumer-generated value.

Companies like LEGO and BMW are harnessing the creativity of their consumers, and sometimes they are even encouraging consumers to produce consumer-generated media content (CGM). MasterCard also asked consumers to play a role in their 'Priceless' advertising campaign. The company showed two vague storylines – in one of them a man sitting in a field with a typewriter – and asked consumers to complete the ads by filling in blanks that appeared on the screen. Over 32,000 videos were submitted in the first few months and the winning ad was aired on TV.[21]

Value from society's perspective

We must also consider how marketing transactions add or subtract value from society. In many ways, we are at the mercy of marketers because we trust them: to sell us products that are safe and perform as promised, to price and distribute these products fairly. Conflicts often arise in business when the pressure to succeed in the marketplace provokes dishonest business practices – the 'NatWest Three', a trio of businessmen who skimmed off £3.7 million in profits through a fraudulent deal between NatWest and Enron in 2000, were jailed for 37 months.[22] Enron filed for bankruptcy in 2001 after a scandal revealed the firm's irregular accounting practices that did not report many of its debts and losses in its financial statements. As the scandal was revealed, the company's shares dropped from $90 to 50¢ before it went bankrupt.

Companies usually find that stressing ethics and social responsibility is also good business, at least in the long run. Some find out the hard way. For example, the Chrysler Corporation was accused of resetting the odometers of new cars that managers had actually driven prior to sale. The company admitted the practice only after some managers tried to get out of paying speeding tickets by claiming that their speedometers – and odometers – didn't work because the cables were disconnected.[23] These actions caused the company great embarrassment, and it took years of hard work to restore the public's trust.

In contrast, in 2007, after salmonella was found in two of the Marks & Spencer houmous range, the company voluntarily removed all other unaffected houmous products from the shelves as a precaution. The company reported the incident to the Food Standards Agency and the Food Safety Authority of Ireland and started a thorough investigation with the suppliers to find out what exactly had happened. The recall cost the firm millions of pounds in revenues.[24]

The dark side of marketing and consumer behaviour

Intentionally or not, some marketers do violate their bond of trust with consumers, and the 'dark side' of marketing is often the subject of harsh criticism.[25] In some cases, these violations are illegal, such as when a retailer adopts a 'bait-and-switch' selling strategy, luring consumers into the shop with promises of inexpensive products with the sole intent of getting them to switch to higher-priced goods. In other cases, marketing practices have detrimental effects on society even though they are not actually illegal. Some alcohol and tobacco companies advertise in low-income areas where abuse of these products is a big problem. Others sponsor commercials depicting groups of people in an unfavourable light or sell products that encourage antisocial behaviour.

Sometimes consumers' worst enemies are themselves, and their desires, choices and actions result in negative consequences to individuals and the society in which they live. Some harmful consumer behaviours such as excessive drinking or cigarette smoking stem from social pressures, and the cultural value placed on money encourages activities such as shoplifting or insurance fraud. Exposure to unattainable ideals of beauty and success can create dissatisfaction with the self. 'The dark side' of consumer behaviour includes:

Did you hear the one about the fat guy suing the restaurants?

It's no joke.
He claims the food was too cheap so he ate too much!

Learn more about the erosion of personal responsibility and common sense. Go to:

ConsumerFreedom.com

Photo 1.6 Some people feel that marketers manipulate consumers, while others argue that people should be responsible for their own choices. This ad is critical of the current trend of lawsuits brought against fast food companies by people who blame their eating problems on the fast food industry. What do you think?
Source: The Center for Consumer Freedom

Addictive consumption: Consumer addiction is a physiological or psychological dependency on products or services. These problems include alcoholism, drug addiction and cigarettes – and many companies profit from addictive products or by selling solutions. Also 'shopaholics' turn to shopping in much the same way addicted people turn to drugs or alcohol, which can result in massive credit card debt, loan consolidations and even bankruptcy.[26]

Exploited people: Sometimes people are used or exploited, willingly or not, for commercial gain in the marketplace; these situations range from travelling road shows that feature dwarves and midgets to the selling of body parts and babies on eBay. Consumed consumers are people who themselves become commodities.

Illegal activities: The cost of crimes committed against business has been estimated at around £4 billion per year.[27] This includes attempts to put false items on an insurance bill to cover the amount deducted because the item was old, to sneaking into a theatre to avoid paying admission or to download music files from illegal file-sharing systems on the internet.[28]

Shrinkage: A retail theft is committed every five seconds. Shrinkage is the industry term for inventory and cash losses from shoplifting and employee theft. This is a massive problem for businesses that is passed on to consumers in the form of higher prices. However, 40 per cent of the losses can be attributed to employees rather than shoppers.

Marketing ethics and sustainability

Ethical voices on marketing's value creation

Whereas marketers often emphasise that marketing is about satisfying needs, critics of marketing sometimes argue on behalf of consumers that marketing just satisfies needs marketers themselves have created and imposed on consumers–sometimes even by applying manipulating strategies and techniques. Is it ethical for diet manufacturers to play on women's fear of becoming fat? Is it ethical for marketers to create a market for Nintendo which didn't exist or to introduce SMS and text messaging to teenagers? Some of these activities have contributed to marketers' sometimes poor reputation.

However, in order to answer these questions we have to resort to what criteria are being used to measure the ethics involved. Marketers operate within a legal framework they should abide by. Second, they also operate within the standards of other regulatory bodies such as the Advertising Standards Authority and codes of conduct from the Chartered Institute of Marketing and Direct Marketing. Third, they also take note of powerful lobbying groups on issues of marketing to children and alcohol advertising. Fourth, they would be foolish to ignore the ethics of their own customers who might desert them if they behaved unethically in their eyes. The question is whose ethical standards should marketers adhere to? The second point to note is that marketers can be responsible for creating people's perceived needs. It is true that, if you need a cold drink, marketers can influence you to think you want Coca-Cola. However, even if they exert this influence, they still can't make you buy it! This would be truly unethical, but it is almost never the case. Thus consumers purchase products of their own free will. Moreover, nowadays the average consumer is more marketing savvy and well aware of the fact that marketing is not only conducted in order to satisfy his or her needs. As stated at the beginning of the book, marketing is not a one-way, but a two-way road.

Debate, discuss, disagree

1 What's your opinion on how much marketers create or simply serve needs?

Marketing as a process

Our definition of marketing refers to processes. This means that marketing is not a one-shot operation. When it's done right, marketing is a decision process in which marketing managers determine the strategies that will help the firm meet its long-term objectives and then execute those strategies using the tools they have at their disposal. In this section, we'll look at how marketers make business decisions and plan actions and the tools they use to execute their plans.

Marketing planning

Objective

6

The basics
of marketing
planning and
the marketing
mix tools used
in the marketing
process

A big part of the marketing process is to engage in what is called marketing planning. The first phase of marketing planning is analysing the marketing environment. This means understanding the firm's current strengths and weaknesses by assessing factors that might help or hinder the development and marketing of products. The analysis must also take into account the opportunities and threats the firm will encounter in the marketplace, such as the actions of competitors, cultural and technological changes, and the economy.

Firms (or individuals) engaging in marketing planning ask questions such as the following:

- What product benefits will our customers be looking for in three to five years in, for example, chocolate consumption?

- What capabilities does our firm have that set it apart from the competition, e.g. Cadbury has established brand and chocolate making expertise?

- What additional customer groups might provide important **market segment**s for us in the future, e.g. would older consumers prefer less sweet chocolate?

- How will changes in technology affect our production process, our communication strategy, and our distribution strategy, e.g. to produce the fine bubbles in Cadbury's Wispa a new procedure was invented.

- What changes in social and cultural values are occurring that will affect our market in the next few years, e.g. will people be more health conscious about chocolate snacks?

- How will customers' awareness of environmental issues affect their attitudes towards our manufacturing facilities, e.g. how will Cadbury's disposal of factory waste have to alter?

- What legal and regulatory issues may affect our business in both domestic and global markets, e.g. might the government add restrictions on the sale of chocolate to young children like banning it in schools?

Answers to these and other questions provide the foundation for developing an organisation's **marketing plan**. This is a document that describes the marketing environment, outlines the marketing objectives and strategy, and identifies who will be responsible for carrying out each part of the marketing strategy. A major marketing decision for most organisations is which products to market to which consumers without turning off other consumers at the same time. Some firms choose to reach as many customers as possible by offering their goods or services to a **mass market** that consists of all possible customers in a market regardless of the differences in their specific needs and wants. Marketing planning then becomes a matter of developing a basic product and a single strategy for reaching everyone.

Although this approach can be cost effective, the firm risks losing potential customers to competitors whose marketing plans are directed at meeting the needs of specific groups within the market. A market segment is a distinct group of customers within a larger market who are similar to one another in some way and whose needs differ from other customers in the larger market. Car makers such as Rover, Fiat and Volvo offer different automobiles for different market segments. Depending on its goals and resources, a firm may choose to focus on one segment. A product's **market position** is how the target market perceives the product in comparison to competitor's brands.

Marketing's tools: the marketing mix

In determining the best way to present a good or service for consumers' consideration, marketers have a toolbox called the **marketing mix**. The elements of the marketing mix are commonly known as the Four Ps: product, price, promotion and place. However, for services there are three more Ps, as we shall see in later chapters. As Figure 1.5 shows, each P is a piece of the puzzle that must be combined with other pieces. Just as a radio DJ puts together a collection of separate songs (a musical mix) to create a certain mood, the idea of a mix in this context reminds us that no single marketing activity is sufficient to accomplish the organisation's objectives.

Although we talk about the Four Ps as separate parts of a firm's marketing strategy, in reality, product, price, promotion and place decisions are totally interdependent. Decisions about any single one of the four are affected by and affect every other marketing mix decision. For example, assume that a firm is introducing a superior quality product,

Figure 1.5	The marketing mix
	What marketing is all about! The marketing mix is a combination of the Four Ps – product, price, place and promotion – all used together to satisfy customer needs. However, thoughout this book we will refer to the 7 Ps model you'll find in Chapter 9

one that is more expensive to produce than its existing line of products. The price the firm charges for this new product must cover these higher costs, but in addition the firm must create advertising and other promotional strategies to convey a top-quality image. At the same time, the price of the product must cover not only the costs of production but also the cost of advertising. Furthermore, the firm must include up-market retailers in its distribution strategy. The elements of the marketing mix therefore work hand in hand.

We'll examine these components of the marketing mix in detail later in this book. For now, let's briefly look at each P to gain some insight into its meaning and role in the marketing mix.

Product

We've already seen that the **product** is a good, a service, an idea, a place, a person – whatever is offered for sale in the exchange. This aspect of the marketing mix includes the design and packaging of a good, as well as its physical features and any associated services, such as free delivery. So we can see that the product is a combination of many different elements, all of which are important to the product's success. For example, when the UK firm Virgin introduced Virgin Cola in the United States, the company attempted to make the product stand out from the competition through its distinctive packaging. Advertising that introduced the brand told customers about the curved squeezable bottles. 'If all you got is Va Va, You got to get some Voom; It's in the curvy bottle, Yeah, Virgin Drinks' got Voom. . . . Virgin puts the Voom in your Va Va.'[29] We're not quite sure what that means, but it does get your attention. Whether the focus is on the bottle or some other element, the product is an important part of the marketing mix.

Price

Price is the amount the consumer must exchange to receive the offering. A price is often used as a way to increase consumers' interest in a product, for example when an item is put on sale, but in other cases marketers try to sell a product with a higher price than people are used to if they want to communicate that it's high quality or cutting edge. For example, the Adidas 1 computerised running shoe got a lot of attention in the media. Some of the fuss was that the shoe was billed as the first 'smart shoe' because it contained a computer chip that adapted its cushioning level to a runner's size and stride. But a lot of the press coverage also revolved around the hefty price tag of €195 per pair, which made the shoe a status symbol for the hardcore runner.[30]

Marketing misstakes

Spellling mistakes

As part of a joint venture with a Turkish company, a US-based telephone directory production company prepared and printed special telephone directories for the Turkish market. In the telephone directory for Bolu, a city situated between Ankara and Istanbul, the last name of a highly regarded and well-known businessman wrongly featured as 'Yarak'. If this misprint was not bad enough, to add insult to injury, 'Yarak' means male genital organ in Turkish slang. While typographical errors are not uncommon in the printing business throughout the world, special attention should have been paid during typing and proofreading given the company's lack of familiarity with the language of interest and the fact that printing was its core business.[31]

Why do you think this might be a marketing misstake?

Promotion

Promotion includes all the activities marketers undertake to inform consumers about their products and to encourage potential customers to buy these products. Promotions can take many forms, including for example personal selling, direct marketing, buzz and viral marketing, television advertising, sponsorship, shop coupons, billboards, magazine ads and publicity releases. Marketing messages often communicate **myths**, stories containing symbolic elements that express the shared emotions and ideals of a culture.[32] Consider, for example, how McDonald's takes on mythical qualities. To some, the golden arches are virtually synonymous with American culture. They offer sanctuary to Europeans in foreign lands who are grateful to know exactly what to expect once they enter. Basic struggles of good versus evil are played out in the fantasy world of McDonald's advertising, as when Ronald McDonald confounds the Hamburglar. McDonald's even runs Hamburger University, where fast-food students learn how to make the perfect burger.

Place

Place refers to the availability of the product to the customer at the desired time and location. This P is related to a channel of distribution – the set of firms working together to get a product from a producer to a consumer. For clothing or electronics, this channel includes local retailers as well as other outlets, such as retail websites that strive to offer the right quantity of products in the right styles at the right time, for example Amazon's next day delivery.

Now that you've read the chapter on how marketers create value for customers and heard the advice read 'Real people, real decisions' to see which strategy Steve selected to maximise the value created for banks around Europe.

Marketing ethics and sustainability

Playboy using play toys for children

A furious vicar took direct action against Playboy stationery products aimed at children – by sweeping them off the shelves.

He was appalled when he found items carrying Playboy's bunny logo on the shelves at his local Stationery Box shop in York next to Winnie-the-Pooh and Mickey Mouse products. Playboy commented: 'Playboy's target audience is 18- to 34-year-olds, so we clearly did not authorise or approve the placement of our product next to such well-known children's characters. We will be reviewing this situation immediately.'

Catherine Hanly, editor of the parents website raisingkids. co.uk, said many mothers had condemned the sale of Playboy products in WH Smith shops on a recent discussion forum. 'They are perceived as targeting children', she added.

Playboy's stationery range, which is widely sold in high street shops, includes pink pencil cases, notebooks, folders, diaries, gel pens and ring binders. Playboy claims that all its products are aimed at adults only. Three years ago, WH Smith was attacked for selling the same Playboy range to children. Argos sells the Playboy stationery range in the section of its catalogue which includes 'toys and gifts'. But WH Smith defended the sale of the Playboy items, saying it aimed to strike the right balance to meet the needs of all its customers 'whilst not acting as a censor'.

Source: Adapted from 'Vicar's war on "wicked" Playboy, Brooke, C., Daily Mail, 21 May 2008

Debate, discuss, disagree

1   Do you think it is ethical or unethical to distribute these products in these shops?

2   Who is more in the right? The vicar? Playboy? The shops?

Real people, real decisions

How it worked out at Visa Europe . . .

With regards to the German market, Steve decided to go for Option 3, the opportunistic approach, and target the banks one by one. Visa Europe set about creating a business case for each bank in order to convince them of the economic benefits of V PAY (in terms of cost efficiencies, greater cross-border usage and decreased fraud). They then constructed a case around the political and governance considerations of adopting V PAY (creating V PAY Deutschland as a national decision-making body responsible for the ongoing management and development of V PAY in Germany). In other countries, such as Luxembourg, where Visa Europe already benefited from strong relationships and centralised decision-making mechanisms, it was more appropriate to work with Option 2. And, in others, such as Italy, it was effective to take a more hybrid approach, working with both individual banks and with national forums.

Irrespective of approach, Visa Europe helped banks to sell the V PAY concept to retailers and consumers alike by local marketing campaigns supported by Visa Europe, waiving certain fees, helping to co-fund advertising, incentives for bank personnel to sell the product to customers, and promotions to encourage retailers to display V PAY signs in their premises. To further attune to local market requirements, Visa Europe was not prescriptive about how the V PAY product is actually configured. In some countries, for example, banks did not want V PAY to be used on the internet, whereas secure e-commerce functionality was enabled in other countries

Marketing metrics

Measuring Visa Europe's success

Things can move slowly in the business-to-business market. In Germany, for example, it took two years to get the first bank to issue V PAY. Since then, more than 100 German banks have begun to migrate. This includes a whole variety of small cooperative banks and savings banks, along with some much larger institutions such as Deutsche PostBank (the country's largest debit card issuer), and TARGOBANK (one of Germany's newest banking brands with more than 3 million customers).

Across Europe, meanwhile, V PAY cards are now being issued in six countries, and Visa Europe has received commitments for more than 60 million cards. This means that the projected market share already exceeds 25 per cent in most target countries and exceeds 50 per cent in key countries such as Italy. As more and more banks declare their commitment and begin to issue V PAY, the momentum behind Europe's new debit card solution grows.

Chapter summary

Now that you have finished reading this chapter, you should be able to understand:

1. **Who marketers are, where they work and marketing's role in the firm.** Marketers come from many different backgrounds and work in a variety of locations, from consumer goods companies to non-profit organisations to financial institutions to advertising and public relations agencies. Marketing's role in the firm depends on the organisation. Some firms are very marketing oriented, whereas others do not focus on marketing. Therefore, no matter what firm marketers work in, their decisions affect and are affected by the firm's other operations.

2. **What marketing is and how it provides value to everyone involved in the marketing process.** Marketing is an organisational function and a set of processes for creating, communicating and delivering value to customers, and for managing customer relationships in ways that benefit the organisation and its stakeholders. Therefore, marketing is all about delivering value to everyone who is affected by a transaction (stakeholders).

3. **The range of services and goods that are marketed.** Any good, service, idea that can be marketed is a product, even though what is being sold may not take a physical form. Consumer goods are the tangible products that consumers purchase for personal or family use. Services are intangible products that we pay for and use but never own. **Industrial goods** are those goods sold to businesses and other organisations for further processing or for use in their business operations. Not-for-profit organisations, places and people can also be marketed.

4. **Value from the perspectives of the customers, producers and society.** Value is the benefits a customer receives from buying a product or service. Marketing communicates these benefits as the value proposition to the customer. For customers, the value proposition includes the whole bundle of benefits the product promises to deliver, not just the benefits of the product itself. Sellers determine value by assessing whether its transactions are profitable, whether it is providing value to stakeholders by creating a competitive advantage, and whether it is providing value through its value chain. Society receives value from marketing activities when producers and consumers engage in ethical, profitable and environmentally friendly exchange relationships. One of the newest developments in marketing is that consumers themselves are playing an increasingly greater role in generating value on behalf of marketers in addition to consuming it.

5. **The basics of marketing planning and the marketing mix tools used in the marketing process.** The strategic process of marketing planning begins with an assessment of factors within the organisation and in the external environment that could help or hinder the development and marketing of products. On the basis of this analysis, marketers set objectives and develop strategies. Many firms use a target marketing strategy in which they divide the overall market into segments and then target the most attractive one. Then they design the marketing mix to gain a competitive position in the target market. The marketing mix includes product, price, place and promotion. The product is what satisfies customer needs. The price reflects the customer assigned value or amount to be exchanged for the product. The place or channel of distribution gets the product to the customer. Promotion is the organisation's efforts to persuade customers to buy the product.

6. **The evolution of the marketing concept.** Early in the twentieth century, firms followed a production orientation in which they focused on the most efficient ways to produce and distribute products. Beginning in the 1930s, some firms adopted a selling orientation that encouraged salespeople to aggressively sell products to customers. In the 1950s, organisations adopted a consumer orientation that focused on customer satisfaction. This led to the development of the marketing concept. Today, many firms are moving toward a New Era orientation that includes not only a commitment to quality and value, but also a concern for both economic and social profit.

Key terms

Chapter review

Marketing concepts: testing your knowledge

1. Where do marketers work, and what role does marketing have in a company?

2. Briefly explain what marketing is.

3. Explain needs, wants and demands. What is the role of marketing in each of these?

4. What is utility? How does marketing create different forms of utility?

5. Define the terms consumer goods, services and industrial goods.

6. What does the lifetime value of the customer refer to, and how is it calculated?

7. What does it mean for a firm to have a competitive advantage? What gives a firm a competitive advantage?

8. What is involved in marketing planning?

9. List and describe the elements of the marketing mix.

10. Trace the evolution of the marketing concept.

Marketing concepts: discussing choices and ethical issues

1. Have you ever pirated software? How about music? Is it ethical to give or receive software instead of paying for it? Does the answer depend on the person's motivation and/or if he or she could otherwise afford to buy the product?

2. The marketing concept focuses on the ability of marketing to satisfy customer needs. As a typical college student, how does marketing satisfy your needs? What areas of your life are affected by marketing? What areas of your life (if any) are not affected by marketing?

3. In both developed and developing countries, not all firms have implemented programmes that follow the marketing concept. Can you think of firms that still operate with a production orientation? A selling orientation? What changes would you recommend for these firms?

4. Successful firms have a competitive advantage because they are able to identify distinctive competencies and use these to create differential benefits for their customers. Consider your business school or your university. What distinctive competencies does it have? What differential benefits does it provide for students? What is its competitive advantage? What are your ideas as to how your university could improve its competitive position? Write an outline of your ideas.

5. Ideally, each member of a value chain adds value to a product before someone buys it. Thinking about a music CD

you might buy in a shop, what kind of value does the music retailer add? How about the label that signs the artist? The public relations firm that arranges a tour by the artist to promote the new CD? The production company that shoots a music video to go along with the cut?

6. User-generated commercials seem to be part of a broader trend towards user-generated content of all sorts. Examples include YouTube, Pinterest (where users post photos and comment on others' pictures), blogging and video sharing sites like YouTube.com. Do you think this is a passing fad or an important trend? How (if at all) should marketers be dealing with these activities?

7. Some marketing or consumption activities involve the (literal) consumption of people – voluntarily or not. In one recent controversial incident, a man in Germany advertised on the internet to find someone who wanted to be killed and eaten (we are not making this up). He actually found a willing volunteer and did just what he promised – and was jailed for manslaughter. If a person consents to be 'consumed' in some way, is this still an ethical problem? What of value is being exchanged here? Would it be different if a person ate part of themselves?

Marketing practice: applying what you've learned

1. An old friend of yours has been making and selling vitamin-fortified smoothies to acquaintances and friends of friends for some time. He is now thinking about opening a shop in a small city with a university, but he is worried about whether he'll have enough customers to keep a business going. Knowing that you are a marketing student, he's asked you for some advice. What can you tell him about product, price, promotion and place (distribution) strategies that will help him get his business off the ground?

2. Assume that you are employed by your city's chamber of commerce. One major focus of the chamber is to get industries to move to your city. As a former marketing student, you know that there are issues involving product, price, promotion and place (distribution) that can attract business. Next week you have an opportunity to speak to the members of the chamber, and your topic will be 'Marketing a City'. Develop an outline for that presentation.

3. As a marketing professional, you have been asked to write a short piece for a local business newsletter about the state of marketing today. You think the best way to address this topic is to review how the marketing concept has evolved and to discuss the New Era orientation. Write a short article to submit to the editor of the newsletter.

4. As university students, you and your friends sometimes discuss the various courses you are taking. One of your friends says to you, 'Marketing's not important. It's just dumb advertising.' Another friend says, 'Marketing doesn't really affect people's lives in any way.' As a role-playing exercise, present your arguments against these statements to your class.

Marketing miniproject: learning by doing

The purpose of this miniproject is to develop an understanding of the importance of marketing to different organisations.

1. Work as a team with two or three other students in your class to select an organisation in your community that practises marketing. It may be a manufacturer, a service provider, a retailer, a not-for-profit organisation – almost any organisation will do. Then schedule a visit with someone within the organisation who is involved in the marketing activities. Arrange for a short visit in which the person can give your group a tour of the facilities and explain the organisation's marketing activities.

   Divide the following list of topics among your team and ask each person to be responsible for developing a set of questions to ask during the interview to learn about the company's programme:

   ● What customer segments the company targets.

   ● How it determines needs and wants.

   ● What products it offers, including features, benefits and goals for customer satisfaction.

   ● What its pricing strategies are, including any discounting policies it has.

   ● What promotional strategies it uses and what these emphasise to position the product(s).

   ● How it distributes products and whether it has encountered any problems.

   ● How marketing planning is done and who does it.

   ● Whether social responsibility is part of the marketing programme and, if so, in what ways.

2. Develop a team report of your findings. In each section of the report, describe what you learned that is new or surprising to you compared with what you expected.

3. Develop a team presentation for your class that summarises your findings. Conclude your presentation with comments on what your team believes the company was doing that was particularly good and what was not so good.

Real people, real surfers

Exploring the web

H&M sells clothing and other merchandise both in its shops and on its website (www.H&M.com). Visit its website, and also identify the website of a competitor. *Hint*: You can do this by Googling the term 'fashion clothing'. Follow the links to find out as much as you can about the companies. Then, on the basis of your experience, answer the following questions:

1. Which firm has the better website? What makes it better?

2. Do you think the firms are targeting specific market segments? If so, what market segments? What features of the website give you that idea?

3. What are your major criticisms of each of the websites? What would you do to improve each site?

Now, take a look at the website at www.pearsoned.co.uk/solomon to see some videos from YouTube relating to aspects of this chapter.

Marketing plan exercise

A key to long-term business success lies in a firm's ability to offer value to customers through its product offerings. The task of communicating that value proposition rests largely with the company's marketers. A marketing plan not only must clarify the sources of value, but also must specify how the value message gets out.

Pick a product or service you like – one that you believe has a strong value proposition. Identify the specific source(s) of value.

That is, what leads you to conclude the product or service offers value?

How is that value communicated? What other sources of value might be developed for the product or service you identified? How might these new value-adding properties be communicated to customers?

Delve deeper into developing market orientation

Dr Lloyd C. Harris

Professor of Marketing and Strategy

The motivation that drove this study centred on my desire to understand more fully the processes and dynamics of developing market orientation. In the early 1990s, key articles defined and operationalised measures of market orientation. Academics across the globe got very excited and spent lots of time doing big surveys and getting increasingly hot and bothered about things that could be found to correlate with these new measures. While some of these studies were really interesting to theorists and scholars, on reflection I felt that academia had rather over-concentrated on *what* should be changed to facilitate the development of market orientation to the notable deficit of explaining *how* such market-oriented change is managed. In an earlier study, drawing on culture theory (Harris and Obonna, 1999) we had argued that, while appearing deceptively simple, developing market orientation was likely to be fraught with difficulties and, in some cases, almost impossible. Indeed, in 2002 I published a study which explored how and why some managers actively sabotage market orientation development. I would encourage interested readers to incorporate these articles into their background reading and to be critical in their reflections on the processes and dynamics of market orientation.

Best wishes

Professor Lloyd C. Harris, Warwick Business School

References

Lloyd C. Harris and Emmanuel Ogbonna (1999), 'Developing A Market Oriented Culture: A Critical Evaluation', *Journal of Management Studies*, 36, no.2, 177–96, ISSN: 0022-2380.

Lloyd C. Harris (2002), 'Sabotaging Market-Oriented Culture Change: An Exploration of Justifications and Approaches', *Journal of Marketing Theory and Practice* 10, no. 3, 58–72, ISSN: 1069-6679.

Marketing in action case

Real decisions at Ocado

The market

Only 3.4 per cent of UK grocery sales are online but this was worth £4.7 billion in 2010 and is expected to grow to over 5 per cent by 2015 (Datamonitor 2010; IGD 2010). Grocery is Britain's biggest retail market, accounting for £140 billion of annual spending, or half of all retail spending. Hence the growth potential is large – already 20 per cent of customers do a weekly online shop, with 7 per cent using online shopping for all of their groceries. Ocado had 20 per cent of Britain's online grocery sales in 2009, putting it third, behind Tesco and Sainsbury's but competition is intensifying. ASDA has gained market share and a new entrant, Amazon.co.uk Grocery launched in the UK on 7 July 2010. However, it is not a full service, for example not offering 'shopping list' features or a full range of food products. Ocado is differentiated by its approach to innovation (Datamonitor 2010) but it lacks the size of global firms such as Tesco and ASDA or Amazon, if the latter enters the UK market.

busy people a true alternative to going to the supermarket. 'It's like how shopping used to be done', says co-founder Tim Steiner. 'Historically, the grocer would know what you wanted and then deliver it. Now we can use the processing power on your desktop to let you choose items for the same price as going to the supermarkets – and get them delivered.'

Ocado aims to provide a more sustainable alternative to supermarket shopping, from 'closed-loop' recycling (Ocado collect, recycle and reuse plastic grocery bags) to popular initiatives like 'green van slots'. It has managed to lower carbon emissions to the point where shopping with Ocado is now greener than walking to your local supermarket, according to Greenstone, the carbon management consultancy. Deliveries are made to the front door of properties or to the kitchen if customers prefer. Ocado will offer substitute goods where the original is out of stock but customers are given the option to reject them with an instant refund.

The offer

Ocado provides 'clicks and mortar' – an online ordering and physical delivery service for grocery goods. It was conceived with one simple objective in mind: to offer

The business model

The founders of Ocado argue that their very ignorance of the grocery business led to them questioning every aspect of online grocery operations. This innovatory outlook provides competitive differentiation. Ocado shows virtually live inventory on its webshop. From the ten miles of conveyor belts at its warehouse in Hatfield, Hertfordshire, Ocado made 80,000 deliveries a week in 2009, offering 19,500 Waitrose grocery lines. This increased to 124,000 deliveries in 2010 with plans to increase to 180,000. Deliveries are supported by unique logistics software and satellite navigation systems in vans, to ensure that the right goods are delivered at the right time. A variable charge applies for delivery from free to £5.99 (or £9.99 a month for unlimited deliveries), depending on the time and day of delivery However, customers must spend at least £40 on an order. Van drivers are equipped with handheld data devices which allow them to correct orders on customer premises if items are missing from the order or are damaged.

Ocado's business has shown strong growth since it launched in 2002. In spring 2011 service was available to over 70 per cent of households across the South East, the Midlands, the North West, the South Coast and, more recently, South Wales. It now:

- has 1.6 million registered customers in England and Wales;
- employs over 4000 staff which will grow by 2000 after the second centre opens in 2012;
- turns over £550 million a year;
- earned £8 million for the half year up to June 2010 (EBITDA);
- is growing by 25 per cent annually.

Growth is being supported by major infrastructure investment, with Ocado starting work on a second warehouse in Warwickshire, scheduled to open in late 2012. This will handle an additional 120,000 customer orders per week, increasing to 180,000, doubling overall capacity. This rate of growth poses both operational and marketing problems. Can Ocado maintain its differentiation while doubling its capacity?

Marketing intelligence

Understanding customers is important if growth is to be achieved – for example do Ocado's customers want the same service as those of Tesco and Sainsburys? Online shoppers show some important differences:

- Ocado consumers show some distinct preferences for order placing speed (maximum 20 minutes).

- Ocado shoppers rate quality as important.
- Ocado customers rate delivery time and delivery time reliability as third and fourth most important to them.

This concern about delivery could be explained by Ocado's original offer, which promoted shorter delivery time slots and hence may have attracted consumers for whom this is a key factor. However, these are online shoppers and it is those currently shopping 'offline', i.e at stores, who need to be persuaded. Grocery retailers' offline and online customer profiles are significantly different, indicating that there is not a direct, straightforward transfer of loyalty from offline to online shopping. Research suggests that these differences are more marked for Waitrose/Ocado and for ASDA than for Sainsbury's and Tesco. The finding that Mosaic Group B (Happy Families) accounts for a much higher proportion of Ocado shoppers than Waitrose may be caused by this customer segment aspiring to be Waitrose shoppers, but not having the opportunity due to branch locations.

Research among the 'offline' revealed that the factors that they rated as important in home delivery were 'ordering time' followed by 'quality'. Delivery time reliability was rated less important than by those who had ordered online, although offline shoppers may become more time sensitive if poorly timed deliveries are experienced. This suggests that a customer acquisition strategy will need to be different to a retention strategy as consumers' needs and fears seem to be different.

The future

Ocado's original agreement with Waitrose prevented the latter from offering an online delivery service. This ended in 2010 and Waitrose is rolling out a competitive service to Ocado. However, the supply agreement with Waitrose was renewed to provide products for Ocado until 2017. There is a need to broaden its offer with new product lines, but the latest supply agreement with Waitrose is reported to include some restrictions on Ocado own-brand products. The problem facing Ocado's founders is how they can maintain their innovatory approach and compete with much bigger players such as Tesco and ASDA.

Things to think about

1. What are some of the environmental factors which are increasing the use of online shopping?

2. What are some of the ways the more traditional supermarkets compete and which Ocado has undertaken?

3. How could Ocado update prior research to understand its customer needs better and identify customer segments for targeted marketing?

4. What problems do Ocado face in matching supply and demand?

5. What are some ways to implement your recommendations?

Case study written by Dr Paul Harborne, City University, London

References

1. John W. Schouten, 'Selves in Transition: Symbolic Consumption in Personal Rites of Passage and Identity Reconstruction', *Journal of Consumer Research*, 17 March 1991, 412–25; Michael R. Solomon, 'The Wardrobe Consultant: Exploring the Role of a New Retailing Partner', *Journal of Retailing* 63 (1987), 110–28; Michael R. Solomon and Susan P. Douglas, 'Diversity in Product Symbolism: The Case of Female Executive Clothing', *Psychology and Marketing* 4 (1987), 189–212; Joseph Z. Wisenblit, 'Person Positioning: Empirical Evidence and a New Paradigm', *Journal of Professional Services Marketing* 4, no. 2 (1989), 51–82.

2. www.cim.co.uk, 2006.

3. www.cim.co.uk/NewsAndEvents/MediaCentre/NewsRelease/ Leading%20body%20calls%20for%20a%20new%20 definition%20.aspx, 2007.

4. Adapted from N. Bendle, P. Farris, Phillip Pfeifer and D. Reibstein, 'Metrics that Matter – to Marketing Managers', *Marketing JRM* 1 (2010) 18–23.

5. Michael R. Solomon, 'Deep-Seated Materialism: The Case of Levi's 501 Jeans', in *Advances in Consumer Research*, ed. Richard Lutz (Las Vegas, NV: Association for Consumer Research, 1986), 13, 619–22.

6. Peter F. Drucker, *Management: Tasks, Responsibilities, Practices* (New York: Harper & Row, 1972), 64–5.

7. Evan Shannon, '3BR w/VU of Asteroid Belt', *Wired* (April 2006), 130.

8. Ch. Gronroos, 'Marketing Redefined', *Management Decisions* 28 no. 8 (1990), 5–9.

9. 'Henry Ford and The Model T', in *Forbes Greatest Business Stories* (New York: John Wiley & Sons, 1996), www.wiley.com/legacy/products/subject/business/forbes/ford.html.

10. Theodore Levitt, 'Marketing Myopia', *Harvard Business Review*, July – August 1960, 45–56.

11. Liz Morrell, 'Your Retailer Needs You', *Retail Week*, 24 March 2006.

12. www.google.com/support/jobs/bin/static.py?page=about. html&about=eng.

13. Based on BBC Watchdog, 'What Does Green Actually Mean?', 10 May 2010. Available at: http://www.bbc.co.uk/blogs/ watchdog/2011/05/green_wash.html. Accessed 11 July 2011.

14. PR Newswire Europe, 'M&S @ Fashioning Change and Changing Fashion', 13 July 2006.

15. Philip R. Cateora, *Strategic International Marketing* (Homewood, IL: Dow Jones-Irwin, 1985).

16. Lee D. Dahringer, 'Marketing Services Internationally: Barriers and Management Strategies', *Journal of Service Marketing* 5 (1991), 5–17.

17. Paul Beckett, 'Picking Side in Scotland's Battle of the Buzz', *The Wall Street Journal*, 11 August 2006.

18. http://blogs.pcworld.com/staffblog/archives/001763.html.

19. Michael E. Porter, *Competitive Advantage: Creating and Sustaining Superior Performance* (New York: Free Press, 1985).

20. P. Farris, N. Bendle, Phillip Pfeifer and D. Reibstein, *Marketing Metrics*: The Definitive Guide to Measuring Marketing Performance, 2nd ed. (New Jersey: FT Press 2011).

21. http://blog.searchenginewatch.com/blog/061013-100808; http://blogs.guardian.co.uk/organgrinder/2007/06/cannes_ the_impact_of_consumer.html; http://current.com/s/news/ news_usatoday032706.htm.

22. www.guardian.co.uk/business/enron.

23. 'Dear Chrysler: Outsiders' Advice on Handling the Odometer Charge', *Wall Street Journal*, 26 June 1987, 19.

24. http://news.bbc.co.uk/1/hi/uk/6367331.stm.

25. Parts of this section are adapted from Michael R. Solomon, *Consumer Behavior: Buying, Having, and Being* 7th ed. (Upper Saddle River, NJ: Prentice Hall, 2007).

26. Thomas C. O'Guinn and Ronald J. Faber, 'Compulsive Buying: A Phenomenological Explanation', *Journal of Consumer Research* 16 (September 1989), 154.

27. www.chamberonline.co.uk/policy/issues/businesscrime /crimereport.pdf.

28. 'Advertisers Face up to the New Morality: Making the Pitch', *Bloomberg*, 8 July 1997.

29. Gerry Khermouch, 'Virgin's "Va Va" Bottle Has "Voom": First Ads via Long Haymes Carr', *Brandweek*, 10 July 2000, 13.

30. http://abclocal.go.com/kgo/business/050704ap_business_ adidas.html.

31. Adapted from T. Dalgic and R. Heijblom, 'Educator Insights: International Marketing Blunders Revisited', *Journal of International Marketing* 4, no. 1 (1996), 81–91

32. Sal Randazzo, 'Advertising as Myth-Maker; Brands as Gods and Heroes', *Advertising Age*, 8 November 1993, 32.

Chapter 2
Strategy and environment

Meet Kevin Parkin,
A decision maker
at DavyMarkham

Q & A with Kevin Parkin

First job out of school?
Trainee Accountant With Dormer Tools in Sheffield

Career high?
Being given a plc Board Position at 34 years of age

Business book I'm reading now
Eli Goldratt's *The Critical Chain*

My hero
My Father who was a Production Director in a Sheffield Engineering Company (Ernest H Hill Ltd) – he walked me round the shop floor every Saturday morning and taught me a great deal

Don't do this when interviewing with me.
Fail to answer the question in no more that three minutes

My pet peeve
People who are constantly negative at work and in life generally

Favourite T.V. programme?
Country File

Holiday resort?
Provence

Hobby/Sport?
Watching Rugby/Motor Racing

Drink?
Fizzy water (and not champagne)

Food?
Very little food I don't enjoy as I have had to eat whatever was available, for example Bull's Testicles in Inner Mongolia!

Kevin Parkin is former Managing Director of DavyMarkham. He studied engineering and business before becoming professionally qualified in both Accounting (Chartered Institute of Management Accounting) and Marketing (Chartered Institute of Marketing). He is also a Member of the prestigious Institute for Turnaround. He has over 30 years of management experience which has tended to be in the manufacturing, engineering and chemicals sectors. For the last 20 years he has specialised in business turnarounds and management buy-outs.

Kevin was appointed in 2006 and was given the task of using his marketing and finance expertise to derive a successful marketing strategy to take the company forward. Kevin failed his 11 plus and studied at the famous Central Technical School which taught practical engineering, maths and science skills. He is currently president of the school's old boys association. He is recently re-married with two grown-up children. One is an apprentice at the highly successful AES SEALS in Rotherham where he is studying a Mechanical Engineering Degree on a part time basis. His other son is a computer expert and is learning the commercial aspects of business life at Backup Technologies in Leeds.

Real people, real decisions
Decision time at DavyMarkham

The history of DavyMarkham dates back to the 1830s. Markham was originally founded in Chesterfield, Derbyshire in 1838, as a company that specialised in supplying to the energy sector. Exactly 100 years later, in 1938, the company was acquired by John Brown and around 50 years after (1986) was acquired by Trafalgar House. Davy, however, was established in Sheffield just eight years earlier than Markham, in 1830, and has a history of metal engineering. It was not until 1996, when both Davy and Markham were acquired by Kvaerner ASA, that some synergy began to take place between these two companies. As a result, in 1997 a combined manufacturing facility was established in Sheffield. Following this, the metals technology division was sold to a company called VAI in 1998, and another company E & C (UK) Ltd, which was part of the Kvaerner group, then took control of the remainder of the company in 2000. In 2003, they decided to re-name the company AK Heavy Engineering.

The company has a tradition of supplying high-specification heavy engineering capability and has provided solutions to among the largest and most famous companies worldwide, including General Electric, Rolls-Royce and TATA. Specifically, the company has the expertise to move bridges, provide high-spec machining, design and build bridges and structures as well as provide vertical boring machinery for huge projects, such as for the Channel Tunnel. As well as producing such heavy engineering components, the company also provides repairs and refurbishment services to the metal engineering sector at large.

At the time of his appointment, Kevin was given the task of using his marketing and finance expertise to derive a successful marketing strategy to take the company forward. The company had been losing money for the previous 15 years and, as a result of rapid and sequential takeovers which had made it a small part of a large group (Kvaerner), staff morale was low, the workforce was demotivated and they felt neglected. At the time of Kevin's appointment, it was probably the last straw for many of the company's staff and there was doom and gloom associated with the appointment of an accountant, who the workers felt had come to close down the factory.

In addition to this, whilst the company's sales representatives appeared to be rushed off their feet and were taking lots of orders, many of these could not be successfully realised and whilst they were useful in keeping the factory workforce employed, they could not generate sufficient profit to cover full company overheads. Relatively few sales orders were appearing and, to put it bluntly, the company was 'strapped for cash'. Whilst at the time of his appointment Kevin was considered to be the 'hatchet man', he soon realised that this could be a stark reality. He was also conscious of the fact that he could easily be seen as a bully, who frightened staff and then simply walked off, and these two perceptions were not necessarily independent of one another.

Despite the rumours, Kevin had to engage in a plan and think quickly about the future. The economic climate was not helping things and recession had hit key markets in Europe and North America. The future looked bleak, but being a local chap, Kevin was determined to try and keep the business solvent and safeguard as much employment as possible. He had three major options that he could consider:

Kevin considers his options . . .

Option 1 Consolidate during the recession with a view that things would become brighter in a couple of years. The company could therefore look to provide more customised service work to the domestic engineering sector and focus purely on high-end key accounts, in order to minimise costs

This option was possible, particularly during the recession, as many companies were looking to outsource to those with expertise, like DavyMarkham, rather than employ their own workers. It also seemed possible for the company to marginalise on sales orders that did not generate sufficient profit and thus be more selective on the nature and type of business customers they deal with. These approaches could also help Kevin reduce the cost of sales associated with servicing and supplying less profitable clients. The downside, of course, is that if the recession worsened there just would not be any service work or profitable customers in the market.

Option 2 Consider adopting internal marketing techniques, in a bid to stimulate workers

During his studies, Kevin had attended a lecture about internal marketing. The idea being that the entire company i.e. top management to the shop floor, would buy into a process whereby employees would be treated as internal customers and jobs would be supplied to meet the needs and requirements of the workers. The aim of internal marketing was to motivate the workforce to provide better service to one another, which could later be transferred to external customers and stimulate better financial returns in terms of increased repeat business, word-of-mouth referrals etc. Whilst in theory Kevin thought this seemed a good idea, in practice he was sceptical, bearing in mind the workers' hostile mentality and the current organisational culture.

Option 3 Expand globally by looking for a corporate buyer to acquire the operation from an emerging international market

This option again presented a feasible option. Kevin could use his expertise in management buy-outs to manage the process. The benefits could be lucrative, as whilst North America and Europe had been struggling, other countries of the world, such as China and India, had been better able to weather the storm of the recession. Although such countries were not experiencing the same growth rate as previously enjoyed, there was still sufficient potential in these countries and significant demand for infrastructure projects, which DavyMarkham could serve. Whilst Kevin realised that this option may well save the heads of his workforce, he knew that he could ultimately pay, as he would probably be replaced.

Now, put yourself in Kevin's position. Which option looks most feasible? Which one would you go for, and why?

Objectives

When you finish reading this chapter, you will be able to:

1 Describe the steps in marketing planning

2 Explain the strategic planning process

3 Discuss some of the important aspects of an organisation's internal environment and understand how factors in the external business environment influence marketing strategies and outcomes

4 Understand the big picture of international marketing, including trade flows, market scope and global competitive advantage

5 Explain the role of implementation and control in marketing planning

6 Explain operational planning

7 Explain the strategies that a firm can use to enter global markets

Business planning: composing the big picture

Objective

1

Describe the steps in marketing planning

Kevin Parkin understands that planning is everything. Part of Kevin's role is to help develop a plan to take the company forward. Careful planning enables a firm to speak in a clear voice in the marketplace so that customers understand what the firm is and what it has to offer that competitors don't – especially as it decides how to create value for customers, shareholders, employees and society. We think this process is so important that we're launching into our exploration of marketing with a discussion about what planners do and the questions they need to ask to be sure they keep their companies and products on course. Then we'll come full circle and see how DavyMarkham answers these questions to maintain its advantage.

Whether a firm is a well-established industrial company like DavyMarkham or a services-based group like Hilton Hotels, planning for the future is key to prosperity. Sure, it's true that a firm can be successful even if it makes some mistakes in planning and there are times when even the best planning cannot anticipate the future accurately. It's also true that some seat-of-the-pants businesses are successful. But without good planning for the future, firms will be less successful than they could be. In the worst-case scenario, a lack of planning can be fatal for both large and small businesses. So, like a Boy Scout, it's always better to be prepared.

Business planning is an ongoing process of making decisions that guide the firm both in the short term and for the long haul. Planning identifies and builds on a firm's strengths, and it helps managers at all levels make informed decisions in a changing business environment. Planning means that an organisation develops objectives before it takes action. In large firms like Sony and Kodak that operate in many markets, planning is a complex process involving many people from different areas of the company's operations. At a small business like Antonio's Pizza Palace, however, planning is quite different. Antonio himself is chief cook, occasional dishwasher, and the sole company planner. With entrepreneurial firms like Innocent drinks, the planning process falls somewhere in between, depending on the size of the firm and the complexity of its operations.

A firm's business model is analogous to capturing the right information in the lens of your mobile phone camera, positioning the image correctly and snapping the picture you'll need to set things in motion. A business plan is a lot like that. In this chapter, we'll look at the different steps in an organisation's planning. First, we'll see how managers develop a **business plan** which includes the decisions that guide the entire organisation or its business units. Then we'll examine the entire marketing planning process and the stages in that process that lead to the development and implementation of a **marketing plan** – a document that describes the marketing environment, outlines the marketing objectives and strategies, and identifies how the strategies embedded in the plan will be implemented and controlled.

The three levels of business planning

We all know what planning is – we plan for a holiday or a Saturday night out. Some of us even plan how we're going to study and get our assignments completed on time. When businesses plan, the process is more complex. As Figure 2.1 shows, planning occurs at three levels: strategic, functional and operational.

What It Is	Strategic Planning	Functional Planning (In Marketing Department, called Marketing Planning)	Operational Planning
Who Does It	Planning done by top-level corporate management	Planning done by top functional-level management such as the firm's marketing director.	Planning done by supervisory managers
What They Do	1. Define the mission 2. Evaluate the internal and external environment 3. Set organisational or business unit objectives 4. Establish the business portfolio (if applicable) 5. Develop growth strategies	1. Perform a situation analysis 2. Set marketing objectives 3. Develop marketing strategies 4. Implement marketing strategies 5. Monitor and control marketing strategies	1. Develop action plans to implement the marketing plan 2. Use marketing metrics to monitor how the plan is working

Figure 2.1 | Levels of planning

During planning, an organisation determines its objectives and then develops courses of action to accomplish them. In larger firms, planning takes place at the strategic, functional and operational levels

- **Strategic planning** is the managerial decision process that matches the firm's resources (such as its financial assets and workforce) and capabilities (the things it is able to do well because of its expertise and experience) to its market opportunities for long-term growth. In a strategic plan, top management – usually the chief executive or managing director, chairman and other top executives – define the firm's purpose and specify what it hopes to achieve over the next five or so years. For example, a firm's strategic plan may set an objective of increasing its total revenues by 20 per cent in the next five years. For large firms such as the Walt Disney Company that have a number of self-contained divisions or strategic business units (such as the theme park, movie, television network and cruise line divisions), strategic planning occurs both at the overall corporate level (Disney headquarters planning for the whole corporation) and at the individual business unit level (at the theme park, movie studios, television networks and cruise line level). We'll discuss these two levels later in the chapter.

- The next level of planning is **functional planning** (sometimes called 'tactical planning'). This level gets its name because it is accomplished by the various functional areas of the firm, such as marketing, finance and human resources. Functional directors usually do this. The functional planning the marketing department conducts is referred to as *marketing planning*. The person in charge of such planning may have the title of Marketing Director or Marketing Manager. Marketers like Kevin Parkin might set an objective to gain 40 per cent of a particular market by introducing three distribution and service outlets during the coming year. This objective would be part of a *functional area plan*. Functional planning typically includes both a broad five-year plan to support the firm's strategic plan and a detailed annual plan for the coming year.

- Still further down the planning ladder are the first-line managers. In the marketing department, first-line managers include people such as sales managers, marketing communications managers and marketing research managers. These managers are responsible for planning at a third level called **operational planning**. This level of planning focuses on the day-to-day execution of the functional plans and includes detailed annual, semi-annual or quarterly plans. Operational plans might show exactly how many units of a product a salesperson needs to sell per month or how many television commercials the firm will place on certain channels during a season. At the operational planning level for DavyMarkham, the marketing manager may develop plans to introduce several new industrial services to specific customers, while the sales manager may develop a quarterly plan for the company's sales force. Both of these activities are forms of operational planning.

Of course, marketing managers don't just sit in their offices dreaming up plans without any concern for the rest of the organisation. Even though we've described each layer separately, *all business planning is an integrated activity*. This means that the organisation's strategic, functional and operational plans must work together for the benefit of the whole, i.e. there is a cascade effect from strategic which feeds into functional which feeds into operational. So, planners at all levels must consider good principles of accounting, the value of the company to its stockholders and the requirements for staffing and human resource management – that is, they must keep the 'big picture' in mind even as they plan for their corner of the organisation's world.

In short, the different functional- and operational-level planners within an organisation have to make sure that their plans support the organisation's overall mission and objectives and that they work well together. A marketer like Kevin Parkin can't go off and develop a successful plan for the marketing side of the firm without fully understanding

Marketing metrics

Norwich Union's marketing resource management system

The UK's biggest insurer, Norwich Union, part of Aviva, uses marketing resource management technology from Aprimo to plan and control marketing strategies, drive down costs, track results and enhance the customer experience. Historically, staff managed marketing ideas, plans and finances using myriad different methods such as spreadsheets, databases and documents. The company's acquisition of motoring organisation RAC prompted it to rethink this approach. The system establishes standardised processes and a central repository of relevant data and a full archive history of past marketing that will aid internal governance and regulatory compliance.

that what he's doing fits within the whole organisation's strategic direction and resource constraints. In the case of DavyMarkham, this means Kevin's plan must fit in with the overall strategic direction of the company. In the next sections, we'll further explore planning at each of these three levels: strategic, functional and operational.

Objective

2

Explain the strategic planning process

Strategic planning: framing the picture

Many large firms realise that relying on only one product can be risky, so they have become multiproduct companies with self-contained divisions organised around products or brands. As mentioned earlier, firms such as Disney operate several distinctly different businesses. These self-contained divisions are called **strategic business units** (SBUs) – individual units representing various areas of business within the firm that are each different enough to have their own mission, business objectives, resources, managers and competitors. As we pointed out earlier, Disney's SBUs include its theme parks, movie studios, television networks and cruise line.

In firms with many SBUs, the first step in strategic planning is for top management to establish a mission for the entire corporation. Top managers then evaluate the internal and external environment of the business and set corporate-level objectives that guide decision making within each individual SBU. In small firms that are not large enough to have separate SBUs, strategic planning simply takes place at the overall firm level. Whether or not a firm has SBUs, the process of strategic planning is basically the same. Let's look at the planning steps in a bit more detail.

Step 1: Define the mission

Theoretically, top management's first step in the strategic planning stage is to answer such questions as: What business are we in? What customers should we serve? How should we develop the firm's capabilities and focus its efforts? In many firms, the answers to questions such as these become the lead items in the organisation's strategic plan. The answers become part of a **mission statement** – a formal document that describes the organisation's overall purpose and what it hopes to achieve in terms of its customers, products and resources. For example, the mission of Mothers Against Drunk Driving (MADD) is 'to stop drunk driving, support the victims of this violent crime and prevent underage drinking'.[1]

The ideal mission statement is not too broad, too narrow, or too shortsighted. It also needs to be: market focused on customer needs and how these will be met; enduring in the face of a changing environment; motivational in the sense that mission statements have value in setting the boundaries (e.g. which new opportunities will be pursued).

A mission that is too broad will not provide adequate focus for the organisation. It doesn't do much good to claim, 'We are in the business of making high-quality products', as it's hard to find a firm that doesn't make this claim. However, a mission statement that is too narrow may inhibit managers' ability to visualise possible growth opportunities. If, for example, a firm sees itself in terms of its product only, consumer trends or technology can make that product obsolete – and the firm is left with no future. If Xerox had continued to define its mission in terms of just producing copy machines instead of providing 'document solutions', the shift to electronic documents would have left the company in the dust, the same way as Ford's Model T replaced the horse and cart. It's important to remember that the need for a clear mission statement applies to virtually any type of organisation, even those like MADD, whose objective is to serve society rather than to sell goods or services.

Step 2: Evaluate the internal and external environment

Objective

3

Discuss some of the important aspects of an organisation's internal environment and understand how factors in the external business environment influence marketing strategies and outcomes

The second step in strategic planning is to assess the firm's internal and external environments. This process is referred to as a situation analysis, *environmental analysis* or sometimes a *business review*. The analysis includes a discussion of the firm's internal environment, which can identify a firm's strengths and weaknesses, as well as the external environment in which the firm does business so it can identify opportunities and threats. By internal environment, we mean all the controllable elements inside a firm that influence how well the firm operates. Internal strengths may lie in the firm's technologies. What is the firm able to do well that other firms would find difficult to duplicate? What patents does it hold? A firm's physical facilities can be an important strength or weakness, as can its level of financial stability, its relationships with suppliers, its corporate reputation, its ability to produce consistently high-quality products and its ownership of strong brands in the marketplace.

Internal strengths and weaknesses often reside in the firm's employees – the firm's human and intellectual capital. What skills do the employees have? What kind of training have they had? Are they loyal to the firm? Do they feel a sense of ownership? Has the firm been able to attract top researchers and good decision makers? Pret A Manger has always been very focused on hiring and developing employees who reflect the 'Pret Spirit' to customers.

The external environment consists of elements outside the firm that may affect it either positively or negatively. External forces are largely uncontrollable (although the firm may be able to bring some influence to bear, e.g. by lobbying) and a key challenge for firms is to attempt to predict these. The role of the controllable internal environment is as a mechanism for a firm to be able to accommodate the uncontrollable external environment. The external environment for today's businesses is global, so managers/marketers must consider Political, Economic and competitive, Socio-cultural, Technological, Legal and Environmental trends – sometimes known as a PESTLE analysis. Unlike elements of the internal environment that management can control to a large degree, the firm can't directly control these external factors, so management must respond to them through its planning process. Also, different forces have different impacts. For example, in health-related products, legislation and political impacts are greater than in the computer industry where technology rules or in fast-moving consumer goods (fmcg), where competition is often king.

Marketing misstakes

Korean autos in the UK

In the UK, Korean cars have not enjoyed the same level of affection as their Japanese counterparts. To own a Honda or Toyota, it is viewed as being progressive and cutting-edge, whereas owning a Kia, until recently at least, was not necessarily perceived by the public in the same way. However that all changed in 2009 when the UK government launched a scrappage incentive scheme, thus offering consumers of vehicles more than nine years old a guaranteed £2000 part exchange against new purchases. While some manufacturers were sceptical, Korean sister brands Hyundai and Kia pounced on the opportunity and developed a wide range of marketing activity to cater for such customers.

Remarkably, Hyundai ended up increasing its sales through the scrappage scheme more than any other. As a result over 46,000 cars were sold, beating even Ford and placing the company in second place for the total number of cars sold that year. This temporarily provided Hyundai with a close to 5 per cent share of the UK market. However, towards the end of the scheme Hyundai struggled to maintain the momentum of sales and its UK share then plummeted to around pre-scrappage levels of 3 per cent.

With a new global head of marketing, Won-hong Cho, the vehicle manufacturer is aiming to unveil a 'modern premium' brand positioning strategy with an imminent advertisement push. However, it remains questionable whether British drivers will respond positively.

Why do you think this might be a marketing misstake?

 ## The global marketing environment

Once a marketer makes the initial decision about whether or not to go global and about what country or countries provide attractive opportunities, the company must gain a good understanding of the local conditions in the targeted country or region. As we saw earlier in this chapter, successful planning depends upon a clear understanding of the environment. In this section, we'll see how economic, competitive, technological, political and cultural factors affect marketers' global strategies.

 ## The economic environment

Objective 4

Understand the big picture of international marketing, including trade flows, market scope and global competitive advantage

Understanding the economy of a country in which a firm does business is vital to the success of marketing plans. Marketers need to understand the state of the economy from two different perspectives: the overall economic health/level of development of a country and the current stage of its business cycle.

Indicators of economic health

One way to gauge the market potential for a product is to look at a country's economic health. The most commonly used measure of economic health of a country is the **gross domestic product (GDP)**; the total value of goods and services a country produces within its borders in a year. A similar but less frequently used measure of economic health is the **gross national product (GNP)**, which measures the value of all goods and services produced by a country's individuals or organisations, whether located within the country's borders or not. Table 2.1 shows the GDP and other economic and demographic characteristics for a sample of countries. In addition to total GDP, marketers may also compare countries on the basis of per capita GDP: the total GDP divided by the number of people (population) in a country.

	Sweden	Netherlands	UK	European Union	United States	China
Total GDP	$354.7 billion	$676.9 billion	$2.17 trillion	$14.82 trillion	$14.66 trillion	$10.09 trillion
Per capita GDP	$39,100	$40,300	$34,800	$32,700	$47,200	$7600
Population below poverty line	NA	10.5%	14%	See individual member state entries	15.1%	2.8%
Inflation rate	1.3%	1.3%	3.3%	1.9%	1.6%	3.2%
Unemployment rate	8.4%	5.5%	7.8%	9.5%	9.6%	4.3%
Population	9.09 million	16.84 million	62.7 million	493.39 million	313.23 million	1.34 billion
Birth rate per 1000 population	10.18	10.23	12.29	9.83	13.83	12.29
Population aged 0–14	15.4%	17%	17.3%	15.4%	20.1%	17.6%
Population aged 15–64	64.8%	67.4%	66.2%	67.2%	66.8%	73.6%
Population aged 65 and over	19.7%	15.6%	16.5%	17.3%	13.1%	8.9%

Table 2.1 Comparisons of several countries on economic and demographic characteristics

Source: CIA World Factbook 2010, www.cia.gov/library/publications/the-world-factbook/index.html

Still, such comparisons may not tell the whole story. Per capita GDP can be deceptive because the wealth of a country may be concentrated in the hands of a few. Furthermore, the costs of the same goods and services are much lower in some global markets. For example, goods and services valued at €30,000 in say Belgium would cost only €5,100 in Uganda. Of course, GDP alone does not provide the information needed by marketers in deciding if a country's economic environment makes for an attractive market. Marketers also need to consider whether they can conduct 'business as usual' in another country. The **economic infrastructure** is the quality of a country's distribution, financial and communications systems.

Level of economic development

These are just some of the issues a marketer must think about when determining whether a country will be a good prospect. However, there are other economic conditions that marketers must understand as well, including the broader economic picture of a country, called its **level of economic development**. When marketers travel around the world to seek opportunities, it helps if they consider a country's level of economic development in order to understand the needs of people who live there and the infrastructural conditions with which they must contend. Economists look past simple facts such as growth in GDP to decide this; they also look at what steps are being taken to reduce poverty, inequality and unemployment. Economists describe the following three basic levels of development.

A country at the lowest stage of economic development is a **less developed country (LDC)**. In most cases, its economic base is agricultural. Many nations in Africa and South America are considered LDCs. A country's **standard of living** is an indicator of the average quality and quantity of goods and services a country consumes. In these

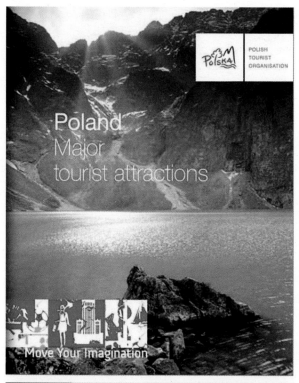

Photo 2.1	Many developing countries rely heavily on tourism to build their economies

Source: Courtesy of Polish National Tourist Office

countries, the standard of living is low, as are literacy levels. Opportunities to sell many products, especially luxury items such as diamonds and caviar, are minimal because most people don't have enough disposable income. They grow what they need and barter for the rest. These countries are attractive markets for inexpensive items. They may also export important raw materials such as minerals or rubber to industrial nations.

When an economy shifts its emphasis from agriculture to industry, standards of living, education and the use of technology rise. These are **developing countries**, and in such markets there may be a viable middle class, often largely composed of entrepreneurs working hard to run successful small businesses. Because over three-quarters of the world's population lives in developing countries, the number of potential customers and the presence of a skilled labour force attracts many firms to these areas. Eastern Europe, with its more than 300 million consumers, is an important region that includes a number of developing countries. Similarly, the countries of Latin America are emerging from decades of state control, and their economies are opening to foreign business.[2] Finally, the Pacific Rim countries of China, South Korea, Malaysia, Indonesia, Thailand, Singapore and Hong Kong are nicknamed the 'Tigers of Asia' because of their tremendous economic growth. For example, in China, consumer spending on products such as mobile phones is encouraging economic growth. Nokia estimates that more than 70 per cent of Beijing residents and more than 60 per cent of Shanghai residents have mobile phone subscriptions.[3]

A **developed country** boasts sophisticated marketing systems, strong private enterprise, and market potential for many goods and services. Such countries are economically advanced, and they offer a wide range of opportunities for international marketers. The United Kingdom, France and Germany are among the most economically developed countries in the EU and the world.

The business cycle

The overall pattern of changes or fluctuations of an economy is called the **business cycle**. All economies go through cycles of prosperity (high levels of demand, employment and income), recession (falling demand, employment and income) and recovery (gradual improvement in production, lowering unemployment and increasing income). A severe recession is a depression, a period in which prices fall but there is little demand because few people have money to spend and many are out of work. Inflation occurs when prices and the cost of living rise while money loses its purchasing power because the cost of goods escalates. During inflationary periods, incomes may increase, but real income – what your currency will buy – decreases because goods and services cost more.

The business cycle is especially important to marketers because of its effect on consumer buying behaviour. During times of prosperity, consumers buy more goods and services. Marketers are busy trying to grow their business, maintain inventory levels and develop new

Marketing in recession

The rise and fall of Woolworths

During 2008, faced with severe competition, the effects of the credit crunch and after nearly a century of British high street presence, the once famous Woolworths retailer entered administration and closed all of its 807 stores. This resulted in 27,000 job losses. A few months later it was announced that Shop Direct Group had purchased the brand to re-launch it as an internet/catalogue-based company (providing an option of collecting items ordered at over 3,500 local pick-up points across the UK).

Discuss, debate, disagree

1   Discuss the future of Woolworths.

2   How can the firm increase sales revenue?

Source: Based on www.guardian.co.uk/business/2008/nov/19/woolworths-retail-department-stores

---

products to meet the demands of customers with the willingness to spend. During periods of recession, consumers simply buy less. The challenge to most marketers is to maintain their firm's level of sales by convincing customers who are buying to select their firm's product over the competitors' offerings. Of course, even recessions aren't bad for all businesses. Although it may be harder to sell luxury items, firms that make basic necessities are not likely to suffer significant losses. It is important to note that when firms assess the economic environment, they evaluate all factors that influence consumer and business buying patterns, including the amount of confidence people have in the health of the economy. This 'crystal ball' must be a global one because events in one country can affect the economic health of other countries.

The competitive environment

A second important element of a firm's external environment is the competitive environment. For all products, firms must keep abreast of what the competition is doing so they can develop new product features, new pricing schedules, or new advertising to maintain or gain market share.

Analysing the market and the competition

Before a firm can begin to develop strategies that will create a competitive advantage in the marketplace, it has to know who its competitors are and what they're doing. Marketing managers analyse competitors according to their strengths and weaknesses, monitor their marketing strategies and try to predict their moves. An increasing number of firms around the globe engage in **competitive intelligence (CI)** activities, the process of gathering and analysing publicly available information about rivals. Most of the information that companies need to know about their competitors is available from rather mundane sources, including the news media, the internet and publicly available governmental documents. Successful CI implies that a firm learns about a competitor's new products, its manufacturing, or the management styles of its executives. Then the firm uses this information to develop superior marketing strategies.

Photo 2.2	Rapidly developing countries like China provide great opportunities for European retailers such as Tesco to expand *Source*: Corbis/EPA/ANDY RAIN

Competition in the micro-environment

To be successful in a competitive marketplace, marketers must have a clear understanding of exactly who their competition is. Competition in the micro-environment means the product alternatives from which members of a target market may choose. We can think of these choices at three different levels. At a broad level, many marketers compete for consumers' **disposable income** – the amount of money people have left after paying for necessities such as housing, utilities, food and clothing. Few consumers are wealthy enough to buy anything and everything, so each of us is constantly faced with choices: do we plough 'leftover' money into a new mobile phone, donate it to charity, or turn over a new leaf and lose those extra pounds by investing in a healthy lifestyle? Thus, the first part of understanding who the competition is means understanding all the alternatives that consumers consider for their discretionary income – not just the brands against which we directly compete within a product category.

A second type of choice is **product competition**, in which competitors offering different products attempt to satisfy the same consumers' needs and wants. So, for example, if a couch potato decides to use some of his discretionary income to get fit, he may join a health club or buy equipment/machinery in order to exercise at home. Starbucks is successfully competing against tea in England. In a country known as much for its afternoon tea as for Manchester United, there are already close to 500 Starbucks outlets (more in London than New York), as well as fast-growing local chains such as Café Nero and Coffee Republic. As a consequence, tea sales in the United Kingdom fell 12 per cent from 2000 to 2005.[4]

Marketing ethics and sustainability

Wal-Mart gets smart

Giant retailers such as Wal-Mart and Tesco are increasingly criticised for forcing scores of independent competitors to go out of business. But Wal-Mart has begun a programme to help its smaller rivals. The US-based programme offers hardware shops, dress shops and bakeries near its new urban shops financial grants, training on how to survive with Wal-Mart in town, and even free advertising in Wal-Mart shops. Of course, Wal-Mart hopes to benefit from the programme in cities like Los Angeles and New York where its plan to build new shops in urban neighbourhoods has met high resistance.[5]

Debate, discuss, disagree

1 What do you think about Wal-Mart's motives?

2 How would such a strategy work in the UK (where Wal-Mart controls ASDA) and Scandinavia?

The third type of choice is **brand competition**, in which competitors offering similar goods or services fight for a share of the consumer's wallet. So, if our flabby friend decides to join a gym, he still must choose among competitors within this industry. He may forgo the exercise thing altogether and count on a Greek seafood diet to work its magic.

Competition in the macro-environment

When we talk about examining competition in the macro-environment, we mean that marketers need to understand the big picture, that is, the overall structure of their industry. This structure can range from one firm having total control to numerous firms that compete on an even playing field. Four structures describe differing amounts of competition. Let's review each structure, beginning with total control by one organisation.

1. It's not just a board game, but a **monopoly** exists when one seller controls a market. Because the seller is the only player in town, it feels little pressure to keep prices low or to produce quality goods or services. In the old days, the state-run postal service had a monopoly on the delivery of documents. Nowadays, the monopoly status has been eroded, as postal services must now compete with couriers such as FedEx and DHL, as well as electronic mail for a share of the market.

2. In an **oligopoly** there is a relatively small number of sellers, each holding substantial market share in a market consisting of many buyers. Because there are few sellers, each is very conscious of the others' actions. Oligopolies most often exist in industries requiring substantial investment in equipment or technology to produce a product. This means that only a few competitors have the resources to enter. The airline industry is an oligopoly. It is pretty hard for an entrepreneur with little start-up cash to be successful entering the airline industry. It's left to billionaires like Richard Branson who have the resources to launch a new airline like Virgin Atlantic.

3. In a state of *monopolistic competition*, there are many sellers who compete for buyers in a market. Each firm, however, offers a slightly different product, and each has only a small share of the market. For example, many sports shoe manufacturers, like Nike, Reebok and Adidas, vigorously compete with one another to offer consumers some unique benefit.

4. Finally, *perfect competition* exists when there are many small sellers, each offering basically the same good or service. In such industries, no single firm has a significant impact on quality, price or supply. Although true conditions of perfect competition are rare, agricultural markets in which there are many individual farmers each offering the same produce come the closest. Even in the case of food commodities, there are opportunities for marketers to distinguish their offerings on quality, service and delivery.

 ## The technological environment

Firms today see technology as an investment they can't afford not to make: it provides firms with important competitive advantages. Many technological developments profoundly affect marketing activities. Free phone numbers, easy computer access to customer databases and, of course, the web have made it possible for people to buy almost anything they want without ever leaving their homes. Distribution has also improved because of automated stock control as a direct result of such advancements.

Changes in technology can dramatically transform an industry. Successful marketers continuously scan the external business environment in search of ideas and trends to spark their own research efforts. They also monitor ongoing research projects in government and private organisations. When inventors feel they have come across something exciting, they usually want to protect their exclusive right to produce and sell the invention by applying for a patent. A **patent** is a legal document issued from a country's patent office that gives inventors or individuals and firms the exclusive rights to produce and sell a particular invention in a country (or countries). Marketers monitor government patent applications to discover innovative products they can purchase from the inventor.

 ## The political and legal environment

The political and legal environment refers to the local, state, national and global laws and regulations that affect businesses. Legal and regulatory controls can be prime motivators for many business decisions. While firms that choose to remain at home have to worry about only local regulations, global marketers must understand more complex political issues that can affect how they do business and their potential for success.

Table 2.2 outlines some of the major EU legislation that protects and serves the rights of consumers within the European Union member states. Several legal institutions also exist within the European Union that monitor business activity and enforce how laws are practised throughout the EU (see Table 2.3).

Competition law

Four main policies of the antitrust law include:

Cartels, or control of collusion in other anti-competitive practices which has an effect on the EU. This is covered under Article 101 of the Treaty on Functioning of the European Community (TFEU).

Monopolies, or preventing the abuse of firms' dominant market positions. This is governed by Article 102 of the TFEU.

Mergers, control of proposed mergers, acquisitions and joint ventures involving companies which have a certain, defined amount of turnover. This is governed by the Council Regulation 139/2004 of the EC Treaty (the EC Merger Regulation).

State aid, control of direct and indirect aid given by EU member states to companies. Covered under Article 107 of the TFEU.

Table 2.2 Areas of EU activities concerning businesses

Consumers

The European policy in favour of consumers aims to safeguard the health, safety and interests of consumers, as set out in Articles 153 and 95 of the Treaty establishing the European Community, by promoting openness, fairness and transparency in the internal market.

Culture

The Maastricht Treaty (1993) enabled the European Union, which is historically geared towards the economy and trade, to take action in the field of culture in order to safeguard, disseminate and develop culture in Europe. However, the EU's role is limited to promoting cooperation between the cultural operators of the different member states or to complementing their activities in order to contribute to the flowering of the cultures of the member states, while respecting their national and regional diversity, with a view to highlighting the shared cultural heritage. With this aim in mind, the EU implements measures in support of cultural initiatives such as the Culture Programme and the European Capital of Culture initiative.

Employment and social policy

In the Treaty of Rome, social and employment policy was practically neglected. In fact, most of the provisions in this field related to the creation of freedom of movement for workers and freedom of establishment for the purpose of the common market. In contrast, the Treaty of Amsterdam attached importance to social policy in the fight against all types of discrimination, and the policy for the promotion of employment finally moved to the top of the agenda, becoming a 'matter of common interest'. Given the need for a Europe capable of sustainable economic growth accompanied by a quantitative and qualitative improvement in employment and greater social cohesion, the interlinking of employment, social affairs and equal opportunities is evident today. In this respect, the European Union provides major impetus for the convergence of Community and national policies through the 'open coordination method'.

Enterprise

Under Article 157 of the Treaty establishing the European Community, the European Union has set itself the goal of creating the best possible conditions for competitiveness.

Maintaining competitiveness is a constant challenge. This is why the EU aims to encourage an environment favourable to initiative, to the development of businesses, to industrial cooperation and to improving the exploitation of the industrial potential of innovation, research and technological development policies. These policies are of vital importance in the context of global competition.

Environment

Since the early 1970s Europe has been firmly committed to the environment: protection of air and water quality, conservation of resources and protection of biodiversity, waste management and control of activities which have an adverse environmental impact are just some of the areas in which the EU is active, at both member state level and internationally. Whether through corrective measures relating to specific environmental problems or cross-cutting measures integrated within other policy areas, European environment policy, based on Article 174 of the Treaty establishing the European Community, aims to ensure the sustainable development of the European model of society.

Food safety

The objective of the European Union's food safety policy is to protect consumer health and interests while guaranteeing the smooth operation of the single market. In order to achieve this objective, the EU ensures that control standards are established and adhered to as regards food and food product hygiene, animal health and welfare, plant health and preventing the risk of contamination from external substances. It also lays down rules on appropriate labelling for these foodstuffs and food products.

This policy underwent reform in the early 2000s, in line with the approach 'From the Farm to the Fork', thereby guaranteeing a high level of safety for foodstuffs and food products marketed within the EU, at all stages of the production and distribution chains. This approach involves both food products produced within the European Union and those imported from third countries.

Product labelling and packaging

The objective of foodstuff labelling is to guarantee that consumers have access to complete information on the content and composition of products, in order to protect their health and their interests. Other information may provide details on a particular aspect of the product, such as its origin or production method. Some foodstuffs, such as genetically modified organisms, allergenic foods, foods intended for infants or even various beverages, are also subject to specific regulations.

Labelling of certain non-food products must also contain particular information, in order to guarantee their safe use and allow consumers to exercise real choice. In addition, the packaging of foodstuffs must adhere to production criteria in order to avoid contaminating food products.

Table 2.2 Areas of EU activities concerning businesses (*continued*)

Fight against fraud

Protecting the financial interests of the European Community is a priority for the European institutions. It is estimated that nearly a billion euros out of an annual budget of more than €100 billion is misappropriated. The European Union combats fraud with a series of regulations to fight currency counterfeiting, violations of intellectual property rights and corruption both in Europe and internationally. The legal basis for the fight against fraud is Article 280 of the Treaty establishing the European Community.

Taxation

Tax policy in the European Union consists of two components: direct taxation, which remains the sole responsibility of member states, and indirect taxation, which affects free movement of goods and the freedom to provide services. With regard to direct taxation, member states have taken measures to prevent tax avoidance and double taxation. Tax policy ensures that competition between member states on the internal market is not distorted by differences in indirect taxation rates and systems. Measures have also been adopted to prevent the adverse effects of tax competition if companies transfer money between European Union member states.

Table 2.2   Areas of EU activities concerning businesses (*continued*)

Sources: Competition law summary, http://en.wikipedia.org/wiki/European_Community_competition_law; all other summaries, http://europa.eu/index_en.htm

European Parliament

The European Parliament is the only directly elected body of the European Union. The 785 members of the European Parliament are there to represent you, the citizen. They are elected once every five years by voters right across the 27 member states of the European Union on behalf of its 492 million citizens.

Each revision of the Treaties has seen an increase in the power of the European Parliament in relation to the other institutions. Today the European Parliament is firmly established as a co-legislator, has budgetary powers and exercises democratic controls over all the European institutions.

Council of the EU

The acts of the Council can take the form of regulations, directives, decisions, common actions or common positions, recommendations or opinions. The Council can also adopt conclusions, declarations or resolutions.

European Commission

The European Commission represents and upholds the interests of Europe as a whole. It is independent of national governments. It drafts proposals for new European laws, which it presents to the European Parliament and the Council. It manages the day-to-day business of implementing EU policies and spending EU funds. The Commission also keeps an eye out to see that everyone abides by the European treaties and laws. It can act against rule breakers, taking them to the Court of Justice if necessary.

The Court of Justice

The job of the Court of Justice is to make sure that EU law is interpreted and applied in the same way in all EU countries, thereby ensuring that the law is equal for everyone. It ensures, for example, that national courts do not give different rulings on the same issue. The Court also makes sure that EU member states and institutions do what the law requires them to do.

The European Economic and Social Committee

The 344 members of the European Economic and Social Committee represent a wide range of interests: from employers to trade unionists, from consumers to ecologists. The Committee is an advisory body which must give its opinion on proposed EU decisions about employment, social spending, vocational training, etc.

The European Central Bank

Based in Frankfurt, the Central Bank is responsible for managing the euro – for example, by setting interest rates. Its prime concern is ensuring price stability so that the European economy is not damaged by inflation. The Bank takes its decisions independently of governments and other bodies.

Table 2.3   EU institutions (relevant for businesses)

Sources: EU Parliament, www.europarl.europa.eu/parliament/public/staticdisplay.do?language=en&id=146; council of the EU, www.consilium.europa.eu/showpage.asp?lang=en; rest, http://europa.eu/abc/panorama/howorganised/index_en.htm#commission

Sometimes firms learn the hard way that government watchdog activities can put a stop to their marketing plans. Warner-Lambert, the manufacturer of Listerine antiseptic, went on US television in the 1970s with advertising claims that its germ-killing properties help reduce the incidence and severity of the common cold. Unfortunately, the firm lacked data to substantiate the claim. The company stopped making this claim in its advertising only after it was forced to do so. However, Warner-Lambert learned from its mistake, as a few years later the company funded medical research that resulted in new claims based on scientific evidence that Listerine was effective against such gum and dental problems like plaque and gingivitis. These claims continue to be a cornerstone of Listerine's advertising message to this day.

Political constraints on trade

Global firms know that political actions taken by a government can drastically affect the business operations of outsiders. At the extreme, of course, it goes without saying that when two countries go to war, the business environment changes dramatically. Often people overseas dislike the actions of another country. This was the case when the United Kingdom sent troops to Iraq. Short of war, a country may impose economic sanctions that prohibit trade with another country so access to some markets may be cut off. In some situations, the government may decide to take over the operations of foreign companies doing business within its borders. It is called **nationalisation** when the domestic government reimburses a foreign company (often not for the full value) for its assets after taking it over. It is called **expropriation** when a domestic government seizes a foreign company's assets. To keep track of the level of political stability or instability in foreign countries, firms often engage in formal or informal analyses of the potential political risk in various countries.

Regulatory constraints on trade

Governments and economic communities impose numerous regulations about what products should be made of, how they should be made, and what can be said about them. For example, sometimes a company has no choice but to alter product content to comply with local laws. Heinz sauce tastes quite different in Europe simply because of different legal restrictions on preservatives and colour additives.[6]

Other regulations are more focused on ensuring that the host country gets a piece of the action. **Local content rules** are a form of protectionism stipulating that a certain proportion of a product must consist of components supplied by industries in the host country or economic community. For example, under NAFTA (North American Free Trade Agreement) rules, cars built by Mercedes-Benz in the US must have 62.5 per cent of their components made in North America to be able to enter Mexico and Canada duty free.[7] These types of rules also help to explain why Japanese car producers such as Toyota and Nissan have heightened their local presence by opening manufacturing plants within the EU

 ## The socio-cultural environment

Another element of a firm's external environment is the socio-cultural environment. This term refers to the characteristics of the society, the people who live in that society, and the culture that reflects the values and beliefs of the society. Whether at home or in global markets, marketers need to understand and adapt to the customs, characteristics and practices of its citizens. Basic beliefs about such cultural priorities as the role of family or proper relations between the sexes affect people's responses to products and promotional messages in any market.

Disney learned the hard way about the importance of being sensitive to local cultures after it opened the Disneyland Resort Paris in 1992 (then EuroDisney). The company was criticised for creating an entertainment venue that re-created its American locations without catering to local customs. More recently, the company applied the lessons it learned in cultural sensitivity to its new Hong Kong Disneyland. Executives decided to shift the angle of the front gate by 12 degrees after consulting a *feng shui* specialist, who said the change would ensure prosperity for the park. Disney also put a bend in the walkway from the train station to the gate, to make sure the flow of positive energy, or *chi*, did not slip past the entrance and out to the China Sea. Cash registers are close to corners or along walls to increase prosperity. And, since the Chinese consider the number four to be bad luck, you won't find any fourth-floor buttons in hotel lifts.[8] Disney eventually discovered that understanding consumer attitudes, beliefs and ways of doing things in different parts of the world is especially important to firms when developing a marketing strategy.

Demographics

The first step towards understanding the characteristics of a society is to look at its **demographics**. These are statistics that measure observable aspects of a population, such as size, age, gender, ethnic group, income, education, occupation and family structure. Demographic studies can be of great value to marketers in helping to predict the size of markets for many products.

Values

More than 8.2 million women in 50 countries read versions of *Cosmopolitan* in 28 different languages. However, because of local norms about modesty, some women have to hide the magazine from their husbands. Adapting the *Cosmo* credo of a 'Fun, Fearless Female' in some cultures may be tricky. Different cultures emphasise varying belief systems that define what it means to be female, feminine, appealing, and what is considered appropriate to see in print on these matters. For example, whilst in India and China *Cosmo* may have articles relating to sex replaced with stories about youthful dedication, there isn't much of this material in the Swedish edition either – because the culture is so open about this topic that it doesn't grab readers' attention.[9]

As this example shows, every society has a set of **cultural values**, or deeply held beliefs about right and wrong ways to live, that it imparts to its members.[10] Those beliefs influence virtually every aspect of our lives, even the way we mark the time we live them. For example, in Hong Kong time is a core value. Indeed, time is money, and business meetings tend to be precise and start promptly. In other countries, like Latin America, this is not at all the case. If you schedule a business meeting at 10 a.m. you can be assured most people will not arrive until around 10.30 or later.

Differences in values often explain why marketing efforts that are a big hit in one country can flop in another. For example, Italian housewives spend about five times as many hours per week as do their US counterparts on household chores. This dedication should make them perfect customers for cleaning products, but when Unilever launched an all-purpose spray cleaner about six years ago, the product failed. The reason is that the company did not realise that the benefit of labour-saving convenience is a huge turnoff to Italian women, who want products that are tough cleaners, not timesavers. As a result, Unilever had to make big adjustments in order to clean up in the Italian market, including making the bottles 50 per cent bigger because Italians clean so frequently.[11]

Marketing ethics and sustainability

Seeing the investor value in being green

Jamestown, an acquisition and management firm based in Cologne Germany and Atlanta, has invested $12 billion in commercial properties in the United States since 1983 through private equity funds for German investors. Matt M. Bronfman, the company's managing director and chief operations officer, said Jamestown's executives believed that real estate holdings, new and existing, would be increasingly valued by their sustainability and environmental impact. 'We come at things from a bit of a European perspective, and Europe is far ahead of the United States in the environmental movement', Mr. Bronfman said. Sustainability 'will become a key factor to the point where, if you haven't taken environmental measures you will have trouble', he added. The company said it would spend $3 million to $10 million to retrofit all of its properties. 'It depends on who buys the investment at the end', Mr. Phillips, Jamestown's creative director, said. 'An insurance company or pension fund typically wants to buy buildings that offer the most modern technology. Green technology is considered the most progressive.' He continued, 'the advantages of being green might be less about a premium, and more about offering a wider pool of buyers'.

Source: From *The New York Times,* 3 March, Business/Financial Desk, p. 6, Alison Gregor. © 2010 The New York Times. All rights reserved. Used by permission and protected by the Copyright Laws in the United States. The printing, copyright, redistribution, or retransmission of this Content without express written permission is prohibited.

Discuss, debate, disagree

1   What are the advantages and disadvantages of being 'green'?

2   Discuss the costs involved for implementing such 'green' concepts.

Photo 2.3   The Body Shop was one of the first beauty companies to recognise sustainability, fair trade and organic products which is in-line with environmental trends
Source: Getty Images/Bennett Raglin 2011

One important dimension on which cultures differ is their emphasis on collectivism versus individualism. In **collectivist cultures**, such as those found in Turkey, Greece and Portugal, people tend to subordinate their personal goals to those of a stable community. In contrast, consumers in **individualist cultures**, such as Great Britain and the Netherlands, tend to attach more importance to personal goals, and people are more likely to change membership when the demands of the group become too costly.[12] This difference can be important to marketers who are appealing to one extreme or the other. For example, try selling a garment that is 'sure to stand out' to consumers who would much prefer to 'fit in'.

Norms and customs

Values are general ideas about good and bad behaviour. From these values flow **norms**, or specific rules dictating what is right or wrong, acceptable or unacceptable. Some specific types of norms include the following:[13]

- A **custom** is a norm handed down from the past that controls basic behaviour, such as the division of labour in a household.

- **Mores** are customs with a strong moral overtone. Mores often involve a taboo, or forbidden behaviour, such as incest or cannibalism. Violation of mores often meets with strong punishment from other members of a society.

- **Conventions** are norms regarding the conduct of everyday life. These rules deal with the subtleties of consumer behaviour, including the 'correct' way to furnish one's house, wear one's clothes, host a dinner party, and so on.

All three types of norms may determine what behaviour is appropriate in different countries. Mores may tell us what kind of food it is permissible to eat. For example, whilst Hindus would turn down a steak, Muslims avoid pork products. Local customs also dictate the appropriate hour at which a meal should be served. In some European countries, and in the Middle East, dinner tends not to be served until around 9 p.m. or later. People in such countries are amused by British visitors whose stomachs are rumbling around 7 p.m. Conventions tell us how to eat the meal, including such details as the utensils, table etiquette and even the appropriate clothes to wear for dining. Conflicting customs can be a problem when Western marketers try to conduct business in other countries where executives have different ideas about what is proper or expected. These difficulties even include body language. People in Latin countries tend to stand much closer to each other than do Anglo-Saxons, and are often insulted if their counterpart tries to stand further away. Understanding such customs is important as these may be the difference between a firm's success and failure on the global stage.

Language

The language barrier is one obvious problem confronting marketers who wish to break into foreign markets. Travellers abroad commonly encounter signs in poor, yet often humorous English – such as a note to guests at a Tokyo hotel saying, 'You are invited to take advantage of the chambermaid', a notice at a hotel in Acapulco reassuring people that 'The manager has personally passed all the water served here', or a dry cleaner in Majorca who urged passing customers to 'drop your pants here for best results'.

These barriers are not just potentially embarrassing; they can affect product labelling and usage instructions, advertising and personal selling. It's vital for marketers to work with local people who understand the subtleties of language so as to avoid the confusion that may result. For example, the meaning of a brand name, one of the most important signals a marketer can send about the character and quality of a product, can get mangled as it travels around the world. Local product names often raise eyebrows of visitors who may be surprised to stumble on a Japanese coffee creamer called Creap, a Spanish bread named Bimbo, or even a Scandinavian product that unfreezes car locks called Super Piss.[14]

Ethnocentrism

Even if a firm succeeds in getting its products to a foreign market, there's no guarantee that local consumers will be interested. Sometimes a willingness to try products made elsewhere comes slowly. In marketing, the tendency to prefer products or people of one's own culture over those from other countries is called **ethnocentrism**. For example, the French tend to have a strong preference for their own cuisine, and they evaluate food products from other countries critically. Despite this, the upscale British department store Marks & Spencer had moderate success in France selling English-style sandwiches like egg and watercress on wholemeal bread. For now, it is important for you to be aware that opportunities and threats can come from any part of the external environment. On the one hand, trends or currently unserved customer needs may provide opportunities for growth. On the other hand, if changing customer needs or buying patterns mean customers are turning away from a firm's products, it's a signal of possible danger or threats down the road.

What is the outcome of an analysis of a firm's internal and external environments? Managers often synthesise the results of a situation analysis into a format called a **SWOT analysis**. A SWOT analysis allows managers to focus clearly on the meaningful strengths (S) and weaknesses (W) in the firm's internal environment and opportunities (O) and threats (T) coming from outside the firm (the external environment). A SWOT analysis enables a firm to develop strategies that make use of what the firm does best in seizing opportunities for growth, while at the same time avoiding external threats that might hurt the firm's sales and profits. Table 2.4 shows an example of a partial SWOT analysis for McDonald's. The idea is to decide on how to match strengths to opportunities or to convert weaknesses to strengths or threats to opportunities.

Table 2.4 SWOT analysis for McDonald's

Strengths	• World-class research and product development • Global franchise system that is second to none • Strong cash position • Consistency of product and service quality around the globe
Weaknesses	• Until recently, slow to react to consumer trends and preferences
Opportunities	• Changing consumer tastes and dining preferences signal opportunities to remake some of the locations as more upmarket • Reconnecting with Baby Boomers and Gen X while cultivating Gen Y and younger provides opportunity for product innovation and more flexibility by market area • Rising cost of petrol means more people want to eat closer to home
Threats	• The general degeneration of the image of Americans globally, especially in Europe may affect sales • Strongly negative PR surrounding unhealthy eating has tarnished the brand • Burger King has emerged as an edgy innovator, especially with the younger crowd

Source: Compilation of research by the authors

Internationalisation

Visa Europe

One of the largest partners and sponsors of the 2012 London Olympics Games is the Visa Credit Card Company. Visa Europe signed a multi-million pound deal with News International (NI) for the publisher's titles to become the first official sponsor of the British Olympic team. The company also spends an enormous amount on its advertising campaigns, featuring five-time gold medallist Sir Steve Redgrave and Paralympics veteran Dame Tanni Grey-Thompson and other well-known stars including Jessica Ennis for their TV commercials, press and outdoor advertisements.

If you feel impressed by the company's generous sponsorship and advertisement campaigns for the London Olympic Games, then you would be even more impressed by its 21 years of sponsorship history associated with the Olympic Games (staged all over the world). Moreover, Visa not only sponsors big events, but also local events, and even plans for its staff to volunteer to work at local schools and help local students with mathematics and other subjects. All of these activities not only enhance the internal value for employees, but also improve the company's international image.

Discuss, debate, disagree

1   What are the key environmental factors that influence Visa Europe's marketing?

2   What advantages are associated with Visa Europe's localisation strategy?

Step 3: Set organisational or SBU objectives

After constructing a mission statement, top management translates that mission statement into organisational or SBU objectives. These goals are derived from the mission statement and broadly identify what the firm hopes to accomplish within the general time frame of its long-range business plan. If the firm is big enough to have separate SBUs, each SBU will have its own objectives relevant to its operations. Here we need to link our actions on the marketing mix with how that translates into securing more competitive advantage.

To be effective, objectives need to be SMART, *Specific*, *Measurable* (so firms can tell whether they've met them or not). To ensure measurability, objectives are often stated in numerical terms. For example, a firm might have as an objective a 10 per cent increase in profitability. It could reach this objective by increasing productivity, by reducing costs or by selling off an unprofitable division. Or it might meet this 10 per cent objective by developing new products, investing in new technologies, or entering a new market. They also need to be *Attainable*. Attainability is especially important – firms that establish 'pie in the sky' objectives can't realistically obtain them, which can create frustration for their employees (who work hard but get no satisfaction of accomplishment) and other stakeholders in the firm, such as sales representatives and shareholders who are affected when the firm doesn't meet its objectives. Objectives also need to be *Relevant* to the company's objective and may relate to revenue and sales, profitability, the firm's standing in the market, return on investment, productivity, product development, customer relations and satisfaction, and social responsibility. Finally, objectives are best if they are *Time* bound, for example to increase sales by 10 per cent over a one-year period.

For many years, Procter & Gamble (P&G) had an objective of having a number one brand in every product category in which it competed. This objective was specific and clearly it was attainable, since P&G could boast of such market leaders as Crest in the toothpaste category, Pampers for nappies, and Head & Shoulders – shampoo. It was also measurable in terms of the share of market of P&G's products versus those sold by competitors. However, in the long run such an objective is very difficult to sustain because of competitive activity and ever-changing consumer tastes. Sure enough, over time, some P&G brands continued to hold a respectable market share, but they dropped from the number one position. Should P&G not sell in a product category simply because its brand is not number one? Management realised the answer to this question was clearly 'no', and the objective moved from category leadership into one focused on profitability for each brand.

 ## Step 4: Establish the business portfolio

For companies with several different SBUs, strategic planning includes making decisions about how best to allocate resources across these businesses to ensure growth for the whole organisation. As Figure 2.2 illustrates, each SBU has its own focus within the firm's overall strategic plan, and each has its own target market and strategies for reaching its objectives. Just like an independent business, each SBU is a separate *profit centre* within the larger corporation – that is, each SBU within the firm is responsible for its own costs, revenues and profits.

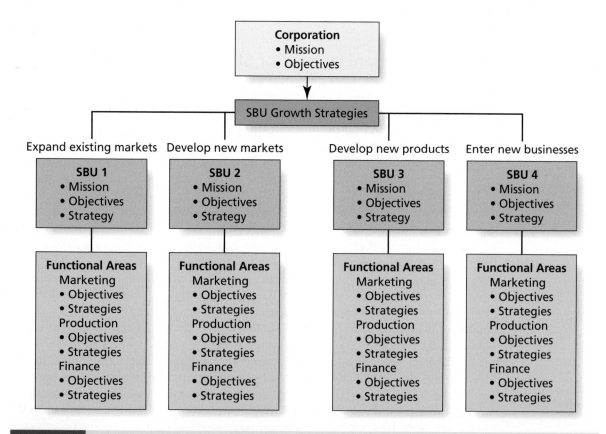

Figure 2.2	Role of strategic business units (SBUs)

Very large corporations are normally divided into self-contained divisions, or SBUs. SBUs represent different major areas of the overall firm's business. For example, General Electric has a jet engine division, a lighting division, an appliance division and numerous other divisions. At GE, as with most corporations, each SBU operates as an independent business with its own mission and objectives – and its own marketing strategy

Marketing metrics

Who uses metrics most?

A survey of leading marketing firms in five countries (United States, United Kingdom, France, Germany and Japan) found that market share is the metric that managers are most likely to report to the company's board of directors. This is because it's the most useful single metric to signal brand strength and financial and competitive performance. Other commonly used metrics include the following:

- Perceived product/service quality;
- Customer loyalty/retention;
- Customer/segment profitability;
- Relative price.

Across the five countries, German companies are the heaviest users of metrics and Japanese firms the lightest. Of the companies surveyed, 97 per cent of German firms said they reported their market share to their boards compared with 79 per cent of American firms and only 57 per cent of Japanese firms. Overall, firms that do business in several countries and those that have above-average marketing budgets are more likely to rely on metrics.[15]

Just as the collection of different stocks an investor owns is called a portfolio, the range of different businesses that a large firm operates is called its **business portfolio**. These different businesses usually represent very different product lines, each of which operates with its own budget and management. Having a diversified business portfolio reduces the firm's dependence on one product line or one group of customers. For example, if travel suffers and Disney has a bad year in theme park attendance and cruises, its managers hope that the sales will be made up by stay-at-homers who go to Disney movies and watch Disney's television networks.

Portfolio analysis is a tool management used to assess the potential of a firm's businesses portfolio. It helps management decide which of its current SBUs should receive more – or less – of the firm's resources, and which of its SBUs are most consistent with the firm's overall mission. Several models are available to assist management in the portfolio analysis process. Let's examine one popular model that the Boston Consulting Group (BCG) developed: the **BCG growth–market share matrix**. The BCG model focuses on determining the potential of a firm's existing successful SBUs to generate cash that the firm can then use to invest in other businesses. In the BCG matrix, as Figure 2.3 shows, the vertical axis represents the attractiveness of the market, the *market growth rate*. Even though the figure shows 'high' and 'low' as measurements, marketers might ask whether the total market for the SBU's products is growing 10, 50, 100 or 200 per cent annually.

The horizontal axis in Figure 2.3 shows the SBU's current strength in the market through its *relative market share*. Here, marketers might ask whether the SBU's share is 5, 25 or perhaps 75 per cent of the current market. Combining the two axes creates four quadrants representing four different types of SBUs. Each quadrant of the BCG grid uses a symbol to designate business units that fall within a certain range for market growth rate and market share. Let's take a closer look at each cell in the grid:

- **Stars** are SBUs with products that have a dominant market share in high-growth markets. Because the SBU has a dominant share of the market, stars generate large revenues, but they also require large amounts of funding to keep up with production and promotion demands. Because the market has a large growth potential, managers design strategies to maximise market share in the face of increasing competition. The firm aims at getting the largest share of loyal customers so that the SBU will generate profits that can then be put into other parts of the company. For example, in recent

Figure 2.3	BCG growth – market share matrix
	The Boston Consulting Group's (BCG) growth–market share matrix is one way a firm can examine its portfolio of different products or SBUs. By categorising SBUs as stars, cash cows, question marks, or dogs, the matrix helps managers make decisions about how the firm should grow

years Disney has viewed its movie brand for grown-ups, Touchstone Studios, as a star. Its strategy of investing in expanding that brand is based on the huge market potential of adult cinemagoers.

- **Cash cows** have a dominant market share in a low-growth potential market. Because there's not much opportunity for new companies, competitors don't often enter the market. At the same time, the SBU is well established and enjoys a high market share that the firm can sustain with minimal funding. Firms usually milk cash cows of their profits to fund the growth of other SBUs. Of course, if the firm's objective is to increase revenues, having too many cash cows with little or no growth potential can become a liability. For Disney, its Disney Pictures unit, which focuses on family films and animated features, fits into the cash cow category. In fact, Disney periodically recycles even its oldest animated films such as *Snow White* back into the cinemas to delight another generation of fans.

- **Question marks** – sometimes called *problem children* – are SBUs with low market shares in fast-growth markets. When a business unit is a question mark, it suggests that the firm has failed to compete successfully. Perhaps the SBU's products offer fewer benefits than competing products. Or maybe its prices are too high, its distributors are ineffective, or its advertising is too weak. The firm could pump more money into marketing the product and hope that market share will improve. But the firm may find itself 'throwing good money after bad', gaining nothing but a negative cash flow and disappointment. For Disney, its Disney Stores may be in the question mark category, as their performance has lagged behind the overall speciality retail market in recent years.

- **Dogs** have a small share of a slow-growth market. They are businesses that offer specialised products in limited markets that are not likely to grow quickly. When possible, large firms may sell off their dogs to smaller firms that may be able to nurture them – or they may take the SBU's products off the market. Disney, being a very savvy strategic planner, does not appear to have any businesses that are currently in the dog house (so to speak).

Like Disney, Kevin Parkin at DavyMarkham may use the BCG matrix to evaluate his product/service lines to understand which ones are primarily cash generators and which are primarily cash users. This analysis will lead him to important decisions about where to invest for the future growth of his business.

 ## Step 5: Develop growth strategies

Although the BCG matrix can help managers decide which SBUs they should invest in for growth, it doesn't tell them much about *how* to make that growth happen. Should the growth of an SBU come from finding new customers, from developing new variations of the product, or from some other growth strategy? Part of the strategic planning at the SBU level entails evaluating growth strategies. Marketers can use the product – market growth matrix shown in Figure 2.4 to analyse different growth strategies first devised by Ansoff. The vertical axis in Figure 2.4 represents opportunities for growth, either in existing markets or in new markets, which vary in their degree of riskiness, with the most risky being new products and new markets to the least risky being existing products in existing markets. The horizontal axis considers whether the firm would be better off putting its resources into existing products or if it should acquire new products. The matrix provides four different fundamental marketing strategies: market penetration, market development, product development and diversification:

- **Market penetration strategies** seek to increase sales of existing products to existing markets such as current users, non-users and users of competing brands within a market. For example, Campbell's can advertise new uses for soup in lunches and dinners, encourage current customers to eat more soup and prod non-users to find reasons to

	Product Emphasis	
	Existing Products	**New Products**
Existing Markets	**Market penetration strategy** • Seek to increase sales of existing products to existing markets	**Product development strategy** • Create growth by selling new products in existing markets
New Markets	**Market development strategy** • Introduce existing products to new markets	**Diversification strategy** • Emphasise both new products and new markets to achieve growth

Market Emphasis

Figure 2.4   Growth strategies

buy soup. The firm might try to increase sales by cutting prices, improving distribution or conducting promotions aimed at attracting users of competing soup brands.

- **Market development strategies** introduce existing products to new markets. This strategy can mean expanding into a new geographic area, or it may mean reaching new customer segments within an existing geographic market. For example, Red Bull, the 'energy' drink that had its beginnings in the 1990s as a cult favourite among the emerging young club crowd, is trying to move up the generational chain to attract older users as well. To do this, Red Bull has recently switched some of its marketing efforts from edgy ads to more mainstream messages. Founder and largest shareholder Dietrich Mateschitz understands the monetary power of the older generation, and to appeal to them he has broadened Red Bull's distribution into shops, restaurants and clubs where they regularly visit. Mateschitz is betting on the vast numbers of clubbers' parents to prop up sales, especially now that the heavyweights like Coca-Cola, Pepsi and Anheuser-Busch are trying to make inroads into fans of energy drinks.[16]

- **Product development strategies** create growth by selling new products in existing markets. Product development may mean extending the firm's product line by developing new variations of the item, or it may mean altering or improving the product to provide enhanced performance. Take the humble mattress for example. Business hotels like Sheraton and Marriott have engaged in something of a 'mattress war'. That is, each one is trying to convince the traveller that its bed is softer, more comfortable and more inviting than the competition (and in some cases if you fall in love with the bed you can actually buy it and take it home!). This 'sleeper' strategy appears to be effective: Radisson Hotels' research with guests told it that the mere fact that a bed was 'upgraded' would allow the chain to charge an additional €7.50 more per room. These new-age beds even carry their own brand names – 'Heavenly Bed' at Westin, 'The Revive Collection' at Marriott and 'Sweet Sleeper' at Sheraton. Radisson's 'Sleep Number' beds even allow each occupant to adjust the firmness of each side with a remote control device.[17] Such a product development strategy is waking up the hotel industry, as the major players (and some smaller luxury hotels) now are scrambling to turn other room elements such as toiletries into products that can be sold.

Marketing ethics and sustainability

Back to basics . . .

McDonald's is the largest operator in the UK fast food market, and has 1225 outlets. Customers can choose from a variety of burgers. The Big Mac is a double beef burger in a bun with melted cheese and a calorie content of almost 500. Another popular product on the menu, a Double Quarter Pounder with Cheese, contains 710 calories, i.e. more than a third of the recommended daily energy intake for women. In 2004, due to heavy criticism of the menu, McDonald's decided on a new strategy and launched a number of what it described as healthier options, such as salads with low-fat dressings, fruit bags containing pieces of fresh fruit, organic milk and a range of toasted sandwiches. However, as part of its 'back-to-basics' policy, the fast food giant launched a new burger in June 2006 that is 40 per cent bigger than a Big Mac.

Debate, discuss, disagree

1   Who do you think should regulate the food sector and how?

2   Is it fair to communicate a healthier strategy to the customers and launch unhealthy products at the same time?

Real people, other voices

Andrew Whalley

School of Management, Royal Holloway, University of London

The problem here is that we have a resource-poor business in a highly competitive world, with less than favourable economic conditions. As such, trying to fund expansion or a relatively risky overseas strategy really isn't attractive. Add to that the issue with internal morale, which is the result of already being treated as a 'hand-me-down' in a series of acquisitions, and option three may well produce a talent exodus long before any potential buyer can be found, and I would expect at best a 'here we go again' feeling that will entrench negative attitudes. As such I would discount option three immediately.

I personally like option two, but if the culture of the company isn't such that internal marketing has already been in place – which seems to be the scenario presented – then it is likely to be relatively ineffective as the workforce is already cynical of the new MD's motives; it will be seen as 'spin'. As such whilst this is attractive from a theoretical viewpoint it may not deliver much 'bang for the bucks'.

Option one is by far the quickest to implement, and could be used to generate liquidity into the business to fund further research and development into marketing. As a part of this I would bring in Recency-Frequency-Monetary value (RFM) cell analysis and use this to apply resources to those customers most likely to generate profit in return. I would also look at core competencies of the firm and use these in a tailored segmentation to develop targeting for the business, which in turn should deliver better positioning and as a result better brand equity and profits. These could then be re-invested to deliver option two in a climate more receptive to constructive change.

- **Diversification strategies** emphasise both new products and new markets to achieve growth. After a long period of sluggish performance in the fast food market, McDonald's has re-energised itself over the past few years through successful strategic planning. For example, feeling that there was little growth potential in the hamburger business in the late 1990s, McDonald's sought to attract different customers with lines of business to diversify its portfolio of food offerings. Among those are Donatos Pizza, Boston Market and a controlling interest in Chipotle Mexican Grills. Interestingly, now that its core business is back on track, McDonald's has begun to divest some of these other brands and is shifting from diversification back to more of a product development strategy around the core McDonald's brand.[18]

For Kevin Parkin of DavyMarkham, using the product–market growth matrix can be a very important way to analyse where his future opportunities lie. To what degree does he want to focus on increasing current customers, taking share away from potential competitors and solidifying his position in his core market space? Or will he quickly expand the service side, perhaps to cover new markets? These are fundamental issues in planning for future growth. To review what we've learned so far, strategic planning includes developing the mission statement, assessing the internal and external environment (resulting in a SWOT analysis), setting objectives, establishing the business portfolio and developing growth strategies. In the next section, we'll look at marketers' functional plans – marketing planning.

Marketing planning: selecting the camera setting

Up until now, we have focused on strategic plans. The strategic plan, however, does not provide details about how to reach the objectives that have been set. Strategic plans 'talk the talk' but put the pressure on lower-level functional area managers, such as the marketing manager, production manager and finance manager, to 'walk the walk' by developing the functional plans – the nuts and bolts – to achieve organisational and SBU objectives.

Thus, marketers develop functional plans (for example, marketing plans) – the next step in planning as Figure 2.1 showed.

The Four Ps of the marketing mix we discussed in Chapter 1 remind us that successful firms must have viable *products* at *prices* consumers are willing to pay, the means to get the products to the *place* consumers want to buy, and a way to *promote* the products to the right consumers. Making this happen requires a tremendous amount of planning by the marketer. The steps in this marketing planning process are quite similar to the steps at the strategic planning level. An important distinction between strategic planning and marketing planning, however, is that marketing professionals focus much of their planning efforts on issues related to the firm's product, its price, promotional approach and distribution (place) methods. In the end, as you learned in Chapter 1, marketing focuses on customer value and customer relationships, and marketing planning plays a central role in making these critical components of marketing successful. Let's look at the steps involved in the marketing planning process in a bit more detail.

Step 1: Perform a situation analysis

The first step in developing a marketing plan is for marketing managers to conduct an analysis of the *marketing* environment. To do this, managers build on the company's SWOT analysis by searching out information about the environment that specifically affects the marketing plan. For example, for Kevin Parkin at DavyMarkham to develop an effective marketing communications programme, it's not enough for him to have a general understanding of the target market. He needs to know specifically what media scope potentially exists for him to connect with his business-to-business (B2B) customers, what messages about the product are most likely to make them buy, and how they prefer to communicate with his firm about upgrades, product servicing and customer support. Kevin must also know how his competitors are marketing to customers so that he can plan effectively.

Step 2: Set marketing objectives

Once marketing managers have a thorough understanding of the marketing environment, the next step is to develop specific marketing objectives. How are marketing objectives different from corporate objectives? Generally, marketing objectives are more specific to the firm's brands, sizes, product features and other marketing mix-related elements. Think of the connection between business objectives and marketing objectives this way: business objectives guide the entire firm's operations, while marketing objectives state what the marketing function must accomplish if the firm is ultimately to achieve these overall business objectives. So, for Kevin Parkin at DavyMarkham, setting marketing objectives means deciding what he wants to accomplish in terms of marketing mix-related elements, such as the development of distribution channels or specific sales figures.

Step 3: Develop marketing strategies

In the next stage of the marketing planning process, marketing managers develop their actual marketing strategies. That is, they make decisions about what activities they must accomplish to achieve the marketing objectives. Usually this means deciding which markets to target and actually developing the marketing mix strategies (product, price, promotion and distribution) to support how the product is positioned in the market. At this stage, marketers must figure out how they want consumers to think of their product compared to competing products.

Selecting a target market

The target market is the market segment selected because of the firm's belief that its offerings are most suited to winning those customers. The firm assesses the potential demand – the number of consumers it believes are willing and able to pay for its products – and decides it has the distinctive competencies that will create a competitive advantage in the marketplace among target consumers. The mission statement for DavyMarkham provides insight about what businesses it is in. From this mission statement, Kevin Parkin can rest assured that he is responsible for focusing resources on developing target markets for DavyMarkham's products and services.

Developing marketing mix strategies

Marketing mix decisions identify how marketing will accomplish its objectives in the firm's target markets by using product, price, promotion and place. It's important to note that these should be mutually reinforcing and supporting and not decisions taken in isolation.

Get an Eiffel of this...

Luton to
Paris
from
£24.99
single inc. taxes

easyJet.com
Flights · Hotels · Cars · Holidays

We fly to Paris, Charles de Gaulle

Hurry, book now

Price correct as of 07/07/2008 – Base on summer flying July to October

Photo 2.4 easyJet's adverts reinforce its image as a low-priced airline in the market
Source: easyJet

- Because the product is the most fundamental part of the marketing mix, firms simply can't make a profit without something to sell. Carefully developed *product strategies* are therefore essential to achieving marketing objectives. Product strategies include decisions such as product design, packaging, branding, support services (such as maintenance), if there will be variations of the product, and what product features will provide the unique benefits targeted customers want. For example, product planners for Virgin Atlantic decided to include in-seat video games and television as a key product feature during the flight. Their planes get you from point A to point B just as fast (or slow) as the other airlines, i.e. the basic product is the same, but the flight seems shorter because there is more to do while you are in the air.

- The *pricing strategy* determines how much a firm charges for a product. Of course, that price has to be one that customers are willing to pay. If not, all the other marketing efforts are futile. In addition to setting prices for the final consumer, pricing strategies usually establish prices that will be charged to wholesalers and retailers. A firm's pricing strategies may be based on costs, demand or the prices of competitor offerings. EasyJet uses a pricing strategy to successfully target customers who could not previously afford air travel. It does not compete solely on price. However, consumers do perceive easyJet as a low-priced airline compared to others, and the airline reinforces this theme regularly in its ads.

- A *promotion strategy* is how marketers communicate product benefits and features to the target market. Marketers use promotion strategies to develop the product's message and the mix of advertising, sales promotion, public relations and publicity, direct marketing and personal selling that will deliver the message. Many firms use all these elements to communicate their message to consumers. British

Airways (BA) strives to portray an image of quality and luxury for the serious business traveller. To do so, it combines television ads focused on that target with sales promotion in the form of BA's loyalty programme, personal selling to companies and conventions to promote usage of British Airways as the 'official carrier' for groups, direct marketing via mail and email providing information to loyal users, and, its managers hope, positive publicity through word of mouth about the airline's good service and dependability.

- *Distribution strategies* outline how, when and where the firm will make the product available to targeted customers (the place component). In developing a distribution strategy, marketers must decide whether to sell the product directly to the final customer or whether to sell through retailers and wholesalers. The choice of which retailers to involve will depend on the product, pricing and promotion decisions. For example, if the firm is producing a luxury good, it may wish to avoid being seen on the shelves of 'discount shops' for fear that it will cheapen the brand image. In recent times, the airline industry has undertaken major changes in its distribution strategy. For many years, most customers bought their airline tickets through travel agencies or at ticket counters of the major airlines. Today, many airlines such as easyJet actually penalise customers who don't opt for online purchase of 'ticketless' flight reservations by charging them a 'ticketing fee' or forcing them to call a premium rate helpline. This strategy has moulded the behaviour of many consumers to go online 24/7 to save money as well as experience the convenience of scheduling the flight they want.

Step 4: Implement and control the marketing plan

Objective

5

Explain the role of implementation and control in marketing planning

Once the plan is developed, it's time to get to work and make it successful. In practice, marketers spend much of their time managing the various elements of the marketing plan. For DavyMarkham, once Kevin Parkin and his group understand the marketing environment, determine the most appropriate objectives and strategies, and get their ideas organised and on paper in the formal plan, the plan really begins to gain traction. Like all firms, how DavyMarkham implements its plan is usually what makes or breaks the success of the firm in the marketplace.

During the implementation phase, marketers must have some means to determine to what degree they are actually meeting their stated marketing objectives. Often called **control**, this formal process of monitoring progress entails the three steps of (1) measuring actual performance, (2) comparing this performance to the established marketing objectives or strategies, and then (3) making adjustments to the objectives or strategies on the basis of this analysis. This issue of making adjustments brings up one of the most important aspects of successful marketing planning: marketing plans aren't written in stone, and marketers must be flexible enough to make such changes when changes are warranted.

Effective control requires appropriate *marketing metrics*, which, as we discussed in Chapter 1, are concrete measures of various aspects of marketing performance. You will note throughout the book a strong emphasis on metrics within each chapter. Today's business leaders are keen on quantifying just how an investment in marketing affects the firm's success, financially and otherwise. Think of this overall notion as **return on marketing investment (ROMI)**. Considering marketing as an investment rather than an expense is critical because this distinction drives firms to use marketing more strategically to enhance the business. The ROMI concept heightens the importance of identifying and tracking appropriate marketing metrics.[19] Table 2.5 provides some example metrics that are applied across an array of marketing planning situations including all the marketing mix variables.

Table 2.5 Example marketing metrics

Cost of a prospect
Value of a prospect
Return on investment of a campaign
Value of telesales
Conversion rates of users of competitor products
Long-term value of a customer
Customer commitment to relationship/partnership
Referral rate
Response rates to direct marketing
Perceived product quality
Perceived service quality
Customer loyalty/retention
Customer turnover
Customer/segment profitability
Customer mindset/customer orientation
Customer satisfaction
Company/product reputation
Customer word-of-mouth (buzz) activity
Salesperson perceived self-efficacy
Timeliness and accuracy of competitive intelligence
Usage rates of technology in customer initiatives
Reach and frequency of advertising
Recognition and recall of message
Sales calls per day/week/month
Order fulfilment efficiency/stock-outs
Timeliness of sales promotion support

Kevin Parkin at DavyMarkham has to establish appropriate metrics related to his marketing objectives and then track those metrics to know how successful his marketing strategy is, as well as whether he needs to make changes in the strategy along the way. For example, what happens if DavyMarkham sets an objective to increase market share in the service operations market by 25 per cent in a given year, but after the first quarter, sales turnover is only even with the previous year? The control process means that Kevin and his crew would have to look carefully at why they were not meeting their objectives. Is it due to internal factors, external factors, or a combination of both? Depending on the cause, Kevin would then have to either adjust the marketing plan's strategies (such as to increase advertising or implement product alterations) or adjust the marketing objective so that it reflects realistic goals. This scenario illustrates the important point made earlier in our discussion of strategic planning that objectives must be specific and measurable, but also *attainable* in the sense that if an objective is not realistic it can become very demotivating for everyone involved in the marketing plan.

Action plans

How does the implementation and control step actually manifest itself within a marketing plan? One very convenient way is through the inclusion of a series of **action plans** in support of the various marketing objectives and strategies within the plan. Action plans are also sometimes referred to as *marketing programmes*. The best way to utilise action plans is by including a separate action plan for each important element involved in implementing the marketing plan. Table 2.6 provides a template for an action plan.

For example, let's consider the use of action plans in the context of supporting Kevin Parkin at DavyMarkham in increasing market share of the machinery service operations side of his business by 25 per cent this year. The marketing plan would probably include a variety of strategies related to how he will employ the marketing mix elements to accomplish this. Important questions will be: Who is his target market? How will the service be positioned in this market? What will be his product/service and branding strategies? What will be his pricing strategy for this group? How will the product/service be promoted to them? And what is the best distribution strategy to access this market? Any one of these important strategic issues may require several action plans to implement.

Table 2.6 Action plan template

Title of action plan Give the action plan a relevant name
Purpose of action plan What do you hope to accomplish by the action plan? That is, what specific marketing objective and strategy within the marketing plan does it support?
Description of action plan Be succinct, but still thorough, in explaining the action plan. What are the steps involved? This is the core of the action plan. It describes what must be done in order to accomplish the intended purpose of the action plan
Responsibility for the action plan What person(s) or organisational unit(s) are responsible for carrying out the action plan? What external parties are needed to make it happen? Most importantly, who specifically has final 'ownership' of the action plan – that is, who is accountable for it?
Timeline for the action plan Provide a specific timetable of events leading to the completion of the plan. If different people are responsible for different elements of the timeline, provide that information
Budget for the action plan How much will implementation of the action plan cost? This may be direct costs only, or may also include indirect costs depending on the situation. The sum of all the individual action plan budget items will ultimately be aggregated by category to create the overall budget for the marketing plan
Measurement and control of the action plan Indicate the appropriate metrics, how and when they will be measured, and who will measure them

Action plans provide an additional convenience for developing assignment of responsibilities, timelines, budgets, and measurement and control processes for marketing planning. Notice in Table 2.6 that these four elements are the final four items to be documented in an action plan. Sometimes when a marketing plan is viewed in total it can seem daunting and nearly impossible to actually implement. Like most big projects, implementation of a marketing plan is best done one step at a time, paying attention to maximising the quality of that step. In practice, what happens is that the input from these last four elements of each action plan can be aggregated to form the overall implementation and control portion of the marketing plan. Let's examine each a bit further.

Responsibility

A marketing plan can't be implemented without people and not everybody who will be involved in implementing a marketing plan is a marketer. The truth is, marketing plans touch most areas of an organisation. Upper management and the human resource department will need to be involved in deploying the necessary human resources to accomplish the plan's objectives. Reviewing the various action plans needed for implementation is a great way to develop an overall human resource deployment strategy for accomplishing the marketing plan. You learned in Chapter 1 that marketing isn't just the responsibility of a marketing department. Nowhere is that idea more vivid than in marketing plan implementation. Sales, production, quality control, shipping, customer service, finance, information technology – the list goes on – all will probably have a part in making the plan successful.

Timeline

Notice that each action plan requires a *timeline* for accomplishment of the various tasks which is essential in the overall marketing plan. Most marketing plans portray the timing of tasks in a flow chart form, so it is easy to visualise when the pieces of the plan will come together. Marketers often use workflow tools such as *Gantt charts* or *PERT charts*, popular in operations management, and the same type of tools might be used to map out the different elements of building a house from the ground up. Ultimately, budgets and the financial management of the marketing plan are developed around the timeline so that managers know when cash outlays are required.

Budget

Each action plan carries a budget item, assuming there are costs involved in carrying it out. Forecasting the needed expenditures related to a marketing plan is difficult, but one way to improve accuracy in the budgeting process overall is to ensure as accurate as possible estimates of the individual action plans. At the overall marketing plan level, a master budget is created and tracked throughout the market planning process. Variances from the budget are reported to the parties responsible for each budget item throughout the process. For example, a firm's director of sales might receive a weekly or monthly report showing each sales area's performance against their budget allocation. The director would note patterns of budget and contact affected sales managers to determine what, if any, action should be taken to get the budget back on track. The same approach would be repeated across all the different functional areas of the firm affected by the budget. In this manner, the budget itself becomes a critical element of control.

Measurement and control

Earlier we described the concept of control as a formal process of monitoring progress through measuring actual performance, comparing the performance to the established marketing objectives or strategies, and making adjustments to the objectives or strategies

Across the hall

Anurag Saxena

Managing Director,
LINKCOZ Ltd.

Recession has made people make difficult choices to manage all stakeholders and deliver value to the shareholders. There are no signs that the recession in the western world is going away in a hurry. So while Kevin can use Option 1 to get short-term respite from declining cash flows, for the long term he may have to innovate and I dare say even find a different business model.

There is no harm in engaging the employees in Option 2. Being a high-end business, highly dependent on the economy, that is unlikely to result in higher revenues, but by all means keeping morale high is crucial in tough times. Option 3 is interesting but very time-consuming and to realise any synergies in a M&A easily takes at least 18 months.

I would recommend a variation of Option 3 or a new option in itself, that of international partnerships and tying up with his customers, who must be taking up infrastructure projects in emerging BRIC economies as well as in vibrant Africa. His experienced, competent staff could be trained to become project managers because of their familiarity with the equipment and he can increase revenue quite fast without incurring additional costs.

He could partner with different companies for various projects/industries in different countries and this could even help him decide if any of them are the right partner for the company for the future, if the need arises. Also, in doing so, he can develop cheaper delivery processes, closer to the customers, thereby reducing costs, but maintaining the same quality. He could also explore tying up with funding institutions that finance such big projects, as they need experts to advise and guide them. This would create additional fee income for the company and even result in a preferred partner status.

on the basis of this analysis. The metric(s) a marketer uses to monitor and control individual action plans ultimately forms the overall control process for the marketing plan. It is an unfortunate fact that many marketers do not consistently do a good job of measurement and control, which of course compromises their marketing planning. Pay close attention throughout the remainder of the book to look at marketing metrics and how they are used to assess the effectiveness of the different components of marketing. Learning these metrics will help you make good choices as a marketer and move up the corporate ladder.

Creating and working with a marketing plan

A marketing plan should provide the best possible guide for the firm to successfully market its products. In large firms, top management often requires such a written plan because putting the ideas on paper encourages marketing managers to formulate concrete objectives and strategies. In small entrepreneurial firms, a well-thought-out marketing plan is often a key factor in attracting investors who will help turn the firm's dreams into reality.

Make your life easier: use the marketing planning template

Ultimately, the planning process we've described in this section gets documented into a formal written marketing plan. You'll find a handy template for a marketing plan to download from the book's website (www.pearsoned.co.uk/solomon). The template will come in handy as you make your way through the book, as each chapter will give you information you can use to 'fill in the blanks' of a marketing plan. You will note that the template is cross-referenced with the questions you must answer in each section of the plan and that it also provides you with a general outline of the topics covered in each chapter. By the time you've finished, we hope that all these pieces will come together and you'll understand how real marketers make real decisions.

 ## Operational planning: day-to-day execution of marketing plans

Objective

6

Explain operational planning

In the previous section, we discussed marketing planning – the process by which marketing planners perform a situation analysis, set marketing objectives, and develop, implement and control marketing strategies. However, the best plan ever written is useless if it's not properly implemented. That's what **operational plans** are for. They really make it happen by focusing on the day-to-day execution of the marketing plan. The task falls to the first-line supervisors we discussed earlier, such as sales managers, marketing communications managers and marketing research managers. Operational plans generally cover a shorter period of time than either strategic plans or marketing plans, perhaps only one or two months, and they include detailed directions for the specific activities to be carried out, who will be responsible for them and timelines for accomplishing the tasks. In reality, the action plan template we provide in Table 2.6 is most likely to be applied at the operational level.

Importantly, many of the marketing metrics managers employ to gauge the success of plans actually get used at the operational planning level. Sales managers in many firms are charged with the responsibility of tracking a wide range of metrics related to the firm – customer relationship such as number of new customers, sales calls per month, customer turnover and customer loyalty. The data are collected at the operational level and are later sent to management for use in planning at the functional level and above.

 ## The value of a marketing culture

A central issue for marketers is gaining a good understanding of the environment in which their planning must take place. That is, how well marketers understand the situation, or environment, in which their firm operates. This is central to the success of marketing planning. Earlier in the chapter, we defined the internal environment as being the controllable elements inside an organisation that influence how well the organisation operates. We also mentioned that internal strengths and weaknesses may lie in a firm's technologies, physical facilities, financial stability, reputation, quality of its products and services, and employees. Marketers must analyse and document all these elements in the SWOT analysis part of the marketing plan.

Ultimately, a firm's **corporate culture** determines much of its internal environment. By this we mean the values, norms and beliefs that influence the behaviour of everyone in the organisation. Corporate culture may dictate whether new ideas are welcomed or discouraged, the importance of individual ethical behaviour, and even the appropriate dress code for work. For many years, IBM was known as 'the white shirt company' because of its unwritten rule that all employees must wear white shirts to look the part. Fortunately, corporate cultures do evolve over time, and even radical changes such as blue shirts are now tolerated. In contrast, Microsoft has always prided itself on having a more casual dress code, reflecting its roots as an entrepreneurial upstart (at least compared with IBM). If you visit Microsoft's corporate headquarters, you will immediately notice everyone's informal attire. However, don't make the mistake of equating informal dress with low work productivity. Microsoft hasn't evolved into the corporate giant it is today by hiring lazy workers.

Photo 2.5 Employees at CAP, a Christian debt counselling charity that operates through a network of 72 church-based centres, voted it the best small company to work for in a *Sunday Times* 2008 survey
Source: Christians Against Poverty

Some corporate cultures are more inclined to take risks than others. These firms value individuality and creativity; they recognise that by nurturing these characteristics their employees are more likely to create important competitive advantages. A risk-taking culture is especially important to the marketing function because firms must continually improve their products, their distribution channels, and their promotion programmes to remain successful in a competitive environment. In firms with more traditional corporate cultures, getting managers to buy into a new way of doing things is like inviting the board of directors to go on a skydiving mission. If a firm is totally focused on economic profit, increasing revenues and decreasing costs, then management attitudes will be profit-centred, often at the expense of employee morale. Firms that harbour a concern for employees, customers and society, as well as shareholder profits, produce a corporate culture that is much more appealing for employees and other stakeholders in the business. In which corporate culture would *you* rather work?

The Sunday Times publishes an annual list of the best companies to work for based on a variety of criteria, including company philosophy and practices, employee trust in management, pride in work and the company, and camaraderie. In 2007, Goldman Sachs International was the best company to work for according to the Times Best Companies Survey. What keeps employees happy is strong leadership, close teamwork, being stretched professionally and the buzz of working for the leading company in its field. Among the top 20 big companies Goldman Sachs staff returned the highest positive scores for 34 of the 70 points that make up the employee survey. These include having pride in working for the firm (88 per cent), happiness with pay and benefits (76 per cent), having a job that is good for personal growth (84 per cent), having confidence in the leadership skills of senior management (83 per cent) and confidence in the abilities of team-mates (84 per cent).

In 2008, Bradford-based Christians Against Poverty (CAP) won the Best Small Company to work for. Chief executive Matt Barlow looks after the Bradford head office and the 72 church-based centres in the UK and, along with founder John Kirkby, provides inspiring leadership, which resulted in the charity's employees giving them a top and near perfect positive score of 98 per cent for leadership. Employees love working for CAP (95 per cent) and have confidence in the leadership of senior managers (98 per cent), another top score. Every day in the Bradford office work begins with a staff meeting to pray and discuss company news.

Playing on an international stage: the complicated world of global marketing

The global marketing game is exciting, the stakes are high and it's easy to make mistakes. Competition comes from both local and foreign firms, and differences in national laws, customs and consumer preferences can make life difficult. The successful global business needs to set its sights on diverse markets around the world, but it needs to act locally by

Objective

7

Explain the strategies that a firm can use to enter global markets

being willing to adapt business practices to unique conditions in other parts of the globe. For example, in the mid-1990s, Nike had to adjust its global strategy to increase its business in foreign markets. The company attempted to appeal to football fans worldwide and actively pursued new customers in Europe, the Far East and South America. This was a major change for a company that had made its mark in sports such as basketball and American football. Nike's president claimed that in order to be a global company, there was a need to focus on football.[20] With the acquisition of Reebok by Adidas in 2006, Nike had to work even harder to achieve its goal. Perhaps that's why Nike won a bidding war with Adidas in 2006 for the sponsorship of the Indian national cricket team, in a five-year deal worth around €50 million.[21]

World trade

World trade refers to the flow of goods and services among different countries, i.e. the value of all the exports and imports of the world's nations. World trade activity is steadily increasing year by year. In 2004, merchandise exports of all countries totalled €9.15 trillion, up 9 per cent from 2003. Similarly, world exports of commercial services totalled €2.13 trillion, up 17 per cent.[22] This growth was the largest in nearly ten years and was the second year of growth since the world economy was sent into a tailspin by the US terrorist attacks in 2001.[23] Of course, not all countries participate equally in the trade flows among nations. Understanding the 'big picture' of who does business with whom is important to marketers when they devise global trade strategies. One British businessman, when posed questions on his internationalisation strategy, said 'the international marketplace is forever dynamic and complex, with wars and S.A.R.S. we have to really think long and hard about planning'.

Having customers in far-away places is important, but it requires some flexibility since business must be done differently to adapt to local social and economic conditions. For example, firms engaged in global marketing must be able to accommodate the needs of trading partners when those foreign firms can't pay cash for the products they want to purchase. Believe it or not, the currency for as many as 70 per cent of all countries is not convertible. This implies it cannot be spent or exchanged outside the country's borders. In other countries, because sufficient cash or credit is simply not available, trading firms work out elaborate deals in which they trade (or barter) their products with each other, or even supply goods in return for tax breaks from the local government. This **counter trade** accounts for about 25 per cent of all world trade. For instance, the Philippine International Trading Corporation agreed to import Vietnamese rice which was paid for with fertiliser, coconuts and coconut by-products produced in the Philippines.[24]

Making the decision to go global

When firms consider 'going global', they must make a number of decisions. As you can see in Figure 2.5, the first two highly related decisions are (1) 'go' or 'no go' – whether it is in the best interest of the firm to remain in its home market or to go where there are good opportunities, and (2) which global markets are most attractive. Although the prospect of millions of consumers purchasing your goods in other countries is very tempting, not all firms can or should go global, and not all markets around the world are alike. In making these decisions, firms need to consider a number of factors that may enhance or detract from their possible success abroad.

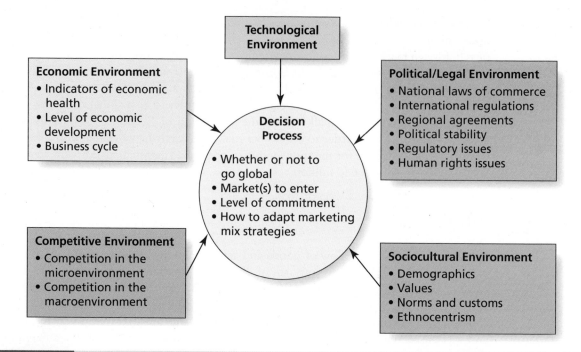

Figure 2.5	Decision model for entering foreign markets
	Entering foreign markets involves a complex decision process. Marketers must fully understand market conditions and environmental factors in order to determine the best strategy for entering the market and to create a successful marketing mix

One key factor, and it's a fairly broad one, is domestic and foreign market conditions, particularly those that affect a firm's ability to develop a competitive advantage in foreign markets. A second key factor is identifying which markets are attractive given the firm's unique capabilities. Finally, the company must consider the extent to which opportunities for success may be hampered by regulations or other constraints on trade that local governments or international bodies impose.

Market conditions

Many times, a firm makes a decision to go global because domestic demand is declining while demand in foreign markets is growing. For example, the market for personal computers has matured in Europe, where more sales come from people replacing old or obsolete machines than from those buying a new personal computer for the first time. In examining the market potential abroad for computers, the demand is much greater in some other parts of the world where consumers and businesses are only now beginning to tune into the power of the web. So it's no coincidence that in 2005 IBM sold its entire personal computing business to Lenovo, a Chinese company.

Of course, it isn't only Western countries that are going global. Countries such as China that have been a vast market for Western firms to expand in are now fighting to win a larger share of business in the global marketplace. Dozens of Chinese companies have global ambitions, including Chery Automobile, which plans to export 250,000 low-priced cars a year to North America. Chery, founded in 1997, realises that growth in its home Chinese market has slowed down while competition has increased. The company sees the US as an attractive new market. Other Chinese car makers such as Great Wall and Geely are also looking in the same direction.[25]

Competitive advantage

In Chapter 1, we saw how firms seek to create competitive advantage, a means to outperform the competition. When firms compete in a global marketplace, this challenge is even greater because there are more players involved and typically some of these local firms have a home advantage. In practice, firms need to capitalise on their home country's assets and avoid competing in areas in which they are at a disadvantage. For example, German firms have trouble keeping production costs down because of the high wages, relatively short working weeks and long vacations that their skilled factory workers enjoy. As a result, they are obliged to compete on high quality rather than on low price. Developing countries typically have a large labour force and low wage rates, but have relatively little in the way of highly trained workers or high-tech facilities. In response they tend to compete better for handmade goods and low-cost manufacturing.

Some of the most significant European exports include healthcare equipment, food, industrial supplies and services, such as tourism and entertainment, plus other industries where consumers around the world value European brands and products. The success of these industries shows that a firm's prospects for success depend not only on its own abilities, but also on its home country's competitive advantage. As we'll see next, barriers to trade and membership in economic communities also affect a firm's success overseas.

Trading blocks at the borders

Even the best of competitive advantages may not allow a firm to be successful in foreign markets if the opportunities for success are not available. People like to think of it as one large, open marketplace where companies from every country are free to compete for business by meeting customers' needs better than the next. Although countries seem to be moving towards such an ideal of free trade, they're not quite there yet. Often a company's efforts to expand into foreign markets are hindered by trade blocs designed to favour local businesses over outsiders.[26]

Of course, marketers who operate in a global environment must consider not only the legal, regulatory and political environments of their own home market, but other individual countries simultaneously. In recent years a number of initiatives have had a major impact on how marketers do business in markets around the globe. The World Trade Organization has made significant strides in creating a single open world market, while economic communities encourage regional groups of countries to trade among themselves.

Global trade agreements: GATT and later the WTO   Established under the United Nations after the Second World War, the **General Agreement on Tariffs and Trade (GATT)** did a lot to reduce the problems that protectionism creates. This regulatory group is now known as the **World Trade Organization (WTO)**. The WTO was established during GATT's 1986–94 Uruguay Round and effectively replaced GATT in 1995. During the 50-plus years of GATT/WTO, world trade exports increased by 6 per cent annually. With nearly 150 members (and around 30 more negotiating membership), the WTO member nations account for over 97 per cent of world trade. The WTO's decisions are made by their entire membership, and all participating governments must ratify agreements.

Through a series of trade negotiations (known as rounds) that set standards for how much countries are allowed to favour their own goods and services, the WTO has become a global referee for trade.[27] The objective of the WTO is to 'help trade flow smoothly, freely, fairly, and predictably'. With over three-quarters of its membership drawn from the world's poorer countries, negotiations in recent years have largely focused on issues concerning economic development.[28] One important issue that the WTO tackles is the protection of copyright and patent rights. This protection will help firms prevent copied versions of software, books and music from being sold in other countries. *Pirating* is a serious problem for many companies, as their profits are eroded by illegal sales. According to a senior Microsoft executive based in Asia, 'Piracy is clearly our number one competitor, and not only Microsoft's number one competitor but also a big impediment to the growth of the local software industry'.[29]

Groups of countries may also band together to promote trade among themselves and make it easier for member nations to compete elsewhere. These **economic communities** coordinate trade policies and ease restrictions on the flow of products and capital across their borders. Economic communities are important to marketers because they set policies in such areas as product content, package labelling and advertising regulations that influence strategic decisions when doing business in these areas (see Table 2.7). An even larger American free trade zone may be in the making. While talks stalled in November 2005, there is still hope that the Free Trade Area of the Americas (FTAA) will eventually be a reality. If and when the parties reach an agreement, FTAA will include 34 countries in North, Central and South America with a population of 800 million and a combined output of equivalent to around €11 trillion.[30]

Protected trade: quotas, embargoes and tariffs

In some cases, a government adopts a policy of **protectionism** in which it enforces rules on foreign firms designed to give home companies an advantage. Many governments set **import quotas** on foreign goods to reduce competition for their domestic industries. Quotas are limitations on the amount of a product allowed to enter or leave a country. Quotas can make goods more expensive to a country's citizens because the absence of cheaper foreign goods reduces pressure on domestic firms to lower their prices. For example, Russia placed import quotas on meat products to protect its own meat production industry.[31] An **embargo** is an extreme quota that prohibits specified foreign goods completely. In the 1990s many of the UK's trading partners in Europe placed an embargo on British beef due to the fear of contracting 'mad cow' disease (bovine spongiform encephalopathy–BSE). Governments also use **tariffs**, or taxes on imported goods, to give domestic competitors an advantage in the marketplace by making foreign competitors' goods more expensive than their own goods.

Table 2.7
Economic communities that have now been created around the world (each economic community includes a number of countries)

- **South America** includes two economic communities: (1) Mercado Común del Sur known as the Southern Common Market (MERCOSUR) and includes five countries; and (2) the Andean Community which includes Bolivia, Columbia, Ecuador, Peru and Venezuela

- **Central America** has the Central American Free Trade Agreement (CAFTA) that includes Costa Rica the Dominican Republic, El Salvador, Guatemala, Honduras, Nicaragua and the United States

- **Africa** has the Common Market for Eastern and Southern Africa (COMESA) which includes 20 African countries

- **Asia** has three groups: the Asia-Pacific Economic Cooperation (APEC) includes 22 countries, the Association of Southeast Asian Nations (ASEAN) includes ten nations and the South Asia Association for Regional Cooperation (SAPTA) includes seven countries

- **Europe** has two economic communities: the Central European Free Trade Agreement (CEFTA) includes seven countries and the European Union (EU) includes 27 members. The EU now represents 450 million consumers, 300 million of whom use the euro as their currency

- **North America** has the North American Free Trade Agreement (NAFTA), which includes the United States, Canada and Mexico

How global should a global marketing strategy be?

Going global is not a simple task. As you have seen, understanding all the economic, legal and cultural differences around the world can be difficult. However, if a firm decides to expand beyond its home country, it must make important decisions about how to structure its business and whether to adapt its product marketing strategy to accommodate local needs. First, the company must decide on the nature of its commitment, including whether the company will partner with another firm or go it alone. Then it must make specific decisions about the marketing mix for a particular product or service. In the next section, we'll consider issues related to global strategy at these two levels: the company and the product.

Choosing a market-entry strategy

Just like a romantic relationship, a firm deciding to go global must determine the level of commitment it is willing to make to operate in another country. This commitment can range from a casual involvement to a full-scale 'marriage'. At one extreme, the firm can simply export its products, while at the other extreme it can directly invest in another country by buying a foreign subsidiary or opening its own production site or retail shops. The decision about the extent of commitment entails a trade-off between control and risk. Direct involvement gives the firm more control over what happens in the country, but risk also increases if the operation is not successful.

Let's review four strategies representing increased levels of involvement: exporting, contractual arrangements, strategic alliances and direct investment. Figure 2.6 summarises these.

Exporting

If a firm chooses to export, it must decide whether it will attempt to sell its products on its own or rely on intermediaries to represent it in the target country. These representatives are specialists known as export merchants (including agents/distributors) who understand the local market and who can find buyers and negotiate terms.[32] An exporting strategy allows a firm to sell its products in global markets and cushions the firm against downturns in its domestic market. Because the firm actually makes the products at home, it is able to maintain control over design and production decisions.[33] Sometimes, exporting

Figure 2.6	Market-entry strategies
	Choosing a market-entry strategy is a critical decision for companies that want to go global. Choosing whether to operate the new venture versus sharing responsibility with organisations in the local market involves a trade-off between control and risk

is the best way to be successful in a foreign market. Frontier Foods Ltd has developed a thriving business exporting cheese to China, where wealthy Chinese consumers are developing an unprecedented taste for it. Because there is so little open farmland in China for large herds of dairy cows, China can't produce enough milk to sustain a domestic cheese industry. Hence, it is easier to import cheese than to make it in China.[34]

Contractual agreements

The next level of commitment a firm can make to a foreign market is a contractual agreement with a company in that country to conduct some or all of its business there. These agreements can take several forms. Two of the most common are licensing and franchising. In a **licensing** agreement, a firm (the licenser) gives another firm (the licensee) the right to produce and market its product in a specific country or region in return for royalties. Because the licensee produces the product in its home market, it can avoid many of the barriers to entry that the licenser would have encountered. However, the licenser also loses control over how the product is produced and marketed, so if the licensee does a poor job, this may tarnish the company's reputation. Licensers also have to accept the possibility that local licensees will alter its product to suit local tastes. **Franchising** is a form of licensing that gives the franchisee the right to adapt an entire way of doing business in the host country. Again, there is a risk to the parent company if the franchisee does not use the same quality ingredients or procedures, so firms monitor these operations carefully. For example, in India, where Hindus do not eat beef, all McDonald's have vegetarian and non-vegetarian burger cooking lines and offer customers such vegetarian specialities as Pizza McPuff and McAloo Tikki (a spiced-potato burger).[35]

Strategic alliances

Firms seeking an even deeper commitment to a foreign market can develop a **strategic alliance** with one or more domestic firms in the target country. These relationships often take the form of a **joint venture** whereby two or more firms create a new entity to allow the partners to pool their resources for common goals. Strategic alliances also allow companies easy access to new markets, especially because these partnerships often bring with them preferential treatment in the partner's home country.

Direct investment

An even deeper level of commitment occurs when a firm expands internationally by buying a business outright in the host country. Instead of starting from scratch in its quest to become multinational, direct investment allows a foreign firm to take advantage of a domestic company's political know-how and market position in the host country. The Chinese appliance maker Haier recently chose this route when it became the first Chinese company to set up facilities in the United States to manufacture some of its 96 product lines ranging from refrigerators and water heaters to mobile phones and flat screen TVs.[36] Ownership gives a firm maximum freedom and control, and it can also overcome import restrictions. Direct investment also carries greater risk. Firms that own businesses in foreign countries could suffer losses of their investment if economic conditions deteriorate or if political instability leads to nationalisation or expropriation.

Born-global firms

The appeal of catering to a global market is so strong that it's even spawning a breed of start-up companies called **born-global firms**.[37] These are companies that deliberately try to sell their products in several countries from the moment they're created rather than taking the usual path of developing business in their local market and then slowly expanding into other countries. For example, Logitech International is a Swiss company that quite possibly made your computer mouse. In addition to having a US base, the company has local subsidiaries in Switzerland, Taiwan and Hong Kong. The company also has offices throughout other major cities in Europe, Asia and North America. In total the company employs over 4500 people worldwide. It's truly a 'born global' company.

Product-level decisions: choosing a marketing mix strategy

In addition to 'big picture' decisions about how a company will operate in other countries, managers must decide how to market the product in each country. The famous Four Ps, i.e. product, price, promotion and place, may need to be modified to suit local conditions. To what extent will the company need to adapt its marketing communications to the specific styles and tastes of each local market? Will the same product appeal to people there? Will it have to be priced differently? How does the company get the product into people's hands? Let's consider each of these questions in turn.

Standardisation versus localisation

When top management makes a company-level decision to expand internationally, the firm's marketers have to answer a crucial question: How necessary is it to develop a customised marketing mix for each country, i.e. a localisation strategy? Gillette decided to offer the same products in all its markets, a standardisation strategy. In contrast, Procter & Gamble (P&G) adopted a localised strategy in Asia, where consumers like to experiment with different brands of shampoo. Most of P&G's shampoos sold in Asia are now packaged in single-use sachets to encourage people to try different kinds.[38]

So, which strategy is right? Advocates of standardisation argue that the world has become so small, with tastes so homogenised, that basic needs and wants are the same everywhere.[39] A focus on the similarities among cultures certainly is appealing. After all, if a firm didn't have to make any changes to its marketing strategy to compete in foreign countries, it would realise large economies of scale because it could spread the costs of product development and promotional materials over many markets. Reebok, realising this, created a new centralised product development centre to develop shoe designs that can easily cross borders.[40] Widespread and consistent exposure also helps create a global brand by forging a strong, unified image all over the world. Coca-Cola signs are visible on billboards throughout London or on metal roofs deep in the forests of Thailand. In contrast, those in favour of localisation feel that the world is not that small and that products and promotional messages should be tailored to local environments. These marketers feel that each culture is unique and that each country has a national character, a distinctive set of behavioural and personality characteristics.[41]

Product decisions

A firm seeking to sell a product in a foreign market has three choices: sell the same product in the new market, modify it for that market, or develop a brand-new product to sell there. Let's take a closer look at each possibility: A **straight extension strategy** retains the same product for domestic and foreign markets. For generations, proper etiquette in Japan was for girls to bow and never raise their eyes to a man.[42] However, the new generation of

Japanese women want to look straight at you, showing their eyes and eyelashes. Japanese eyelashes are very short, so they have to be curled to show. To meet this need, L'Oréal introduced its Maybelline brand Wonder Curl that dramatically thickens and curls lashes as it is applied. The launch was such a success in Japan that local television news showed Japanese girls standing in queues to buy the product. A **product adaptation strategy** recognises that in many cases people in different cultures do have strong and different product preferences. Sometimes these differences can be subtle yet important.

A **product invention strategy** means a company develops a new product as it expands to foreign markets. For example, firms that wish to market household appliances in Japan, where apartments are very small by Western standards, must design and manufacture smaller products. In some cases, a product invention strategy takes the form of *backward invention*. A firm may find it needs to offer a less complex product than it sells elsewhere, such as a manually operated sewing machine or a hand-powered clothes washer for people without access to a reliable source of electricity.

Promotion decisions

Marketers must also decide whether it's necessary to modify their product promotions in a foreign market. Some firms endorse the idea that the same message will appeal to everyone around the world, while others feel the need to customise it. The 2006 FIFA World Cup was broadcast in 189 countries to one of the biggest global television audiences ever. This major event illustrates how different marketers make different decisions, even when they're creating ads to be run during the same game. MasterCard ran ads that appeared in 39 countries, so its ad agency came up with a spot called 'Fever', in which 100-odd fans from 30 countries appear cheering. There's no dialogue so it works in any language. At the end, the words 'Football fever. Priceless' appeared under the MasterCard logo. Gillette, in contrast, ran an ad in over 20 countries that it digitally altered to reflect local differences. The spot shows cheering fans, wearing the colours and carrying the flags of their national team. The colours were changed depending on the country where the ad was shown.[43]

Price decisions

Costs associated with transportation, tariffs, differences in currency exchange rates and even bribes paid to local officials often make the product more expensive for the company to manufacture for foreign markets than in its home country. To ease the financial burden of tariffs on companies that import goods, some countries have established free trade zones. These are designated areas where foreign companies can store goods without paying taxes or customs duties until the goods are moved into the marketplace.

One danger of pricing too high is that competitors will find ways to offer their products at a lower price, even if they do this illegally. **Grey market goods** or (parallel imports) are items that are imported without the consent of the trademark holder. While grey market goods are not counterfeits, they may be different from authorised products in warranty coverage and compliance with local regulatory requirements.[44] Another unethical and often illegal practice is **dumping**, in which a company prices its products lower than they are offered at home – often removing excess supply from home markets and keeping prices high there.

Distribution decisions

Getting the product to consumers in a remote location is half the battle. Thus, establishing a reliable distribution system is essential if a marketer is to succeed in a foreign market. Marketers used to dealing with a handful of large wholesalers or retailers may have to rely instead on thousands of small shops or distributors, some of whom transport goods to remote rural areas in a primitive fashion. In less developed countries, marketers may run into problems finding a way to package, refrigerate or store goods for long periods of time.

Even the retailing giant Wal-Mart has occasionally stumbled at going global. When Wal-Mart attempted to ease its entry into the German market by buying local retailers, it underestimated the problems it would face in dealing with local distributors. When the chain tried to force the distributors to switch from supplying individual shops to utilising Wal-Mart's new centralised warehouse system, the distributors refused and left Wal-Mart with empty shelves. Wal-Mart has had to work hard to understand local business cultures and to work more closely with suppliers.[45]

To summarise what we've discussed in this chapter, business planning, a key element of a firm's success, occurs in several different stages. Strategic planning takes place at both the corporate and the SBU level in large firms and in a single stage in smaller businesses. Marketing planning, one of the functional planning areas, comes next. Operational planning ensures proper implementation and control of the marketing plan.

Now that you've learned the basics of marketing strategy and read the advice, read 'Real people, real decisions' to see which strategy Kevin Parkin selected to develop for DavyMarkham.

Real people, real decisions

How it worked out at DavyMarkham

Before telling you which strategy Kevin decided upon, we thought we would inform you firstly that he did manage to turn the company around, to the tune of a turnover in excess of €20 million and safeguarding more than 200 full-time workers. So how was it achieved?

If you selected any of the three options then you were not entirely wrong! Actually Kevin worked with all three in mind. He first decided to go for Option 2 by adopting an internal marketing ethos. Kevin soon realised that in order to succeed he had to quickly win the hearts and minds of his staff. Remember that he was perceived by the workers as the hatchet man who had been sent to close down the firm. He therefore decided to demonstrate to his new team that he was here for the long term by investing in apprentices. The tactic was an instant winner with staff, as they immediately realised that Kevin was committed to investing in the firm with a view to recruiting, rather than shedding staff. He is actually passionate about apprentices and the education of young people. He not only revived the company's apprenticeship scheme but revolutionised it. He

also pioneered a scheme called work-wise for immersing young people in a company over a three-year period, giving them exposure to the working environment and the disciplines of each of the company's departments whilst still at school.

Kevin realised that the organisational structure represented a blame culture that had been de-motivating staff. He wanted to inspire his workers to take their own decisions, be responsible for their actions and fulfil duties to the best of their potential. In order to do this, he wanted to be seen to make changes, regardless of size. Therefore, if workers presented ideas to improve quality or job design, he would guarantee that a response would be provided instantly, i.e. written feedback within 24 hours. Therefore, everyone had a say in improving the structure of the firm.

To facilitate trust, Kevin also made it his prerogative to be at work each day at the start of shift to welcome and show appreciation to his staff, as well as walking the factory and office floor four times daily and visiting the canteen during breaks. His aim was clearly not to dismiss comments from the shop floor, but to be available to offer guidance on actions. Much of his emphasis was on finding effective ways for listening and communicating. He therefore decided to stop all 'round robin' emails, as these led to scare-mongering and unpleasant rumours. Instead he wanted people to speak more personally with one another either on the phone, in person at night, in the car or wherever.

To stimulate efficient and effective communication, rather than having weekly planning meetings, Kevin successfully introduced the 8.30 a.m. stand-up meeting. Each department could send a representative to the meeting where instead of sitting at a table, everyone stood. He said: 'it is amazing to see how quickly decisions get made when people are not sat down drinking coffee.' Everyone is provided with a chance to speak at the meeting and present his or her issue. Each concern is then managed during that day. In addition to stand-up meetings, Kevin implemented a policy to remove all minutes from meetings, the only exception being board meetings. His rationale was that he felt minutes created a 'blame culture'. He did however, encourage individuals to write up their own minutes and use these accordingly. This, he believes creates a sense of ownership for managing tasks.

Kevin also developed a phrase related to the marketing term 'post-purchase dissonance', calling it 'post-employment dissonance'. Whereas with the former, the consumer considers whether or not a substantial purchase has been worthwhile, the latter term is used by Kevin relating to the employee's decision to join the company. He therefore works hard to make the experience as positive as possible, so employees feel they made the right decision to join his company. Finally he provided us with a list of other items that he had implemented on the internal marketing side, which he believes were useful in the turnaround of the business. These included:

- Working with the Institute of Work Psychology to assess motivation in the workplace, thus trying to improve the work environment for everyone.

- Sharing good news and thanking employees when company Awards were achieved.

- Sponsoring an employee of the year prize.

- Thanking employees for working long hours in achieving delivery deadlines etc.

After firstly addressing employee issues, Option 1 was also implemented to some extent based on good internal marketing practice. Kevin encouraged all employees to take a 'bottom-up' review of profitability and working capital drivers. In response, the shop floor were able to initially advise on those jobs that were heavily time-consuming and, along with the sales team, Kevin was later able to use this information to weed out less profitable and non-profitable sales orders. The sales team soon began to realise where the most profit came from and were able to work more closely with such key accounts. This spiralled into a healthier situation whereby more attention and activity was focused on relatively fewer and more profitable customers than lots of loss-making ones. More devoted attention and service was provided to such customers, which also generated further orders through representatives cross-selling additional customised service work. Finally, Kevin has not ruled out Option 3, as he realises that over the long term, the market opportunities for this type of specialised engineering is heading East. Only recently a number of companies have visited from this area of the world with a vested interest in DavyMarkham – so watch this space!

Chapter summary

Now that you have finished reading this chapter, you should be able to answer any of the following potential examination questions:

1. **Explain the strategic planning process.** Strategic planning is the managerial decision process in which top management defines the firm's purpose and specifies what the firm hopes to achieve over the next five or so years. For large firms that have a number of self-contained business units, the first step in strategic planning is for top management to establish a mission for the entire corporation. Top managers then evaluate the internal and external environment of the business and set corporate-level objectives that guide decision making within each individual SBU. In small firms that are not large enough to have separate SBUs, strategic planning simply takes place at the overall firm level. For companies with several different SBUs, strategic planning also includes making decisions about how to allocate resources across these businesses to ensure growth for the whole organisation and developing growth strategies.

2. **Describe the steps in marketing planning.** Marketing planning is one type of functional planning. Marketing planning begins with an evaluation of the internal and external environments. Marketing managers then set marketing objectives usually related to the firm's brands, sizes, product features and other marketing mix-related elements. Next, marketing managers select the target market(s) for the organisation and decide what marketing mix strategies they will use. Product strategies include decisions about products and product characteristics that will appeal to the target market. Pricing strategies state the specific prices to be charged to channel members and final consumers. Promotion strategies include plans for advertising, sales promotion, public relations, publicity, personal selling and direct marketing used to reach the target market. Distribution strategies outline how the product will be made available to targeted customers when and where they want it. Once the marketing strategies are developed, they must be implemented. Control is the measurement of actual performance and comparison with planned performance.

Maintaining control implies the need for concrete measures of marketing performance called *marketing metrics*.

3. **Understand how factors in the external business environment influence marketing strategies and outcomes.** The economic environment refers to the economic health of a country that may be gauged by its gross domestic product and its economic infrastructure, its level of economic development, and its stage in the business cycle. Marketers use competitive intelligence to examine brand, product and discretionary income competition in the micro-environment and in the structure of the industry within the macro-environment. A country's political and legal environment includes laws and regulations of individual countries that affect business, international regulations developed by the World Trade Organization (WTO) and regional agreements among countries that form economic communities. In addition, marketers must understand the local political situation, the prospects for nationalisation or expropriation of foreign holdings, regulations such as local content rules, and labour and human rights regulations. Marketers also examine a country's socio-cultural environment including demographics, values, norms and customs, language and ethnocentricity.

4. **Explain operational planning.** Operational planning is done by first-line supervisors such as sales managers, marketing communication managers, and marketing research managers and focuses on the day-to-day execution of the marketing plan. Operational plans generally cover a shorter period of time and include detailed directions for the specific activities to be carried out, who will be responsible for them, and timelines for accomplishing the tasks.

5. **Explain the key role of implementation and control in marketing planning.** Any plan is only as good as its ability to actually be implemented. To ensure effective implementation, a marketing plan must include individual action plans, or programmes,

that support the plan at the operational level. A template for documenting action plans within a marketing plan is included as Table 2.6. Each action plan necessitates providing a budget estimate, schedule or timeline for its implementation, and appropriate metrics so that the marketer can monitor progress and act on discrepancies or variation from the plan. Sometimes variance from a plan requires shifting or increasing resources to make the plan work; at other times, it requires changing the objectives of the plan to recognise changing conditions. The key is that marketing plans aren't written in stone and marketers must be flexible enough to make such changes when warranted.

6. **Discuss some of the important aspects of an organisation's internal environment.** The internal environment includes the controllable elements inside an organisation that influence how well the organisation operates, including the firm's technologies, its physical facilities, its financial stability, its reputation, the quality of its products and services, and its employees. Ultimately, much of the internal environment of a firm is related to its corporate culture.

7. **Explain how countries seek to protect local industries by establishing barriers to foreign companies and by bonding together into economic communities.** Some governments adopt policies of protectionism with rules designed to give home companies an advantage. Such policies may include trade quotas, embargoes or tariffs that increase the costs of foreign goods. The World Trade Organization works to reduce such protectionism and encourage free trade. Many countries have come together to form economic communities to promote free trade.

8. **Explain how factors in the external business environment influence marketing strategies and outcomes.** The economic environment refers to the economic health of a country that may be gauged by its gross domestic product and its economic infrastructure, its level of economic development, and its stage in the business cycle. Marketers use competitive intelligence to examine brand, product and disposable income competi-

tion in the micro-environment and in the structure of the industry within the macro-environment. A country's political and legal environment includes laws and regulations of individual countries that affect business, international regulations developed by the World Trade Organization and regional agreements among countries that form economic communities. In addition, marketers must understand the local political situation, the prospects for nationalisation or expropriation of foreign holdings, regulations such as local content rules, and labour and human rights regulations. Marketers also examine a country's socio-cultural environment including demographics, values, norms and customs, language and ethnocentricity.

9. **Explain the strategies that a firm can use to enter global markets.** Different foreign market entry strategies represent varying levels of commitment for a firm. Exporting of goods entails little market commitment and exerts an exporter has less overall control on how products are sold. Contractual agreements such as licensing or franchising allow greater control. With strategic alliances through joint ventures, commitment increases. Finally, the firm can choose to invest directly by buying an existing company or starting a foreign subsidiary in the host country.

10. **What are the arguments for standardisation versus localisation of marketing strategies in global markets?** Firms that operate in two or more countries can choose to standardise their marketing strategies by using the same approach in all countries or choose to localise by adopting different strategies for each market. The firm needs to decide whether to sell an existing product, change an existing product, or develop a new product. In many cases, the promotional strategy must be tailored to fit the needs of consumers in another country. The product may need to be priced differently, especially if income levels are not the same in the new market. Finally, different methods of distribution may be needed, especially in countries lacking a solid infrastructure that provides adequate transportation, communications, and storage facilities.

Key terms

Action plans 80
BCG growth-market share matrix 71
Born-global firms 90
Brand competition 60
Business cycle 57
Business plan 51
Business planing 51
Business portfolio 71
Cash cows 72
Collectivist cultures 67
Competitive intelligence (CI) 58
Control 78
Conventions 67
Corporate culture 83
Counter trade 85
Cultural values 65
Custom 67
Demographics 65
Developed country 57
Developing countries 57
Disposable income 59
Dogs 73
Dumping 92
Economic communities 88

Economic infrastructure 56
Embargo 88
Ethnocentrism 68
Expropriation 64
Franchising 90
Functional planning 52
General Agreement on Tariffs and Trade (GATT) 87
Grey market goods 92
Gross domestic product (GDP) 55
Gross national product (GNP) 55
Import quotas 88
Individualistic cultures 67
Joint venture 90
Less developed country 56
Level of economic development 56
Licensing 90
Local content rules 64
Market development strategies 74
Market penetration strategies 73
Marketing plan 51
Mission statement 53
Monopoly 60
Mores 67

Nationalisation 64
Norms 67
Oligopoly 60
Operational planning 52
Operational plans 83
Patent 61
Portfolio analysis 71
Product adaptation strategy 92
Product development strategies 74
Product invention strategy 92
Protectionism 88
Question mark 72
Return on marketing investment (ROMI) 78
Standard of living 56
Stars 71
Straight extension strategy 91
Strategic alliance 90
Strategic business units (SBUs) 53
Strategic planning 52
SWOT analysis 68
Tariffs 88
World trade 85
World Trade Organization (WTO) 87

Chapter review

 ## Marketing concepts: testing your knowledge

1. What is strategic functional and operational planning? How does strategic planning differ at the corporate and the SBU levels?
2. What is a mission statement? What is a SWOT analysis? What role do these play in the planning process?
3. What is a strategic business unit (SBU)? How do firms use the Boston Consulting Group matrix for portfolio analysis in planning for their SBUs?
4. Describe the four business growth strategies: market penetration, product development, market development and diversification.
5. Explain the steps in the marketing planning process.
6. How does operational planning support the marketing plan?
7. What are the elements of a formal marketing plan?
8. What is an action plan? Why are action plans such an important part of marketing planning? Why is it so important for marketers to break the implementation of a marketing plan down into individual elements through action plans?

9. What is return on marketing investment (ROMI)? How does considering marketing as an investment instead of an expense affect a firm?
10. Give several examples of marketing metrics. How might a marketer use each metric to track progress of some important element of a marketing plan?
11. What is corporate culture? What are some ways in which the corporate culture of one organisation might differ from that of another? How does corporate culture affect marketing decision making?
12. Describe the market conditions that influence a firm's decision to enter foreign markets.
13. What is protectionism? Explain import quotas, embargoes and tariffs.
14. Explain how GDP, the categories of economic development and the business cycle influence marketers' decisions in entering global markets.
15. What is a monopoly, an oligopoly, monopolistic competition and pure competition?

16. What aspects of the political and legal environment influence a firm's decision to enter a foreign market?
17. Why do marketers need to understand these environments in a global marketplace?
18. What is ethnocentricity? How does ethnocentricity affect a firm that seeks to enter a foreign market?
19. How is a firm's level of commitment related to its level of control in a foreign market? Describe the four levels of involvement that are options for a firm: exporting, contractual agreements, strategic alliances and direct investment.
20. What are the arguments for standardisation of marketing strategies in the global marketplace? What are the arguments for localisation? What are some ways a firm can standardise or localise its marketing mix?

Marketing concepts: discussing choices and ethical issues

1. The Boston Consulting Group matrix identifies products as stars, cash cows, question marks and dogs. Do you think this is a useful way for organisations to examine their businesses? What are some examples of product lines that fit in each category?
2. In this chapter we talked about how firms do strategic, functional and operational planning. Yet some firms are successful without formal planning. Do you think planning is essential to a firm's success? Can planning ever hurt an organisation?
3. Most planning involves strategies for growth. But is growth always the right direction to pursue? Can you think of some organisations that should have contraction rather than expansion as their objective? Do you know of any organisations that have planned to get smaller rather than larger in order to be successful?
4. When most people think of successful marketing, internal firm culture doesn't immediately come to mind as a contributing factor. What are some reasons a firm's corporate culture is important to the capability to do good marketing? Give some examples of what you consider to be a good corporate culture for marketing.

5. Most marketers today feel pressure to measure (quantify) their level of success in marketing planning. Is it easy to measure marketing's success (compared with, say, measuring the success of a firm's financial management or production quality)? Explain your viewpoint.
6. The World Trade Organization seeks to eventually remove all barriers to world trade. Do you think this will ever be a reality? What do you think are the positive and negative aspects of a totally free marketplace? Which countries will win and which will lose in such a world?
7. In recent years, terrorism and other types of violent activities around the globe have made the global marketplace seem very unsafe. How concerned should firms with international operations be about such activities? Should these firms consider abandoning some global markets? How should firms weighup concerns about terrorism against the need to help the economies of developing countries? Would avoiding countries such as those in the Middle East make good sense in terms of economic profit? What about in terms of social profit?

Marketing practice: applying what you've learned

1. Assume that you are the marketing director for a small firm that manufactures educational toys for children. Your boss, the company president, has decided to develop a mission statement. He's admitted that he doesn't know much about developing a mission statement and has asked that you help guide him in this process. Write a memo outlining what exactly a mission statement is, why firms develop such statements, how firms use mission statements, and your thoughts on what the firm's mission statement might be.
2. As a marketing student, you know that large firms often organise their operations into a number of strategic business units (SBUs). A university might develop a similar structure in which different academic schools or departments are seen as separate businesses. Working with a group of four to six classmates, consider how your university might divide its total academic units into separate SBUs. What would be the problems with implementing such a plan? What would be the advantages and disadvantages for students and for faculty? Present your analysis of the university's SBUs to your class.
3. An important part of planning is a SWOT analysis, understanding an organisation's strengths, weaknesses, opportunities and threats. Choose a business in your community with which you are familiar. Develop a brief SWOT analysis for that business.
4. As an employee of a business consulting firm that specialises in helping people who want to start small businesses, you have been assigned a client who is interested in introducing a new concept in health clubs, one that offers its customers both the usual exercise and weight training opportunities, as well as certain related types of medical assistance such as physical therapy, a weight loss physician and diagnostic testing. As you begin thinking about the potential for success for this client, you realise that developing a marketing plan is going to be essential. In a role-playing situation, present your argument to the client as to why she needs to invest in formal marketing planning.

5. Assume that your firm is interested in the global market potential for a chain of coffee shops in the following countries: Italy, the UK and the Netherlands. You recognise that an understanding of the external environments in each of these potential markets is essential. First, decide which environmental factors are most important to your business. Then, use your library to gather information about the environments of each of these countries. Finally, tell how the differences among the environments might affect marketing strategies for coffee shops.

6. Although most large firms have already made the decision to go global, many small to medium-sized firms are only now considering such a move. Consider a small firm that manufactures gas barbecue grills.

   a. What type of market entry strategy (exporting, contractual agreement, strategic alliance or direct investment) do you feel would be best for the firm? Why?

   b. How would you recommend that the firm implement the strategy? That is, what type of product, price, promotion and distribution strategies would you suggest? What role can the internet play?

Marketing miniprojects: learning by doing

The purpose of this miniproject is to gain an understanding of marketing planning through actual experience.

1. Select one of the following for your marketing planning project:
   - yourself (in your search for a career);
   - your university;
   - a specific department in your university.

2. Next, develop the following elements of the marketing planning process:
   - a mission statement;
   - a SWOT analysis;
   - objectives;
   - a description of the target market(s);
   - a positioning strategy;
   - a brief outline of the marketing mix strategies, i.e. the product, pricing, distribution and promotion strategies that satisfy the objectives and address the target market.

3. Prepare a brief outline of a marketing plan using the template provided on the book's website as a guide.

The purpose of this second mini-project is to begin to develop an understanding of a culture other than your own and how customer differences lead to changes in the ways marketing strategies and socially responsible decision making can be implemented in that culture.

1. As part of a small group, select a country you would like to know more about and a product you think could be successful in that market. As a first step, gather information about the country. If possible, find a fellow student from the country and talk with him or her about the country. You will probably also wish to investigate other sources of information, such as books and magazines found in your library, or access information from the web.

2. Prepare a summary of your findings that includes the following:

   a. An overall description of the country, including such factors as its history, economy, religions and so on, that might affect marketing of the product you have selected.

   b. A description of the cultural values and business ethics dominant in the country.

   c. The current status of this product in the country.

   d. Your recommendations for a product strategy (product design, packaging, brand name, price and so on).

   e. Your recommendations for promotional strategies.

   f. A discussion of the ethical and social responsibility issues present in the recommendations you have made.

Further reading

Marketing Strategy and Competitive Positioning, 5th Edition, Graham Hooley, Brigitte Nicoulaud and Nigel F. Piercy, Financial Times/Prentice Hall , 2011

First and foremost we are increasingly seeing both public and private sector organisations raising the importance and seriousness they attach to their environmental and social responsibilities. Motor manufacturers, for example, are now competing vigorously to produce low-emission vehicles such as hybrids and electric cars, and the emphasis for many firms is on reducing waste and using raw inputs more efficiently as well as effectively. This fifth edition attempts to identify new approaches to doing business that will promote sustainability, both for the organisations adopting them and the environments (economic, social and natural) in which they operate. The focus remains, however, on creating and sustaining superior performance in the marketplace through clearly targeting and positioning the organisation's offerings.

Real people, real surfers

Exploring the web

Visit the home pages of one or more firms you are interested in. Follow the links to find out about the company's products, pricing, distribution, and marketing communications strategies. Do a search of the web for other information about the company. Based on your findings, answer the following questions:

1. What is the organisation's business? What is the overall purpose of the organisation? What does the organisation hope to achieve?

2. What customers does the business want to serve?

3. What elements of the web page specifically reflect the business of the organisation? How is the web page designed to attract the organisation's customers?

4. Do you think the marketing strategies and other activities of the firm are consistent with its mission? Why do you feel this way?

5. Develop a report based on your findings and conclusions about the firm. Present your report to your class.

Assume that you are the director of marketing for a firm that manufactures small household appliances such as mixers, coffee makers, toasters and so forth. You are considering entering (the country you have selected). You recognise that businesses must carefully weigh up opportunities for global marketing. Use the internet to gather information that would be useful in your firm's decision.

Write a report that answers the following questions:

1. What are the physical characteristics of the country (geography, weather, natural resources and so forth)?

2. Describe the economy of the country.

3. What is the country's investment climate?

4. What trade regulations will your firm face in entering the country?

5. What is the country's political climate? Are there obvious political risks?

6. Based on this information, what overall market entry strategy do you recommend for your firm, i.e. exporting, contractual agreement, strategic alliance or direct investment?

7. What are your specific recommendations for implementing the strategy?

As a final part of your report, describe the websites you used to gather this information. Which sites were most useful and why?

Now, take a look at the website at www.pearsoned.co.uk/solomon to see some videos from YouTube relating to aspects of this chapter.

Marketing plan exercise

The airline industry has experienced a lot of turbulence in recent years that inhibits its ability to plan for the future. Pick your favourite airline and help it plan by doing the following:

1. See if you can locate its mission statement, then develop a few marketing objectives that you believe would nicely support it.

2. Take a look at Figure 2.4, the product–market growth matrix, and the accompanying discussion. How might your chosen airline go about developing some strategies in each of the boxes: penetration, market development, product development and diversification? (Hint: Remember that airlines are in

the business of providing a service. The strategies you come up with will probably entail adding new or modified services in their targeted markets.)

3. Considering the strategies you identified in question 2, identify some specific marketing metrics that are appropriate for use in control.

4. What are some important global marketing issues that one must be mindful of when developing a marketing plan? Why do these issues need to be considered separately from a firm's domestic plan?

Delve deeper into strategic and international marketing

Professor Costas Katsikeas

The Arnold Ziff Research Chair in Marketing and International Management at the University of Leeds

It is useful for students that this chapter focuses on both strategy and international marketing. In response, I provide reference to three publications in leading journals for further reading that build on these two key areas and are particularly relevant in today's business climate as they each provide empirical evidence relating to performance outcomes. The first article by Cavusgil and Zou (1994) analyses the internal and external forces that can influence marketing strategy, which in turn enhances performance. The second article, which is developed by Morgan, Kaleka and myself (2004), builds on the role of company resources and capabilities in influencing competitive strategy pursued and positional advantages achieved that, depending on the contingent role competitive intensity of the market, affect performance. Finally, in the most recent article of the three, developed by myself, Samiee and Theodosiou (2006), we discover that the degree of marketing strategy standardisation is significantly related to the similarity between different international markets with respect to several key macro- and micro-environmental factors. I sincerely hope that these readings will encourage your studies and motivate you to continue with academic research in this challenging area.

References

Cavusgil, S.T. and Zou, S. (1994) 'Marketing Strategy-Performance Relationship: An Investigation of the Empirical Link in Export Market Ventures', *Journal of Marketing*, 58, no.1, 1–21.

Katsikeas, C.S., Samiee, S. and Theodosiou, M. (2006) 'Strategy Fit and Performance Consequences of International Marketing Standardization', *Strategic Management Journal*, 27, 867–90.

Morgan, N.A., Kaleka, A. and Katsikeas, C.S. (2004) 'Antecedents of Export Venture Performance: A Theoretical Model and Empirical Assessment', *Journal of Marketing*, 68, no. 1, 90–108.

Marketing in action case

Real decisions at Mattel Toys

In 1945 Mattel's founders, Ruth and Elliott Handler, were manufacturing picture frames out of a garage workshop. The couple also ran a side business making dollhouse furniture from the frame scraps; this became so successful that they turned to making toys. In 1955, Mattel began advertising its toys through the *Mickey Mouse Club* TV show and thus revolutionised the way toys are sold. In 1959, Ruth Handler, noting her own daughter Barbara's love for cut-out paper dolls, created the idea of a three-dimensional paper doll. Barbie was born and very quickly propelled Mattel to the forefront of the toy industry.

The 1960s saw Mattel grow with such new products as Barbie's boyfriend Ken, See-and-Say toys and Hot Wheels toy cars. In the 1980s Mattel became a global company with the purchase of Hong Kong-based ARCO industries, Correlle, SA, a maker of collector-quality dolls based in France, a British company, Corgi Toys Ltd, and a joint venture with Japan's largest toy company, Bandai. Mattel stresses social responsibility. Its Sustainability Mission states: 'We regard the thoughtful management of the environment and the health and safety of our employees, customers, and neighbours as among our highest priorities and as key elements of our responsibility to be a sustainable company.'

In 2006, Mattel's Children's Foundation donated approximately $4.8 million in cash grants and approximately

$10 million in toys to organisations serving children around the world. Over 2500 Mattel employees volunteered for charitable activities and Special Olympics programmes in 13 countries. In 2007 trouble arrived in Toyland. Like many other toy makers, in recent years Mattel commissioned Chinese companies to produce its products. In August, Mattel was forced to recall 1.5 million of its Fisher-Price toys, including such favourites as Elmo and Big Bird, because they were suspected of containing hazardous levels of lead paint. Later in August, Mattel recalled over 19 million more Chinese-made toys because they contained magnets that could be swallowed by children or because they were made with dangerous lead paint.

Following the second recall the company purchased full-page ads in the *New York Times* and the *Wall Street Journal* to assure parents that it understands how they feel. CEO Robert Eckert, a father of four, appeared on an online video to state, 'I can't change what has happened in the past, but I can change how we work in the future.' Mattel pledged to test the paint in every batch of paint delivered to all of its toy producers and to take other safety measures. Consumers, however, were not all convinced. Video clips appeared on YouTube mocking the company's efforts. One video referred to the recall of 'Tickle Me Lead-Mo.' The recall dramatically cut into Mattel's revenues. Sales of Dora the Explorer toys fell 21 per cent internationally. Barbie sales fell 19 per cent in the United States, and Brazil banned imports of all Mattel products while it evaluated whether or not the company was complying with its safety regulations.

Again in 2010, Mattel recalled over 10 million of its Fisher-Price products including about 7 million Fisher-Price Trikes and Tough Trikes. The tricycles have a plastic ignition key near the seat that kids can sit on or fall onto, potentially leading to injuries. Fisher-Price offered customers free repair or replacements. Mattel must continue to work hard to recover from these disasters. Are apologies and claims for new safety regulations enough? Since some but not all of the recalls were because of production in other countries, should the company stop producing its toys in China and other developing countries where costs are low? Or should Mattel return to its roots and produce the millions of Polly Pockets, 'Sarge' toy cars and Barbie play sets in the United States, where costs are substantially higher, but standards are tougher?

Things to think about

1. What is the decision facing Mattel?

2. What factors are important in understanding this decision and situation?

3. What are the alternatives?

4. What decision(s) do you recommend?

5. What are some ways to implement your recommendation?

Sources: www.mattel.com/about_us/history/default.asp; Nicholas Casey and Nicholas Zamiska, 'Mattel Does Damage Control after Recall', *The Wall Street Journal*, 17 August 2007, http://on-line.wsj.com/article/SB11870956721897168.html (accessed 16 January 2008); 'Key Dates in China Export Scares,' *The Wall Street Journal*, 21 October , 2007, http://on-line.wsj.com/ article/SB118606827156686195.html (accessed January 16, 2008); Roger Parloff, 'Not Exactly Counterfeit,' *Fortune* 1, May 2006, 108–16; 'Mattel, Battered by Recalls, Posts Quarterly Profit Drop,' *The International Herald Tribune*, 16, October 2007, 19; Associated Press, 'Fisher-Price Recalls 10 Million Items', *New York Times*, 6, September, 2010, B6.

References

1. www.madd.org (accessed 30 May 2006).

2. 'Peru: Privatization Is Principal Policy for Attracting Foreign Investment', *Wall Street Journal*, 27 October 1993, B7.

3. Keith Bradsher, 'Consumerism Grows in China, with Beijing's Blessing', *New York Times*, 1 December 2003, www.bdachina .com/content/about/pressquotes/P1070443598/en?portal_ skin=printable.

4. Deborah Ball, 'Lattes Lure Brits to Coffee; Tea Sales Fall as Starbucks Draws the Young', *The Wall Street Journal*, 20 October 2005, B1.

5. Michael Barbaro, 'Wal-Mart Offers Aid to Rivals', *New York Times*, 5 April 2006, Section C, page 1, http://web.lexis-nexis .com/universe/document?_m=a65b59dd05c3bc4cd6408663 bf954224 &_docnum=5&wchp=dGLbVzb-zSkVb&_md5=9d 53d563cc5228449eebb4a230887f3f.

6. Sara Hope Franks, 'Overseas, It's What's Inside That Sells', *Washington Post National Weekly Edition*, 5–11 December 1994, 21.

7. William C. Symonds, 'Border Crossings', *Business Week*, 22 November 1993, 40.

8. Adapted from Michael R. Solomon, *Consumer Behavior: Buying, Having, and Being*, 7th ed. (Upper Saddle River, NJ: Prentice Hall, 2007).

9. David Carr, 'Romance, In *Cosmo*'s World, Is Translated in Many Ways', *New York Times*, 26 May 2002, sec. 1, p. 1, adapted from Michael R. Solomon, *Consumer Behavior: Buying, Having, and Being*, 6th ed. (Upper Saddle River, NJ: Prentice Hall, 2003).

10. Richard W. Pollay, 'Measuring the Cultural Values Manifest in Advertising', *Current Issues and Research in Advertising* 6 (1983), 71–92.

11. Deborah Ball, 'Women in Italy Like To Clean but Shun the Quick and Easy', *Wall Street Journal*, 25 April 2006, A1.

12. Daniel Goleman, 'The Group and the Self: New Focus on a Cultural Rift', 25 December 1990, www.nyt.com, 37; Harry C. Triandis, 'The Self and Social Behavior in Differing Cultural Contexts', *Psychological Review* 96 (July 1989), 506; Harry C. Triandis *et al.*, 'Individualism and Collectivism: Cross-Cultural Perspectives on Self-Ingroup Relationships', *Journal of Personality and Social Psychology* 54 (February 1988), 323.

13. George J. McCall and J.L. Simmons, *Social Psychology: A Sociological Approach* (New York: Free Press, 1982).

14. Adapted from Solomon, *Consumer Behavior: Buying Having, and Being*, 7th ed.

15. Patrick Barwise and John U. Farley, 'Which Marketing Metrics Are Used and Where?', *Working Paper Series*, Report No. 03-111 (Cambridge, MA: Marketing Science Institute, 2003).

16. Kerry A. Dolan, 'The Soda with Buzz', *Forbes*, 28 March 2005, 126.

17. Christina Binkley, 'Hotels "Go to the Matresses"; Marriott is Latest to Make Huge Bet on Better Bedding', *Wall Street Journal*, 25 January 2005, D1.

18. Pallovi Gogoi, 'Chipolte's IPO: One Hot Tamale', *Business Week Online*, 23 September 2005.

19. Gordon A. Wyner, 'Beyond ROI: Make Sure the Analytics Address Strategic Issues', *Marketing Management* 15 (May/June 2006), 8–9.

20. Nike, 'Nike Reports Second Quarter Earnings Up Nine Percent; Worldwide Futures Orders Increase Eight Percent', press release, 20 December 2001, www.nikebiz.com/media/n_q202.shtml.

21. Michael Barbaro, 'Cricket Anyone? Sneaker Makers on Fresh Turf', *The New York Times Online*, 28 January 2006.

22. 'World Trade in 2004 – Overview', www.wto.org/english/ res_e/ststis_e/its2005_e/its05_overvoew_e.pdf.

23. World Trade Organization, 'stronger Than Expected Growth Spurs Modest Trade Recovery', press release, 5 April 2004, www.wto.org/english/news_e/pres04_e/pr373_e.htm.

24. 'Phillippines Implements Countertrade Program for Vietnamese Rice', *Asia Pulse*, 27 April 2005, http://web.lexis-nexis. com/universe/document?_m=39eaf11285f8163c2b36a2ad0 a15af9f&_docnum=3&wchp=dGLbVzb-zSkVb&_md5=8af52 9d535ea2a669565a8be3399ef0e.

25. www.usatoday.com/money/autos/2005-12-15-china-cars-usat5_x.htm.

26. Michael R. Czinkota and Masaaki Kotabe, 'America's New World Trade Order', *Marketing Management* 1 (3) (1992), 47–54.

27. World Trade Organization, 'The WTO in Brief', www.wto.org/ english/thewto_e/whatis_e/inbrief_e/inbr02_e.htm.

28. Ibid.

29. Nic Hopkins, 'software Piracy Microsoft's Big Threat', *CNN. com*, 7 February 2001, www.cnn.com/2001/WORLD/asiapcf/ east/02/07/hongkong.microsoft.

30. Geri Smith, Elisabeth Malkin, Jonathan Wheatley, Paul Magnusson and Michael Arnds, 'Betting on Free Trade', *Business Week*, 23 April 2001, 60–62; Free Trade Area of the Americas, 'Antecedents of the FTAA Process' (accessed 20 March 2006), www. ftaa-alca.org/View_e.asp#PREPARATORY; Johathan Wheatley, 'Bush and Lula Try to Paper Over Divisions Seen at Summit of Americas', *Financial Times*, 7 November 2005, http://web .lexis-nexis.com/universe/document?_m=621ddc7a6d8e970d 0c1068f13f4da39b&_docnum=88&wchp=dGLbVzb-zSkVb&_ md5=7dd29a69c250e36cf7a13cf6cf73539d.

31. 'Russia: Introduction of Mean Import Quotas', www.iet.ru/ afe/english/apk/january03.pdf.

32. Alexander Hiam and Charles D. Schewe, *The Portable MBA in Marketing* (New York: John Wiley & Sons, 1992).

33. Harvey S. James Jr. and Murray Weidenbaum, *When Businesses Cross International Borders* (Westport, CT: Praeger, 1993).

34. Rebecca Buckman, 'China's Cheeseman Is No Longer Alone', 11 December 2003, www.wsj.com.

35. Saritha Rai, 'Tastes of India in U.S. Wrappers', 29 April 2003, www.nyt.com.

36. 'Haier's Global Ambitions Demand Flexible Advice', *Managing Intellectual Property*, February 2006, 1.

37. P.D. Harveston and P.S. Davis, 'Entrepreneurship and the Born Global Phenomenon: Theoretical Foundations and a Research Agenda', in *E-Commerce and Entrepreneurship: Research in Entrepreneurship and Management*, vol. 1, ed. John Butler (Information Age Publishing, 2001), 1–30; text adapted from www.campbell.berry.edu/faculty/pharveston/bornglobal.html.

38. Jeremy Kahn, 'The World's Most Admired Companies', *Fortune*, 26 October 1998, 206–16.

39. One of the most influential arguments for this perspective can be found in Theodore Levitt, 'The Globalization of Markets', *Harvard Business Review* (May–June 1983), 92–102.

40. Juliana Koranteng, 'Reebok Finds Its Second Wind as It Pursues Global Presence', *Advertising Age International* (January 1998), 18.

41. Terry Clark, 'International Marketing and National Character: A Review and Proposal for an Integrative Theory', *Journal of Marketing* 54 (October 1990), 66–79.

42. Richard C. Morais, 'The Color of Beauty', *Forbes*, 27 November 2000, 170–76.

43. Aaron O. Patrick, 'World Cup's Advertisers Hope One Size Fits All: Month-Long Tournament Sets Off Scramble to Reach Huge Global TV Audience', *The Wall Street Journal*, 28 March 2006, B7.

44. Better Business Bureau, 'Gray Market Goods', www.newyork. bbb.org/library/publications/subrep45.html.

45. Wendy Zellner, 'How Well Does Wal-Mart Travel?', *BusinessWeek*, 3 September 2001, 82, no. 2, 82–4.

Chapter 3
Marketing research

Meet Ryan Garton,
Consumer Insights Director at Discover Financial Services

Q & A with Ryan Garton

What I do when I'm not working
Activities with my three kids – soccer, dance, swimming and music lessons. Restoring our 1910 home (I am a bit of a carpenter! Think of This Old House)

First job out of school?
Marketing research for The Gallup Organization

Business book I'm reading now.
Buyology by Martin Lindstrom

My motto to live by
'Make no small plans, for they have not the power to stir the hearts and minds of men.' Daniel Burnham

My management style
Competitive – strategic – achiever – individualisation – relator

Don't do this when interviewing with me
Make excuses

My pet peeve
Others not taking ownership of their actions

Promoted to his current position in January 2008, Ryan and the Consumer Insights team are responsible for all market research activities for the firm including brand and advertising tracking/effectiveness, new product development/innovation screeners, financial attitudes and usage studies, overall voice of the customer, and other ad hoc quantitative and qualitative studies as requested by business lines. Prior to joining Discover Financial Services, Ryan had an 11-year career at United Airlines, which spanned several marketing leadership roles in international marketing – STAR Alliance, market research, product development and brand marketing strategy. He and his team were responsible for all United branding, the new United aircraft livery, development of airport lounge products, EasyCheck-in, sub-brand development (TED) and overall partnership strategy (Starbucks, Pepsi and AOL). His assignment prior to joining the Marketing Division was as the marketing and sales manager for the Midwest Region–Chicago, where he was responsible for revenue and profitability within United's largest North American Region.

Before his airline career, Ryan worked for The Gallup Organization in survey research and political tracking. He worked with several key accounts including Volkswagen, NationsBank, CNN News and numerous political polls. He has an MBA from the University of Nebraska with an emphasis on international marketing and strategy, and an undergraduate degree from St. Olaf College in economics and political science.

Real people, real decisions
Decision time at Discover

Ryan's problem at Discover Financial was simple: too much of a good thing. The company had a lot of very good new product and services ideas: new card products, new technologies to help people manage their finances/bills, enhancements to its website, new insurance products and new banking products. However, Ryan lacked an integrated approach to determine which of the ideas would be most likely to fit cardholders' desires, fit with the Discover brand image as the card that is all about cashback and other rewards to cardholders, and fit with company resources (financial and technical). In fact, Ryan had such a good thing that he didn't have the internal resources to evaluate each product idea. In particular, he was missing a crucial piece of the puzzle: customer input. Typically Discover would prioritise new product ideas using metrics such as revenue projections, resource consumption estimates, and internal assessments of strategic fit. But these estimates largely occur in a vacuum because they don't include the 'reality check' that actual users could provide. Ryan knew he had to seriously consider whether it was worthwhile to invest crucial resources to develop a system that could screen a large number of new product ideas with input from current or potential users of these products. He convened a cross-functional team of colleagues from Consumer Insights, Brand Strategy and New Product Strategy to outline what this new screening process might look like. The 'old' process was one where Ryan would gather these business partners together to look at the financial information available and the technology resources available. They would then determine the best course of action, typically without necessarily considering consumers' needs.

Things to understand

Like many companies, Discover Financial collected a lot of data from different sources to stay on top of changes in the financial services industry and to monitor the types of credit card options competitors offered to customers. But (also like many companies), the recognition that consumers' preferences should play a role when decisions are made regarding which products to take to market is a fairly new one for Discover. The marketing research process also gets more complicated when more input is included, so Ryan has to decide if his internal organisation has the resources to make the best use of all the information. He also recognises that internal decision–making often has a 'political' side to it, as executives frequently have a vested interest in which paths the company will choose to follow.

Ryan considers his options . . .

Option 1 Don't muddy the waters

Continue to use the same project prioritisation process that Discover had been using for many years. A passive approach would not put additional roadblocks in front of project timelines; new card features and other offerings could get to market faster because they wouldn't have to undergo another evaluation. Decision makers wouldn't have to learn a new process. But decisions about new features would continue to rely on internal projections and the intuition of managers without benefiting from input by actual consumers.

Option 2 Modify the current process to include existing consumer input that Discover can easily access

The team could look more carefully at feedback the company received in blogs, letters and telephone calls to help it gauge the likelihood of success. Again, this extra layer of information wouldn't significantly hold up the progress of product ideas in the pipeline. And, if the information contradicted management's priorities, at least this would be a red flag to force decision makers to take a second look. However, some of the new ideas broke new ground so there was no primary or syndicated research to indicate if they would fly. Consumers can't spontaneously provide feedback about products that don't yet exist.

Option 3 Engage an outside firm to assist Discover in developing a new process

Ideally Ryan wanted to test consumers' reactions to several key measures: market potential, consumer likeability, brand fit and comparisons with launches by other financial services companies. This new process would involve hiring an outside firm to apply a standardised set of measures to assess all potential offerings so Discover could use an 'apples to apples' comparison. Decision makers could access one score for each concept that encompasses all relevant research results. They could more easily identify how a concept might be improved so that cardholders would think more highly of it. And the score would include an assessment of how well each concept fits with the Discover brand. But this radical new approach would be politically challenging within the organisation because it would challenge some internal stakeholders' existing beliefs and priorities regarding which offerings they would like to develop. And a new approach would involve a big financial investment, most likely in the region of $100,000. There would also be a potential cost in that it would add weeks to the decision-making process so a competitor might get to market with the idea first.

Put yourself in Ryan's shoes. Which option do you think is best and why?

Objectives

When you finish reading this chapter, you will understand and be able to identify and evaluate:

1 The role of the marketing information system and the marketing decision support system in marketing decision making

2 The marketing research process

3 The differences among exploratory, descriptive and causal research techniques available to marketers

4 The different types of data-collection methods and types of consumer samples that researchers use

5 The growing use of online research

Knowledge is power

In Chapter 1, we talked about how marketing is a decision process in which marketing managers determine the strategies that will help the organisation meet its long-term objectives. In Chapter 2, we said that successful planning meant that managers made good decisions for guiding the organisation. But how do marketers make good decisions? How do they go about developing marketing objectives, selecting a target market, positioning (or repositioning) their product, and developing product, price, promotion and place strategies?

The answer is *information*. Information is the fuel that runs the marketing engine. To make good decisions, marketers must have information that is collectable and accessible as well as accurate, up to date and relevant. Information is also indispensable for effective customer relationship management (CRM). Only with access to the best possible information are companies able to identify truly valuable customers and satisfy them on a long-term basis. As you'll see in Figure 3.1, we are now in the second section of the book, 'Understanding Consumers' Value Needs'. Part of the marketer's role in understanding these needs is to conduct *marketing research* in order to identify them. In this chapter, we will discuss some of the tools that marketers use to get that information. In the chapters that follow, we will look at consumer behaviour, at how and why organisations buy, and then at how marketers sharpen their focus through target marketing strategies. But first let's talk about the marketing information system.

 The marketing information system

One of the ways in which firms collect information is through a **marketing information system (MkIS)**. The MkIS is a process that first determines what information marketing managers need and then gathers, sorts, analyses, stores and distributes relevant and timely marketing information to system users. Another possible definition comes from the American Marketing Association, which describes an MkIS as 'a set of procedures and methods for the regular, planned collection, analysis, and presentation of information

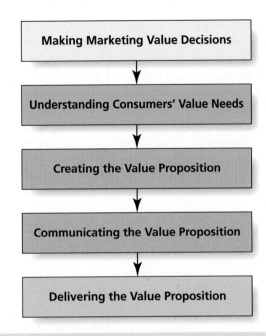

| Figure 3.1 | Making and delivering value |

Objective

1

The role of
the marketing
information
system and
the marketing
decision
support system
in marketing
decision making

for use in making marketing decisions'.[1] As you can see in Figure 3.2, the MkIS system
includes three important components:

- four types of data;

- computer hardware and software to analyse that data and to create reports;

- information and the decision makers who use it.

| Figure 3.2 | The marketing information system |

A firm's marketing information system (MkIS) stores and analyses data from a variety of
sources and turns the data into information for making marketing decisions

Where exactly do all the data come from? Information to feed the system comes from four major sources: these are internal company data, marketing intelligence data on competition and other elements in the firm's business environment, information gathered through marketing research and acquired databases.

The data are stored and accessed through computer hardware and software. Based on an understanding of managers' needs, MkIS personnel generate a series of regular reports for various system users. For example, supermarket chain Tesco gains most of the market insights through information from its Tesco Clubcard loyalty scheme. The research specialist firm Dunnhumby, which is responsible for Tesco's database management, receives 5 billion bits of information per week through the Clubcards and is able to convert the data into regular, valuable reports about sales figures, customer preferences and shopping patterns.

Let's take a closer look at each of the four different data sources for the MkIS.

1. Internal company data

The internal company data system uses information from within the company to produce reports on the results of sales and marketing activities. Internal company data consists of a firm's internal records of sales, basic information which every company possesses – information such as which customers buy which products in what quantities and at what intervals, what items are in stock and which ones are back-ordered because they are out of stock, when items were shipped to the customer, and what items have been returned because they are defective.

Often, an MkIS allows salespeople and sales managers in the field to access internal records through a company intranet. An **intranet** is an internal corporate communications network that uses internet technology to link company departments, employees and databases. Intranets are secured so that only authorised employees have access. When the MkIS is made available to managers, they can serve their customers better by having immediate access to information on pricing, inventory levels, production schedules, shipping dates, and the customer's sales history.

But equally important – because salespeople and sales managers are the ones in daily direct contact with customers – their reports are entered directly into the system via the company intranet. This means the reports can provide an important source of information to upper management on changes in sales patterns or new sales opportunities.

Marketing metrics

BP Lubricants intranet-based data repository

Global oil company BP has a lubricants division active in 60 countries. Maintaining an accurate picture of these markets is challenging. Historically, marketing data had been manually transcribed onto spreadsheets and then manually consolidated into one master spreadsheet, often with the need for re-keying of data or cutting and pasting. The company decided to standardise its global marketing data and as a first step defined and agreed a set of data standards. Next it created a standard data collection system that could be used by all 60 countries. Then a set of macro programs was written that loaded the country data into a master spreadsheet which was hosted on the corporate intranet. Users globally can access a set of reports from their web browsers that enable them to compare and rank their performance against that in the 59 other countries; they can also press a button that automatically generates a PowerPoint slide show with the latest figures.

From the internal company data system, marketing managers can get daily or weekly sales data for a brand or product line. They can also get monthly sales reports which help them to measure progress toward sales goals and market share objectives. For example, managers and buyers at many large retailers use up-to-the-minute sales information obtained from shop cash registers around the country so they can detect problems with products, promotions, and even the firm's distribution system.

2. Marketing intelligence

As we saw in Chapter 2, to make good decisions marketers need to have information about the marketing environment. Possessing up-to-date and relevant information is absolutely crucial for successful knowledge management which is seen as a vital tool for achieving competitive advantage. Thus, a second important element of the MkIS is the **marketing intelligence system**, a method by which marketers get information about everyday happenings in the marketing environment. The name intelligence may suggest cloak-and-dagger spy activities, but in reality nearly all the information companies need about their environment – including the competitive environment – is available by monitoring everyday sources: newspapers, trade publications or simple observations of the marketplace. And because salespeople are the ones 'in the trenches' every day, talking with customers, distributors and prospective customers, they can provide valuable information as well.

In recent years, the web has become a major source of marketing intelligence. Tremendous amounts of information are available on company web pages, including those of competitors, through news sources from around the globe, through government reports and on trade association sites. The ease of accessing and searching the web and individual sites makes the internet an attractive source of marketing intelligence.

Sometimes companies engage in specific activities to gain intelligence. For example, retailers often hire 'mystery shoppers' to visit their shops and those of their competitors posing as customers to see how people are treated. (Imagine being paid to shop for a living!) When McDonald's set up a quality improvement scheme, its managers sent mystery shoppers to visit restaurants on a regular basis to collect information about the shop environments and service. Other information may come from speaking to organisational buyers about competing products, attending trade shows, or simply purchasing competitors' products.

Marketing managers may use marketing intelligence data to predict fluctuations in sales due to economic conditions, political issues, and events that heighten consumer awareness or to forecast the future so that they will be on top of developing trends. For example, knowledge of trends in consumer preferences, driven by the younger teen generation, prompted Avon to create an entirely new brand of cosmetics called Mark. While traditional Avon salesladies (and buyers) are 30+, Mark is sold and bought by tweens, teens and 20-somethings.[2] The cosmetic industry, for example, is currently experiencing a new trend concerning beauty and skincare products for men. Firms like Biotherm or L'Oréal which were able to forecast this trend gained an extraordinary advantage as they could launch profitable product lines and attract customers before the competition became aware of the trend.

Photo 3.1 L'Oréal was able to forecast the popularity of skincare products for men
Source: Getty Images/Lintao Zhang

Marketing metrics

Nokia consumer insights

World leader in mobile communications, Nokia, has a consumer insights division of 30 people. It was established in 2001, and absorbed the old market research function. Its remit includes product conception and design and interpreting attitudes and behaviour of consumers. They try to track and forecast changes in long-term consumer motivation. Their aim is to provide internal consultancy to Nokia's managers. Market research firms are retained for their data collection and tabulation roles, but are not expected to provide added value.

Indeed, some marketing researchers, known as *futurists*, specialise in predicting consumer trends to come. They try to forecast changes in lifestyles that will affect the wants and needs of customers in the coming years by engaging in scenario planning. Futurists try to imagine different **scenarios**, or possible future situations, that might occur and assign a level of probability to each.

A scenario can be shaped by a number of key outcomes. For example, deregulation laws could shape the future of the banking or telecommunications industries. In those cases, a futurist might develop different scenarios for different levels of deregulation, including forecasts assuming no deregulation, moderate deregulation and complete deregulation. Each scenario allows marketers to consider the impact of different marketing strategies and to come up with plans based on which outcomes they consider are most likely to happen. No one can predict the future with certainty, but it's better to make an educated guess than no guess at all and be caught totally unprepared. Even something as seemingly simple as accurately predicting the price of a gallon of petrol next year greatly affects business success.

In some cases, companies are enlisting consumers' help to predict the success or failure of different products. The online stock exchange Ball Street (http://ball-street.ftd.de /view/) is a virtual project from the *Financial Times Germany* and Dresdner Bank which was launched for the World Cup in 2006, where football fans could trade stocks, for example of national teams, and by doing so forecast the results of the tournament. The predictions of Ball Street turned out to be quite precise and were of great interest for sponsors and investors. The stock exchange game was so popular that it was kept alive after the World Cup and now predicts the German premier league.[3]

Of course, collecting marketing intelligence data is just the beginning. An effective MkIS must include procedures to ensure that the marketing intelligence data are translated and combined with internal company data and other marketing data to create useful reports for marketing managers.

3. Marketing research

Marketing research refers to the process of collecting, analysing and interpreting data about customers, competitors and the business environment to improve marketing effectiveness. It is defined by the American Marketing Association (AMA) as the function that links consumer, customer and public to the marketer through information. Although marketing intelligence data are collected continuously to keep managers abreast of happenings in the marketplace, marketing research is called for when unique information is needed for specific decisions. Whether their business is selling cool clothes to teens or coolant to factories, firms succeed by knowing what customers want, when they want it, where they want it – and what competing firms are doing about it. In other words, the better a firm is at obtaining valid marketing information, the more successful it will be. Therefore, virtually all companies rely on some form of marketing research, though the amount and type of research they conduct varies dramatically. Although marketing research offers many potential benefits, a firm must not lose sight of the costs involved. Conducting effective marketing research can be very expensive and time-consuming and therefore should not be undertaken in every case. If a company faces serious budget deficits, if managers cannot agree what information they need for decision making, or if poor timing would result in irrelevant research results, it is very likely that the costs of the research will outweigh its benefits. A careful cost–benefit analysis will therefore help the company to find out whether marketing research can be beneficial in a certain situation or not. In general, marketing research available in an MkIS include syndicated research reports and custom research reports.

Syndicated research is general research collected by firms on a regular basis, then sold to other firms. The QScores Company, for instance, reports on the familiarity and appeal of over 1700 celebrity performers and provides information about how they are being perceived by customers. The obtained research can serve as a decision basis for companies that are interested in using a performer in their advertising. The services of the QScores Company include ratings of cartoon characters, sports stars and even deceased celebrities, so that the client could, for example, gain insights into the demographic appeal of Elvis Presley and Marilyn Monroe and determine whether they would be a valuable input for an advertising campaign.[4] The Broadcasters' Audience Research Board (BARB), for example, conducts research on the estimated number of people watching certain television shows and sells this audience data to the TV channels and advertisers.[5] Another example is the British Marketing Research Bureau (BMRB), which conducts a variety of syndicated research ranging from social policy and public interest research, environmental and climate change research to reports on in-store advertising, giving information about customer perceptions, shopping behaviours and the most useful media to use for advertising.

Alternative examples of syndicated research techniques are consumer panels, where members receive periodic invitations to participate in a survey, or retail audits, which are the continuous monitoring of product flows from supplier to consumer. As valuable as it may be, syndicated research doesn't provide all the answers to marketing questions because the information collected typically is broad but shallow; it gives good insights about general trends, such as who is watching what television shows or what brand of perfume is hot this year.

Often firms need to undertake custom marketing research. **Custom research** is research conducted for a single firm to provide answers to specific questions. This kind of research is especially helpful for firms when they need to know more about why certain trends have surfaced.

Some firms maintain an in-house research department that conducts studies on its behalf. Many firms, however, hire outside research companies that specialise in designing and conducting projects based on the needs of the client. These custom research reports are another kind of information that is included in the MkIS.

Marketers may use marketing research to identify opportunities for new products, to promote existing ones, or to provide data about the quality of their products, who uses them and how. Sometimes a company will even do research to counter a competitor's claim. Procter & Gamble (P&G), for example, challenged rival Revlon's claim that its ColorStay line of cosmetics wouldn't rub off. P&G researchers wanted to answer a specific question: was ColorStay's claim true? Because that kind of question can't be answered by buying a syndicated report, P&G commissioned 270 women to provide the specific information needed to support its case against Revlon. The women rubbed their

Marketing misstakes

Getting the basics wrong

Daf Trucks, a major Dutch vehicle manufacturer, was looking to expand into the Saudi Arabian market and entered the
market with its standard line of trucks. After years of hard
work and marketing effort, sales were still proving hard to
come by. In the end, the company decided to conduct some
in-depth consumer research which identified several issues. To
start with, Saudi truck owners had strong loyalties towards a
well-established German brand of trucks – Mercedes. Second,
Saudi buyers liked trucks with a 'torpedo' like front as opposed
to a 'flat' front. While Daf had invested in an extensive dealer
network equipped with modern facilities, Saudi truck owners actually preferred the services of the older, smaller service
stations which they had grown to know well. These were perceived as more flexible with friendlier mechanics. Finally, Daf
trucks had only two front seats instead of the four that were
standard in the German models. These better suited Saudi
truckers who have a habit of carrying a number of passengers
and family members in their driver cabs.[6]

Why do you think this might be a marketing misstake?

cheeks against their shirts while wearing ColorStay and reported that, in fact, most of the
shirts did get stained. Revlon, however, countered that P&G's test was flawed because
the women might have been encouraged to rub too hard. Revlon did its own test on 293
women who were told to use 'the pressure they use when caressing someone else's face'.
This time the women found few stains. To avoid further controversy, Revlon now says
that ColorStay won't rub off under 'normal circumstances'.[7] (Aren't you relieved?)

4. Acquired databases

A large amount of information that can be useful in marketing decision making is available in the form of external databases. Firms may acquire databases from any number of
sources. For example, some companies are willing to sell their customer database to non-
competing firms. Government databases, including the massive amounts of economic and
demographic information compiled by the statistics offices of the respective country, are
available at little or no cost.

Recently, the use of such databases for marketing purposes has come under increased
government scrutiny. Using the data for analysing consumer trends and product planning is one thing – using it for outbound mailings and unsolicited phone calls and emails
has evoked a backlash resulting in 'do-not-call' lists and anti-spam laws. Maybe you have
noticed that when you sign up for a credit card or have other occasion to give a seller
your contact information, you receive an invitation to 'opt out' of receiving promotional
mailings from them or from others who may acquire your contact information from them
later. By law, if you decide to opt out, companies cannot use your information for marketing purposes.

 ## Marketing decision support systems

A firm's marketing information system generates regular reports for decision makers on
what is going on in the internal and external environment. But sometimes these reports
are inadequate. Different managers may want different information, and in some cases

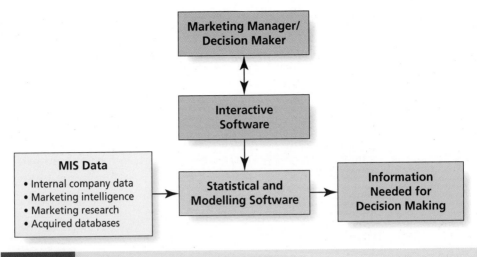

Figure 3.3	The marketing decision support system
	Although an MkIS provides many reports managers need for decision making, it doesn't answer all their information needs. The marketing decision support system (MDSS) is an enhancement to the MkIS that makes it easy for marketing managers to access the system and find answers to their questions

the problem that must be addressed is too vague or unusual to be easily answered by the MkIS process. As a result, many firms take the vital step to beef up their MkIS with a **marketing decision support system (MDSS)**. An MDSS includes analysis and interactive software that allows marketing managers, even those who are not computer experts, to access MkIS data and conduct their own analyses, often over the company intranet. Figure 3.3 shows the elements of an MDSS.

Modelling software, 'perceptual maps' and 'what-if' questions

Typically, an MDSS includes sophisticated statistical and modelling software tools. Statistical software allows managers to examine complex relationships among factors in the marketplace. For example, a marketing manager who wants to know how consumers perceive her company's brand in relation to the competition's brand might use a sophisticated statistical technique called multidimensional scaling to create a 'perceptual map', or a graphic presentation of the various brands in relationship to each other. You'll see an example of a perceptual map in Chapter 6 on segmentation and positioning.

Marketing metrics

Deciding which ice cream

Famous ice cream producer Ben & Jerry's, owned by consumer product giant Unilever, was looking for a technology system which would give managers and marketing executives easy access to customer information collected by the different departments. The IT (information technology) department chose a business intelligence software called BusinessObjects which offered the possibility to easily and quickly receive, analyse and act on consumer information data. This made it a lot easier for the company to discover buying patterns and taste preferences and react to customer comments. Any cream and chocolate sprinkles with your data?[8]

Table 3.1
Examples of
questions that might
be answered by an
MkIS and an MDSS

Questions Answered with an MkIS	Questions Answered with an MDSS
What were our company sales of each product during the past month and the past year?	Have our sales declines simply reflected changes in overall industry sales, or is there some portion of the decline that cannot be explained by industry changes?
What changes are happening in sales in our industry, and what are the demographic characteristics of consumers whose purchase patterns are changing the most? Are the same trends seen in our different product categories?	Are the changes in consumer trends very similar among all our products? What are the demographic characteristics of consumers who seem to be the most and the least loyal?
What are the best media for reaching a large proportion of heavy, medium or light users of our product?	If we change our media schedule by adding or deleting certain media buying, will we reach fewer users of our product?

Modelling software can be used for scenario planning, as mentioned before, and helps decision makers to examine possible or preconceived ideas about correlations in the data – to ask cause and effect questions. For example, media modelling software allows marketers to see what would happen if they made certain decisions about where to place their advertising. A manager may be able to use sales data and a model to find out how many consumers stay with his brand and how many switch, thus developing projections of market share over time. *Contingency planning* is the sister tool of scenario planning and is especially concerned with developing alternatives for the main plan in case of threats or emergencies – events which are foreseen but unlikely to occur. Table 3.1 gives some examples of the different marketing questions that an MkIS and an MDSS might answer.

Searching for gold: data mining

As we have explained, most MkIS systems include internal customer transaction databases and many include acquired databases. Often these databases are extremely large. To take advantage of the massive amount of data now available, sophisticated analysis techniques called data mining are becoming a priority for many firms. **Data mining** is a process in which analysts sift through data (often measured in terabytes – much larger than kilobytes or even gigabytes) to identify unique patterns of behaviour among different customer groups. This allows the company to get to know its customers inside out and aids successful and tailored customer relationship management.

British Airways, for example, uses data mining to create customised services for its travellers. The company receives a lot of information through customers who sign up for a frequent traveller programme or for newsletters as they have to fill out some questionnaires before joining. Through data mining the company can segment its customer base into different groups of interest concerning price, destination and dates of flights. Those customers can then receive specific promotional offers tailored to their needs.[9]

Data mining uses supercomputers that run sophisticated programs so that analysts can combine different databases to understand relationships among buying decisions, exposure to marketing messages and in-store promotions. These operations are so complex that companies often need to build a data warehouse (sometimes costing more than £5 million) simply to store and process the data.[10]

What marketers can do with data mining

Data mining has four important applications for marketers:[11]

1. **Customer acquisition:** Many firms work hard to include demographic and other information about customers in their database. For example, a number of supermarkets offer weekly special price discounts for shop loyalty card holders. These shops' membership application forms require that customers indicate their age, family size, address and so on. With this information, the supermarket can determine which of its current customers respond best to specific offers and then send the same offers to non-customers who share the same demographic characteristics.

2. **Customer retention and loyalty:** The firm can identify big-spending customers and then target them for special offers and inducements other customers won't receive. Keeping the most profitable customers coming back is a great way to build business success because keeping good customers is less expensive than constantly finding new ones.[12]

3. **Customer abandonment:** Strange as it may sound, sometimes a firm wants customers to take their business elsewhere because servicing them actually costs the firm too much. Today, this is popularly called 'firing a customer'. For example, a department store may use data mining to identify unprofitable customers – those who are not spending enough or who return most of what they buy. Top luxury fashion brand Burberry has experienced a major crisis since its well-known checked products became highly demanded by a new customer segment – the so-called 'chavs', who are associated with tracksuits, fake jewellery and rowdy behaviour. Football hooligans and unpopular ex-reality soap stars wearing Burberry hats and outfits were regarded as a nightmare by Burberry, whose real desired target customers are the rich and famous. Throughout the last few years Burberry has been fighting rigorously to 'fire' its unwanted customers and re-establish its luxury image. Measures of customer abandonment undertaken by the company included removing baseball caps, which were extremely popular among the chavs, from its product line and replacing items with the eye-catching checked pattern by ones with a more 'classy' and plain design.[13]

Marketing ethics and sustainability

Supermarkets 'use loyalty cards to kill off local shops'

Supermarkets have been accused of using information gleaned form loyalty cards to drive small local retailers out of business. The use of loyalty card schemes came under the spotlight during the Commons home affairs select committee's latest hearing into Britain's surveillance society. For example, Loyalty Management Group (LMG), which operates the Nectar card on behalf of Sainsbury's, confirmed that the chain could access data on where its customers lived, where and when they shopped and how much they spent.

Daily Telegraph, 8 June 2007

Debate, discuss, disagree

1. Is it a legitimate business practice for big retail companies to use their databases to gain competitive advantage over other retailers?

Marketing metrics

How to measure car capabilities

Companies like BMW often use a market research concept called 'car clinics' in which customers can spend a day driving, testing and evaluating not only the car of the specific company but also the ones of their competitors. Several questionnaires, interviews and group discussions are being carried out in order to find out as much valuable information as possible. To avoid biases and make the research more reliable, the company often uses an independent agency which invites the customers to the clinic and all the cars are made unrecognisable so that the customers do not actually know which company is carrying out the research. If, for example, the research reveals that the perception of the car is better than the competitor's car, it can be used in advertising against competitors and in order to counter their claims.

4. **Market basket analysis:** Firms can develop focused promotional strategies based on their records of which customers have bought certain products. Hewlett-Packard, for example, carefully analyses which of its customers have recently bought new printers and targets them to receive emails about specials on ink cartridges and tips on getting the most out of their machines.

So far, we have looked at the MkIS and the MDSS, the overall systems that provide the information marketers need to make good decisions. We've seen how the data included in the MkIS and MDSS include internal company data, marketing intelligence data gathered by monitoring everyday sources, acquired databases and information gathered to address specific marketing decisions through the marketing research process. In the rest of the chapter, we'll look at the steps that marketers must take when they conduct marketing research.

Steps in the marketing research process

Objective

2

The marketing research process

The collection and interpretation of strategic information is hardly a one-shot deal that managers engage in 'just out of curiosity'. Ideally, marketing research is a continual process, a series of steps marketers take to learn about the marketplace. Whether a company conducts the research itself or hires another firm to do it, the goal is the same: to help managers make informed marketing decisions and reduce risks of taking actions which could harm the business. Figure 3.4 shows the steps in the research process, and we'll go over each of these now.

Step 1: Define the research problem

The first step in the marketing research process is to clearly understand what information managers need. This step is referred to as defining the research problem. You should note that the word 'problem' here does not necessarily refer to 'something that is wrong' but instead to the overall questions for which the firm needs answers. Defining the problem has three components:

1. **Specifying the research objectives:** What questions will the research attempt to answer?

2. **Identifying the consumer population of interest:** What are the characteristics of the consumer groups of interest?

3. **Placing the problem in an environmental context:** What factors in the firm's internal and external business environment might be influencing the situation?

Define the Research Problem

- Specify the research objectives
- Identify the consumer population of interest
- Place the problem in an environmental context

Determine the Research Design

- Determine whether secondary data are available
- Determine whether primary data are required
  —Exploratory research
  —Descriptive research
  —Causal research

Choose the Method for Collecting Primary Data

- Determine which survey methods are most appropriate
  —Postal questionnaires
  —Telephone interviews
  —Face-to-face interviews
  —Online questionnaires
- Determine which observational methods are most appropriate
  —Personal observation
  —Unobtrusive measures
  —Mechanical observation

Design the Sample

- Choose between probability sampling and non-probability sampling

Collect the Data

- Translate questionnaires and responses if necessary
- Combine data from several sources (if available)

Analyse and Interpret the Data

- Tabulate and cross-tabulate the data
- Interpret or draw conclusions from the results

Prepare the Research Report

- In general, the research report includes:
  —An executive summary
  —A description of the research methods
  —A discussion of the results of the study
  —Limitations of the study
  —Conclusions and recommendations

Figure 3.4	Steps in the marketing research process

The marketing research process includes a series of steps that begins with defining the problem or the information needed and that ends with the finished research report for managers

Providing the right kind of information for each of these pieces of the problem is not as simple as it seems. For example, suppose a luxury car manufacturer wants to find out why its sales have fallen off dramatically over the past year. The research objective could revolve around any number of possible questions: Is the firm's advertising failing to reach the right consumers? Is the right message being sent? Do the firm's cars have a particular feature (or lack of one) that's turning customers away? Is there a problem with the firm's reputation for providing quality service? Do consumers believe the price is right for the value they get? The particular objective chosen depends on a variety of factors, such as the feedback the firm is getting from its customers, the information it receives from the marketplace, and sometimes even the intuition of the people designing the research.

Often the focus of a research question is driven by feedback from the marketplace that identifies a possible problem. Mercedes-Benz is a great example of a firm that, for years, has continually monitored drivers' perceptions of its cars. When the company started getting reports from its dealers in the 1990s that more and more people were viewing Mercedes products as 'arrogant' and 'unapproachable', even to the point at which they were reluctant to sit in showroom models, the company undertook a research project to understand the reasons for this perception.

The research objective determines the consumer population the company will study. In Mercedes' case, the research could have focused on current owners to find out what they especially liked about the car. Or it could have been directed at non-owners to understand their lifestyles, what they looked for in a luxury automobile, or their beliefs about the company itself that kept them from choosing its cars. So what did Mercedes find out? Research showed that although people rated its cars very highly on engineering quality and status, many were too intimidated by the elitist Mercedes image to consider buying one. Mercedes dealers reported that a common question from visitors to showrooms was, 'May I actually sit in the car?'[14] Based on these findings, Mercedes has in recent years worked hard to adjust perceptions by projecting a slightly more down-to-earth image in its advertising, and it ultimately created new downsized classes of vehicles to appeal to consumers who wanted something a little less ostentatious.[15]

Placing the problem in the context of the firm's environment helps to structure the research, determine the specific types of questions to ask and identify factors it will need to take into account when measuring results. Environmental conditions also matter. For

Marketing ethics and sustainability

Making a song and a dance of it

According to *Marketing*'s annual poll, conducted exclusively by TNS, Gocompare.com's television commercials have been named the most irritating in the UK for the second year running. The survey reveals that 59 per cent of respondents rated Gocompare.com as the most irritating ad of 2010, a rise from 56 per cent in 2009. The campaign, which features the rotund opera singer character Gio Compario, surpassed used-car purchasing site Webuyanycar.com to the top spot. The latter was rated by 48 per cent of those surveyed as the year's most irritating ad. Nick Hall (Go compare) said to the magazine: 'The strategy and objective of the campaign is to raise awareness of the gocompare brand and ensure that it is front of mind, and we have certainly achieved that. www.tellymix.co.uk,17 January 2011[16]

Debate, discuss, disagree

1   Is it an acceptable strategy to gain brand awareness by irritating and annoying?

Figure 3.5	Marketing research design
	For some research problems, the secondary research may provide the information needed. At other times, one of the primary research methods may be needed

example, when the economy is tight and sales of luxury cars are generally declining, researchers may narrow the population to be studied down to a select group of consumers who are still willing and able to indulge in a luxury vehicle. Today, many car consumers are moving away from status-conscious materialism and more towards functionality. In addition, as petrol prices have skyrocketed in recent years, drivers' sensitivity to miles per gallon translates even to luxury brands and huge sport-utility vehicles like a mighty BMW X5. Thus, a research question might be to see how consumers react to different promotional strategies for luxury goods that go beyond simply 'snob appeal'.

Step 2: Determine the research design

Once marketers have isolated specific problems, the second step of the research process is to decide on a 'plan of attack'. This plan is the **research design**, which specifies exactly what information marketers will collect and what type of study they will do. Figure 3.5 summarises many of the types of research design in the researcher's arsenal. As you can see, research designs fall into two broad categories: secondary research and primary research. All marketing problems do not call for the same research techniques, and marketers solve many problems most effectively with a combination of techniques.

Secondary research

The very first question marketers must ask themselves when determining their research design is whether the information required to make a decision already exists. For example, a coffee producer in the US who needs to know the differences in coffee consumption among different demographic and geographic segments of the market may find that the information needed is already available from a study conducted by the National Coffee Association. Data that have been collected for some purpose other than the problem at hand are called **secondary data**.

Many marketers thrive on going out and collecting new, 'fresh' data from consumers. However, if secondary data are available, it saves the firm time and money because the expense of designing and implementing a study has already been incurred. It is often helpful to start off with secondary research as a first step in the research process. Even if it does not lead to the actual solution, it may give a better understanding of the research problem or aid in the design of further primary research. Sometimes the data that marketers need may even be 'hiding' right under the organisation's nose in the form of company reports; previous company research studies; feedback received from customers, salespeople or shops; or even in the memories of long-time employees. More typically, though, researchers need to look elsewhere for secondary data. They may obtain reports published in the popular and business press, studies that private research organisations or government agencies conduct, and published research on the state of the industry from trade organisations.

For example, many companies gain market and consumer knowledge by subscribing to reports from the Mintel International group which researches many different business problems ranging from 'opportunities for retailing in emerging markets' to 'new trends in the health food sector'.[17]

Another very effective way of acquiring useful secondary data, which gives the company new ideas, is to partner up with an academic institution such as a well-known university. Both sides benefit from this partnership as the university improves its reputation and importance and the company receives a useful, scientifically backed insight into the market and business problems. An example is the creation of the 'Audi Lab for Market Research' where German car manufacturer Audi partnered up with the prestigious Swiss university St. Gallen to create a leading research centre for customer needs, product improvement and development into new markets.[18]

On the downside, however, secondary research data may be outdated, inaccurate or not available for specialised markets and products. Before relying on secondary information, the researcher needs to assess its usefulness and the trustworthiness of the source, as well as filter out the truly relevant sources from an overload of data.

Table 3.2 lists a number of websites helpful to marketers looking for secondary research topics.

Table 3.2
Helpful websites for marketing research

URL	Description
www.statistics.gov.uk	The Office for National Statistics (ONS) collects and publishes official statistics about the UK's society and economy
www.gfk.com/group/index.en.html	The GfK group is one of the world's largest market research organisations, specialising in custom retail, retail and technology, consumer tracking, and media and healthcare
www.mintel.co.uk	The Mintel International Group is a global supplier of consumer, media and market research and publishes reports on various business topics
www.bmrb.co.uk	The British Marketing Research Bureau (BMRB) provides different kinds of research solutions such as syndicated and proprietary research
www.lexis-nexis.co.uk	Lexis-Nexis is a large database featuring information from all major newspapers, trade journals and magazines and reports

Primary research

Of course, secondary research is not always the answer. When a company needs to make a specific decision, it often needs to conduct research to collect **primary data** – that is, information collected directly from respondents to specifically address the question at hand. Primary data include demographic and psychological information about customers and prospective customers, customers' attitudes and opinions about products and competing products, as well as their awareness or knowledge about a product and their beliefs about the people who use those products. In the next few sections, we'll talk briefly about the various designs useful in conducting primary research.

Exploratory (qualitative) research

Marketers use **exploratory research** to generate topics for future, more rigorous studies to come up with ideas for new strategies and opportunities or perhaps just to get a better handle on a problem they are currently experiencing with a product. Besides, exploratory research also plays an assisting role in designing subsequent research. The studies are usually carried out on a small scale, are less costly than other techniques and often provide a deep insight into consumer behaviour. Quantitative research, by contrast, is rather concerned with testing hypotheses, for example with the help of large-scale surveys and other quantifiable methods. This explains why marketers may use exploratory research to test their hunches about what's going on without too much risk.

Exploratory studies often involve in-depth probing of a few consumers who fit the profile of the 'typical' customer. Researchers may interview consumers, salespeople or other employees about products, services, ads or shops. They may simply 'hang out' and watch what people do when choosing among competing brands in a shop aisle. Or they may locate places where the consumers of interest tend to be and ask questions in these settings. For example, some researchers find that members of Generation Y – those born between 1977 and 1994 – are too suspicious or sceptical in traditional research settings, so they may interview young people queueing to buy concert tickets or in clubs.[19] Firms like the trendy sportswear manufacturer Puma employ so-called 'coolhunters', young people who observe and record crowds in metropolitan areas with cameras and try to forecast upcoming trends. By doing so, Puma hopes to always stay one step ahead of competition and gain a leadership position regarding trends and style.[20]

Most exploratory research is referred to as qualitative in nature: that is, the results of the research project tend to be non-numeric and instead might be detailed verbal or visual information about consumers' attitudes, feelings and buying behaviours in the form of words rather than in numbers. For example, when Beiersdorf, producer of the well-known Nivea product range, wanted to introduce a new deodorant, it conducted a 'blind test' where people used the Nivea deodorant on one armpit and a conventional deodorant on the other without knowing which was which. The tested people were questioned about the comfort and smell of the deodorant and this made it possible for Beiersdorf to improve the product.[21]

Exploratory research can take many forms. **Consumer interviews** are one-on-one discussions in which an individual shares his or her thoughts in person with a researcher. The mobile phone maker Nokia has used consumer interviews in the past to identify important changes in consumer behaviour. They were able to spot a trend in customers wanting to move away from fixed line phones towards using a wireless headset service for all calls. With this new knowledge it became easier for Nokia to develop innovative product lines and stay ahead of the competition.[22]

Nestlé used personal interviews to find out reasons for the decline in sales of the Maggi brand. The interviews revealed that consumers perceived both the design of the bottle and the flavour of the product as uninteresting and old-fashioned. When consumers explained that

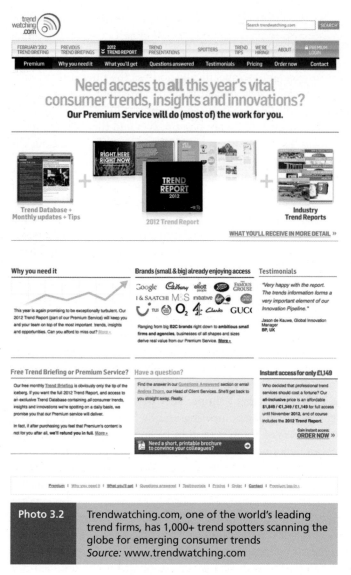

| Photo 3.2 | Trendwatching.com, one of the world's leading trend firms, has 1,000+ trend spotters scanning the globe for emerging consumer trends
Source: www.trendwatching.com |

they were longing for fresher ingredients and a younger design, Nestlé was able to reposition its Maggi brand and add 'more natural qualities in terms of taste, smell, look and texture'.[23]

The **focus group** is the technique that marketing researchers use most often for collecting exploratory data. Focus groups typically consist of five to nine consumers who have been recruited because they share certain characteristics. These people sit together to discuss a product, ad or some other marketing topic introduced by a discussion leader. Focus group facilitation is a real art that requires discipline, patience and a strong sense of when to sit back and listen and when to jump in and direct discussion. Typically, the leader video- or audio-records these group discussions, which may be held at special interviewing facilities that allow for observation by the client, who watches from behind a one-way mirror.

In addition to getting insights from what the participants say about a product, a good moderator can sometimes learn by carefully observing other things such as body language. While conducting focus groups on bras, an analyst noted that small-chested women typically reacted with hostility when discussing the subject. The participants would unconsciously cover their chests with their arms as they spoke and complained that they were ignored by the fashion industry. To meet this overlooked need, the company introduced a line of A-cup bras called 'A-OK' that depicted these women in a positive light.[24]

Researchers use **projective techniques** to get at people's underlying feelings, especially when they think that people will be unable or unwilling to express their true reactions. A projective test asks the participant to respond to some object, often by telling a story about it. For example, Georgia-Pacific, a manufacturer of paper kitchen towels, was locked in a struggle with ScotTowels (made by Kimberly-Clark) for the number two position in the US behind leading seller Bounty (made by Procter & Gamble). The company decided to re-examine its brand identity, which was personified by a 60-foot character named Brawny who held an axe. Georgia-Pacific managers were afraid that their brand was too old-fashioned or that women were confused about why a man was selling paper towels in the first place. Researchers asked women in the focus groups questions such as, 'What kind of woman would he go out with?' and 'What is his home life like?' Then the researchers asked the women to imagine how he would act in different situations and even to guess what would happen if they were locked in a lift with him for 20 minutes.

Responses were reassuring: the women saw the Georgia-Pacific kitchen towel as a knight in shining armour who would get them out of the lift – a good spokesman for a product that's supposed to be reliable and able to get the job done. The character kept his job and in fact since he was originally introduced in 1975 he has had two makeovers to keep his look modern.

| Photo 3.3 | This is the 'Mini United' festival where Mini owners and fans come together to socialise
Source: Alamy Images/Chris Warham |

The idea of creating brand personalities and finding out what customers think about the character was taken to a new level with the 'Volcanicity' campaign of bottled water producer Volvic. The company created a profile for the TV ad character 'Mr. Volcano' in the virtual community MSN Live Spaces (volcanogeorge.spaces.live.com). Just like a real person, 'Mr. Volcano' published pictures, blogs and news about himself, and by the reactions which he received from other Live Space users the company could gain information about how the brand was perceived by customers.[25]

The **case study** is a comprehensive examination of a particular firm or organisation. In business-to-business marketing research in which the customers are other firms, for example, researchers may try to learn how one particular company makes its purchases. The goal is to identify the key decision makers, to learn what criteria they emphasise when choosing among suppliers and perhaps to learn something about any conflicts and rivalries among these decision makers that may influence their choices.

An **ethnography** is a different kind of in-depth report. It is a technique borrowed from anthropologists who go to 'live with the natives' for months or even years. This approach has been adapted by some marketing researchers who visit people's homes or participate in real life consumer activities to get a handle on how they really use products. Imagine having a researcher follow you around while you shop and then while you use the products you bought to see what kind of consumer you are.

Of course, unlike anthropologists living with indigenous tribes, marketing researchers usually don't have months or years to devote to a project, so they devise shortcuts to get the information they need. For example, when Nissan was preparing for the $60 million launch of its first full-size truck, the Titan, its ad agency (TBWA/Chiat/Day) deployed researchers in the field to understand the psyche of such US truck owners. Team members hung out for several months at hunting expos, gun shows, cross-country events and even fishing spots – places that target consumers frequented. Results from the observations, supported by results from focus groups and interviews, provided strong ammunition for Nissan to communicate its message of what the Titan could do. Ultimately, to portray a rough-and-tumble image the ads showed dirty Titans in action, sloshing through mud and driving up inclines.[26] Another example is the 'Mini United 2007' festival which took place in June 2007 in Zandfoort, Holland. True to the motto 'Friends. Festival. Challenge', thousands of Mini fans and Mini Classic fans from all over the world came together to party, socialise and exchange experiences about their favourite car. Apart from being a great PR event, this festival gave the car manufacturer excellent opportunities to mingle among the fans, conduct market research and spot trends in customer behaviour.[27]

Descriptive (quantitative) research

We've seen that marketers have many tools in their arsenal, including focus groups and observational techniques, to help them better define a problem or opportunity. These are usually modest studies of a small number of people, enough to get some indication of what is going on but not enough for the marketer to feel confident about generalising what he or she observes to the rest of the population.

The next step in marketing research, then, is to conduct **descriptive research**, which probes systematically into the marketing problem and bases its conclusions on a large sample of participants. Descriptive research is typically expressed in quantitative terms – averages, percentages or other statistics summarising results from a large set of measurements. In such quantitative approaches to research, the project can be as simple as counting the number of Listerine bottles sold in a month in different regions of the country or as complex as statistical analyses of responses to a survey mailed to thousands of consumers. In each case, marketers conduct the descriptive research to answer a specific question in contrast to the 'fishing expedition' that may occur in exploratory research.

Marketing researchers who employ descriptive techniques most often use a **cross-sectional design**. This approach usually involves the systematic collection of responses to a consumer survey instrument, such as a questionnaire, from one or more samples of respondents at one point in time. The data may be collected on more than one occasion but generally not from the same pool of respondents.

In contrast to these one-shot studies, a **longitudinal design** tracks the responses of the same sample of respondents over time. Market researchers sometimes create consumer panels to get information; in this case a sample of respondents representative of a larger market agrees to provide information about purchases on a weekly or monthly basis. Procter & Gamble, for instance, recruits consumer advisory panels on a market-by-market basis to keep its finger on the pulse of local shoppers. Since P&G acquired the Gillette line of razors and blades, for the first time it had to recruit special all-male consumer panels to contribute to the development of new products such as the Fusion line of razors.[28]

Causal research

It's a fact that purchases of both nappies and beer peak between 5.00 and 7.00 p.m. Can we say that purchasing one of these products caused shoppers to purchase the other as well – and, if so, which caused which? Or is the answer simply that this happens to be the time that young fathers stop at the shop on their way home from work to pick up some brew and Pampers?[29]

The descriptive techniques we've examined do a good job of providing valuable information about what is happening in the marketplace, but descriptive research, by its very nature, can only *describe* a marketplace phenomenon – it cannot tell us why. Sometimes marketers need to know if something they've done has brought about some change in behaviour. For example, does placing one product next to another in a shop mean that people will buy more of each? We can't answer this question through simple observation or description.

Causal research attempts to understand cause-and-effect relationships. Marketers use causal research techniques when they want to know if a change in something (for example, placing cases of beer next to a nappy display) is responsible for a change in something else (for example, a big increase in nappy sales). They call the factors that might cause such a change independent variables and the outcomes dependent variables. The independent variable(s) cause some change in the dependent variable(s). In our example, then, the beer display is an independent variable, and sales data for the nappies are a dependent variable. That is, the study would investigate whether an increase in nappy sales 'depends' on the proximity of beer. Another example for the use of causal research would be to examine a rise in sales after the implementation of a 'buy-one-get-one-free' offer. Did sales really go up because of this offer or was the rise caused by some other, external, factors? Researchers can gather data and test the causal relationship statistically.

To rule out alternative explanations, researchers must carefully design **experiments** that test predicted relationships among variables in a controlled environment. Because this approach tries to eliminate competing explanations for the outcome, respondents may be brought to a laboratory so that the researcher can control precisely what respondents should see. For example, a study testing whether the placement of nappies in a supermarket influences the likelihood that male shoppers will buy them might bring a group of men into a testing facility and show them a 'virtual store' on a computer screen. Researchers would ask the men to fill a grocery trolley as they click through the 'aisles'. The experiment might vary the placement of the nappies – next to shelves of beer in one scenario, near paper goods in a different scenario. The objective is to see which placement gets the men to put nappies into their carts.

Although a laboratory allows researchers to exert control over what test subjects see and do, marketers don't always have the luxury of conducting this kind of 'pure' research. But it is possible to conduct field studies in the real world, as long as the researchers can control the independent variables.

For example, a nappy company might choose two supermarkets that have similar customer bases in terms of age, income and so on. With the cooperation of the supermarket's management, the company might place its nappy display next to the beer in one shop and next to the paper goods in the other and then record nappy purchases made by men over a two-week period. If a lot more nappies were bought by guys in the first shop than in the second (and the company was sure that nothing else was different between the two shops, such as a money-off coupon for nappies being distributed in one shop and not the other), the nappy manufacturer might conclude that the presence of beer in the background does indeed result in increased nappy sales.

Step 3: Choose the method for collecting primary data

Objective

4

The different types of data-collection methods and types of consumer samples that researchers use

When the researcher decides to collect primary data, the next step in the marketing research process is to figure out just how to collect it. Primary data collection methods can be broadly described as either survey or observation. There are many ways to collect data, and marketers are trying new ones all the time. Today, a few marketing researchers are even turning to sophisticated brain scans to directly measure our brains' reactions to various advertisements or products. These 'neuromarketers' hope to be able to tell companies how people will react to their brands by scanning consumers' brains rather than collecting data the old-fashioned way – by asking them.[30] These techniques are still in their infancy, so for now we'll still rely on other methods to collect primary data.

Survey methods

Survey methods involve some kind of interview or other direct contact with respondents who answer questions. Questionnaires can be administered on the phone, in person, through the mail or over the internet. Table 3.3 summarises the advantages and disadvantages of different methods for collecting data.

Questionnaires

Questionnaires differ in their degree of structure. With a totally unstructured questionnaire, the researcher loosely determines the questions in advance. Questions may evolve from what the respondent says to previous questions. At the other extreme, the researcher uses a completely structured questionnaire. He or she asks every respondent exactly the same questions and each participant responds to the same set of fixed choices. You have probably experienced this kind of questionnaire, where you might have had to respond

Table 3.3
Advantages and disadvantages of data-collection methods

Data-Collection Method	Advantages	Disadvantages
• Mail questionnaires	• Respondents feel anonymous • Low cost • Good for ongoing research	• May take a long time for questionnaires to be returned • Low rate of response; many may not return questionnaires • Inflexible questionnaire • Length of questionnaire limited by respondent interest in the topic • Unclear whether respondents understand the questions • Unclear who is responding • No assurance that respondents are being honest
• Telephone interviews	• Fast • High flexibility in questioning • Low cost • Limited by interviewer	• Decreasing levels of respondent cooperation • Limited questionnaire lenght • High likelihood of respondent misunderstanding • Respondents cannot view materials • Cannot survey households without phones • Consumers screen calls with answering machines and caller ID • Do-not-call lists allow many research subjects to opt out of participation
• Face-to-face interviews	• Flexibility of questioning • Can use long questionnaires • Can determine whether respondents have trouble understanding questions • Can use visuals or other materials	• High cost • Interviewer bias a problem • Take a lot of time
• Online questionnaires	• Instantaneous data collection and analysis • Questioning very flexible • Low cost • No interviewer bias • No geographic restrictions • Can use visuals or other materials	• Unclear who is responding • No assurance that respondents are being honest • Limited questionnaire length • Unable to determine whether respondent is understanding the question • Self-selected samples

to a statement by saying if you 'strongly agree', 'somewhat agree' and so on. Moderately structured questionnaires ask each respondent the same questions, but the respondent is allowed to answer the questions in his or her own words.

Mail questionnaires are easy to administer and offer a high degree of anonymity to respondents. This removes the interviewer bias and lowers the social desirability bias. Respondents are given the opportunity to answer the questions at their own pace. On the downside, because the questionnaire is printed and mailed, researchers have little flexibility in the types of questions they can ask and little control over the circumstances under which the respondent is answering them. The researcher cannot ask any probing questions or clarify responses. Mail questionnaires also take a long time to get back to the company and are likely to have a much lower response rate than other types of data collection methods because people tend to ignore them. In addition, because they use paper, they may be perceived as being less environmentally friendly.

Telephone interviews usually consist of a brief phone conversation in which an interviewer reads a short list of questions to the respondent. Although telephone interviews are relatively cheap, reach a large number of people quite easily, and a random sample can be generated by using random digital dialling, there are several problems with this data collection method. One problem with this method is that the growth of **telemarketing**, where businesses sell directly to consumers over the phone, has eroded consumers' willingness to participate in phone surveys (especially during dinnertime!). In addition to aggravating people by barraging them with telephone sales messages, some unscrupulous telemarketers have 'poisoned the well' for legitimate marketing researchers by hiding their pitches behind an illusion of doing research. They contact consumers under the pretence of doing a research study when in fact their real intent is to sell the respondent something or to solicit funds for some cause. In the US, the act of selling under the guise of doing market research is called 'sugging', and 'frugging' is the practice of fundraising under the pretence of doing market research (see Marketing ethics and sustainability box). The respondent also may not feel comfortable speaking directly to an interviewer, especially if the survey is about a sensitive subject, and the researcher cannot use any visual aids during the interview or try building up a rapport with the interviewee. Besides, body language and non-verbal clues cannot be observed. Collectable information therefore often stays limited and it only makes sense to use a short questionnaire. Of course, increasing numbers of people use voicemail and caller ID to screen calls, further reducing the response rate. Besides, some numbers may not be listed, which can lead to an unrepresentative sample. And, as noted earlier, do-not-call lists allow many would-be research subjects to opt out of participation both in legitimate marketing research and unscrupulous telemarketing.[31]

Using *face-to-face interviews*, a live interviewer asks questions of one respondent at a time. Although in 'the old days' researchers often went door to door to ask questions, which allowed the interviewer to adapt questions to the specific situation and possibly gain deeper insights, that's much less common today because of fears about security and because the large numbers of dual-income families make it less likely to find people at home during the day. Other disadvantages are that this research method is very time-consuming, expensive, slow to complete and that there is a high likelihood of bias, for example that the respondent will answer in a socially desirable way. Typically, today's face-to-face interviews occur in a shopping centre intercept study in which researchers recruit shoppers in shopping centres or other public areas. You've probably seen this going on in your local shopping centre where a smiling person holding a clipboard stops shoppers to see if they are willing to answer a few questions.

Shopping centre intercepts offer good opportunities to get feedback about new package designs, styles or even reactions to new foods or fragrances. Besides, this method is easy to supervise and less time-consuming than, for example, in-house interviews. However, because only certain groups of the population frequently shop at shopping centres, a shopping centre intercept study does not provide the researcher with a representative sample of the population (unless the population of interest is shopping centre shoppers). In addition to being more expensive than mail or phone surveys, respondents may be reluctant to answer questions of a personal nature in a face-to-face context.

Online questionnaires are growing in popularity, mainly due to their ability to reach a large number of people, speed of distribution and collection and low cost. However, the use of such questionnaires is not without concerns. Many researchers question the quality of responses they will receive – particularly because (as with mail and phone interviews) no one can be really sure who is typing in the responses on the computer. In addition, it's uncertain whether savvy online consumers are truly representative of the general population.[32] Response rates are often rather low since consumers might perceive them as spam, have technical problems or are worried about data security issues. As a result it can be argued that although online surveys become easier to do, good online surveys become increasingly harder to do.[33] However, these concerns are rapidly evaporating as research firms devise new ways to verify identities; present surveys in novel formats, including the use of images, sound and animation; and recruit more diverse respondents.[34] The importance and impact of online surveys will be covered in more depth later on in this chapter.

Observational methods

The second major primary data collection method is observation. Observation is a type of data collection that uses a passive instrument in which the researcher simply records the consumer's behaviour – often without their knowledge. On the one hand, observational research offers the advantage of being able to measure behaviour in a direct and flexible way. On the other hand, however, it can be rather difficult to interpret and generalise the observed patterns. Researchers might tend to 'see what they want to see' in the observed behaviours. Besides, disguised research, for example with hidden cameras, might cause some difficulties regarding legal issues. Researchers do this through personal observation, unobtrusive measures and mechanical observation.

When researchers use *personal observation*, they simply watch consumers in action to understand how they react to marketing activities. Household goods manufacturer Vileda gained insight into customer behaviour by sending researchers into their homes and observing their cleaning techniques. It was discovered that there is a large customer group with a rather easygoing attitude towards cleaning; this helped the company develop its Magic Mop which makes cleaning fast and convenient.

Marketing ethics and sustainability

Have you ever been sugged or frugged?

The Labour Party and some charities have been accused of 'selling under guise' or 'sugging'. Sugging is something that appears to be market research questionnaires at first, and actually is little more than direct marketing, soliciting the names, addresses and ideally cash from participants. It relies on the fact that there are plenty of people who are willing to cooperate with market research, but who don't want to get involved in a sales approach. Frugging is fund raising under the guise of doing market research. So a cancer charity might ask people about their perceptions on the risks of getting cancer and end up by asking for a donation. Ultimately, the important thing is not to mislead the consumer. If you haven't, it's up to the consumer whether they want to fill out a questionnaire and give money.

Debate, discuss, disagree

1 Have you ever been sugged or frugged?

2 Should sugging and frugging activities be allowed?

3 If so, when in the direct mail, email or street interview should the respondent be told they will be asked for money?

A shopping centre in Texas became a laboratory for the workplace of the future when it put a 'Connection Court' in the middle of the shopping centre. In an observational project sponsored by the internet Home Alliance, a group of mostly high-tech companies including Cisco Systems, Microsoft and IBM, workers installed chairs and couches, set up desks with laptops, flat-panel monitors and printers, and hooked up a high-speed wireless internet network. This space is free for use by people who want to work in a more casual – and public – setting. The motivation: to understand if and how people want to work outside their homes and offices. With the spread of wireless internet by companies like McDonald's and Starbucks that are setting up networks to let their customers work, these companies are doing observational research to understand just how to structure the physical environment so that their customers can work more comfortably.[35]

Researchers use **unobtrusive measures** that measure traces of physical evidence which remain after some action has been taken when they suspect that people will probably alter their behaviour if they know they are being observed. For example, instead of asking a person to report on the alcohol products which they currently stock at home, the researcher might go to the house and perform a 'pantry check' by actually counting the bottles in the drinks cabinet. Another option for collecting primary data is to sift through garbage, searching for clues about each family's consumption habits. The 'garbologists' can tell, for example, which soft drink accompanied what kind of food. As one garbologist noted, 'The people in this study don't know that we are studying their garbage so the information is totally objective.'[36] Smelly, too!

Mechanical observation is a primary data-collection method that relies on non-human devices to record behaviour. For example, one well-known application of mechanical observation is A.C. Nielsen's famous use of 'people meters' – boxes attached to the television sets of selected viewers, to record patterns of television watching. Data obtained from these devices indicate who is watching which shows. These 'television ratings' help the networks determine how much to charge advertisers for commercials and which shows to cancel or renew, although critics claim that there are problems of undercounting minorities, Arbitron has recently deployed thousands of 'portable people meters', or PPMs. PPMs resemble pagers and automatically record the wearer's exposure to any media that has inserted an inaudible code into its promotion (TV ad, shelf display and so on). Thus, when the consumer is exposed to a broadcast commercial, cinema ad, internet banner ad or other form of commercial exposure, the PPM registers, records and time-stamps the signal. At day's end, the media history is downloaded by a home docking station that simultaneously recharges the PPM. Portability ensures that all exposures register, eliminating obtrusive people meters and written diaries that participants often

| Photo 3.4 | IPA TouchPoints is a relatively new survey. IPA Touch-Points 1 was published in 2006, followed by IPA Touch-Points 2 in 2008. The hub survey is conducted by TNS who questioned 5,000 people for both surveys using a substantial self-completion questionnaire and a PDA time-based diary that collected data every half hour for a week on how they were spending their time, their opinions, and the role of the media in their lives
Source: IPA TouchPoints |

forget to fill out.[37] The Institute of Practitioners in Advertising developed 'IPA Touchpoints' which measure the exposure of an individual to media streams with a PDA (personal digital assistant) in combination with a self-completion questionnaire. The Touchpoint project is designed to get an insight into how consumers move through the media jungle and to improve overall industry media research. This form of market research helps with answering questions like 'is TV still the dominant form of media?' or 'how much time do consumers in the Greater London area spend shopping on the internet?'[38]

Of course, many research firms are developing techniques to measure which websites are being visited and by whom. As we'll see shortly, there are ways for companies to tell where you've travelled in virtual space, so be careful about the sites you surf!

Data quality: garbage in, garbage out

We've seen that a firm can collect data in many ways, including focus groups, ethnographic approaches, observational studies, and controlled experiments. But how much faith should marketing managers place in what they find out from the research?

All too often, marketers who have commissioned a study assume that because they have a massive report full of impressive-looking numbers and tables, they must have the 'truth'. Unfortunately, there are times when this 'truth' is really just one person's interpretation of the facts. At other times, the data used to generate recommendations are flawed. As the expression goes, 'garbage in, garbage out!'[39] That is, bad data mean bad managerial decisions. Typically, three factors influence the quality of research results – validity, reliability and representativeness.

Validity is the extent to which the research actually measures what it was intended to measure. This was part of the problem underlying the famous New Coke fiasco in the 1980s in which Coca-Cola underestimated people's loyalty to its flagship soft drink after it replaced 'Old Coke' with a new, sweeter formula. In a blind taste test, the company assumed testers' preferences for one anonymous cola over another was a valid measure of consumers' preferences for a cola brand. Coca-Cola found out the hard way that measuring taste only is not the same as measuring people's deep allegiances to their favourite soft drinks. After all, Coke is a brand that elicits strong consumer loyalty and is nothing short of a cultural icon. Tampering with the flavours was like assaulting Mum and her Sunday roast. Sales eventually recovered after the company brought back the old version as 'Coca-Cola Classic'.[40]

Reliability is the extent to which the research measurement techniques are free of errors. Sometimes, for example, the way a researcher asks a question creates error by biasing people's responses. Imagine that an attractive female interviewer working for Trojans condoms stopped male college students on campus and asked them if they used contraceptive products. Do you think their answers might change if they were asked the same questions on an anonymous survey they received in the mail? Most likely, their answers would be different because people are reluctant to disclose what they actually do when their responses are not anonymous. Researchers try to maximise reliability by thinking of several different ways to ask the same questions, by asking these questions on several occasions, or by using several analysts to interpret the responses. Thus, they can compare responses and look for consistency and stability.

Reliability is a problem when the researchers can't be sure that the consumer population they're studying even understands the questions. For example, kids are difficult subjects for market researchers because they tend to be undependable reporters of their own behaviour, they have poor recall and they often do not understand abstract questions. In many cases, the children cannot explain why they prefer one item over another (or they're not willing to share these secrets with grown-ups).[41] For these reasons, researchers have

Figure 3.6	**Completion test**
	It can be especially difficult to get accurate information from children. Researchers often use visuals such as this Japanese completion test to encourage children to express their feelings. The test asked boys to write in the empty balloon what they think the boy in the drawing will answer when the girl asks, 'What programme do you want to watch next?'

had to be especially creative when designing studies on younger consumers. Figure 3.6 shows part of a completion test used to measure children's preferences for television programming in Japan.

Representativeness is the extent to which consumers in the study are similar to a larger group in which the organisation has an interest. This criterion for evaluating research underscores the importance of **sampling**, the process of selecting respondents for a study. The issue then becomes how large or small the sample should be and how these people are chosen. The requirements regarding representativeness have to be adapted slightly depending on what type of research the marketers use. When a large-scale survey is being conducted as part of a quantitative research project, representativeness is absolutely crucial. When dealing with qualitative research, such as a focus group, marketers will much rather look for in-depth information about this small group of consumers than for representativeness across the whole population. In order to ensure representativeness, it is important to select an experiment group, which receives a certain stimulus, as well as a control group, which does not receive any stimulus. Afterwards, the results can be compared. We'll talk more about sampling in the next section.

Online research

Objective

5

The growing use of online research

The growth of the internet is rewriting some of the rules of the marketing research process. As more and more people have access to the web, many companies are finding that the internet is a superior way to collect data – it's fast, it's relatively cheap and it lends itself well to forms of research from simple questionnaires to focus groups.

Fifty per cent of European researchers state that they have replaced face-to-face interviews with online research.[42] Seventy-five per cent of research decision makers in the US have tried online research and expect to use it again in the future. In 2005, some researchers predicted that within two years, online surveys would have an average predicted share of business of 39.6 per cent, more than telephone (30.7 per cent), face-to-face (23.9 per cent) or mail surveys (5.7 per cent).[43] Developments in online research are happening quickly, so let's take some time now to see where things are heading.

The web is revolutionising the way many companies collect data and use them to guide marketing decisions. There are two major types of online research. One type is information gathered by tracking consumers while they are surfing. The second type is information gathered through questionnaires on websites, through email or from moderated focus groups conducted in chat rooms.

The internet offers an unprecedented ability to track consumers as they search for information. Marketers can better understand where people go to look when they want to learn about products and services – and which advertisements they stop to browse along the way. How can marketers do this? One way is by the use of cookies. Beware the Cookie Monster! **Cookies** are text files inserted by a website sponsor into a user's hard drive when the user connects with the site. Cookies remember details of a visit to a website, typically tracking which pages the user visits. Some sites request or require that visitors 'register' on the site by answering questions about themselves and their likes and dislikes. In such cases, cookies also allow the site to access these details about the customer.

This technology allows websites to customise services, such as when Amazon.co.uk recommends new books to users on the basis of what books they have ordered in the past. Most consumers have no idea that cookies allow websites to gather and store all this information. You can block cookies or curb them, although this can make life difficult if you are trying to log on to many sites, such as online newspapers or travel agencies that require this information to admit you.

This information generated from tracking consumers' online journeys has become a product as well – companies sell these consumer data to other companies that are trying to target prospects. But consumers have become increasingly concerned about the sharing of these data. In a study of 10,000 web users, 84 per cent objected to the reselling of their information to other companies. Although internet users can delete cookie files manually or install anti-cookie software on their computers, there are many people who feel there is a need for privacy regulation and for cookie regulation in order to limit potential abuses.

Online research applications

The internet offers a faster, less expensive alternative to traditional communication data collection methods. Here are some ways companies are using the internet to get feedback from consumers:

- **New-product development:** In the 1990s, Procter & Gamble spent more than five years testing products such as Febreze, Dryel and Fit Fruit & Vegetable Wash the old-fashioned way before launching in the US. Using online tests, its Crest MultiCare Flex & Clean toothbrush was launched in less than a year. General Motors and Nissan are two car makers that now gather online consumer reactions to forthcoming products. Such research allows manufacturers to learn what consumers want in future vehicles.[44]

- **Estimating market response:** A few cutting-edge companies are creating virtual worlds and using them to test consumers' responses to brands. Using 'There-bucks', people who sign up to join the virtual community at There.com can choose to 'buy' products like Levi's Type I jeans or Nike's high-end Zoom Celar shoes on the site. Companies can then analyse who chose to buy which brands and which activities they engaged in while on the site (for example, do people who select the Levi's style tend to spend a lot of time socialising in There clubs that are available on the site?).[45]

- **Exploratory research:** Online focus groups have mushroomed in popularity in recent years. Firms such as itracks.com offer complete focus group capabilities via the web, claiming that 'online research does not mean you lose the human touch. The online environment elicits honest responses, uninfluenced by peer pressure or group dominance'. To achieve this comfort level, all participants and the moderator log in anonymously using password protection. Of course, with online groups it is impossible to observe body language, facial expressions and vocal inflection. But marketers continue to develop new ways to talk to consumers in virtual space, including software that allows online focus group participants to indicate non-verbal responses. For example, an online participant can register an expression of disgust by clicking on the command to 'roll eyes'.[46]

- **Instant messaging:** A few forward-thinking marketers are starting to take advantage of the fact that 75 per cent of teens who go online use IM (instant messaging) and 48 per cent trade IM messages at least once a day. These researchers link IM to online focus groups: a moderator can conduct a chat with a respondent using IM technology in order to probe his or her answers more deeply in a separate conversation.[47]

Advantages and disadvantages of online data collection

Many marketing research companies are running, not walking, to the web to conduct studies for clients. Why? For one thing, replacing traditional mail consumer panels with internet panels allows marketers to collect the same amount of data in a weekend that used to take six to eight weeks. And consumers can complete surveys when it is convenient – even at 3 a.m. in their pyjamas. There are other advantages: companies can conduct large studies at low cost. International borders are not a problem either, since in many regions (such as Scandinavia) internet use is very high and it's easy to recruit respondents. web-based interviews eliminate interviewer bias or errors in data entry.

However, no data collection method is perfect, and online research is no exception – although many of the criticisms of online techniques also apply to offline techniques. One potential problem is the representativeness of the respondents. Although the number of internet users continues to grow, many segments of the consumer population, mainly the poor and elderly, do not have equal access to the internet. In addition, in many studies (just as with mail surveys or shopping centre intercepts) there is a self-selection bias in the sample in that respondents have agreed to receive invitations to take part in online studies, which means they tend to be the kind of people who like to participate in surveys. As with other kinds of research such as live focus groups, it's not unusual to encounter 'professional respondents' – people who just enjoy taking part in studies (and getting paid for it). Online firms such as Harris Interactive, Survey Sampling or Greenfield online address this problem by monitoring their participants and regulating how often they are allowed to participate in different studies over a period of time.

There are other disadvantages of online research. Hackers can actually try to influence research results. Even more dangerous may be competitors who can learn about a firm's marketing plans, products, advertising and so forth by intercepting information used in research. Despite the potential drawbacks, online research has a bright future. This research has the potential to take off even faster as a result of the 2001 terrorist attacks, since many Americans are more hesitant to answer questions from strangers, drive to focus group facilities or open mail surveys from sources they don't recognise.

Step 4: Design the sample

Once the researcher has defined the problem, decided on a research design and determined how to collect the data, the next step is to decide from whom to obtain the needed data. This is the main problem namely, 'who should they interview?' Of course, you could collect the information from every single customer or prospective customer. But this collection, known as a consensus, would be extremely expensive and time-consuming, if possible at all. Instead, researchers collect most of their data from a sample of the population of interest. Based on the answers from this sample, researchers hope to generalise to the larger population. Whether such inferences are accurate or inaccurate depends on the type and quality of the study sample. There are two main types of sample: probability and non-probability samples.

Probability sampling

With a **probability sample**, each member of the population has some known chance of being included in the sample. Using a probability sample ensures that the sample is representative of the population and that inferences about the population made from the sample are justified. For example, if a larger percentage of males than females in a probability sample say they prefer action movies to 'chick flicks', one can infer with confidence that a larger percentage of males than females in the general population also would rather see a character get sliced and diced.

Simple random sampling. The most basic type of probability sample is a simple random sample in which every member of a population has a known and equal chance of being included in the study. For example, if we simply take the names of all students in your class – let's assume there are 40 students for now – and put them in a hat and draw one out, each member of your class has a 1 in 40 chance of being included in the sample. In most studies, the population from which the sample will be drawn is too large for a hat, so marketers generate a random sample from a list of members of the population using a computer program.

Systematic sampling. Sometimes researchers use a systematic sampling procedure to select members of a population in which they pick the *n*th member of a population after a random start. For example, if we want a sample of 10 members of your class, we might begin with the second person on the register and select every fourth name after that, that is, the 2nd, the 6th, the 10th, the 14th and so on. Researchers know that studies that use systematic samples are just as accurate as with simple random samples. Unless a list of members of the population of interest is already in a computer data file, it's a lot simpler to create a systematic sample.

Stratified sampling. Yet another type of probability sample is a stratified sample in which a researcher divides the population into segments that are related to the study's topic. For example, imagine that you are interested in studying what types of films are most liked by members of a population. You have learned from previous studies that men and women in the population differ in their attitudes toward different types of movies – men like action flicks and women like romances. To create a stratified sample, you would first divide the population into male and female segments. Then respondents from each of the two segments would be selected randomly in proportion to their percentage of the population. In this way, you have created a sample that is proportionate to the population on a characteristic that you know will make a difference in the study results.

Non-probability sampling

Sometimes researchers do not believe the time, effort and costs required to develop a probability sample are justified, perhaps because they need an answer quickly or they just want to get a general sense of how people feel about a topic. They may choose a **non-probability sample**, which entails the use of personal judgement in selecting respondents – in some cases just asking whomever they can find. With a non-probability sample, some members of the population have no chance at all of being included in the sample. Thus, there is no way to ensure that the sample is representative of the population. Results from non-probability studies can be generally suggestive of what is going on in the real world but not necessarily definitive.

A **convenience sample** is a non-probability sample composed of individuals who just happen to be available when and where the data are being collected. For example, if you simply stand in front of the student union and ask students who walk by to complete your questionnaire, that would be a convenience sample.

Quota sampling

Finally, researchers may also use a quota sample that includes the same proportion of individuals with certain characteristics as is found in the population. For example, if you are studying attitudes of students in your university, you might just go on campus and find bachelor, master and PhD students in proportion to the number of members of each class in the university. The quota sample is much like the stratified sample except that with a quota sample, the researcher uses his or her individual judgement to select respondents.

Step 5: Collect the data

At this point, the researcher has determined the nature of the problem that needs to be addressed. He or she has decided on a research design that will specify how to investigate the problem and what kinds of information (data) will be needed. The researcher has also selected the data collection and sampling methods. Once these decisions have been made, the next task is to actually collect the data.

Although collecting data may seem like a simple process, researchers are well aware of its critical importance to the accuracy of research. There are several criteria which affect how successful the chosen research collection method will be. A precise timescale can help, for example accurate decision making and the access to relevant skills and expertise can speed up the collection process. When interviewers are involved, researchers know that the quality of research results is only as good as the poorest interviewer collecting the data. Careless interviewers may not read questions exactly as written, or they may not record respondent answers correctly. So marketers must train and supervise interviewers to make sure they follow the research procedures exactly as outlined. In the next section, we'll talk about some of the problems in gathering data and some solutions.

Challenges to gathering data in foreign countries

Conducting market research around the world is big business for many firms. However, market conditions and consumer preferences vary worldwide, and there are major differences in the sophistication of market research operations and the amount of data available to global marketers. In Mexico, for instance, because there are still large areas where native Indian tribes speak languages other than Spanish, researchers may bypass these groups in surveys.

Another example for 2003 (the last year for which figures are available), estimated expenditures for research by marketing research companies – $387 million – rank China number two in Asia Pacific markets, topped only by Japan. In fact, money spent on marketing research in China is growing faster than in any other country in the world, with increases of over 25 per cent a year. The reason for such expenditures is obvious: China is an emerging market of more than 1.3 billion potential consumers. Interestingly, however, there's an erroneous impression among foreign marketers that most of the population lives in large cities. Coupled with real infrastructure and transportation challenges, this demographic misconception has left large portions of the vast Chinese countryside virtually untouched by modern marketing – so far.[48]

For these and other reasons, choosing an appropriate data collection method is difficult. In some countries, many people may not have phones, or low literacy rates may interfere with mail surveys. *Local customs* can be a problem as well. Offering money for interviews is generally considered rude in Latin American countries.[49] Saudi Arabia bans gatherings of four or more people except for family or religious events, and it's illegal to stop strangers on the street or knock on the door of someone's house.[50]

Cultural differences also affect responses to survey items. Both Danish and British consumers, for example, agree that it is important to eat breakfast, but the Danish sample may be thinking of fruit and yogurt while the British sample is thinking of toast and tea. Sometimes marketers can overcome these problems by involving local researchers in decisions about the research design.

Another problem with conducting marketing research in global markets is *language*. Sometimes translations just don't come out right. In some cases entire subcultures within a country might be excluded from the research sample. In fact, this issue is becoming more and more prevalent inside the United States as non-English speakers increase as a percentage of the population.

To overcome language difficulties, researchers use a process called **back-translation**, which requires two steps. First, a native speaker translates the questionnaire into the language of the targeted respondents. Then this new version is translated back into the original language to ensure that the correct meanings survive the process. Even with precautions such as these, however, researchers must interpret data obtained from other cultures with care. The European Society for Opinion and Marketing Research (ESOMAR, www.esomar.org) is a world organisation which publishes codes and guidelines for conducting market research. Look at their website. Why is such an organisation useful? Which standards do you regard as most necessary?

Step 6: Analyse and interpret the data

To understand the important role of data analysis, let's take a look at a hypothetical research example. In our example, a company that markets frozen foods wishes to better understand consumers' preferences for varying levels of fat content in their diets. They have conducted a descriptive research study in which they collected primary data via telephone interviews. Because companies recognise that gender is related to dietary preferences, they have used a stratified sample that includes 175 males and 175 females.

Table 3.4
Examples of data tabulation and cross-tabulation tables

Fat Content Preference (number and percentage of responses)		
Questionnaire Response	Number of Responses	Percentage of Responses
Do you prefer a meal with high fat content, medium fat content, or low fat content?		
High fat	21	6
Medium fat	179	51
Low fat	50	43
Total	350	100

Fat Content Preference by Gender (number and percentage of responses)						
Questionnaire	Number of Females	Percentage of Females	Number of Males	Percentage of Males	Total Number	Total Percentage
Do you prefer a meal with high fat content, medium fat content, or low fat content?						
High fat	4	2	17	10	21	6
Medium fat	68	39	111	64	179	51
Low fat	103	59	47	27	150	43
Total	175	100	175	100	350	100

Tabulating and cross-tabulating

Typically, marketers first tabulate the data as Table 3.4 shows – that is, they arrange the data in a table or other summary form so they can get a broad picture of the overall responses. The data in this table show that 43 per cent of the sample prefers a low-fat meal. In addition, there may be a desire to cross-classify or cross-tabulate the answers to questions by other variables. Cross-tabulation means that the data are examined by subgroups, in this case males and females separately, to see how results vary between categories. The cross-tabulation in Table 3.4 shows that 59 per cent of females versus only 27 per cent of males prefer a meal with low fat content. In addition, researchers may wish to apply additional statistical tests.

Based on the tabulation and cross-tabulations, the researcher must then interpret or draw conclusions from the results and make recommendations. For example, the study results shown in Table 3.4 may lead to the conclusion that females are more likely than males to be concerned about a low-fat diet. The researcher might then make a recommendation to a firm that it should target females in the introduction of a new line of low-fat foods.

 ## Step 7: Prepare the research report

The final step is to prepare a report of the research results. In general, a research report must clearly and concisely tell the readers what they need to know in a way that they can understand. A typical report includes the followings:

- An executive summary of the report that covers the high points of the total report.
- An understandable description of the research methodology.

- A complete discussion of the results of the study, including the tabulations, cross-tabulations and additional statistical analyses.
- Limitations of the study (no study is perfect).
- Conclusions and recommendations for managerial action based on the results.

Now you've learned about marketing research, and read 'Real people, real decisions' to see which marketing strategies Ryan Garton could go for at Discover, here's how it worked out.

Real people, real decisions

How it worked out at Discover Financial

Ryan chose Option 3.

The firm's leadership decided it was worth taking on additional costs and delays to maximise the chances that consumers would adopt new card offerings. After all, a new product that bombs can cost a company millions of dollars, so investing up-front to prevent this can be well worth the money and time. Ryan's team undertook the first Innovation Screening in Discover's history. The company interviewed numerous marketing research companies and eventually selected Ipsos, which had impressive prior experience in working with clients from the financial services industry. This company also maintained an online panel that would allow them to create a statistically representative panel of over 1600 respondents who were current customers of Discover as well as those who used competing card products. The consumer panelists evaluated a total of 16 concepts: three benchmark cards (card products that Chase, Citibank and American Express already had in the market), seven new product ideas and six new feature ideas. Each respondent evaluated three concepts, for a total of about 300 evaluations per concept. In order to get at the true potential of the ideas, participants assessed them without being told which card company was thinking about introducing them. At a later point in the study they rated the attractiveness of these ideas when they were paired with actual card companies. The consumer research showed that in fact some of management's initial estimates about the likely appeal of new products was significantly off the mark. Some were less appealing than sponsors assumed, while some showed evidence of greater demand than Discover's internal finance teams predicted – one potential product moved from the back of the list to be Discover's highest priority based on this work. In addition, when the team tested some new offerings that competing card companies had recently launched, it found that they weren't all that appealing – and indeed, about a year later the other companies closed these down. Ryan was gratified that Discover lived up to its name and invested in discovering what its customers actually liked and disliked.

Marketing metrics

Measuring success at Discover Financial

Discover Financial developed a number of key metrics for its evaluation process. Consumers rated each new concept on these dimensions:

- Intent to sign up for the new product.
- Intensity of liking for the product.
- Price vs. perceived value.
- Uniqueness of the product versus competitive offers.
- Believability.
- Whether the concept fulfilled a need compared to the card product already in use.

The team went on to develop an IPP (intent for product purchase) index score that combined a consumer's responses to several of the key variables. It created a second index it called 'Brand Right', which combined measures of brand fit and customer need. Brand fit is crucial – the team knew from past research that the best new offerings still require more marketing funds (advertising, direct mail, incentives, etc.) to gain acceptance if customers don't believe that they are consistent with an existing brand's image. It measured customer need through some questions in the study that related to whether respondents felt the product Discover was considering would fill a need that one of the cards they already used wasn't filling. For example, the respondent would be asked to indicate if 'this is a new idea that solves a problem for me today.' Then Ryan and the team plotted the IPP index against the 'Brand Right' index to highlight to leadership which proposed products and services were likely to be a hit with consumers *and* to be best fits with Discover.

Chapter summary

Now that you have finished reading this chapter, you should understand:

1. **The role of the marketing information system and the marketing decision support system in decision making.** A marketing information system (MkIS) is composed of internal data, marketing intelligence, marketing research data, acquired databases, and computer hardware and software. Firms use an MkIS to gather, sort, analyse, store and distribute information needed by managers for marketing decision making. The marketing decision support system (MDSS) allows managers to use analysis software and interactive software to access MkIS data and to conduct analyses and find the information they need.

2. **The marketing research process.** The research process begins by defining the problem and determining the research design or type of study. Next, researchers choose the data collection method, that is, whether there are secondary data available or if primary research with a communication study or through observation is necessary. Then researchers determine what type of sample is to be used for the study and then collect the data. The final steps in the research are to analyse and interpret the data and prepare a research report.

3. **The differences among exploratory, descriptive and causal research and some research techniques available to marketers.** Exploratory research typically uses qualitative data collected by individual interviews, focus groups or observational methods such as ethnography. Descriptive research includes cross-sectional and longitudinal studies. Causal research goes a step further by designing controlled experiments to understand cause-and-effect relationships between marketing independent variables, such as price changes, and dependent variables, such as sales.

4. **The different types of data-collection methods and types of samples that researchers use.** Researchers may choose to collect data via survey methods and observation approaches. Survey approaches include mail questionnaires, telephone interviews, face-to-face interviews or online questionnaires. A study may utilise a probability sample such as a simple random or stratified sample in which inferences can be made to a population on the basis of sample results. Non-probability sampling methods include a convenience sample and a quota sample. The research tries to ensure that the data are valid, reliable and representative. Validity is the extent to which the research actually measures what it was intended to measure. Reliability is the extent to which the research measurement techniques are free of errors. Representativeness is the extent to which consumers in the study are similar to a larger group in which the organisation has an interest.

5. **The growing use of online research.** Online research accounts for more than 25 per cent of all marketing research. Online tracking uses cookies to record where consumers go on a website. Consumers have become increasingly concerned about privacy and how this information is used and made available to other internet companies. The internet also provides an attractive alternative to traditional data collection methods because of its speed and low cost.

Key terms

Chapter review

Marketing concepts: testing your knowledge

1. What is a marketing information system (MkIS)? What types of information are included in a marketing information system? How does a marketing decision support system (MDSS) allow marketers to easily get the information they need?

2. What is data mining? How is it used by marketers?

3. What are the steps in the marketing research process? Why is defining the problem to be researched so important to ultimate success with the research project?

4. What techniques are used to gather data in exploratory research? How can exploratory research be useful to marketers?

5. What are some advantages and disadvantages of telephone interviews, postal questionnaires, face-to-face interviews and online interviews?

6. When considering data quality, what are the differences among validity, reliability and representativeness? How do you know data have high levels of these characteristics?

7. How do probability and non-probability samples differ? What are some types of probability samples? What are some types of non-probability samples?

8. What is a cross-tabulation? How are cross-tabulations useful in analysing and interpreting data?

9. What is a cookie? What ethical and privacy issues are related to cookies?

10. What important issues must researchers consider when planning to collect their data online?

Marketing concepts: discussing choices and ethical issues

1. Some marketers attempt to disguise themselves as marketing researchers when their real intent is to sell something to the consumer. What is the impact of this practice on legitimate researchers? What do you think might be done about this practice?

2. Do you think marketers should be allowed to conduct market research with young children? Why or why not?

3. Are you willing to divulge personal information to marketing researchers? How much are you willing to tell, or where would you draw the line?

4. What is your overall attitude toward marketing research? Do you think it is a beneficial activity from a consumer's perspective? Or do you think it merely gives marketers new insights on how to convince consumers to buy something they really don't want or need?

5. Sometimes firms use data mining to identify and abandon customers who are not profitable because they don't spend enough to justify the service needed or because they return a large proportion of the items they buy. What do you think of such practices? Is it ethical for firms to prune out these customers?

6. Many consumers are concerned about online tracking studies and their privacy. Do consumers have the right to 'own' data about themselves? Should governments limit the use of the internet for data collection?

7. One unobtrusive measure mentioned in this chapter involved going through consumers' or competitors' garbage. Do you think marketers should have the right to do this? Is it ethical?

8. Consider the approach to tracking consumers' exposure to promotions via portable people meters, or PPMs. How would you feel about participating in a study that required you to use a PPM? What would be the advantage of a PPM approach versus keeping a written diary of television shows you watched and ads you saw?

Marketing practice: applying what you've learned

1. Your firm is planning to begin marketing a consumer product in several markets. You have been given the responsibility of developing plans for marketing research to be conducted in South Africa, in Spain and in China In a role-playing situation, present the difficulties you expect to encounter, if any, in conducting research in each of these areas.

2. As an account executive with a marketing research firm, you are responsible for deciding on the type of research to be used in various studies conducted for your clients. For each of the following client questions, list your choices of research approaches.

   a. Will television or magazine advertising be more effective for a local bank to use in its marketing communication plan?

   b. Could a new package design for breakfast cereal do a better job at satisfying the needs of buyers and thus increase sales?

   c. Are consumers more likely to buy brands that are labelled as environmentally friendly?

   d. How do female consumers determine if a particular perfume is right for them?

   e. What types of people read the local newspaper?

   f. How frequently do consumers switch brands of soft drinks?

   g. How will an increase in the price of a brand of laundry detergent affect sales?

   h. What are the effects of advertising and sales promotion in combination on sales of a brand of shampoo?

3. Your marketing research firm is planning to conduct surveys to gather information for a number of clients. Your boss has asked you and a few other new employees to do some preliminary work. He has asked each of you to choose three of the topics (from among those listed next) that will be included in the project and to prepare an analysis of the advantages and disadvantages of these communication methods of collecting data: mail questionnaires, telephone interviews, face-to-face interviews and online questionnaires.

   a. The amount of sports nutrition drinks consumed in a city.

   b. Why a local bank has been losing customers.

   c. How heavily the company should invest in manufacturing and marketing home fax machines.

   d. The amount of money spent on euro lottery tickets in Denmark, Sweden, Holland and the UK.

   e. What local doctors would like to see changed in the hospitals in the city.

   f. Consumers' attitudes toward several sports celebrities.

4. For each of the topics you selected in item 3, how might a more passive (observation) approach be used to support the communication methods employed?

Marketing miniproject: learning by doing

The purpose of this miniproject is to familiarise you with marketing research techniques and to help you apply these techniques to managerial decision making.

1. With three other students in your class, select a small retail business or fast-food restaurant to use as a 'client' for your project. (Be sure to get the manager's permission before conducting your research.) Then choose a topic from among the following possibilities to develop a study problem:

   ● Employee–customer interactions.

   ● The busiest periods of customer activity.

   ● Customer perceptions of service.

   ● Customer likes and dislikes about offerings.

   ● Customer likes and dislikes about the environment in the place of business.

   ● The benefits customers perceive to be important.

   ● The age groups that frequent the place of business.

   ● The buying habits of a particular age group.

   ● How customer complaints are handled.

2. Develop a plan for the research:

   a. Define the problem as you will study it;

   b. Choose the type of research you will use;

   c. Select the techniques you will use to gather data;

   d. Develop the mode and format for data collection.

3. Conduct the research.

4. Write a report (or develop a class presentation) that includes four parts:

   a. Introduction: a brief overview of the business and the problem studied.

   b. Methodology: the type of research used, the techniques used to gather data (and why they were chosen), the instruments and procedures used, the number of respondents, duration of the study, and other details that would allow someone to replicate your study.

   c. Results: a compilation of the results (perhaps in table form) and the conclusions drawn.

   d. Recommendations: a list of recommendations for actions management might take based on the conclusions drawn from the study.

Further reading

Marketing Research: An Applied Approach. 4th European Edition, Naresh Malhotra, David Birks and Peter Wills, Pearson, 2012

A key feature throughout this book that matches the ethos of 'Real People, Real Decisions', are the 'Real Research' sections present in all chapters. These sections show how research is used to support contemporary marketing decisions. They reinforce the relevance and value of well-crafted research to decision-makers. The book covers quantitative data analysis (with SPSS and SAS illustrations) and qualitative data analysis. It incorporates the major international communications, ethical and digital developments in marketing research that are impacting upon how decision-makers are supported. The growth of online research and social media research methods are changing the nature of marketing research. They are shaping the breadth of skills demanded of researchers that command the respect of decision-makers. The nature, scope and future developments in marketing research, primarily as practised in Europe are clearly set out in this book.

Real people, real surfers

Exploring the web

As discussed in this chapter, monitoring changes in demographics and other consumer trends is an important part of the marketing intelligence included in an MkIS. Today, much of this information is gathered by government research and is available on the internet.

The UK National Statistical Office provides tabled data for cities and counties across the nations at its site, www.statistics.gov.uk. Statistics Netherlands is a governmental institution which collects and provides data about the Netherlands at its site, www.cbs.nl/en-GB/default.htm. A similar statistics website exists for Denmark, at www.dst.dk/homeuk.aspx.

On the homepage, click on population. You should be able to locate the statistical data for your area by using a search engine such as Google, and entering something like 'Utrecht Statistical Abstract'. Using both state data and Statistics Netherlands data, develop a report on a city or county of your choice that answers these questions:

1. What is the total population of your city or town?

2. Describe the population of the area in terms of age, income, education, ethnic background, marital status, occupation and housing.

3. How does your city or town compare to the demographic characteristics of the entire UK or Dutch or Danish population?

4. What is your opinion of the different websites you used? How useful are they to marketers? How easy were they to navigate? Was there information that you wanted that was not available? Was there more or less information from the sites than you anticipated? Explain.

Now, take a look at the website at www.pearsoned.co.uk/solomon to see some videos from YouTube relating to aspects of this chapter.

Marketing plan exercise

Select a company that makes a product that you use and with which you are familiar. For the company to make decisions about developing new products and attracting new customers, it must rely on marketing research. These decisions feed into the company's marketing plan. For the firm you selected:

1. Undertake preliminary secondary research, for example by looking at company and market reports in order to get a better initial insight into the company. Try to identify problems which the company is facing and areas where performance could be improved. Now pick and define one specific problem they could address through marketing research.

2. What type of research design do you recommend for addressing that problem, and why?

3. What is the most appropriate way to collect the data? Justify your choice.

4. How will you ensure high validity, reliability, and representativeness of the data?

5. Design an appropriate sampling plan.

Delve deeper into market research

Udo Wagner, PhD

Chaired Professor of Management and Marketing, University of Vienna

Market research is a fascinating topic bridging empirical and conceptual areas. Whereas, typically, descriptive research designs, the development of data collection forms, issues of sample design as well as sample collection and more statistically orientated topics of data analysis are dominating contents of textbooks on market research, I would like to point out three other areas which appear to be very interesting:

1. Given the increasing popularity of exploratory research design the sound evaluation of *qualitative data* usually lags behind. In addition, qualitative research might contribute considerably to improving conceptual insights and theory building. The paper by Laurent (2000) pinpoints this aspect.

2. Data on consumer behaviour collected by means of communication are frequently affected by social desirability biases but are nevertheless all too frequently used. *Observational designs* offer powerful alternatives. Hodock's (1991) paper makes a very strong point on this issue.

3. Market research data are used as a basis for validating models used by marketing science *models*. Discrete choice models in general, and logit models in particular, are nice examples of such approaches. One of the most cited papers in this area is the article by Guadagni and Little (1983), which gives a flavour of the research.

I always encourage my students to deepen their knowledge in market research and to study the relevant literature. The readings provided here are good examples of the huge diversity covered by our field. Enjoy studying market research, it is fascinating!

References:

P.M. Guadagni and J.D.C. Little (1983) 'A Logit Model of Brand Choice Calibrated on Scanner Data', *Marketing Science*, 2, no. 3, 203–38.

C.L. Hodock (1991) 'The Decline and Fall of Marketing Research in Corporate America', *Marketing Research*, June, 12–22.

G. Laurent (2000) 'Improving the External Validity of Marketing Models: A Plea for More Qualitative Input', *International Journal of Research in Marketing*, 17 no. 2/3, 177–82.

Marketing in action case

Neuromarketing – taking a peek inside the consumer's mind

Ever wondered what mysterious forces of attraction make us prefer some brands over others despite never having actually tried any of their products? Why Pepsi wins endless taste tests, yet Coca-Cola remains many's preferred choice? Believe it or not, recent advances in the neurosciences might soon be providing the answers to such mindboggling questions. Neuromarketing is the new kid on the block and is promising to revolutionise marketing research. Its proponents, who include some of the greatest minds in the field of cognitive neuroscience argue that by bypassing language and going straight to the source, the consumer's brain, neuromarketing has the potential to provide objective and unparalleled knowledge about customer perceptions and decision making.[1] It has in fact been used to measure and better understand a whole variety of marketing phenomena such as advertisement effectiveness (for message recall and emotional response), product appeal and pricing, brand engagement and brand/logo selection.[2] It has even been used by film makers to refine characters, scripts and special effects.[3]

Marketers have long been telling us that the key to customer loyalty lies in the quality of the customer experience, but little did we know that this has the potential to actually alter our brain chemistry. Functional magnetic resonance imaging or fMRI, is the most advanced of the neuroscientific techniques and can precisely pinpoint the origin of brain activity. It produces pretty, colourful images of the working brain and different images are associated with different emotional states or cognitive functions such as reward, empathy and the sense of self.[4]

Thanks to such technological advances, firms worldwide are now offering neuromarketing solutions to companies' marketing dilemmas.[5] In the UK, Neurosense has been a major pioneer, making the benefits of neuroscience available to its clients for over a decade – McDonald's, GMTV, Procter & Gamble and Uniliver.[6]

Yet, perhaps the most compelling study to date has been the re-enactment of the iconic Pepsi/Coca-Cola blind taste challenge assessing the impact of brand perception on consumer product preference.[7] During the blind tasting fMRI scans revealed participant brain activity was concentrated in the ventral medium putanen, a region of the brain known to be associated with seeking reward (i.e. good taste). Readings were strong for both drinks, but the majority of participants ultimately expressed a taste preference for Pepsi. However, in the brand-cued test, where participants were aware of what they were consuming, it was a different story, brand familiarity seemingly kicked in and most participants ended up choosing in favour of Coke. On this occasion neural activity was mainly recorded in the hippocampus, midbrain and dorsolateral prefrontal cortex – zones of the brain associated with memory, emotions and cognitive control. Researchers concluded that Coke's superior brand image coupled with participants' memories and emotional ties to the brand produced a brand recognition effect which trumped peoples' actual taste preference for Pepsi.

Yet neuromarketing is not without its sceptics and critics; doubts have been voiced regarding the efficacy of the technology.[8] Consumer groups such as Commercial Alert in the US have expressed ethical concerns, fearing that neuromarketing may lead to an increased incidence in marketing-related pathologies such as alcoholism, gambling and child obesity[9]. It is feared that as businesses learn to read consumers' minds, at a deep subconscious level, we will become defenceless against their power to control our perceptions and behaviour, signifying the end of free will and decision making.[10] At which point the real question is, when does influence become blatant manipulation? This promises to be a tougher nut to crack than the Pespsi/Coca-Cola challenge, and ironically, neuromarketing could well help provide the answer.

Things to think about

1. What advantages does neuromarketing offer over more traditional marketing research methods and for which type of consumer behaviour questions might this type of methodology be most appropriate?

2. Can you identify the limitations presently effecting neuromarketing research and make suggestions to improve future research?

3. Neuromarketing has been criticised on ethical grounds with concerns relating to the use of neuroscience for commercial gains and its detrimental effects for consumer behaviour. Can you think of ways in which neuromarketing can be used to better serve the discipline of marketing and society?

Case study written by Leandro Galli, Warwick Business School

References

1. N. Carr, *'Neuromarketing Could Make Mind Reading the Ad-Man's Ultimate Tool'*, The Guardian, http://www.guardian.co.uk/technology/2008/apr/03/news.advertising (accessed 7 June 2011), T. Grose, *'Brain Sell'*, Time Magazine, (2006), http://www.time.com/time/magazine/article/0,9171,1533381,00.html (accessed 6 June 2011); Martin Lindstrom, 'What is Neuromarketing?' http://www.martinlindstrom.com/index.php/cmsid__buyology_what_is_neuromarketing (accessed 6 June 2011).

2. D.L. Fugate, 'Neuromarketing: A Layman's Look at Neuroscience and its Potential Application to Marketing Practic', *Journal of Consumer Marketing*, 24, no. 7 (2007) .385 – 94.

3. Branding Strategy Insider, 'Neuromarketing and the Oscars', http://www.brandingstrategyinsider.com/2011/03/neuromarketing-and-the-oscars.html (accessed on 6 June 2011).

4. Z. Eser, B. Isin, and M. Tolon, 'Perceptions of Marketing Academics, Neurologists and Marketing Professionals about Neuromarketing' (*Journal of Marketing Management* (2010), 1–15.

5. N. Lee, A. Broderick and L. Chamberlain, 'What is "Neuromarketing"? A Discussion and Agenda for Future Research', *International Journal of Psychophysiology* 63 (2007), 199–204.

6. Neurosense (2011), http://www.neurosense.co.uk/our_clients.html (accessed 8 June 2011).

7. S. M. McClure, J. Li, D. Tomlin, K.S. Cypert, L.M. Montague and P.R. Montague, 'Neural Correlates of Behavioural Preference for Culturally Familiar Drinks', *Neuron* 44, no. 2 (2004) 379–87.

8. S. James, 'Neuromarketing is no Brainwave if You Think About It', *Precision Marketing* 24 (September 2004), 12–13; J. Medina, 'The Neurobiology of the Decision to Buy', *Psychiatric Times* (October 2004), 31–4; T. Perrachione and J. Perrachione, 'Brains and Brands: Developing Mutually Informative Research in Neuroscience and Marketing', *Journal of Consumer Behaviour* 7 2008), 303–18; M. Sutherland, 'Using our Brains: Neuromarketing, No-hands Gaming and the Arrival of the EEG Headset' (2011), http://www.gizmag.com/eeg-headsets-gaming-neuromarketing/18693/ (accessed 6 June 2011).

9. R. Harris, 'Brain Waves', *Marketing Magazines* 111, no. 20 (2006), 15–17; C. Witchalls. 'Pushing the Buy Button' (2004) http://www.commercialalert.org/issues/culture/neuromarketing/pushing-the-buy-button (accessed 6 June 2011); C. Madam, 'Neuromarketing: The Next Step in Market Research', *Eureka* 1, no. 1.

10. N. Carr, *The Guardian*, 'Neuromarketing Could Make Mind Reading the Ad-man's Ultimate Tool', http://www.guardian.co.uk/technology/2008/apr/03/news.advertising (accessed 7 June 2011).

References

1. www.marketingpower.com/mg-dictionary.php?SearchFor=Marketing+Research& Searched=1 American Marketing Association Website, (accessed 24 January 2008).

2. www.foxnews.com/story/ 0,2933, 136233,00.html Megan Dowd, 'Avon's Daughters Make their "Mark"', (accessed 17 February 2006).

3. http://ball-street.ftd.de/view/'Ball Street Börsenspiel', *Financial Times Deutschland*,(accessed 8 June 2007).

4. www.qscores.com 'The Q Scores Company', Marketing Evaluations, (accessed 15 February 2006).

5. www.barb.co.uk/about.cfm?flag= about 'About BARB', Broadcasters' Audience Research Board, accessed 13 June 2007).

6. Adapted from T. Dalgic and R. Heijblom, Educator Insights: International Marketing Blunders Revisited. *Journal of International Martketing*, 4, (1996) 81–91.

7. Yumiko Ono, 'An Ad for Smudge-Proof Makeup Rubs a Big Marketer Wrong Way', *Wall Street Journal*, 12 April 1996, B1.

8. www.businessobjects.com/company/customers/company.asp?industryid=2&productid=&companyid=83 'Consumer Products: Ben & Jerry's', Business Objects, (accessed 14 June 2007).

9. www.britishairways.com/travel/fullpp/public/en_gb, 'Privacy Policy', British Airways, (accessed 4 June 2007).

10. Pan-Ning Tan, Michael Steinbach and Vipin Kumar, *Introduction to Data Mining*, 1st ed. (New York: Addison Wesley, 2005).

11. Ibid.

12. Frederich F. Reichheld, *Loyalty Rules! How Leaders Build Lasting Relationships in the Digital Age* (Cambridge, MA: Harvard Business School Press, 2001).

13. http://news.bbc.co.uk/2/hi/business/4381140.stm Claire Bothwell (2005): 'Burberry versus the chavs'. *BBC Money Programme*, (accessed 13 June 2007).

14. Robert Baxter, Mercedes-Benz North America, personal communication, June 1996.

15. Hamilton Nolan, 'Mercedes Launches PR Push,' *PR Week*, 6 February 2006, 3.

16. Adapted from Telly mix we love it, *Go compare car insurance telly ad named most annoying of 2010* (2011), http://tellymix.co.uk/2011/news/25252-gocompare-car-insurance-telly-ad-named-most-annoying-of-2010.html (accessed 21 July 2011).

17. www.mintel.com/frontpage/Mintel International, 'Consumer Media and Market Research' (accessed 5 June 2007).

18. www.audi.de/audi/de/de2/unternehmen/news/ pressemitteilungen/_Audi_Lab_for_Market_Research_an_der_Universitaet_St_Gallen_gegruendet.html 'Audi Lab for Market research an der Universität St. Gallen gegründet', Audi Website, Press Release, 23 August 2006, (accessed 4 June 2007).

19. Michael R. Solomon, *Conquering Consumerspace: Marketing Strategies for a Branded World* (New York: Amacom Books, 2003).

20. Paul English, 'So Cool, It Hurts: Paul English gets Hip to the Glamorous Work, of Professional Trendsetters', *Daily Record*, 20 October 2001, 6–7; Don Hedley, 'Trendspotter: The Uber-Sexual Man', *Brand Strategy*, 8, 12 June 2007.

21. 'Nivea Deodorant. How Market Research Supports the New Product Development Process' *The Times* and MBA Publishing (eds), Edition 12. 105–8, www.thetimes100.co.uk/downloads/nivea/nivea_12_full.pdf.

22. Nokia Website, 'Consumers Increasingly Giving Up Their Fixed Line Phones', Press Release 21 October 2004, (accessed 6 June 2007) http://press.nokia.com/PR/200410/ 965166_5.html.

23. 'Nutrition, Health and Wellness: New Product Development at Nestlé' *The Times* and MBA Publishing (eds), Edition 11, 113–16, www.thetimes100.co.uk/downloads/nestle/nestle_11_full.pdf.

24. Michael R. Solomon, *Consumer Behavior: Buying, Having and Being*, 5th ed. (Upper Saddle River, NJ: Prentice Hall, 2001).

25. 'Volvic Puts TV Ad Character on MSN Spaces', *New Media Age*, 17 May 2007, 2.

26. Jean Halliday, 'Nissan Delves into Truck Owner Psyche', *Advertising Age*, 1 December 2003, 11.

27. www.mini.de/de/de/mini_united/index.jsp?refType=teaser Homepage&refPage=/de/de/general/homepage/content_specials.jsp Mini: 'Mini United: Friends Challenge Festival: Are you Ready for Amsterdam', (accessed 14 June 2007).

28. Jack Neff, 'Six-Blade Blitz', *Advertising Age*, 19 September 2005, 3.

29. Srikumar Rao, 'Diaper–Beer Syndrome', *Forbes*, 6 April 1998, 161, (no. 7) 128–30.

30. Clive Thompson, 'There's a Sucker Born in Every Medial Prefrontal Cortex', NYTimes.com, 26 October 2003, http://query.nytimes.com/gst/fullpage.html?res=9B07E1DE113EF935A15753C1A9659C8B63.

31. Direct Marketing Association, 'Where Marketers Can Obtain State Do-Not-Call Lists', Accessed 7 February 2006, www.the-dma.org/government/donotcalllists.shtml.

32. Kim Bartel Sheehan, 'Online Research Methodology: Reflections and Speculations', *Journal of Interactive Advertising*, 3, no. 1 (Fall 2002), (accessed 7 February 2006) www.websm.org/ index.php?fl=2&lact=1&bid=631&cat= 351&p1=1123&p2= 82&id=520&page=1&parent=12.

33. Mick P. Cooper, 'Web Surveys. A Review of Issues and Approaches', *Public Opinion Quarterly*, 64(4) (2001), 464–94.

34. Basil G. Englis and Michael R. Solomon, 'Life/Style OnLine: A Web-Based Methodology for Visually-Oriented Consumer Research', *Journal of Interactive Marketing* 14, no. 1 (2000), 2–14; Basil G. Englis, Michael R. Solomon, and Paula D. Harveston, 'Web-Based, Visually Oriented Consumer Research Tools', in *Online Consumer Psychology: Understanding How to Interact with Consumers in the Virtual World*, ed. Curt Haugtvedt, Karen Machleit and Richard Yalch (Hillsdale, NJ: Lawrence Erlbaum Associates, 2005.

35. Matt Richtel, 'A New On-the-Job Hazard: Turning into a Mall Rat', NYTimes.com, 3 May 2004, (accessed 7 February 2006). www.internethomealliance.com/press_room/in_the_news/docs/NewYorkTimesMay32004.pdf.

36. Mike Galetto, 'Turning Trash to Research Treasure', *Advertising Age*, 17 April 1995, 1–16.

37. Linda Dupree and John Bosarge, 'Media on the Move: How to Measure In- and Out-of-Home Media Consumption', (accessed 16 February 2006). http://us.acnielsen.com/pubs/ documents/media_000.pdf.

38. IPA. 'The IPA TouchPoints initiative', (accessed 11 June 2007) www.ipa.co.uk/touchpoints.

39. Bruce L. Stern and Ray Ashmun, 'Methodological Disclosure: The Foundation for Effective Use of Survey Research', *Journal of Applied Business Research* 7 (1991), 77–82.

40. Alan E. Wolf, 'Most Colas Branded Alike by Testy Magazine', *Beverage World*, 31 August 1991, 8.

41. Gary Levin, 'New Adventures in Children's Research', *Advertising Age*, 9 August 1993, 17.

42. Greenfield/Ciao Online Research Barometer 2005, www.greenfield-ciaosurveys.com/.

43. Nicolas Metzke and Katherine Allan (2005). 'Researching the Researchers: The Online Barometer', *Esomar Panel Conference Proceedings*, April 2005.

44. Jean Halliday, 'Automakers Involve Consumers', *Advertising Age*, 31 January 2000, 82.

45. Tobi Elkin, 'Virtual Test Market', *Advertising Age*, 27 October 2003, 6.

46. James Heckman, 'Turning the Focus Online', *Marketing News*, 28 February 2000, 15; Judith Langer, '"On" and "Offline" Focus Groups: Claims, Questions', *Marketing News*, 5 June 2000, H38.

47. Deborah L. Vence, 'In an Instant: More Researchers Use IM for Fast, Reliable Results', *Marketing News*, 1 March 2006: 55, no. 3.

48. 2004 Honomichl Top 50 Report, *Marketing News*, 15 June 2004, H4.

49. Jack Honomichl, 'Research Cultures Are Different in Mexico, Canada', *Marketing News*, 10 May 1993, 12.

50. Esomar, Amsterdam, reported in *Marketing News*, 15 July 2005, 24.

Chapter 4
Consumer behaviour

Meet Julie Cordua,
Vice President of
Marketing at (RED)

Q & A with Julie Cordua

What do I do when I'm not working?
Read, travel, and spend time with friends and family

First job out of school
Account coordinator at Hill & Knowlton Public Relations

Career high
Two: introducing the MOTO RAZR and introducing (RED)

Business book I'm reading now
The End of Poverty by Jeff Sachs

My management style
Give your team the tools it needs to do its best job and trust it

Don't do this when interviewing with me
Ask about the salary in the first part of the interview

Julie Cordua is the Vice President of Marketing at (RED), a new brand created By U2 lead singer Bono and Bobby Shriver to engage business in the fight against AIDS in Africa. (RED) partners with the world's best brands to make uniquely branded products from which up to 50 per cent of the profits are directed to the Global Fund to finance African HIV/AIDS programmes with a focus on women and children. In her role at (RED), she is responsible for building the (RED) brand through innovative marketing programmes including public relations, advertising, events and co-branding. Prior to joining (RED), Julie spent the bulk of her career in marketing in the wireless industry. Most recently, she was the senior director of buzz marketing and part of the start-up team at HELIO, a new mobile brand for young, connected consumers. Before HELIO, Julie spent five years at Motorola in the mobile devices division in Chicago. At Motorola, she led the global category marketing group and was part of the team that orchestrated the RAZR launch in 2002. Julie started her career in public relations at Hill & Knowlton in Los Angeles. She holds a BA in communications with an emphasis in business administration from UCLA and an MBA from the Kellogg School at Northwestern University. She currently lives in Manhattan Beach, California, with her husband.

Real people, real decisions
Decision time at (RED)

(RED) works with the world's best brands to make unique (PRODUCT) RED-branded products and directs up to 50 per cent of its gross profits to the Global Fund to invest in African AIDS programmes with a focus on the health of women and children. (RED) is not a charity or 'campaign.' It is an economic initiative that aims to deliver a sustainable flow of private sector money to the Global Fund. Launch product partners included Converse, Gap, Motorola, Emporio Armani, Apple and American Express (UK only). In its first year, (RED) added Hallmark, Dell and Microsoft as partners. These companies were chosen because they were strong international consumer brands that could drive significant awareness and sell large volumes of products. And, more importantly, they were the few brave companies that were willing to take a risk on the idea of (RED) before it was a proven concept. By autumn 2007, with a successful first year behind it, (RED) was evaluating how to ensure sustained success for the brand. One of the main inputs Julie needed was more consumer insights about how shoppers related to the (RED) concept and to cause marketing where purchases are linked to donations to a non-profit organisation in general. The company had not done this research before launch, so Julie decided it was time to do an extensive consumer research study in the United States. Specifically, Julie wanted to know what consumers thought about the following (and how their beliefs affected their purchasing/participationm actions):

- A corporation's role in solving social issues.
- Churches/community organisations' roles in solving social issues.
- An individual's role in solving social issues (via donation or volunteering).
- Government's role in solving social issues.
- Celebrity involvement in solving social issues.
- The idea of combining charity with capitalism (buying and contributing at the same time).

The research project included three stages: (1) interviews with a variety of consumers to qualitatively understand major issues on people's minds, how consumers relate to shopping and charity, and what people know about (RED); (2) a nationwide quantitative survey to identify major attitudinal and behavioural trends across the population; and (3) ethnographies where researchers actually spent time with people as they went about their daily lives, which helped bring some of the key insights from the survey to life. The research showed that teens were most open to the idea of cause marketing. This finding made sense to Julie; this is a group that has grown up with the idea of 'creative capitalism' and doesn't understand why doing good and having what you want should be separated. Also, this group looked up to celebrities more than any other age segment; they cited famous people across music, film, TV and sports as major influences on their opinions and behaviours. However, when describing how they relate to (RED), they often commented that the brands that were current partners were not relevant to them.

A surprisingly large portion of the population rejected the idea of combining charity and capitalism. These 'traditionalists' believed that social issues were best taken care of by the government or churches and community organisations. They were highly sceptical of corporations that promoted an ability to do good by buying a product. These consumers wanted a more traditional way to get involved – through donations, volunteering or simply through paying taxes and allowing their government to address the issues. With these insights in hand, Julie and her colleagues, including the head of business development, several outside advisers, and the CEO, had to decide if the (RED) model – partnering with mass market international brands for long-term deals – was the optimal way to generate the most money for the Global Fund.

Julie considers her options . . .

Option 1 Expand the (RED) model based on what the research revealed about the teen market

Complement the bigger deals involving mainstream brands with the introduction of smaller 'special edition' deals with younger, more relevant brands. Engage celebrities that specifically appeal to the younger demographic. If young people buy into the concept now, this would build loyalty and they would remain long-term fans of the brand. On the downside, this extra investment in smaller brands would require additional resources and divert (RED)'s small staff from its primary task of working with larger companies.

Option 2 Stick with the existing (RED) model

Continue to partner only with large, international brands that make significant marketing and contribution commitments. Use celebrity engagement to draw attention to the brand. This option would let (RED) tap into the growing sentiment toward combining charity and capitalism. It would provide opportunities for significant exposure for (RED) through large-scale marketing programmes. On the other hand, this approach might alienate those who prefer more traditional avenues of giving to charity; these people might not give to the Global Fund under these circumstances. And, with such a mass market approach, (RED) might not maximise engagement with the high-potential teen segment, which might be valuable long term.

Option 3 Expand the (RED) model to include more traditional non-profit aspects, such as donation and volunteering, in order to appeal to all consumer groups and increase engagement

This would allow (RED) to expand its reach to a much broader audience and potentially drive more revenue for the Global Fund through donations. But such an expansion might create brand confusion since (RED) is all about shopping and doing good at the same time. Julie feared that the company might not be able to be 'all things to all people' by appealing to those who endorse the idea of 'creative capitalism' and to those who want to contribute via more traditional avenues.

Things to remember: A sizeable portion of consumers have strong negative attitudes toward big corporations. They don't necessarily want to deal with companies now aligned with (RED) as part of their charitable activities

Now, put yourself in Julie's shoes: Which option would you choose to be a winner, and why?

Objectives

When you finish reading this chapter, you will be able to:

1 Define consumer behaviour and explain why consumers buy what they buy
2 Describe the pre-purchase, purchase and post-purchase activities that consumers engage in when making decisions
3 Explain how internal factors influence consumers' decision-making processes
4 Show how situational factors at the time and place of purchase influence consumer behaviour
5 Explain how consumers' relationships with other people influence their decision-making processes
6 Show how the internet offers consumers opportunities to participate in consumer-to-consumer marketing

Objective

1

Define consumer behaviour and explain why consumers buy what they buy

Decisions, decisions

Compelling new products, clever packaging and creative advertising surround us, clamouring for our attention – and our money. But each of us is unique, with our own reasons for choosing a product. Recall that the focus of the marketing concept is to satisfy consumers' wants and needs and therefore we need to understand what those wants and needs are. **Consumer behaviour** is the process individuals or groups go through to select, purchase, use and dispose of goods, services, ideas or experiences to satisfy their needs and desires.

Let's look at an example of consumer purchase which is probably very familiar to you: breakfast cereal. Marketers need to understand why and where you buy your cereal. Do you go to a large hypermarket in order to buy big boxes of cereal at a cheaper price? Or do you just go to the local corner shop if you get the urge for cereal in the middle of the night? Then there is the decision of the type of cereal. Do you eat only low-fat, high-fibre bran cereals, or do you go for the sugar-coated varieties or maybe you like to vary between all of them?

Marketers also need to know how and when you consume their products. Do you eat cereal only for breakfast, or do you snack on it while sitting in front of the TV at night?

Do you eat certain kinds of cereal only at certain times (like sugary 'kids' cereals' that serve as comfort food when you're staying up late)? What about storing the product? Do you have a kitchen pantry where you can store the super-size box, or is space an issue?

Actually, there's lots more marketers also need to understand, such as factors at the time of purchase (how it was displayed) and the social influences of people around us (who was with us at the time). In this chapter, we'll talk about the ways in which all these factors influence how and why consumers do what they do. But first we'll look at the types of decisions consumers make and the steps in the decision-making process.

Steps in the consumer decision process

Extended problem solving versus habitual decision making

Objective

2

Describe the pre-purchase, purchase and post-purchase activities that consumers engage in when making decisions

Researchers realised that decision makers actually possess a set of approaches ranging from painstaking analysis to pure whim, depending on the importance of what they are buying and how much effort the person is willing to put into the decision. Marketers have found it convenient to think in terms of an 'effort' continuum that is anchored on one end by habitual decision making, such as deciding to purchase a box of cereal, and at the other end by extended problem solving, such as deciding to purchase a new car.

When consumers make very important decisions – such as buying a new house or a car – they engage in extended problem solving and carefully go through the steps. Figure 4.1 outlines problem recognition, information search, evaluation of alternatives, product choice and post-purchase evaluation.

When they make habitual decisions, however, consumers make little or no conscious effort, they don't search for information, and they don't compare alternatives. Rather, they make purchases automatically. For example, you may simply throw the same brand of cereal in your shopping trolley week after week without thinking about it. Consumers are also often tempted to make impulse purchases, for example when they are waiting in the queue for the supermarket checkout and grab, on a sudden impulse, a cereal bar or chewing gum from the till next to them. Figure 4.2 provides a summary of the differences between extended problem solving and habitual decision making. Many decisions fall somewhere in the middle and are characterised by limited problem solving, such as deciding on a new pair of running shoes. Two factors often dictate the type of decision-making process: these are involvement and perceived risk.

Knowing the level of involvement and perceived risk involved

The answer to just how much effort we put into our buying decisions depends on our level of involvement – the importance of the perceived consequences of the purchase to the person and if we think the product is risky in some way. **Perceived risk** may be present if the product is expensive, complex and hard to understand, such as a new computer, or highly socially visible like some new trendy clothes where the risk of embarrassment or social rejection is present. For example, wearing a pair of Adidas trainers on a job interview may be fashion suicide and jeopardise the job, unless of course the job is with Adidas. In fact there are five main types of risk: time risk, i.e. the time needed to make the purchase; financial risk, i.e. the money required; social risk, i.e. what people think of us buying this; psychological risk, i.e. what we think of ourselves buying this; and physical risk, i.e. the risk to consumers' health or appearance.

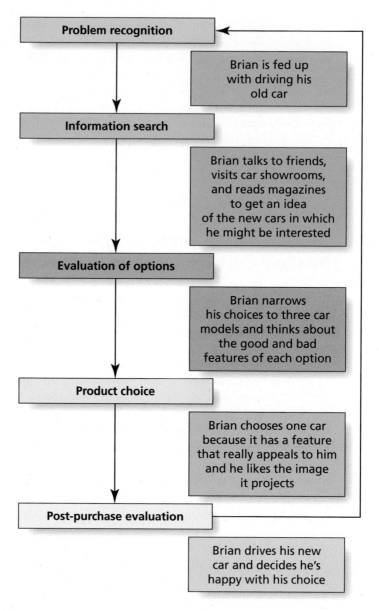

Figure 4.1	The consumer decision-making process
	The consumer decision-making process involves the series of steps summarised here

When perceived risk is low, as in buying a box of cereal, consumers feel low **involvement** in the decision-making process and are often more influenced by environmental cues, such as in special offers or whether the cereal is prominently displayed at the end of the supermarket aisle. Knowing this, a cereal marketer may decide to spend extra money to be sure its cereal stands out at a shop display or to change the packaging so consumers notice it.

For high-involvement purchases, such as buying a new TV or a car, a consumer will spend a lot of time thinking about the decision and evaluating the alternatives, as the consequences of a bad decision may result in significant financial losses, aggravation or embarrassment. Therefore, managers must start to reduce perceived risk by educating the

	Extended Problem Solving	*Habitual Decision Making*
Product	New car	Box of cereal
Level of involvement	High (important decision)	Low (unimportant decision)
Perceived risk	High (expensive, complex product)	Low (simple, low-cost product)
Information processing	Careful processing of information (search advertising, magazines, car dealers, websites)	Respond to environmental cues (shop signage or displays)
Learning model	Cognitive learning (use insight and creativity to use information found in environment)	Behavioural learning (ad shows product in beautiful setting, creating positive attitude)
Needed marketing actions	Provide information via advertising, salespeople, brochures, websites. Educate consumers to product benefits, risks of wrong decisions, etc.	Provide environmental cues at point of purchase, such as product display

Figure 4.2   Extended problem solving versus habitual decision making

consumer about why their product is the best choice well in advance of the time that the consumer is ready to make a decision.

To understand each of the steps in the decision-making process better, in the next section we'll follow the fortunes of a consumer named Brian, who, as Figure 4.1 shows, is in the market for a new car – a highly involving purchase decision, to say the least.

Step 1: What's my problem?

Problem recognition occurs whenever a consumer sees a significant difference between their current state of affairs and some desired or ideal state. For example, you like your car, but it eats up too much petrol and is not economical or eco friendly, or a man might think that he would have a better chance with women if he drove a sports car rather than his current Skoda. Brian falls into the latter category – his old Skoda runs okay, but he wants some sporty wheels that will get him more admiring stares instead of laughs.

So do marketers have a role in consumers' problem recognition? Well, although most problem recognition occurs spontaneously or when a true need arises, marketers often develop creative advertising messages that stimulate consumers to recognise that their current state – that old car – just doesn't equal their desired state – a shiny, new sports convertible. Figure 4.3 provides examples of marketers' responses to consumers' problem recognition and the other steps in the consumer decision-making process.

Step 2: What information is there about alternative solutions?

Once Brian recognises his problem (that he wants a new sports car), he needs information to resolve it. **Information search** is the step of the decision-making process in which the consumer checks his memory and surveys the environment to identify what options are out there that might solve his problem. Brian's evoked set of alternatives consists

Stage in the Decision Process	Marketing Strategy	Example
Problem recognition	Encourage consumers to see that existing state does not equal desired state	• Create TV commercials showing the excitement of owning a new car
Information search	Provide information when and where consumers are likely to search	• Book advertising around TV programmes with high target-market viewership • Provide sales training that ensures knowledgeable salespeople • Make new-car brochures available in dealer showrooms • Design exciting, easy-to-navigate, and informative websites
Evaluation of alternatives	Understand the criteria consumers use in comparing brands and communicate own brand superiority	• Conduct research to identify most important evaluative criteria • Create advertising that includes reliable data on superiority of a brand (e.g., miles per litre, safety, comfort)
Product choice	Understand choice heuristics used by consumers and provide communication that encourages brand decision	• Advertise 'Made in Germany' (country of origin) • Stress long history of the brand (brand loyalty)
Post-purchase evaluation	Encourage accurate consumer expectations	• Provide honest advertising and sales presentations

Figure 4.3　Marketer's responses to decision-making stages

of all the car brands and models which come immediately to his mind. For most of the brands, he will have some form of specific associations and possess some information about them. However, this form of internal information search might not be enough and Brian then needs to turn to external sources. Advertisements in newspapers, on TV or the radio, in the Yellow Pages or on the internet often provide valuable guidance during this step. Brian might rely on television ads about different cars, recommendations from his friends, and additional information he finds in media reports, at www.whatcar.co.uk, in brochures from car dealerships, or on the manufacturers' websites.

The internet as a search tool

Increasingly, consumers are using web search engines, portals or 'shopping robots' to find information. Search engines, sites such as Google (www.google.co.uk) and Excite (www.shopping.net), help consumers locate useful information by searching millions

Real people, other voices

Advice for Julie Cordua

Katrin Horn
Senior Lecturer in Marketing,
Leeds Metropolitan University

Option 1 is definitely the one that is most promising. Julie has identified a powerful potential target group that could drive (RED) forward: young people. As a target group, teens command a very large disposable income. Due to their position in the family life cycle, they don't have the commitments of older consumer groups and can spend the income they have on things they like. This is also an age group that often shows a great deal of enthusiasm and engages deeply with the brands they perceive to be relevant to them.

If a brand is able to connect with consumers at a young age, there is the distinct possibility that they can stay with them and accompany consumers as they grow older and make the transition into different stages of the life cycle, which will then impact on the lifestyle they pursue. For (RED) is would be a great opportunity to build up loyalty at a young age and then follow their customers – due to the fact that

they comprise different brands under the (RED) label, they certainly offer enough variety to stay relevant even if people's circumstances and needs change. On the other hand, (RED) needs to take care that they pick the right brands for the teen target group, who are wary of grown-ups trying too hard to be a part of their world.

Teens and young people are also the generation called digital natives, and are connected to each other in ways which make word-of-mouth communication quicker and more powerful than ever before – for example through social networks and mobile phones. While this is a two-edged sword for (RED) – teens will disseminate positive as well as negative communication equally fast in their networks – it also opens up new chances of communicating, engaging with, and being relevant for their target group.

Finally, the teens are probably the target group who embrace the concept of a consumer society most fully: growing up in a branded world, they are familiar not only with signalling their group membership through brands, but also with the notion of communicating their self-perception, their values and attitudes through their consumption choices. Teens will therefore be the ideal target group to accept that you can buy branded items and do some good at the same time.

of web pages for key words and returning a list of sites that contain those key words. Shopping portals such as Yahoo! (www.yahoo.co.uk) simplify searches by organising information from many websites into topics or categories. Shopping robots, also called 'shopbots', are software programs some websites use to find internet retailers selling a particular product (e.g. www.pricerunner.co.uk or www.kelkoo.co.uk). The programs trawl the web for information and then report back to the host site. Some sites also provide information on competitors' prices and ask customers to rate the retailers that they have listed on their site; this enables consumers to view both positive and negative feedback from other consumers (e.g. www.reviewcentre.com).

Marketing metrics

Measuring web stickiness

Conventional internet metrics have relied on counting the number of people viewing a website. Research has shown, however, that conversion rates and average order value are better measures for a website's success. A new method allows companies to conduct funnel-based analysis of where revenue is lost when consumers drop-off. One such method is **clickstream analysis**, which helps companies analyse where customers enter their websites and where they exit. The managers

at some companies are using clickstream data to increase site subscription and convert free visitors into paying members. They can now examine exactly where on the website customers are converted and where they lose them by tracking each user's movements around the website. The company receives reports from the clickstream provider about how traffic comes in from other websites, how the site compares with competitors and where conversions are failing.

The role of marketers during the information search step of the consumer decision-making process is to make the information consumers want and need about their product easily accessible. For example, car manufacturers make sure that information about their newest models is on the web, in magazines, radio and TV, and, of course, are available in dealer showrooms. To fine-tune this, some marketers have started to experiment with so-called **behavioural targeting** techniques; Amazon is a good example. The basis for this approach is that by watching what you do online, marketers can deliver advertisements for products and services you are actually looking for. So, for example, if you are surfing at several motoring sites you might start to notice pop-up ads on your monitor for a new car model.[1] What a coincidence!

Step 3: How do I evaluate all the options?

Once Brian has identified his options, it's time to decide on a few true contenders. First, armed with information, a consumer identifies a small number of products in which he is interested. Second, he narrows down the choices by deciding which of all the options are feasible and by comparing the pros and cons of each remaining option.

Brian has always wanted a red Ferrari, but knows that, realistically, he couldn't afford one right now. As he looks around, he decides that the cars he and his friends like in his price range are the Renault Clio Sport, Ford Focus and Honda Civic. He's narrowed down his options by considering the criteria of affordability and what his friends suggest.

Evaluative criteria

Now Brian has to choose. It's time for him to look more systematically at each of the three possibilities and identify the important characteristics, or **evaluative criteria**, he will use to decide among them. The criteria may be power, space, comfort and price, as well as the style of the car, insurance costs, safety and especially the driving experience. Keep in mind that marketers often play a role in educating consumers about which product characteristics they should use as evaluative criteria – usually, they will emphasise the dimensions on which their product excels. Understanding what criteria consumers use and which are more or less important helps sales and advertising professionals to point out a brand's superiority on the most important criteria. After Brian has examined his alternatives and gone on a few test drives, it's time to make a decision.

Step 4: Making the final choice

Deciding on one product and acting on this choice is the next step in the decision-making process. Choices such as Brian's are often difficult because it's hard to juggle all the product characteristics in your head. One car may be more eco-friendly, another is €1000 cheaper, while another boasts a better safety record or a better driving experience. So how do we make sense of all these characteristics and arrive at a decision?

Heuristics

Consumers often rely on decision guidelines when weighing the claims that companies make. These **heuristics**, or rules, help simplify the decision-making process. One such heuristic is 'price = quality', so many people willingly buy the more expensive brand because they assume that if it costs more, it must be better.

Perhaps the most common heuristic is **brand loyalty**, where people buy from the same company over and over because they believe that the company makes superior products. Consumers who have strong brand loyalty feel that it's not worth the effort to consider competing options. Creating this allegiance is a prized goal for marketers because once some people form preferences for a favourite brand, they may never change their minds in the course of a lifetime, making it extremely difficult for rivals to persuade them to switch. That explains why many companies are working harder to woo consumers early on. For example, it's hard to find an adult in Helsinki, home to the Finnish company Nokia, who doesn't have a mobile phone – 92 per cent of its households have at least one, if not several. But while the phones have been an accepted part of daily life for grown-ups and teenagers for over a decade, the latest boom in phone use is occurring among young children. Many of them get their first phone around the age of seven when they start to engage in activities like soccer practice where their parents aren't present. Now there's an expanding market for accessories like phone covers decorated with pictures of Donald Duck or Star Wars characters.[2] Another good example would be how designer clothes companies try to create a bond with customers from early age by offering exclusive child collections (e.g. D&G Junior or Prada Kidswear).

Still another heuristic is based on *country of origin*. We assume that a product has certain characteristics if it comes from a certain country. For example, Brian assumed that the Japanese-made Honda Civic would be a bit more reliable than the Ford Focus or Renault Clio Sport, so he factored that into his decision. Sometimes a marketer wants to encourage a country association even when none exists. Anheuser-Busch, for example, introduced a new beer brand into the US that it hopes customers will think of as an import, even though it's not. Anheuser World Select comes in a Heineken-style green bottle and a tagline that reads: 'Ten Brewmasters. Four Continents. One Beer.' The label on the neck of the bottle lists the home countries of the brewmasters involved in the beer's production, such as Japan, Ireland, Canada and Spain, but the reality is that the beer is actually made in the US.[3] Marketers must not forget that there is often a further pre-purchase evaluation step involved in the decision-making process. This step concerns thoughts about the possible disposal or recyclability of the product. If the consumer wants to buy a soft drink, he might choose an environmentally friendly glass bottle, which is easily recyclable. This also applies to Brian's decision-making process. Thinking ahead, he will ask himself how easy will it be to re-sell or recycle the car once he has driven it for several years.

Marketing metrics

Brand loyalty metrics

Brand loyalty is grounded in a number of factors such as satisfied and influential customers, in the hidden values or emotional benefits of the brand and strong product image and usage experience. Measures include share of requirements, willingness to pay a price premium, willingness to search and willingness to recommend.

Willingness to search (percentage) in particular, also called 'accept no substitutes', is regarded as the acid test for measuring brand loyalty. It is defined as the percentage of customers willing to delay purchases, change stores or reduce purchase quantities to avoid switching brands.

Even though consumers may manifest one aspect of brand loyalty, such as rarely switching to substitutes, they may or may not manifest other aspects such as a willingness to recommend the brand to their friends. In practice, behavioural loyalty can also be difficult to distinguish from habit or inertia and, when asked, consumers may not know what they would do in new circumstances or be able to recall past purchasing behaviour. There are therefore methodological issues associated to the measurement of brand loyalty that marketers need to account for.[4]

After agonising over his choice, Brian decides that even though the Renault Clio Sport and the Honda Civic have attractive qualities, the Ford Focus has the affordability he needs and its carefree image is the way he wants others to think about him. All this thinking about cars was 'driving' him crazy, and he's relieved to make a decision to buy the Ford Focus and get on with driving his new car and seeing what others think.

Step 5: Using and evaluating the purchase

In the last step of the decision-making process, the consumer evaluates just how good a choice it was. The evaluation of the product results in a level of **consumer satisfaction/dissatisfaction**, which is determined by the overall feelings, or attitude, a person has about a product after purchasing and using it.

How do consumers decide if they're satisfied with their purchases? When we buy a product, we have some expectations of product performance created by a mixture of information from marketing communications, informal information sources such as friends and family, and their own experience with the product category. Consumers then judge

Marketing metrics

Customer satisfaction metrics

Seventy-one per cent of marketing managers find customer satisfaction very useful and it is the most used metric in marketing. Customer satisfaction captures the view of current customers, not lost customers, and is a function of expectations. It is perhaps the best indicator of how likely customers are to make further purchases in the future, but how is satisfaction measured? Satisfaction scores are generally based on survey data and measured on a scale of 1–5 (sometimes 1–10)' according to which customers state their level of satisfaction with the brand in general or with specific product/service attributes or dimensions. It is generally measured at the individual level, but almost always reported at an aggregate level. Satisfaction levels are usually reported as either the percentage of participants who checked either the 'top box' (customers who rate their experience as 5) or more commonly, the 'top two boxes'.

Satisfaction can also be measured by other means, such as by noting the number of complaints during a given time frame, or captured by related concepts and metrics, such as the net promoter score metric, and willingness to recommend metric, which measure the degree to which current customers will recommend a product or company.

$$\text{Net Promoter Score (I)} = \text{Percentage of Promoter (\%)} - \text{Percentage of Detractors (\%)}$$

Promoters: customers who are willing to recommend the company to others (who gave the company a rating of 9 or 10 on a 10-point scale).

Passives: satisfied but unenthusiastic customers (ratings of 7 or 8).

Detractors: customers who are unwilling to recommend the company to others (ratings of 0–6).

Willingness to recommend: the percentage of surveyed customers who state they would recommend a brand to friends.[5]

Very Dissatisfied	Somewhat Dissatisfied	Neither Satisfied nor Dissatisfied	Somewhat Satisfied	Very Satisfied
1	2	3	4	5

Figure 4.4 A typical 5-point scale

the product performance against these expectations. That's why it's very important that marketers create accurate expectations of their product in advertising and other communications. However, everyone has experienced regret after making a purchase ('what *was* I thinking?') and this is called cognitive dissonance. Reducing this dissonance between what you wanted to happen and what the product actually does for you is in consumers' as well as the marketers' interests. If the consumer comes to the conclusion that his purchase was a mistake, he is not only very unlikely to return to the company, but might also engage in negative word of mouth. This highlights the crucial importance of the post-evaluation stage. The marketer needs to gain as many insights as possible about how the consumer feels after the purchase and try to reinforce his feeling of having made the right decision. Cognitive dissonance can often occur when two alternatives are similarly attractive, but you can only buy one. Hence, you often feel regret at not buying the other. So, even though Brian's new Ford Focus is not exactly as powerful as a Ferrari, he's still happy with the car because he never really expected a fun little car to streak up the motorway like a high-performance sports car which costs ten times as much.

Influences on consumers' decisions

Apart from understanding the mechanics of the consumer decision-making process, marketers also try to ascertain what influences in consumers' lives affect this process. There are three main categories: internal, situational and social influences. In Brian's case, the evaluative criteria which he used to compare cars and his feelings about each car were influenced by internal factors such as the connection he learned to make between a name like Ford Focus and an image of 'slightly hip yet safe and solid', situational factors such as the way he was treated by the Ford salesperson, and social influences such as his prediction of what his friends would say when they saw him cruising down the road in his new wheels.

Figure 4.5 shows the influences in the decision-making process and emphasises that all these factors work together to affect the ultimate choice each person makes. Let's consider how each of these three types of influences work, starting with internal factors.

Objective

3

Explain how internal factors influence consumers' decision-making processes

Internal influences on consumers' decisions

Car manufacturers know that one consumer's ideal car can be quite different from that of another consumer. You may think the ideal car is a sporty Porsche, while your best friend dreams of a classic Mercedes and your father is set on owning a big BMW. Some of these

---

Marketing metrics

Limitations of customer satisfaction metrics

Due to 'response bias', it is often difficult to judge the true level of customer satisfaction; disappointed or angry customers are often keener to complete a survey and they might therefore be disproportionally represented among respondents. This can in part be overcome by reviewing survey data over time for changes in broad trends. Because it is only the current customers that are surveyed, a company's scores may be inflated as deeply dissatisfied customers have already left. Also, normative differences between populations have to be accounted for: some populations are more frank and demanding than others and more inclined to complain. To allow for this, measures are taken within the same market.[6]

Figure 4.5	Influences on consumer decision making
	A number of different factors in consumers' lives influence the consumer decision-making process. Marketers need to understand these influences and which ones are important in the purchase process to make effective marketing decisions

differences are due to the way in which consumers internalise information about the outside world such as perception, exposure, attention and interpretation.

Perception

Perception is the process by which people select, organise and interpret information from the outside world. We receive information in the form of sensations, the immediate response of our sensory receptors – eyes, ears, nose, mouth and fingers – to such basic stimuli as light, colour and sound. Our impressions about products are often based on their physical qualities. We try to make sense of the sensations we receive by interpreting them in light of our past experiences. For example, people associate the textures of fabrics and other surfaces with product qualities, and some new plastic containers for household beauty items incorporate 'soft touch' resins that provide a soft, friction-like resistance when held. US focus group members who tested one such package for Clairol's Daily Defense shampoo described the sensations as 'almost sexy' and were actually reluctant to let go of the containers![7] That's a powerful impact for a piece of plastic.

Consumers are bombarded with information on products – thousands of ads, in-store displays, special offers, opinions of their friends, and on and on have led to some consumers becoming confused by either too much information, too similar information (e.g. look-alike products), or ambiguous or conflicting information such as what's healthy to eat. Therefore, some consumers see all brands within a category as similar even when they are not. The perception process has implications for marketers because, as consumers absorb and make sense of the vast quantities of information competing for their attention, the odds are that any single message will get lost in the clutter. And, if they do notice it, there's no guarantee that the meaning they give it will be the same one the marketer intended. The issues that marketers need to understand during this process include exposure, attention and interpretation.

The stimulus must be within range of people's sensory receptors to be noticed; in other words, people must be physically able to see, hear, taste, smell or feel the stimulus. For example, the lettering on a hoarding by the motorway must be big enough for a passing motorist to read easily, or the message will be lost. **Exposure** is the extent to which a stimulus is capable of being registered by a person's sensory receptors.

Many people believe that even messages they can't see will persuade them to buy advertised products. Claims about **subliminal advertising**, which means that messages are hidden in advertisements in order to affect consumers in their subconsciousness, have been surfacing since the 1950s. Coca-Cola tried using subliminal advertising by very quickly flashing pictures of a Coke bottle during films shown in a cinema, hoping that this would result in a sudden craving for the drink among the cinema-goers. A survey of US consumers found that almost two-thirds believed in the existence of subliminal advertising, and over one-half were convinced that this technique could get them to buy things they did not really want.[8] In 2007, the American Food Network show *Iron Chef* apparently mistakenly aired a single frame of the McDonald's logo and the 'I'm lovin it' slogan during the final few moments of a show which was captured on video by two boys and exposed. The network denies it was an attempt at subliminal advertising.

In 2006 in the US, ABC rejected a commercial for KFC that invited viewers to slowly replay the ad to find a secret message, citing the network's longstanding policy against subliminal advertising. The ad (which other networks aired), was a seemingly ordinary pitch for KFC's 99-cent Buffalo Snacker chicken sandwich. But if replayed slowly on a digital video recorder or VCR, it revealed a message that viewers could visit KFC's website to receive a coupon for a free sandwich. Ironically, this technique was really the *opposite* of subliminal advertising because instead of secretly placing words or images in the ad, KFC blatantly publicised its campaign by informing viewers that it contained a message and how to find it.[9] But stunts like this certainly can make consumers pay more attention to an ad, which is the second crucial element.

As you drive down the road, you pass hundreds of other cars. But how many do you pay attention to? Probably only one or two – the bright pink and purple VW and the Honda with the broken rear light that cut you up at the motorway exit. **Attention** is the extent to which mental processing activity is devoted to a particular stimulus. Consumers are more likely to pay attention to messages that speak to their current needs. For example, you're far more likely to notice an ad for a fast-food restaurant when you're hungry, while smokers are more likely than non-smokers to block out messages about the health hazards of smoking.

Grabbing consumers' attention is getting harder than ever, because people's attention spans are shorter than ever. Now that people are accustomed to *multitasking*, flitting back and forth between their emails, TV, Instant Messenger, SMS, mobile, Blackberry, iPod and so on, advertisers have to be more creative in the mix and type of messages they send. That's why we're seeing on the one hand long (60 second) commercials that almost feel like miniature movies and,

ABSOLUT SUBLIMINAL.

| Photo 4.1 | One company's play on subliminal advertising. If you look hard enough you can see Absolute Vodka in the ice cubes *Source:* The Absolut Company |

on the other hand, short (some as brief as five seconds) messages that are meant to have surprise value: they are usually over before commercial-haters can zap or zip past them. Indeed, brief blurbs that are just long enough to tantalise viewers but just short enough not to bore them are becoming commonplace – in contrast to the old days when most commercials on US television networks were 30-second spots, today more than a third run for only 15 seconds.[10]

Another cutting-edge strategy to grab attention by increasing the relevance of ads is to actually customise them to the audience that's viewing them. Uniquely for now, in the US a TV station called Fox plans to offer *tweakable ads*, which can be digitally altered to contain elements relevant to particular viewers at the time they are seen. By changing voiceovers, scripts, graphic elements or other images, for instance, advertisers could make an ad appeal to teens in one instance and retired people in another. As this approach is refined, for example, a cola company could have actors refer to the particular teams in a sporting event. Or a soup company could direct viewers' attention to a snowstorm brewing outside to encourage people to stock up on soup.[11] However, all these techniques rely on the consumer interpreting the message in the way the company wants.

Interpretation is the process of assigning meaning to a stimulus based upon prior associations a person has with it and assumptions he or she makes about it. A Pepsi drink called 'Pepsi Blue' flopped despite heavy marketing and advertising campaigns. Consumers didn't associate its blue colour with a fruity and refreshing beverage (as the marketing department hoped) but rather with too many artificial ingredients and chemicals. Another example would be the BMW C1, which is a motorcycle with a roof and the possibility for the driver to wear a seatbelt, which made it much safer than other motorcycles and reduced the risk of severe injury in accidents. BMW therefore specifically stressed this safety aspect in all of its marketing and advertising approaches. However, the company did not consider that many consumers who drive motorcycles are rather looking for fun and speed than for protection and thought that the C1 was a boring vehicle. If we don't interpret the product the way it was intended because of other experiences, the best marketing ideas will be 'wasted'.

Motivation

Motivation is an internal state that drives us to satisfy needs. Once we activate a need, a state of tension exists that drives the consumer toward some goal that will reduce this tension by eliminating the need.

For example, think about Brian and his old car. Brian began to experience a gap between his present state (owning an old car) and a desired state (having a car that gets him noticed and is fun to drive). The need for a new car is activated, motivating Brian to test different models, to talk with friends about different makes, and finally to buy a new car.

Psychologist Abraham Maslow developed an influential approach to motivation.[12] He formulated a **hierarchy of needs** that categorises motives according to five levels of importance, the more basic needs being at the bottom of the hierarchy and more sophisticated needs at the top. The hierarchy suggests that before a person can meet needs at a given level, he must first meet the lower level's needs – somehow those hot new Diesel jeans don't seem so enticing when you don't have enough money to buy food.

As you can see from Figure 4.6, people start at the lowest level with basic physiological needs for food and sleep and then progress to higher levels to satisfy more complex needs, such as the need to be accepted by others or to feel a sense of accomplishment. Ultimately, people can reach the highest level such as self-fulfilment. Brian's need for

Marketing ethics and sustainability

Cruel consumer cost of the human egg trade

One of the most basic needs is the need to procreate and British women who desperately want to have babies are being sent to Eastern Europe and Cyprus. There, clinics are thriving on the profits of fertility tourism. But donors in this egg harvest run hidden health risks. Women from countries like the Ukraine are told that the process of donating eggs is straightforward and that they will be given $300. But the process is not a straightforward matter like donating sperm. It can be a lengthy, painful and potentially dangerous procedure involving the injection of a powerful drug, a follicle-stimulating hormone. In today's global market, a healthy human egg from a young white European woman is more valuable than gold. The human need to reproduce and to have mothering and fathering needs met is very powerful. While there is no denying the joy of an infertile woman who has been able to have a baby using an overseas donor, there can be an unsavoury underside to the process where poor young women are exploited, injected with potentially dangerous hormones and treated like 'battery hens' being farmed for their eggs.

Adapted from *The Observer*, 20 April 2006

Debate, discuss, disagree

1   Who should be responsible/ blamed for the situation?

2   What would you suggest to put a stop to the illegal human egg trade?

a new car would be an example of the fourth level of Maslow's hierarchy, referring to esteem needs. Brian hopes to gain prestige and to be admired while taking a ride in his new car. If marketers understand the level of needs relevant to consumers in their target market, they can tailor their products and messages to them.

Higher-Level Needs

Hobbies, travel, education (UK Army–'Be the best')

Cars, furniture, credit cards, shops, country clubs (Royal Ascot–'Henley Regatta')

Clothing, grooming products, clubs, drinks (Pepsi–'You're in the Pepsi generation')

Insurance, alarm systems, retirement investments (Insurance–'You're in safe hands with US')

Medicines, staple items, generics (All Bran–'Be good to your heart')

Self-Actualisation
Self-fulfilment, enriching experiences

Ego Needs
Prestige, status, accomplishment

Belongingness
Love, friendship, acceptance by others

Safety
Security, shelter, protection

Physiological
Water, sleep, food

Lower-Level Needs

Figure 4.6	Maslow's hierarchy of needs and related products
	Abraham Maslow's proposed hierarchy of needs that categorises motives. Savvy marketers know they need to understand the level of needs that motivates a consumer to buy a particular product or brand

Learning

Learning is a change in behaviour caused by information or experience. Learning about products can occur deliberately, as when we set out to gather information about different MP3 players before buying one brand. We also learn even when we are not trying. Consumers recognise many brand names and can hum many product jingles, for example, even for products they themselves do not use. Learning theories to explain the learning process are important because a major goal for marketers is to 'teach' consumers to prefer their products. Let's briefly review the most important perspectives on how people learn.

Behavioural learning   **Behavioural learning theories** assume that learning takes place as the result of connections that form between events that we perceive. In the first type of behavioural learning, **classical conditioning**, a person perceives two stimuli at about the same time. After a while, the person transfers his response from one stimulus to the other. This theory was primarily developed by Ivan Pavlov, a Russian scientist who executed an experiment in which his dog received two stimuli in the form of dog food and the ringing sound of a bell at the same time. After a while the dog did indeed transfer his response from one stimuli to the other, because he started salivating when the bell was ringing, even when there was no food in sight. Marketers also try to make use of this phenomenon. For example, an ad shows a product and a breathtakingly beautiful scene so that (the marketer hopes) you will transfer the positive feelings you get from looking at the scene to the advertised product. (Did you ever notice that ads often show a new car on a beautiful beach at sunset or speeding down a mountain road with brightly coloured leaves blowing across the pavement?)

Another common form of behavioural learning is called **operant conditioning**, which occurs when people learn that their actions result in rewards or punishments. This influences how they will respond in similar situations in the future. Just as a rat in a maze learns the route to a piece of cheese, consumers who receive a reward, such as a prize in the bottom of a box of cereal, will be more likely to buy that brand again. We don't like to think that marketers can train us like lab mice, but that kind of prize feedback does reward us for our behaviour.

These acquired associations in classical and operant conditioning have a tendency to transfer to similar things in a process called **stimulus generalisation**. This means that the good or bad feelings associated with a product will 'rub off' on other products that resemble it. For example, some marketers create *product line extensions* in which new products share the name of an established brand so that people's good feelings about the current product will transfer to the new one. Dove, which is associated with gentle soap, was able to also establish itself as a producer of bodylotions and moisturisers without great difficulty. The consumer already trusted the product and mentally connected it with soothing body care. More on this in Chapter 7.

Cognitive learning   In contrast to behavioural theories of learning, **cognitive learning theory** views people as problem solvers who do more than passively react to associations between stimuli. Supporters of this point of view stress the role of creativity and insight during the learning process. Cognitive learning occurs when consumers make a connection between ideas or by observing things in their environment. **Observational learning** occurs when people watch the actions of others and note what happens to them as a result. They store these observations in memory and at some later point use the information to guide their own behaviour. Marketers often use this process to create advertising and other messages that allow consumers to observe the benefits of using their products. Health clubs and manufacturers of exercise equipment feature well-muscled men and women using their products, while mouthwash makers show that fresh breath is the key to romance.

The results of the internal processes of perception, motivation and learning influence how consumers absorb and interpret information. This also depends on some unique consumer characteristics. Let's talk next about some of these characteristics: existing consumer attitudes, the personality of the consumer and consumer age groups.

Attitudes

An **attitude** is someone's lasting evaluation of a person, object, or issue.[13] Consumers have attitudes towards brands, such as whether McDonald's or Burger King has the best beefburgers, as well as towards more general consumption-related behaviours, for example whether high-fat foods including beefburgers are a no-no in a healthy diet. A person's attitude has three components: affect, cognition and behaviour:

Affect refers to the overall emotional response a person has to a product. Affect, the feeling component, is usually dominant for expressive products such as perfume. In this case, our attitude towards the product is simply determined by our immediate reaction of whether we like the smell of the perfume or not. Some marketing researchers are trying to understand how consumers' emotional reactions influence how they feel about products. A company called Sensory Logic, for example, studies videotape of people's facial reactions – to products and commercials – in increments as fleeting as 1/30th of a second. Staffers look for the difference between a so-called true smile (which includes a relaxation of the upper eyelid) and a social smile (which occurs only around the mouth). Whirlpool hired the company to test consumers' emotional reactions to a yet-to-be-launched generation of its Duet washers and dryers. Its perhaps ambitious goal was to design appliances that would actually make people happy. The research led Whirlpool to change some design options on the Duet products, including geometric patterns and certain colour combinations.[14] Research has also concluded that while smiling has little effect in service encounters, employees displaying authentic emotions does affect consumers' emotional states.[15]

Cognition, the knowing component, is the beliefs or knowledge a person has about a product and its important characteristics. You may believe that a Mercedes is built better than most cars or that a Volvo is very safe. Cognition is especially important for complex products, such as computers, where we may develop beliefs on the basis of technical information.

Behaviour, the doing component, involves a consumer's intention to do something, such as the intention to purchase or use a certain product. For products such as cereal, consumers purchase and try the product on the basis of limited information and then form an evaluation of the product simply on the basis of how the product tastes or performs.

Depending on the nature of the product, one of these three components – feeling, knowing or doing – will be the dominant influence in creating an attitude towards

Marketing metrics

Consumer intention metrics

When measuring consumer intention, some of the metrics which can be used have been rated by marketing managers. Here are those metrics and what percentage of marketing managers found them 'very useful'. Consumer Beliefs 48 per cent, Purchase Habits 43 per cent, Purchase Intentions 39 per cent, Willingness to Search 20 per cent, Trial Volume 19 per cent and Net Promoter Score 19 percent.[16]

a product. Marketers need to decide which part of an attitude is the most important driver of consumers' preferences. For example, Pepsi's advertising focus changed from its typical emotional emphasis on celebrities, jingles and music to an attempt which offers rational reasons to drink the beverage. The new campaign portrayed the soft drink as the perfect accompaniment to foods and social situations like football matches and dates.[17]

Personality

Personality is the set of unique psychological characteristics that consistently influence the way a person responds to situations in the environment. One adventure-seeking consumer may always be on the lookout for new experiences and cutting-edge products, while a different consumer may prefer familiar surroundings, and wants to use the same brands over and over again. The German brewery Beck's, for example, tries to position its product as a beer for thrill-seeking consumers. Its commercials always show young, outgoing people who are looking for the ultimate adventure in exotic locations and the slogan invites consumers to join the 'Beck's Experience'.[18] A contrasting example would be Nivea, which puts its main focus on pointing out the long tradition, experience and expertise with skincare products. Nivea tries to create a very close bond with its customers and consumers voted it to be one of the most trusted brands in the 'European Trusted Brand' studies 2006.[19]

Photo 4.2 Observational learning means we learn by observing the behaviour of others
Source: Alamy Images/Richard Naude

For marketers, differences in *personality traits* such as thrill seeking underscore the potential value of considering personality when they are crafting their marketing strategies. The following are some specific personality traits relevant to marketing strategies:

- **Innovativeness:** The degree to which a person likes to try new things. Cutting-edge products such as radical new fashions or the latest iPhone might appeal to innovative women.

- **Materialism:** The amount of emphasis placed on owning products. Materialistic consumers focus on owning products simply for the sake of ownership. For example, many people buy D&G designer handbags not because they urgently need a place to store keys and wallet but rather for the mere sake of owning them and showing off.

- **Self-confidence:** The degree to which a person has a positive evaluation of her abilities, including the ability to make good decisions. People who don't have much self-confidence are good candidates for services like image consultants, who help clients select the right outfit for a job interview. People who do have a lot of self-confidence are more likely to travel alone or go on independent holidays.

- **Sociability:** The degree to which a person enjoys social interaction. Sociable people might respond to entertainment-related products, like pub quiz nights or group outings to the cinema that claim to bring people together or make parties more fun.

- **Need for cognition:** The degree to which a person likes to think about things and expend the necessary effort to process brand information.[20] Such people are likely to buy *Which? Guides* or *What Car* magazine when purchasing products to get as much information as possible about them.

The self: are you what you buy?   It makes sense to assume that consumers buy products that are extensions of their personalities. That's why marketers try to create brand personalities that will appeal to different types of people. For example, consider the different 'personalities' invented by fragrance marketers: a brand with a 'wholesome, girl-next-door' image such as Clinique's Happy would be hard to confuse with the sophisticated image of Christian Dior's Dolce Vita. We'll talk more about this in Chapter 8.

A person's **self-concept** is his attitude towards the self and is composed of a mixture of beliefs about one's abilities and observations. This includes, for example, behaviour and feelings (both positive and negative) about one's personal attributes, such as body type or facial features. The extent to which a person's self-concept is positive or negative can strongly influence his buying decision.

Marketing ethics and sustainability

Frenzied footwear

When a new product is hot, it's hot – but the burning desire to get hold of it can make it too hot to handle. Athletic shoe manufacturers compete fiercely to produce dynamically continuous innovations that children want. For example, Puma, Nike, Reebok and other manufacturers introduce new models every year, and with each new version the products become more and more desirable to young children. News of a new model's arrival date in shops sometimes causes frenzy. Children go so far as to gamble for money with their friends or try all means to beg their parents to be the first to buy the latest shoe.

Debate, discuss, disagree

1   Do you think marketers should feel good or bad about kids being so anxious to buy their new products?

Dove, a marketer for body and skincare products, recognised that many girls and women suffer from a lack of self-confidence because they feel they cannot compete with those perfect size-zero supermodels which they see in magazines and on TV. The company therefore launched a global marketing campaign called 'Campaign for Real Beauty', which aims to help women to gain more self-esteem and make them feel beautiful the way they are.[21] This technique is also used in ads for Clairol ('You're not getting older, you're getting better'), Budweiser in the US ('For all you do, this Bud's for you'), and L'Oréal ('Because you're worth it').

Age group

A person's age is another internal influence on purchasing behaviour. Many of us feel that we have a closer connection with people of our own age because we share a common set of experiences and memories about cultural events, whether these involve the student revolts in the 1960s or the introduction of the euro.

As people are attracted to products that remind them of past experiences, marketers of products from cereals to cars are banking on nostalgia to draw in customers. Audi, for example, created a commercial for its model Audi A6, which showed a short, humorous remake of the classic film *The Graduate*. The commercial was very popular among consumers who were reminded of their 'old favourite classic movie'.[22]

Goods and services often appeal to a specific age group. Although there are exceptions, most buyers of Lady Gaga CDs are younger than those who buy Elton John discs. Thus, many marketing strategies appeal to the needs of such different age groups as children, teenagers, the middle-aged and the elderly.

Young people are among the most enthusiastic users of the internet. In fact, teens spend over €1 billion online each year using their own or their parents' cards, so many firms are working hard to develop websites that will capture their interest. What do teens do online? Approximately three out of four teens do research, and nearly two out of three use the internet for email, while far fewer use it for finding or buying products. For marketers, this means that the web may be a great way to get information about their goods and services to teens but not so good for sales.

The family life cycle

Marketers know that the process of change continues throughout consumers' lives. Interestingly, the purchase of goods and services may depend more on consumers' current

Marketing ethics and sustainability

An unhealthy need for the beauty industry

The rise of an image-conscious, celebrity-obsessed society has led to massive growth in the health and beauty industries, and cosmetic surgery is reaping the benefits. The cosmetic surgery industry was worth £359 million in the UK in 2005 and it was expected to top £1 billion by 2010. As consumer attitudes change and procedures become less invasive, cosmetic surgery providers have shifted their positioning to become more holistic. Bupa Cosmetic Surgery and Transform Medical Group, the largest provider of cosmetic surgery in the UK, has been promoting its services as 'enhancements' that improve self-esteem and confidence.

Debate, discuss, disagree

1 What do you think?

2 How great a role should plastic surgery have in promoting better self-esteem and confidence?

Photo 4.3	This ad targets an older generation, later in the family life cycle

Source: Alamy Images/David TW Gee

position in the **family life cycle** – the stages through which family members pass as they grow older – than on chronological age. Singles of any age are more likely to spend money on expensive cars, entertainment and recreation than married people. Couples with small children purchase baby furniture, insurance and a larger house, while older couples whose children have 'left the nest' are more likely to buy a retirement home in the south of France.

Lifestyle

A **lifestyle** is a pattern of living that determines how people choose to spend their time, money and energy and that reflects their values, tastes and preferences. Lifestyles are expressed in a person's preferences for activities such as sports, interests such as music, and opinions on politics and religion. Consumers often choose goods, services and activities that are associated with a certain lifestyle. Brian may drive a Ford Focus, hang out in internet cafés and go snowboarding during the Easter holidays because he views these choices as part of a cool university student lifestyle.

Marketers often develop marketing strategies which recognise that people can be grouped into market segments based on similarities in lifestyle preferences.[23] Many kids happily fork out €20 for T-shirts and more than €50 for skate shoes in addition to the hundreds they may spend on the latest skateboards. In fact, kids spend well over €3 billion a year on skateboard 'soft goods', like T-shirts, shorts and sunglasses, while actual skateboarding equipment 'only' sells over €600 million.[24]

If lifestyles are so important, how do marketers identify them? How can they reach consumers who share preferences for products they associate with a certain lifestyle? Demographic characteristics, such as age and income, tell marketers what products people buy, but they don't reveal why. Two consumers can share the same demographic characteristics yet be completely different from each other – all 20-year-old male university students are hardly identical. That's why it is often important to further profile consumers in terms of their passions and how they spend their leisure time.

| Photo 4.4 | Our choices of clothing, furniture and other products often reflect our commitment to a consistent lifestyle
Source: IKEA Ltd. |

We'll look further at how marketers identify and find these kinds of specialised consumer groups in Chapter 6.

Psychographics   To breathe life into demographic analyses, marketers turn to **psychographics**, which groups consumers according to psychological and behavioural similarities. One way to do this is to describe people in terms of their activities, interests and opinions (known as **AIOs**). These AIOs are based on preferences for holiday destinations, club memberships, hobbies, political and social attitudes, tastes in food and fashion, and so on. Using data from large samples, marketers create profiles of customers who resemble each other in terms of their activities and patterns of product use.[25]

For example, US marketers looking at people who wanted walking shoes assumed that all recreational walkers were just burned-out joggers. Subsequent psychographic research that examined the AIOs of these walkers showed that there were actually several psychographic segments within the larger group who engaged in the activity for very different reasons, including walking for fun, walking to save money and walking for exercise. This research resulted in the creation of walking shoes aimed at different segments, from Footjoy Walkers to Nike Healthwalkers.

 ## Situational influences on consumers' decisions

We've seen that internal factors such as how people perceive marketing messages, their motivation to acquire products, and their unique personalities influence the decisions they make. In addition, when, where and how consumers shop – what we call *situational*

Objective
4

Show how situational factors at the time and place of purchase influence consumer behaviour

influences – shape their purchase choices. Some important situational cues are our physical surroundings and time pressures.

Marketers know that dimensions of the physical environment, including such factors as decor, smells, lighting, music and even temperature, can significantly influence consumption. If you don't believe this, consider that one study found that pumping certain odours into a Las Vegas casino actually increased the amount of money patrons fed into slot machines.[26] Let's see how situational factors influence the consumer decision-making process.

The physical environment

It's no secret that people's moods and behaviours are strongly influenced by their physical surroundings. Despite all their efforts to sway consumers through advertising, marketers know that the shop environment strongly influences many purchases. For example, consumers decide on about two out of every three of their supermarket product purchases while standing in the aisles (so always eat before you go to the supermarket). The messages they receive at the time and their feelings about being in the shop influence their decisions.[27]

Two dimensions, arousal and pleasure, determine whether a shopper will react positively or negatively to a shop environment. In other words, the person's surroundings can be either dull or exciting (arousing) and either pleasant or unpleasant. Just because the environment is arousing doesn't necessarily mean it will be pleasant – we've all been in crowded, loud, hot shops that are anything but pleasant. Maintaining an upbeat feeling in a pleasant context is one factor behind the success of theme parks such as Disney World, which tries to provide consistent doses of carefully calculated stimulation to visitors.[28]

The importance of these surroundings explains why many retailers focus on packing as much entertainment as possible into their shops. For example, IKEA creates its shops in such a way that they appeal to the whole family. Huge children's playgrounds, restaurants, special workshops or events such as visits from Santa Claus during Christmas time are only some of the features which make the shopping at IKEA a special experience.

Another example is the Easy Everything café in London, which welcomes about 5000 people every day, including backpackers who can check their email on the café's computers. This cyber-hangout is trying to increase traffic with computer game competitions, training seminars and wine tastings.[29] Whether through entertainment, email or information services, it increases sales if a company provides surroundings that consumers want.

In-store displays are a marketing communication tool that attracts attention. Although most displays consist of simple racks that dispense the product or related coupons, some marketers use elaborate performances and scenery to display their products. And advertisers are also being more aggressive about hitting consumers with their messages, wherever they may be. A **place-based media** strategy is a growing way to target consumers in non-traditional places. Today, messages can pop up in airports, doctors' offices, college cafeterias and health clubs. An example of this would be the TV screens that you see at the checkout in a Tesco supermarket while waiting in the queue for the cashier.

Photo 4.5 As consumers are exposed to more and more advertising, advertisers must work harder than ever to get their attention. Place-based media, in this case a Kitkat advert offers a way to reach consumers when they are a 'captive audience'.
Source: Alamy Images/Jeffrey Blackler

Time

In addition to the physical environment, time is another situational factor. Marketers know that the time of day, the season of the year and how much time one has to make a purchase affect decision making. Time is one of consumers' most limited resources. We talk about 'making time' or 'spending time', and are frequently reminded that 'time is money'.

Indeed, many consumers believe that they are more pressed for time than ever before.[30] This sense of **time poverty** makes consumers responsive to marketing innovations that allow them to save time, including such services as one-hour photo processing, drive-through lanes at fast-food restaurants and ordering products on the web.[31] Many websites, including Apple's iTunes, Virgin Digital and even Tesco, now offer consumers the speed and convenience of downloading music. These sites allow consumers to browse through thousands of titles, listen to selections, and order and pay for them – all without setting foot inside a shop. This saves the customer time, plus the 'shop' is always open.

Social influences on consumers' decisions

www.pearsoned.co.uk/Solomon

Objective

5

Explain how consumers' relationships with other people influence their decision-making processes

Our discussion of consumer behaviour so far has focused on factors that influence us as individuals, such as the way we learn about products. Although we are all individuals, we are also members of many groups that influence our buying decisions. Families, friends and classmates often influence our decisions, as do larger groups with which we identify, such as ethnic groups and political parties. Now let's consider how social influences such as culture, social class and influential friends and acquaintances affect the consumer decision-making process.

Culture

Think of **culture** as a society's personality. It is the values, beliefs, customs and tastes produced or practised by a group of people. However, what people in one culture find desirable or appropriate will not necessarily be appreciated in other cultures as well. The producers of the Middle Eastern version of the hit reality show *Big Brother* had to realise this when a male character kissed a female character on the cheek in the first few minutes of an episode. In conservative Bahrain, the Persian Gulf island where the show was filmed, a social kiss between a young man and a young woman meeting for the first time suggested rampant moral depravity. In the wake of street protests, the show was pulled.[32]

Rituals and values Thus, a consumer's culture influences buying decisions. For example, cultures have their own rituals, such as weddings and funerals, that have specific activities and products associated with them. Some companies are more than happy to help us in these efforts. Consider the elaborate weddings Disney stages for couples who want to re-enact their own version of a popular fairy tale: at Disney World, the princess bride wears a tiara and rides to the park's lakeside wedding pavilion in a horse-drawn coach, complete with two footmen in grey wigs and gold lamé trousers. At the exchange of vows, trumpets blare as Major Domo (he helped the Duke in his quest for Cinderella) walks up the aisle with two wedding rings gently placed in a glass slipper on a velvet pillow. Disney stages about 2000 of these extravaganzas in the US each year.[33]

Even corporations sometimes have myths and legends as a part of their history, and some make a deliberate effort to be sure that newcomers to the organisation learn these. Nike designates senior executives as 'corporate storytellers' who explain the company's heritage to other employees, including the hourly workers at Nike shops. They tell stories about the founders of Nike, including the coach of the Oregon track team who poured rubber into his family waffle iron to make better shoes for his team – the origin of the Nike waffle sole. The stories emphasise the dedication of runners and coaches involved with the company to reinforce the importance of teamwork.

Marketing ethics and sustainability

What's your favourite skin colour?

Compared to European customers, Asian female customers are more concerned about their skin being fairer and if it is moisturised adequately. European customers are more likely to buy tanning products since they consider a tan as a healthier colour. As a result, the most popular products of French international brand Clarins in Europe are foaming cleanser (deep clean) followed by self-tanning cream and lastly anti-wrinkle eye cream. In contrast, the brand's best-selling products in Asia are whitening sun cream, body firming and moisturising cream.

Debate, discuss, disagree

1 To what degree do you think the beauty industry in these two countries have shaped consumer preferences as opposed to simply reflecting them?

As we also saw in Chapter 2, cultural values are deeply held beliefs about right and wrong ways to live.[34] For example, one culture might feel that being a unique individual is preferable to subordinating one's identity to a group, whereas another culture may emphasise the importance of the group over individuality. That's not to say, however, that values can't change. A recent study showed that both baby-boomer women (born between 1946 and 1964) and Generation X men (born between 1965 and 1976) and Generation Y men (born after 1976) are more likely to seek balance than to seek only material success.[35]

Marketers who understand a culture's values can tailor their product offerings accordingly. For example, cigarette brands Salem Pianissimo and Virginia Slims One, which emit less smoke than other brands, flopped in the United States yet sell well in Japan. Why? Because the Japanese culture values the welfare of others more than it values individual pleasure. The cigarettes that emit less smoke won't offend others (especially non-smokers) quite as much, so the Japanese prefer to buy them. An industry executive observed: 'Japanese are much more concerned about people around them. If you develop a product which helps them address these concerns, then you have a good chance of developing a hit product.'[36]

Subculture

A subculture is a group coexisting with other groups in a larger culture whose members share a distinctive set of beliefs or characteristics. Each of us belongs to many subcultures. These subcultures could be religious groups, ethnic groups or regional groups as well as those that form around music groups such as fans of the Rolling Stones, media creations such as Trekkies (*Star Trek* fans) or leisure activities such as extreme sports. The hip-hop subculture has had enormous influence as many marketers relied on young trendsetters to help decide what brands were off the hook (good) and which were wack (bad). Successful hip-hop artists like P. Diddy, Jay-Z, Nelly and Usher are slowly but surely becoming major players in the marketing world. Nelly has branched out into the beverage business by creating 'Pimp Juice', a hip-hop inspired energy drink, Usher has created his own fragrances and Gwen Stefani started her own clothing line.[37]

For marketers, some of the most important subcultures are racial and ethnic groups because many consumers identify strongly with their heritage and are influenced by products that appeal to this aspect of their identities. Some racial differences in consumption preferences can be subtle but important.

Social Class

Social class is the overall rank of people in a society. People who are within the same class work in similar occupations, have similar income levels, and usually share tastes in clothing, decorating styles and leisure activities. These people also share many political and religious beliefs as well as ideas regarding valued activities and goals.

Many products and shops are designed to appeal to people in a specific social class.[38] Working class women often are less likely to experiment with new products or styles, such as modern furniture or coloured appliances, because they tend to prefer predictability to novelty.[39] Marketers need to understand these differences and develop product and communication strategies that appeal to the different groups.

Luxury goods often serve as **status symbols**, visible markers that provide a way for people to flaunt their membership in higher social classes (or at least to make others believe they are members). Marketers of high-end products often seek out rich people (or those who want others to think they are) to buy their brands. For example, Mercedes teamed up with designer Giorgio Armani to produce a line of products for the well-heeled, including a new car with sand-coloured leather seats, jet-black dashboard and brown leather steering wheel designed by Armani.[40]

However, it's important to note that, over time, the importance of different status symbols rises and falls. Today, wealthy consumers who want to let the world know of their success are likely to choose a Mercedes or Porsche. The 'in' car five years from now is anyone's guess.

In addition, traditional status symbols today are available to a much wider range of consumers around the world with rising incomes, so this change is fuelling demand for mass-consumed products that still offer some degree of panache or style. Think about the success of companies like Nokia, H&M, Zara, ING, Dell Computers, Gap, Nike, easyJet or L'Oréal. They cater to a consumer segment that analysts have labelled **mass-class**: the hundreds of millions of global consumers who now enjoy a level of purchasing power that's sufficient to let them afford high-quality products – except for expensive items like college education, housing or luxury cars. The mass-class market, for example, has spawned several versions of affordable cars: Latin Americans had their Volkswagen Beetle (affectionately called *el huevito*, the little egg), Indian consumers have their Maruti 800 (selling for as little as US$4860), and the Fiat Palio, the company's 'world car', is aimed

Across the hall

Advice for Julie Cordua

Professor Cary L. Cooper, CBE

Distinguished Professor of Organisational Psychology and Health, Lancaster University Management School

Option 2 doesn't appeal to me because it is sticking to the big corporates, and not thinking creatively about other novel markets. Option 3 is too broad a concept, it is giving by all means, and will, I believe, confuse 'direct giving' with the (RED) model of indirect giving, which may turn off either or both potential consumers. I think the best option is Option 1, because (RED)

is expanding into a market that understands both 'doing good' and the world of gadgets and youth-orientated products. The young are active consumers and shoppers, but also have a conscience and would like to think of themselves as helping others, while they help themselves. This option will have to be well thought through, with the brands carefully chosen to reflect the lifestyle of the Y generation or even Z generations! The (RED) concept has real value in the world that many of the Y generation will find themselves in, where they will have little time to volunteer and little money to donate in the traditional mode (as we have seen in the decline of charitable contributions over recent years), until the recession and its aftermath dies down and growth occurs again. Option 1 has real possibilities if well researched and implemented.

at emerging countries such as Brazil, Argentina, India, China and Turkey. Today the Fiat Palio is marketed in 40 countries.[41]

Group membership

Anyone who's ever 'gone along with the crowd' knows that people act differently in groups than they do on their own. There are several reasons for this phenomenon. With more people in a group, it becomes less likely that any one member will be singled out for attention, and normal restraints on behaviour may be reduced (think about the last wild party you attended). In many cases, group members show a greater willingness to consider riskier alternatives than they would if each member made the decision alone.[42]

Since many of the things we buy are consumed in the presence of others, group behaviours are important to marketers. Sometimes group activities create new business opportunities. Consider, for example, the Olympic Games which took place in London in summer 2012. This event gave ideal opportunities for companies to benefit from the huge popularity and immense media presence. Not only main sponsors made good profits but also smaller companies which sold fan articles such as banners, T-shirts and hats or souvenirs from Great Britain.

Reference groups   A **reference group** is a set of people a consumer wants to please or imitate. Consumers 'refer to' these groups in evaluating their behaviour – what they wear, where they go, what brands they buy and so on. Unlike a larger culture, the 'group' can be composed of one person, such as your significant other, or someone you've never met, such as a statesman like Winston Churchill, a star like Gwyneth Paltrow or a sophisticated man of the world like James Bond. The group can be small, such as your immediate family, or it could be a large organisation, such as Greenpeace.

Conformity   Consumers often change their behaviour to gain acceptance into a particular reference group. **Conformity** is at work when a person changes as a reaction to real or imagined group pressure. For example, a student getting dressed to go to a college ball may choose to wear clothing similar to what he knows others will be wearing so that he's accepted by the group.

Marketing ethics and sustainability

Greenpeace praises Nokia, slams Nintendo in 'green' study

Greenpeace rated 18 major electronics companies for their progress on phasing out hazardous substances, recycling electronic waste and improving energy efficiency to avert global warming. Nintendo came out bottom according to Greenpeace. Nokia took the top spot and Sony Ericsson came second. Philips edged up to third place from fourth in December, followed by Motorola, up from eighth place, and Apple, which remained unchanged in fifth place. However, the report targets the elimination of two toxic chemicals in particular – polyvinyl chloride (PVC) and brominated flame retardants (BRFs) – because they are persistent in the environment and can accumulate in human bodies. More companies such as HP, Acer and two Indian brands, Wipro and HCL, are now rolling out products which are free of PVCs and BRFs.

Source: Based on www.greenpeace.org/international/en/campaigns/climate-change/cool-it/Campaign-analysis/Guide-to-Greener-Electronics

Debate, discuss, disagree

1   Who should be policing the reduction of toxic substances in the production of consumer products if not Greenpeace?

2   Apart from producing reports and naming and shaming, what other actions could Greenpeace and other organisations take?

Home shopping parties, as epitomised by the Tupperware party that we will encounter in Chapter 12, capitalise on group pressures to boost sales. A company representative makes a sales presentation to a group of people who have gathered in the home of a friend or acquaintance. Participants model the behaviour of others who can provide them with information about how to use certain products, especially because the home party is likely to be attended by a relatively homogeneous group (for example, neighbourhood homemakers). Pressures to conform may be intense and may escalate as more group members begin to 'cave in' (this process is sometimes termed the *bandwagon effect*). Even though Tupperware has moved into new sales venues, including a website (www.tupperware.co.uk), the Home Shopping Network and kiosks in shopping centres, it hopes the shopping party remains a popular means of generating sales.[43]

Opinion leaders   If, like Brian, you are in the market for a new car, is there someone you know you would seek out for advice? Some individuals are particularly likely to influence others' product decisions. An **opinion leader** is a person who influences others' attitudes or behaviours because others perceive them as possessing expertise about the product.[44] Opinion leaders usually exhibit high levels of interest in the product category and may continuously update their knowledge by reading, talking to salespeople and so on. Because of this involvement, opinion leaders are valuable information sources and, unlike commercial endorsers who are paid to represent the interests of just one company, they have no axe to grind and can impart both positive and negative information about the product. In addition, opinion leaders are often among the first to buy new products, so they absorb much of the risk, reducing uncertainty for others who are not as courageous.

Today, many shrewd marketers appreciate the value of coaxing opinion leaders – and especially celebrities – to be seen using or wearing their products so that others will follow suit. For example, the sport clothing company Puma used this approach in order to enhance the popularity of its products. It looked for opinion leaders such as popular DJs or barkeepers in clubs who generally have a big influence on young people and equipped them with Puma clothes and shoes. As a result, the brand image improved and suddenly everybody wanted to wear those hip 'speedcat trainers'.

Gender roles

Some of the strongest pressures to conform come from our **gender roles**, society's expectations regarding the appropriate attitudes, behaviours and appearance for men and women. These assumptions about the proper roles of men and women, flattering or not, are deeply ingrained in marketing communications.[45] For example, men are far less likely than women to see a doctor regularly, and 25 percent say they would delay seeking help as long as possible. Experts suggest that this may be because boys playing sports are taught to 'ignore pain and not ask for help'.[46]

Many products take on masculine or feminine attributes, and consumers often associate them with one gender or another.[47] For example, many women downplay their femininity at work by wearing masculine clothing such as trouser suits. These women feel that feminine dress in the workplace hurts their chances of being promoted – that the corporate world still rewards men more than women. Trouser suits, in this case, take on a masculine attribute. A different example of how gender differences influence consumer behaviour is the insight that the female online population in the UK spends far more time surfing websites with health and beauty content than one would predict by simply looking at their share of the total population. Marketers can use such information to reach their target audience and tailor their marketing plan.[48]

'Sex-typed' products   Marketers play a part in teaching us how society expects us to act as men and women. As consumers, we see women and men portrayed differently in marketing communications and in products promoted to the two groups. And these

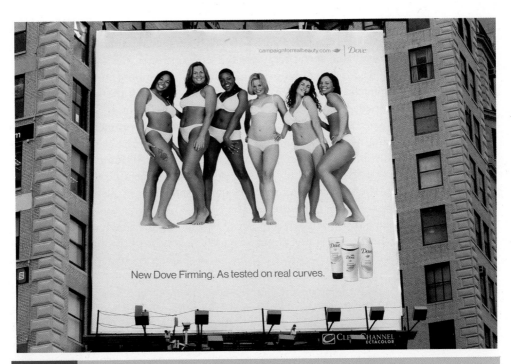

Photo 4.6	In terms of gender roles, Dove's real beauty campaign challenges the conventional size zero model beauty which helps to define what is attractive in women *Source:* Redux/Ruby Washington/The New York Times

influences teach us what the 'proper' role of women or men is and, in addition, which products are appropriate for each gender. Some of these 'sex-typed' products have come under fire from social groups. For example, feminists have criticised the Barbie doll for reinforcing unrealistic ideas about what women's bodies should look like – even though a newer version of the doll isn't quite as skinny and buxom. Other Barbie protests erupted when Mattel introduced a shopping-themed version called Cool Shoppin' Barbie. The doll comes with all the equipment kids need to pretend Barbie is shopping – including a Barbie-size MasterCard. When the card is pressed into the card scanner, her voice says, 'Credit approved!' Although Mattel includes a warning about sticking to a budget, some critics fear the doll sends the wrong message to girls about the desirability of shopping.[49]

Objective

6

Show how the internet offers consumers opportunities to participate in consumer-to-consumer marketing

Consumer-to-consumer e-commerce

Of course, not all consumer behaviour is related to marketers offering goods and services to consumers. **Consumer-to-consumer (C2C) e-commerce** refers to online communications and purchases that occur among individuals without directly involving the manufacturer or retailer. The most famous of such sites, eBay, provides an opportunity for consumers (and an increasing number of small businesses) to sell everything from comic books to a vintage trombone. In 2005, eBay ranked number 14 in Fortune's 100 Fastest-Growing Tech companies list, had websites in 23 countries and 8000 employees.[50]

Much of C2C e-commerce is far less sensational. It's more about groups of 'netizens' around the world with similar interests united through the internet by a shared passion. These virtual communities meet online and share their enthusiasm for a product, recording artist, art form, celebrity and so on.[51] In fact, over 40 million people worldwide participate in such virtual communities. How many consumers actually visit these sites? Let's review the most popular online C2C formats:[52] gaming, chat rooms, boards and blogs.

Gaming   The emergence of gaming as an online, shared experience opens new vistas to marketers. Consider this: Toyota's digital racing game Tundra Madness attracts 8000 consumers who spend an average of eight minutes on the site daily. The company's research showed that the campaign raised brand awareness among consumers by 28 per cent and intent to purchase by 5 per cent. Heartened by the success of this experiment, Toyota launched games to promote other models. To target first-time car buyers the company created the Matrix Video Mixer game, which it promoted through sites like RollingStone .com, GetMusic.com and Launch.com. The effort was tied to a Gravity Games sponsorship and an in-cinema commercial campaign. About three in ten registered users forwarded videos created through the game to their friends.

The secret behind the appeal of this format is the huge chunks of time people spend immersed in these games. The average online player logs 17 hours per week, and firms like Sony, Microsoft and Sega are building their own virtual worlds to get a piece of the action. This is not a genre of game but a breakthrough new medium which provides a completely new social, collaborative shared experience. As a result such companies are in the internet community business.

Sony online's EverQuest is among the most successful of the Massively Multiplayer online Role-Player Games that allow people to live shadow lives. More than 430,000 registered players worldwide belong to 'guilds' in a never-ending journey to slay monsters and earn points. EverQuest combines the stunning graphics of advanced gaming with the social scene of a chat room. Like The Sims, players create a character as a virtual alter-ego, which may be a wise elf or a backstabbing rogue. Some players sell powerful characters on eBay for $1000 or more.

Chat rooms, rings and lists   These include internet relay chat (IRC), otherwise known as chat rooms. Rings are organisations of related home pages, and lists are groups of people on a single mailing list who share information.

Boards   Boards are online communities organised around interest-specific electronic bulletin boards. Active members read and post messages sorted by date and subject. There are boards devoted to musical groups, movies, wind, cigars, cars, comic strips, even fast-food restaurants.

The Japanese have embraced chat rooms as a way to express themselves bluntly in a society where face-to-face confrontation is avoided. Channel 2 is Japan's largest internet bulletin board – the place where disgruntled employees leak information about their companies, journalists include tidbits they cannot get into the mainstream news media, and the average salaryman attacks with ferocity and language unacceptable in daily life. It is also the place where gays come out in a society in which they mostly remain in the closet. About 5.4 million people come to Channel 2 each month (www.2ch.net), many of them several times a day. Founded in 1999, *ni-channeru*, as the Japanese call it, has become part of Japan's everyday culture. News organisations follow it closely to gauge the public mood; big companies meticulously monitor how their products or companies are portrayed on it; and the police react immediately to threats posted on the site. As with any bulletin board, anonymous users start threads on myriad subjects and post comments. Unlike the real Japanese world, where language is calibrated according to one's social position, the wording on Channel 2 is often stripped of social indicators or purposefully manipulated to confuse readers. Language is also raw. 'Die!' is a favourite insult.

Blogs   The fastest growing form of online community is the 'weblog', or **blog**. These online personal journals are building an avid following among people who like to dash off a few random thoughts, post them on a website, and read similar musings by others. Although these sites are similar to web pages offered by Geocities and other free services, they employ a different technology that lets people upload a few sentences without going through the process of updating a website built with conventional home page software.

Bloggers can fire off thoughts on a whim, click a button, and quickly have them appear on a site. Weblogs frequently look like online diaries, with brief musings about the days' events, and perhaps a link or two of interest. This burgeoning **Blogosphere** (the name given to the universe of active weblogs) is starting to look like a force to be reckoned with.

At the start of the chapter, you met Julie Cordua from (RED). She needs to work out which one of the options was best. Having read 'Real people, other voices' to learn how others advised Julie, now see how it worked out at (RED).

Real people, real decisions

How it worked out at (RED)

Julie chose Option 1. (RED) continued to seek major international brands to partner with, but it is now complementing those partnerships with smaller special editions that appeal to a younger age group. The company decided that this expansion of its business model is necessary to keep (RED) fresh and relevant in the consumer marketplace. Teens are clearly the emerging consumer group that will drive (RED)'s success in the future. One of the first examples of this strategy was the release of a (PRODUCT) RED skateboard in the spring of 2008. (RED) is also looking at adding other action sports products and teen-focused fashion brands to the collection.

Marketing metrics

Measuring success at (RED)

(RED) implemented a brand-tracking study that will allow the organisation to measure awareness, consideration, preference and brand momentum with its key consumer targets over time. Through this study Julie can determine whether (RED)'s investment in key consumer groups via new partnerships and marketing programmes is paying off. Are these consumers more aware of (RED)? Do they prefer (RED) products over non-(RED) products? Are they more likely to choose brands that join (RED)? If (RED) is able to move the needle on these measures, this feedback will give Julie powerful ammunition when she pitches the idea to brands that haven't yet signed up for the programme.

Chapter summary

Now that you have finished reading this chapter, you should be able to

1. **Define consumer behaviour and explain why consumers buy what they buy.** Consumer behaviour is the process individuals or groups go through to select, purchase, use and dispose of goods, services, ideas or experiences to satisfy their needs and desires. Consumer decisions differ greatly ranging from habitual, repeat (low involvement) purchases to complex, extended problem-solving activities for important, risky (high involvement) purchases.

2. **Describe the pre-purchase, purchase and post-purchase activities that consumers engage in when making decisions.** When consumers make important purchasing decisions, they go through a set of five steps. First, they recognise there is a problem to be solved and search for information to make the best decision. They then evaluate a set of alternatives and judge them on the basis of various evaluative criteria. At this point, they are ready to make their purchasing decision. Following the purchase, consumers decide whether it matched their expectations.

3. **Explain how internal factors influence consumers' decision-making processes.** Several internal factors influence consumer decisions. Perception is how consumers select, organise and interpret stimuli. Motivation is an internal state that drives consumers to satisfy needs. Learning is a change in behaviour that results from information or experience. Behavioural learning results from external events, while cognitive learning refers to internal mental activity. An attitude is a lasting evaluation of a person, object or issue and includes three components: affect, cognition and behaviour. Personality traits such as innovativeness, materialism, self-confidence and sociability and the need for cognition may be used to develop market segments. Marketers seek to understand a consumer's self-concept in order to develop product attributes that match some aspect of the consumer's self-concept.

The age of consumers and their lifestyle also are strongly related to consumption preferences. Marketers may use psychographics to group people according to activities, interests and opinions that may explain reasons for purchasing products.

4. **Situational influences include our physical surroundings and time pressures.** Dimensions of the physical environment including decor, smells, lighting, music and even temperature can influence consumption. The time of day, the season of the year and how much time one has to make a purchase also affect decision making.

5. **Explain how consumers' relationships with other people influence their decision-making processes.** Consumers' overall preferences for products are determined by the culture in which they live and their membership in different subcultures. Social class, group memberships and opinion leaders are other types of social influences that affect consumer choices. A reference group is a set of people a consumer wants to please or imitate, and this affects the consumer's purchasing decisions. Purchases also often result from conformity to real or imagined group pressures. Another way social influence is felt is in the expectations of society regarding the proper roles for men and women. Such expectations have led to many sex-typed products.

6. **Show how the internet offers consumers opportunities to participate in consumer-to-consumer marketing.** Consumer-to-consumer (C2C) e-commerce includes marketing communication and purchases between individuals. C2C activities include virtual communities that allow consumers to do such things as share their enthusiasm or dislike for a product or company. Virtual communities and other C2C e-commerce activities provide both a source of information about the market and about competitors for marketers and an opportunity to communicate with consumers.

Key terms

Chapter review

 ## Marketing concepts: testing your knowledge

1. What is consumer behaviour? Why is it important for marketers to understand consumer behaviour?

2. Explain habitual decision making, limited problem solving and extended problem solving. What is the role of perceived risk in the decision process?

3. What are the stages of the decision-making process?

4. What is perception? Explain the parts of the perception process: exposure, attention and interpretation. For marketers, what are the implications of each of these components?

5. What is motivation? What is the role of motivation in consumer behaviour?

6. What is behavioural learning? What is cognitive learning? How is an understanding of behavioural and cognitive learning useful to marketers?

7. What are the three components of attitudes? What is personality? What are some personality traits that may influence consumer behaviour?

8. Explain what is meant by lifestyle. What is the significance of family life cycle and lifestyle in understanding consumer behaviour and purchasing decisions?

9. How do culture and subculture influence consumer behaviour? What is the significance of social class to marketers?

10. What are reference groups, and how do they influence consumers? What are opinion leaders?

11. How does the physical environment influence consumer purchasing behaviour?

12. What is consumer-to-consumer (C2C) e-commerce? What are virtual communities, and how are they related to consumer behaviour?

Marketing concepts: discussing choices and issues

1. Demographic or cultural trends are important to marketers. What are some current trends that may affect the marketing of the following products?
   a. Housing
   b. Food
   c. Education
   d. Clothing
   e. Travel and tourism
   f. Cars.

2. What are the core values of your culture? How do these core values affect your behaviour as a consumer? What are the implications for marketers?

3. Consumers often buy products because they feel pressure from reference groups to conform. Does conformity exert a positive or a negative influence on consumers? With what types of products is conformity more likely to occur?

4. Millions of consumers around the globe use eBay to supplement their incomes or as their primary source of income. What do you think of the future of sites such as eBay? What opportunities does eBay provide for twenty-first century entrepreneurs?

5. Retailers often place impulse purchase items such as magazines and chocolate bars near the entrance to the shop or near the checkout area. How would you describe the decision process for these products? Why are these locations effective?

6. In different cultures, perceptions about the proper roles for men and women, that is, sex roles, can vary greatly. What are some ways you think sex roles may differ in the following countries, and what are the implications for global marketers?
   a. UK
   b. Bahrain
   c. Japan
   d. Holland.

7. We noted in this chapter that consumers often use country-of-origin as a heuristic to judge a product. Sometimes this tendency can backfire. While one study found that around the world 'the Golden Arches are now more widely recognised than the Christian cross',[53] the strong link between McDonald's and the USA has been a liability for the food chain in recent years. As anti-war protests in many countries give vent to raw anti-US sentiment, the familiarity of McDonald's has made it a widespread target. In Quito, Ecuador, protesters burned a Ronald McDonald statue. In Paris, demonstrators smashed a McDonald's window. South Korean activists calling for an end to the war sought attention by climbing up a McDonald's sign. Other McDonald's outlets – in Karachi, in Buenos Aires – have been ringed with police officers to stave off trouble. Should a company that takes credit for its association with its country-of-origin in good times have to take its blame in bad times? What steps can marketers take to avoid these problems?

8. Behavioural targeting involves tracking where people go online and then feeding them advertising information that's related to what they're looking for. While proponents of this approach argue that it's a very efficient and convenient way for people to conduct an information search, others who are concerned about a potential invasion of privacy aren't so enthusiastic. What's your opinion – do you mind having marketers know what sites you visit in return for having a better sense of the competing products available while you're searching?

9. Online games like The Sims and EverQuest attract thousands of people around the world, many of whom spend virtually all of their free time hunched over their computer monitors. Advocates of online gaming point to the social benefits, including an outlet for creativity and the opportunity to interact (at least electronically) with other like-minded people. Critics argue that the games are antisocial because they reduce the amount of time gamers spend in 'the real world'. What do you think?

Marketing practice: applying what you've learned

1. Assume that you are the vice president of marketing for a car maker. You know that internal factors such as perception, motivation, learning, attitudes and personality influence consumers' decision making. Develop a report that describes these internal factors, why each is important in the purchase of a car and how you might use these factors in developing marketing strategies for your firm.

2. This chapter indicated that consumers go through a series of steps (from problem recognition to post-purchase evaluation) as they make purchases. Write a detailed report describing what you would do in each of these steps when deciding to choose one of the following products:
   a. Mobile telephone
   b. A university
   c. A fast-food lunch.

3. Using one of the products in question 2, what can marketers do to make sure that consumers going through each step in the consumer decision process move towards the purchase of their brand? Hint: think about product, place, price and promotion strategies.

4. Sometimes advertising or other marketing activities cause problem recognition to occur by showing consumers how much better off they would be with a new product or by pointing out problems with products they already own. For the following product categories, what are some ways marketers might try to stimulate problem recognition?
   a. Life insurance
   b. Mouthwash
   c. A new brand of laundry detergent
   d. An airline.

5. Assume that you are a marketing manager for a large hotel chain with outlets in popular tourism sites around the world. You are concerned about the effects of current consumer trends, including changing ethnic populations, changing roles of men and women, increased concern for time and for the environment, and decreased emphasis on status goods. Others in your firm do not understand or care about these changes. They believe that the firm should continue to do business just as it always has. Develop a role-playing exercise with a classmate to discuss these two different points of view for your class. Each of you should be sure to include the importance of each of these trends to your firm and offer suggestions for marketing strategies to address these trends.

Marketing miniproject: learning by doing

The purpose of this miniproject is to increase your understanding of the roles of personal, social and situational factors in consumer behaviour.

1. With several other members of your class, select one of the following product categories (or some other product of your choice):
   - Hairstyling
   - Large appliances such as refrigerators or washing machines
   - Children's clothing
   - Banking
   - Fine jewellery.

2. Visit three shops or locations where the product may be purchased. (Try to select three that are very different from each other.) Observe and make notes on all the elements of each retail environment.

3. At each of the three locations, observe people purchasing the product. Make notes about their characteristics (e.g. age, race, gender and so on), their social class and their actions in the shop in relation to the product.

4. Prepare a report for your class describing the situational variables and individual consumer differences between the three shops and how they relate to the purchase of the product.

5. Present your findings to your class.

Further reading

Consumer Behaviour: A European Perspective, 4th Edition, Michael Solomon, Gary Bamossy, SorenAskegaard, Margaret Hogg, Financial Times/Prentice Hall, 2009

Consumer behaviour is about much more than just buying things; it also embraces the study about how having (or not having) things affects our lives, and how our possessions influence the way we feel about ourselves and about each other – our state of being. In addition to understanding why people buy things, we also try to appreciate how products, services and consumption activities contribute to the broader social world we experience. Whether shopping, cooking, cleaning, playing football or hockey, lying on the beach, emailing or texting friends, or even looking at ourselves in the mirror, our lives are touched by the marketing system.

Real people, real surfers

Exploring the web

Visit two or three virtual communities such as the ones listed in this chapter's discussion of C2C e-commerce. Based on your experience, answer the following questions for each site you visit:

1. What is the overall reason for the site's existence?

2. What is your opinion of the site?

3. What type of consumer do you think would be attracted to the site?

4. How easy or difficult is it to navigate each site?

Now, take a look at the website at www.pearsoned.co.uk/solomon to see some videos from YouTube relating to aspects of this chapter.

Marketing plan exercise

An important key to success for marketers is understanding consumers and how they go about selecting the products they buy. Pick a product, either a good or a service, that you like and that perhaps you've purchased in the past. As part of developing a marketing plan for this product, do the following;

1. Make a list of the many things you need to know about the consumers of your product and how they make the decision to purchase so that you can help to devise where you should sell your product, as well as how and what you should communicate to them.

2. What are some of the ways you might go about gathering the information?

3. Which consumer information is most useful in developing the marketing plan?

Delve deeper into consumer behaviour

Professor Margaret K. Hogg

Chair in Consumer Behaviour and Marketing, Lancaster University Management School

Consumer behaviour involves choices; and similarly any recommendation of further reading also involves choices. What has been exciting about the academic debates in consumer behaviour research over the past 40 years is how they have drawn on an increasingly wide range of disciplines in order to understand the psychological and sociological contexts for consumer behaviour. The field is so varied in terms of theoretical and empirical coverage. My selection begins with a paper which highlights the considerable disagreements about what constitutes consumer research. Simonson et al. (2001) review how researchers' attention has switched from the original concern with comprehensive models of consumer behaviour; to behavioural decision theory (BDT) and social cognition; and then to postmodern approaches to consumer research. My second suggestion is Fournier and Mick's (1999) 'Rediscovering Satisfaction', which examines a variety of different research approaches to investigating consumer satisfaction that is 'central to the marketing concept' (Fournier and Mick 1999: 5). These authors show how insights from different research approaches (both positivist and non-positivist paradigms) can inform our understanding of consumer behaviour. My third suggestion is Arnould and Thompson's (2005) paper on consumer culture theory, which provides an excellent overview of what Simonson et al. (2001) would probably classify as the postmodern, i.e. the 'sociocultural, experiential, symbolic and ideological aspects of consumption' (Arnould and Thompson 2005: 868) although this is probably rather too narrow a classification of the approaches captured in the studies reviewed by Arnould and Thompson.

If reading these articles excites you to pursue this topic further, two other good sources of material are the *Journal of Consumer Research* and six volumes which I edited (Hogg 2005, 2006) for the Sage Library in Business and Management on *Consumer Behavior: Research and Influences* (Vols. 1–3) and *Consumer Behavior: The Meaning of Consumption* (Vols. 4–6). These volumes contain selected readings which cover such varied topic areas as: consumer behaviour as a field of study; consumer decision-making; consumer socialisation: childhood, children and families; advertising and consumption; possessions, brands and the self; (sub)cultures of consumption.

The best of luck with your reading

Dr Margaret K Hogg

References

Eric J. Arnould and Craig J. Thompson (2005) 'Consumer Culture Theory (CCT): Twenty Years of Research', *Journal of Consumer Research* 31 (March), 868–82.

Susan Fournier and David G. Mick (1999) 'Rediscovering Satisfaction' *Journal of Marketing* 63, no. 4, 5–23.

M.K. Hogg, ed. (2005) *Consumer Behavior Research 1: Research and Influences in Consumer Behavior*, Sage Library of Business and Management (London: Sage):

Vol I: *Consumer Behavior as a Field of Study*;
Vol II: *Consumer Decision-making*;
Vol III: *Consumer Socialization: Childhood, Children and Families.*

M.K., Hogg ed. (2006) Consumer Behavior Research 2: The Meaning of Consumption', Sage Library of Business and Management (London: Sage):

Vol IV: *Advertising and Consumption*;
Vol V: *Possessions, Brands and the Self*;
Vol VI: *(Sub)cultures of consumption*.

Itamar Simonson, Ziv Carmon, Ravi Dhar, Aimee Drolet and Stephen M. Nowlis (2001) 'Consumer Research: In Search of Identity' *Annual Reviews in Psychology* 52, 249–75.

Marketing in action case

Real decisions at ASDA – it's all about customer–oriented philosophy

The popularity of ASDA as an organisation positioned to meet the needs of its target customers is well acknowledged. Although it has faced challenges like many other organisations since it was formed in 1965, its transactions have significantly expanded to cover a number of areas which include food, clothing, books, housewares, music and videos. Having gone through some strategic changes, it eventually emerged as the second largest food retailer in the UK in 2003. If asked to highlight the secrets of this success, as expected, the management will have a long list, but the overarching factor is its customer-oriented philosophy.

It is noteworthy that ASDA devotes considerable attention to having an in-depth understanding of its customers in terms of how they select, purchase, use and dispose of goods, ideas or experience to satisfy their needs and desires. It provides a variety of products to give its customers the opportunity to select. This covers products requiring extended problem solving and those associated with habitual decision making. For example, in response to the growing needs for different products by its customers, under its new parent's guidance, it has been adding photo departments, jewellery, opticians and pharmacies to its stores. Its customer-focused approach is what propelled the supermarket into the relaunching of its mid-tier own-brand food products under the new name 'Chosen by You' in an investment worth over £100 million, as a way of improving product quality across its stores. In this special promotional programme, an independent company – Cambridge Market Research – conducted over 325,000 blind taste tests and when ASDA's products were certified by customers as meeting their high standards, then it labelled them 'Chosen by You'. In addition, it has introduced more than 1000 new and improved products to its offerings. It has been reported that the supermarket is expanding the 'Chosen by You' range into meat and fish with the hope of boosting the brand name, generating additional annual sales of £20 million and more profits in 2011. This scheme has been described by ASDA as the largest, single own-brand launch in British retailing history. This is not surprising as own brands account for half of ASDA's turnover. Besides, the scheme is meant to communicate to its target audience that ASDA is not undermining quality even as it aims to offer Britain's best value weekly shop at prices that could be independently confirmed to be lower than its main rivals. In the words of Andy Clarke, the president and chief executive of the company, 'When it comes to our food, we've taken a long, hard look at our products, done a lot of listening to our customers, and invested a significant amount of time, effort and money'.

While the organisation is conscious of various influences on consumers' decisions which could be internal, social or situational, its exploitation of social factors in its marketing strategies is especially spot-on. Factors like culture, subculture, social class, group membership and gender roles are carefully incorporated into the planning of its various marketing stimuli. For instance, one of the intriguing aspects of its 'Chosen by You' promotion is the accompanying ad messages. It chooses the lucky ones among those who have tried, tasted and chosen its products to feature in its TV advertisements. This is carefully designed such that it covers all of the major categories of this team of 'professional testers' – a term used by ASDA to describe the real people that have a passion for their favourite products and have given their seal of approval to its 'Chosen by You' products. As children appear in TV ads for products like lollies, breakfast cereals and cake, elderly consumers also communicate their love for products like ASDA's teabags and BBQ in some of the associated ad series. Similarly, while women are featured to promote some products, their male counterparts also appear in ads that will appeal to people of their group. In other words, ASDA pays attention to the match-up between those that feature in the marketing communication messages and the target audience who are in similar social groups.

One of the key objectives of ASDA is to assist its customers in the buying decision process. The display of the products in the stores is done in such a way as to assist consumers while shopping to remember some of the products they need. Since it is aware that consumers usually rely on both personal and commercial sources for information during the search stage of the process, it provides useful information in the form of integrated marketing communications through the website, newspaper, magazine, television and other relevant media. The idea is that even if customers will rely on information and recommendations from friends and relatives, they will still find those provided by the company useful while evaluating their options towards reaching the stage of making the relevant decisions.

Knowing that post-purchase evaluation done by the customers will be pivotal to whether they make a repeat purchase or not, ASDA introduced a number of measures to gauge the views of its customers. Apart from the popular 'Chosen by You' scheme, it believes that asking customers about their experience of using its products after purchases will indicate whether they are satisfied or dissatisfied with the status quo, and what could be done to remediate the unpalatable experience. The rationale is simple. *The customer is the king!* Closely related to this is the existing customer complaints management in the organisation. Presently, it uses two systems to collect relevant data – one involves using an internal web-based system, email, telephone and letters to log the complaints, and using the information as an input for suppliers to track and correct the issues in question. The other involves making it easy for customers to return any item bought and found to be defective. Overall, it aims at ensuring that its customers do not only pass through these stages, but also make repeat purchases, and eventually become loyal to the organisation.

Things to think about

1. Explain why and how ASDA's consumers would behave differently when buying low involvement products compared to buying high involvement products.

2. Discuss the implications of ASDA's use of social factors in the planning and implementation of its marketing strategies for its sale of market offerings including the 'Chosen by You' range.

3. With the assumption that ASDA's competitor would fight back in reaction to its launch of 'Chosen by you', what alternative decisions do you think the management will likely be confronted with towards maintaining and improving its customers' satisfaction?

4. What are your recommendations to ASDA on how to increase its market share without jeopardising its customer-oriented philosophy?

Case Study written by Dr Tunji Gbadamosi, University of East London.

Sources: ASDA Mission, Purpose and Values, www.asdasupplier.com/what-is-asda (accessed 2 June 2011); 'Pounds or Kilos – How do you Think when you're Buying Fruit and Veg?', http://your.asda.com/2011/5/27/pounds-or-kilos (accessed 2 June 2011); ASDA: Private Labels, www.asdasupplier.com/what-is-asda/private-label (accessed 2 June 2011); ASDA: Customer & Market, www.asdasupplier.com/what-do-i-need-to-do-next/ethnic-local-suppliers/customer-market/ (accessed 2 June 2011); ASDA Group Ltd., FundingUniverse, www.fundinguniverse.com/company-histories/ASDA-Group-Ltd-Company-History.html (accessed 2 June, 2011); 'ASDA Chosen by You', http://groceries.asda.com/asda-estore/banneroffers/banneroffercontainer.jsp?listId=1214989084579&utm_source=Google&utm_medium=PPC&utm_campaign=Homepage&utm_term=chosen%20by%20youP&referrer=cookiesDetecting (accessed 17 June 2011); www.facebook.com/Asda?sk=app_121320344614512 (accessed 17 June 2011); R. Baker, 'Asda Own Brand is Chosen by You', *Marketing Week* (2010), www.marketingweek.co.uk/sectors/retail/asda-own-brand-is-chosen-by-you/3018416.article (accessed 17 June 2011); BBC 'Asda Staff to Share £27m Bonus Pool', 22 February 2011, www.bbc.co.uk/news/business-12543568, (accessed on 17 June 2011); M. Canning, 'Asda Begins Fightback Against Tesco', *Belfast Telegraph*, Wednesday, 22 September 2010, www.belfasttelegraph.co.uk/business/business-news/asda-begins-fightback-against-tesco-14955308.html (accessed 17 June 2011); A. Felsted, 'Asda to Spruce Up Own-label Range', 21 September 2010, www.ft.com/cms/s/0/14fb53a8-c5a2-11df-ab48-00144feab49a.html#axzz1PWtFfXNS, (accessed 17 June 2011); Z. Wood, 'Asda Relaunches Own-brand Range', Guardian, 21 September 2010, www.guardian.co.uk/business/2010/sep/21/asda-relaunches-own-brand (accessed 17 June 2011); 'Asda Relaunches £8billion Own Label Food Range', *Food and Drink Business*, 22 September 2010, http://foodanddrinkbusiness.com/?tag=asda (accessed 17 June 2011); 'Meat and Fish are Added to ASDA Chosen by You', *The Food & Drink Innovation Network*, 10 may 2011, www.fdin.org.uk/2011/05/meat-and-fish-are-added-to-asda-chosen-by-you (accessed 17 June 2011); 'Asda's Latest Chosen By You Adverts Broadcast', *The Drum*, 31 May 2011, http://www.thedrum.co.uk/news/2011/05/31/22001-asda-s-latest-chosen-by-you-adverts-broadcast (accessed 17 June 2011); R. Ford, 'Meat and Fish Added to Asda Chosen by You', *The Grocer*, 6 May 2011, www.thegrocer.co.uk/articles.aspx?page=articles&ID=217818 (accessed 17 June 2011).

References

1. David Kesmodel, 'Marketers Push Online Ads Based on Your Surfing Habits', *The Wall Street Journal Interactive Edition,*5 April 2005.

2. Michael R. Solomon, *Consumer Behavior: Buying, Having, and Being,* 7th ed. (Upper Saddle River, NJ: Prentice Hall, 2007).

3. Christopher Lawton, 'Pushing Faux Foreign Beer in U.S.: Can Anheuser-Busch Tap Imports' Growth with Beers Produced in Land of Budweiser?', 27 June 2003, www.wsj.com.

4. P. Farris, N. Bendle, Phillip. Pfeifer, and D. Reibstein, *Key Marketing Metrics: The 50+ Metrics Every Manager Needs to Know* (Harlow: Financial Times Prentice Hall); P. Farris, N. Bendle, Phillip. Pfeifer, and D. Reibstein, *Marketing Metrics: The Definitive Guide to Measuring Marketing Performance,* 2nd ed. (Upper Saddle River, NJ: FT Press); N. Bendle, p. Farris, Phillip. Pfeifer, and D. Reibstein, 'Metrics that Matter – to Marketing Managers', *Marketing JRM,* (2010) 18–23.

5. Farris et al., *Key Marketing Metrics;* Bendle et al., 'Metrics that Matter'.

6. Farris et al., *Key Marketing Metrics;* Bendle et al., 'Metrics that Matter'.

7. 'Touch Looms Large as a Sense That Drives Sales', *Brand Packaging* (May/June 1999), 39–40.

8. Michael Lev, 'No Hidden Meaning Here: Survey Sees Subliminal Ads', *New York Times*, 3 May 1991, D7.

9. 'ABC Rejects KFC Commercial, Citing Subliminal Advertising', *The Wall Street Journal Interactive Edition,* 2 March 2006.

10. Stuart Elliott, 'TV Commercials Adjust to a Shorter Attention Span', *The New York Times Online*, 8 April 2005.

11. Brian Sternberg, 'Next Up on Fox: Ads that can Change Pitch', *The Wall Street Journal*, 21 April 2005, B1.

12. Abraham H. Maslow, *Motivation and Personality*, 2nd ed. (New York: Harper & Row, 1970).

13. Robert A. Baron and Donn Byrne, *Social Psychology: Understanding Human Interaction*, 5th ed. (Boston: Allyn & Bacon, 1987).

14. Jeffrey Zaslow, 'Happiness Inc.: Science is Exploring the Roots of Joy – and Companies are Putting the Findings to Work.

How it's Changing your Appliances and Cheering up your Sales Clerks', *The Wall Street Journal*, 18 March 2006, P1.

15. Thorsten Hennig-Thurau, Markus Groth, Michael Paul and Dwayne D. Gremler, 'Are All Smiles Created Equal? How Emotional Contagion and Emotional Labor Affect Service Relationships', *Journal of Marketing*, 70 no.3 (2006), 58–73.

16. Adapted from Bendle et al., 'Metrics that Matter'.

17. Stuart Elliott, 'Pepsi's New Campaign Leaves Left Brain for Right', 20 November 2003, www.nyt.com.

18. www.becks.co.uk.

19. www.nivea.co.uk; www.rdtrustedbrands.com/ TrustedBrands2006.

20. Richard E. Petty and John T. Cacioppo, 'Need for Cognition and Advertising: Understanding the Role of Personality Variables in Consumer Behavior', *Journal of Consumer Psychology* 1, No. (3) (1992), 239–60.

21. www.campaignforrealbeauty.com/press.asp?id=4737&section =news&target=press.

22. www.audiworld.com/news/05/hoffman/content.shtml.

23. Benjamin D. Zablocki and Rosabeth Moss Kanter, 'The Differentiation of Life-Styles', *Annual Review of Sociology* (1976), 269–97.

24. Damien Cave, 'Dogtown U.S.A.', *The New York Times Online*, 12 June 2005.

25. Alfred S. Boote, 'Psychographics: Mind Over Matter', *American Demographics* (April 1980), 26–9; William D. Wells, 'Psychographics: A Critical Review', *Journal of Marketing Research* 12 (May 1975), 196–213.

26. Alan R. Hirsch, 'Effects of Ambient Odors on Slot-Machine Usage in a Las Vegas Casino', *Psychology and Marketing* 12, no. 7) (October 1995), 585–94.

27. Marianne Meyer, 'Attention Shoppers!', *Marketing and Media Decisions* 23 (May 1988), 67.

28. See Eben Shapiro, 'Need a Little Fantasy? A Bevy of New Companies Can Help', *New York Times*, 10 March 1991, F4.

29. Stephanie Grunier, 'An Entrepreneur Chooses to Court Cafe Society (Cyber Version, Actually)', 24 September 1999, www .wsj.com.

30. John P. Robinson, 'Time Squeeze', *Advertising Age* (February 1990), 30–33.

31. Leonard L. Berry, 'Market to the Perception', *American Demographics* (February 1990), 32.

32. Neil MacFarquhar, 'A Kiss Is Not Just a Kiss to an Angry Arab TV Audience', 5 March 2004, www.nyt.com.

33. Adapted from Solomon, *Consumer Behavior: Buying, Having, and Being* 7th ed.

34. Richard W. Pollay, 'Measuring the Cultural Values Manifest in Advertising', *Current Issues and Research in Advertising*, 2, No. (1), (1983), 71–92.

35. Becky Ebenkamp, 'Chicks and Balances', *Brandweek*, 12 February 2001, 16.

36. Norihiko Shirouzu, 'Japanese "Hygiene Fanatics" Snap Up Low-Smoke Cigarette', 8 September 1997, www.wsj.com.

37. Adapted from Solomon, *Consumer Behavior: Buying, Having, and Being,* 7th ed.

38. J. Michael Munson and W. Austin Spivey, 'Product and Brand-User Stereotypes among Social Classes: Implications for Advertising Strategy', *Journal of Advertising Research* 21 (August 1981), 37–45.

39. Stuart U. Rich and Subhash C. Jain, 'Social Class and Life Cycle as Predictors of Shopping Behavior', *Journal of Marketing Research* 5 (February 1968), 41–9.

40. Alessandra Galloni, 'Armani, Mercedes to Form Marketing, Design Venture', 30 September 2003, www.wsj.com.

41. Adapted from Solomon, *Consumer Behavior: Buying, Having, and Being*, 7th ed.

42. Nathan Kogan and Michael A. Wallach, 'Risky Shift Phenomenon in Small Decision-Making Groups: A Test of the Information Exchange Hypothesis', *Journal of Experimental Social Psychology* 3 (January 1967), 75–84; Arch G. Woodside and M. Wayne DeLozier, 'Effects of Word-of-Mouth Advertising on Consumer Risk Taking', *Journal of Advertising* (Fall 1976), 12–19.

43. Jack Neff, 'Door-to-Door Sellers Join the Party Online', *Advertising Age*, 27 September 1999, www.adage.com/news. cms?newsId=1100.

44. Everett M. Rogers, *Diffusion of Innovations*, 3rd ed. (New York: Free Press, 1983).

45. Kathleen Debevec and Easwar Iyer, 'Sex Roles and Consumer Perceptions of Promotions, Products, and Self: What Do We Know and Where Should We Be Headed', *in Advances in Consumer Research*, vol. 13, ed. Richard J. Lutz (Provo, Utah: Association for Consumer Research, 1986), 210–14; Lynn J. Jaffe and Paul D. Berger, 'Impact on Purchase Intent of Sex-Role Identity and Product Positioning', *Psychology and Marketing* (Fall 1988), 259–71.

46. Becky Ebenkamp, 'Battle of the Sexes', *Brandweek*, 17 April 2000, www.findarticles.com/p/articles/mi_m0BDW/is_16_41/ ai_61860406.

47. Debevec and Iyer, 'Sex Roles and Consumer Perceptions of Promotions, Products and Self'; Deborah E.S. Frable, 'Sex Typing and Gender Ideology: Two Facets of the Individual's Gender Psychology That Go Together', *Journal of Personality and Social Psychology* 56 (1989), 95–108; Jaffe and Berger, 'Impact on Purchase Intent of Sex-Role Identity and Product Positioning'; Keren A. Johnson, Mary R. Zimmer and Linda L. Golden, 'Object Relations Theory: Male and Female Differences in Visual Information Processing', in *Advances in Consumer*

Research, vol. 14, ed. Melanie Wallendorf and Paul Anderson (Provo, Utah: Association for Consumer Research, 1986), 83–7; Leila T. Worth, Jeanne Smith and Diane M. Mackie, 'Gender Schematicity and Preference for Gender-Typed Products', *Psychology & Marketing* 9 (January 1992), 17–30.

48. VITALSTATS, 'Behaviourally Targeted Advertising', *Media Week*, 4–11 March 2008, 15.

49. Kara K. Choquette, 'Not All Approve of Barbie's MasterCard', *USA Today*, 30 March 1998, 6B.

50. Adam Lashinsky, 'Meg and the Machine', *Fortune*, 11 August 2003, 2–3.

51. This section adapted from Solomon, *Consumer Behavior: Buying, Having and Being*, 7th ed.

52. This section adapted from Solomon, *Consumer Behavior: Buying, Having, and Being* 7th, ed.

53. Quoted in Rob Walker, 'McDonald's: When a Brand Becomes a Stand-In for a Nation', *The New York Times Online*, 30 March 2003.

Chapter 5
Business-to-business marketing

Meet Paul Baxter-Gibson,
a decision maker at Lucore

Paul Baxter-Gibson is Director of Professional Services at Lucore. He joined the company in 2009, having previously spent 13 years working on providing IT business solutions and services in the business-to-business arena. After being brought up in England and Hong Kong, Paul returned to the UK for his secondary and further education at the Royal Hospital School in Ipswich and later went on to study Leisure Management. Paul began his career with The Employment Service, where he worked as a Project Manager. He later moved into IT services in the private sector and now oversees the service offering that Lucore provides to its client base.

Specifically Paul's role is to work with the company's commercial sales team and manage Lucore's resources to develop global IT solutions for a range of business clients. Paul lives with Wendy and his three daughters – Emily, Sophie and Maddie – on the edge of the Peak District. He is a mad football fan and plays regularly for and manages his local team, The Bull's Head, on Sunday mornings.

Real people, real decisions
Decision time at Lucore

Founded in 2009 by John F. Hudson, Lucore provides risk management/control systems and retail management solutions which serve as end-to-end business software solutions designed to help business customers ensure compliancy and increase their productivity. Specifically, such solutions are designed around workflow procedure systems to help management by reporting on areas of noncompliance and inefficiency. Such systems can help companies to incorporate smart decisions based on efficiency gains, so they can remain competitive in the marketplace.

Lucore's Professional Service model has been designed and is based on years of experience in implementing IT systems in large multinational organisations with varying degrees of complexity. In order to offer such IT solutions to business customers, Lucore rely heavily on its sales, professional services and customer experience teams to successfully project manage and consult with business to offer end-to-end business solutions. The aim of the end-to-end business solutions function at Lucore is not to purely sell the IT system, but to effectively manage the business relationship over a company's lifespan and leverage greater business opportunities for all parties. Developing, maintaining and improving business relationships is extremely important for Lucore, and to advance the customer experience the company employs a range of consultants including professionally accredited project and programme managers. These employees have a wealth of experience in managing and implementing IT systems with varying degrees of complexity within both public and private sector organisations, both over time and through journeys of change. Providing commercial off the shelf (COTS) and bespoke IT systems often brings about changes and refinements to existing business processes. Lucore's consultants therefore need to use their experience to identify changes in existing business processes as a result of the changing dynamic business environment and provide new solutions accordingly.

This case looks at a particular business relationship between Lucore and a client that consisted of a team of three entrepreneurs, which Paul was tasked with managing. The company client had identified a new business opportunity in the healthcare sector and this specifically involved the automation and completion of assessments on behalf of a range of adult social care organisations for the purpose of the regulator – the Care Quality Commission (CQC). The three entrepreneurs involved in the development constituted an existing risk management consultant in the UK, a managing director of a successful UK-based organisation that delivered consulting services around CQC assessments and a professor of learning at the Concordia University in Montreal, Canada. The three had entered into a collaborative joint venture to create a new company called Care2Standard (C2S).

On a regular basis adult social care organisations are required to complete assessments for the Care Quality Commission based on the range of services that they provide. The CQC is the independent regulator of health and social care in England. It regulates care provided by the NHS, local authorities, private companies and voluntary organisations. The CQC aims to make sure that a high level of care is provided for everyone, in hospitals, care homes and people's own homes.

Prior to the formation of C2S and the provision of technology to assist with the completion of CQC assessments, these were completed and submitted in hard copy format, often with the assistance of trained and accredited consultants who helped with the process. This case will therefore focus on a series of potential service outcomes that Paul had to consider for making an important decision relating to how he pitched for business with these three entrepreneurs. Historically, Lucore had a good working relationship with all three entrepreneurs. Through the formation of C2S, an opportunity had arisen for all parties to work together with the aim of developing business over the long term and rolling out new technology to other parts of the healthcare industry at large. The nature of the business relationship was therefore considered a true partnership that would be seen as a 'win–win' for all parties concerned, as the success of this project would create opportunities for C2S to take a major stake in this sector and for Lucore to break into a new industry at large.

As part of establishing the business (C2S), and in conjunction with developing and implementing various aspects of the business strategy, C2S approached Lucore and asked for advice on how best to deliver the technology side of the business and tasked Lucore with developing and delivering the IT software itself. Clearly the three entrepreneurs had a variety of knowledge and skills in the care sector and had varying ideas regarding system requirements and the approach for implementing IT software. Three options came to mind, which Paul considered when pitching for the business:

Option 1 Use Lucore's existing IT COTS (commercial off the shelf) products in their current format to enable customers to complete CQC assessment

There are a number of advantages with this approach: not only will the product be available in the marketplace sooner, but the development cost and risk would be minimal, as this approach calls for no configuration changes and the use of core technology that is fairly standard. Whilst the technology is well established and has been successfully tried and tested, it is firmly based around generic uses and procedures. Such a system is not customised or tied to a specific industry or the needs of particular regulatory bodies. The use of COTS products, whilst cost effective in their procurement and implementation do rely heavily on re-engineering business processes, policies and/or procedures to utilise the IT software – in contrast to changing the software to meet the requirements of current business processes. Achieving business process re-engineering often requires heavy investment with stakeholders, good relationship management and the application of a variety of change management principals. These combined with industry and organisational wide commitment to 'buy in' to change are likely to raise further unforeseen mid-term implications.

Option 2 Use existing IT products in the marketplace including open source IT software products that enable customers to complete CQC assessments

This approach shares many benefits with Option 1 with regard to the speed and ease with which this software can be implemented. There is a wide range of open source (free) software that is available in the marketplace that is easy to download and access. Such software provides a wide range of functionality, but again this tends to be generic to cover a wide range of markets and uses. The flexibility, freedom and cost benefits are, however, well documented. The other benefits of going down this route is that more often than not, open source software comes with a certain amount of free training, which Lucore could look to build on and provide further hands-on support, thus complementing the service offer.

When considering implementing open source software, Paul also realises that some degree of assessment would be needed in order to accurately reflect on the functionality of each service and select one that is best aligned to the requirements of C2S's customers. This is a daunting task, bearing in mind that so many products are available in the marketplace, so Paul would in fact have to charge a fee for his time involved in shopping around to find the best solution. There is also a need for Paul to further research such technology, make sure it is stable, and there is a clear accountability support framework in place, and whichever solution is purchased can be integrated easily. Depending on the way that the task is approached, this may bring about further time and cost implications.

However, despite such drawbacks, using existing technologies means that much of the costly consultation, testing, marketing and product refinement stages of development have already been conducted. The cost of implementation can therefore be minimised to a large extent.

Option 3: Encourage C2S to develop a new fully integrated system to enable customers to complete CQC assessment and in parallel develop the software so it can be applied to other business processes

Option 3, although costly and time-consuming, would potentially give C2S more control over its business and product offering. By restructuring its systems it may also be possible for C2S to engage more with potential customers and utilise their input to shape the direction of its future services. Developing completely new IT software is not without risk either. Because the technology is not fully tested in the marketplace, this can lead to identification of software errors, so some degree of after-sales support would be needed that would impact on Lucore's resources. Establishing a 'pioneering' status in the marketplace will not evolve overnight and requires a great deal of time and investment to cultivate and manage customer relationships and establish expectations with end users, who may not wish to develop a 'true' partnership relationship.

Now, put yourself in Paul's shoes: Which option should he pitch for and why?

Objectives

When you finish reading this chapter, you will be able to:

1 Describe the general characteristics of business-to-business markets

2 Explain the unique characteristics of business demand

3 Describe how business or organisational markets are classified

4 Explain the business buying situation and describe business buyers

5 Explain the roles in the business buying centre (decision-making unit)

6 Understand the stages in the business buying decision process

7 Understand the growing role of B2B e-commerce

Business markets: buying and selling when the stakes are high

Objective

1

Describe the general characteristics of business-to-business markets

You might think most marketers spend their days dreaming up the best way to promote cutting-edge web browsers or trendy shoes – not really. Many marketers know that the 'real action' more likely lies in industrial solutions like Lucore offers, or in office supplies, work safety shoes, group medical insurance, machine components or construction products that other companies sell to businesses and organisations. In fact, some of the most interesting and lucrative jobs for young graduates are in industries you've probably never heard of because these businesses don't deal directly with consumers.

Like an end consumer, a business buyer makes decisions – but with an important difference: the purchase may be worth millions of euros, and both the buyer and the seller have a lot at stake. A consumer may decide to buy two or three T-shirts at one time, each showing a different design. Leading companies such as British Airways, Shell and Pizza Hut buy hundreds, even thousands of employee uniforms embroidered with their corporate logos in one single order.

Consider these transactions: IBM produces computer network servers to sell to its business customers. Unilever has contracts with several advertising agencies to promote its brands at home and around the globe. The London Theatre Company buys costumes, sets and programmes. The EU in Brussels places orders for thousands of new computers.

All these exchanges have one thing in common: they're part of **business-to-business (B2B) marketing**. This is the marketing of goods and services that businesses and other organisations buy for purposes other than personal consumption. Some firms resell these goods and services, so they are part of a channel of distribution. Other firms use the goods and services they buy to produce other goods and services that meet the needs of their customers or to support their own operations. These **business-to-business markets**, or *organisational markets*, include manufacturers, wholesalers, retailers and a variety of other organisations, such as hospitals, universities and governmental agencies.

To put the size and complexity of business markets into perspective, let's consider a single product – a pair of jeans. A consumer may browse through several racks of jeans and ultimately purchase a single pair, but the store at which the consumer shops has purchased many pairs of jeans in various sizes, styles and brands from different manufacturers. Each of these manufacturers purchases fabrics, zips, buttons and cotton thread from other manufacturers – that in turn purchase the raw materials to make these components. In addition, all the firms in this chain need to purchase equipment, electricity, labour, computer systems, legal and accounting services, insurance, office supplies, packing materials and countless other goods and services. So even a single purchase of the latest style of Diesel jeans represents the culmination of a series of buying and selling activities among many organisations.

In this chapter, we'll look at the big picture of the business marketplace, a world in which the success of business buyers and sellers can hang in the balance of a single transaction. Then we'll examine how marketers categorise businesses and other organisations to develop effective business marketing strategies. We'll look at business buying behaviour and the business buying decision process. Finally, we'll talk about the important world of business-to-business e-commerce.

Characteristics that make a difference in business markets

Objective

2

Explain the unique characteristics of business demand

In theory, the same basic marketing principles hold in both consumer and business markets – firms identify customer needs and develop a marketing mix to satisfy those needs. For example, take the company that made the desks and chairs at your university. Just like a firm that markets consumer goods, the furniture company that supplies university establishments first must create an important competitive advantage for its target market of universities. Next the firm develops a marketing mix strategy beginning with a product – the lecture/seminar room furniture that will withstand years of use by thousands of students while providing a level of comfort required for a good learning environment. The firm must offer the furniture at prices that universities can afford and that will allow the firm to make a reasonable profit. Then the firm must develop a sales force or other marketing communications strategy to make sure your university (and many others) consider and hopefully choose its products when it furnishes classrooms.

Although marketing to business customers does have a lot in common with consumer marketing, there are differences that make this basic process more complex.[1] Figure 1.1 provides a quick look at some of these differences.

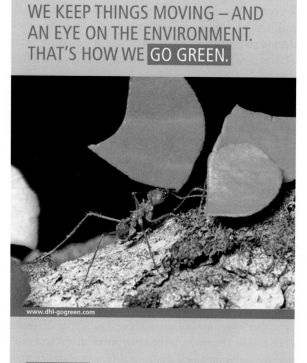

WE KEEP THINGS MOVING – AND AN EYE ON THE ENVIRONMENT. THAT'S HOW WE GO GREEN.

www.dhl-gogreen.com

GOGREEN
Climate Protection with DHL

DHL

Photo 5.1 With Go Green, DHL differentiates itself in the B2B marketplace
Source: DHL

Large buyers

In business markets, products often have to do more than satisfy an individual's needs. They must meet the requirements of everyone involved in the company's purchase decision. If you decide to buy a new chair for your room or apartment, you're the only one who has to be satisfied. For the lecture/seminar room, the furniture must satisfy not only students but also faculty, administrators, campus planners, financial controllers and the people at your institution who actually do the purchasing. In some cases the furniture may also have to meet certain governmental and safety standards.

Organisational Markets	Consumer Markets
• Purchases made for some purpose other than personal consumption	• Purchases for individual or household consumption
• Purchases made by someone other than the user of the product	• Purchases usually made by ultimate user of the product
• Decisions frequently made by several people	• Decisions usually made by individuals
• Purchases made according to precise technical specifications based on product expertise	• Purchases often based on brand reputation or personal recommendations with little or no product expertise
• Purchases made after careful weighing of alternatives	• Purchases frequently made on impulse
• Purchases based on rational criteria	• Purchases based on emotional responses to products or promotions
• Purchasers often engage in lengthy decision process	• Individual purchasers often make quick decisions
• Interdependencies between buyers and sellers; long-term relationships	• Buyers engage in limited-term or one-time-only relationships with many different sellers
• Purchases may involve competitive bidding, price negotiations and complex financial arrangements	• Most purchases made at 'list price' with cash or credit cards
• Products frequently purchased directly from producer	• Products usually purchased from someone other than producer of the product
• Purchases frequently involve high risk and high cost	• Most purchases are low risk and low cost
• Limited number of large buyers	• Many individual or household customers
• Buyers often geographically concentrated in certain areas	• Buyers generally dispersed throughout total population
• Products often complex; classified based on how organisational customers use them	• Products: consumer goods and services for individual use
• Demand derived from demand for other goods and services, generally inelastic in the short run, subject to fluctuations, and may be joined to the demand for other goods and services	• Demand based on consumer needs and preferences, is generally price-elastic, steady over time and independent of demand for other products
• Promotion emphasises personal selling	• Promotion emphasises advertising

Figure 5.1	Differences between organisational and consumer markets
	There are many major and minor differences between organisational and consumer markets. To be successful, marketers must understand these differences and develop strategies that can be effective with organisational customers

 ## Number of customers

Organisational customers are few and far between compared with end consumers. In Europe, there are several million consumer households but significantly fewer businesses or organisations. Dutch giant Philips Medical, which markets sophisticated electrical products to hospitals, health maintenance organisations and other medical groups, has a limited number of potential customers compared with its consumer electronics division. This means that business marketing strategies may be quite different from consumer marketing strategies. For example, in consumer markets Philips may use TV advertising, but in its business markets a strong sales force is vital for promoting the product.

Size of purchases

Business-to-business products can influence consumer purchases, both in the quantity of items ordered and in the price of individual purchases. A company that hires out uniforms to other businesses, for example, buys huge volumes of washing detergent each year to clean its uniforms. In contrast, even a hard-core football mother dealing with piles of dirty socks and shorts is likely to use just one box every few weeks. Organisations purchase many products, such as highly sophisticated manufacturing equipment or computer-based marketing information systems that can cost millions of euros. Recognising such differences in the size of purchases allows marketers to develop effective marketing strategies. Although it makes perfect sense to use mass-media advertising to sell laundry detergent to consumers, selling laundry detergent worth thousands of euros or a million-euro machine tool is often best handled by a strong personal sales force.

Geographic concentration

Another difference between business markets and consumer markets is geographic concentration. Business customers are often located in a small geographic area rather than being spread out across a country. Whether they live in the heart of Paris or in a small fishing village in Greece, consumers buy toothpaste and televisions. Business-to-business customers may be almost exclusively located in a single region of a country. Birmingham in the UK is home to a significant number of companies that supply steel and engineering components. For business-to-business marketers who wish to sell to these markets, this means that they can concentrate their sales efforts and perhaps even locate distribution centres nearby.

Business-to-business demand

Demand in business markets differs from consumer demand. Most demand for business-to-business products is derived, inelastic, fluctuating and joint. Understanding these differences in business-to-business demand is important for marketers in forecasting sales and in planning effective marketing strategies.

Derived demand

Consumer demand is based on a direct connection between a need and the satisfaction of that need. However, business customers don't purchase goods and services to satisfy their own needs. Business-to-business demand is **derived demand** because a business's demand for goods and services comes either directly or indirectly from consumer demand.

Consider an airline carrier such as KLM (from the Netherlands). Demand for the purchase of aircraft (Boeing or Airbus orders) comes from the demand for air travel and holidays. Likewise, demand for a marketing textbook is likely to come from the demand for business and marketing education. As a result of derived demand, the success of one company may depend on another company, and it could be in a different industry. The derived nature of business demand means that marketers must be constantly alert to changes in consumer trends that ultimately will have an effect on business-to-business sales. To help understand some of the issues associated with derived demand, consider the example below based on derived demand among commercial uses of gas.

Marketing misstakes

Derived demand in B2B sales promotions

The Sun and the *News of the World* newspapers have long-standing experience in running large-scale promotions. For example, they ran a special offer for their readers in association with LEGO toys. Over nine days they planned to give away more than 27 million pieces of LEGO. A voucher from each day's paper could be exchanged for a toy character based on recent blockbuster films like the *Pirates of the Caribbean* and *Toy Story*. The promotion proved a huge success, so much that

WH Smiths and Toys R Us, the stores participating in the promotion, ran out of pieces. According to BBC's 'Watchdog' (a consumer's complaints TV programme), this left many children bitterly disappointed and the show received complaints from angry viewers who had tried to exchange their vouchers only to be told by both stores that they had run out. On the promotion it did say in VERY tiny letters 'subject to availability', but this was of little consolation to those affected.

Why do you think this might be a marketing misstake?

Source: Based on www.bbc.co.uk/blogs/watchdog/2011/05/the_sun_and_news_of_the_world.html

 ## Inelastic demand

Inelastic demand means that it usually doesn't matter if the price of a business-to-business product goes up or down – business customers still buy the same quantity. Demand in business-to-business markets is mostly inelastic because what is being sold is often just one of many parts or materials that go into producing the consumer product. It is not unusual for a large increase in a business product's price to have little effect on the final consumer product's price.

For example, you may be able to buy a BMW Z4 Roadster 3.0i 'loaded' with options for about €60,000. To produce the car, BMW purchases thousands of different parts. If the price of tyres, batteries or stereos goes up or down, BMW will still buy enough to meet consumer demand for its cars. As you might imagine, increasing the price by €30, €40 or even

Marketing in recession

The derived demand for gas!

British Gas Business – the largest energy supplier to businesses in the UK – is using its own purchasing power to negotiate substantial deals and pass on those discounted rates to its small business customers. It has enlisted the support of eight companies, including household names such as Royal Mail, AXA and the AA. The scheme, called Purchase Power, could help UK businesses save thousands of pounds each year. Those

companies that have signed up to offer exclusive savings and benefits to British Gas Business customers provide a range of essential services to small and medium sized businesses. The package is free to join for British Gas customers and could save members up to £4500 each year.

Source: Based on www.britishgas.co.uk/business/what-we-do/ our-business/bgb-news.html

Discuss, debate, disagree

1   Consider the factors that influence business transactions relating to the consumption of gas.

€100 won't change consumer demand for this type of car, so demand for parts remains the same (if you have to ask how much it costs, you probably can't afford one).

But business-to-business demand isn't always inelastic. Sometimes producing a consumer good or service relies on only one or a few materials or component parts. If the price of the part increases, demand may become elastic if the manufacturer of the consumer good passes the increase on to the consumer. Steel, for example, is a major component in cars. Vehicle manufacturers will need to pay a lot more for steel should its price rise. An increase in the price of steel can drive up the price of vehicles so greatly that consumer demand drops, and eventually decreases the demand for steel.

Fluctuating demand

Business demand is also subject to greater fluctuations than consumer demand. There are two reasons for this. First, even small changes in consumer demand can create large increases or decreases in business demand. Take air travel for example – even a small increase in demand for air travel can cause airlines to order new equipment, creating a dramatic increase in demand for planes.

A product's life expectancy is another reason for fluctuating demand. Business customers tend to purchase certain products infrequently. Some types of large machinery may need to be replaced every 10 or 20 years. Thus demand for such products fluctuates. It may be very high one year when a lot of customers' machinery is wearing out, but low the following year because everyone's old machinery is working fine. One solution for keeping production more constant is to use price reductions to encourage companies to order products *before* they actually need them.

Joint demand

Joint demand occurs when two or more goods are necessary to create a product. For example, the BMW Z4 needs tyres, batteries and spark plugs (a range of products). If the supply of one of these parts decreases, BMW may find it difficult to manufacture as many vehicles, and the company may not buy as many of the other items either.

Types of business-to-business markets

Objective

3

Describe how business or organisational markets are classified

As we noted earlier, many firms buy products in business markets so they can produce other goods. Other business-to-business customers resell, rent or lease goods and services. Still other customers, including governments and not-for-profit institutions such as the Red Cross or a local church, serve the public in some way. In this section, we'll look at the three major classes of business-to-business customers – producers, resellers and organisations (Figure 5.2). Then we'll look at how marketers classify specific industries.

Producers

Producers purchase products for the production of other goods and services that they in turn sell to make a profit. For this reason, they are customers for a vast number of products from raw materials to goods manufactured by still other producers. For example, in

Figure 5.2	**The business marketplace**
	The business marketplace consists of three major categories of customers: producers, resellers and organisations. Business-to-business marketers need to understand the different needs of these customers if they are to build successful relationships

our introductory case, Lucore purchases a range of generic software and adds value to these by transferring them into highly customised systems for its customers. Airbus buys engines, high-tech navigation systems, passenger seats and a host of other component parts to put into its planes. The French hotel chain Accor purchases linens, furniture and food to produce the ambiance and meals its guests expect.

Resellers

Resellers buy finished goods for the purpose of reselling renting or leasing to other businesses. Although resellers do not actually produce goods, they do provide their customers with the time, place and possession, by making goods available to consumers when and where they want them. For example, French supermarket chain Carrefour buys toothpaste, soft drinks, clothing and thousands of other product lines to sell in its retail shops.

Organisations

Governments may be the only customers for certain products – Tornado fighter jets for example. But much governmental expenditure is for more familiar and less expensive items. In any one year, the national government in any one of the largest EU countries is likely to purchase a range of goods and services, ranging from thousands of notepads and paintbrushes, to rail tickets, hotel rooms and the like.

To inform possible vendors about purchases they are about to make, governments regularly make information on forthcoming purchases available to potential bidders. The EU government provides information on business opportunities and tenders through the *Official Journal of the European Union*, and suppliers can easily seek opportunities through scanning the journal.

Not-for-profit institutions are organisations with educational, community and other public service goals, such as hospitals, churches, universities, museums and charitable and lobby groups. These institutions tend to operate on low budgets. Because non-professional part-time buyers who have other duties often make purchases, these customers may rely on marketers to provide more advice and assistance before and after the sale.

The Standard Industry Classification (SIC) system

In addition to looking at business-to-business markets within these three general categories, marketers can identify potential customers using the **Standard Industrial Classification system (SIC)**. This is a numerical coding system whereby companies that operate within specific industrial sectors (their SIC code) can be identified.

Firms may therefore use the SIC system to find new customers. A marketer might first determine the SIC industry classifications of his current customers and then evaluate the sales potential of other firms occupying these categories. For example, Paul at Lucore may find that several of his large customers are in the environmental consulting sector. To find new customers, he could contact other firms in the same industrial group.

The nature of business buying

www.pearsoned.co.uk/Solomon

Objective

4

Explain the business buying situation and describe business buyers

So far we've talked about how business-to-business markets are different from consumer markets and about the different types of customers that make up business markets. In this section, we'll discuss some of the important characteristics of business buying. This is important because just like companies that sell to end consumers, a successful business-to-business marketer needs to understand how his or her customers make decisions. Armed with this knowledge, the company is able to participate in the buyer's decision process from the start. Take a firm that sells equipment to hospitals. Understanding that doctors who practise at the hospital (rather than buyers who actually purchase medical supplies) often initiate new equipment purchases means that the firm's salespeople have to be sure that they establish solid relationships with such individuals as well as with the hospital's buyers – if they expect their products to be taken seriously.

The buying situation

Like end consumers, business buyers spend more time and effort on some purchases than on others. Devoting such effort to a purchase decision usually depends on the complexity of the product and how often the decision has to be made. A **buy class** framework identifies the degree of effort required by the firm's personnel to collect information and make a purchase decision. These classes, which apply to three different buying situations, are called straight re-buys, modified re-buys and new-task buys.

Straight re-buy

A **straight re-buy** is the routine purchase of items that a business-to-business customer regularly needs. The buyer has purchased the same items many times before and routinely reorders them when supplies are low, often from the same suppliers. Reordering takes little time. Buyers typically maintain a list of approved suppliers that have demonstrated their ability to meet the firm's criteria for pricing, quality, service and delivery. Such products could include paper or stationery.

Because straight re-buys often contribute the 'bread and butter' revenue a firm needs to maintain a steady stream of income, many business marketers go to great lengths to cultivate and maintain relationships with customers who submit reorders on a regular basis. Salespeople regularly call on these customers to handle orders personally and to see if there are additional products the customer needs. The goal is to be sure that the customer doesn't even think twice about just buying the same product every time he or she is running low. Re-buys keep a supplier's sales volume up and selling costs down.

Modified re-buy

Life would be sweet for companies whose customers automatically do straight re-buys. Unfortunately, these situations do not last forever. A **modified re-buy** occurs when a firm wants to shop around for suppliers with better prices, quality or delivery times. This situation also can occur when the organisation has new needs for products it already buys. A buyer who has purchased many office printers in the past, for example, may have to evaluate several lines of printers if the firm has a new need for office equipment.

Modified re-buys require more time and effort than straight re-buys. The buyer generally knows the purchase requirements and a few potential suppliers. Marketers know that modified re-buys can mean that some vendors get added to a buyer's approved supplier list while others may be dropped. Astute marketers routinely call on buyers to detect and define problems that can lead to winning or losing in such situations.

New-task buy

A first-time purchase is a **new-task buy**. Uncertainty and risk characterise buying decisions in this classification, and they need the most effort because the buyer has no previous experience on which to base a decision.

Your university, for example, may decide (if it hasn't done so already) to go into the 'distance learning' business, which is delivering courses to off-site students. Buying the equipment to set up classrooms with two-way video transmission is an expensive and complex new-task buy. The buyer has to start from scratch to gather information on purchase specifications that may be highly technical/complex and require detailed input from others. In new-task buying situations, not only do buyers lack experience with the product, but they also are often unfamiliar with firms that supply the product. Supplier choice is critical, and buyers gather much information about quality, pricing, delivery and service from several potential suppliers.

A prospective customer's new-task buying situation represents both a challenge and an opportunity. Although a new-task buy can be significant in itself, often the chosen supplier gains the added advantage of becoming an 'in' supplier for more routine purchases that will follow. A growing business that needs an advertising agency for the first time, for example, may seek exhaustive information from several firms before selecting one, but then it may continue to use the chosen agency's services for future projects without exploring other alternatives. We can see through 'Marketing metrics' how Dow Chemicals has invested in identifying ways of retaining business customers – trying to influence them to move towards a straight re-buy.

Marketers know that to get the order in a new-buy situation, they must develop a close working relationship with the business buyer. Keep in mind that these relationships aren't just important in sectors like industrial services. There are in fact many situations where marketers focus on selling their product or service through inspiring people to recommend their products – over and above the end consumers who actually buy them. To use an example, think about all of the products and services that make up the higher education

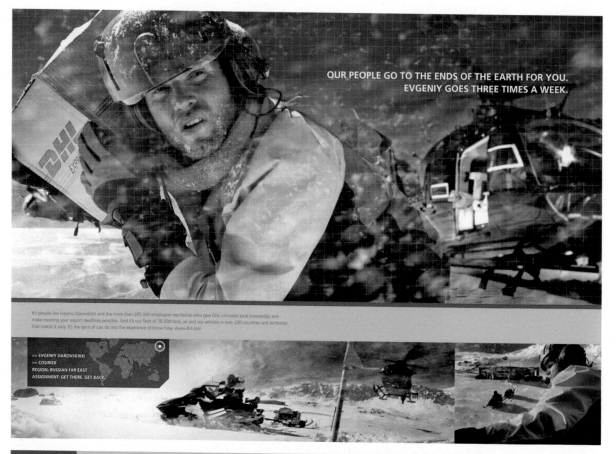

OUR PEOPLE GO TO THE ENDS OF THE EARTH FOR YOU.
EVGENIY GOES THREE TIMES A WEEK.

It's people like Evgeniy Darovskikh and the more than 285,000 employees worldwide who give DHL unrivaled local knowledge and make meeting your export deadlines possible. And it's our fleet of 76,000 land, air and sea vehicles in over 220 countries and territories that makes it easy. It's the spirit of can do and the experience of know how. www.dhl.com

\>\> EVGENIY DAROVSKIKH
\>\> COURIER
REGION: RUSSIAN FAR EAST
ASSIGNMENT: GET THERE. GET BACK.

| Photo 5.2 | DHL aims to appeal to its routine business customers and discourage them from 'shopping around' through providing more reach
Source: DHL |

industry. For instance, even though you are perhaps the one who paid the money for this textbook, your tutor was the one who made the wise decision to assign it. He or she may have made their choice only after carefully considering numerous textbooks and talking to several publishing sales representatives.

At the start of the chapter, you met Paul Baxter-Gibson of Lucore. He needs to figure out a strategy. Read the 'Real people, other voices' box to learn how other people advise Paul.

Marketing metrics

Dow Chemicals

Dow Chemicals is one of the world's biggest science and technology companies. It produces more than 3000 products at over 200 sites in 40 countries, and has over 40,000 industrial customers. Management wanted to know how to improve customer retention and commissioned a programme of surveys that involved more than 10,000 interviews. They used these to build a detailed quantitative picture of the factors driving loyalty and retention. Factors studied included flexible credit, invoice accuracy, price stability, on-time delivery, technical staff availability, wide range of products, and health and safety support. Using this data they have identified customer segments and their specific loyalty drivers. This is used to inform business unit strategy, marketing plans and also account plans for major accounts.

The professional buyer

Objective

5

Explain the roles
in the business
buying centre
(decision-
making unit)

Just as it is important for marketers of consumer goods and services to understand their customers, it is essential that business-to-business marketers understand who handles the buying for business customers. Trained professional buyers frequently carry out buying in business-to-business markets. These people typically have a title such as *purchasing manager*, *purchasing director* or *head of purchasing*.

While some consumers like to shop till they drop almost every day, most of us spend far less time roaming the aisles. However, professional purchasers do it all day, every day. These individuals focus on economic factors beyond the initial price of the product, including transportation and delivery charges, accessory products or supplies, maintenance and other costs. They are responsible for selecting quality products and ensuring their timely delivery. They shop as if their jobs depend on it – and they do.

 ## The buying centre or decision-making unit (DMU)

Often in business buying situations several people work together to reach a decision. Depending on what they need to purchase, these participants may be production workers, supervisors, engineers, secretaries, shipping clerks or financial controllers. In a small organisation, everyone may have a voice in the decision. The group of people in the organisation who participate in the decision-making process is referred to as the **buying centre**. Although this term may conjure up an image of offices buzzing with purchasing activity, a buying centre is not a place at all. Instead, it is a cross-functional team of decision makers. Generally, the members of a buying centre have some expertise or interest in the particular decision, and as a group they are able to make the best decision.

Real people, other voices

**Advice for
Paul Baxter-Gibson**

Zubin Sethna

Westminster Business School,
University of Westminster

This is a complex situation, and one in which there are many potential stakeholder views! From the very beginning I would recommend that Paul chooses Option 3. However, we know that companies rarely make proactive choices; rather [they] usually go through a process of elimination. So let's first of all look at why we should eliminate two of the options. Option 1 by its very nature of being a COTS product means that its use is totally generic and hence it competes with a plethora of similar products, all vying for business. There is absolutely no USP here whatsoever. Whilst the potential free training which comes with Option 2 could be a useful addition to 'complement the service offering', it once again is very generic and its applicability to a 'wide range of markets and uses' does nothing for Lucore to help differentiate C2S in the

healthcare sector. In addition, there is a very real issue of technological instability which is inherent with such open source products. Add to this the issues surrounding integration with and into existing systems and we have more problems than perhaps initially envisaged.

Therefore we are 'left with' Option 3; the option which I would have chosen from the outset. Developing a sepecialism is the key here. The way to do this is to engage with potential customers and to utilise their user-expertise to further develop a product which demonstrates C2S's commitment to working with the most technologically advanced tools in ensuring that their customers operate in accordance with the CQC's requirements. So the 'specialism and USP' revolves around a product which is the conduit for quality and compliance tasks, based on the CQC Standards of Quality, one which provides the methodology for reporting and one which is suitable for all roles and responsibilities. A solution which would most definitely give C2S ultimate control over their business offering, and position them as the leader in customised CQC IT software.

Hospitals, for example, frequently make purchase decisions through a large buying centre. When making a decision to purchase disposable oxygen masks, one or more doctors, the director of nursing and purchasing personnel may work together to determine quantities and select the best products and suppliers. A separate decision regarding the types of pharmaceutical supplies to stock might need a different group of employees to advise the purchasing manager. Marketers must continually identify which employees in a firm take part in every purchase and develop relationships with them all.

Depending on the complexity of the purchase and the size of the buying centre or decision-making unit, a participant may assume one, several, or all of the six roles (Figure 5.3).

- The *initiator* begins the buying process by first recognising that the firm needs to make a purchase. A production employee, for example, may notice that a piece of equipment is not working properly and notify a supervisor. At other times, the initiator may suggest purchasing a new product because it will improve the firm's operations. Depending on the initiator's position in the organisation and the type of purchase, the initiator may or may not influence the actual purchase decision. For marketers, it's important to make sure that individuals who might initiate a purchase are aware of improved products they offer.

- The *user* is the member of the buying centre who actually needs the product. The user's role in the decision-making unit varies. For example, an administrative assistant may give his input on the features needed in a new copier that he will be 'chained to' for several hours a day. Marketers need to inform users of their products' benefits, especially if the benefits outweigh those that competitors offer.

- The *gatekeeper* is the person who controls the flow of information to other members. Typically the gatekeeper is the purchasing agent who gathers information and materials from salespeople, schedules sales presentations and controls suppliers' access to other participants in the buying process. For salespeople, developing and maintaining strong personal relationships with gatekeepers is critical to being able to offer their products to the buying centre.

Role	Potential Player	Responsibility
• Initiator	• Production employees, sales manager, almost anyone	• Recognises that a purchase needs to be made
• User	• Production employees, secretaries, almost anyone	• Individual(s) who will ultimately use the product
• Gatekeeper	• Buyer/purchasing agent	• Controls flow of information to others in the organisation
• Influencer	• Engineers, quality control experts, technical specialists, outside consultants	• Affects decision by giving advice and sharing expertise
• Decider	• Purchasing agent, managers, chief executive	• Makes the final purchase decision
• Buyer	• Purchasing agent	• Executes the purchase decision

Figure 5.3   Roles in the buying centre (or DMU)

A buying centre is a group of individuals brought together for the purpose of making a purchasing decision. Marketers need to understand that the members of the DMU play a variety of roles in the process

- An *influencer* affects the buying decision by dispensing advice or sharing expertise. By virtue of their expertise, engineers, quality control specialists and other technical experts in the firm generally have a great deal of influence in purchasing equipment, materials and component parts used in production. The influencers may or may not end up using the product. Marketers need to identify key influencers in the DMU and work to persuade them of their product's superiority.

- The *decider* is the member of the buying centre who makes the final decision. This person usually has the greatest power within the decision-making unit. He or she often has power within the organisation to authorise spending the company's money. For a routine purchase, the decider may be the purchasing officer. If the purchase is complex, a manager, director or chief executive may be the decider. Quite obviously, the decider is key to a marketer's success and deserves a lot of attention in the selling process.

- The *buyer* is the person who has responsibility for executing the purchase. Although the buyer often has a role in identifying and evaluating alternative suppliers, this person's primary function is handling the details of the purchase. The buyer obtains competing bids, negotiates contracts, and arranges delivery dates and payment plans.

Internationalisation

Business in China

In building effective business-to-business relationships in China, Western firms are advised to nurture their business relationships with a range of influential parties and these include local partners, top-level executives in local firms and government officials. Local partners are suggested as one of the most important targets for good relationship connections (*guanxi*). Building good *guanxi* with locals can also help foreign firms obtain more precise and up-to-date information regularly and efficiently. This will help increase a foreign firm's understanding of local market conditions and provide better access to local channels and overcome some of the constraints associated with conducting business in a Chinese context (language, dialect, customs, norms and values).

Top executives from local firms should also be targeted for foreign firms to establish *guanxi* with. Such parties can often be instrumental for initiating contacts with other local firms, and establishing personal friendship. Through nurturing such links, foreign businesses are more likely to obtain preferential treatment, which can smooth out transactions, lower costs and improve performance. In addition to developing relations with local partners and business executives, government officials should also be targets for good relationship building. This is because Chinese governmental officials often have influential power that can help in terms of resource allocation and legislative decisions. However, foreign firms should bear in mind that establishing contact and maintaining good *guanxi* with such officials requires significant investment. Using local parties and intermediaries to establish *guanxi* with government officials is therefore a useful approach for tackling the market. Whilst government officials are considered an important key target for such firms, establishing good *guanxi* with appropriate personnel may often take years to develop.

Discuss, debate, disagree

1 Why is it important for Western firms to develop relationships when attempting to do business in a Chinese context?

2 Who are the key relationship parties in China and do you think this is likely to change in the future?

3 What are the key implications for Western firms wishing to develop *guanxi* in a Chinese context?

Source: Based on Dorothy Ai-Wan Yen, Bradley R. Barnes and Cheng Lu Wang, 'The Chinese Notion of Guanxi' in *Handbook of Contemporary Marketing in China*, ed. Cheng Lu Wang (New York: NovaScience Publishers, 2011)

Once a firm makes the purchase decision, marketers turn their attention to negotiating the details of the purchase with the buyer. Successful marketers are well aware that providing exemplary service in this stage of the purchase can be key to future sales.

 # The business buying decision process

www.pearsoned.co.uk/Solomon

Objective

6

Understand the stages in the business buying decision process

We've seen there are several players in the business buying process, beginning with an initiator and ending with a buyer. To make matters even more challenging to marketers, members of the buying team go through several stages in the decision-making process. The business buying decision process, as Figure 5.4 shows, is a series of steps similar to those in the consumer decision process. To help understand these steps, let's say you've just started working at the 'Big Skateboard Company' and you've been assigned to be in the buying centre for the purchase of new web page design computer software (a new-task buy) for your firm.

Step 1: Problem recognition

As in consumer buying, the first step in the business buying decision process occurs when someone sees that a purchase can solve a problem. For straight re-buy purchases, this step may result because the firm has run out of paper, pens or bin bags. In these cases, the

Step 1: Problem Recognition
- Purchase requisition or request made
- Buying centre formed if needed

Step 2: Information Search
- Product specifications developed
- Potential suppliers identified
- Proposals and quotations obtained

Step 3: Evaluation of Options
- Proposals evaluated
- Samples obtained and evaluated

Step 4: Product and Supplier Selection
- Purchase order issued

Step 5: Post–purchase Evaluation
- Users surveyed
- Performance documented

Figure 5.4 Steps in the business buying process

The steps in the business buying decision process are the same as those in the consumer decision process. But for business purchases, each step may be far more complex and require more attention from marketers buyer places the order, and the decision-making process ends. Recognition of the need for modified re-buy purchases often comes from wanting to replace outdated equipment, from changes in technology, or from an ad, brochure or some other marketing communication that offers the customer a better product or one at a lower price. Two events may occur in the problem recognition step. First, a firm makes a request or requisition, usually in writing. Depending on the complexity of the purchase, the firm may form a DMU.

The need for new-task purchases often occurs because the firm wants to enhance its operations in some way, or when a smart salesperson tells the business customer about a new product that will increase the efficiency of the firm's operations or improve the firm's end products. In the case of Big Skateboard's new software purchase, your marketing department has previously had its web page designed and maintained by an outside agency. The company has become dissatisfied with the outside supplier and has decided to move the design function in-house. Now the company needs new software to create a website.

Step 2: Information search

In the second step of the decision process (for purchases other than straight re-buys) the buying centre searches for information about products and suppliers. Members of the DMU may individually or collectively refer to reports in trade magazines and journals, seek advice from outside consultants, and pay close attention to marketing communications from different manufacturers and suppliers. As in consumer marketing, it's the job of marketers to make sure that information is available when and where business customers want it. This can be achieved by placing ads in trade magazines, through mailing out brochures and other printed material to prospects, and via having a well-trained, enthusiastic sales force regularly call on customers. For Big Skateboard's purchase, you may try to find out what software your outside supplier has been using (if the supplier will tell you), talk to the information technology experts in your firm or review ads and articles in trade magazines.

There are thousands of specialised publications out there that cater for just about any industry you can think of, and each is bursting with information from competing companies that cater to a specific niche.

Developing product specifications Business buyers often develop **product specifications**. That is a written description of the quality, size, weight, colour, features, quantity, training, warranty, service terms and delivery requirements for the purchase. When the product needs are complex or technical, engineers and other experts are the key players in identifying specific product characteristics and determining whether standard off-the-shelf or customised made-to-order goods and services are needed. Although there is excellent web design software available, for some computer applications custom-designed software is necessary.

Identifying potential suppliers and obtaining proposals Once the product specifications are in hand, the next step may be to identify potential suppliers and obtain written or verbal proposals, or bids, from one or more of them. For standardised or branded products in which there are few if any differences in the products of different suppliers, this may be as simple as an informal request for pricing information, including discounts, shipping charges and confirmation of delivery dates. At other times, the potential suppliers will receive a formal written request for a proposal, or ask for a quotation that requires specific detail such as price and terms for supplying the product. For the Big Skateboard's software, which is likely to be a standardised package, you would probably just ask for general pricing information.

Step 3: Evaluation of options

At this stage of the business decision process, the DMU assesses the proposals. Total spending for goods and services can have a major impact on the firm's profitability, so all other things being equal, price is the primary consideration. Pricing evaluations must take into account discount policies for certain quantities, returned-goods policies, the cost of repair and maintenance services, terms of payment and the cost of financing large purchases. For capital equipment – such as large machinery, cost criteria can also include the life expectancy of the purchase, the expected re-sale value, as well as the disposal costs. In some cases, the buying centre may negotiate with the preferred supplier to match the lowest bidder.

Although a firm often selects a bidder because it offers the lowest price, there are times when the buying decision is based on other factors, and these may be related to a number of factors including reputation, quality, previous experience, history or even environmental concerns, as explained in 'Marketing ethics and sustainability'. See how Marks & Spencer has been inspired to consider 'green' issues.

The more complex and costly the purchase, the more time buyers will spend searching for the best supplier (and the more marketers must try to win the order). In some cases, a company may even ask one or more of its current customers to participate in a *reference programme* where they recommend products to others. For example, Siebel Systems once asked over 350 corporate buyers of its computer systems to explain to new prospects how

| Photo 5.3 | You don't see too many everyday consumers driving Volvo trucks, but plenty of manufacturers and retailers buy them
Source: Courtesy of Volvo Car Corporation |

their system worked and why they chose Siebel's products. The payoff for customers was that they could network with other existing customers to gain insights about how to use the company's products. As a Siebel executive observes, customers become heroes – and by involving them in speaking engagements and articles in trade magazines, a real win–win scenario is evident for everyone.[2]

Marketers often make formal presentations and product demonstrations to the DMU. In the case of installations and large equipment, marketers sometimes arrange for buyers to speak to or even visit other customers to examine how the product performs. For less complex products, the buying firm may ask potential suppliers for samples of the products to evaluate alternatives. For the Big Skateboard Company website, your buying centre may ask salespeople from various companies to demonstrate their software for your group, so that you can compare the capabilities of different products.

Step 4: Product and supplier selection

Once buyers have assessed all proposals, the next step in the buying process is the purchase decision, that is the selection of the best product and supplier to meet the firm's needs. Reliability and durability rank especially high for equipment and systems that keep the firm's operations running smoothly without interruption. For some purchases, warranties, repair service and regular maintenance after the sale are important. For the Big Skateboard Company, the final decision may be based not only on the capabilities of the software itself, but also on the technical support provided by the software company. What kind of support is available and at what cost to the company?

One of the most important decisions of a buyer is how many suppliers can best serve the firm's needs. Sometimes a single supplier is more beneficial to the organisation than having several suppliers. **Single sourcing** occurs when a buyer and seller work quite closely together. It is particularly important when a firm needs frequent deliveries or specialised products. However, reliance on a single source means that the firm is at the mercy of the chosen supplier to deliver the needed goods or services without interruption.

In contrast, **multiple sourcing** means buying a product from several different suppliers. Under this system, suppliers are more likely to remain price competitive. If one supplier has problems with delivery, the firm has others to fall back on. However, using one or a

Marketing ethics and sustainability

Many GreenPac Products Hangon the Selves [sic] of Top Retailers

It takes a lot of bottle to do what Simon Lee has achieved. Four years ago, he quit his job at a leading packaging supplier and bet everything he had to create a business to pioneer innovative recycling products. In 2007 he convinced Marks & Spencer to manufacture some of its range of fleeces in Greenspun, a fabric made from 100 per cent recycled plastic bottles. One of the biggest problems has been finding products that can be commercialised. 'We have seen some fantastic environmental innovations. Some of it is not fit for purpose. Some is not right for the market.' Making sure that the product meets environmental standards and does not have any unethical skeletons in the closet is crucial.

Source: Adapted from Many GreenPac products hang on the selves of top retailers by Jonathan Moules, *Financial Times* (London), 12 May 2007. © The Financial Times Limited 2007. All Rights Reserved.

Debate, discuss, disagree

1 What would you suggest for GreenPac to maximise its profits without having to change its company philosophy?

few suppliers rather than many has its advantages. A firm that buys from a single supplier becomes a large customer with a lot of clout when it comes to negotiating prices and contract terms. Having one or a few suppliers also lowers the firm's administrative costs because it has fewer invoices to pay, fewer contracts to negotiate and fewer salespeople to see than if it used many sources. Many large organisations work with a number of preferred suppliers for certain goods. For example, companies use preferred suppliers when purchasing IT products and solutions or business travel. For the marketer, this often presents a challenge, as becoming a preferred supplier may pose many difficulties. Obtaining approval can be a long-drawn-out process and may involve careful scrutiny by the decision-making unit. However, once approval has been granted, business can often evolve as in a straight re-buy situation. Many hospitals are now moving towards single sourcing where possible. Historically, hospital buyers have had to negotiate with hundreds of suppliers for a vast range of products from disposable gloves to surgical implants. Some hospitals have more recently tried to reduce their supplier lists by only working with specific suppliers that can provide a diverse range of items.

Sometimes supplier selection is based on *reciprocity*, which means that a buyer and seller agree to be each other's customers by saying essentially, 'I'll buy from you, and you buy from me'. For example, a firm that supplies mechanical component parts to a company that manufactures vans would agree to buy their fleet vans only from that company.

Reciprocal agreements between firms often limit the effect of free market competition. New suppliers simply don't have a chance against the preferred suppliers. In certain less developed countries, reciprocity or countertrade is a practice that is common and even expected in business-to-business marketing.

Outsourcing occurs when firms obtain outside suppliers to provide goods or services that might otherwise be supplied in-house. Outsourcing is an increasingly popular strategy, but also a controversial one. Many critics object when companies contract with firms or individuals in remote places like China or India to perform work that used to be done at home. These tasks range from complicated jobs like writing computer code to fairly simple ones like manning reservation desks and call centres for telephone sales. Controversy aside, many companies are finding that it may be both cost-efficient and productive to call upon outsiders from around the world to provide such assistance. However, they must ensure that service is not compromised by moving their operations to less developed economies. The experience gained is now leading some companies to reconsider their initial strategies.

Yet another type of buyer–seller partnership is **reverse marketing**. Instead of sellers trying to identify potential customers and then 'pitching' for business, buyers try to find suppliers capable of producing specific needed products and then attempt to 'sell' the idea to the suppliers. The seller aims to satisfy the buying firm's needs. Through advertising in well regarded international trade directories, like *Kompass*, European companies have been able to receive unsolicited business orders from buyers as far away as Saudi Arabia that are keen to acquire supply of a European standard.

Step 5: Post-purchase evaluation

Just as consumers evaluate purchases, an organisational buyer assesses whether the performance of the product and the supplier is living up to expectations. The buyer surveys users to determine their satisfaction with the product as well as the installation, delivery and service provided by the supplier. For producers of goods, this may relate to the level of satisfaction of the final consumer of the buying firm's product. Has demand for the manufacturer's product increased, decreased or stayed the same? By documenting and reviewing supplier performance, a firm decides whether to keep or drop the supplier. Many

Across the hall

Shane Redding

is founder of Think Direct Ltd, experts in business-to-business marketing and Chair of the Institute of Direct Marketing's B2B Council

This is a clear case where Lucore needs to decide what business it is in, not just now but to develop a successful strategy to secure future profitable growth. Option 1 allows the business to sweat its existing asset of off-the-shelf-IT packages, selling through C2S; Option 2 doesn't create software IP, but instead leverages the expertise of the new partnership to build a revenue stream around implementation and consultancy; and Option 3 requires a longer term commitment to an untested market with a new system.

If you apply the Ansoff model, Option 3 is the most risky for Lucore and unless the business is confident that there is sufficient market demand from the healthcare sector for bespoke software, this is not an option that I would recommend Paul pursues. Option 1, whilst attractive if Lucore is confident of alternative growth sources, is unlikely to deliver longer term benefits.

Instead, with the pressure on organisations supplying the NHS to move towards open source systems as a way of both controlling costs and ensuring more competition from vendors, this would seem an appropriate time to diversify into these tools. The USP that Lucore can build on is the adaptation of open source software for the specialist requirements to complete CQC assessments. The partnership with C2S will allow more focus on selling 'add-ons', including potentially profitable training alongside the consultancy and business change processes, which in turn could lead to more software module development for Lucore.

suppliers recognise the importance of conducting their own performance reviews on a regular basis. Measuring up to a customer's expectations can mean winning or losing a big account. Many a supplier has lost business because of a past history of late deliveries or poor equipment repairs and maintenance.

Business-to-business e-commerce

Objective

7

Understand the growing role of B2B e-commerce

The internet has brought about massive changes in marketing, from the creation of new products to providing more effective and efficient marketing communications, as well as assisting with the actual distribution of certain products. This is particularly true in business markets. **Business-to-business (B2B) e-commerce** refers to an online exchange between two or more businesses or organisations. B2B e-commerce includes the exchange of information, products, services and payment. It's not as flashy as consumer e-commerce, but it has changed the way businesses operate. Multinational enterprises are now saving significant amounts through obtaining supplies over the internet. For sellers, e-commerce also provides remarkable advantages. Boeing, for example, received orders worth over €100 million in spare parts in the first year that its website was established.[3]

Using e-commerce allows business marketers to link directly with suppliers, factories, distributors and their customers. It radically reduces the time necessary to order and deliver goods, track sales and obtain customer feedback.

In the simplest form of B2B e-commerce, the internet provides an online catalogue of products and services that businesses need. Companies find that their website is important for delivering online technical support, product information order status information and customer service to corporate customers. Many companies, for example, save thousands of euros equivalent a year by replacing hard-copy manuals with electronic downloads.

As with the growth of social network sites such as Facebook and LinkedIn, many businesses have experienced success through the growth of online networking in business markets. Sites such as Alibaba.com provide a comprehensive range linking industrial suppliers to business customers and others such as ConnectBuzz and bizmeed provide the opportunity for businesses to network with one another. Even the Round Table has developed a site to encourage online networking (www.roundtable.co.uk). As social media continues to expand in consumer markets, it will become more prevalent in business markets with time.

Intranets, extranets and private exchanges

Although the internet is the primary means of B2B e-commerce, many companies maintain intranets, which provide a more secure means for conducting business. The *intranet* is an internal corporate computer network that uses internet technology to link company departments, employees and databases. Intranets give access only to authorised employees. They allow companies to process internal transactions with greater control and consistency because of stricter security measures than those they can use on the entire web. Businesses also use intranets for video-conferencing, distributing internal documents, communicating with geographically dispersed branches and training employees.

In contrast to an intranet, an **extranet** allows certain suppliers, customers and others outside the organisation to access a company's internal system. A business customer that a company authorises to use its extranet can place orders online. Extranets can be especially useful for companies that need to have secure communications between the company and its channel members like dealers, distributors and/or franchisees.

Intranets and extranets can prove to be very cost efficient. Prudential Health Care's extranet allows its corporate customers to enrol new employees and check the eligibility and claim status themselves. This saves Prudential money because it can hire fewer customer service personnel. There are also no packages of insurance forms to mail back and forth, and Prudential doesn't even have to input policyholder data into the company database.[4]

In addition to saving companies money, extranets allow business partners to collaborate on projects (such as product design) and build relationships. Hewlett-Packard and Procter & Gamble swap marketing plans and review ad campaigns with their advertising agencies through extranets. They can exchange ideas quickly without having to spend money on travel and meetings.

Some of the most interesting online activity in the B2B world is taking place on **private exchanges**. These are systems that link a specially invited group of suppliers and partners over the web. A private exchange allows companies to collaborate with suppliers they trust – without sharing such sensitive information with others.

Security threats

There are several security threats related to B2B e-commerce. You may be concerned about someone obtaining your credit card number and charging even more to your account. However, companies have even greater worries. When hackers break into company sites, they can destroy company records and steal trade secrets. Both B2C and B2B e-commerce companies worry about *authentication* and ensuring that transactions are secure. This means making sure that only authorised individuals are allowed to access a site and place an order. Maintaining security also requires firms to keep the information transferred as part of a transaction, such as a credit card number, from criminals' hard drives.

Well-meaning employees also can create security problems. They can give out unauthorised access to company computer systems and be careless about keeping their passwords secret. For example, hackers can guess at obvious passwords, such as nicknames, birth dates, hobbies or a spouse's name. To increase security of their websites and transactions, most companies now have safeguards in place, firewalls and encryption devices, to name the two most common methods.

Firewalls

A *firewall* is a combination of hardware and software that ensures that only authorised individuals gain entry into a computer system. The firewall monitors and controls all traffic between the internet and the intranet to restrict access. Companies may even place additional firewalls within their intranet when they wish only designated employees to have access to certain parts of the system. Although firewalls can be fairly effective (even though none is foolproof), they require costly and constant monitoring.

Encryption

Encryption means scrambling a message so that only another individual (or computer) that has the right 'key' for deciphering it can unscramble it. Otherwise, the message is unreadable. The message is inaccessible without the appropriate encryption software. Without encryption, it would be easy for unethical people to get your credit card number by creating a 'sniffer' program that intercepts and reads messages. A sniffer finds messages with four blocks of four numbers, copies the data, and voilà – someone else has your credit card number. Even with basic encryption software, hackers have been able to steal thousands of credit card numbers from various online retailers.

Despite these and other measures, web security for B2B marketers remains a problem. The threat to intranet and extranet usage goes beyond competitive espionage. The increasing sophistication of hackers and internet criminals who create viruses, worms and other means for disrupting individual computers as well as entire company systems means that all organisations and consumers are vulnerable to attacks and need to remain vigilant.

Now that you've learned the basics of B2B commerce, read 'Real people, real choices' to see which strategy Paul decided upon.

Real people, real choices

How it worked out at Lucore

Paul and his colleagues went for Option 3, and encouraged Care2Standard to invest in the development of a new IT system that could better reflect the requirements of customers, regulatory bodies and C2S's strategic growth plans. Although initially this appeared to require the most time and largest resource investment to establish industry best practice software, Lucore's service team were still able to develop the solution quite quickly and efficiently. Once the system was available, it provided C2S with the opportunity to undertake comprehensive customer consultation and testing at an early stage, and enabled the organisation to further develop this software based on real time feedback from clients to identify concerns. The process helped C2S to build and strengthen existing relationships with its customer base, as it allowed the company to forge ongoing partnerships, gather customer views and use real testimonies to create case studies and fully integrate customers into the development process so as to build working relationships within the industry itself. Through end-user consultation, this provided the opportunity for C2S to stay in touch with customers and use their feedback to aid future developments. This in itself ensured value for money as C2S was able to assess future software investment based on customer feedback and demand. Through spending more time with C2S and conducting a full internal requirements audit, Paul was also able to utilise this relationship to improve the future of Lucore. He therefore developed a list of requirements to identify industry-wide generic requirements so that Lucore could look at providing similar solutions to others operating in the industry at large. This became a good starting point for servicing the healthcare industry and outlining the future strategic direction for the company entering a growing market.

Chapter summary

Now that you have finished reading this chapter, you should be able to answer any of the following potential examination questions:

1. **Describe the general characteristics of business-to-business markets.** Business-to-business markets include business or organisational customers that buy goods and services for purposes other than for personal consumption. Business customers are usually few in number, may be geographically concentrated and often purchase higher-priced products in larger quantities.

2. **Explain the unique characteristics of business demand.** Business demand is derived from the demand for another good or service. It is generally not affected by price increases or decreases, is subject to great fluctuations, and may be tied to the demand and availability of some other good.

3. **Describe how business or organisational markets are classified.** Business customers include producers, resellers, governments and not-for-profit organisations. Producers purchase materials, parts and various goods and services needed to produce other goods and services to be sold at a profit. Resellers purchase finished goods to resell at a profit as well as other goods and services to maintain their operations. Governments and other not-for-profit organisations purchase the goods and services necessary to fulfil their objectives. The Standard Industrial Classification (SIC) system provides a numerical coding system that is widely used in business and organisational markets.

4. **Explain the business buying situation and describe business buyers.** The business buy class identifies the degree and effort required to make a business buying decision. Purchase situations can be straight re-buy, modified re-buy and new-task buying. Business buying is usually handled by trained professional buyers.

5. **Explain the roles in the business buying centre.** A buying centre or DMU is a group of people who work together to make a buying decision. The roles in the DMU are (1) the initiator who recognises the need for a purchase, (2) the user who will ultimately use the product, (3) the gatekeeper who controls the flow of information to others, (4) the influencer who shares advice and expertise, (5) the decider who makes the final decision and (6) the buyer who executes the purchase.

6. **Explain the stages in the business buying decision process.** The stages in the business buying decision process are similar to, but more complex than, the steps in consumer decision making. These steps include problem recognition, information search during which buyers develop product specifications and obtain proposals from prospective sellers, evaluating the proposals, selecting a supplier and formally evaluating the performance of the product and the supplier. A firm's purchasing options include single or multiple sourcing. In outsourcing, firms obtain outside vendors to provide goods or services that otherwise might be supplied in-house. Other business buying activities include reciprocity and reverse marketing.

7. **Explain the growing role of B2B e-commerce.** Business-to-business (B2B) e-commerce refers to the online exchange of information, products, services or payments between two or more businesses or organisations and allows business marketers to link directly to suppliers, factories, distributors and their customers. An intranet is a secure internal corporate network used to link company departments, employees and databases. Extranets link a company with authorised suppliers, customers or others outside the organisation. Companies can address security issues by using firewalls and encryption.

Key terms

Chapter review

Marketing concepts: preparing for the examination and testing your knowledge

1. How do business-to-business markets differ from consumer markets? How do these differences affect marketing strategies?

2. Explain the unique characteristics of business demand.

3. How are business-to-business markets generally classified? What is the SIC system?

4. Describe new-task buys, modified re-buys and straight re-buys.

5. What are the characteristics of business buyers?

6. What is a buying centre or DMU? What are the roles of the various people in the DMU?

7. What are the stages in the business buying decision process? What happens in each stage?

8. How are the stages in the business buying decision process similar to the steps in the consumer buying process? How are they different?

9. What is single sourcing? Multiple sourcing? Outsourcing?

10. Explain how reciprocity and reverse marketing operate in business-to-business markets.

11. Explain the role of B2B e-commerce in today's marketplace.

Marketing concepts: discussing choices

1. E-commerce is dramatically changing the way business-to-business transactions take place. What are the advantages of B2B e-commerce to companies? To society? Are there any disadvantages of B2B e-commerce?

2. The practice of buying business products based on sealed competitive bids is popular among all types of business buyers. What are the advantages and disadvantages of this practice to buyers? What are the advantages and disadvantages to sellers? Should companies always give the business to the lowest bidder? Why or why not?

3. When firms implement a single sourcing policy in their buying, other possible suppliers do not have an opportunity. Is this ethical? What are the advantages to the company? What are the disadvantages?

4. Many critics of government say that strict engineering and other manufacturing requirements for products purchased by governments increase prices unreasonably and that taxpayers end up paying too much because of such policies. What are the advantages and disadvantages of such purchase restrictions? Should governments loosen restrictions on their purchases?

5. In the buying centre, the gatekeeper controls information flow to others in the centre. Thus, the gatekeeper determines which possible sellers are heard and which are not. Does the gatekeeper have too much power? What policies might be implemented to make sure that all possible sellers are treated fairly?

6. The chapter discussed how Siebel Systems operated a reference programme where previous purchasers of products were encouraged to discuss their experiences of a product with potential new customers. What are the advantages and disadvantages of such progress for companies like Siebel Systems? For previous customers? For prospective customers? For competitor firms?

7. Some critics complain that outsourcing sends much-needed jobs to competitors overseas while depriving our own national workers of these opportunities. Should a company consider this factor when deciding where to obtain raw materials or brainpower in order to compete efficiently?

Real people, real surfers

Exploring the web

Lucore isn't the only company that provides bespoke IT systems and services. Visit Lucore's website (www.lucore.com). Then explore the websites of one or more other similar business-to-business service providers.

On the basis of your experience, answer the following questions:

1. Who are Lucore's main competitors?

2. In general, how do the competitors' websites compare? Which are easier to navigate, and why? Which are more innovative and attractive, and why?

3. Evaluate each site from the perspective of a potential client. What feature in each site would be useful? What information is available that a manager might need? Overall, which site do you feel would be most useful to the manager? Why?

Now, take a look at the website at www.pearsoned.co.uk/solomon to see some videos from YouTube relating to aspects of this chapter.

Delve deeper into business-to-business marketing

Professor Peter Naudé

Deputy Dean of Manchester Business School

How you see business-to-business marketing really depends on where you start looking from. If you are a traditional marketing person, with a point of view that is heavily grounded in the early work of Kotler and many other North Americans, then marketing to you is what a company or a person (typically a brand manager working in a FMCG environment) does in order to win more customers. Marketing takes place in a company, and is essentially all about optimising a set of variables – the well-known 4Ps – in order to win customers. Customers, in this view, are rather anonymous things 'out there' with whom you have little direct contact (does Coke have a relationship with you?), and who decide whether to react positively or negatively to the 4Ps stimulus you have aimed at them. If this is your view of marketing, then your unit of analysis is the customer – that is what you have to try and understand.

But there are other views. For many of us working in the field of B2B marketing, we sometimes see a different reality. We see firms where just five or ten customers may account for 50 per cent or perhaps 80 per cent of their sales. We find empirical evidence for the on-going importance of these buyer–seller relationships, where relationships between companies often last for decades and where, crucially, there is a high level of mutual dependence between the companies. If this kind of environment reflects the reality that you see, then you need to think about marketing rather differently. For a start, facets such as the levels of commitment and trust between the two parties play a far more important role (hence the article by Morgan and Hunt). Crucially, in studying such markets, your unit of analysis may have to be the relationship itself, rather than the customer – here marketing is something that takes place between companies, rather than in the selling company alone. I leave it for you to

(continued on the next page)

think about whether such long-lasting interactions between two companies involve just products or perhaps services too, and hence to what extent the acclaimed article by Vargo and Lusch (see Academic Insights Chapter 9) does or does not represent a radically new idea in (B2B) marketing.

Sometimes, though, even this relationship-based view of marketing is insufficient. Any relationship between a buying and a selling organisation is embedded in a wider network, where what goes on between organisations A and B is often influenced by the interactions between other parties C and D – where they may be upstream suppliers, downstream customers, legal partners, consultants, lobby groups etc. In such cases your unit of analysis in order to understand 'the market' may need to be the network itself.

It is for this reason that I have included the papers by Anderson et al. and Turnbull et al. – they give some insights into these two other views of marketing. For those interested, you may find The Industrial Marketing and Purchasing Group's website (www.impgroup.org) to be of interest.

References

J.C. Anderson, H. Håkansson and J. Johanson (1994) 'Dyadic Business Relationships within a Business Network Context', *Journal of Marketing* 58, no. 4, 1–15.

R.M. Morgan and S.D. Hunt (1994) 'The Commitment–Trust Theory of Relationship Marketing', *Journal of Marketing* 58, no. 3, 20–38.

P. Turnbull, Ford, D., and Cunningham, M. (1996) 'Interaction, Relationships and Networks in Business Markets: An Evolving Perspective', *Journal of Business and Industrial Marketing* 11, no. 3/4, 44–62.

Marketing in Action Case

The Filter

How often do website recommendations work for the average customer? Yahoo.com offers advice as customers browse its music and video catalogue and suggests selections based on what other shoppers chose. In many cases, however, the connections it proposes aren't very helpful. Many businesses develop proprietary algorithms to make suggestions for their customers. However, others choose not to take on this task and outsource this activity to firms that specialise in recommendation engine technology. Recommendation engines apply the information collected from user activity to suggest other items for consumption. The type of items can range from music to television content, videos, books, news, web pages and so on. Operating in a business-to-business environment, the companies that develop recommendation engines have to carefully consider the specific needs of their diverse clients in order to be successful.

The Filter is a company that thinks it can do a better job for those companies that need this type of functionality,

like Yahoo.com. Doug Merrill, current director and a former chief information officer at Google, says, 'Recommendations from friends, from newspapers, from colleagues are the most common way to find new content. However, there is more information available than there are people to recommend. The Filter analyses data to provide measurably better, more relevant recommendations, automatically.'

Based in Bath, UK, The Filter is a privately held company that provides recommendation technology for various companies on the web. Its founder is Martin Hopkins, a physicist who is also a passionate music fan. In 2004, he started The Filter due to his own frustration as he tried to keep track of his digital music collection of over 10,000 tracks. Hopkins developed an algorithm using artificial intelligence that learned his likes and dislikes and then suggested playlists. This software would later become the foundation for the decision-making procedure that controls The Filter's recommendation engine. The Filter's client list includes firms such as Sony Music, Nokia and Comcast. In 2010, The Filter entered into a deal with Dailymotion, a website of over 66 million monthly users, to make video-to-video recommendations.

During the trial and optimisation period, the company's software captured over 5 billion video views and delivered over 1 billion recommendations. Just as Netflix uses its extensive database of customers' posted opinions to help locate movies they might not have thought of on their own, The Filter guides customers toward music and video choices that are not obvious. One of the program's advantages over other recommendation engines is that it only deals with digital media that can be tracked after a customer actually purchases a song online. This advantage allows The Filter to monitor post-purchase consumption behaviour. For instance, some customers only listen to or watch parts of the media they download, so this behaviour may signal

that the customer is not truly interested in all the material he or she purchased. This type of knowledge could make a significant difference in what the software recommends the next time the user accesses the system.

Initially The Filter aimed its services at individual consumers; however, it did not win enough business to be profitable. As a result, the company shifted direction to a business-to-business environment and began to promote its recommendation engine to media firms, which utilised the service to make recommendations for visitors at their websites. The pressure is on to prove that its recommendation algorithms do provide the kind of improvements it claims. The ultimate goal for The Filter is to market its service to companies in industries other than media, entertainment and technology. The firm has to define its long-term strategy and find ways to ensure profitability well into the future.

Things to consider

1. What is the decision facing The Filter?
2. What factors are important in understanding this decision situation?
3. What are the alternatives?
4. What decision(s) do you recommend?
5. What are some ways to implement your recommendation?

Sources: Devin Leonard, 'Tech Entrepreneur Peter Gabriel Knows What You Want', *Bloomberg Businessweek*, 8 April 2010, www.businessweek.com/magazine/content/10_16/b4174046688330.htm; The Filter, Wikipedia, http://en.wikipedia.org/wiki/The Filter (accessed 22 June 2010); Rachel Carr and Arielle Himy, 'The Filter Recommendation Engine Launched on Dailymotion to Further Boost User Engagement', *Marketwire*, 2 March 2010, www.marketwire.com/press-release/Filter-Recommendation-Engine-Launched-on-Dailymotion-Further-Boost-User-Engagement-1124739.htm; Erick Schonfeld, 'The Filter Reboots as Recommendation Engine for Hire, Ex-Googler Doug Merrill Joins Board', *TechCrunch*, 8 February 2010, http://techcrunch.com/2010/02/08/the-filterreboots-doug-merrill/.

References

1. F. Robert Dwyer and John F. Tanner, *Business Marketing: Connecting Strategy, Relationships, and Learning* (Boston, MA: McGraw-Hill, 2005); Edward F. Fern and James R. Brown, 'The Industrial/Consumer Marketing Dichotomy: A Case of Insufficient Justification', *Journal of Marketing* (Spring 1984), 68–77.
2. Catherine Arnold, 'Reference Programs Keep B-to-B Customers Satisfied', *Marketing News*, 18 August 2003, 4.
3. Faye W. Gilbert, Joyce A. Young and Charles R. O'Neal, 'Buyer–Seller Relationships in Just-in-Time Purchasing Environments', *Journal of Organizational Research*, 29 February 1994, 111–20.
4. Andy Reinhardt, 'Log On, Link Up, Save Big', *Business Week*, 22 June 1998, 132–8.

Chapter 6
Segmentation, targeting, positioning and CRM

Meet Jochen Barth
A decision maker
at &samhoud

Q & A with Jochen Barth

First job out of school?
Tutor at Maastricht University

Career high?
Young investigator award from the American Psychological Association

Business book I'm reading now
Delivering Happiness by Tony Hsieh

My hero
Charles Darwin

My pet peeve
Slow driving

Favourite TV programme?
'Top Gear'

Holiday resort?
Ishigaki-jima, Japan

Hobby?
Playing drums in a heavy metal band

Drink?
Beer

Food?
Anything my wife cooks

Jochen Barth holds the position of organisational assessment consultant at &samhoud, where he has worked for five years. Before joining &samhoud Jochen spent several years of working in academia. First as a research assistant and PhD student at the Max Planck Institute for Evolutionary Anthropology in Leipzig, Germany and later as a post-doc at the University of Louisiana at Lafayette. Having studied for his first degree in Psychology at Maastricht University, he received his PhD in 2005 from the same university. He was appointed to the post at &samhoud in 2006, where he currently holds responsibility for the company's organisational assessment activities together with three other colleagues. Specifically, Jochen's remit is to advise clients and consultants at &samhoud regarding all aspects of organisational assessment in the areas of employee and customer attitudes, organisational culture and development, and multisource feedback. Jochen has worked with over 50 organisations spanning all sectors, SMEs as well as multinationals. Jochen has extensive experience as project manager of large-scale research projects and makes a vast contribution to knowledge development at &samhoud on a diversity of topics.

Jochen has an active interest in academic developments and is also a visiting fellow at the Institute of Work Psychology (IWP), University of Sheffield. He currently lives in Maastricht in the Netherlands, with his wife Sanae Okamoto-Barth, who is an assistant professor in neuroeconomics at Maastricht University.

Real people, real decisions
Decision time at &samhoud

n 2009 &samhoud celebrated its twentieth year in business. The company's headquarters are in Utrecht, the Netherlands and in total &samhoud employs over 160 full-time staff in Europe and Asia. The history of the company dates back to 1989 when Salem Samhoud came into contact again with a former student friend, Kees Arends. The pair was a little disillusioned with their current work life experiences. Salem was almost bankrupt after struggling to establish two medical centres and Kees had lost confidence in the product market that he was working in.

As a result, the two joined forces to establish a business in the service sector. Armed only with a video camera, Salem and Kees thought that it would be a good idea to film the driver of a bus company as he rudely interacted with passengers. When the video evidence was presented to management of the transport company, they were startled with what they saw. They instantly offered Salem and Kees their first ever business contract and subsequently Arends & Samhoud Dienstenmarketing was established. This first contract proved decisive for Salem and Kees as it provided the two budding entrepreneurs with an opportunity to establish their name as a service consulting business to the public transportation sector. It became a springboard for further business and in the future lucrative projects emerged with Schiphol Airport (Amsterdam) and several other transportation companies. This led the company to expand and lease office facilities approximately 40 kilometres south of Amsterdam in a city called Utrecht. By 1995 the company was regularly in the national press through being innovative in terms of its workplace dynamics and was renowned for its excellence with employees.

During 1998, Kees and Salem decided to part company and go their own separate ways. With the departure of his co-founder, Salem rather pragmatically decided to rename the company &samhoud. The '&' representing major stakeholders in the company i.e., clients, employees and suppliers, thus placing them before the company's name, to epitomise Salem's beliefs of how the company should be positioned. Following this restructure, Salem had intentions to grow the business further and expand into other international markets including Germany, the US, Sweden and Spain.

Despite early promise in these markets, Salem probably bit off more than he could chew and for various reasons all the international offices later closed, except for the Spanish office. The next couple of years saw the company consolidate, with Salem deciding to re-focus on the business's core competency. Several divisions were therefore merged and others were closed, as Salem had aspirations to focus the company on its mission to create breakthroughs by inspiring and connecting people. From 2006 &samhoud focused more and more on vision creation. From 2008 onwards the company experienced significant growth, in terms of sales, staff employed and bottom-line financial profitability. In 2010 &samhoud was awarded first place in Europe on the 'Great Place to Work' list after having won first place already three consecutive times in the Netherlands. Additionally &samhoud was named Employer of the Year by the European Business Awards 2010 in London.

Having made it through a difficult consolidation stage of the company's evolvement, &samhoud was also discussing the future of the firm's information provision and consultancy. Founded in 2000 by &samhoud employees, the 'tools' devision of &samhoud had been a separate company for seven years and built up a solid annual revenue of about half a million euros by serving a highly diverse client portfolio. Most clients were returning clients who measured employee or customer satisfaction on an annual basis. However, due to an unclear growth strategy and several changes in personnel, annual revenue was not increasing but stayed around half a million euros. In 2006 discussions emerged in the company whether to sell the tools section of the company or integrate it into &samhoud consulting. The decision was made to integrate tools into &samhoud, because the synergy and cross-selling opportunities from tools to consulting seemed to have enormous potential. However, the choice to brand the tools division as &samhoud tools created new problems. After all, &samhoud's higher goal is 'Achieving breakthroughs by inspiring and connecting people'. The consultancy part of the company lived up to this promise, facilitating large change projects, often spanning several years, in major organisations, mostly financial services and government. Tools, on the other hand, had become a service provider for delivering survey reports to a very broad range of businesses ranging from small family businesses to multinational enterprises. For tools, in most cases the end result delivered to the client was a collection of reports. For &samhoud, on the other hand, the end result was a lasting culture change and organisational transformation. When the decision was made to integrate the separate tools company into the &samhoud consultancy firm, Jochen and his team now had to serve clients with two different profiles i.e., those that received pure reports (tools-only) and clients that were seeking 'a breakthrough'. It became apparent that the expectations and value propositions of tools and consulting were difficult to combine. The synergy and cross-selling opportunities that seemed a no-brainer proved to be extremely difficult in practice. The tools team rarely succeeded in scaling up tools projects to larger consulting projects, partially because their clients were not at the strategic decision level. Clients were mostly coming from HR and marketing departments, rarely from board level; in contrast, consultants rarely sold tools in their projects, because they were focused on consulting. Clearly, a change was needed and yet again a decision had to be made about the strategy that &samhoud wanted to follow with the integration of its tools services. The tools team came up with three different scenarios, each with a different market and target segment.

Jochen considers his options . . .

Option 1 Tools-only: Segment on organisational size, then target small and medium sized enterprises (SMEs) and provide them with organisational assessment services

The existing client base of returning customers provides a solid revenue that may only need the right marketing strategy to finally grow revenue over the half a million euros mark. After all, &samhoud had carved out a niche in servicing this market segment. Revenue could be maximised through increasing automation and efficiency. Instead of providing in-depth, highly customised consulting services, the company had started and been successful in providing SMEs with a range of 'off the shelf' company reports. SMEs could afford to purchase several of these reports annually. This represented a good option for the company to pursue, as relatively fewer competitors were operating in this segment and &samhoud had acquired a 'unique selling proposition' of providing reports and being able to follow up with consulting if desired by the client.

Option 2 Consulting only: Segment on organisational size, then target only large business-to-business markets, like multinational enterprises, key financial service providers and public sector providers

The advantage of this option is that Jochen can align the tools with the core business of &samhoud and provide services to a relatively smaller number of high fee paying consulting clients. Rather than trying to follow up tools projects with consulting, tools would become (and only be sold) as part of consulting projects. The main disadvantage is that this choice would mean that a lot of the current (satisfied) clients did not fit with this strategy and needed to be dropped, resulting in an immediate revenue loss of several thousand euros. Also dropping clients is not in line with the strong relationship that &samhoud wants to establish with clients (one of the core values of the company is 'friendship'). This segmentation could also mean missing out on a lot of business opportunities by closing the door for interested potential clients. Also sales responsibility would entirely depend on consultants not the tools team.

Option 3 Both tools-only and consulting: Segment on organisational size, then target both SMEs and large business-to-business markets. This would imply combining Options 1 and 2 to provide service propositions to cater for these two segments

Staying with the same strategy seemed attractive at first. Keeping the target group open would mean business opportunities at large and being able to tap into a diverse population of potential clients. Cross-selling opportunities clearly existed but had not worked well in the past. Also, this strategy does not move the business away from the company's current position of basically providing a service for everyone. The different expectations between tools and consulting clients conflicts with developing a clear value proposition. Whilst staying put may be an option, Jochen was not so sure that this would reflect well on what &samhoud wanted to achieve. Second, from a resource perspective, &samhoud as a company was known for its 'usual unusual' consulting service and increasing automation did not fit with the services consulting provided. Thus, through continuing to service all businesses in a similar vein, the company was evidently 'stuck in the middle' which may be a recipe for disaster.

Now, put yourself in Jochen's shoes: which option would you choose, and why?

Objectives

When you finish reading this chapter, you will be able to:

1 Understand the need for market segmentation in today's business environment

2 Know the different dimensions that marketers use to segment consumer and business-to-business markets

3 Show how marketers evaluate and select potential market segments

4 Explain how marketers develop a targeting strategy

5 Understand how a firm develops and implements a positioning strategy

6 Explain how marketers increase long-term success and profits by practising customer relationship management

Target marketing strategy: selecting and entering a market

Objective

1

Understand the need for market segmentation in today's business environment

By now, we've heard over and over again that the goal of the marketer is to create value, build customer relationships and satisfy needs. In our modern, complex society, it is naive to assume that everyone's needs are the same. Understanding people's needs is an even more complex task today because technological and cultural advances in modern society have created a condition of **market fragmentation**. This condition occurs when people's diverse interests and backgrounds divide them into numerous different groups with distinct needs and wants. Due to this diversity, the same good or service will not appeal to everyone.

Consider, for example, the effects of fragmentation in the health and fitness industry. Back in the 1960s, dieting was simple. Pritikin was a best-selling weight loss system emphasising very low fat and high fibre, and health-conscious consumers thought that this combination would surely yield a lean body and good health. Today's consumers, however, have a wide range of diets from which to choose. There's Weight Watchers, Slim Fast and the Atkins diet, to name a few, and dozens of herbal remedies for people with weight problems. Calories, fat, carbohydrates or all of the above – which to cut? The fact is that people have different requirements.

Marketers must balance the efficiency of mass marketing, serving the same items to everyone, with the effectiveness of offering each individual exactly what he or she wants. Mass marketing is certainly the most efficient plan. It costs much less to offer one product to everyone because that strategy eliminates the need for separate advertising campaigns and distinctive packages for each item. However, consumers see things differently; from their perspective, the best strategy would be to offer the perfect product for each individual. Unfortunately, that's often not realistic.

Instead of trying to sell something to everyone, marketers select a **target marketing strategy** in which they divide the total market into different segments based on customer characteristics, select one or more segments, and develop products to meet the needs of those specific segments. Figure 6.1 illustrates the three-step process of segmentation, targeting and positioning, and it's what we will build on in this chapter. Let's start with the first step – segmentation.

Step 1: Segmentation

www.pearsoned.co.uk/solomon

Segmentation is the process of dividing a larger market into smaller pieces based on one or more meaningful, shared characteristics. Segmentation is a way of life for marketers. The truth is that you can't please everyone all the time, so you need to do your best. How do marketers segment a population? How do they divide the whole pie into smaller

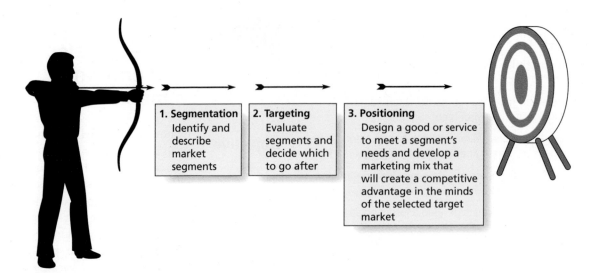

Figure 6.1	Steps in the target-marketing process
	Target marketing strategy consists of three separate steps. Marketers first divide the market into meaningful segments, then select segments, and finally design a unique marketing mix for each segment

slices they can 'digest'? Segmenting the market is often necessary in both consumer and business-to-business markets. In each case, the marketer must decide on one or more useful **segmentation variables**. These represent dimensions that divide the total market into fairly homogeneous groups, each with different needs and preferences. In this section, we'll take a look at this process, beginning with the types of segmentation variables that marketers use to divide up end consumers.

Segmenting consumer markets

Objective

2

Know the different dimensions that marketers use to segment consumer and business-to-business markets

At one time, it was sufficient to divide the sports shoe market into athletes and non-athletes. However, a walk through any sports shop today reveals that the athlete market has fragmented in many directions – trainers designed for jogging, playing football, basketball, tennis, etc.

During the 1990s, obscure makers of such footwear focused their products on **Generation Y consumers** (those born between 1977 and 1994), and as a result managed to gain a significant share of the market. Several segmentation variables can slice up the market for all the shoe variations available today. First, not everyone is willing to pay €150 for the latest sports shoes, so marketers need to consider income. Second, whilst men may be more interested in football trainers, women may look to buy the latest aerobics style, so marketers need to consider gender. Because not all age groups are going to be equally interested in buying specialised sport shoes, the large consumer 'pie' can be sliced into smaller pieces in a number of ways, including demographic, psychological and behavioural differences. Let's consider each variable in turn.

Segmenting by demographics: age

Demographics are measurable characteristics such as gender and age. Demographics are vital to identify the best potential customers for a good or service. These objective characteristics are usually easy to identify, and then it's just a matter of tailoring messages and products to relevant groups. The demographic dimensions that marketers usually look at

Figure 6.2   **Segmenting consumer markets**
Consumer markets can be segmented by demographic, psychographic or behavioural criteria

Objective

3

Show how
marketers
evaluate and
select potential
market
segments

are age, gender, family structure, income and social class, race and ethnicity, and geography (where people live). Let's take a quick look at how marketers can use each of these dimensions to slice up the consumer pie.

Consumers of different age groups have different needs and wants. Members of a generation tend to share the same outlook and priorities. A focus on such segments is often called **generational marketing**. Marketers need to know about the characteristics of such sub-segments in order to effectively market to them. During the famous 'cola wars' of the 1970s and 1980s, Pepsi managed to convince a generation (the 'Pepsi Generation') that its product reflected their core values of youth, idealism and casting off old ways. By default, Coca-Cola became identified as their parents' drink.[1]

Children have become an attractive age segment for marketers. Although kids obviously have a lot to say about purchases of toys and games, they influence other family purchases as well (just watch them at work in the supermarket, or look how excited they often are when they enter McDonald's – having convinced their poor parents to eat fast food so they can acquire a kid's meal, perhaps only for the giveaway toy!). Teenagers/adolescents are also an attractive market segment. Much of the money spent by this segment goes towards 'feel-good' products, such as cosmetics, posters and fast food – see how Apple tries to appeal to this segment through the 'feel good' factor (Photo 6.1). Because they are so interested in many different products and have the resources to obtain them, many marketers focus on the teen market.[2] Of course, there are subgroups within the teen market with their own music idols and distinct styles, etc.

As we said, Generation Y consists of those consumers born between the years 1977 and 1994. Sometimes referred to as the baby 'boomlet', Generation Y is made up of the children of the baby boomer generation.[3] They are the first generation to grow up online and are more ethnically diverse than earlier generations. Generation Y is an attractive market for a host of consumer products, as it is significant in size and is free-spending in nature. But Generation Y consumers may be hard to reach because they resist reading and increasingly turn the TV off. As a result, many marketers have had to develop other ways of reaching this generation, including online chat rooms, email promotions and some of the more unusual 'guerrilla marketing' techniques we'll talk about later in this book. A significant proportion of Generation Y consumers are known as DINKYs (dual income no kids yet). Whilst such couples are often faced with a dilemma between continuing to rent a home and considering a mortgage to enter the property ladder, those in rental accommodation often have high levels of disposable income as they are not influenced by the '*pester power*' of children or teenagers.

The group of people born between 1965 and 1978 is sometimes known as **Generation X** consumers. Many of these people have a cynical attitude towards marketing. A chapter in a book called *Generation X* is 'I am not a target market!'[4] As one 20-year-old Japanese Xer commented, 'I don't like to be told what's trendy. I can make up my own mind.'[5] Despite this tough reputation, members of Generation X, the oldest of whom are now entering their mid 40s, have mellowed with age. In retrospect, they also have developed an identity for being entrepreneurial. An industry expert observed, 'Today's Gen Xer is both values-oriented and value-oriented. This generation is really about settling down.'[6] Many people in this segment seem to be determined to have stable families after being latchkey children themselves. Seven out of ten regularly save some portion of their income, a rate comparable to that of their parents. Xers tend to view the home as an expression of individuality rather than material success. More than half are involved in home improvement and repair projects.[7]

Baby boomers – consumers born between 1946 and 1964 and who are now in their 40s, 50s and 60s, are an important segment to many marketers, if for no other reason than because there are so many of them who are making a lot of money. Boomers were the result of their parents wanting to start families after the Second World War interrupted their lives. Back in the 1950s and 1960s, couples started having children younger and had more of them than the previous generation. The resulting number of kids really changed the market infrastructure, resulting in the need for more single family houses, more schools, migration to suburban areas and so on. One aspect of boomers for marketers to always remember is that they never tend to age. At least, that's the way they look at it. Boomers are willing to invest significant money, time and energy to maintain their youthful image, hence the growth of cosmetic surgery and nip and tucks for those in their 50s. This may also help to explain why women boomers in their 50s are becoming a hot new market for what the motor industry calls 'reward cars, i.e. sexy and extravagant vehicles. These consumers say that for years they had let their roles of wife and mother restrict them. Many consumers that fit into this segment are also known as *SKIs* (sod

Photo 6.1

Apple is a masterful marketer to teens, yet its product line appeals to other age groups as well. The iPod in its various forms enables teens to be content creators and empowers them to be master of their own music world. This satisfies a strong need among this age group for individuality. The iphone is coveted by youth as the smartphone du jour – any other brand is viewed as subpar. Teens don't particularly like to be marketed to, which is a great fit for apple's approach of letting fans and the media do their marketing for them. The iPod and iPhone are iconic symbols of modern youth – stylish, nonconforming, and an expression of a clear difference from the past
Source: Alamy Images/Sergio Azenha

the kids' inheritance), and as their kids grow up and leave home it's reward time. As one woman who bought a sporty Mercedes convertible for herself stated, 'I don't have the disease to please any more . . . I'm pleasing me.' This lady is not alone as the number of women over 45 who purchased such medium-sized sporty models has risen significantly since 2000. Among women of 45 and over earning at least €80,000, purchases of smaller luxury cars like the BMW 3 Series and the Audi A4 have also grown.[8]

Another important aspect of boomers, a connection with the socio-cultural trends discussed in Chapter 2, is that because there are so many of them they are clogging the upward mobility pipeline in employment. Generation Xers especially complain that the boomers hold all the power and position, and that the sheer number of boomers in managerial spots impedes promotion opportunities for Xers. This has fuelled the entrepreneurial spirit among the generations following boomers. Generation Xers and younger have no expectation of long-term employment with any one firm and are cynical about their prospects of ever receiving social security as a retirement benefit. These generations have had to very much make their own opportunities.

A significant percentage of the population in Western Europe is now 65 years and older – and this segment known as the '*silver*' or '*grey*' market is increasingly growing in size. Many older consumers are enjoying leisure time and continued good health. A key question nowadays is, what is a senior citizen/old age pensioner? As we will see later in the chapter, perhaps it isn't age but rather lifestyle factors, including mobility, that best define this group. More and more marketers are offering products that have strong appeal to those with able and active lifestyles. Disney challenges such consumers to re-live their youth by visiting their theme parks or joining one of their cruise liners – with or without their grandchildren. UK based company Saga actively

Photo 6.2	See how Honda attempts to capture the imagination of 'would-be' buyers
	Source: Honda (UK)

targets this segment of the market by providing a range of services, from insurance to holidays.

Segmenting by demographics: gender

Many products, from fragrances to footwear, appeal to men or women either because of the nature of the product or because the marketer chose to appeal to one sex or the other. Segmenting by gender starts at a very early age, even nappies come in pink for girls and blue for boys. In some cases, manufacturers develop parallel products to appeal to each gender. For example, male grooming products have traditionally been Gillette's priority since the company introduced the safety razor in 1903. Today the company offers the five-bladed Fusion for men and at the same time offers women a soothing shave from the Venus Vibrance system.

Whilst the ways in which products have been marketed to men and women have traditionally been very clear-cut, it may vary with subject, trends and fashion. For example, **'Metrosexual'** is a marketing buzzword you may have heard of. While many men are reluctant to identify with a metrosexual lifestyle, a renewed interest in personal care products, fashion accessories and other 'formerly feminine' product categories is creating many marketing opportunities. This term describes a man who is heterosexual, sensitive, educated and an urban dweller who is in touch with his feminine side.[9] This web posting from *The Urban Dictionary* sums up the metrosexual stereotype:[10]

You may be 'metrosexual' if:

1. You just can't walk past a Banana Republic shop without making a purchase.
2. You own 20 pairs of shoes, half a dozen pairs of sunglasses, just as many watches and you carry a man-purse.
3. You see a hair stylist instead of a barber, because barbers don't do highlights.
4. You can make her lamb shanks and risotto for dinner and Eggs Benedict for breakfast . . . all from scratch.
5. You only wear Calvin Klein boxer-briefs.
6. You shave more than just your face. You also exfoliate and moisturise.
7. You would never, ever own a pickup truck.
8. You can't imagine a day without hair styling products.
9. You'd rather drink wine than beer . . . but you'll find out what estate and vintage first.
10. Despite being flattered (even proud) that gay guys hit on you, you still find the thought of actually getting intimate with another man truly repulsive.

An interesting trend related to gender segmentation has been fuelled by the recent recession. Men are now increasingly likely to marry wives with more education and income than they have, and the reverse is true for women. In recent decades, with the rise of well-paid working wives, the economic gains of marriage have been a greater benefit for men. The education and income gap has grown even more in the latest recession, when men held about three in four of the jobs that were lost.

Segmenting by demographics: family life cycle

Because family needs and expenditures change over time, one way to segment consumers is to consider the stage of the family life cycle they occupy. Not surprisingly, consumers in different life cycle segments are unlikely to need the same products, or at least they

Photo 6.3	David Beckham epitomises the celebrity lifestyle that appeals to many metrosexual men

Source: Getty Images

may not need these things in the same quantities.[11] For example, Procter & Gamble introduced a brand of instant coffee for people who live alone and don't need to brew a full pot of coffee at a time.[12]

As families age and move into new life stages, different product categories ascend and descend in importance. Young bachelors and newlyweds are the most likely to exercise, go to bars and the cinema, and consume alcohol. Older couples and bachelors are more likely to use maintenance services. Old age pensioners are a prime market for exclusive second home apartments and golf products. Marketers need to discern the family life cycle segment of their target consumers by examining purchase data by family life cycle group.

Segmenting by demographics: income and social class

The distribution of wealth is of great interest to marketers because it determines which groups have the greatest buying power. It should come as no surprise that many marketers yearn to capture the hearts and wallets of high-income consumers. Perhaps that explains a recent proliferation of ultra-high-end bottled waters such as Voss, which claims the water is extracted from a real Norwegian glacier (to taste this delicacy in gourmet restaurants and mini-bars, there is an expectation to pay for the privilege). At the same time, other marketers target lower-income consumers. Certainly, several European retailers such as Lidl and Aldi sell generic bottled water at a fraction of the price of Voss!

After a 50-year run during which the truly wealthy just kept getting richer, the current recession has taken some of the wind out of their sails due to heavy investment losses. Just how much poorer the rich will ultimately end up is unclear. Any major shift in the financial status of the rich could have implications for certain marketers. For example, a drop in their income and wealth would complicate life for elite universities and others that receive significant donations from such benefactors. Governments may also struggle, as they rely on taxes paid by the rich segment to fund public services.

In the past, it was popular for marketers to consider social class segments, such as upper class lower class, and the like. However, many consumers buy not according to where they may fall in that framework but rather according to the image they wish to portray. For example, readily available credit has facilitated many a sale of a BMW to a consumer who technically falls into the middle or lower class segment. Six years of making payments later, they finally own the car.

Segmenting by demographics: ethnicity and place of residence

A consumer's national origin is often a strong indicator of preferences for specific magazines or TV shows, foods, clothing and choice of leisure activities. Marketers need to be aware of these differences and sensitivities in order to try to appeal to consumers of diverse races and ethnic groups. Consider the metropolitan City of London, which is home to hundreds of different nationalities. Each, ethnic subgroup has its own cultural traits which dictate what can and cannot be consumed and what is appropriate to the societal norms within each culture. This has implications for example in the type of clothes worn by different groups and the types of food eaten on a daily basis. Whilst perhaps the English may have a reputation for eating fish and chips, roast beef and Yorkshire pudding, it may be surprising for readers of non-UK origin to discover that the most popular food that is consumed in the UK is now Indian, closely followed by Chinese. Maybe ethnicity has broader implications for people as societies embrace different cultures.

Recognising that people's preferences often vary depending on where they live, many marketers tailor their offerings to appeal to different regions. This is known as **geographic segmentation**. For example, whilst traditional beer drinkers in the south-east of England prefer to see their pint with little or no head of froth, this would not be accepted in some parts of the north, where consumers expect to see a head of a centimetre or more. When marketers want to segment regional markets even more precisely, they sometimes combine geography with demographics by using a technique called **geodemography**. A basic assumption of geodemography is that 'birds of a feather flock together', i.e. people who live near one another share similar characteristics. Sophisticated statistical techniques identify geographic areas that share the same preferences for household items, magazines and other products. Through geodemography, marketers construct segments of households with a common pattern of preferences. This way the marketer can focus on those customers who are most likely to be interested in its specific offerings – in some cases so precisely that families living on one road will be included in a segment, while those on the next may not. Companies can even customise web advertising by **geocoding** so that people who log on from different places will see ad banners for local businesses. Just check it out when you log on to your hotmail or Yahoo account!

Segmenting by psychographics

Demographic information is useful, but it does not always provide enough information to divide consumers into meaningful segments. Although we can use demographic variables to discover, for example, that the female student segment uses perfume, we won't be able to tell whether certain women prefer perfumes that express an image of, say, sexiness rather than athleticism. The **personality** of consumers may therefore be used as a base to segment the market. Perhaps this is a reason why certain celebrities are often used to endorse specific brands of goods, for example, tennis star Roger Federer, golfer Tiger Woods and footballer Thierry Henry were all used by Gillette to publicise their razors. We can use psychographic data to understand differences among consumers who may be statistically similar to one another but whose needs and wants vary.

Psychographics can be used to segment consumers in terms of shared activities, interests and opinions (*AIOs*).[13] Psychographic segments usually include demographic information such as age or gender, but the richer descriptions that emerge go well beyond these characteristics and relate to consumer **lifestyle**, which can also be used as a base to segment the market. For example, most people are happy driving at the speed limit (or a little over) on the motorway, but others enjoy danger. To appeal to this lifestyle, there is a variety of unique product offerings, including a tour of the sunken Titanic at 12,500 feet below the surface of the ocean, getting behind the wheel of a Formula One racing car, parachuting or swimming with sharks.

Over the years, Harley-Davidson has done a great job of understanding buyers on the basis of psychographic lifestyles. A Harley user's profile includes both thrill seeking and affinity for a counter-cultural image. In fact, your doctor, banker, accountant or even marketing professor may be a member of HOG (the Harley Owners Group). However, demographics also come into play. Over the past decade, the age of the typical Harley owner has risen to about 46. This is significantly older than the motorcycle industry average of 38. But because the company knows the psychographics of its target buyers, it isn't lulled by age stereotypes of safety and conservatism. Harley-Davidson knows that in spite of the older age demographic, its buyers are still a thrill-seeking bunch. Although some advertising agencies and manufacturers develop their own psychographic techniques to classify consumers, other agencies subscribe to services that divide the entire population into segments and then sell pieces of this information to clients for specific strategic applications.

German research firm Sigma developed a segmentation system using personality and lifestyle bases. As a result, the system paved the way for BMW's highly publicised reinvention and expansion of its car range. It included 'upper liberals' (socially conscious, open-minded professionals who prefer roominess and flexibility), 'post-moderns' (high-earning innovators like architects, entrepreneurs and artists who like the individualistic statements made by driving convertibles and sports cars), 'upper conservatives' (made up of wealthy, traditional thinkers who like the upper crust) and 'modern mainstream' (family-oriented up-and-comers who want a luxury brand but probably can't afford more than the lowest priced model). Using this segmentation scheme as an anchor, BMW created vehicles for each category and also acquired Rolls Royce and the Mini to serve the extreme ends, with phenomenal success.[14]

Social class is another base that can be used to segment customers and it is one thing that visitors from overseas find quite peculiar about UK culture. For example, upper class members of society are often less inclined to mix and associate themselves with lower levels of society. They will eat in different restaurants, play different sports and seek a different education for their children. Even newspapers in England are highly differentiated to appeal to different groups of society. On one extreme *The Sun* newspaper has been successful in appealing to working class males, particularly builders, factory workers and the likes, whereas *The Guardian* appeals to a relatively more educated middle class leafy suburb reader. Marketers of consumer goods and services can therefore use such media to better target customers with their newspaper ads and promotions.

Segmenting by behaviour

In addition to demographics and psychographics, it is useful to study what consumers actually do with a product. **Behavioural segmentation** slices consumers on the basis of how they act towards, feel about or use a product. Fairtrade provides a range of products that appeal to consumers who want the benefits of consuming such produce, at the same time contributing to others in less developed regions. Segmentation based on the type of **benefits sought** is one way of slicing up the market. As a very simple example, consider different people and the benefits they seek from a particular toothpaste. A heavy smoker may opt to purchase Eucryl (smokers) to try and alleviate the yellow stains left from tobacco. A single mother with several children may select to purchase any brand that offers the best value in terms of price and quantity at a given time; children, meanwhile, may pester for a specific blue gel toothpaste, that incidentally has their comic book hero on the box and tube.

Another way to segment based on behaviour is to divide the market based on **usage** frequency. Marketers may therefore attempt to reward current users, and try to win over infrequent users. Typically marketers often distinguish between users and non-users by segmenting their current customers further into groups of heavy, moderate and light users. Emirates airline, for example, segments its customers this way by providing different levels of service for its Blue, Silver and Gold members. For example, when travelling via Dubai, which is always an exciting place to stop off to break up a long journey, it is evident that Emirates provide a different class of lounge for its members. Silver members can only use a certain lounge, whilst gold members have the choice and Blue members are not entitled to complimentary use of such facilities. Most hotels, airlines and retailers now operate such loyalty schemes by providing points or miles with the intention of segmenting their customer base further, cross-selling other services and providing rewards to those that consume heavily.

In contrast, and often frustrating to loyal customers, a range of service providers are now doing the opposite and through segmenting the market on **user status**, they are targeting non-users, ex-users or potential users with exclusive offers that reward them for switching from other service providers. British Gas, for example, has offered better priced service contracts to new users than existing customers. Santander has also offered excellent rates of interest over the short term to entice new customers to open a current bank account with them.

Many marketers abide by a rule of thumb called the **80/20 or Pareto rule**: 20 per cent of purchasers account for 80 per cent of the sales revenue (the ratio is an approximation, not gospel). This rule means that it often makes more sense to focus on the smaller number of people who are really into a product rather than on the larger number who are just casual users. Perhaps this is the reason why Emirates airline takes such pride in looking after its Gold members, who pay huge amounts of money when travelling with them. While the 80/20 rule still holds in the majority of situations, the web's ability to offer an unlimited choice of goods to billions of people is starting to change how marketers think about segmentation. A new approach called the **long tail** is turning traditional thinking about the virtues of selling in high volume on its head. The basic idea is that we need no longer rely solely on big hit sales (like blockbuster movies or best-seller books) to generate profits. Companies can also make money by selling small amounts of items that only a few people want – if they sell enough different items.

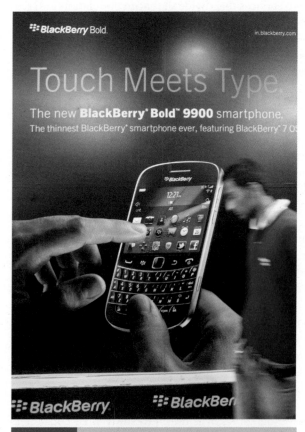

Photo 6.4	Increasingly popular for today's busy lifestyle segment is a Blackberry
	Source: Getty Images/Bloomberg

Marketing in recession

M&S profits soar 13 per cent

Marks & Spencer, a retail chain with 600 stores in the UK and 300 overseas has resisted the trend in retail gloom after revealing a 12.9 per cent rise in its annual profit 2011, pre-tax profits of £714 million, despite challenging high street conditions and rising cotton prices.

With the help of an advertising campaign featuring former X Factor judge Dannii Minogue and ex-Liverpool and England footballer Jamie Redknapp, the retailer managed to increase its clothing market share by 0.5 per cent to 11.7 per cent. Food market share also rose by 0.1 per cent to 3.9 per cent with the success of the 'Dine in for £10' promotion, which sold 15 million meals during the year.

Marc Bolland, chief executive, unveiled a strategic review for the business which involved increasing the rate of overseas expansion as well as revamping various labels to create 'proper brands'. He said 'we traded well in a challenging environment, growing our market share in both clothing and food' and 'we did this by offering great quality and value, and more choice through innovation'. The company will start testing new store formats at the end of 2011 in a bid to tailor them more to their location and demographic.

Metro, 25 May 2011

Discuss, debate, disagree

1   How does M&S segment the marketplace?

2   To what extent does the use of in-store promotions and celebrity endorsements help M&S target its customers?

For example, Amazon.com maintains a stock of some 3.7 million books compared with the 100,000 or so you'll find in a Barnes & Noble bookshop. Most of these will sell only a few thousand copies (if that), but the 3.6 million books that Barnes & Noble does not carry make up a quarter of Amazon's revenue!

Another way to segment a market based on behaviour is to look at **usage occasions**, or when consumers use the product most. Many products are associated with specific occasions, whether time of day, holidays, business functions or casual get-togethers. Businesses often divide up their markets according to when and how their offerings are in demand. Similarly, Google enables its advertising clients to target specific ads at certain behavioural usage consumers via their Google domain, query entered, IP address and preferred language. This way, companies can have Google automatically sort and send the intended ad to particular market segments. Thus, it is possible for advertisers on Google to tailor their automated ads based on seasonality and behavioural traits.

Segmenting business-to-business markets

We've reviewed the segmentation variables marketers use to divide up the consumer pie, but how about all those business-to-business marketers out there? Adding to what we learned about business markets in Chapter 5, it's important to know that segmentation also helps them slice up the pie of their customers. Though the specific variables may differ, the underlying logic of classifying the larger market into manageable pieces that share relevant characteristics is the same whether the product being sold is pasta or potatoes.

Organisational demographics also help a business-to-business marketer to understand the needs and characteristics of its potential customers – just look at our Real people &Samhoud case for example. These classification dimensions include the size of the firms either in total sales or number of employees, the number of factories, whether they are a domestic or a multinational company, policies on how they purchase and the type of business they are in. Business-to-business markets may also be segmented on the basis of the production technology they use and whether the customer is a user or a non-user of the product. General Electric's Aviation division is one of the world's largest producers of jet engines. GE divides its customers by the types of jets they fly: commercial, corporate, military, and marine and industrial. The final category, in fact, doesn't include planes at all but rather large ships and other applications of jet engine technologies.[15]

Many industries use the Standard Industrial Classification (SIC) system discussed in Chapter 5 to obtain information about the number of companies operating in a particular industry. Business-to-business marketers often consult information sources. For example, the likes of Dun & Bradstreet and Kompass provide subscribers with up-to-date information on private and public companies worldwide.

Step 2: Targeting

www.pearsoned.co.uk/Solomon

Objective

4

Explain how marketers develop a targeting strategy

We've seen that the first step in developing a target marketing strategy is segmentation, in which the firm divides the market into smaller groups that share certain characteristics. The next step is **targeting**, in which marketers evaluate the attractiveness of each potential segment and decide which of these groups they will invest resources in to try to turn them into customers. The customer group or groups selected are the firm's **target market**. In this section, we'll review how marketers assess these customer groups, and we'll discuss selection strategies for effective targeting.

Evaluating market segments

Just because a marketer identifies a segment does not necessarily mean that it's a useful target. A viable target segment should satisfy the following requirements:

Are members of the segment similar to each other in their product needs and wants and, at the same time, different from consumers in other segments? Without real differences in consumer needs, firms might as well use a mass-marketing strategy. For example, it's a waste of time to develop two separate lines of skincare products for working women and non-working women if both segments have the same complaints about dry skin.

Can marketers measure the segment? Marketers must know something about the size and purchasing power of a potential segment before deciding if it is worth their efforts.

Is the segment large enough to be profitable now and in the future? For example, a graphic designer hoping to design web pages for Barbie doll collectors must decide whether there are enough hard-core interested parties to make this business worthwhile and whether the trend will continue.

Can marketing communications reach the segment? It is easy to select television programmes or magazines that will efficiently reach older consumers, those with certain levels of education or residents of major cities because the media they prefer are easy to identify.

Can the marketer adequately serve the needs of the segment? Does the firm have the expertise and resources to satisfy the segment better than the competition? Please read the Marketing ethics and sustainability box, as it is interesting to see how McDonald's appeals to the very young – a 'significant' market segment.

At the start of the chapter, you met Jochen Barth of &Samhoud. He needs to capture the attention of a specific segment of business customer. Read 'Real people, other voices' to learn how others advise Jochen.

Real people, other voices

Benny Sweeney

University of West Scotland

I think Option 3 should be the preferred one. The &samhoud consultancy is a successful division with repeat customers and relationships/ projects that last for several years so this should not be abandoned. The tools division also has repeat business with customers coming back annually for customer service reports. So the consultancy division should focus on the needs of the larger organisations as at present, offering an unrivalled service and helping develop these through managing strategic change and delivering culture change and growth. Sub-segments within this market can be identified and particular change-management projects undertaken in each different environment.

The tools division should focus on SME's etc. but should look at the various segments within their market and identify those, such as the multinationals for example, where the opportunity may exist to get to know their needs better and boost revenue and the relationship by tracking customer service and satisfaction levels on a more regular basis. The opportunity may arise then to turn these annual 'reports' into bigger culture change projects where these are deemed necessary.

For each division the opportunity to continue working with the founder's values of improving the quality of the workplace will remain, and this value can be the way to position the company in the eyes of its clients: improving the workplace in order to improve the quality of service given to customers.

 ## Developing segment profiles

Once a marketer has identified a set of usable segments, it is helpful to generate a profile of each to really understand segment members' needs and to look for business opportunities. This segment profile is a description of the 'typical' customer in that segment. A **segment profile** might, for example, include customer demographics, location, lifestyle information and a description of how frequently the customer buys the product.

Marketing ethics and sustainability

'Half of all children aged four don't know their own name – but two-thirds of three-year-olds can recognise the McDonald's golden arches'

There is an industry worth at least £70 million every year: advertising aimed directly at children. The value of indirect marketing – ads that are not made expressly for kids but are seen by them anyway – runs into the hundreds of millions. The result is that today's average British child is familiar with up to 400 brand names by the time they reach the age of ten. One study found that 69 per cent of all three-year-olds could identify the McDonald's golden arches, while half of all four-year-olds did not know their own name. Schools are no longer a refuge from this commercial onslaught. There are poster sites promoting new films by the assembly hall. Until Education Secretary Ruth Kelly banned them in 2005, school vending machines were a prime outlet of crisps, chocolates and fizzy drinks. The marketing of food to young consumers is not only a matter of when, but how. The techniques are tried, tested and familiar. The appeal to young children is obvious: bright, primary colours, friendly, elastic faces. Except these lovable creations are not there to amuse or entertain but to sell.

Source: Adapted from The onslaught: Half of all children aged four don't know their own name - but two thirds of three-year-olds can recognise the McDonald's golden arches by Jonathan Freedland, *The Guardian*, 25 October 2005. Copyright Guardian News & Media Ltd 2005.

Debate, discuss, disagree

1   What is your opinion about the fact that 'half of all children aged four don't know their own name – but two-thirds of three-year-olds can recognise the McDonald's golden arches'?

Choosing a targeting strategy

A basic targeting decision is how finely tuned the target should be. Should the company go after one large segment or focus on meeting the needs of one or more smaller segments? Let's look at four targeting strategies, which are summarised in Figure 6.3.

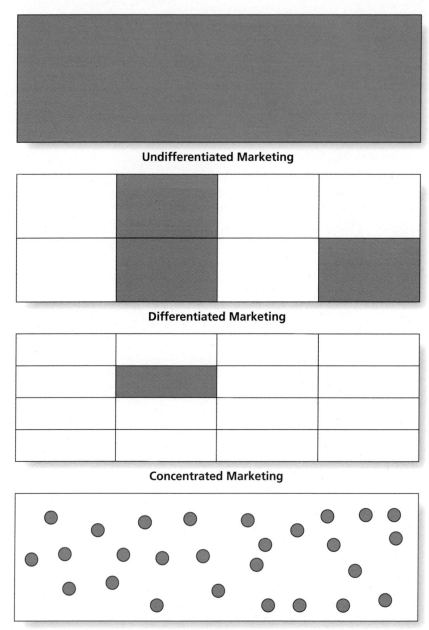

Undifferentiated Marketing

Differentiated Marketing

Concentrated Marketing

Customised Marketing

Figure 6.3	Choosing a target marketing strategy
	After the market is divided into meaningful segments, marketers must decide on a target marketing strategy. Should the company go after one total market, one or several market segments, or even target customers individually?

A company such as Asda Wal-Mart that selects an **undifferentiated targeting strategy** is appealing to a broad spectrum of people. If successful, this type of operation can be very efficient, especially because production, research and promotion costs benefit from economies of scale. It's cheaper to develop one product or one advertising campaign than to choose several targets and create separate products or messages for each. The company must however be willing to gamble that people have similar needs, or that any differences among them will be so trivial that they will not matter so that the same product and message will appeal to many customers.

A company that chooses a **differentiated targeting strategy** develops one or more products for each of several customer groups with different product needs. A differentiated strategy is called for when consumers are choosing among well-known brands that have distinctive images and the company can identify one or more segments that have distinct needs for different types of products. The cosmetics giant L'Oréal follows this philosophy. The company has the resources to offer several product lines at a variety of prices. It targets the luxury market with such brands as Georgio Armani, Lancôme and Helena Rubinstein, while less expensive L'Oréal branded products are targeted to large department stores and discount stores, with Redken and Biotherm brands serving a more professional market.[16] Differentiated marketing can also involve connecting one product with different segments by communicating differently to appeal to those segments. VW has successfully achieved this in Europe through appealing to different segments via SEAT and Skoda.

When a firm focuses its efforts on offering one or more products to a single segment, it is using a **concentrated targeting strategy**. Smaller firms that do not have the resources or the desire to be all things to all people often use a concentrated strategy. For example, as commented on earlier, UK tour operator Saga purely markets its holidays at the growing segment of over 55s.

Ideally, marketers should be able to define segments so precisely that they can offer products and services that exactly meet the unique needs of each individual or firm. This level of concentration frequently does occur in the case of personal or professional services from doctors, law firms and hairstylists. A **custom marketing strategy** is common in an industrial context whereby a supplier often works with one or a few large clients and develops products and services that only these clients will use, such as in the case of a design and build construction project.

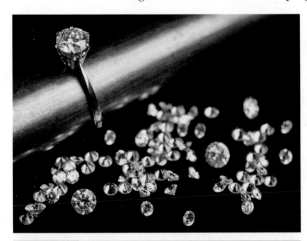

Of course, in most cases this level of segmentation is neither practical nor possible when mass-produced products such as computers or cars enter the picture. However, advances in computer technology, coupled with new emphasis on building solid relationships with customers, have focused managers' attention on devising a new way to tailor specific products and the messages about them to individual customers. Thus, some forward-looking, consumer-oriented companies are moving toward **mass customisation**, in which they modify a basic product or service to meet the needs of an individual.[17] Dell does this by offering customised computer products over the internet at Dell.com. Users can create their own computers – everything from personal computers to networking systems. We'll return to the issue of customisation later in this chapter when we introduce the idea of customer relationship management.

Photo 6.5 The diamond industry practises mass customisation; couples can create their own specific designs, diamond sizes and shapes, mounting styles and so forth
Source: PhotoDisc/Photolink/F. Schussler

Step 3: Positioning

www.pearsoned.co.uk/solomon

Objective

5

Understand how
a firm develops
and implements
a positioning
strategy

The final stage of developing a target marketing strategy process is to provide consumers who belong to a targeted market segment with a product or service that meets their unique needs and expectations. **Positioning** means developing a marketing strategy aimed at influencing how a particular market segment perceives a good or service in comparison to the competition. To position a brand, marketers have to clearly understand the criteria target consumers use to evaluate competing products and then convincing them that their product, service or organisation will meet those needs. In addition, the organisation has to come up with a way to communicate this 'position' to its target market.

 ## Steps in positioning

Figure 6.4 illustrates four stages that marketers can use to decide how to position their product or service, i.e. Stage 1 – Analyse competitors' positions, Stage 2 – Offer a good or service with competitive advantage, Stage 3 – Match elements of the marketing mix to the selected segment and Stage 4 – Evaluate the target market's responses and modify strategies if needed. We will now take a closer look at each of these positioning strategies.

Analyse competitors' positions

The first step is to analyse competitors' positions in the marketplace. To develop an effective positioning strategy, marketers must understand the current state of the market. What competitors are out there, and how does the target market perceive them? Aside from direct competitors in the product category, are there other products or services that provide similar benefits?

Sometimes the indirect competition can be more important than the direct, especially if it represents an emerging consumer trend. For years, McDonald's developed positioning strategies based only on its direct competition, i.e. other fast-food chains (such as Burger King and KFC). McDonald's failed to realise that consumers' needs for a quick, tasty, convenient meal was being fulfilled by a plethora of indirect competitors, ranging from supermarket

Figure 6.4   Positioning decision
Four key elements comprise the decision-making process in positioning

delicatessens and frozen microwavable single-serving meals to telephone order takeaways and full-service restaurants, such as T.G.I. Friday's, Pizza Hut and the like. Only recently has McDonald's begun to understand that it must react to this indirect competition by serving up a wider variety of adult-friendly and healthy food, as well as improving service.

Define your competitive advantage

The second stage is to offer a good or service with a competitive advantage to provide a reason why consumers will perceive the product as being better than the competition. If the company only offers a 'me-too product', then it can only look to induce people to buy based on a lower price. Other forms of competitive advantage include offering a superior image like Giorgio Armani, a unique product feature like Levi's 501 button-fly jeans, better service like Singapore Airlines, or more experienced sales assistance like retailer B&Q.

Finalise the marketing mix

Once a positioning strategy has been established, the third stage is for marketers to finalise the marketing mix by putting all the pieces into place. The elements of the marketing mix must match the selected segment. This means that the good or service must deliver benefits that the segment values, such as convenience or status. Put another way, it must add value and satisfy consumer needs. Furthermore, marketers must price this offering at a level these consumers will pay, make the offering available at places consumers are likely to go, and correctly communicate the offering's benefits in locations where consumers are likely to take notice.

Evaluate responses and modify as needed

In the fourth and final stage, marketers evaluate the target market's responses so they can modify strategies as needed. Over time, the firm may find that it needs to change which segments it targets, or even alter a product's position to respond to marketplace changes. Lucozade was originally positioned as a drink that should be consumed when you were ill, in order to provide the body with increased energy. Nowadays, and through the use of high-profile celebrity endorsements from Olympic athletes like Jessica Ennis, the product is positioned as a sports drink that can improve endurance. This type of change in strategy is called **re-positioning**, and it's fairly common to see a company try to modify its brand image to keep up with changing times. Re-positioning can also occur when brands once thought to be dead or near death get revived. Sometimes these products arise from their deathbeds to ride a wave of nostalgia and return to the marketplace as **retro brands** – both Fred Perry (polo shirts) and Lyle & Scott (sportswear) have recently received a new lease of life in the fashion industry.

Brands are almost like people in that we can often describe them in terms of personality traits. We may use adjectives such as cheap, elegant, sexy or cool when talking about a shop, a perfume, a car and so on. That's why a positioning strategy often tries to create a **brand personality** for a good or service – a distinctive image that captures its character and benefits. An advertisement for *Elle* magazine once said, 'She is not a reply card. She is not a category. She is not shrink-wrapped. Elle is not a magazine. She is a woman.'

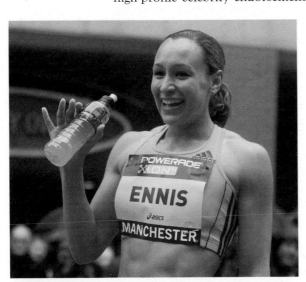

Photo 6.6   Powerade use the Olympic gold medal winner, sheffield's Jessica Ennis, to help position their brand
Source: Rex Features/Andrew Schofield

Marketing ethics and sustainability

Oxfam's vintage

Oxfam is positioning itself as a fashion brand in recent campaigns such as 'Beating poverty with style'. Oxfam's boutiques are aiming to create a new benchmark for sustainable fashion. They provide shoppers with unique style, beautiful one-off clothes and the assurance that every item will raise money to fight poverty around the world. Along with the recent launch of the Oxfam Curiosity Shop, over a ten-day period, Selfridges hosted a fabulous collection of unique, handpicked vintage pieces, designer samples and stunning garments that were generously donated by style icons including Livia Firth, Kate Moss and Lily Allen. Fashion icons, journalists, stylists and bloggers were also invited to attend the store by Oxfam, in order to share their styling wisdom and know-how with customers and to create some stunning, and sustainable, Oxfam fashion looks!

www.oxfam.org.uk/shop/content/secondhandstore/
fashion/boutiques/defaultp.html

www.oxfam.org.uk/applications/blogs/fashion/?p=771

http://fashion.telegraph.co.uk/news-features/TMG3364886/
Jane-Shepherdson-from-Topshop-to-Oxfam.html

Discuss, debate, disagree

1 Discuss Oxfam's re-positioning strategy.

2 What are the advantages and disadvantages of re-positioning an established brand such as Oxfam?

Products as people? It seems funny to say, yet marketing researchers find that most consumers have no trouble describing what a product would be like 'if it came to life'. People often give clear, detailed descriptions, including what colour hair the product would have, the type of house it would live in, and even whether it would be thin, overweight or somewhere in between.[18] If you don't believe us, try doing this yourself.

Part of creating a brand personality is developing an identity for the product that the target market will prefer over competing brands. How do marketers determine where their products actually stand in the minds of consumers? One solution is to ask consumers what characteristics are important and how competing alternatives would rate on these attributes too. Marketers use this information to construct a **perceptual map** – a vivid way to construct a picture of where products or brands are 'located' in consumers' minds.

For example, suppose you wanted to construct a perceptual map of women's magazines as perceived by women in their 20s to give you some guidance while developing an idea for a new magazine. After interviewing a sample of female readers, you might determine questions women ask when selecting a magazine: (1) Is it 'traditional', that is oriented towards family, home or personal issues, or is it 'fashion forward', oriented towards personal appearance and fashion? (2) Is it for 'upmarket' women who are older and established in their careers or for relatively downmarket women who are younger and just starting out in their careers?

The perceptual map, Figure 6.5 illustrates how these ratings might look for a set of major women's magazines. The map provides some guidance as to where you might position your new magazine. You might decide to compete directly with either the cluster of 'service magazines' in the lower left or the traditional fashion magazines in the upper right. In this case, you would have to determine what benefits your new magazine might offer that these existing magazines do not. Condé Nast, for example, postioned *Allure* to compete against fashion magazines by going into more depth than they do on beauty issues, such as the mental, physical and emotional dangers of cosmetic surgery.

You might try to locate an unserved area, for example there may be room for a magazine aimed at 'cutting-edge' fashion for college-age women. An unserved segment is a

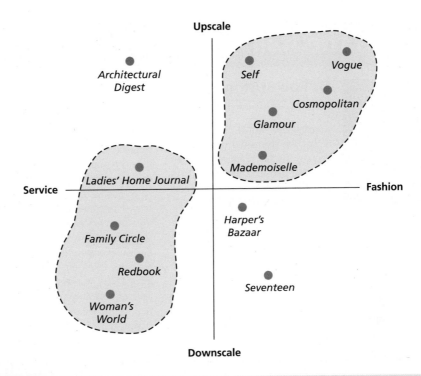

Figure 6.5	**Perceptual Map** Perceptual mapping allows marketers to identify customers' perceptions of their brand in relation to the competition

Internationalisation

Coco Mademoiselle

Mintel data suggest that the majority of women own one to three bottles of fragrance, with two in five owning two to three, and a third owning four or more (Strutton, 2010). With these statistics in mind, it shows there is a large market for fragrances. Jacques Polge, master perfumer at Chanel, wanted to create a scent that would appeal to the granddaughters of women who use the brand's most popular perfume, Chanel No. 5. Based on psychographics, Mintel research also suggests that women purchase premium fragrances to 'give themselves a lift' during economic downturns, with Chanel's Coco

Mademoiselle being an obvious choice. Based on Mintel's research, the heaviest users of Coco Mademoiselle perfume are single women, under 25 that are in full-time employment. Through pioneering work the company has managed to successfully create a scent that portrays the very essence of Chanel through its appeal to a significant segment of the market. The company has also continued to promote Coco Chanel's spirit by pushing the brand forward with modern times and, at the same time, not alienating any of Chanel's existing users.

Discuss, debate, disagree

1   Identify other appropriate STP strategies that may be available to Chanel?

2   In order to maintain long-term success and profits, what must Chanel consider?

References

Sources: Based on J. Polge, sourced from A. Chiles (2001) 'Lunch Lesson 12 – Brands', Paris, BBC, http://news.bbc.co.uk (accessed 1 December 2010); M. Strutton (2010) *Women's Fragrances* (London: Mintel).

Across the hall

Advice for Jochen Barth

Dr Rob Britton

is Principal at AirLearn, Inc.

I recommend Option 3. My sense is that the teams did not try hard enough the first time round, after the 2006 decision to integrate Tools into the consulting practice. It seems that neither team had sufficient information, a coherent marketing strategy or, crucially, financial incentives to sell the other products. Moreover, the effort appeared polarised or at least binary: no one seemed to be working to identify and market consulting services or other products 'in the middle', between the relatively formulaic offerings of Tools and the somewhat ethereal (to this reader at least) lines of the consulting business. Either/or thinking is responsible for a lot of business mistakes, in strategy and in execution.

There are clearly many opportunities in the middle, between the research and reports business of Tools and the breakthrough-oriented consulting business, and these would not only offer revenue opportunities, but would be like stepping stones between the two lines of business, making upselling and downselling easier and more rewarding. The previous gap between the two was just too great.

To address the concern that Option 3 had already been tried, I recommend that &samhoud establish some flexible milestones to measure progress toward integration. Too often, strategic decisions are taken without any way to measure intermediate progress. No need for rigidity, but four or five simple measures taken quarterly would provide a basis for assessment. Finally, as part of this measurement process, a firm time limit for achieving one or more of these measures would prevent the rudderless drift that often develops. If progress is not evident in 9–15 months, it's time to re-assess. There's nothing wrong with making mistakes as long as you learn from them!

gift for marketers: with luck, they can move quickly to capture a segment and define the standards of comparison for the category. This tactic paid off for European retailer Netto which identified a niche in the UK market to provide branded goods at lower prices.

Customer relationship management

www.pearsoned.co.uk/solomon

Objective

6

Explain how marketers increase long-term success and profits by practising customer relationship management

We've talked about identifying a unique group of consumers and developing products specifically to meet their needs. We also talked about how marketers can build products to meet the needs of individual consumers with mass customisation. Today many highly successful marketing firms embrace **customer relationship management (CRM)** programmes that allow companies to talk to individual customers and adjust elements of their marketing programmes in light of how each customer reacts to elements of the marketing mix.[19] In a nutshell, CRM aims to identify profitable customers and find effective ways to develop relationships with them, so that business is nurtured and expanded upon over the long term. However, the problem is that very often executives have a wide range of different views relating to what constitutes CRM. In reality, and as a result, the lack of a universal definition for CRM may actually lead to the failure of such well intended projects. In implementing CRM, marketers may find it useful to follow those steps offered by Don Peppers and Martha Rogers[20] in relation to one-to-one marketing. The later subsection on CRM implementation will explore this specific issue in further detail.

Four steps in one-to-one marketing

Peppers and Rogers have identified four steps in one-to-one marketing:[21]

1. Identify customers and get to know them in as much detail as possible.

2. Differentiate among these customers in terms of both their needs and their value to the company.

3. Interact with customers and find ways to improve cost efficiency and the effectiveness of the interaction.
4. Customise some aspect of the products or services that you offer to each customer. This means treating each customer differently based on what has been learned through customer interactions.

Peppers and Rogers define CRM as 'managing customer relationships. If I'm managing customer relationships, it means I'm treating different customers differently, across all enterprises . . . The relationship develops a context over time, it drives a change in behaviour . . . [this] means that I have to change my behavior as an enterprise based on a customer'.[22] A CRM strategy allows a company to identify its best customers, stay on top of their needs and increase their satisfaction.

Is CRM for all companies? Should producers of consumer goods that target the entire market adopt CRM strategies? Of course, CRM seems to make more sense for firms such as business-to-business companies and consumer products companies that have a limited number of customers. But, as we'll see in the next section, a range of companies have used CRM to build customer relationships and brand loyalty.

CRM: a new perspective on an old problem

CRM is about communicating with customers and about customers being able to communicate with a company one to one. CRM systems are applications that use computers, CRM computer software, databases and often the internet to capture information at each

Table 6.1
Four steps to one-to-one marketing

Step	Suggested Activities
Identify	Collect and enter names and additional information about your customers.
	Verify and update, deleting outdated information
Differentiate	Identify top customers
	Determine which customers cost the company money
	Find higher-value customers who have complained about your product more than once
	Find customers who buy only one or two products from your company but a lot from other companies
	Rank customers into A, B and C categories based on their value to your company
Interact	Call the top three people in the top 5 per cent of dealers, distributors and retailers that carry your product and make sure they're happy
	Call your own company and ask questions; see how hard it is to get through and get answers
	Call your competitors and compare their customer service with yours
	Use incoming calls as selling opportunities
	Initiate more dialogue with valuable customers
	Improve complaint handling
Customise	Find out what your customers want
	Personalise your direct mail
	Ask customers how and how often they want to hear from you
	Ask your top ten customers what you can do differently to improve your product
	Involve top management in customer relations

Source: Reprinted by permission of *Harvard Business Review*. From 'Is Your Company Ready for One-to-One Marketing?' by Peppers, D., Rogers, H., and Dorf, B. January–February 1999, pp. 151–60. Copyright © 1999 by Harvard Business Publishing; all rights reserved.

touch-point (or interaction) between customers and companies to allow for overall better customer care. These systems include everything from websites that let you check on the status of a bill or package to call centres that solicit your business. When you log on to a website to track, for example, the expected delivery time for a product – that's part of a CRM system. When you get a phone message from the dentist reminding you about that filling appointment tomorrow, that's CRM. When you get a call from the car dealer asking how you would like your new vehicle, that's also CRM. In a nutshell, CRM helps firms communicate with and serve customers by understanding their needs. Remember how in Chapter 3 we said information is the fuel that runs the marketing engine? CRM is how much of that customer information is managed and acted on.

To fully appreciate the value of a CRM strategy, consider the following. In general, an investment banker needs to manage accounts as well as open new ones – often 30 to 50 per month. Just opening the account can take 45 minutes, not a satisfying process for the banker or for the customer. But with an automated CRM system, the banker can open an account, issue a welcome letter and produce an arbitration agreement in 10 minutes. He or she can create a unique marketing campaign for each client based on that person's life cycle – including such variables as when a person opened an account, their annual income, family situation, desired retirement age and so on. The marketer can generate a happy anniversary letter to clients and include an invitation to update their investment objectives. These firms have found that this level of individualised attention results in a much higher rate of customer retention and satisfaction, so CRM creates a win–win situation for everyone.[23] That success helps explain why CRM has become a driving philosophy in many successful firms. Industry sources estimated that in 2005 companies spent about €20 billion worldwide on CRM.[24]

The airline industry has experienced financial problems over the last decade, but it relies on customer relations and has invested heavily in CRM systems. These systems help flyers by automating crucial information and reducing the number of incoming phone calls.[25] CRM also helps identify flying patterns, favoured destinations and loyal users so that extra perks (upgrades, tailored special offers and so on) can be sent their way. CRM systems may also help reduce the number of angry customers and marketers can use CRM systems to monitor the behaviour of their valued customers.

Perhaps the most important aspect of CRM is that it presents a new way of looking at how to compete in the marketplace. This begins with looking at customers as partners. CRM proponents suggest that the traditional relationship between customers and marketers is an adversarial one where marketers try to sell their products to customers and customers seek to avoid buying.[26] The customer relationship perspective sees customers as partners, with each partner learning from the other every time they interact. Successful firms compete by establishing relationships with individual customers on a one-to-one basis through dialogue and feedback. What does this customer really want? That's one-to-one marketing.

 ## Characteristics of CRM

In addition to having a different mind-set, companies that practise CRM have different goals, use different measures of success, and look at customers in some different ways. So, CRM marketers look at their share of the customer, at the lifetime value of a customer, at customer equity and at focusing on high-value customers.

Share of customer

Historically, marketers have measured success in a product category by their share of market. For example, if there are 100 million pairs of sports shoes sold each year, a firm that sells 10 million of them has a 10 per cent market share. If the manufacturer's marketing objective is to increase market share, it may lower the price of its shoes, increase its advertising, or offer customers a free football with every pair purchased. Such tactics may increase sales in the short run, but unfortunately may not do much for the long-term success of the firm. In fact, such tactics may actually decrease the value of the brand by weakening its image with giveaways.

Because it is always easier and less expensive to keep an existing customer than to get a new customer, CRM firms focus on increasing their **share of customer**, not share of market. Let's say that a consumer buys six pairs of shoes a year, two pairs from three different manufacturers. Let's assume one shoemaker has a CRM system that allows it to send letters to its current customers inviting them to receive a special price discount or a gift if they buy more of the firm's shoes during the year. If the firm can get the consumer to buy three, maybe four or perhaps all six pairs from them, the firm has increased its share of the customer. Incidentally, this may not be too difficult because the customer already buys and presumably likes the supplier's shoes. Without the CRM system, the shoe company would probably use traditional advertising in an attempt to increase sales, which would be far more costly than the direct-mail campaign. So the company can increase sales and profits at a much lower cost than it would spend to get one, two or three new customers.

Lifetime value of the customer

As you'll recall from Chapter 1, the **lifetime value of a customer** is the potential profit generated by a single customer's purchase of a firm's products over the customer's lifetime. With CRM, a customer's lifetime value is identified as the true goal, not an individual transaction. It just makes sense that a firm's profitability and long-term success are going to be far greater if it develops long-term relationships with its customers so that those customers buy from it again and again. Costs will be far higher and profits lower if each customer purchase is a first-time sale.

How do marketers calculate the lifetime value of a customer? They first estimate a customer's future purchases across all products from the firm over the next 20 or 30 years. The goal is to try to figure out what profit the company could make from the customer in the future. For example, a car dealer might calculate the lifetime value of a single customer by first calculating the total revenue that could be generated by the customer over his lifetime: the number of cars he would buy multiplied by their average price, plus the service the dealership would provide over the years, and even possibly the income from vehicle financing. The lifetime value of the customer would be the total profit generated by the revenue stream.

Customer equity

Today an increasing number of companies are considering their relationships with customers as financial assets. Such firms measure success by calculating the value of their **customer equity** – the financial value of customer relationships throughout the lifetime of the relationships.[27] To do this, firms compare the investments they make in acquiring customers, retaining customers and relationship enhancement with the financial return on those investments. The goal is to reap a high return on the investments made in customer relationships and maximise the value of a firm's customer equity. Please analyse the Marketing metrics case, to see how lifetime value and customer equity came into play at BCA.

Focusing on high-value customers

Using a CRM approach, customers must be prioritised and communication customised accordingly. For example, any banker will tell you that not all customers are equal – when

Marketing metrics

Book Club Associates example

BCA is one of the world's biggest book clubs. Its business model, that of selling books by mail order to people who join its clubs, is one that has been around for a long time, but recent changes in its markets and channels have put it under severe financial pressure. The company decided to construct a customer equity optimisation model of the business, a spreadsheet which ran on data from their membership database and handled data for 30 book clubs (allowing a few extra for new clubs), 15 media channels and allowed for 450 different recruitment/spend decisions. The use of the optimisation model gave it guidance on:

- Targeting of marketing expenditure that maximises customer lifetime value;
- Clubs that were candidates for closure;
- Profitability over five years that will result from customer equity strategy and the use of the model resulted in a substantial growth in the company's profitability.

it comes to profitability. So banks use CRM systems to generate a profile of each customer based on factors such as value, risk and interest in buying new financial products. This automated system helps the bank decide which current or potential customers it will target with certain communications, or how much effort to spend on retaining a person's account – whilst at the same time cutting its costs by as much as a third.[28] It just makes sense to use different types of communication contacts based on the value of each individual customer. For example, personal selling (the most expensive form of marketing communication per contact) may constitute 75 per cent of all contacts with high-volume customers, while direct mail or telemarketing is more often the best way to contact low-volume customers.

The Strategic implementation of CRM

In attempting to illustrate how CRM can be implemented, Payne and Frow warn that many CRM projects are doomed for failure as they have not appropriately defined CRM, or have simply defined it from a limited technology perspective. They suggest that:

Marketing misstakes

Customer relationship management's evil twin

Marks & Spencer customers must have received a shock when they were told by the leading high street retailer to expect an increase in their spam email because Epsilon, the company M&S uses to send emails to customers, had its customer email addresses accessed without authorisation. According to its website, the marketing company sends over 40 billion emails annually and serves around 2500 clients. The breach had affected 2 per cent of clients including major banks and retailers worldwide, most of them in the US.

Marks & Spencer assured its customers that no other personal information such as account details had been obtained or were ever at risk. However, the fear is that once scammers get hold of their victims' names and email addresses, along with the companies that they do business with, they can design targeted email attacks that attempt to deceive victims into releasing more sensitive information such as passwords or account details. It is customer relationship management turned on its head.

Why do you think this might be a marketing misstake?

Source: Based on www.bbc.co.uk/news/technology-12983177

CRM is a strategic approach that is concerned with creating improved shareholder value through the development of appropriate relationships with key customers and customer segments. CRM unites the potential of relationship marketing strategies and IT to create profitable, long term relationships with customers and other stakeholders.[29]

These researchers propose a continuum, where at one end CRM can be defined narrowly and tactically – it is about the implementation and use of technology to create and develop relationships. At the opposite end, CRM is considered to be broader and has more of a strategic purpose in managing relationships to create shareholder value. In the middle of the spectrum, CRM is concerned with the implementation of an integrated series of customer-oriented technology solutions.

Based on a series of inductive case study investigations, the researchers provide a useful framework for implementing CRM strategies. Whilst the fine detail is too broad to include here, the idea of the framework is that CRM begins as a Strategy Development Process that feeds into (and from) the Value Creation Process (providing benefits for customers and companies); and then links into a firm's Multichannel Integration Process for managing relationships at the customer interface; which in turn feeds back to the Value Creation Process and feeds forward for enhancing Performance Assessment Processes, i.e. shareholder results and performance monitoring. Running parallel with these processes is the Information Management Process which feeds in and out of all these.

The framework is particularly useful for marketers, as it (a) helps to better define the arena surrounding CRM activities, (b) outlines the significance of cross-functional processes that are involved in CRM implementation and (c) illustrates key elements within each process. Whilst the authors acknowledge that much research remains to be done regarding the multifaceted nature of CRM, their work provides a useful starting point for marketers to follow. To fully appreciate CRM, organisations therefore need to look beyond simply using IT systems to develop customer relationships and, instead, need to be more proactive in effectively utilising their organisation's complete resources to engage and facilitate with customers and other stakeholders of strategic importance, which in turn will lead to positive effects on performance.

Now that you've learned more about segmentation, targeting and relationship building, read 'Real people, real decisions' to see which strategy Jochen opted for.

Real people, real decisions

How it worked out at & Samhoud

Jochen decided to be bold and supported Option 2. It was not an easy decision, as it would have been much easier to simply continue providing company reports that satisfied the needs of a large number of clients. He could have easily gone with Option 3, which was also quite a safe option. Selecting Option 2, however, seemed like a much better fit, allowing for more consistency by enabling Jochen to firmly position &samhoud as a corporate consultancy firm that aims at achieving breakthroughs. Tools is then not positioned as a product in itself but rather as an incremental part contributing to organisational change efforts. The decision meant letting go of several hundred thousand euros of annual turnover and guaranteed repeat turnover, because most clients used such services on an annual basis. However, an analysis of all projects from the previous five years revealed that projects at larger companies returned a higher efficiency profit. Also the lifetime value of larger organisations was better because they simply have more resources. Also, since the price for many services offered by &samhoud depends on the number of people an organisation employs (such as employee surveys), it made sense to focus on fewer projects with larger organisations and higher profit potential. Last but not least, &samhoud is a vision-driven company with a strong desire to grow internationally. Focusing on large organisations and multinationals clearly seemed the way forward to create the right degree of excitement for the company's employees. Due to the segmentation and targeting strategy employed, this business unit of &samhoud has experienced growing success. This has been achieved through making the shift in sales responsibility from tools to consulting and focusing on large organisations within several target sectors, i.e. financial services, government, healthcare and multinationals. Through a clear focus on targeting larger organisations in well-defined markets, Jochen was able to successfully develop a strategy for segmenting the market based on organisational size. He then targeted key players in several business markets, i.e. financial service providers, government markets, multinationals and large private firms that service care homes. The outcome reflected on a lesson that Jochen had learned during a visit to Harvard Business School, i.e. most companies only ask who they want as their customer. A question that is just as important is who you do not want as your customer. Segmentation can help you decide who falls in which category.

Chapter summary

Now that you have finished reading this chapter, you should be able to answer any of the following potential examination questions:

1. **Is market segmentation needed in today's business environment?** Market segmentation is often necessary in today's marketplace because of market fragmentation. That is, the splintering of a mass society into diverse groups due to technological and cultural differences. Most marketers can't realistically do a good job of meeting the needs of everyone, so it is more efficient to divide the larger pie into slices in which members of a segment share some important characteristics and tend to exhibit the same needs and preferences.

2. **What are the different dimensions marketers use to segment consumer and business-to-business markets?** Marketers frequently find it useful to segment consumer markets on the basis of demographic characteristics, including age, gender, family life cycle, social class, race or ethnic identity and place of residence. A second dimension, psychographics, uses measures of psychological and social characteristics to identify people with shared preferences or traits. Consumer markets may also be segmented on the basis of how consumers behave towards the product. For example, their brand loyalty, usage rates (heavy, moderate or light) and usage occasions. Business-to-business markets are often segmented on the basis of industrial demographics, type of business, i.e. their Standard Industrial Classification (SIC) codes, and geographic location.

3. **Describe how marketers evaluate and select potential market segments.** To choose one or more segments to target, marketers examine each segment and evaluate its potential for success as a target market. Meaningful segments have wants that are different from those in other segments, can be identified, can be reached with a unique marketing mix, will respond to unique marketing communications, are large enough to be profitable, have future growth potential and possess needs that the organisation can satisfy better than the competition.

4. **Explain how marketers develop a targeting strategy.** After marketers identify the different segments, they estimate the market potential of each segment. The relative attractiveness of segments also influences the firm's selection of an overall marketing strategy. The firm may choose an undifferentiated, differentiated, concentrated or custom strategy based on the company's characteristics and the nature of the market.

5. **Describe how a firm develops and implements a positioning strategy.** After marketers select the target market(s) and the overall strategy, they must determine how they wish customers to perceive the brand relative to the competition. That is, should the brand be positioned with, against or away from the competition? Through positioning, a brand personality is developed. Marketers can compare brand positions by using such research techniques as perceptual mapping. In developing and implementing the positioning strategy, firms analyse the competitors' positions, determine the competitive advantage offered by their product, tailor the marketing mix in accordance with the positioning strategy, and evaluate responses to the marketing mix selected. Marketers must continually monitor changes in the market that might indicate a need to reposition the product.

6. **Explain how marketers increase long-term success and profits by practising customer relationship management.** Companies using customer relationship management (CRM) programmes establish relationships and differentiate their behaviour towards individual customers on a one-to-one basis through dialogue and feedback. Success is often measured one customer at a time using the concepts of share of customer, lifetime value of the customer and customer equity. In CRM strategies, customers are prioritised according to their value to the firm, and communication is customised accordingly.

Key terms

Chapter review

Marketing concepts: testing your knowledge

1. What is market segmentation, and why is it an important strategy in today's marketplace?
2. List and explain the major demographic characteristics frequently used in segmenting consumer markets.
3. Explain consumer psychographic segmentation.
4. What is behavioural segmentation?
5. What are some of the ways marketers segment industrial markets?
6. List the criteria used for determining whether a segment may be a good candidate for targeting.
7. Explain undifferentiated, differentiated, concentrated and customised marketing strategies. What is mass customisation?
8. What is product positioning? Describe the three approaches that marketers use to create product positions.
9. What is CRM? How do firms practise CRM?
10. Explain the concepts of share of customer, lifetime value of a customer and customer equity.

Marketing concepts: discussing choices

1. One of the criteria for a usable market segment is its size. This chapter suggested that to be usable, a segment must be large enough to be profitable now and in the future and that some very small segments get ignored because they can never be profitable. So, how large should a segment be? How do you think a firm should go about determining if a segment is profitable? Have technological advances made it possible for smaller segments to be profitable?
2. Customer relationship management (CRM) focuses on share of customer, lifetime value of the customer, customer equity and high-value customers. What do you think are some problems with replacing earlier concepts such as share of market with these concepts?

Marketing practice: applying what you've learned

1. Assume that a firm has hired you to develop a marketing plan for a small regional brewery. In the past, the brewery has simply produced and sold a single beer brand to the entire market – a mass-marketing strategy. As you begin work, you feel that the firm could be more successful if it developed a target marketing strategy. The owner of the firm, however, is not convinced. Write a memo to the owner outlining the following:

   a. The basic reasons for target marketing.
   b. The specific advantages of a target marketing strategy for the brewery.

2. As the marketing director for a company that is planning to enter the business-to-business market for photocopy machines, you are attempting to develop an overall marketing strategy. You have considered the possibility of using mass marketing, concentrated marketing, differentiated marketing and custom marketing strategies.
   a. Write a report explaining what each type of strategy would mean for your marketing plan in terms of product, price, promotion and distribution.
   b. Evaluate the desirability of each type of strategy.
   c. What are your final recommendations for the best type of strategy?

3. As an account executive for a marketing consulting firm, your newest client is a university – your university. You have been asked to develop a positioning strategy for the university. With a group of classmates, develop an outline of your ideas, including the following:
   a. Who are your competitors?
   b. What are the competitors' positions?
   c. What target markets are most attractive to the university?
   d. How will you position the university for those segments relative to the competition? Present the results to your class.

4. Assume that a firm hires you as marketing manager for a chain of bookshops. You feel that the firm should develop a CRM strategy. Outline the steps you would take in developing that strategy.

 ## Marketing miniproject: learning by doing

This miniproject will help you to improve your understanding of how firms make target marketing decisions. The project focuses on the market for women's beauty care products.

1. Gather ideas about different dimensions useful for segmenting the women's beauty products market. You may use your own ideas, but you probably will also want to examine advertising and other marketing communications developed by different beauty care brands.

2. Based on the dimensions for market segmentation that you have identified, develop a questionnaire and conduct a survey of consumers. You will have to decide which questions should be asked and which consumers should be surveyed.

3. Analyse the data from your research and identify the different potential segments.

4. Develop segment profiles that describe each potential segment.

5. Generate several ideas for how the marketing strategy might be different for each segment based on the profiles. Develop a presentation (or write a report) outlining your ideas, your research findings and your marketing strategy.

Further reading

Customer Relationship Management, Ed Peelen, Financial Times/ Prentice Hall, 2005

The period of grandiose promises for Customer Relationship Management is far behind us, but the ambition to develop mutually beneficial relationships with the right customers remains. It requires the realisation of an infrastructure that enables customers and suppliers to communicate with one another, freed from the constraints of place and time. Also knowledge of individual customers has to be built by recording the right data in databases, updating it, enriching it, and using it. A customer-oriented organisation will have to be created which incorporates the proper culture, structure and procedures. CRM has far-reaching implications for organisations. Reason enough to examine all of the aspects of CRM further in this book and to share the experiences and research results obtained.

Real people, real surfers

Exploring the web

In this chapter, we learned about the importance of segmentation and targeting at &samhoud. Please go on to the company's website www.samhoud.com/en/home and try to answer the following:

1. How does &samhoud segment its customer base?

2. Look closely at the services offered by &samhoud and identify which particular businesses it aims to target.

Now, take a look at the website at www.pearsoned.co.uk/solomon to see some videos from YouTube relating to aspects of this chapter.

Marketing plan exercise

Check out a website for a company that manufacturers a product that you like and are familiar with. Pay special attention to the company's product lines and how it describes products and product uses. Select one particular product and answer the following questions:

1. What market segmentation approaches do you believe are most relevant for your chosen product given the type of product it is? Why do you recommend these over other possible approaches?

2. Describe the top three target markets for the product you selected. What makes these particular targets so attractive?

3. From your review of the website as well as your knowledge of the product, write out a positioning statement for the product. Keep it to a few sentences; start out with 'Product X is positioned as . . .'

4. In what ways could CRM help the company conduct successful target marketing and positioning of the product?

Delve deeper into market segmentation, targeting, positioning and CRM

Professor Caroline Tynan

Nottingham University Business School

CRM is one on the interesting battlefields of marketing, one of those few places where its advocates among academics and practitioners meet with varying degrees of disagreement. It is big business and therefore a rich territory for practitioners, particularly consultants, and those companies which sell CRM systems and technology-based customer solutions. To its many adherents in academia, CRM is seen as the practical application of relationship marketing. This more purist approach frequently conflicts with the requirements of producing an economical and efficient IT solution. So these various perspectives give rise to a measure of confusion about what exactly constitutes CRM, whether it is tactical or strategic, whether it is successful or failing to achieve its promise and how it should be implemented.

To give you some feel for these debates, and an update of current understandings, I have selected three papers to cover the spectrum of the discussions. The first paper by Russell Winer sets out a useful process model for CRM. This addresses the key tactical decision points for managers of creating the database, analysis and decisions about which customers to target, a review of tools for targeting, how to build relationships with targeted customers, privacy issues and metrics to measure the success of the programme. In doing this it sets out the basic practice of CRM with lots of real world examples to illustrate the issues. In the second paper, Payne and Frow's study focuses on understanding CRM as a value creation process for both customer and company and sets out a strategic approach to increase shareholder value. The future of CRM lies in its application and practice in a global marketplace, an issue which is addressed in the final paper by Ramaseshan et al. These authors review the challenges of successfully implementing Global CRM (GCRM) across more and more diverse groups of customers spanning nations and cultures, suggesting issues for future research. These three papers show that CRM is complex and challenging but, if well managed, an extremely valuable approach to marketing which will be with us for many years to come.

References

B. Ramaseshan, David Bejou, Subhash C. Jain, Charlotte Mason, and Joseph Pancras (2006) 'Issues and Perspectives in Global Customer Relationship Management', *Journal of Service Research* 9, no. 2, 195–207.

Adrian Payne, and Penny Frow (2005) 'A Strategic Framework for Customer Relationship Management', *Journal of Marketing*, 69, no. 4 (October), 167–176.

Russell S. Winer (2001) 'A Framework for Customer Relationship Management', *California Management Review* 43, no. 4, 89–105.

Professor Francis Buttle

Leading CRM author

Customer relationship management (CRM) is concerned with the deployment of technology to support the customer-facing business functions of sales, marketing and service. There is plenty of research conducted by technology analysts like Forrester and Gartner. Gartner is renowned for its analysis of the CRM technology marketplace, especially through its Magic Quadrant vendor comparisons, and its Hype Cycle studies which track the maturity of various technologies. Forrester provides similarly branded research, known as the Forrester Wave. Forrester's Emerging Trends research delivers insight into new technologies. If you wanted to find out how new technology platforms are empowering peer-to-peer communication, or how collaborative software enables knowledge workers to work in partnership across organisational boundaries, you'd look to these analysts. Academic research on CRM is both rare and insignificant in comparison. Because there are no journals focussed on CRM, per se, academic research is sprinkled amongst marketing, sales and customer service journals. As you'd expect, academic research addresses different questions from those tackled by the analysts. Academic research will help you understand how organisational culture is associated with CRM performance and whether the implementation of CRM technologies strengthens and lengthens customer relationships, but it won't deliver any insight into the technologies that support customer management strategies. There are a number of good books on CRM. The second edition of Francis Buttle's book *Customer Relationship Management: Concepts and Technologies* provides a solid and highly regarded overview of the field; Adrian Payne's book *The Handbook of CRM* is organised around a unique conceptual model that identifies a number of core CRM processes; Ed Peelen's book *Customer Relationship Management* takes relationship marketing principles and grafts on technology considerations. They all have something useful to say.

Marketing in action case

Real decisions at PizzaExpress

Peter Boizot founded PizzaExpress in 1965 after determining the need for a UK-based pizza restaurant with quality food comparable to that found in other parts of Europe. What is now an international chain began as a small, private restaurant in London. Boizot demanded absolute authenticity, which led him to purchase an Italian pizza oven, a Signora Notaro. With this genuine Italian machinery, Boizot teamed up with Margaret Zampi, the only mozzarella maker in London, and set out to make the first great pizzeria in the UK. Together they created a unique product for the city. The delicious and authentic Italian food of PizzaExpress immediately became a hit amongst Londoners. The business continued to grow and now consists of over 320 locations in the UK and 61 abroad.

Nearly half a century after its grand opening, PizzaExpress is currently a casual, sit-down eatery that caters to a full range of customers. The décor utilises glass, chrome, marble, fresh flowers and live plants, which radiate a sophisticated atmosphere that encourages diners to eat out. The menu features classic Italian bread, salad, pasta, wine and dessert, complete with a large selection of pizzas. Because the establishment focuses on combining authentic taste, service and creativity, PizzaExpress is constantly releasing new menu items with customer-led innovation. This means PizzaExpress must demonstrate consistent creativity and style with its service and food. To better suit families loyal to the restaurant chain, a one of a kind kids' menu has been designed. This menu aims to keep children occupied with four small courses presented one after another, while adult courses come at a regular and steady pace. The success of the new children's menu brought another target market to light: women, specifically weight-conscious women over 45 who tend to eat out twice a month with their female friends, partners and children.

PizzaExpress understood the dilemma many women face. They are torn between the desire to eat delicious food and the desire to lose weight. In most cases these wants do not come hand in hand. Seizing the opportunity to satisfy both, PizzaExpress began to brainstorm healthy options for the menu. Marketers understood that customers consider eating out as a treat and do not want to be reminded of their diet. Therefore, the PizzaExpress team focused on designing a healthy dish that did not compromise great taste for those who want to enjoy eating out, while managing their weight. Development chefs and marketers worked together to generate ideas for a food range that would satisfy these needs. After consulting the Foods Standards Agency and qualified nutritionists, PizzaExpress determined a cap of 500 calories for a pizza worthy of a weight-conscious consumer's appetite. Given the driven lifestyles and trendy, young-at-heart characteristics of its customers, PizzaExpress' management needed to balance both calorie control and style in an imaginative way.

Action taken by PizzaExpress

Executive Development Chef Antonio Romani realised that a majority of the calories in a pizza are from the dough. From there, he discovered the basis of a new idea, traditional fresella bread, which is made by removing the center. This bread became the inspiration for Leggera ('light' in Italian). Launched in 2009, Leggera is a food range designed for those who want to enjoy the benefit of eating out without the consequence of gaining weight. It became endorsed by Weight Watchers and includes starters, wine, dessert and pizza, all of which are labelled as Leggera items on the menu. The Leggera pizzas are composed of a ring of authentic Italian pizza, based on fresella, with low fat cheese and a fresh salad replacing the dough in the centre, delivering a pizza of around 500 calories. The Leggera contributes to 10 per cent of the restaurant chain's pizza sales, making the reduced-calorie pizzas the second-biggest sellers next to its classic Margherita pizza. In addition to offering a healthy alternative, the Leggera pizzas also save resources by requiring only half the amount of dough as a regular pizza and are priced on average 49p more than a classic pizza. Thus, according to James Hall of *The Telegraph*, 'It is ingenious marketing by PizzaExpress. The less dough it puts in, the more dough it makes.' Unlike the pizza, the Leggera wines cost nearly the same as the regular wine. By harvesting the grapes early, before they're fully sweetened, a lighter and less calorific wine has been created. The wine possesses fewer than 100 calories per small (175ml) glass, with an alcohol level just below 9.5 per cent, making it a popular selection amongst weight-watching customers and a complement to the pizza. A Leggera meal of pizza and wine would fall just below 600 calories. Emma Woods, Marketing Editor at Pizza Express, commented, 'The thing I am really proud of is that it is distinctive and memorable and it solves the eternal "shall I order a pizza or a salad?" conundrum.'

Prior to commercialising the Leggera brand, PizzaExpress underwent rigorous market testing. The campaign spanned a period of three months from July to September 2009. This included print advertisements, digital escalator panels, Facebook posts and social media, all of which apply a creative strategy, 'Leggera is more than a pizza. It's an opportunity to lunch again.' This instilled a sense of security within its customers, resulting in one in nine adult customers ordering Leggera immediately after its launch. In order to generate online conversation and word of mouth, PizzaExpress invited influential food and lifestyle bloggers to free Leggera Lunch events, during which they sampled the new menu and were able to create their own low-calorie pizzas. After the event, guests talked about the food online. PizzaExpress marked September as 'Blogger Lunch Month', which encouraged participants to invite fellow bloggers to join in on Leggera Lunches held throughout the month. As a result, Leggera appeared in 60 blogs and over 1,000,000 people were reached by this online word of mouth. PizzaExpress teamed up with Weight Watchers to execute additional events, showing members of Weight Watchers that not even pizza is off-limits. In 2010, the Marketing Society Awards for Excellence honoured PizzaExpress for its new campaign and this innovative brand experience. Thus fuelling the stage for PizzaExpress' idea generation and market research, in addition to catering directly to consumer needs with new products.

Things to think about

1. What is/are the decision(s) facing PizzaExpress?

2. What factors are important in understanding these decisions?

3. Which types of segmentation and targeting strategies are PizzaExpress implementing in this case?

4. What suggestion(s) for a health conscious product do you recommend?

5. What steps should be followed to implement your suggestion?

Case study prepared by Kristy Xu, Madeleine Aaron and Anastasia Stathopoulou

References

1. Stanley C. Hollander and Richard Germain, *Was There a Pepsi Generation before Pepsi Discovered It? Youth-Based Segmentation in Marketing* (New York: NTC Business Books, 1992).

2. Amy Barrett, 'To Reach the Unreachable Teen', *Business Week*, 18 September 2000, 78–80.

3. Bruce Horovitz, 'Gen Y: A Tough Crowd to Sell', *USA Today*, 21 May 2002, www.usatoday.com/money/covers/2002-04-22-geny.htm.

4. Douglas Coupland, *Generation X: Tales for an Accelerated Culture* (New York: St. Martin's Press, 1991).

5. Quoted in Karen Lowry Miller, 'You Just Can't Talk to These Kids', *Business Week*, 19 April 1993, 104.

6. Robert Scally, 'The Customer Connection: Gen X Grows Up, They're in Their 30s Now', *Discount Store News*, 25 October 1999, 38, www.findarticles.com/p/articles/mi_m3092/is_20_38/ai_57443548.

7. Ibid.

8. Alex Williams, 'What Women Want: More Horses', *New York Times Online*.

9. Michael Flocker, *The Metrosexual Guide to Style: A Handbook for the Modern Man* (Cambridge, MA: Da Capo Press, 2003).

10. www.urbandictionary.com/define.php?term=metrosexual.

11. Charles M. Schaninger and William D. Danko, 'A Conceptual and Empirical Comparison of Alternate Household Life Cycle Markets', *Journal of Consumer Research* 19 (March 1993), 580–94.

12. Christy Fisher, 'Census Data May Make Ads More Single-Minded', *Advertising Age*, 20 July 1992, 2.

13. See Lewis Alpert and Ronald Gatty, 'Product Positioning by Behavioral Life Styles', *Journal of Marketing* 33 (April 1969), 65–69; Emanuel H. Demby, 'Psychographics Revisited: The Birth of a Technique', *Marketing News*, 2 January 1989, 21; and William D. Wells, 'Backward Segmentation', in *Insights into Consumer Behavior*, ed. Johan Arndt (Boston: Allyn & Bacon, 1968), 85–100.

14. Neal E. Boudette, 'Navigating Curves: BMW's Push to Broaden Line Hits Some Bumps in the Road', *Wall Street Journal*, 10 January 2005, A1.

15. www.ge.com/en/product/business/aviation.htm.

16. L'Oréal, 'Our Brand Portfolio', www.loreal.com.

17. Chip Bayers, 'The Promise of One to One (a Love Story)', *Wired* (May 1998), 130.

18. For an example of how consumers associate food brands with a range of female body shapes, see Martin R. Lautman, 'End-Benefit Segmentation and Prototypical Bonding', *Journal of Advertising Research* (June/July 1991), 9–18.

19. 'A Crash Course in Customer Relationship Management', *Harvard Management Update*, March 2000 (Harvard Business School reprint U003B).

20. Don Peppers and Martha Rogers, *The One-to-One Future* (New York: Doubleday, 1996).

21. Don Peppers, Martha Rogers and Bob Dorf, 'Is Your Company Ready for One-to-One Marketing?', *Harvard Business Review* (January–February 1999), 151–60.

22. Quoted in Cara B. DiPasquale, 'Navigate the Maze', Special Report on 1:1 Marketing, *Advertising Age*, 29 October 2001, S1(2).

23. Jim Middlemiss, 'Users Say CRM Is Worth the Effort', www.wallstreetandtech.com, third quarter 2001, 17–18.

24. Mary Jo Nott, 'CRM Spending Forecast and Analysis 2001–2005', *DM Review*, www.dmreview.com/specialreports/20020806/5607-1.html.

25. Marc L. Songini, 'Dimmed Utilities Plug into CRM', *Computer World*, 6 August 2001.

26. Susan Fournier, Susan Dobscha and David Glen Mick, 'Preventing the Premature Death of Relationship Marketing', *Harvard Business Review* (January–February 1998), 42–4.

27. Robert C. Blattberg, Gary Getz and Mark Pelofsky, 'Want to Build Your Business: Grow Your Customer Equity', *Harvard Management Update* (August 2001, Harvard Business School reprint U0108B), 3.

28. Tonia Bruyns, 'Banking on Targeted Marketing', 7 November 2001, www.business2.co.za.

29. Adrian Payne and Pennie Frow, 'A Strategic Framework for Customer Relationship Management', *Journal of Marketing* 69, no. 4, 168.

Chapter 7
Creating the product

Meet Fraser Chisholm
Head of Media Propositions and Communications, Royal Mail

Q & A with Fraser Chisholm

What I do when I'm not working
Skiing and triathlon

First job out of school?
Tractor driver

Career high?
Delivering £51m of new revenue for Royal Mail or putting together a campaign for Poggenpohl Kitchens featuring Jamie Oliver

Best business book you've read?
The Telegraph

My hero
My Dad

My motto to live by
Trust your instinct

What drives me
Pleasing customers

My management style
Empowering

Don't do this when interviewing with me
Talk too much

Favourite drink?
Fizzy Water

Favourite management motto?
Bring me solutions not problems

Best holiday you've ever had?
Verbier 2007

F raser joined the Media Markets team at Royal Mail in 2002 to provide support and education in the use of Mail Media for the creative agency sector. He was instrumental in setting up Royal Mail's unique 'Mail Media Centre' near Covent Garden, where this information can be accessed.

Fraser has worked within the marketing industry for more than 20 years. He started his career with telemarketing firm Sitel, and positions at creative agencies Sutcliffe Reynolds Fitzgerald and TMO followed, before he joined Royal Mail. Fraser has experience in all areas of the direct marketing industry across sectors including automotive, financial services and pharmaceuticals.

Real people, real decisions
Decision time at Royal Mail

I n 2008 Royal Mail unveiled the 'Matterbox' (Photo 7.1), a quirky marketing tool to give nice things to people so they'll tell their friends. Antony Miller, Head of Media Business Development at Royal Mail, said: 'Advertisers are no longer able to rely only on consumers seeing or hearing their messages to boost sales – they now have to really engage people to stand out. Matter harnesses the marketing power of direct mail – communicating one-to-one with targeted recipients – and allows brands to physically place their products into people's hands.' John Willshire, Chief Innovation Officer at Cadbury's, defined Matterbox as, 'The most effective route we have developed to engage players for the Spots v Stripes campaign'.

The box was an instant hit after a trial box sent to 1000 18–24-year-old males created a storm of online interest, with Matterbox featuring on more than 100 blogs and websites, as well as YouTube. Today subscribers total more than 200,000.

Matterbox had stagnated a little with no large-scale buy-in from major brands; it wasn't despatched often enough to keep the buzz going and make its subscribers happy. The lack of buy-in from potential stakeholders created a Catch 22 situation. Lack of partners limits the number of sample products to be distributed and a lack of products to be distributed limited the powerful word-of-mouth recruitment strategy for new subscribers to send them to. Despite Matterbox being an innovative route to market, marketers preferred to spend their budgets on established media – the old model isn't broken yet.

Brand marketers cited both the lack of targeting – anyone can join Matter – and the lack of reach. This misses the point of Matter: it's based on the idea that enthusiasm and engagement will generate better responses (in an overcrowded media market) and reach can be achieved by people getting excited and telling their friends. Nonetheless, based on advertiser feedback, it was concluded that Matterbox needs to increase the breadth of subscribers both to have a bigger pool to target from and to achieve better reach. Three options were considered to improve the channel.

Option 1 To go for a general increase of the subscriber list, i.e. reach

Matterbox doesn't have a subscriber acquisition problem per se. It's gathered 200,000 UK subscribers with no acquisition activity (or cost) whatsoever and sees significant jumps in subscription whenever a box is issued (which is rare), even though most people don't receive them. A deliberate attempt at driving subscription (i.e. with an advertising campaign) without producing boxes, would most likely create a frustrated and hostile community of subscribers and undermine the goodwill and enthusiasm that underpins the concept.

The alternative would be to subsidise advertisers into the boxes, by either offering the media (box, collation and delivery) free and/or the content (the items). However, it's not that simple. Matter is a complex and sophisticated mechanic that requires an outcome, a suitably engaging item that asks consumers to do something and a response channel in order to deliver a cost-effective ROI. Offering it cheap or free still requires the advertisers and agencies to put all these in place, and generally, they're set up to do other things (i.e. make TV ads).

Or it could do both (subsidy and subscriber acquisition)?

Option 2 Get more information on both businesses and end consumers to improve targeting

This would solve the targeting problem, but would create very small audiences and would, inevitably, require more subscribers to create a bigger pool (back to Option 1).

An alternative would be to produce boxes around specific interests, i.e. gardening, cooking etc. Matter already asks its subscribers to share details about their interests and some of these groups are already quite large (e.g. 60,000+ interested in Health and Beauty). It might

Photo 7.1   An example of a typical Matterbox
Source: Image reproduced with kind permission of Royal Mail Group Ltd.

require some adjustments to the data questions, with an inherent problem of changing the questions after so many have already joined (getting people to go back and answer more questions is a lot harder than asking them to answer them when they join).

It would also require a more rigorous sales process of identifying enough suitable advertisers who all want the same audience at the same time and much of the sales channel problem has been getting sufficient advertiser engagement. So, often, it's like herding cats.

Option 3 Focus on single-brand boxes and build the case studies one at a time

Single-brand editions allow advertisers to have their pick of the audience – who and how many and when the boxes go out, without having to wait for anyone else.

It also eliminates the false-starts, missed deadlines and disappointments of abandoned boxes when not enough advertisers actually commit to doing it.

The disadvantage of single-brand editions is that they're expensive and miss the advantage of sharing the distribution costs amongst multiple advertisers (though, arguably, there's no dissolution of mail revenue for Royal Mail), and thus mean that Matter has to work harder to make its case.

The need to have specific problems to solve, suitably creative and engaging content and a robust and measurable digital response channel remain.

Now put yourself in Fraser's shoes; which option do you think will be most successful and why?

Objectives

When you finish reading this chapter, you will be able to:

1 Explain the layers of a product

2 Describe the classifications of products

3 Understand the importance of new products

4 Show how firms develop new products

5 Explain the process of product adoption and the diffusion of innovations

Build a better mousetrap: the value proposition

'Build a better mousetrap and the world will beat a path to your door.' Although we've all heard that adage, the truth is that just because a product is better is no guarantee it will succeed. For decades, the Woodstream Company (under the brand name 'Victor') built wooden mousetraps. Then the company decided to build a better one. Woodstream's product development people researched eating, crawling and resting habits of mice (hey, it's a living . . .). They built prototypes of different mousetraps to come up with the best possible design and tested them in homes. Then the company unveiled the sleek-looking 'Little Champ', a black plastic miniature inverted bathtub with a hole. When the mouse went in and ate the bait, a spring snapped upward and the mouse was history.

Sounds like a great new product (unless you're a mouse), but the Little Champ failed. Woodstream studied mouse habits, *not* consumer preferences. The company later discovered that husbands set the trap at night, but wives were left in the morning to dispose of the trap holding the dead mouse. Unfortunately, wives thought the Little Champ looked too expensive to throw away, so they felt they should empty the trap for reuse. This was a task most women weren't willing to do – they wanted a trap they could happily throw away.[1]

Woodstream's failure underscores the importance of creating products that provide benefits that people seek. It also tells us that any number of products, from low-tech cheese to high-tech traps, potentially deliver these benefits. Despite Victor's claim to be the 'World's Leader in Rodent Control Solutions', in this case cheese and a shoe box could trap a mouse as well as a high-tech trap.

We need to take a close look at how products successfully trap consumers' money. Chapter 1 showed us that the value proposition is consumers' perception of the benefits they will receive if they buy a product or service. So, the marketer's task is twofold: first, to create a better value than what's already out there and then to convince customers that this is true.

As we defined it in Chapter 1, a product is a tangible good, service, idea, place or person or some combination of these that satisfies consumer or business customer needs through the exchange process; a bundle of attributes including features, functions, benefits and uses. A good may be a pack of biscuits, a digital camera, a house, a fancy new computer or a pair of distressed jeans. A **good** is a tangible product, something that we can see, touch, smell, hear, taste or possess. In contrast, intangible products – services, ideas, people, places – are products that we can't always see, touch, taste, smell or possess. We'll talk more about intangible products in Chapter 9.

Marketers think of the product as more than just a thing that comes in a package. They view a product as a bundle of attributes that includes the packaging, brand name, benefits and supporting features in addition to a physical good. The key word here is *creating*, and a large part of the marketer's role in creating the value proposition is developing and *marketing* products appropriately. In this chapter, we'll first examine what a product is and see how marketers classify consumer and business-to-business products. Then we'll go on to look at new products, how marketers develop new products, and how markets accept them. In the chapters that follow, we'll look at issues such as managing and pricing products and services.

 ## Layers of the product concept

www.pearsoned.co.uk/solomon

Objective

1

Explain the layers of a product

No doubt you've heard someone say, 'It's the thought, not the gift that counts.' This means that the gift is a sign or symbol that the gift giver has remembered you. When we evaluate a gift, we may consider the following: Was the gift presented with a flourish? Was it wrapped in special paper? Was it obviously a 're-gift': something the gift giver got as a gift for himself but wanted to pass on to me? These dimensions are a part of the total gift you receive in addition to the actual goodie sitting in the box.

Like a gift, a product is everything that a customer receives in an exchange. As Figure 7.1 shows, we can distinguish among three distinct layers of the product – the core product,

Figure 7.1   Layers of the product
A product is everything a customer receives – the basic benefits, the physical product and its packaging, and the 'extras' that come with the product

the actual product and the augmented product. In developing product strategies, marketers need to consider how to satisfy customers' wants and needs at each of these three layers. Let's consider each layer in turn.

The core product

The **core product** consists of all the benefits the product will provide for consumers or business customers. As we noted in Chapter 1, a benefit is an outcome that the customer receives from owning or using a product. Wise old marketers (and some young ones, too) will tell you, 'A marketer may make and sell a half-inch drill bit, but a customer buys a half-inch hole.' This timeworn saying tells us that people are buying the core product, in this case the ability to make a hole. If a new product such as a laser comes along that provides that outcome in a better way or more cheaply, the drill bit maker has a problem. The moral of this story? Marketing is about supplying benefits, not features. Table 7.1 shows how some marketers rigorously test their products 'in action' to be sure they deliver the benefits they promise.

Many products actually provide several benefits. For example, the primary benefit of a car is transportation – all cars (in good repair) provide the ability to travel from point A to point B. But products also provide customised benefits – benefits customers receive because manufacturers have added additional features to win over customers. Different drivers seek different customised benefits in a car. Some want economical transportation; others want a top-of-the-line, all-terrain vehicle; and still others look for a hot car that will be the envy of their friends.

The actual product

The second layer of the product, the actual product, is the physical good or the delivered service that supplies the desired benefit. For example, when you buy a washing machine, the core product is the ability to get clothes clean, but the actual product is a large, square,

Marketing misstakes

The power of words

Around the world words mean different things. Indeed HSBC, the world's local bank, has conducted a very successful campaign playing on these different meaning for many years. Firms often fail to check linguistic implications of their product names and slogan, thus the direct translation may convey a different message. Take a look at some of these examples from around the world.

1. The famous fried chicken hub KFC's slogan 'finger-lickin good': when marketed in China, the translation was 'eat your fingers off'. Needless to say that it was an embarrassment for the company.

2. GEC and Plessey had a joint company in France which was called GPT. When GPT is pronounced in French 'Jay-Pay-Tay' it sounds similar to 'J'ai pete', which means 'I have farted.'

3. When Ford tried selling its car 'Pinto' in Brazil it was a huge failure. The reason – the word 'Pinto' is slang for small penis in Brazil.

4. When Hunt–Wesson introduced its Big John products in French in Canada as Gros Jos, they forgot to note that Gros Jos is the slang for 'big breasts.'

5. Parker pens' slogan 'Avoid Embarassment – use Quink,' when translated into Spanish, it came out as 'Avoid pregnancy – use Quink.'

Source: Marketing Hackz.com/10-product-and-campaign-blunders-to-learn-from

Table 7.1
Product testing

Product	Testing Procedure	Benefit
Ikea furniture	Ikea puts its products through three years of 'everyday home use' in one week, such as opening and closing the doors of a closet. Only if the product passes this test does it go on the market	Furniture which can survive in turbulent everyday family life and does not collapse after one week
Motorola mobile phones	The phones are exposed to a large variety of tests, such as environmental stress tests, electromagnetic compatibility and reliability tests	A high-quality product which can meet the technological and safety requirements of the consumer
Mercedes A-Class	The car had to pass the so-called 'Elk-test', which examined the stability of the car when it drives into a sharp curve at high speed. This simulated a situation in which an elk runs into the road and the car has to avoid it – a scenario which can be common in Scandinavia. For quite some time the car failed this test and kept falling over in the curve, to the amusement of the press and competitors.	Thanks to this product testing procedure, the company was able to correct mistakes made in the planning process and improve the product

Source: www.motorola.com/testservices/; www.welt.de/motor/article1280688/Mercedes_und_der_Elch_Die_perfekte_Blamage.html

metal apparatus. When you have a medical examination, the core product is maintaining your health, but the actual product is a lot of annoying poking and prodding. The actual product also includes the unique features of the product, such as its appearance or styling, the package and the brand name. Canon makes a wide range of different cameras from inexpensive, disposable cameras to expensive digital models that do everything but take the photo for you – all offering the same core benefit of recording a person or event on film or in a digital format.

The augmented product

Finally, marketers offer customers an **augmented product** – the actual product plus other supporting features such as a warranty, credit, delivery, installation and repair service after the sale. Marketers know that adding these supporting features to a product is an effective way for a company to stand out from the crowd.

For example, Tesco DVD Rental provides rental of DVDs (the actual product) to customers who want access to films (the core product). Tesco successfully competes with video/DVD rental shops by letting customers rent an unlimited number of DVDs, with three titles out at a time, for a small monthly subscription. Unlike renting from a video shop, customers can keep the movies for as long as they want with no late fees, no contracts and you can cancel at anytime. Customers pay no delivery fees in either direction, and they can choose from 56,000 titles – a much more extensive collection than what the largest DVD rental shops can offer. Tesco DVD Rental also offers a movie recommendation service based on each customer's rating of previous discs. Tesco DVD Rental's augmented product (free shipping, no time limits, extensive selection and targeted recommendation) has paid off for the company.

A different example is that membership in a Virgin Active Health Club provides access to pieces of sports equipment and gym classes (the actual product) for customers who want to keep in good shape (the core product). However, as customers purchase the gym membership they also benefit from several additional and supporting features. Those include, for example, a free personal trainer session, the 'V-Club' where children are looked after while their parents exercise, free internet access and a large spa area. The company hopes that this augmented product offer will make customers feel especially well treated and more comfortable at the Health Club and that they will return the favour with loyalty and good word-of-mouth promotion.[2]

 ## Classifying products

Objective

2

Describe the classifications of products

So far, we've learned that a product may be a tangible good or an intangible service or idea and that there are different layers to the product. Now we'll build on that idea by looking at how products differ from one another. Marketers classify products into categories because the categories represent differences in how consumers and business customers feel about products and how they purchase them. Such an understanding helps marketers develop new products and a marketing mix that satisfies customer needs. Table 7.2 summarises these categories.

Generally, products are either consumer products or business-to-business products, although sometimes consumers and businesses buy the same products, such as toilet paper,

Table 7.2
Classification of products

Marketers classify products to help understand how consumers make purchase decisions
Consumer Products

Classified by how long they last

Durable: products that provide a benefit over a long period
- Example: Refrigerator

Non-durable: products that provide a benefit over a short time
- Example: Toothpaste

Classified by how consumers buy them

Convenience Products: products that are frequently purchased with little effort
- Examples: Staples (milk)
              Impulse products (chocolate bars)
              Emergency products (drain cleaner)

Shopping Products: products that are selected with considerable time and effort
- Examples: Attribute-based (shoes)
              Price-based (drain cleaner)

Speciality Products: products that have unique characteristics to the buyer
- Examples: Favourite restaurant, Rolex watch

Unsought Products: products that consumers have little interest in until need arises
- Example: Retirement plans

Business-to-Business Products

Classified by how organisational customers use them

Equipment
- Examples: Capital equipment (buildings)
              Accessory equipment (computer terminals)

Maintenance, Repair and Operating (MRO) Products
- Examples: Maintenance products (lightbulbs, mops)
              Repair products (nuts, bolts)
              Operating supplies (paper, oil)

Raw Materials
- Example: Iron ore

Processed Materials
- Example: Sheets of steel

Specialised Services
- Example: Legal services

Component Parts
- Example: Car water pump

vacuum cleaners and light bulbs. In these cases, though, businesses tend to buy a lot more of them at once. Of course, as we saw in Chapters 4 and 5, customers differ in how they make the purchase decision depending on whether the decision maker is a consumer or a business purchaser. Let's first consider differences in consumer products based on how long the product will last and on how the consumer shops for the product. Then we will discuss the general types of business-to-business products.

Classifying goods: how long does the product last?

Marketers classify consumer goods as durable or non-durable depending on how long the product lasts. You expect a refrigerator to last many years, but a pint of milk will last only a week or so until it turns into a science project. **Durable goods** are consumer products that provide benefits over a period of months, years, or even decades, such as cars, furniture and appliances. In contrast, **non-durable goods**, such as newspapers and food, are consumed in the short term.

We are more likely to purchase durable goods under conditions of high involvement (as we saw in Chapter 4), while non-durable goods are more likely to be low-involvement decisions. When consumers buy a computer or a house, they will spend a lot of time and energy on the decision process. When they offer these products, marketers need to understand consumers' desires for different product benefits and the importance of warranties, service and customer support. So they must be sure that consumers can find the information they need. One way to do this is by providing a 'Frequently Asked Questions (FAQ)' section on a company website. Another way is to host a message board or blog to facilitate a sense of community around the product. When a company itself sponsors such forums, odds are the content will be much more favourable and the firm can police peripheral postings. For example, the section of the Microsoft website called 'Microsoft Technical Communities' allows users to solve problems by typing in any product (or even an error code that popped up on your computer) and then to track through a discussion board on that issue.[3]

In contrast, consumers usually don't consider the details so much when choosing among non-durable goods where there is little if any search for information or deliberation. Sometimes this means that consumers buy whatever brand is available and reasonably priced. In other instances, they base their decisions largely on past experience. Because a certain brand has performed satisfactorily in the past, customers see no reason to consider other brands and they choose the same one out of habit. For example, some consumers buy the box of Persil laundry detergent with that familiar red logotype again and again. In such cases, marketers can probably be less concerned with developing new product features to attract customers; they should focus more on pricing and distribution strategies.

Classifying goods: how do consumers buy the product?

Marketers also classify products based on where and how consumers buy the product. We can think of both goods and services as convenience products, shopping products, speciality products or unsought products. Recall that, in Chapter 4, we talked about how consumer decisions differ in terms of effort from habitual decision making to limited problem solving to extended problem solving. We can tie this classification of products in terms of how consumers buy them to these differences in consumer decision making. By understanding how consumers buy products, marketers have a clearer vision of the buying process that will help them to develop effective marketing strategies based upon the category into which their product falls.

A **convenience product** typically is a non-durable good or service that consumers purchase frequently with a minimum of comparison and effort, e.g. milk. As the name implies, consumers expect these products to be handy and they will buy whatever brands are easy to obtain. In general, convenience products are low priced and widely available. You can buy a litre of milk or a loaf of bread at grocery shops, at corner shops and even at many petrol stations. Consumers generally know all they need or want to know about a convenience product, devote little effort to purchases and willingly accept other brands if their preferred brand is not available in a convenient location. Most convenience product purchases are the results of habitual consumer decision making. What's the most important thing for marketers of convenience products? Unsurprisingly, it's to make sure the product is easily obtainable in all the places where consumers are likely to look for it.

But all convenience product purchases aren't alike. You may stop by a local shop on your way home from university or work to pick up that carton of milk because milk is something you always keep in the refrigerator. As long as you're there, why not grab a chocolate bar for the drive home? Later that night, you dash out to buy something to unblock your kitchen drain – also a convenience product. Marketers classify convenience products as staples, impulse products and emergency products.

Staples such as milk, bread and petrol are basic or necessary items that are available almost everywhere. Most consumers don't perceive big differences among brands. When selling staples, marketers must offer customers a product that consistently meets their expectations for quality and make sure it is available at a price comparable to the competition's prices.

Consider this situation: You are standing in the checkout queue at the supermarket and notice a copy of *Hello!* magazine featuring a photo of Victoria Beckham with a provocative headline. You've got to check out that article! This magazine is an **impulse product** – something people often buy on the spur of the moment. With an impulse product, marketers have two challenges: to create a product or package design that is enticing, that 'reaches out and grabs the customer', and to make sure their product is highly visible, for example by securing prime end-aisle or checkout-till space.

Emergency products are those products we purchase when we're in dire need. Bandages, umbrellas and something to unblock the bathroom sink are examples of emergency products. Because we need the product badly and immediately, price and sometimes product quality may be irrelevant to our decision to purchase. If you're caught out in a sudden downpour, any umbrella at almost any price may do.

What are the challenges to marketers of emergency products? As with any other product, emergency products are most successful when they meet customer needs – you won't sell a drain cleaner that doesn't unblock a drain more than once. And emergency products need to be offered in the sizes customers want. If you cut your finger during a night out on the town you don't want to buy a box of 100 bandages – you want a box of 5 or 10. Of course, making emergency products available when and where an emergency is likely to occur is the real key to success.

In contrast to convenience products, **shopping products** are goods or services for which consumers will spend time and effort gathering information on price, product attributes and product quality. They are likely to compare alternatives before making a purchase. The purchase of shopping products is typically a limited problem-solving decision. Often consumers have little prior knowledge about these products. Because they gather new information for each purchase occasion, consumers are only moderately brand loyal and will switch whenever a different brand offers new or better benefits. They may visit several shops and devote considerable effort to comparing products.

Laptop computers are a good example of a shopping product because they offer an ever-expanding array of new features and functions. There are trade-offs and decisions to make about the price, speed, screen size, weight and battery life. Consumers may ask,

'Does it have an internal DVD drive to play my movies?' 'How much does it weigh?' 'How long is the battery life?' 'Does it have built-in wireless networking?' or 'Does it have enough memory to drive my game?'[4] Designing successful shopping products means making sure they have the attributes that customers want. And it helps to design product packaging that points out those features consumers need to know about to make the right decisions.

Some shopping products have special characteristics. When people shop for *attribute-based shopping products*, such as a new party dress or a pair of designer jeans, they spend time and energy finding the best possible product selection. At other times, when choices available in the marketplace are just about the same, we consider these to be shopping products because of differences in price. For these *price-based shopping products*, such as a new lawnmower, determined shoppers will visit numerous shops in hopes of saving an additional €10 or €20.

In business-to-consumer e-commerce, shopping is easier when consumers use **'shopbots'** or 'intelligent agents': computer programs that find sites selling a particular product. Some of these programs also provide information on competitors' prices, and they may even ask customers to rate the various e-businesses that they have listed on their site so consumers can learn from other shoppers which sellers are good and which are less than desirable. It should be noted, however, that some sites do not wish to compete on price and don't give bots access to their listings.

Photo 7.2	Consumers will spend time and effort comparing shopping products. This MacBook Air advert focuses on its unique benefits – its size and weight – to inform the consumer's decision-making process

Source: Getty Images

Consumers can buy a mop in any supermarket for well under £10, right? Yet the demand for high-tech cleaning robots like the Kärcher RC3000 RoboCleaner is steadily increasing. The RoboCleaner promises 'cleaning at the touch of a button' as it sweeps and vacuums the floor all by itself. The only thing the consumer still needs to do is to switch it on. However, Kärcher charges a hefty price of around €1500 (about £1000) for this little knee and back saver.[5]

The RoboCleaner is a good example of a **speciality product**, as are Rolex watches. Speciality products have unique characteristics that are important to buyers at any price. We can even find speciality products competing in such mundane product categories as drinking water: Voss water has sleek packaging that makes it stand out from other bottled waters. Extracted from an aquifer that was buried under snow and ice for centuries in Norway, Voss markets its water as the purest in the world (for €10 or more a bottle in chic restaurants).

Consumers usually know a good deal about speciality products, and they tend to be loyal to specific brands. Generally, a speciality product is an extended problem-solving purchase that requires a lot of effort to choose. That means that firms selling these kinds of products need to create marketing strategies that make their product stand out from the rest. For example, advertising for a speciality product such as a flat-screen plasma TV may talk about plasma's unique and superior characteristics, attempting to convince prospective customers that savvy shoppers won't accept a substitute such as a mere LCD screen.

Unsought products are goods or services (other than convenience products) for which a consumer has little awareness or interest until a need arises. For university graduates with their first 'real' jobs, retirement plans and disability insurance are unsought products. It requires a good deal of advertising or personal selling to interest people in these kinds of products – just ask any life insurance salesperson. It's a real challenge to find convincing ways to interest consumers in unsought products. One solution may be to make pricing more attractive; for example, reluctant consumers may be more willing to buy an unsought product for 'only pennies a day' than if they have to think about their yearly or lifetime cash outlay.

Business-to-business products

Although consumers purchase products for their own use, as we saw in Chapter 5, organisational customers purchase items to use in the production of other goods and services or to facilitate the organisation's operation. Marketers classify business-to-business products based on how organisational customers use them. As with consumer products, when marketers know how their business customers use a product, they are better able to design products and craft the entire marketing mix. Let's briefly review the five different types of business-to-business products.

Equipment

Equipment refers to the products an organisation uses in its daily operations. Heavy equipment, sometimes called installations or capital equipment, includes items such as buildings and robotics used to assemble cars. Installations are expensive items and last for a number of years. Computers, photocopy machines and water fountains are examples of light or accessory equipment; they are portable, cost less, and have a shorter life span than capital equipment. Equipment marketing strategies usually emphasise personal selling and may mean custom-designing products to meet an industrial customer's specific needs.

MRO products

Maintenance, repair and operating (MRO) products are goods that a business customer consumes in a relatively short time. Maintenance products include light bulbs, mops, cleaning supplies and the like. Repair products are such items as nuts, bolts, washers and small tools. Operating supplies include computer paper and oil to keep machinery running smoothly. Although some firms use a sales force to promote MRO products, others rely on catalogue sales, the internet and telemarketing to keep prices as low as possible.

Raw materials

Raw materials are products of the fishing, lumber, agricultural and mining industries that organisational customers purchase to use in their finished products. For example, a food company may transform soya beans into tofu, and a steel manufacturer changes iron ore into large sheets of steel used by other firms to build cars, washing machines and lawnmowers.

Processed materials and special services

Processed materials are produced when firms transform raw materials from their original state. Organisations purchase processed materials that become a part of the products they make. A builder uses treated timber to add a deck to a house, and a company that creates aluminium cans for Red Bull buys aluminium ingots for this purpose.

Some business customers purchase specialised services from outside suppliers. Specialised services may be technical, such as equipment repair, or non-technical, such as market research and legal services. These services are essential to the operation of an organisation but are not part of the production of a product.

Component parts

Component parts are manufactured goods or subassemblies of finished items that organisations need to complete their own products. For example, a computer manufacturer needs silicon chips to make a computer, and a car manufacturer needs batteries, tyres and fuel injectors. As with processed materials, marketing strategies for component parts usually involve nurturing relationships with customer firms and on-time delivery of a product that meets the buyer's specifications.

Real people, other voices

Advice for Fraser Chisholm

Matthew Wood
University of Brighton

I would go for Option 2. The whole point of this marketing tool is to enable companies to more effectively target customers so this is the most logical option.

More research is required to understand potential consumer segments and their needs and desires. To make this work Royal Mail should work with clients to understand the segments they are trying to reach and to ensure they can be targeted.

The themed idea is a good one, provided competitive rivalries can be avoided (i.e. how to work with companies competing in the same market). I would also recommend Royal Mail work more closely with retailers, who can offer an assortment of branded products in particular categories/themes.

This innovation has a lot of potential if partnerships can be established with retailers and brand manufacturers. In this way Matterbox could be integrated effectively with other marketing and promotional strategies to truly target and engage consumers.

To review, we now understand what a product is. We also know how marketers classify consumer products based on how long they last and how they are purchased, and we've seen how they classify business-to-business products according to how they are used. In the next section we'll learn about the marketing of new products, or innovations.

'New and improved!' The process of innovation

Objective

3

Understand the importance of new products

'New and improved!' What exactly do we mean when we use the term *new product*? One interpretation is that a product must be entirely new or changed significantly to be called new and that a product may be called new for only six months.

That definition is fine from a legal perspective, but from a marketing standpoint, a new product or an **innovation** is anything that customers perceive as new and different. Innovations may be a cutting-edge style like the Motorola RAZR cellphone, a fad like Razor scooters or a new personal care product like the Gillette Fusion razor (starting to see a pattern here?). It can also be a new communications technology such as Skype person-to-person telephony over the internet, or a new way to power a vehicle such as the Toyota Prius hybrid, which addresses consumer demand shifts driven by high petrol prices. An innovation may be a completely new product that provides benefits which were never available before, such as personal computers when they were first introduced, or it may simply be an existing product with a new style, in a different colour, or with some new feature like Kellogg's Special K Red Berries.

It's important to understand how innovations work

If an innovation is successful, it spreads throughout the population. First, it is bought and used by only a few people, and then more and more consumers adopt it. Or (more typically) an innovation can be a flop and it may not be around a year from now.

Understanding the process by which innovations succeed (or not) is critical to the success of firms for at least two reasons. First, technology is advancing at a dizzying pace. Products are introduced and become obsolete faster than ever before. In many industries, firms are busy developing another new-and-better product before the last new-and-better one even hits shop shelves. Nowhere is this more obvious than with personal computers, for which a steady change in technology makes consumers want a smaller, slimmer, faster machine before the dust even settles on the old one. Another reason why understanding new products is important is the high cost of developing new products and the even higher cost of new products that fail. In the pharmaceutical industry, the cost of bringing each new drug to market is over €4.5 billion.[6] Even the most successful firms can't afford many product failures with that kind of price tag.

Marketers must understand what it takes to develop a new product successfully. They must do their homework and learn what it is about existing products consumers find less than satisfactory and exactly what it will take to do a better job satisfying customer needs. Savvy marketers know they'll waste a lot of investment money if they don't.

Finally, new products contribute to society. We would never suggest that everything new is good, but many new products like those Table 7.3 lists allow us to live longer, happier lives of better quality than ever before. Although there are some who disagree, most of us feel that our lives are better because of mobile phones (if that person blabbing on his next to us would shut up . . .), televisions, PDAs, iPods, microwave ovens and laptop computers. And new medical products keep *us* from breaking down: in the near future, doctors

Table 7.3
Some innovations since 1900

Products that have changed how we play	
1900	Kodak Brownie camera
1948	Polaroid camera
1970	Digital music
1976	JVC video recorder
1982	Philips/Sony CD player
1995	DVD player
1998	MP3 players

Products that have changed how we work	
1959	Xerox photocopier
1967	ATMs
1971	Intel microprocessor
1980	3M Post-it Notes
1984	Apple Macintosh
1996	Universal Serial Bus
1998	BlackBerry PDA

Products that have changed how we travel	
1908	Ford Model T
1936	DC-3
1949	de Havilland Comet
1950s	Skateboard
1993	Ryanair
2000	Global Positioning Systems (GPS)
2003	Toyota Prius hybrid car

Products that have changed our health and grooming	
1921	Johnson & Johnson Band-Aid
1928	Penicillin
1931	Tampax tampon
1960	Searle birth control pill
2003	Crest Whitestrips

Products that have changed our homes	
1907	Vacuum cleaner
1918	Frigidaire refrigerator
1955	TV remote
1967	Amana microwave oven
2003	TMIO internet-accessible refrigerated oven

Products that have changed the way we communicate	
1922	British Broadcasting Corporation formed
1936	BBC's first regular TV broadcasts
1991	World Wide Web
2003	Treo cell phone/PDA/camera
2004	Web 2.0

Products that have changed our clothing	
1913	Zipper
1914	Bra
1939	Nylons
1954	Velcro
1961	Procter & Gamble Pampers

Sources: Based on Christine Chen and Tim Carvell, 'Products of the Century,' *Fortune*, 22 November 1999, 133–36; 'Best of What's Next,' *Popular Science*, 13 November 2003; http://inventors.about.com/ library/ inventors/bldvd.htm; www.time.com/time/2003/inventions/list.html; Thomas Hoffman, 'Segway's Tech Plans Look Down the Road to Growth,' *Computer World*, 26 January 2004, 4; Louis E. Frenzel, 'The BlackBerry Reaps the Fruits of Innovation,' *Electronic Design*, 29 March 2004, 41(5); David Stires, 'Rx for Investors,' *Fortune*, 3 May 2004, 158; and 'Procter & Gamble,' *Drug Store News*, 19 January 2004, 57; www.bbc.co.uk/ heritage; www.tnenewsis.com/2006/11/02/10-inventions-that-changed-our-lives

will be able to replace or assist almost every part of the body with bionic products such as replacement spinal discs, insulin pumps that mimic a natural pancreas in diabetes patients by automatically testing blood-glucose levels, microdetectors implanted into retinas allowing patients with retinal damage to see light, and bionic ears that allow the deaf to hear.[7]

 ## Types of innovation

Innovations differ in their degree of newness, and this helps to determine how quickly the target market will adopt them. Because innovations that are more novel require us to exert greater effort to figure out how to use them, they are slower to spread throughout a population than new products that are similar to what is already available.

Marketers classify innovations into three categories based on their degree of novelty: continuous innovations, dynamically continuous innovations and discontinuous innovations. However, it is better to think of these three types as ranges along a continuum that goes from a very small change in an existing product to a totally new product. We can then describe the three types of innovations in terms of the amount of disruption or change they bring to people's lives. For example, the first cars caused tremendous changes in the lives of people who were used to getting to places under 'horse power'. While a more recent innovation like GPS systems that feed us driving directions by satellite are undoubtedly cool, in a relative sense we have to make fewer changes in our lives to adapt to them (other than not having to ask a stranger for directions when you're lost).

Continuous innovations

A **continuous innovation** is a modification to an existing product, such as when Kellogg's introduced Special K Bliss Strawberry and Chocolate versions of its cereal. This type of modification can set one brand apart from its competitors. For example, Volvo cars are known for their safety, and Volvo comes out with a steady stream of safety-related innovations. Volvo was the first car to offer full front and side air bags, and its models come with an extensive menu of air bags, including Inflatable Curtain head-protection air bags for front and rear passengers, torso side air bags for front passengers, and the usual dual-stage front air bags. Additional crash protection for the Volvo V40 comes from whiplash-reducing front seats and seatbelt pretensioners.[8]

The consumer doesn't have to learn anything new to use a continuous innovation. From a marketing perspective, this means that it's usually pretty easy to convince consumers to adopt this kind of new product. For example, Samsung's high-definition plasma flat-screen monitors don't require computer users to change their behaviour. We all know what a computer monitor is and how it works. The system's continuous innovation simply gives users the added benefits of taking up less space and being easier on the eyes.

How different does a new product have to be from existing products before people think it's *too* different? We've all heard that 'imitation is the sincerest form of flattery', but decisions regarding how much (if at all) one's product should resemble those of competitors are often a centrepiece of marketing strategy. Sometimes marketers feel that the best strategy is to follow the competition. For example, the packaging of 'me-too' or lookalike products can create instant market success because consumers assume that similar packaging means similar products.

A **copycat** is a new product that copies, with slight modification, the design of an original product. Firms deliberately create copycats of clothing, jewellery or other items, often with the intent to sell to a larger or different market. For example, companies may copy the *haute couture* clothing styles of top designers and sell them at lower prices to the mass market. It is difficult to legally protect a design (as opposed to a technological invention) because an imitator can argue that even a very slight change – different buttons or a slightly wider collar on a dress or shirt – means the copycat product is not an exact copy.

Dynamically continuous innovations

A **dynamically continuous innovation** is a pronounced modification to an existing product that requires a modest amount of learning or change in behaviour to use it. The history of audio equipment is a series of dynamically continuous innovations. For many years, consumers enjoyed listening to their favourite Frank Sinatra songs on record players. Then, in the 1960s, that same music became available on a continuous-play eight-track tape (requiring the purchase of an eight-track tape player, of course). Then came cassette tapes (oops, now a cassette player is needed). In the 1980s, consumers could hear Metallica songs digitally mastered on compact discs (that, of course, required the purchase of a new CD player).

Photo 7.3	The Toyota Prius is an example of a dynamically continuous innovation
	Source: Courtesy of Toyota (GB) Ltd.

In the 1990s, recording technology moved one more step forward with MP3 technology, allowing music fans to download music from the web or to exchange electronic copies of the music with other fans. Mobile MP3 players hit the scene in 1998, letting music fans download their favourite tunes into a portable player. In November 2001, Apple Computer introduced its first iPod. With the original iPod, music fans could take 1000 songs with them wherever they went. By 2006, iPods could hold 15,000 songs, 25,000 photos and 150 hours of video and now it's integrated into the iPhone.[9] Music fans go to the Apple iTunes music shop or elsewhere to download songs and to get suggestions for new music they might enjoy. Even though each of these changes required learning how to operate new equipment, consumers were willing to buy the new products because of the improvements in music reproduction, the core product benefit. Hopefully the music will continue to improve, too.

Convergence is one of the most talked-about forms of dynamically continuous innovations in the digital world. This term means the coming together of two or more technologies to create new systems that provide greater benefit than the original technologies alone. Think about the NeoReader Qode technology we discussed in Chapter 2 that combines mobile phones, cameras and web browsers in a unique way. Similarly, the phone, organiser and camera all come together in the Palm Treo. The Treo 700P Smartphone seamlessly combines a full-feature mobile phone with wireless email and text messaging, web browsing and digital camera into a pocket-sized, totally integrated device that includes a full QWERTY keyboard.[10]

Discontinuous innovations

A **discontinuous innovation** creates major changes in the way we live. To use a discontinuous innovation, consumers must engage in a great amount of learning because no similar product has ever been on the market. Major inventions such as the aeroplane, the car and the television have radically changed modern lifestyles. Another discontinuous innovation, the personal computer, changed the way we shop and allowed more people to work from home or anywhere else. What's the next discontinuous innovation? Is there a

Across the hall

Jim Surguy
Senior Partner, Harvest

Option 1 misses a key point – lack of targeting. A large, general audience may be of interest to some mass market products such as chocolate but not for most. And without the guarantee of the boxes, as has been correctly observed, any attempt to build a general subscription list will cause hostility and bad word of mouth, in social media particularly. So, 'No' to Option 1 and 'No' to Option 3 as well. Single brand boxes would simply be too expensive and miss the distribution cost saving of having multiple advertisers.

Advertisers won't come without a sensible sized audience and when buying an audience they want one which is relevant to their own particular product/service. All advertisers want to target as accurately as possible to minimise wastage. This leads inevitably to Option 2. There is no reason why producing boxes around specific interests would only create small audiences. For example, Matter could consider

co-branding with special interest magazines. For food lovers an example would be Tesco's *Real Food* with a circulation of 1.2 million. For health and beauty *Glamour* magazine – circulation 533,000. For gardeners the RHS magazine *The Garden* with a circulation of 345,000 and so on.

For the magazines it is an 'added value' they can promote editorially to their readers at no cost to them but it targets perfectly for Matter. Cheaper than buying mailing lists. Once a number of successful market sectors are established they can be aggregated to provide a large audience for true mass market products like the aforementioned chocolate.

Putting samples into people's hands is often done via field marketing so it would be interesting for Matter to compare, from the advertiser's point of view, the respective costs versus distributing via Matter.

Finally, and importantly, Matter should exploit social media. Matter needs to build online communities. Existing web word of mouth is good but this whole area does not appear to have been exploited. Encourage conversations online – it helps give advertisers feedback and it helps drive people to the website.

product out there already that will gain that distinction? Usually, marketers only know for sure through 20–20 hindsight; in other words, it's tough to plan for the next big one (what the software industry calls 'the killer application').

Understanding the degree of newness of innovations helps marketers develop effective marketing strategies. For example, if marketers know that consumers may resist adopting a new and radically different product, they may offer a free product trial or place heavier emphasis on a personal selling strategy to convince consumers that the new product offers benefits worth the hassle. When Apple introduced its Macintosh computers (you've seen those in museums!), the company allowed bewildered customers to take them home and use them for a month for free to see their benefits first-hand. Business-to-business marketers often provide in-service training for employees of their customers who invest in new products.

Objective
4
Show how firms develop new products

Developing new products

Building on our knowledge of different types of innovations, we'll now turn our attention to how firms go about developing new products. Product development doesn't simply mean creating totally new products never before on the market. Of course, a lot of companies do that, but for many other firms product development is a continuous process of looking for ways to make an existing product better or finding just the right width of leg for this year's new jean styles. No product category is immune to this process – even a 'boring' product like a toilet is constantly being improved by enterprising companies. Consider, for example, the Neorest toilet the Japanese firm Toto introduced in the EU. For a 'mere' €3000 you get a toilet that solves that age-old problem of toilet seat up versus toilet seat down. Motion sensors automatically open the lid as you approach and close it as you leave. It also has a heated seat, a temperature-controlled water spray and blow dryer, a catalytic air deodoriser, and even a 'white noise' control to mask sounds.[11]

The popular UK TV show *Dragons' Den* illustrates the lengths people and companies will go to come up with 'the next big thing' – whether screwy or sensible. Entrepreneurs with fresh and innovative ideas can pitch their business plans to five top British venture capitalists. After having been grilled by the 'five dragons', and after having shown that their idea has great potential, they hope to convince the venture capitalists to make an investment. Not only is this process quite entertaining for the TV viewers, it is also very important that young entrepreneurs have an opportunity to raise funding and turn their business concepts into reality. Without new business ideas and people who are willing to invest in them, new product development would be much more difficult and the whole business environment would slow down. For several reasons, new product development is increasingly important to firms. First, as we've already mentioned, technology is changing at an ever-increasing rate so that companies develop products, consumers adopt them, and then companies replace them with better products faster and faster. In addition, competition in our global marketplace makes it essential for firms to continuously offer new choices for consumers if they are to compete with companies all around the world rather than just down the street. Firms need to stay on top of current developments in popular culture, religion and politics to develop products that are consistent with consumers' mind-sets. Sometimes new hit products are based on careful research, but in many cases being in the right place at the right time doesn't hurt. For example Aston Martin experienced a big wave of customer recognition after the James Bond films *Casino Royale* and *Quantum of Solace* hit the screens. The 'Bond factor' even helped Aston Martin to the top of the 'list of the UK's coolest brands'.[12]

Unfortunately, most new product introductions need a bit more than good timing to score big in the marketplace. If anything, it's becoming more and more difficult to successfully introduce new products. The costs of research and development are often so huge that firms must limit the number of new products in development. Because products are outdated faster than ever, firms have less time to recover their research-and-development costs. With so many products competing for limited shelf space, retailers often charge manufacturers exorbitant 'slotting' fees to stock a new product, increasing manufacturers' costs even more.[13] Firms must reduce the time it takes to get good products to market and increase the speed of adoption to recover these costs quickly. As Table 7.4 shows, new product development generally occurs in seven phases.

Table 7.4
Phases in new-product development

Phases in Development	Outcome
1. Idea generation	Identify product ideas that will provide important customer benefits compatible with company mission
2. Product concept development and screening	Expand product ideas into more complete product concepts and estimate the potential commercial success of product concepts
3. Marketing strategy, development	Develop preliminary plan for target markets, pricing, distribution and promotion
4. Business analysis	Estimate potential for profit. What is the potential demand, what expenditures will be required, and what is the cost of marketing the product?
5. Technical development	Design the product and the manufacturing-and-production process
6. Test marketing	Develop evidence of potential success in the real market
7. Commercialisation	Implement full-scale marketing plan

Phase 1: idea generation

In the initial *idea generation* phase of product development, marketers use a variety of sources to come up with great new product ideas that provide customer benefits and that are compatible with the company mission. Sometimes ideas come from customers. Ideas also come from salespeople, service providers and others who have direct customer contact. And some companies encourage their designers to 'think outside the box' by exposing them to new ideas, people and places. When Lego decided to revitalise its Mindstorms programmable robotics kit, the Danish company recruited a panel of outside experts who were well known among Lego fans (and fanatics) for creating complex robots using the firm's 2001 version of the kit. These outsiders worked intensively with Lego's in-house design team for a year to create the next generation of Lego robotics and software (Mindstorms NXT) that includes drag-and-drop icons, sophisticated sound sensors and motors to allow the robots to roam free. It's worth noting that these self-proclaimed 'geeks' did all of this work without pay other than being given some Mindstorms prototypes. As one of the panellists observed, 'They're going to talk to us about Legos, and they're going to pay us with Legos? They actually want our opinion? It doesn't get much better than that.'[14] Now *that's* dedication! Often firms use marketing research activities such as the focus groups we discussed in Chapter 3 in their search for new product ideas. For example, a company such as MTV that is interested in developing new channels might hold focus group discussions across different groups of young people to get ideas for new types of programmes.

Phase 2: product concept development and screening

The second phase in developing new products is product concept development and screening. Although ideas for products initially come from a variety of sources, it is up to marketers to expand these ideas into more complete product concepts. Product concepts describe what features the product should have and what benefits they will provide for consumers.

It has been said that McDonald's makes the world's best French fries – a claim that has annoyed arch-rival Burger King for decades. Unfortunately for BK, the chain achieved technical success but not commercial success when it invested heavily to out-fry McD's.[15] BK's food engineers came up with a potato stick coated with a layer of starch that makes the chip crunchier and keeps the heat in to stay fresh longer. Burger King created 19 pages of specifications for its new contender, including a requirement that there must be an audible crunch present for seven or more chews. The €53 million rollout of the new product included a 'Free Fryday' when 15 million orders of fries were given away to customers free, and lavish advertising at major sporting events.

Unfortunately, the new chip was a 'whopper' of a product failure. Burger King blamed the product failure on inconsistent cooking by franchisees and a poor potato crop, but a more likely explanation is that consumers simply did not like the chips as well as those they might find at certain (golden) arch-rivals. Just because it's new doesn't always make it better.

BK's new product failure illustrates the importance of screening ideas for *both* their technical and commercial value. When screening, marketers and researchers examine the chances that a new product concept might be successful, while weeding out concepts that have little chance of making it. Estimating *technical success* means assessing whether the new product is technologically feasible – is it possible to build this product? Estimating *commercial success* means deciding whether anyone is likely to buy the product. The marketing graveyard is piled high with products that sounded interesting but that failed to catch on, including jalapeño pepper soda, aerosol mustard and edible deodorant.[16]

Table 7.5
New products that bit the dust

Product Introduced	Date	Company	Product Description	Why did the product fail?
Electrolux vacuum cleaner	1960s	Electrolux	Vacuum cleaner	Unfortunately the company translated its slogan a bit too literally and marketed its product with 'Nothing sucks like an Electrolux', which is a derogatory statement, especially in American English
Thirsty Dog! Thirsty Cat!	1995	Dr. George Hill Pet Drinks	Flavoured water for pets, such as with tangy beef	Cats and dogs were highly unimpressed and preferred tap water after all
Kellogg's Cereal Mates	1998	Kellogg's	All in one breakfast in a box, including a little packet of cereal, a small pint of milk and a plastic spoon	In the supermarket, the product was stored on the cereal shelf. This made it easy to find the product but it also meant that consumers had to drink warm milk
Clairol Mist Stick	2002	Clairol	Curling Iron	When introducing this product to the German market, the marketers did not know that 'Mist' in German is a slang word for manure. Not surprisingly, customers refused to have a 'manure stick' in their hair

Sources: www.bild.de/BTO/tipps-trends/geld-job/topthemen/allgemein/MARKEN/markenflops/markenflops. html; http://findarticles.com/p/articles/mi_m3289/is_n5_v164/ai_16902133; www.sfgate.com/cgi-bin/article. cgi?file=/ chronicle/archive/2005/02/06/ING0VB42071.DTL; www.failuremag.com/arch_mcmath_kelloggs.htm

Table 7.5 provides other examples of colossal new product failures and the Marketing ethics and sustainability box describes a promotional campaign that hit the dust too.

Today, it's not just new functions that companies look for when they devise new product concepts. A product's *appearance* also plays a huge role – in a marketplace loaded with products that seem to do pretty much the same thing, people are attracted to the options that do what they need to do – but look good while doing it. Two young US entrepreneurs named Adam Lowry and Eric Ryan discovered that basic truth in the early days of 2000. They quit their day jobs to develop a line of house-cleaning products they called Method. Cleaning products – boring, right?

But, think again: for years companies like Procter & Gamble have plodded along, peddling boring boxes of soap powder to generations of housewives. Lowry and Ryan gambled that they could offer an alternative – cleaners in exotic scents like cucumber, lavender and ylang-ylang that come in aesthetically pleasing bottles. The bet paid off. Within two years the partners were cleaning up, taking in more than $2 million in revenue. Mass-market consumers are thirsting for great design, and they're rewarding those companies that give it to them with their enthusiastic patronage and loyalty, from razor blades like the Gillette Sensor to computers like Apple. To meet the demand for design, Maytag introduced lines of stylish home and kitchen equipment products such as refrigerators, (dish)washing machines and cookers. The product ranges not only offer convenience and smooth performance, they are also seen as *aesthetic* design pieces made out of *chic* materials such as stainless steel and glass.[17]

Even P&G is starting to get the idea. Although it's a bit like turning a battleship, Procter & Gamble now recognises the importance of integrating design into every product initiative. In the 'good old days', design was basically an afterthought. Marketing meant appealing to customers in terms of efficiency rather than aesthetics. Since 2002, Chairman-CEO A.G. Lafley has directed P&G to focus on what he calls 'the first moment of truth'–winning over consumers in the shop with packaging and displays. As a result, P&G now has a Vice President of design, strategy and innovation who sums up her philosophy as: 'Competitive advantage comes not just from patents, but also from incorporating design into products, much like Apple, Sony or Dell.'[18]

 ## Phase 3: marketing strategy development

The third phase in new product development is to develop a marketing strategy to introduce the product to the marketplace. This means that marketers must identify the target market, estimate its size, and determine how the product can be positioned to address the target market's needs. And, of course, marketing strategy development includes planning for pricing, distribution and promotion expenditures both for the introduction of the new product and for the long run.

 ## Phase 4: business analysis

Once a product concept passes the screening stage, the next phase is to conduct a *business analysis*. Even though marketers have evidence that there is a market for the product, they still must find out if the product can make a profitable contribution to the organisation's product mix. How much potential demand is there for the product? (see the Marketing metrics box for an example). Does the firm have the resources that will be required for successful development and introduction of the product?

Larger firms typically develop new products in-house in their own laboratories, but in some cases even they prefer to scout out new ideas from entrepreneurs and just buy the

Marketing ethics and sustainability

Do kids get enough sleep for adults' liking?

It's the prize no company wants. But the victor in the Bad Products Awards 2007, organised by the US-based Consumers International (CI), certainly deserved to win. Takeda Pharmaceuticals was a worthy overall champion for its promotion of sleeping pills to children. This particular ad was released at the beginning of the school year and used images of children, blackboards, school books and a school bus. The accompanying voiceover stated: 'Rozerem would like to remind you that it's back to school season. Ask your doctor today if Rozerem is right for you.' As CI said, announcing the award: 'It doesn't take a PhD in marketing to see this is an effort to persuade parents to seek out the sleeping drug for their children – help them get through the stress of term starting.' It took six months before government agencies told Takeda to remove the ad. Despite the fact that Takeda is a $10 billion pharmaceutical company and had spent $118 million on advertising Rozerem, it was not fined and not penalised (Consumer International Press briefing, 2007).

Source: Adapted from *New Statesman,* 10 December 2007

Debate, discuss, disagree

1 What is your opinion about Takeda's sleeping pill promotion for children?

2 What do you think authorities should have done to handle this situation?

technology. For example, Church and Dwight Company sell the Crest SpinBrush range of battery-powered toothbrushes. SpinBrush is a technology developed by four entrepreneurs whom Procter & Gamble then bought out (P&G then divested the product after the P&G/Gillette merger in 2005). Unlike electric toothbrushes that typically sell for upwards of €35 each, the SpinBrush sells for just slightly more than a decent old-fashioned toothbrush.[19] Another consideration in this phase may be the need to sell products more cheaply to some countries. See the Marketing ethics box about pharmaceutical drugs.

Phase 5: technical development

If it survives the scrutiny of a business analysis, a new product concept then undergoes *technical development* in which a firm's engineers work with marketers in refining the design and production process. For example, when McDonald's recognised the need to bulk up its breakfast menu by adding something sweeter than its Egg McMuffin, the company's executive chef had to scramble to develop a pancake offering that could be eaten while driving. He first considered a pancake shaped like a muffin, but he decided this would be too confusing to customers – and besides, how could he add in the all-important syrup? Fortunately, one of the company's suppliers had just developed a technology that crystallises syrup – just stir crystals into the batter and the syrup will seep through the entire pancake once it's heated. McDonald's did a lot of laboratory work to adapt this process so the syrup would melt uniformly and produce what the industry calls the correct 'mouth feel'. Enter the McGriddle, a breakfast sandwich that can be customised with combinations of sausage, bacon, egg and cheese. It's served between two 'high-tech syrup-infused' pancakes instead of bread and has become a very successful staple on the company's breakfast menu.[20]

The better a firm understands how customers will react to a new product, the better its chances of commercial success. For this reason, a company's research-and-development (R&D) department will typically develop one or more physical versions or **prototypes** of the product. Prospective customers may evaluate these mockups in focus group or in field trials at home.

Prototypes also are useful for people within the firm. Those involved in the technical development process must determine which parts of a finished good the company will

Marketing ethics and sustainability

Creating products to die for

It is not surprising that pharmaceutical companies' marketing plans call for heavy emphasis on new product development. These companies rely on a stream of new products to stay ahead of competitors. However, developing a new blockbuster drug is expensive in R&D. To recoup the high cost of new product development these companies often charge high prices for their drugs. They do not lower the price even in countries where consumers cannot afford to pay high prices. Critics say that pharmaceutical companies have a moral obligation to subsidise drug prices in poor countries. The companies counter that they would have no incentive to develop life-saving drugs if they subsidised prices.

Debate, discuss, disagree

1 Should pharmaceutical companies be mandated by law to sell their products at lower prices in poor countries?

2 Discuss the pros and cons of this approach.

make and which ones will be bought from other suppliers. If goods are to be manufactured, the company may have to buy new production equipment or modify existing machinery. Someone has to develop work instructions for employees and train them to produce the product. In developing service processes, technical development includes such decisions as which activities will occur within sight of customers and whether parts of the service can be automated to make delivery more efficient.

Technical development sometimes requires application for a patent. Because patents legally prevent competitors from producing or selling the invention, a patent may reduce or eliminate competition in a market for many years, allowing a firm 'breathing room' to recoup investments in technical development.

Phase 6: Test marketing

The next phase of new product development includes **test marketing**. This means the firm tries out the complete marketing plan – the distribution, advertising and sales promotion – but in a small geographic area that is similar to the larger market it hopes to enter.

There are both pluses and minuses to test marketing. On the negative side, test marketing is extremely expensive. It can cost over €1 million to conduct a test market even in a single city. A test market also gives the competition a free look at the new product, its introductory price and the intended promotional strategy – and an opportunity to get to the market first with a competing product. On the positive side, by offering a new product in a limited area of the market, marketers can evaluate and improve the marketing programme. Sometimes test marketing uncovers a need to improve the product itself. At other times, test marketing indicates product failure, allowing the firm to save millions of euros by 'pulling the plug'. Remember Fraser from Royal Mail you met at the beginning of the chapter? He's putting his new Matterbox product out into the marketplace to test market it.

For years, Listerine manufacturer Warner-Lambert wanted to introduce a mint-flavoured version of the product to compete with Procter & Gamble's mouthwash Scope (it originally introduced this alternative under the brand Listermint). Unfortunately, every time Warner-Lambert tried to run a test market, P&G found out and poured substantial extra advertising and coupons for Scope into the cities in which the test market was conducted. This counter-attack reduced the usefulness of the test market results for Warner-Lambert when its market planners were trying to decide whether to introduce Listermint nationwide. As P&G's aggressive response to Listermint's test marketing actually *increased* Scope's market share in the test cities, there was no way to determine how well Listermint would actually do under normal competitive conditions. As a result, Warner-Lambert eventually introduced Listermint nationally, but achieved only marginal success, so the company eventually pulled it from the market.

Because of the potential problems and expense of test marketing, marketers instead may conduct simulated tests that imitate the introduction of a product into the marketplace, using special computer software as we saw in Chapter 3. These simulations allow the company to see the likely effect of price cuts and new packaging – or even to determine where in the shop the product should be placed to maximise sales. The process entails gathering basic research data on consumers' perceptions of the product concept, the physical product, the advertising and other promotional activity. The test market simulation model uses that information to predict the product's success much less expensively (and more discreetly) than a traditional test market. As this simulated test market technology improves, traditional test markets may become a thing of the past.

Phase 7: Commercialisation

The last phase in new product development is **commercialisation**. This means the launching of a new product, and it requires full-scale production, distribution, advertising and sales promotion. For this reason, commercialisation of a new product cannot happen overnight. A launch requires planning and careful preparation. Marketers must implement trade promotion plans that offer special incentives to encourage dealers, retailers or other members of the channel to stock the new product so that customers will find it on shop shelves the very first time they look. They must also develop consumer promotions such as coupons. Marketers may arrange to have point-of-purchase displays designed, built and delivered to retail outlets. If the new product is especially complex, customer service employees must receive extensive training and preparation.

As launch time nears, preparations gain a sense of urgency – like countdown to blast-off. Sales managers explain special incentive programmes to salespeople. Soon the media announce to prospective customers why they should buy and where they can find the new product. All elements of the marketing programme – ideally – come into play like a carefully planned lift-off of the space shuttle.

And there is always a huge element of risk in a new product launch – even for products that seem like a sure thing. For example, car manufacturer BMW introduced the C1 model, a small motorcycle with a roof in 1992. In the eyes of the company, the motorcycle was bound to be a great success, with its emphasis on safety due to the cage roof top and a seatbelt which prevented the driver from hitting the road in case of an accident. Besides, the C1 was supposed to appeal to people who wanted to get around quickly in a crowded city. However, the consumers did not share this view and rather saw a vehicle in it which was less safe than a car, less fun to drive than a normal motorcycle and offered no real protection from rain anyway. As a result, the expected high demand failed to appear.[21]

What do you think about the C1's success or lack of it? Why do you think it didn't take off?

Marketing metrics

AC Nielsen BASES

BASES was founded in the mid-1970s as a method of forecasting sales of new products, and in the years since its inception has evaluated more than 75,000 new product ideas in more than 60 countries. Simulated Test Marketing (STM) is used to combine consumer reaction to new product ideas with marketing plan information to forecast likely sales volumes. STM has supplanted traditional in-market testing as the predominant method used by packaged goods manufacturers to evaluate new products, line extensions and other new business opportunities prior to large-scale in-market introduction. It is faster, less expensive, more secure and more accurate with regard to their forecasting capability and can answer the following questions.

- What is the volume potential for my new product?
- How will a line extension affect my overall brand franchise?
- What elements of my new initiative should be improved to increase the odds for consumer adoption?
- Who will be the core users of my new product and how can I reach them?
- How should I prioritise developing the ideas in my innovation pipeline?
- How should I price my new product?

Objective

5

Explain the
process of
product
adoption and
the diffusion of
innovations

Adoption and diffusion

In the previous section, we talked about the steps marketers take to develop new products from generating ideas to launch. Moving on, we'll look at what happens *after* that new product hits the market – how an innovation spreads throughout a population.

A painting is not a work of art until someone views it. A song is not music until someone sings it. In the same way, new products do not satisfy customer wants and needs until the customer uses them. **Product adoption** is the process by which a consumer or business customer begins to buy and use a new good, service or idea.

The term **diffusion** describes how the use of a product spreads throughout a population. One way to understand how this process works is to think about a new product as if it was a computer virus that spreads from a few computers to infect many machines. A brand like Hush Puppies, for example, might just slog around – sometimes for years and years. It's initially bought by a small number of people, but change happens in a hurry when the process reaches the moment of critical mass. This moment of truth is called the **tipping point**. For example, Sharp created the low-price, home/small-office fax market in 1984 and sold about 80,000 in that year. There was a slow climb in the number of users for the next three years. Then, suddenly, in 1987 enough people had faxes that it made sense for everyone to have one – Sharp sold a million units that year. Along with such diffusion almost always come steep price declines – today you can buy a Sharp fax machine at Amazon for less than £90.[22]

After months or even years spent developing a new product, the real challenge to firms is getting consumers to buy and use the product and to do so quickly to recover the costs of product development and launch. To accomplish this, marketers must understand the product-adoption process. In the next section, we'll discuss the stages in this process. We'll also see how consumers and businesses differ in their eagerness to adopt new products and how the characteristics of a product affect its adoption (or 'infection') rate.

 ## Stages in consumer adoption of a new product

Whether the innovation is better film technology or a better mousetrap, individuals and organisations pass through six stages in the adoption process. Figure 7.2 shows how a person goes from being unaware of an innovation through the stages of awareness, interest, evaluation, trial, adoption and confirmation. At every stage, people drop out of the process, so the proportion of consumers who wind up using the innovation on a consistent basis is a fraction of those who are exposed to it.

Marketing metrics

Market penetration metrics

When measuring market penetration, some of the metrics which can be used have been rated by marketing managers. Here are those metrics and what percentage of marketing managers found them 'very useful'. Dollar Market Share 67 per cent, Unit Market Share 61 per cent, Market Penetration 45 per cent, Relative Market Share 44 per cent, and Penetration Share 22 per cent.[23]

Reinforcing the customer's choice through advertising, sales promotion and other communications

Confirmation

Making the product available
Providing product use information

Adoption

Demonstrations, samples, trial size packages

Trial

Providing information to customers about how the product can benefit them

Evaluation

May use teaser advertising

Interest

Massive advertising

Awareness

Figure 7.2	Adoption pyramid

Consumers pass through six stages in the adoption of a new product – from being unaware of an innovation to becoming loyal adopters. The right marketing strategies at each stage help ensure a successful adoption

Awareness

Learning that the innovation exists is the first step in the adoption process. To make consumers aware of a new product, marketers may conduct a massive advertising campaign, called a **media blitz**. For example, to raise awareness of its entry into the electronic gaming product category, Microsoft launched a massive $500 million marketing campaign when it introduced the original Xbox, promoting the new product through in-store merchandising, retailer incentives, events and sponsorship in addition to traditional advertising.[24] At this point, some consumers will say, 'So there's a new gaming console out there. So what?' Many of these, of course, will fall by the wayside, out of the adoption process. But this strategy works for new products when consumers see a new product as something they want and need and just can't live without.

Interest

For some of the people who become aware of a new product, a second stage in the adoption process is *interest*. In this stage, a prospective adopter begins to see how a new product might satisfy an existing or newly realised need. Interest also means that consumers look for and are open to information about the innovation. Volkswagen's Jetta, for instance, developed a certain panache with the young 20s crowd around 2000 or so. But, as today's 20- and 30-something car buyers started having families and needing bigger cars with more carrying space, their interest in the Jetta declined. To get the lucrative young parent group interested in the product again, Volkswagen reintroduced the 2006 model with great advertising fanfare, touting seven more inches of room from front to back, 25 per cent more boot space and more safety features than the 2005 model. Ads hark back to those of another era, stressing 'German engineering' to make the car seem less frivolous and more appealing to families looking for quality and dependability.[25] Marketers often design teaser advertisements that give prospective customers just enough information about the new product to make them curious and to stimulate their interest. Despite marketers' best efforts, however, some consumers drop out of the process at this point.

Evaluation

In the *evaluation* stage, a prospect weighs the costs and benefits of the new product. On the one hand, for complex, risky or expensive products, people think about the innovation a great deal before trying it. For example, a firm will carefully evaluate spending hundreds of thousands of euros on manufacturing robotics before purchase. Marketers for such products help prospective customers see how such products can benefit them.

But little evaluation may occur with an **impulse purchase**; – a purchase made without any planning or search effort. As an example, consumers may do very little thinking before buying a virtual pet such as the Tamagotchi (Japanese for 'cute little egg'). For these products, marketers design the product to be eye-catching and appealing to get consumers to notice it quickly. Tamagotchis certainly grabbed the attention of consumers – 40 million of them bought the virtual pets. Toymaker Bandai Co. came out with a third generation of Tamagotchis in 2006, this time offering pets that not only communicate with other Tamagotchis via infrared ports, but that can recognise their owners' voices and respond to commands to speak, bark, walk, lie down, shake hands, perform tricks and follow clapping hands. Now the pets can make friends, 'marry' other Tamagotchis and even give birth.[26]

Some potential adopters will evaluate an innovation positively enough to move on to the next stage. Those who do not think the new product will provide adequate benefits drop out.

Trial

Trial is the stage in the adoption process when potential buyers will actually experience or use the product for the first time. Often marketers stimulate trial by providing opportunities for consumers to sample the product.

HMV, for example, opened up shops with a 'new generation' concept that was supposed to keep customers in the shop for longer and make them try out the products. Now it is easier to listen to CDs and watch extracts of DVDs in store by simply scanning the barcode of the product. Bright-coloured walls, a juice bar and free web access round up the home-like atmosphere for the shopper who, according to HMV's plan, will now easily spend hours and hours trying out the products and taking home a full shopping basket afterwards.[27]

Travel through some airports, for example, and you'll see Dell demonstration kiosks – a major departure from the company's usual focus on online direct marketing. That's because there is a drawback to online direct marketing: some consumers just can't stand to buy without first touching, holding, and using a product – in short, conducting a 'trial'. Interestingly, people are also buying right at the kiosks, which in retrospect is not too surprising given that the passenger demographics tend towards an age range of 24–49, most with annual household incomes above €50,000 – just the type of people who want the latest computer.[28]

Based on the trial experience, some potential buyers move on to adoption of the new product. Sometimes prospective customers will not adopt a new product because it costs too much. Initially, this was the case with onboard navigation systems in cars. Consumers could try out the system in rental cars from Hertz and Avis, but the price (over €1500) understandably put off most prospective customers. By 2006, with prices having dipped below €400 and continuing to fall, many more consumers were buying the units for their own cars and ordering them with new vehicles.[29]

Adoption

In the *adoption* stage, a prospect actually buys the product (Hallelujah!). If the product is a consumer or business-to-business good, this means buying the product and learning how to use and maintain it. If the product is an idea, this means that the individual agrees with the new idea.

Does this mean that all individuals or organisations that first choose an innovation are permanent customers? That's a mistake many firms make. Marketers need to provide follow-up contacts and communications with adopters to ensure they are satisfied and remain loyal to the new product over time.

Confirmation

After adopting an innovation, a customer weighs expected versus actual benefits and costs. Favourable experiences contribute to new customers becoming loyal adopters, as their initially positive opinions result in *confirmation*. Of course, nothing lasts forever – even loyal customers may decide that a new product is not meeting expectations and reject it. Some marketers feel that reselling to the customer in the confirmation stage is important. They provide advertisements, sales presentations and other communications to reinforce a customer's choice.

The diffusion of innovations

Diffusion describes how the use of a product spreads throughout a population. Of course, marketers would prefer that their entire target market would immediately adopt a new product, but this is rarely the case. Consumers and business customers differ in how eager or willing they are to try something new, lengthening the diffusion process by months or even years. Based on adopters' roles in the diffusion process, experts have classified them into categories.

Adopter categories

Some people like to try new products. Others are so reluctant you'd think they were afraid of anything new. As Figure 7.3 shows, there are five categories of adopters: innovators, early adopters, early majority, late majority and laggards.[30] To understand how the

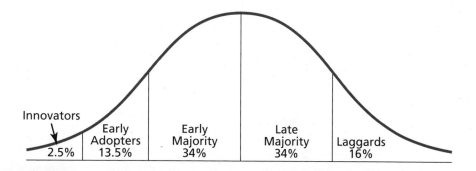

Figure 7.3	**Categories of adopters**
	Because consumers differ in how willing they are to buy and try a new product, it often takes months or years for an innovation to be adopted by most of the population

Photo 7.4	Early adopters of new technology queuing outside an Apple store to be among the first to have the latest iPhone
	Source: Getty Images/PETER PARKS/AFP

adopter categories differ, we'll focus on the adoption of one specific technology, Wi-Fi (wireless fidelity).

Innovators are roughly the first 2.5 per cent of adopters. This segment is extremely adventurous and willing to take risks with new products. Innovators are typically younger and better off financially than others in the population, as well as worldly and well educated. Innovators were the ones who knew all about Wi-Fi before other people, as they were fascinated and enthusiastic about trying this new technology. Because innovators pride themselves on trying new products, they purchased laptops with Wi-Fi cards way back in 1999, when Apple introduced them in its laptops. However, a company must take great care not to anger innovators such as through inconsistent pricing strategies. Apple lowered the prices for its iPhone quite drastically only three months after the launch. The consumers who first purchased the iPhone were very upset and protested heavily through online communities and forums. In the end Apple did indeed give in to the protests and each consumer received $100 back.[31]

Early adopters, approximately 13.5 per cent of adopters, buy product innovations early in the diffusion process but not as early as innovators. Unlike innovators, early adopters have greater concern for social acceptance. Typically, they are heavy media users and often are heavy users of the product category. Others in the population often look to early adopters for their opinions on various topics, making early adopters key to a new product's success. For this reason, marketers often target them in developing advertising and other communications efforts.

Columnists who write about personal technology for popular magazines like *Time* were testing Wi-Fi in mid-2000. They experienced some problems (like PCs crashing when setting up a wireless network at home) but touted the benefits of wireless connectivity. Road warriors adopted the technology as Wi-Fi access spread into airports and hotels. Intel, maker of the Centrino mobile platform, launched a major campaign with Condé Nast's *Traveller* magazine, offering a location guide to T-Mobile hotspots nationwide.

The **early majority**, roughly 34 per cent of adopters, avoid being either first or last to try an innovation. They are typically middle-class consumers and are deliberate and cautious. Early majority consumers have slightly above average education and income levels. When the early majority adopts a product, it is no longer considered new or different – it is, in essence, already established. By 2002, Wi-Fi access was available in many Starbucks cafés, and monthly subscription prices were dropping rapidly.

Late majority adopters, about 34 per cent of the population, are older and more conservative and typically have lower than average levels of education and income. The late majority adopters avoid trying a new product until it is no longer risky. By that time, the product has become an economic necessity or there is pressure from peer groups to adopt. By 2004, Wi-Fi capability was bundled into almost all laptops and you could connect in mainstream venues such as cafés and sports stadiums. Cities like London or Manchester were considering blanket Wi-Fi coverage throughout the entire town through WiMax technology.

Laggards, about 16 per cent of adopters, are the last in a population to adopt a new product. Laggards are typically lower in social class than other adopter categories and are bound by tradition. By the time laggards adopt a product, it may already be superseded by other innovations. By 2006, it would have seemed strange if Wi-Fi or a similar capability was not part of the standard package in even the lowest-priced laptop computer.[32]

By understanding these adopter categories, marketers are able to develop strategies that will speed the diffusion or widespread use of their products. For example, early in the diffusion process, marketers may put greater emphasis on advertising in special interest magazines to attract innovators and early adopters. Later they may lower the product's price or come out with lower priced models with fewer 'bells and whistles' to attract the late majority. We will talk more about strategies for new and existing products in the next chapter.

Product factors affecting the rate of adoption

Not all products are successful, to say the least. As we saw in Table 7.5, all sorts of products litter the marketing graveyard. Other classic boobs include Crystal Pepsi, the Persil Power washing powder that turned out so powerful that it destroyed not only the stains but also the clothes; Thirsty Dog! (bottled water with crispy beef flavour for your pet); the Sony Betamax video player; and Snif-T-Panties (women's underwear that smelled like bananas, popcorn, whisky, or pizza).[33] The reason for such product failures is very simple – consumers did not perceive that they satisfied a need better than competitive products already on the market.

If you could predict which new products will succeed and which will fail, you'd quickly be in high demand as a marketing consultant by companies worldwide. That's because companies make large investments in new products, but failures are all too frequent. Experts suggest that between one-third and one-half of all new products fail. As you might expect, there is much research devoted to making us smarter about new product successes and failures.

Researchers have identified five characteristics of innovations that affect the rate of adoption: relative advantage, compatibility, complexity, trialability and observability.[34] Whether a new product has each of these characteristics affects the speed of diffusion. Think about Fraser's options at Royal Mail in terms of these characteristics to help decide which option might be most successful. It may take years for a new product to become widely adopted. The five factors in Table 7.6 help to explain both why the new product was not adopted during its early years and why adoption sped up later. Let's take a closer look at the microwave oven to understand why these factors are important.

Table 7.6
Adoption-rate
factors – using a
wi-fi example

A variety of product factors cause adoption of the innovation by consumers to be faster or slower. Understanding these factors means marketers can develop strategies to encourage people to try a new product

Product Factors Affecting Rate of Adoption	Product Rated High on Factor	Product Rated Low on Factor	Rating of Wi-Fi on the Factors
Relative advantage	Faster	Slower	Low until consumer lifestyles changed
Compatibility	Faster	Slower	Low – required new PC card and base station
Complexity	Slower	Faster	Early setups were complex
Trialability	Faster	Slower	Low until infrastructure was established
Observability	Faster	Slower	Moderately low: wireless is invisible

Relative advantage is the degree to which a consumer perceives that a new product provides superior benefits. In the case of the microwave oven, consumers in the 1960s did not feel that the product provided significant benefits that would improve their lives. But by the late 1970s, that perception had changed because more women had entered the workforce. In the 1960s a woman had all day to prepare the evening meal, so she didn't need a microwave. In the 1970s, however, when many women left home for work at 8 a.m. and returned home at 6 p.m., an appliance that would 'magically' defrost a frozen chicken and cook it in 30 minutes provided a genuine advantage. However, what do you think the relative advantage was of Dasani? Read the Marketing ethics and sustainability box.

Marketing ethics and sustainability

Bottled water or tap water? Which is better? – Dasani

Coca-Cola is undoubtedly one of the most recognised and successful brands on the planet, but even it pushed marketing into the realms of the ridiculous with its international bottled water – Dasani. In 2004, Coca-Cola was forced to take Dasani off the UK shelves after a public outcry because it contained nothing more than tap water. Coca-Cola itself says that Dasani isn't spring water and that it is sourced from local tap water supplies. But from its marketing and packaging, one could easily think otherwise. Dasani promotional material gushes with terms like:

'Filtered for purity using state of the art processes' and 'enhanced with a special blend of minerals for a pure, crisp, fresh taste.'

What it doesn't say quite as loudly is that Dasani comes from the same local municipal reservoirs as the water out of the tap. Coca-Cola is not doing anything illegal, but advertising which suggested its bottled water is significantly superior to local tap water is misleading. It is simply repackaging in plastic containers a common resource and charging consumers hundreds to thousands of times what it would cost out of the tap.

Source: Consumers International – Press Briefing: International Bad Product Awards 2007, December 2007

Debate, discuss, disagree

1 What do you think about a big multinational company such as Coca-Cola repackaging tap water and selling it to the public at a high price?

2 Do you think it is just a clever strategy of Coca-Cola or it is actually deceiving its consumers?

Photo 7.5	This Smart car advert tries to convey the relative advantage of size over other cars to increase adoption *Source:* Alamy Images/P. Cox

Compatibility is the extent to which a new product is consistent with existing cultural values, customs and practices. Did consumers see the microwave oven as being compatible with existing ways of doing things? Hardly. Cooking on paper plates? If you put a paper plate in a conventional oven, you're likely to get a visit from the fire brigade. By anticipating compatibility issues early in the new product development stage, marketing strategies can address such problems in planning communications programmes, or there may be opportunities for altering product designs to overcome some consumer objections.

Complexity is the degree to which consumers find a new product or its use difficult to understand. Many microwave users today haven't a clue about how a microwave oven cooks food. When appliance manufacturers introduced the first microwaves, they explained that microwaves cause molecules to move and rub together, creating friction, which produces heat. Voilà! Cooked roast beef. But that explanation was too complex and confusing for the homemaker of the early 1980s.

Trialability is the ease of sampling a new product and its benefits. Marketers took a very important step in the 1970s to speed up adoption of the microwave oven – product trial. Just about every place that sold microwaves invited shoppers to pay a visit and sample an entire meal cooked in the microwave.

Observability refers to how visible a new product and its benefits are to others who might adopt it. The ideal innovation is easy to see. For example, for a generation of kids, scooters such as the Micro became the hippest way to get around as soon as one preteen saw his friends flying by. That same generation observed their friends trading Pokémon cards and wanted to join in. In the case of the microwave, it wasn't quite so readily observable for its potential adopters – only close friends and acquaintances who visited someone's home would see it in use by an early adopter. But the fruits of the microwave's labours – tasty food – created lots of buzz at the office and social events and its use spread quickly.

 ## How organisational differences affect adoption

Just as there are differences among consumers in their eagerness to adopt new products, businesses and other organisations are not alike in their willingness to buy and use new industrial products. New or smaller companies may be more nimble and able to jump onto emerging trends. Those that do often are rewarded with higher sales (though, of course, the risks are higher, too). Thus while Samsung recognised early on that colour screens on mobile phones were going to be in demand by consumers, some other companies (Nokia, for example) were slower to pick up on a trend that had originated in Samsung's home turf in Asia. While other firms continued to try to market monochrome screens for months longer than they should have, Samsung made strong gains with its more innovative product.

Firms that welcome product innovations are likely to be younger companies in highly technical industries with younger managers and entrepreneurial corporate cultures (think Apple). Early adopter firms are likely to be market-share leaders that adopt new innovations and try new ways of doing things to maintain their leadership. Firms that adopt new products only when they recognise that they must innovate to keep up are in the early majority. Late majority firms tend to be oriented toward the status quo and often have large financial investments in existing production technology. Laggard firms are probably already losing money.

Business-to-business products, like consumer products, also may possess characteristics that will increase their likelihood of adoption. Organisations are likely to adopt an innovation that helps them increase gross margins and profits. It is unlikely that firms would have adopted new products like voicemail unless they provided a way to increase profits by reducing labour costs. Organisational innovations are attractive when they are consistent with a firm's ways of doing business.

Cost is also a factor in the new products firms will adopt. Recall the concept of value as we introduced it in Chapter 1. For similar reasons, firms and institutions are more likely to accept a new product if they perceive the improvement to be large in relation to the investment they will have to make. This was the case when King's College London changed its IT system and adopted an open source network infrastructure. The advantages of using open source software include the ability to read, alter and improve the software and therefore tailor it to one's specific needs. King's College claims to have saved thousands of pounds through this investment and underlines that 'with open source software they spend their time focusing on education, not hardware or software'.[35] Many firms are starting to turn their attention to the possible advantages of open source software. The European Commission funded a report which states that although open source software may lead to some increased short-term costs, it will reduce long-term costs significantly in almost all cases.[36]

Real people, real decisions

How it worked out at Royal Mail

In December 2010, Matter produced its first single-brand edition (Photo 7.6). Cadbury used Matter with considerable success to engage consumers in its Spots v Stripes campaign as part of its sponsorship of the London 2012 Olympics. The traditional campaign, across TV, press and outdoor, had failed to drive home the underlying message of its Olympic involvement – that playing games is fun (and chocolate = fun). Through the media-planning agency, PHD, the company wanted to put actual games in the hands of consumers with an online games competition, the finalists of which were produced and sent in the Matterbox.

Matter subscribers were asked to play-test the games, pick a winner and vote for it on a specially created microsite. In addition, they were asked how many people they played with, told about and what effect it had on their perception of the Cadbury brand.

Thirty-four per cent (4100 people) voted. Matter succeeded in its objective of putting games in the hands of 36,000 consumers (from a distribution of only 12,000); 66,000 people heard about the games through (primary) word-of-mouth and 57 per cent said it changed their opinion of the brand (very little advertising achieves any kind of uplift).

The Cadbury edition of Matter proved that with the right content, its enthusiastic audience will engage and share their experiences with their friends as a multiple of its audience (and not a fraction) and thus create a workable Reach model.

Other lessons were learned too. The entire Matter audience was emailed initially to request the box (initially, to overcome the problem of a very out-of-date database). Thirty-three per cent responded to the initial email (50,000 for 12,000 boxes) and the returns on the whole mailing was less than 50 items (normal returns from a clean database are circa 3–4 per cent). This also proved that the digital channel is as important as the physical and Matter's unique digital/physical relationship with its audience is very powerful and could be utilised in different ways in the future.

Cadbury is using Matter again, this time to ask Matter subscribers to refine the rules of the winning game – as well as play them and tell all their friends.

Some of the problems remain. Matter still requires advertisers to have a problem to solve and put a complete activity

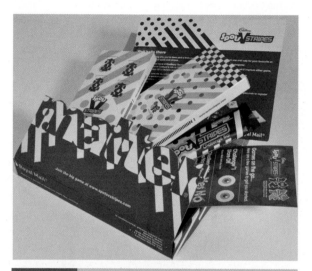

Photo 7.6	Matter single-brand edition
	Source: Image reproduced with kind permission of Royal Mail Group Ltd.

together including compelling content, clear consumer action and a digitial response channel to collect the results. It still faces considerable resistance and inertia from advertisers and agencies who are disincentivised to do something new and different on a day-to-day basis.

The underlying principle that engaged and enthusiastic people are more responsive and thus valuable than an accurately targeted one is a lot to swallow for marketers, especially in an age where data is king. It may be that it needs both – and that Matter will only start to gain traction once it's established it can work for a variety of advertisers.

It's also notable that Matter has found a genuinely enthusiastic consumer engagement (even when they don't get boxes!) at the same time as widespread advertiser apathy. This may have something to do with the disparity of the respective propositions – simple for consumers; complex for advertisers – but also might be to do with the fact that advertising and media often lag behind contemporary consumer behaviour and maybe Matter has revealed that the gulf is as wide as it ever was.

Acknowledgements to Neil McFerran, Tom Willis, Enrico Innocenti, Amine Maddi, who researched and helped to write this case.

Marketing metrics

Measuring the success of matterbox

Return on investment

The Cadbury edition was judged both a strategic and commercial success. The total cost for the Cadbury edition, media and content, was £56K. The ROI was calculated at 156 per cent. The Cadbury edition of Matter proved the underlying concepts of Matter:

- An engaged and enthusiastic audience is more responsive than a purely targeted one (in fact, the audience wasn't profiled at all, merely self-selected).

- Matter generates deep engagement – it asked a lot of its subscribers; they weren't just asked to go to a website.

- Matter can produce competitive ROIs (a similar campaign using conventional DM would have cost three times at much).

- Unlike conventional DM, Matter proved its ability to drive multiple responses (as per Figure 7.4). Not only did it generate direct responses, it also generated WOM and brand uplift.

Direct response with the brand

Tweets about the content

Facebook posts about the content

Matter survey – 'what did you do with it?'

Word-of-mouth

| Figure 7.4 | How Matter creates a flow of viral discussion |

Chapter summary

Now that you have finished reading this chapter, you can:

1. **Explain the layers of a product.** A product may be anything tangible or intangible that satisfies consumer or business-to-business customer needs. Products include goods, services, ideas, people and places. The core product is the basic product category benefits and customised benefit(s) the product provides. The actual product is the physical good or delivered service including the packaging and brand name. The augmented product includes both the actual product and any supplementary services, such as warranty, credit, delivery, installation and so on.

2. **Describe the classifications of products.** Marketers generally classify goods and services as either consumer or business-to-business products. They further classify consumer products according to how long they last and how they are purchased. Durable goods provide benefits for months or years, whereas non-durable goods are used up quickly or are useful for only a short time. Consumers purchase convenience products frequently with little effort. Customers carefully gather information and compare different brands on their attributes and prices before buying shopping products. Speciality products have unique characteristics that are important to the buyer. Customers have little interest in unsought products until a need arises. Business products are for commercial use by organisations. Marketers classify business products according to how they are used, for example, equipment; maintenance, repair and operating (MRO) products; raw and processed materials; component parts; and business services.

3. **Explain the importance of new products.** Innovations are anything consumers perceive to be new. Understanding new products is important to companies because of the fast pace of technological advancement, the high cost to companies of developing new products, and the contributions to society that new products can make. Marketers classify innovations by their degree of novelty. A continuous innovation is a modification of an existing product, a dynamically continuous innovation provides a greater change in a product, and a discontinuous innovation is a new product that creates major changes in people's lives.

4. **Show how firms develop new products.** In new product development, marketers first generate product ideas from which product concepts are developed and then screened. Next they develop a marketing strategy and conduct a business analysis to estimate the profitability of the new product. Technical development includes planning how the product will be manufactured and may mean obtaining a patent. Next, the effectiveness of the new product may be assessed in an actual or a simulated test market. Finally, the product is launched, and the entire marketing plan is implemented.

5. **Explain the process of product adoption and the diffusion of innovations.** Product adoption is the process by which an individual begins to buy and use a new product, whereas the diffusion of innovations is how a new product spreads throughout a population. The stages in the adoption process are awareness, interest, trial, adoption and confirmation. To understand the diffusion process better, marketers classify consumers according to their readiness to adopt new products as innovators, early adopters, early majority, late majority and laggards.

Five product characteristics that have an important effect on how quickly (or if) a new product will be adopted by consumers are relative advantage, compatibility, product complexity, trialability and observability. As with individual consumers, organisations differ in their readiness to adopt new products based on characteristics of the organisation, its management, and characteristics of the innovation.

Key terms

Augmented product 261

Commercialisation 279

Compatibility 287

Complexity 287

Component parts 267

Continuous innovation 270

Convenience product 263

Convergence 271

Copycat 270

Core product 260

Diffusion 280

Discontinuous innovation 271

Durable goods 263

Dynamically continuous innovation 270

Early adopters 284

Early majority 285

Emergency products 264

Equipment 266

Good 259

Impulse product 264

Impulse purchase 282

Innovation 268

Innovators 284

Laggards 285

Late majority 285

Maintenance, repair and operating (MRO) products 267

Media blitz 281

Non-durable goods 263

Observability 287

Processed materials 267

Product adoption 280

Prototypes 277

Raw materials 267

Relative advantage 286

Shopbots 265

Shopping products 264

Speciality product 266

Staples 264

Test marketing 278

Tipping point 280

Trialability 287

Unsought products 266

Chapter review

Marketing concepts: testing your knowledge

1. What is the difference between the core product, the actual product and the augmented product?

2. What is the difference between a durable good and a non-durable good? Provide examples of each.

3. What are the main differences among convenience, shopping and speciality products?

4. What is an unsought product? How do marketers make such products attractive to consumers?

5. What types of products are bought and sold in business-to-business markets?

6. What is a new product? Why is understanding new products so important to marketers?

7. What are the types of innovations?

8. List and explain the steps in developing new products.

9. What is a test market? What are some pros and cons of doing test markets?

10. List and explain the categories of adopters.

Marketing concepts: discussing choices and ethical issues

1. Technology is moving at an ever-increasing speed, and this means that new products enter and leave the market faster than ever. What are some products you think technology might be able to develop in the future that you would like? Do you think these products could add to a company's profits?

2. In this chapter, we talked about the core product, the actual product and the augmented product. Does this mean that marketers are simply trying to make products that are really the same seem different? When marketers understand these three layers of the product and develop products with this concept in mind, what are the benefits to consumers? What are the hazards of this type of thinking?

3. Discontinuous innovations are totally new products – something seldom seen in the marketplace. What are some examples of discontinuous innovations introduced in the past 50 years? Why are there so few discontinuous innovations? What products have companies recently introduced that you believe will end up being regarded as discontinuous innovations?

4. Consider the differences in marketing to consumer versus business markets. Which aspects of the processes of product adoption and diffusion apply to both markets? Which aspects are unique to one or the other? Provide evidence of your findings.

5. In this chapter, we explained that copycats are slightly modified copies of original product designs. Should copycat products be illegal? Who is hurt by them? Is the marketing of such products good or bad for consumers in the short run? In the long run?

6. It is not necessarily true that all new products benefit consumers or society. What are some new products that have made our lives better? What are some new products that have actually been harmful to consumers or to society? Should there be a way to monitor or 'police' new products that are introduced to the marketplace?

 ## Marketing practice: applying what you've learned

1. Assume that you are the director of marketing for a major mobile phone manufacturer. Your company has just developed a new product that does everything but tap dance. How would you go about convincing the late majority to go ahead and adopt this new technology?

2. Assume that you are employed in the marketing department of the firm that is producing a hybrid car. In developing this product, you realise that it is important to provide a core product, an actual product and an augmented product that meets the needs of customers. Develop an outline of how your firm might provide these three product layers in the hybrid car.

3. Firms go to great lengths to develop new product ideas. Sometimes new ideas come from brainstorming in which groups of individuals get together and try to think of as many different, novel, creative – and hopefully profitable – ideas for a new product as possible. With a group of other students, participate in brainstorming for new product ideas for one of the following (or some other product of your choice):

   - An exercise machine with some desirable new features
   - A combination shampoo and body wash
   - A new type of university.

   Then, with your class, screen one or more of the ideas for possible product development.

4. As a member of a new product team with your company, you are working to develop an electric car jack that would make changing tyres for a car easier. You are considering conducting a test market for this new product. Outline the pros and cons for test marketing this product. What are your recommendations?

 ## Marketing miniproject: learning by doing

What product characteristics do consumers think are important in a new product? What types of service components do they demand? Most important, how do marketers know how to develop successful new products? This miniproject is designed to let you make some of these decisions.

1. Create (in your mind) a new product item that might be of interest to university students such as yourself. Develop a written description and possibly a drawing of this new product.

2. Show this new product description to a number of your fellow students who might be users of the product. Ask them to tell you what they think of the product. Some of the questions you might ask them are the following:

   a. What is your overall opinion of the new product?

   b. What basic benefits would you expect to receive from the product?

   c. What about the physical characteristics of the product? What do you like? Dislike? What would you add? Delete? Change?

   d. What do you like (or would you like) in the way of product packaging?

   e. What sort of services would you expect to receive with the product?

   f. Do you think you would try the product? How could marketers influence you to buy the product?

3. Develop a report based on what you found. Include your recommendations for changes in the product and your feelings about the potential success of the new product.

Real people, real surfers

Exploring the web

Go to the Black & Decker website (www.blackanddecker.com). Check out the information on the ScumBuster as well as a few other Black & Decker products that interest you.

Pick any Black & Decker product and describe the core product, the actual product and the augmented product.

In your opinion, is Black & Decker engaged in product innovation? What clues from the website lead you to this conclusion?

What do you think of Black & Decker's 'How To' centre? Did you find the information there relevant and useful? Was it easy to navigate?

Why would a company such as Black & Decker include a 'How To' centre on its website instead of just focusing on the products themselves?

Now, take a look at the website at www.pearsoned.co.uk/solomon to see some videos from YouTube relating to aspects of this chapter.

Marketing plan exercise

Go to the Procter & Gamble website (www.pg.com) and click on 'Products' at the top of the page. Next, find and click on 'Oral Care' and then click on 'Crest'. Look over the information about Crest products, then answer these questions that Procter & Gamble must answer when doing marketing planning for the Crest product line:

1. Crest lists several product innovations, including Whitestrips, and Night Effects. How would you 'classify' each of these products based on the discussion in the chapter? What leads you to classify each as you do?

2. What type of innovation do you consider each of these products? Why?

3. Pick any one of the products and consider the process that Procter & Gamble probably went through when initially developing it. Give an example of how each of the steps in Table 7.4, 'Phases in new product development', might have been utilised for that product.

4. For the same product you selected, what stage in the adoption process do you believe that product currently occupies with most consumers? What leads you to this conclusion? Why is knowledge of the adoption process important in marketing planning?

5. Go to the website www.pcworld.com/printable/article/id125772/printable.html#. Take a look at some of the flops of the IT industry. Pick several examples and using the five product characteristics that have an important effect on how quickly (or if) a new product will be adopted by consumers, explain why they might have failed.

6. Also, take a look at www.springwise.com, a website which features many innovative entrepreneurial ideas. Pick several examples and explain why you think they will or won't work in the future.

Delve deeper into innovation/NPD

Professor Jaideep Prabhu

The Jawaharlal Nehru Professor of Indian Business and Enterprise, Cambridge University

A major question drives most research on innovation and new product development (NPD): what types of firms are good at it and why? A secondary question of relevance is: what are the rewards to innovation? Here are references to three papers in leading journals that address these questions.

The first article by Sorescu, Chandy and Prabhu (2003) finds that a large majority of radical innovations come from a minority of firms. It also finds that the financial rewards of innovation vary dramatically across firms and are tied closely to firms' resource base. The second article by Yadav, Prabhu and Chandy (2007) uses an attentional perspective to argue that chief executive officers (CEOs) have a positive, direct and long-term impact on how firms detect, develop, and deploy new technologies over time. The authors test their arguments on longitudinal data from the US retail banking industry and find that CEOs' attention to the future is a critical driver of innovation. Finally, the third article by Tellis, Prabhu and Chandy (2009) uses survey and archival data from 759 firms across 17 major economies of the world to show that corporate culture is the crucial driver of radical innovation in firms across nations and that the commercialisation of radical innovations is a stronger predictor of financial performance than other popular measures, such as patents.

References

G.J. Tellis, J.C. Prabhu and R.K. Chandy (2009) 'Radical Innovation across Nations: The Preeminence of Corporate Culture', *Journal of Marketing*, 73, no.1, 3–23.

M.S. Yadav, J.C. Prabhu and R.K. Chandy (2007) 'Managing the Future: CEO Attention and Innovation Outcomes,' *Journal of Marketing* 71, no. 4, 84–101.

A.B. Sorescu, R.K. Chandy and J.C. Prabhu (2003) 'Sources and Financial Consequences of Radical Innovation: Insights from Pharmaceuticals.' *Journal of Marketing*, 67, no. 4, 82–102.

Marketing in action case

Real decisions at Starbucks

Starbucks began as a local coffee bean roaster and retailer of whole bean and ground coffee, tea and spices. From 1971, a lone store in Seattle's Pike Place Market has grown into the largest coffeehouse company in the world. The Seattle-based Starbucks Corporation is an international coffee and coffeehouse chain with 16,635 stores in 49 countries, including 11,068 in the United States, nearly 1000 in Canada and more than 800 in Japan. The Starbucks product selection includes drip brewed coffee, espresso-based hot drinks, other hot and cold drinks, coffee beans, salads, hot and cold sandwiches and paninis, pastry, snacks and items such as mugs and tumblers.

One of Starbuck's prominent brands that suffered in the recession at the beginning of the twenty-first century is the Frappuccino™. At its height, annual sales of this speciality drink exceeded $2 billion. However, sales have declined over the past few years. In 2010 the Frappuccino™ brand was estimated to represent between 15 per cent and 20 per cent of annual sales at Starbucks retail outlets. Dunkin' Donuts and McDonald's, along with many other smoothie chains, are gearing up to snatch market share away from Starbucks with their own coffee drinks. Since the Frappuccino™ plays such an important role in Starbucks' product mix, the company takes these challenges very seriously.

Frappuccino™ is a registered trademark of the Starbucks Corporation and it has been a brand for over 15 years. The blended ice beverage is a mixture of frappé and cappuccino, an Italian-style coffee with a topping of frothed milk. Starbucks sells it at the counter and also in bottles. Like the terms 'Kleenex' and 'Band-Aid,' the word 'Frappuccino' has become almost generic and many customers think the product is also available at other coffee purveyors.

Starbucks has tried various strategies to extend the brand name. Two new Frappuccino-flavoured ice creams are available on supermarket shelves. Vanilla Frappuccino Light, a bottled beverage, was created in a joint venture with PepsiCo. In addition, Starbucks globally introduced new blends, such as Black Sesame Frappuccino in China and Red Bean Frappuccino in other Asian markets. Still other plans are in the works including new bottled versions, new 'wacky' ingredients, and other products under the same brand banner.

The chain is also looking closely at a 'however-you-want-it-Frappuccino' customisation programme at a premium price. Customisation empowers the consumer to co-create value by beginning with an empty slate and personalising the beverage with his or her own choice of milk, coffee intensity, syrup and any optional toppings. Annie Young-Scrivner, global chief marketing officer for Starbucks, observes that one of the target markets for the Frappuccino™ is an 18- to 24-year-old woman. The customisation option allows calorie-counting customers to create a non-fat milk, light syrup and no whipped cream version with only

160 calories. According to Young-Scrivner, this market is ideal for the custom-made Frappuccino™. She told the *Wall Street Journal,* 'Millennials (otherwise known as Gen Y) are the iPod age group . . . accustomed to selecting exactly what they want. Now, they can choose an extra shot of espresso, no whipped cream, or a dab more caramel, for instance.'

With any product extension strategy, there are inevitable challenges. The Frappuccino™ has an involved preparation process and takes longer to produce than other Starbucks beverages. This may present a problem if the new programme is successful. The extra time needed for *baristas* to customise each drink may lead to long lines, customer irritation, more complicated employee training and slower than expected sales growth. Starbucks has questions to answer concerning, among other things, pricing, training and competition.

Things to think about

1. What is the decision facing Starbucks?

2. What factors are important in understanding this decision situation?

3. What are the alternatives?

4. What decision(s) do you recommend?

5. What are some ways to implement your recommendation?

Sources: Bruce Horovitz, 'Starbucks' Strategy: Whip It Good,' *USA Today*, 27 April, 2010, 3B; Starbucks Corporation Official website,'Company Profile' www.starbucks.com/about-us/company-information; Starbucks, Wikipedia, http://en.wikipedia.org/wiki/Starbucks (accessed 28 April, 2010); Kevin Helliker, 'At Long Last, Customized Frappuccino,' *Wall Street Journal* (Eastern Edition), New York, 17 March, 2010, D3.

References

1. Woodstream Corp., *Victor*, 27 March 2006, at www.victorpest.com.

2. Virgin Active Health Clubs website 2007, www.virginactive.co.uk

3. Microsoft Corp., 'Communities', 3 April 2006, www.microsoft.com/communities/default.mspx.

4. Walter S. Mossberg, 'Lots of Laptop Choices Mean Shoppers Have to Identify Their Needs', *Wall Street Journal*, 29 April 2004, B1.

5. Kärcher website 2004, wwww.karcher.com

6. Reuters News Service, 'Drugs Cost More, Return Less to Investors – Study', *Forbes.com*, 7 April 2006, www.forbes.com/business/newswire/2003/12/08/rtr1173648.html.

7. 'The Replacements', *Newsweek*, 25 June 2001, 50.

8. '2006 Volvo V40', *Top 100 Muscle Car Sites*, 30 March 2006, www.top100musclecarsites.com/Volvo-V40.html.

9. Steve Traiman, 'Goin' Digital', *Billboard*, 1 May 2004; John Markoff, 'Oh, Yeah, He Also Sells Computers', *New York Times*, 25 April 2004, Section 3, 1; Devin Leonard, 'Songs in the Key of Steve', *Fortune*, 12 May 2003, 52+; Apple Computer, 'The New iPod' 29 March 2006, www.apple.com/ipod/ipod.html.

10. Palm Inc., *The Treo Store*, 30 March 2006, http://web.palm.com/products/communicators/treo600_overview.jhtml.

11. Becky Worley, 'Marriage-Saving Technology: Simple Devices Help Achieve Marital Bliss', *ABC News*, 1 April 2006, http://abcnews.go.com/GMA/Technology/story?id=1390155.

12. M. Sweeny, 'Aston Martin top cool brands list', *Guardian*, 13 September 2007, www.guardian.co.uk/media/2007/sep/13/marketingandpr.business; F. Keenan, 'G.I. Joe Heroics at Hasbro', *Business Week*, 26 November 2001, 16.

13. CBS Broadcasting Inc., 'Getting Products on Store Shelves', *CBS Evening News*, 28 March 2006, www.cbsnews.com/stories/2000/09/14/eveningnews/main233535.shtml.

14. Quoted in Brendan I. Koerner, 'Geeks in Toyland', *Wired* (February 2006), www.wired.com/archive/14.02/lego.html.

15. Jennifer Ordonez, 'Burger King's Decision to Develop French Fry Has Been a Whopper', *Wall Street Journal.com*, 16 January 2001, http://interactive.wsj.com/articles/SB97960472517999878.

16. James Dao, 'From a Collector of Turkeys, a Tour of a Supermarket Zoo', *New York Times*, 24 September 1995, F12.

17. Maytag UK website 2007, www.maytag.co.uk

18. Quoted in Jack Neff, 'P&G Boosts Design's Role in Marketing', *Advertising Age*, 9 February 2004, 52. This section adapted from Michael R. Solomon, *Consumer Behavior: Buying, Having, and Being*, 7th ed. (Upper Saddle River, NJ: Prentice Hall, 2006).

19. Robert Berner, 'Why P&G's Smile Is So Bright', *Business Week*, 12 August 2002, 58–60; Procter & Gamble Co., 'Crest Spin-Brush', 28 March 2006, www.spinbrush.com.

20. Dan Cray and Maggie Sieger, 'Inside the Food Labs', *Time*, 6 October 2003, 56–60; James Norton, 'The McGriddle', *flakmagazine*, 5 April 2006, http://flakmag.com/misc/mcgriddle.html.

21. Jeremy Clarkson, www.timesonline.co.uk/driving/jeremy_clarkson/articles698732.ece.

22. Malcolm Gladwell, *The Tipping Point* (Newport Beach, CA: Back Bay Books, 2002).

23. N. Bendle, P. Farris,, Phillip. Pfeifer and D. Reibstein, (2010) 'Metrics that Matter to Marketing Managers', *Marketing JRM*,1(2010), p. 18–23.

24. Alice Z. Cuneo, 'Microsoft Taps "Puffy" for Xbox', *Advertising Age*, 20 October 2004, 4.

25. Neal E. Boudette and Lee Hawkins, 'Volkswagen Eyes Young Parents with Newest Version of Jetta', *Wall Street Journal*, 11 January 2005, D.9.

26. Polson Enterprises and Amazon.com, 'Virtual Pet Store', 6 April 2006), www.virtualpet.com/pe/books/vpbs/vpbs.htm.

27. K. Allen, 'HMV Unveils Next Generation Stores' *Guardian*, 12 September 2007, www.guardian.co.uk/business/2007/sep/12/media.

28. 'Dell Brings Kiosk-Based Marketing to DFW Airport', *Kiosk Marketplace*, 4 April 2006, www.kioskmarketplace.com/news_story.htm?i=16464.

29. Amy Gilroy, 'More Players Enter Portable Nav Market', *TWICE*, 5 April 2004; Pioneer Electronics Co., 'XM NavTraffic', *Pioneer: Car Electronics*, 4 April 2006, www.pioneerelectronics.com/pna/article/0,,2076_3149_269505659,00.html.

30. Everett Rogers, *Diffusion of Innovations* (New York: Free Press, 1983), 247–51.

31. Steve Jobs, To all iPhone customers, Apple website 2007, www.apple.com/hotnews/openiphoneletter.

32. Sources used in this section: 'Wi-Fi's Big Brother', *Economist*, 13 March 2004, 65; 'Burgers, Fries and Wi-Fi', *Informationweek*, www.informationweek.com/showarticle.jhtml?articleID = 8700269; William J. Gurley, 'Why Wi-Fi Is the Next Big Thing', *Fortune*, 5 March 2001, 184; Joshua Quittner, 'Cordless Capers', *Time*, 1 May 2000, 85; Scott Van Camp, 'Intel Switches Centrino's Gears', *Brandweek*, 26 April 2004, 16; Benny Evangelista, 'SBC Park a Hot Spot for Fans Lugging Laptops', *San Francisco Chronicle*, 26 April 2004, A1; Todd Wallack, 'Santa Clara Ready for Wireless', *San Francisco Chronicle*, 19 April 2004, D1; http://wifinetnews.com.

33. Christine Chen and Tim Carvell, 'Hall of Shame', *Fortune*, 22 November 1999, 140.

34. Everett Rogers (2003) *Diffusion of Innovations*, 5th ed. (New York: Free Press).

35. Clement James, 'UK School Saves Thousands with Open Source Software', *VNUNet* 31 August 2006.

36. Richard Thurston, 'EU: Open Source Almost Always Cheaper Option', *silicon.com* 15 January 2007.

Chapter 8
Managing the product

Meet Mads Kjær,
CEO and Chairman of the board of Kjaer Group

Mads Kjær is the Chairman and majority owner of Kjaer Group A/S. Kjaer Group is the Danish parent company to an international group of automotive companies providing transportation solutions to emerging countries and it is a business partner of Nissan, Land Rover, Ford and Honda. Kjaer Group's focus is on MDG number 6 (Health), specifically Road Safety in Africa. Mads Kjær has been working for the last 25 years in leadership and with a special love and dedication for Africa. Main competences are strong passion for entrepreneurship, people and our world.

Q & A with Mads Kjær

What I do when I'm not working
Spend time with my family, friends, travel, sport, think, learn, read, enjoy, sleep and dream

First job out of school?
Trainee in shipping company, ICO/ASECO in Copenhagen, Denmark

Career high?
Still to come!

A job-related mistake I wish I hadn't made
Giving our African employees Samsonite suitcases for Christmas instead of seeing to it that they should have mosquito bed nets to prevent them and their families from catching malaria

Best business book you've read?
Tom Peters and Jim Collins *From Good to Great*

My hero
Nelson Mandela

My motto to live by
When we can walk on the moon then we can also end poverty

What drives me
To learn – to contribute – to do the impossible!

My management style
Open, passionate, empathy, visionary, talkative!

Don't do this when interviewing with me
Come unprepared

Favourite drink?
Wine and water

Best holiday you've ever had?
Many with my family, I would say all of them

Real people, real decisions
Decision time at the Kjaer Group

In 1962 Mr Christian Kjaer (we shall see later the importance of the last name being pronounced 'care') founded a car sales company in the town of Svendborg, Denmark. The company initially had success by agreeing to deliver cars to customers on the small islands in the archipelago surrounding the town, something other car dealers refused to do. This initial corporate policy about not backing down for distance or logistical reasons contributed to the development of the specialisation that has now secured the company a worldwide presence. No longer selling cars in the neighbourhood, what is today known as Kjaer Group Ltd is a holding company with approximately 200 employees consisting of a number of sub-companies each with a different name. They specialise in providing and servicing cars and special vehicles in disaster areas (e.g. after earthquakes) and in developing countries for customers like the United Nations and Red Cross.

The corporate logo is based on the legend of the hero Beowulf, who sailed with his men to save the Danish king's court from the monster Grendel, which attacked and slaughtered the king's men. In Kjaer Group, Beowulf is interpreted as a symbol of a willingness to expose oneself to risk and trouble in order to help others. In formulating the values of the company, Mads Kjaer, son of the founder, who became chairman in 1986, had been influenced by Maslow's hierarchy of needs. He had seen first hand in Africa, where the company mainly operates, that the satisfaction of the most basic human needs is not something that can be taken for granted. This drive for equality in society led to the company being voted the best workplace in Denmark in 2003 and 2004, and more recently a prize for 'multiplicity in the workplace', which is given to companies that are providing good opportunities for employees regardless of gender, ethnicity, age, handicap, religion or sexual orientation.

Because of its growing involvement in different markets and collaborative partnerships with several car-producing companies, a number of sub-companies and sub-brands had been created. Furthermore, the creative spirit within the company had led to something of an explosion in the number of values that were used to express the philosophy of the company. In short, it was no longer very clear what constituted the unifying element and the core values of the Kjaer Group. Since Mads Kjaer saw it as imperative that the basic values could be founded in a philosophy and a history, and not just the latest advertising agency lingo, he contacted a group of researchers at the unit Brand Base, at University of Southern Denmark. Together, Mads Kjaer and the researchers distilled three alternatives:

Option 1 Accept and support the development of the sub-brands

In this option, the Kjaer Group would be divided into a series of sub-companies each with their own brand and value profile as a result of them operating in different markets with very different conditions. Thus, instead of attempting to maintain a unity which no longer really existed, a better option was to 'let the sub-brands' free. Strategically, they should become more independent and grow and flourish on their own conditions and pursuing their specific values, mission and vision. Focus would consequently shift from the Kjaer Group name and the collective vision and mission to the sub-brands and their visibility and equity in each of the markets within which they operate. The disadvantages of this option is that the Kjaer Group risks putting at stake the strong corporate team spirit that runs across the sub-companies and which has won it prizes and high rankings in national and international competitions of being 'best workplace'.

Option 2 Strengthen the current Kjaer Group value profile by a clean-up process in the values

Basically, this option suggests that there is nothing fundamentally wrong with the current value profile of Kjaer Group that runs through the corporate communication policies, as the success stories of the HRM and corporate communication indicates. Maslow's hierarchy of needs provides a strong theoretical basis for a corporation operating in disaster areas and in Africa, where the fundamental principle of survival is not a given and the basic mission is to provide the logistical means for people to survive. All that it takes is a simplification of the values resulting from the diverse sub-brands. It is more important to keep the strong integrated marketing communication than to provide maximum freedom for all the sub-brands. The disadvantage of this option is that it represents a 'more-of-the-same' solution and potentially does not tackle the main problem of too many values and confusion about the coherence of the sub-brands.

Option 3 Reformulate the corporate vision and mission

This option involves a scrutiny of the values that pervade Kjaer Group in order to find the 'social glue' that really keeps the company a coherent, strong unit and a great place to work. Kjaer Group had already played with the relative similarity between the name Kjaer (remember, the j is almost silent) and 'care'. Caring for the staff, as well as for the people in need of infrastructure and logistics in the world, was a built-in practice of corporate culture as expressed in the corporate slogan: 'Love cars, love life, love people'. The disadvantages of this option were twofold: first of all a fundamental change in value structure, mission and vision is always a risky business

and may be seen as superfluous 'playground activities' for an idle management structure in a company, where the ground floor staff is very happy with the state of things. 'Oh no, another whimsical idea', the saying could go. Thus, such processes may be counterproductive to creating corporate team spirit and a sound foundation for a good integrated marketing communications. Secondly, introducing a more complex model for how and why we act in society or a company, rather than the relatively simple Maslow hierarchy of needs, may contribute more to confusion and disintegration of the company's values.

Now put yourself in Mads' shoes. Which option would you choose and why?

Objectives

When you finish reading this chapter, you will be able to:

1 Explain the different product objectives and strategies a firm may choose

2 Explain how firms manage products throughout the product life cycle

3 Discuss how branding creates product identity and describe different types of branding strategies

4 Explain the roles packaging and labelling play in developing effective product strategies

5 Describe how organisations are structured for new and existing product management

Product planning: taking the next step

Objective

1

Explain the different product objectives and strategies a firm may choose

In 2006, Lexus introduced the GS450h – that's 'h' as in hybrid. It's the first hybrid ever brought to market on a rear-wheel drive car, with an acceleration claim of 0–60 mph in 5 1/2 seconds. The G450h is also the first 'luxury hybrid'; it's out to prove that phrase isn't an oxymoron. With an initial base price of about €41,450, Lexus is banking on re-educating high-end car buyers that they can have their cake and eat it too with fuel economy, comfort and performance.[1]

Toyota's Prius has been a sales phenomenon at the lower end of the emerging hybrid market, although several other Prius rivals have posted more disappointing sales. Will the GS450h succeed? A lot depends on how this innovative product is marketed and managed. What makes one product fail and another succeed? It's worth repeating what we said in Chapter 2: firms that plan well succeed. Product planning plays a big role in the firm's *tactical marketing plans*. The strategies outlined in the product plan spell out how the firm expects to develop a product that will meet marketing objectives.

Today, successful product management is more important than ever. As more and more competitors enter the global marketplace and as technology moves forward at an ever-increasing pace, products are created, grow, reach maturity and decline at faster and faster speeds. Think about how quickly mobile phones are replaced. This means that good product decisions are more critical than ever.

In Chapter 7, we talked about what a product really is and about how companies develop and introduce new products. In this chapter, we'll finish the product focus of the

Develop Product Objectives
- For individual products
- For product ranges and mixes

Design Product Strategies

Make Tactical Product Decisions
- Product branding
- Packaging and labelling design

Figure 8.1	Steps in managing products
	Effective product strategies come from a series of orderly steps

book by seeing how companies manage products and examine the steps in product planning, as Figure 8.1 outlines. These steps include developing product objectives and the strategies required to successfully market products as they evolve from 'new kids on the block' to tried-and-tested favourites – and in some cases finding new markets for these favourites. Next, we'll discuss branding and packaging, two of the more important tactical decisions product planners make. Finally, we'll examine how firms organise for effective product management. Let's start by seeing how firms develop product-related objectives.

Using product objectives to decide on a product strategy

When marketers develop product strategies, they make decisions about product benefits, features, styling, branding, labelling and packaging. But what do they want to accomplish? Clearly stated product objectives provide focus and direction. They should support the broader marketing objectives of the business unit in addition to being consistent with the firm's overall mission. For example, the objectives of the firm may focus on return on investment. Marketing objectives then may concentrate on building market share and/or the unit or sales volume necessary to attain that return on investment. Product objectives need to specify how product decisions will contribute to reaching a desired market share or level of sales.

To be effective, product-related objectives must be SMART, i.e. Specific, Measurable, Achievable, Relevant and Timebound, which means indicating a specific time frame. Consider, for example, how a frozen meal manufacturer might state its product objectives:

- 'In the next financial year, eliminate the product's trans fat content to satisfy consumers' health concerns.'

- 'Introduce three new items this quarter to the product line to take advantage of increased consumer interest in Brazilian foods.'

- 'During the next financial year, improve the chicken main course dishes to the extent that consumers will rate them as tasting better than the competition.'

Planners must keep in touch with their customers so that their objectives accurately respond to customer needs. An up-to-date knowledge of competitive product innovations is also important in developing product objectives. Above all, product objectives should consider the *long-term implications* of product decisions. Planners who sacrifice the long-term health of the firm to reach short-term sales or financial goals may be on a risky course. Product planners may focus on one or more individual products at a time, or they may look at a group of product offerings as a whole. In this section, we'll briefly examine both these approaches. We'll also look at one important product objective: product quality.

Objectives and strategies for individual products

How do you launch a new car that's only 142 inches long and makes people laugh when they see it? BMW did it by calling attention to the small size and poking fun at the car itself.

After the official launch at the Paris motor show in 2000, the Mini Cooper hit the UK market in 2001 with an innovative marketing campaign which targeted young, well-to-do urbanites. The TV advertisement campaign called 'It's a Mini Adventure' wowed not only the car owners, but a plague of zombies and an invading army of Martians as well. One in the series of the TV advertisements was classified as the shortest film ever by the British Film Board, being just 12 seconds long. The Mini also went on a tour at the end of the summer which included ten UK cities, visiting the biggest shopping centres and the most famous amusement park in the country over a five-week period. During the tour BMW organised games, convoys, drive-bys, stunts, plenty of give-aways and a Guinness World Record attempt. The Mini also picked up commuters from bus stops and hitchhikers held up 'Take me to a Mini Adventure' signs. A Sound System Mini – which has enough

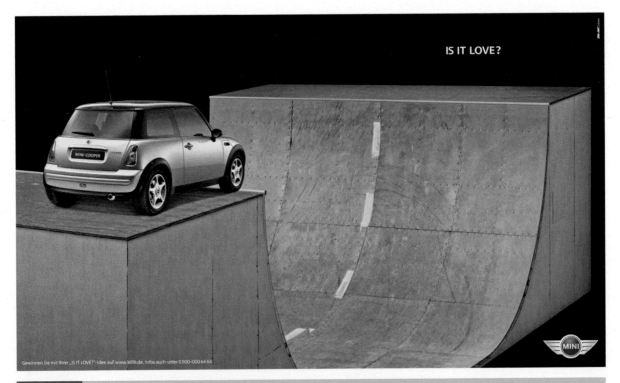

IS IT LOVE?

Photo 8.1	With a relatively tiny budget for a new car model, the marketers of the Mini Cooper had to be very creative
	Source: BMW

Photo 8.2	Actimel's value proposition is to protect your immune system and keep you healthy

Source: RKCR/Y&R/Danone/Coy! Communications

power to entertain a small nightclub – was featured at V music festival 2001 in Stafford, the Notting Hill Carnival and London's Mardi Gras. A remake of *The Italian Job* in 2003 also featured Minis which further helped to popularise BMW's little car in homage to their use in the original *The Italian Job* featuring Michael Caine.[2] If someone didn't know what a 'Mini Adventure' was by the end of the year, there probably wasn't much hope for them . . .[3]

Some product strategies, such as that for the new hybrid Lexus GS450h or the Mini Cooper, focus on a single new product. However, strategies for individual products may be quite different for new products, for regional products and for mature products.

- For new products, not surprisingly, the objectives relate to successful introduction, such as retailer acceptance, 70 per cent awareness of the product, etc.

- After a firm has experienced success with a product in a local or regional market, it may decide to introduce it nationally. Scottish & Newcastle was a local brewer in 1985 focusing on Scotland and the North of England. By 2005 it became the UK's leading brewer. It has covered several markets in the world such as Europe, China and India with well-known beers like Foster's, Baltika and Kronenbourg 1664.[4]

- For mature products like Haribo sweets, originally founded in Germany in 1920,[5] product objectives may focus on breathing new life into a product while holding on to the traditional brand personality. Haribo, the sweets 'Kids and grown-ups love 'em so', has introduced a host of different tastes, such as MagicMix, Starmix, Strawbs, Liquorice and Jelly Beans. Haribo has been around for over 80 years but continues to try to stay fresh with more than 25 varieties offered in its pre-packed range and also selling other ranges.

Objectives and strategies for several products

Although a small firm might make a go of focusing on one product, such as a small English winemaker, a larger firm often markets a set of related products. This means that strategic decisions affect two or more products simultaneously. The firm must think in terms of its entire portfolio of products. As Figure 8.2 shows, product planning means developing *product range* and *product mix* strategies encompassing several offerings. Figure 8.3 illustrates how this works for a selection of Procter & Gamble's products.

Product range strategies

A **product range** is a firm's total product offering designed to satisfy a single need or desire of a group of target customers. For example, Procter & Gamble's cleaning products include three laundry detergent brands: Ace focuses on reviving the brightness of coloured clothes; Ariel delivers outstanding whiteness; and Bounce is designed for tumble driers. To do an even better job of meeting varying consumer needs, each of the three brands comes in more than one formulation. In addition to regular Ariel, you can buy Ariel Sensitive which is gentler to your skin and Ariel Handwash for your delicate fabrics.[6] The number of separate items within the same category determines the *length* of the product line.

A large number of variations in a product range is described as a *full line*, like Heinz soups, which target many customer segments to boost sales potential. A *limited line strategy* with fewer product variations can improve the firm's image if it is perceived as a specialist with a clear,

Figure 8.2	Objectives for single and many products

Product objectives provide focus and direction for product strategies. Objectives can focus on a single product or a group of products

Width of Product Mix

Fabric and Home Care	Beauty Care	Health Care/Baby and Family Care	Snacks and Beverages
Ace Laundry and Bleach	Aussie	Bounty	Millstone
Alomatik	Camay	Charmin	Pringles
Ariel	Clairol's Herbal Essences	Codi	Sunny Delight
Bold	Cover Girl	Crest	Torengos
Bonux	Evax	Didronel	
Bounce	Giorgio	Fixodent	
Dash	Head & Shoulders	Kandoo	
Daz	Hugo Boss	Luvs	
Dryel	Infasil	Macrobid	
Era	Infusion 23	Metamucil	
Fairy	Ivory Personal Care	Pampers	
Febreze	Lacoste	Pepto-Bismol	
Flash	Laura Biagiotti	Puffs	
Gain	Lines Feminine Care	PUR	
Hi Wash	Max Factor	Scope	
Ivory Dish	Mum Always Whisper	Tempo	
Joy	Muse	ThermaCare	
Lenor	Natural Instincts and Hydrience	Vicks	
Mr Clean/Proper	Naturella		
Rindex	Nice 'n Easy		
Salvo	Noxzema		
Tide	Olay		
Viakal	Old Spice		
Vizir	Pantene		
	Physique		
	Rejoice		
	Safeguard		
	Secret		
	SK-II		
	Sure		
	Tampax		
	Vidal Sassoon		
	Wash & Go		
	Zest		

Length of Product Range

Figure 8.3   Product range length and product mix width

A product range is a firm's total offerings that satisfy one need, whereas the product mix includes all the products that a firm offers. Here we see an example of both for a selection of Procter & Gamble's extensive family of products. The figure illustrates the length of Procter & Gamble's product range as well as the width of its product mix

Marketing metrics

Branding in the detergents market

Liquid detergents provide a revealing example of evidence of consumer behaviour towards innovation. Technically, the new products were revolutionary, with seven years' of R&D to develop a fatty acid with water-softening capabilities equivalent to a phosphate, and new 'builders' to prevent redisposition of dirt in the wash. But the key question is how did consumers perceive the innovation? First to market was the new Unilever brand, named Wisk, in the final quarter of 1985. Procter & Gamble responded in the first quarter of 1987, but quite differently from Unilever and the product was launched as Ariel Liquid, a line extension. Unilever responded to the success of Ariel Liquid rather belatedly in the third quarter of 1988, and launched Persil Liquid (chemically identical to Wisk). Eventually, the more strongly differentiated product, Wisk, ended up in the weakest position and by mid-1989, Persil Liquid had 6 per cent share and Persil Powder 23 per cent, Wisk had decayed to 5 per cent, and Ariel Liquid and Powder had 9 and 11 per cent respectively. This suggests that strong differentiation can be less effective than hiding behind an existing identity. The key determinant is whether consumers see the differentiation. Despite all the technical innovation, most consumers saw the liquid as an example of the detergent category, not as a new category.

specific position in the market. A great example of such a strategy is Rolls-Royce Motor Cars, owned by BMW. Rolls-Royce makes expensive, handcrafted cars built to each customer's exact specifications and for decades has maintained a unique position in the automobile industry. Every Phantom and 101EX that rolls out of the factory door is truly a unique work of art.[7]

Organisations may also decide to extend their product range by adding more brands or models when they develop product strategies. For example, Gap extended its reach by adding children's clothing. When a firm stretches its product line, it must decide on the best direction to go. If a firm's current product line includes middle-range and cheaper items, an *upward line stretch* adds new items – higher priced and claiming more quality. For example, Hyundai decided it could tap the market for bigger, more luxurious cars and SUVs, and stretched its line upward in the form of models such as the Grandeur, Coupe SIII and Santa Fe SUVs.[8] Each of these is positioned against top-end products by Toyota and Honda, but costs thousands of euros less.[9]

Conversely, a *downward line stretch* augments a range by adding cheaper items. Here the firm must take care not to blur the images of its higher-priced, upper-end offerings. Rolex, for example, may not want to run the risk of cheapening its image with a new watch line to compete with lower-priced watches such as Swatch.

In some cases, a firm may decide that it is targeting too small a market. In this case, the product strategy may call for a *two-way stretch* that adds products at both the upper and lower ends. Marriott Hotels, for example, added Fairfield Inns and Courtyard at the lower end and J.W. Marriott and Ritz Carlton at the upper end to round out its product line.

A *filling-out strategy* may mean adding sizes or styles not previously available in a product category. Kraft Foods did this by introducing a 4 × 35g multipack version of its Toblerone chocolate. In other cases, the best strategy may be to *contract* a product line, particularly when some of the items are not profitable. For example, Heinz scrapped its 'Bite Me' brand of frozen pizza snacks because of poor sales. The product, targeted to teenagers, failed to meet company expectations.[10]

We've seen that there are many ways a firm can modify its product line to meet the competition or take advantage of new opportunities. To further explore these strategic decisions, let's return to the world of detergents. What does Procter & Gamble do if the objective is to increase market share? One possibility would be to expand its range of laundry detergents. If the line extension meets a perceived consumer need currently not being addressed, such as bobbling on clothes, this would be a good strategic objective.

But whenever a product line or a product family is extended, there is risk of **cannibalisation**, which occurs when sales of an existing brand are eaten up by the new item as the firm's current customers switch to the new product. This is the risk Procter & Gamble took in meeting consumer demands for sensitive or handwash detergents by creating new versions of the existing brand Ariel, which could cannibalise sales of normal Ariel. But better that than consumers swapping to a competitor brand with sensitive properties.

Product mix strategies

Product planning can go beyond a single product item or a product line to entire groups of products. A firm's **product mix** is its entire range of products. For example, in addition to a deep line of shaving products, Procter & Gamble's 2005 acquisition of the Gillette line gave P&G new toiletries such as Old Spice and Secret deodorants, Oral B toothbrushes, Braun oral care products, Duracell batteries and Cricket cigarette lighters.

In developing a product mix strategy, planners usually consider the *width of the product mix*, that is, the number of different product lines produced by the firm. By developing several different product lines, firms can reduce the risk associated with putting all their eggs into one basket. Normally, firms develop a mix of product lines that have some things in common, be it distribution channels or manufacturing facilities.

Wine and spirits distributor Constellation Brands' entry into the mainstream supermarket wine space through its acquisition of Robert Mondavi is an example of a successful product mix expansion strategy. Europeans are drinking more wine of late, and the Mondavi brand gives Constellation the crown jewel in the €2.7 billion supermarket wine channel.[11]

Quality as a product objective

Product objectives often focus on product quality: the overall ability of the product to satisfy customers' expectations. Quality is tied to how customers *think* a product will perform and not necessarily to some technological level of perfection, so it can depend on how the company promotes the product.

In some cases, quality means fanatical attention to detail and also getting extensive input from actual users of a product as it's being developed or refined – this is known as integrating the *voice of the consumer* into product design. The Japanese take this idea a step further with a practice they call **Kansei engineering**, a philosophy that translates customers' feelings into design elements. In one application of this practice, the designers of the Mazda Miata focused on young drivers who saw the car as an extension of their body, a sensation they call 'horse and rider as one'. After extensive research, they discovered that making the gear stick exactly 9.5 centimetres long conveys the optimal feeling of sportiness and control.[12]

Total quality management

As noted in Chapter 1, many firms with a quality focus have adopted the principles and practices of **total quality management (TQM)**, a philosophy that calls for company-wide dedication to the development, maintenance and continuous improvement of all aspects of the company's operations. Indeed, many of the world's most admired, successful companies – top-of-industry firms such as 3M, Boeing and Coca-Cola – have adopted a total quality focus.

Product quality is one way that marketing can add value to customers. However, TQM as an approach to doing business is far more sophisticated and effective than simply paying attention to product quality. TQM firms promote the attitude among employees that *everybody* working there has customers – even employees who never interact with customers outside the firm. In such cases, employees' customers are *internal customers* – other employees with whom they interact. In this way, TQM seeks to ensure customer satisfaction by involving all employees, regardless of their function, in efforts to improve quality continually. For example, TQM firms encourage employees, even the lowest-paid factory workers, to suggest ways to improve products – and then reward employees for good ideas.

But how do you know when you've attained your goal of quality? Other than increased sales and profits, a few key award programmes recognise firms that are doing the job well. For example, in 1989 heads of prominent European businesses established the European Foundation for Quality Management (EFQM) to recognise excellence. The EFQM Excellence Award has been awarded to the best performing firms in Europe since 1992 (see Table 8.1). For example, the reason for Villa Massa's success is its focus on customer satisfaction and the creation of a top quality brand which is internationally recognised. The marketing strategy is to satisfy the consumer needs by offering a strong, unique selling proposition based on 'quality, authenticity and premiumness'. Continuous improvement in activity performance is based on knowledge of customer satisfaction, competences of the people, suppliers, partnerships strengthening, technological innovations and evaluation of all process indicators and trends.

Around the world, many companies look to the uniform standards of the International Organization for Standardization (ISO) for quality guidelines. This Geneva-based organisation developed a set of criteria in 1987 to improve and standardise product quality in Europe. The broad set of guidelines, known as **ISO 9000**, sets established voluntary standards for quality management. This means what the organisation does to achieve the customer's quality requirements, the applicable regulatory requirements, while aiming to enhance customer satisfaction, and achieve continual improvement of its performance in pursuit of these objectives.

The EFQM Excellence Award is Europe's most prestigious recognition for organisational excellence given to Europe's best performing companies and not-for-profit organisations. In 2010, 13 organisations reached the final stage of the award.

The 2010 prize winners and finalists were:

- **Dr. Germain Becker & Associés (Luxembourg)** Private dental medical practice. *Finalist*

- **Bradstow School (UK)** Residential special school for children with autistic disorders and learning disabilities. *Prize Winner in Leading with Vision, Inspiration & Integrity and a Prize Winner in Succeeding through People*

- **Alpenresort Schwarz (Austria)** A private family-run alpine resort. *Finalist*

- **Eskisehir Maternity and Child Illness Hospital (Turkey)** Eskisehir Maternity's mission is to treat mother and child illnesses *Prize Winner in Leading with Vision, Inspiration and Integrity*

- **Domino-World (Germany)** A geriatric caring service provider. *Finalist*

- **Olabide Ikastola Sociedad Cooperativa (Spain)** A not-for-profit private school, part-funded (grant-aided) by the Basque Government. *Prize Winner in Adding Value for Customers and a Prize Winner in Succeeding through People*

- **Liverpool John Moores University (UK)** Higher education provider. *Finalist*

- **Stavropol State Agrarian University (Russia)** A federal state educational institution of higher professional education. *Prize Winner in Nurturing Creativity & Innovation and a Prize Winner in Leading with Vision, Inspiration & Integrity*

- **Osakidetza – Comarca Gipuzkoa Ekialde (Spain)** Healthcare provider. *Finalist*

- **Robert Bosch Fahrzeugelektrik Eisenach (Germany)** The company produces sensors and different components for injection and safety systems as well as for engine management and transmission control in the plant. *Finalist*

- **Vamed KMB (Austria)** A facility management companies providing technical, administrative, and infrastructural services. *Prize Winner in Succeeding through People*

- **Worthington Cylinders (UK)** Steel cylinder producer for a variety of high pressure gas packaging applications. *Finalist*

- **Siemens Congelton (UK)** An operational manufacturing unit within the global Siemens Industry sector Drive Technologies. *Finalist*

Table 8.1 The EFQM Excellence Award winners

Source: Adapted from www.efqm.org/en/Home/theEFQMnetwork/Awardwinners/EFQMExcellenceAward2010/tabid/224/Default.aspx

Quality management ensures that an organisation's products conform to the customer's requirements. In 1996, the ISO developed **ISO 14000** standards, which concentrate on 'environmental management'. This means the organisation works to minimise any harmful effects it may have on the environment. Because members of the European Union and other European countries prefer suppliers with ISO 9000 and ISO 14000 certification, companies must comply with these standards, otherwise other companies won't buy from them.[13]

One way that companies can improve quality is by using the **Six Sigma** methodology. The term *Six Sigma* comes from the statistical term 'sigma', which is a standard deviation from the mean or average. Six Sigma, therefore, refers to six standard deviations from a normal distribution curve. In practical terms, that translates to no more than 3.4 defects per million – getting it right 99.9997 per cent of the time. As you can imagine, achieving that level of quality requires a very rigorous approach (try it on your coursework) – and that's what Six Sigma offers. The methodology involves a five-step process called DMAIC: define, measure, analyse, improve and control. Employees are trained in the methodology and, as in karate, progress towards 'black belt' status by successfully completing all the levels of training. Employees can use Six Sigma processes to remove defects from services, not just products. A 'defect' means failing to meet customer expectations. For example, hospitals can use Six Sigma processes to reduce medical errors, and airlines can use Six Sigma to improve flight scheduling.

Adding a dose of quality to the marketing mix

Marketing people research the level of quality consumers want and need in their products and what price they are willing to pay for them. The price-versus-quality decision is a major aspect of providing value to consumers. Marketing also has to *inform* consumers about product quality through its marketing communications.

But keeping on top of what customers want is just the beginning. Firms also have to deliver a (customer-perceived) quality product at the right place and at the right price. Instead of being satisfied with doing things the same way year after year, marketers must continuously seek ways to improve product, place, price and promotion. Let's see how quality concerns affect the marketing mix:

- **Product:** One way firms can offer quality for their customers is by improving their customer service support. For example, Whirlpool has been steadily improving the repair services it offers on its appliances. In the past, if your washing machine broke down, you'd call Whirlpool, they'd refer you to a service centre, and you'd call the service centre and try to arrange a repair time. Today, technology lets Whirlpool's customer service reps view the schedules of all its repair technicians in your area and then set a repair time that suits you – all during the first phone call. Whirlpool also offers an online service that lets customers schedule service themselves, without even talking with a rep. The easier it is for customers to interact with the company and get results, the more satisfied they will be. And Whirlpool's acquisition of Maytag in 2006 gave the company the opportunity to expand this service to include customers of its products.[14]

- **Place:** Dell has a general approach of manufacturing close to its customers, thus improving delivery time to its clients which in turn improves the quality of its service. In the EU it manufactures in Ireland and Poland, in the US the company has three plants, it also owns three in Asia and one in South America.

- **Price:** Hewlett-Packard (HP) is lowering costs and improving service to customers at the same time. HP developed a 'sure supply' technology that is embedded into its printer cartridges. The technology has a sensor that detects when the ink supply is low, and the networked printer automatically orders a new cartridge. By building an auto-

Figure 8.4	Product quality
	Some product objectives focus on quality or the ability of a product to satisfy customer expectations – no matter what those expectations are

mated cartridge supply service into the printer, HP also reduces its own costs related to processing a customer's phone order.[15]

- **Promotion:** Today's marketing firms realise that customers want information when they need it, not when it's convenient for the marketer. Gap exemplifies this philosophy. At Gap's Old Navy stores, salespeople wear headsets so they can quickly get information to answer customers' questions. Another example is Marks & Spencer – the firm uses Radio Frequency Identification tags on several of its clothing lines which can be monitored to know exactly how many items are on the shop floor or in the store room to improve stock levels in store.[16]

Dimensions of product quality

But what exactly *is* quality? Figure 8.4 summarises some of the many meanings of quality. In some cases, product quality means durability. For example, trainers shouldn't develop holes after their owner plays football for a few weeks. Reliability also is an important aspect of product quality – just consider Toyota, its cars have been ranked among the top performers in reliability surveys for many years.[17]

Marketing misstakes

Lucozade: more than just an energy drink

Lucozade has performed well since it re-positioned itself as a sports drink. However, the Food Standards Agency (FSA) recently revealed that the company has taken the action of withdrawing all its 'sport lite summer berries' flavoured drinks from sale, in response to consumer complaints regarding an unpleasant smell from the bottled drink. A report from the FSA warned of the risk of 'mould growth'.

Why do you think this might be a marketing misstake?
Source: Based on Food Standards Agency

For other products, quality means a high degree of precision. For example, high-tech audio equipment promises clearer music reproduction with less distortion. Quality, especially in business-to-business products, is also related to ease of use, maintenance and repair. Yet another crucial dimension of quality is product safety, e.g. a child's car seat. Finally, the quality of products such as a painting, a film or even a wedding dress relates to the degree of aesthetic pleasure they provide. Of course, evaluations of aesthetic quality differ dramatically among people: to one person, quality TV may mean a BBC period drama such as *Pride and Prejudice*, while to another it's MTV.

Marketing planners often focus product objectives on one or both of two key aspects of quality: level and consistency. Customers often determine the *level of quality* of a product by comparison with other brands in the same product category. A handcrafted Rolls-Royce boasts higher quality than an assembly-line Fiat Punto, but this may be irrelevant to a Punto buyer inclined to compare his car with the quality of a Mini Cooper and not to an elite luxury car.

Consistency of quality means that customers experience the same level of quality in a product time after time, bringing repeat business and free word-of-mouth advertising or buzz. Consistent quality is also one of the major benefits of adopting TQM practices. Consumer perceptions can change overnight when quality is lacking. Ask anybody who's ever bought a new car only to find it back in the garage the following week with problems.

Real people, other voices

Advice for Mads Kjaer

Nigel Bradley

Senior Lecturer at the University of Westminster

I would, with no doubt at all, choose Option 1, accept and support the development of the sub-brands. Let us take stock of the situation. Already the operation is built on a series of brands and there is no unifying brand. The customers are such organisations as the United Nations and Red Cross. The offering is providing and servicing cars and special vehicles in disaster areas (e.g after earthquakes) and in developing countries. Effectively this is a niche product with a great reliance on personal contact and immediate reaction. Branding is useful in that it can communicate those things to customers, so there is certainly a need for branding, but not necessarily an overall brand, Sub-brands are powerful because they can offer multiple identites, and this allows a varied customer base, rather then being seen as a supplier with a single strength. Sub-brands come about because of numerous dedicated individuals and to remove them could demoralise, but more importantly could stifle their motivation and energies. Behind the scenes the individual employees know they belong to a larger group that offers both them and ultimately customers security.

The comparision is not the best, but consider Unilever with over 400 brands; most consumers know their brands rather than the overall company name. The energy and ingenuity of individual product managers make the different brands unique and strong in their respective market. As a whole the different brands play a different role in the portfolio at different times. Similary the Kjaer Group can harness the unique nature of employees who know individual markets. It is called 'not putting all your eggs in one basket' and allows easy future diversification.

Peter Ruddock

University of Central Lancashire

The current policy of the central values has been summed up as 'love cars, love life and love people'. It has been very effective and there is an adage that says 'If it ain't broke don't fix it'. The proliferation of values internally within the subsidiaries, however, poses a threat to these values and they are in danger of becoming both diluted and confused.

The opposing view is that just because something has worked well in the past, it doesn't mean to say that it will continue to do so into the future. This seems to be the root of the problem as the company doesn't want to lose the strong branding achieved from the central values and so will resist making changes. Yet companies need to move with the times and the developments in the environment. The reports from the subsidiaries are that they want to change: no doubt this is based upon good information from the marketplace. So the dilemma that the company faces is to determine which one of these two scenarios applies

When you analyse the situation, what becomes clear is that a strategy is needed which will allow for both! So how can the Kjaer Group retain and reinforce the strong branding based upon the central values and yet at the same time embrace the new values for each subsidiary?

To arrive at a solution, the internal situation should be separated from the external one. The key to this is that these original values do not have to be replaced: they can co-exist with the new ones in the subsidiaries! The central values are essential to the success of the group. The message of caring for people, as the customers, needs to be reinforced internally first. The people in the company need to be sure of this once again.

In association with these central values, winning prizes for the 'best workplace' is a great strength for the 'people' part of the 7Ps: yet this is first and foremost about the internal situation – Kjaer's own people. It fits very well with the values of caring for customers externally too. The strong team spirit will greatly assist the reinforcement of the central values desired internally, and then the dissemination of this to the customers.

The first priority is therefore to reinforce the central values through internal and then external marketing communications. The company needs to continue to hold on to these values into the future. So first, as Stage 1, management need to tell their own people and then their customers that these values are still strong and will remain so as the core foundation of the company and all its subsidiaries. The message is: 'These are the central values we will remain true to.' This looks to be more of an internal situation as the messages seem to have remained consistent externally, but there might have been some dilution of this with customers.

Once they have reinforced the central values they can then proceed to implement changes to allow the sub-brands some independence in stating their own values, but there needs to be a gradual transition toward this. In Stage 2 it needs to be established that it is no longer necessary to tell people about the central values. The message needs to be that 'Everyone knows that this is so – it goes without saying. You can trust that this will always be so.' Having achieved this then, at Stage 3 each subsidiary can start to introduce its new messages alongside this. Over time, at Stage 4, the original values can be given less 'air time' and eventually, at Stage 5, dropped altogether. Thus the sub-brands will have freedom to adapt to their respective market conditions and at the same time the central values will remain strong. It would be a good strategy, however, to reinforce the central values, say once a year, just to ensure that the Kjaer Group's own people and customers don't forget that they are there!

How e-commerce affects product quality

The web has made product quality even more important in product strategies. One of the most exciting aspects of the digital world is that consumers can interact directly with other people – around the corner or around the world. But this form of communication cuts both ways since it lets people praise what they like and criticise what they don't to an audience of thousands. Numerous websites like starbucked.com and microsoftsucks.org let consumers sound off about bad experiences they have had with products.

Marketing throughout the product life cycle

www.pearsoned.co.uk/solomon

Objective

2

Explain how firms manage products throughout the product life cycle

Many products have very long lives, while others are 'here today, gone tomorrow'. The **product life cycle** is a useful way to explain how product features change over the life of a product. In Chapter 7, we talked about how marketers go about introducing new products, but the launch is only the beginning. Product marketing strategies must evolve and change as they continue through the product life cycle.

Alas, some brands don't have long to live. Who can remember the Nash car or Evening in Paris perfume? In contrast, other brands seem almost immortal. For example, Coca-Cola has been the number one cola brand for 120 years and Kleenex has been the number one tissue brand for 82 years.[18]

The introduction stage

Like people, products are born, they 'grow up', and eventually they die. We can divide the life of a product into four separate stages: introduction, growth, maturity and decline. The first stage Figure 8.5 shows is the **introduction stage**. Here customers get the first chance to purchase the good or service. During this early stage, a single company usually produces the product. If it works and is profitable, competitors will follow with their own versions.

During the introduction stage, the goal is to get first-time buyers to try the product. Sales (hopefully) increase at a steady but slow pace. As is also evident in Figure 8.5, the company usually does not make a profit during this stage. Why? Research and development (R&D) costs and heavy spending for advertising and promotional efforts cut into revenue.

During the introduction stage, pricing may be high to recover the R&D costs (demand permitting) or low to attract large numbers of consumers (see Figure 8.6). For example, the introductory base price of the Lexus GS450h described at the beginning of this chapter was €41,450, nearly the same as the BMW 550i's base of €43,050. The price is designed to appeal to consumers who are willing to pay for the GS450h's unique combination of comfort, great mileage and superb performance. The high cost helps Lexus recover its R&D costs for this revolutionary engineering design.

How long does the introduction stage last? As we saw in Chapter 7's Wi-Fi example, it can be quite long. A number of factors come into play, including marketplace acceptance and the producer's willingness to support its product during start-up.

Not all products make it past the introduction stage. For a new product to be successful, consumers must first know about it. Then they must believe that it is something they want or need. Marketing during this stage often focuses on informing consumers about

Figure 8.5	The product life cycle
	The product life cycle helps marketers understand how a product changes over its lifetime and suggests how marketing strategies should be modified accordingly

Characteristic	Introduction	Growth	Maturity	Decline
Goals	Get first-time buyers to try the new product	Encourage brand loyalty	Attract new users	Remain profitable; decide whether to keep or phase out product
Sales	Increase at a steady but slow pace	Rapid increase	Peak, then level off, often decline	Continue to decline
Profits	Negative	Increase and peak	Profit margins narrow	Declining
Product	Single company produces single product	Competitors enter the market creating variations of the product	New features added; sales are mostly replacement products	Number of variations reduced
Pricing	High: recover R&D costs Low: attract large numbers of customers	May need to reduce because of competition	Set price to maintain market share	May be reduced if product can remain profitable
Place	Selected outlets	Increase coverage	Maximum distribution	Fewer outlets
Promotion	Informing customers	Heavy advertising to counter competition	Reminder advertising	Decreased to maintain profitability

Figure 8.6 Marketing mix strategies through the product life cycle
Marketing mix strategies – the Four Ps – change as a product moves through the life cycle

the product, how to use it, and its promised benefits. Think about Apple's iPhone. However, this isn't nearly as easy as it sounds: almost 40 per cent of all new products fail.[19]

The growth stage

In the **growth stage**, sales increase rapidly while profits increase and peak. Marketing's goal here is to encourage brand loyalty by convincing the market that this brand is superior to others. In this stage, marketing strategies may include the introduction of product variations to attract market segments and increase market share. The mobile phone is an example of a product that is still in its growth stage as worldwide sales continue to increase (though they might have peaked in some countries). A large part of its continued growth is due to relentless product innovation and the building in of converging communication features.

When competitors appear, marketers must use heavy advertising and other types of promotion. Price competition may develop, driving profits down. Some firms may seek to capture a particular segment of the market by positioning their product to appeal to a certain group. And, if pricing has initially been set high, it may be reduced to meet the increasing competition.

| Photo 8.3 | Companies continue to modify their products to breathe life into them when in the maturity phase |

Source: Getty Images/Robert Caplin/Bloomberg

 ## The maturity stage

The **maturity stage** of the product life cycle is usually the longest. Sales peak and then begin to level off and even decline while profit margins narrow. Competition grows intense when remaining competitors fight for their share of a shrinking pie. Firms may resort to price reductions and reminder advertising ('did you brush your teeth today?') to maintain market share. Because most customers have already accepted the product, sales are often to replace a 'worn-out' item or to take advantage of product improvements. For example, almost everyone owns a TV, which means most people who buy a new set are replacing an older one. During the maturity stage, firms will try to sell their product through as many outlets as possible because availability is crucial in a competitive market. Consumers will not go far to find one particular brand if satisfactory alternatives are close at hand.

To remain competitive and maintain market share during the maturity stage, firms may tinker with the marketing mix. Competitors may add new 'bells and whistles', as when producers of potato crisps and other snack foods modify their products. When consumers became concerned about carbohydrates and turned to diets such as Atkins, Nestlé introduced new lines of low-carb chocolate, such as the low-carb versions of Rolo and Kit Kat.[20] Unilever likewise rolled out 18 new low-carb products, rejuvenating venerable brands like Ragu spaghetti sauce and Wishbone salad dressing.[21]

Attracting new users of the product can be another strategy that marketers use in the maturity stage. Market development means introducing an existing product to a market that doesn't currently use it. Many UK and Scandinavian firms are finding new markets in developing countries such as China for products whose domestic sales are stagnant. For example, Nokia, the world's largest mobile phone manufacturer, is offsetting stagnated domestic sales with aggressive investment in growth in the Chinese market, where it holds a 35 per cent share of the market.[22]

The decline stage

The **decline stage** of the product life cycle is characterised by a decrease in product category sales. The reason may be obsolescence forced by new technology – where do you see a new typewriter in this computer age or VHS video or a cassette tape? Although a single firm may still be profitable, the market as a whole begins to shrink, profits decline, there are fewer variations of the product and suppliers pull out. In this stage, there are usually many competitors, with none having a distinct advantage.

A firm's major product decision in the decline stage is whether to keep the product at all. An unprofitable product drains resources that could be better used to develop newer products. If the decision is to keep the product, advertising and other marketing communications may be decreased to cut costs, and prices may be reduced if the product can remain profitable. If the decision is to drop the product, it can be eliminated in two ways: phase it out by cutting production in stages and letting existing stocks run out, or simply drop the product immediately. If the established market leader anticipates that there will be some residual demand for the product for a long time, it may make sense to keep the product on the market. The idea is to sell a limited quantity of the product with little or no support from sales, merchandising, advertising and distribution and just let it 'wither on the vine'.

In the web era, some products that otherwise would have died a natural death in the shops continue to sell online to a cadre of fans, backed by zero marketing support. Banana Mojos, Blackcurrant Chewits and Cola Frosties are sold direct to consumers by online purveyors such as handycandy.co.uk. Before the web, those sweets would have been doomed by aggressive marketing budgets for all the new product introductions in the category by competitors such as Haribo or M&M's.

Oil of Olay has been a great example of a product that, like a cat, has had many lives through the product life cycle. The pink moisturiser was developed during the Second World War for Britain's Royal Air Force as a lotion to treat burns. In 1962, another company bought it and started to market it as a 'beauty fluid'. Procter & Gamble acquired that company in 1985 and reinvigorated it by pumping in a lot of advertising spend. In the early 1990s, P&G started to launch line extensions built around the Oil of Olay name. The company also began revamping the product's image to make it more appealing to women. P&G found through research that some consumers were put off by the word 'oil' because they equate it with greasy. Now the €260 million range of skin-care products and cosmetics is known simply as Olay, aimed at women who want to 'love the skin you're in'. The Olay line now includes over a dozen brand extensions such as Total Effects (to diminish middle-aged consumers' fine lines and wrinkles), Complete (an all-day moisturiser with ultraviolet protection), and Ribbons body wash (with your choice of aloe extract, almond oil or jojoba butter). Olay's an example of a product with life cycle staying power![23]

Creating product identity: branding decisions

Objective

3

Discuss how branding creates product identity and describe different types of branding strategies

Marketers keep close tabs on their products' life cycle status, and plan accordingly. Equally important, though, is giving that product an identity, as Ferrero did with Kinder Bueno; which is made of layers of crispy waffle with hazelnut filling and a milk chocolate wrapping. That's where branding comes in. The brand personality connotes pure, unadulterated fun, and the launch featured TV adverts with the animated Nutshells, a band of musical elephants. How important is branding? In 2011 the total amount spent on advertising in the UK was around £15.9 billion, and in 2012 it's expected to be £16.5 billion. The government spent £113 million on advertising in 2010, down from £227 million in 2009.[24]

We said earlier that nearly 40 per cent of all new products fail, but for new brands the failure rate is even higher – up to 80 to 90 per cent.[25] Branding is an extremely important (and expensive) element of product strategies. In this section, we'll examine what a brand is and how certain laws protect brands. Then we'll discuss the importance of branding and how firms make branding decisions.

 ## What's in a name (or a symbol)?

How do you identify your favourite brand? By its name? By the logo (how the name appears)? By the packaging? By some graphic image or symbol, such as the Guinness harp? A **brand** is a name, a term, a symbol or any other unique element of a product that identifies one firm's product(s) and sets it apart from the competition. Consumers easily recognise the Coca-Cola logo, and the illuminated golden arches of McDonald's when driving at night. Branding provides the recognition factor products need to succeed in regional, national and international markets.

There are several important considerations in selecting a brand name, brand mark or trade character. First, it must have a positive connotation and be memorable. Kentucky Fried Chicken changed its name to KFC in 1991. The reasons for the name change included the move to de-emphasise 'chicken' as the company started to offer more varied menus that included other types of food, to eliminate the word 'fried' because it had a negative connotation as consumers became more health-conscious, and to use an abbreviation to make the brand name more memorable.[26]

A brand name is probably the most used and most recognised form of branding. Coca-Cola and Disney are sometimes two of the first words children learn. Smart marketers use brand names to maintain relationships with consumers 'from the cradle to the grave'. For example, McDonald's now markets Salads Plus to appeal to adults who live a healthy lifestyle or are on a diet.

A good brand name may position a product by conveying a certain image or personality (Nature Valley, crunchy granola bar) or by describing how it works (Kleenoff, Vanish). Brand names such as Palmolive and Shield help position these different brands of bath soap by saying different things about the benefits they promise. Carex handwash provides an unerring image of gentle hand cleaning. The Nissan Xterra combines the word *terrain* with the letter X, which many young people associate with extreme sports, to give the brand name a cutting-edge, off-road feel.

How does a firm select a good brand name? Good brand designers say there are four 'easy' tests: easy to say, easy to spell, easy to read and easy to remember – like Daz, Bold, Lenor and Head & Shoulders. And the name should also 'fit' four ways: fit the target market, fit the product's benefits, fit the customer's culture and fit legal requirements.

When it comes to graphics for a brand symbol, name or logo, the rule is that it must be recognisable and memorable. No matter how small or how large, the triangular Nabisco logo in the corner of the box is a familiar sight. In addition, it should have visual impact.

Marketing metrics

Brand perception metrics

When measuring consumer brand perceptions, some of the metrics which can be used have been rated by marketing managers. Here are those metrics and what percentage of marketing managers found them 'very useful'. Brand Awareness 61 per cent, Top of Mind 50 per cent, Likeability 43 per cent, Consumer Knowledge 40 per cent, Ad Awareness 23 per cent, Hierarchy of Effects 43 per cent.[27]

Marketing metrics

Millward Brown brand dynamics

Millward Brown tracks the importance of over 50,000 brands in 60 countries. It offers summary measurements under the name Brand Dynamics, which it describes as measures of past performance (called Brand Presence) and future potential (called Brand Voltage); these two figures are distilled from research data using proprietary formulae. The company has also used its Brand Dynamics scores to estimate the brand valuations of the world's top brands, which it publishes every year in its BrandZ survey (www.brandz.com). For 2008 the top three brands were Google (valued at $86,057 million), General Electric ($71,379 million) and Microsoft ($70,887 million).

That means that from across a shop or when you are quickly flicking through the pages in a magazine the brand will catch your attention. Some marketers enhance brand recognition by creating a trade character such as the Pillsbury Dough Boy or the Playboy Bunny.

Trademarks

A **trademark** is the legal term for a brand name, brand mark or trade character. The symbol for legal registration in the UK is a capital 'R' in a circle: ® Marketers register trademarks to make their use by competitors illegal. Because trademark protection applies only in individual countries where the brand has been registered, unauthorised use of marks on counterfeit products made in foreign countries is a huge headache for many companies.

A firm can have protection for a brand even if it has not legally registered it. In the UK, *common-law protection* exists if the firm has used the name and established it over a period of time. Although a registered trademark prevents others from using it on a similar product, it may not bar its use for a product in a completely different type of business. Consider the range of 'Quaker' brands: Quaker Oats (cereals), Quaker Funds (mutual funds), Quaker State (motor oil), Quaker Bonnet (gift food baskets) and Quaker Safety Products Corporation (firemen's clothing). This principle was recently applied when Apple Corp., the Beatles' music company, sued Apple Computers in 2006 over its use of the Apple logo. The plaintiff wanted to win an injunction to prevent Apple Computers from using the Apple logo in connection with its iPod and iTunes products; it argued that the application to music-related products came too close to the Beatles' musical products. The judge didn't agree; he ruled that the logo was clearly used in relation to the download service, not to the music itself.[28]

 ## The importance of branding

A brand is a lot more than just the product it represents – the best brands build an emotional connection with the consumer. Strong brands don't just meet rational needs, they create an emotional reaction. Think about the most popular nappy brands – they're named Pampers and Huggies, not some functionally descriptive name like AbsorbancyMaster. The point is that Pampers and Huggies evoke the joys of parenting, not the utility of the nappy.

Marketers spend huge amounts of money on new product development, advertising and promotion to develop strong brands. When they succeed, this investment creates **brand equity**, which is a brand's value to its organisation over and above the value of the generic version of the product (that is, how much extra will you pay for a golf shirt with a Ralph Lauren logo on it than for the same shirt with no logo?). (See the Marketing metrics boxes on the subject for what they get back for their money.) We can identify different levels of loyalty or lack thereof by assessing how customers feel about the product. At the lowest level, customers really have no loyalty to a brand and will change brands for any reason, often jumping ship if they find something else at a lower price. At the other extreme, some brands command fierce devotion, and loyal users will go without rather than buy a competing brand.

Figure 8.7 shows one way to think about these escalating levels of attachment to a brand. At the lowest level of the 'brand equity pyramid', consumers are aware of a brand's existence. Moving up the pyramid, they might look at the brand in terms of what it literally does for them or how it performs relative to competitors. Going up still further, they may think more deeply about the product and form beliefs and emotional reactions to it. The truly successful brands, however, are those that make the long climb to the top of the pyramid – they 'bond' with their customers so that people feel they have a real relationship with the product. Here are some of the types of relationships a person might have with a product:

- **Self-concept attachment:** The product helps establish the user's identity. (For example, do you feel more like yourself in Ralph Lauren or Diesel clothing?)

- **Nostalgic attachment:** The product serves as a link with a past self. (Does eating the inside of a Cadbury Creme Egg remind you of childhood?)

- **Interdependence:** The product is a part of the user's daily routine. (Could you get through the day without a Starbucks or Caffe Nero coffee?)

- **Love:** The product elicits emotional bonds of warmth, passion or other strong emotion. (Ever been to a match between Arsenal and Manchester United?)[29]

As the pyramid in Figure 8.7 shows us, the way to build strong brands is to build strong bonds with customers – bonds based on *brand meaning*. Try and apply this to Innocent drinks. What attachments spring to mind? This concept encompasses the beliefs and associations

Figure 8.7	The brand equity pyramid
	The brand equity pyramid shows one way to think about escalating levels of attachment to a brand

Source: Kevin Lane Keller, *Building Customer-Based Brand Equity: A Blueprint for Creating Strong Brands*, Working Paper Series, Report 01–107 (Cambridge, MA: Marketing Science Institute, 2001), 7

Dimension	Example
Brand identification markers	Coca-Cola's red and white colours, the Nike logo, Harley-Davidson's characteristic sound
Product attribute and benefit associations	Starbucks as good coffee; BMW as the ultimate driving machine
Gender	World Wrestling Forum, Harley-Davidson, Marlboro and masculinity; Laura Ashley and femininity
Social class	Mercedes and the old-guard elite; Primark and the lower classes
Age	Nokia and the iPod
Reference group	Marks & Spencer and the smart-casual workforce; B&Q and the serious home improver
Life stage	Dewar's and the coming of age; Fisher Price and babies
Lifestyles and taste subcultures	BMW and the 'yuppie'; Red Bull and the club culture
Place	Coke and America; Chelsea FC and London
Time and decade	Marylin Monroe and the 1950s; VW and the 1960s' countercultural revolution
Trends	John Lewis and cocooning; Pret A Manger and small indulgences
Traditions and rituals	Häagen-Dazs ice cream and the pampering of self

Table 8.2   Dimensions of brand meaning

Source: Adapted from Susan Fournier, Michael R. Solomon, Basil G. Englis and Jeff Green, 'How Brands Mean: Resonance as a Mediator of the Brand Meaning–Brand Strength Connection', unpublished manuscript, March 2004

that a consumer has about the brand. In many ways, the practice of brand management revolves around the management of meanings. Brand managers, advertising agencies, package designers, name consultants, logo developers and public relations firms are just some of the collaborators in a global industry devoted to the task of meaning management. This complex and synergistic system is based on one simple but critical truth: strong brands are built on strong meanings. The corollary: brands die when their meanings lose value in consumers' worlds. Table 8.2 shows some of the dimensions of brand meaning.

Brand equity means that a brand enjoys customer loyalty because the customers are not only aware of it but they also perceive it to be superior to the competition. For a firm, brand equity provides a competitive advantage because it gives the brand the power to capture and hold on to a larger share of the market and to sell at prices with higher profit margins. For example, among pianos, the Steinway name has such brand equity that 95 per cent of concert pianists use a Steinway.[30]

What makes a brand successful? Here are ten characteristics of the world's top brands:[31]

1. The brand excels at delivering the benefits customers truly desire.

2. The brand stays relevant.

3. The pricing strategy is based on consumers' perceptions of value.

4. The brand is properly positioned.

5. The brand is consistent.

6. The brand portfolio and hierarchy make sense.

Marketing ethics and sustainability

Waste it and want it more?

The four elements of the marketing mix which the world's largest luxury-goods groups LVMH focus on are: product, distribution, communication and price, which of course they try to get people to forget about. One of its brands, Louis Vuitton, LVMH's star company, has yielded consistent profit margins of around 40–45%, which is one of the highest of any luxury-goods brand.

So what explains Vuitton's resilience? There are several reasons, but some are that it never puts its products on sale at a discount; instead it destroys stock and keeps a close eye on the proportion it ends up scrapping. Also, unlike most other luxury brands, Vuitton never gives licences to other firms, to avoid brand degradation, and its factories use techniques from other industries, such as car manufacturing, to drive costs down.

Source: Based on The Economist (Online) 17th March 2009.[32]

Debate, discuss, disagree

1 What are the ethics involved in such tactics as stock destruction as opposed to price reduction?

---

7. The brand makes use of and coordinates a full repertoire of marketing activities to build brand equity.

8. The brand's managers understand what the brand means to consumers.

9. The brand is given proper support, and that support is sustained over the long run.

10. The company monitors sources of brand equity.

Products with strong brand equity provide enticing opportunities. A firm may leverage a brand's equity with **brand extensions**: new products sold with the same brand name. For example, in 2004 premium ice cream maker Häagen-Dazs decided to get into the growing 'low fat' ice cream market. Its choices were to create a new brand or modify the existing one. It chose to introduce the line as Häagen-Dazs Light, sold as having 'all the taste and texture of original Häagen-Dazs with only half the fat'. The brand extension was an immediate success, and soon 14 flavours carried the Light banner, many of which were available only as Light. More generally, this success highlights the potential value of a strong brand name: although many people assume the European-sounding name assures high quality, in reality the name is made up. The company started in the Bronx, New York, and today Pillsbury owns it![33]

Playboy also expanded its brand to increase recognition of the magazine and to support its sales. It sells a wide range of merchandise. You can find Playboy branded cushions, cosmetics, lingerie, mobile phone and party accessories in high street Playboy Stores in Oxford Street, London, or in other retailers like Argos.

Because of the existing brand equity, a firm is able to sell its brand extension at a higher price than if it had given it a new brand, and the brand extension will attract new customers immediately. Of course, if the brand extension does not live up to the quality or attractiveness of the original brand, brand equity will suffer, as will brand loyalty and sales. Having read this section, how does it help you to decide which of the options at the start of the chapter fits in with the company's brand image?

Marketing misstakes

Innocent curry?

The market-leading smoothie brand expanded into food in 2008, with the launch of Innocent Veg Pots, a range of four microwaveable meals containing three portions of vegetables to count towards the five-a-day total.

The new range comes in several flavours including Tuscan bean stew and Thai coconut curry, and has been developed by the chefs at Michelin-starred restaurant The Fat Duck. The meals are low in salt and fat, and were first available in Waitrose stores for £3.49.

However, sales are not comparable to innocent's best-selling smoothies, the drastic change in product extension may cause consumers to question the credibility of the veg pots as it may be difficult to associate fresh fruity drinks with hearty high-protein food pots.

Source: Adapted from Marketing Magazine (Online) 23 September 2008.[34]
Why do you think this might be a marketing misstake?

 ## Branding strategies

Because brands are important to a marketing programme's success, branding strategies are a major part of product decision making. Marketers have to determine whether to create individual or family brands, national or shop brands, or co-brands – it's not that easy.

Individual brands versus family brands

Part of developing a branding strategy is deciding whether to use a separate, unique brand for each product item – an *individual brand strategy* – or market several items under the same brand name – a **family brand** or *umbrella brand* strategy. Individual brands may do a better job of communicating clearly and concisely what attributes, values and benefits the consumer can expect from the specific product while a well-known company like Apple may find that its high brand equity in other categories (like computers) can sometimes 'rub off' on a new brand (like the iPod). The decision of whether to use an individual or family branding strategy often depends on characteristics of the product and whether the company's overall product strategy calls for introduction of a single, unique product or for the development of a group of similar products. For example, Microsoft serves as a strong umbrella brand for a host of diverse individually branded products such as Office, internet Explorer, Xbox and MSN Web Search, while Procter & Gamble prefers to brand each of its household products separately.

National and own-label brands

Retailers today often are in the driver's seat when it comes to deciding what brands to stock and push. In addition to choosing from producers' brands, called **national or manufacturer brands**, retailers decide whether to offer their own versions. **Own-label brands**, also called **private-label** or *own brands*, are the retail shop's or chain's exclusive trade name. Tesco, for example, sells own brand Tesco Healthy Living ready meals and Tesco Diet Cola along with national brands such as Weight Watchers and Coca-Cola. Own brands are gaining in popularity for many value-conscious shoppers. Retailers continue to develop new ones, and some are adding services to the mix: Asda now has opticians and pharmacies in its shops and Sainsbury's is planning to offer an out-of-hours GP walk-in service.

Retailers choose an own-label branding strategy because they generally make more profit on these than on national brands. Even mid-range retailers such as John Lewis now offer private-label clothing to lure millions of customers away from more upmarket

Marketing metrics

Pros and cons of brand equity metrics

Each of the following approaches to measuring brand equity has some good points and some bad points:

1. *Customer mind-set metrics* focus on consumer awareness attitudes and loyalty towards a brand. However, these metrics are based on consumer surveys and don't usually provide a single objective measure that can be used to assign a financial value to the brand. An example is Young and Rubicam's Brand Asset Evaluator, which surveys consumers' perspectives along four dimensions:

   Differentiation: the defining characteristics of the brand and its distinctiveness relative to the competition.
   Relevance: the appropriateness and connection of the brand to a given consumer.
   Esteem: Consumers' respect and attraction for the brand.
   Knowledge: Consumers' awareness of the brand and understanding of what it represents.

2. *Product-market outcomes metrics* focus on the ability of a brand to charge a higher price than the one charged by an unbranded equivalent. This usually involves asking consumers how much more they would be willing to pay for a certain brand compared with others. These measures often rely on hypothetical judgements and can be complicated to use. Conjoint Analysis is one of the popular methods used and it measures consumers' preference for various product attributes such as design, price or location. The premise of conjoint analysis is that consumers' preferences can be broken into a set of attributes that are weighed to form an overall evaluation. By including brand and price as two of the attributes, insights are gained into consumers' relative evaluation of a brand.

3. *Financial market metrics* consider the purchase price of a brand if it is sold or acquired. They may also include subjective judgements about the future stock price of the brand. A good example is the Brand Evaluation Model used by Interbrand. The model analyses brands according to three aspects: financial contribution of the brand, the role of the brand within the company strategy and the brand strength, i.e. awareness of what the brand stands for. By reviewing companies' financial statements and the role of the brand in income generation it can separate those earnings attributable to tangible assets (capital, product packaging etc.) from the residual which is attributed to the brand. It then forecasts future earnings and discounts these according to brand strength and risk.[35]

Source: Farris, Paul W.; Bendle, Neil T.; Pfeifer, Phillip E.; Reibstein, David J., *Marketing Metrics: The Definitive Guide to Measuring Marketing Performance, 2nd,* © 2010. Printed and Electronically reproduced by permission of Pearson Education, Inc., Upper Saddle River, New Jersey.

department stores as well as lower end discounters. John Lewis' own-label shirts, trousers and coats for men have become a significant competitive force against national brands like French Connection, fcuk, Timberland and Levi's.

In addition, if you stock a unique brand that consumers can't find in other shops it makes it much harder for shoppers to compare 'apples with apples' across shops and simply buy the brand where they find it sold for the lowest price. Tesco, the UK's largest supermarket chain, developed its own Tesco Finest 'premium quality' own-label brand. Tesco sells over 1100 food items under the Tesco Finest label, from biscuits to beef, olive oil, copying paper and kitchen utensils. Under the own-label, Tesco can introduce new products at high quality but lower prices than brand names. It can also keep entire categories profitable by its mix of pricing options. Competitors that sell only national brands can cut prices on those brands, but that hurts their overall profitability. Tesco can bring prices down on national brands but still make money on its own-label products.[36]

Generic brands

An alternative to either national or store branding is **generic branding**, which is basically no branding. Generic branded products are typically packaged in white with black lettering that name only the product itself (for example, 'green beans'). Generic branding is one strategy to meet customers' demand for the lowest prices on standard products such as dog food or kitchen towels. Generic brands were first popularised during the inflationary period of the 1980s, when consumers became especially price conscious because of rising prices. However, today generic brands account for very little consumer spending.

Licensing

Some firms choose to use a **licensing** strategy to brand their products. A licensing agreement means that one firm sells another firm the right to use a legally protected brand name for a specific purpose and for a specific period of time. Firms do this for a variety of reasons. Licensing can provide instant recognition and consumer interest in a new product, and this strategy can quickly position a product for a certain target market by trading on the high recognition of the licensed brand among consumers in that segment. For example, distiller Brown-Forman licensed its Jack Daniels bourbon name to T.G.I. Friday's for use on all sorts of menu items from shrimp to steak to chicken. The menu partnership has been highly successful, contributing to a turnaround in sales at Friday's in the highly competitive mid-range family restaurant space.[37]

Much better known, however, is the licensing of entertainment names, such as when film producers license their properties to manufacturers of a seemingly infinite number of products. Each time the blockbuster Harry Potter films hit the screens, a plethora of Potter products packed the shops. In addition to toys and games, you can buy Harry Potter sweets, clothing, all manner of back-to-school items, home items, and even wands and cauldrons.

| Photo 8.4 | Adverts for Celebrations are a good example of ingredient branding as they focus on the strength of the component brands within the product
Source: Rex Features/Martin Lee |

Co-branding

Co-branding examples include Nat West and Mastercard credit card, Ford and *Elle* magazine to form Ford Focus Elle, Brita on Electrolux fridge freezers. Strange marriages? No, these are examples of **co-branding**, as is the Jack Daniels/T.G.I. Friday's combination. This branding strategy benefits both partners when combining the two brands provides more recognition power than either enjoys alone. For example, Panasonic markets digital cameras that use Leica lenses. Leica lenses are legendary for their superb image quality. Panasonic is known for its consumer electronics. Combining the best in traditional camera optics with a household name in consumer electronics helps both brands.

A new and fast-growing variation on co-branding is **ingredient branding**, in which branded materials become 'component parts' of other branded products.[38] This was the strategy behind the classic 'Intel inside' campaign that encouraged millions of consumers to ask by name for a highly technical computer part (a processor) that they wouldn't otherwise recognise if they fell over it.[39] Today, consumers can buy Häagen-Daz Bailey's Ice Cream, Carl Zeiss lenses in Sony cameras or Scotchguard in fabrics. The ultimate co-branding deal for chocolate lovers may be a box of Celebrations sweets, which includes up to six brands in a single package. Mars, Bounty, Snickers, Galaxy, Malteaser and MilkyWay are all part of the package. Brand heaven!

The practice of ingredient branding has two main benefits. First, it attracts customers to the host brand because the ingredient brand is familiar and has a strong brand reputation for quality. Second, the ingredient brand's firm can sell more of its product, not to mention the additional revenues it gets from the licensing arrangement.[40]

Creating product identity: packaging and labelling decisions

How do you know if the cola you are drinking is 'normal' or 'caffeine free'? How do you keep your low-fat grated cheese fresh after you have used some of it? Why do you always leave your bottle of Kylie's new perfume out on your dresser so everyone can see it? The answer to all these questions is effective packaging and labelling. So far, we've talked about how marketers create product identity with branding. In this section, we'll learn that packaging and labelling decisions are also important in creating product identity.

Packaging functions

Objective

4

Explain the roles packaging and labelling play in developing effective product strategies

A **package** is the covering or container for a product, but it's also a way to create a competitive advantage. The important functional value of a package is that it protects the product. For example, packaging for computers, TV sets and stereos protects the units from damage during shipping, storage and shelf life. Cereal, crisps or packs of grated cheese wouldn't be edible for long if packaging didn't provide protection from moisture, dust, odours and insects. The chicken broth in Figure 8.8 is protected (before opening) from spoilage by a multilayered soft box. In addition to protecting the product, effective packaging makes it easy for consumers to handle and store the product. Figure 8.8 shows how packaging serves a number of different functions.

Over and above these utilitarian functions, however, the packaging plays an important role in communicating brand personality. Effective product packaging uses colours, words, shapes,

Marketing ethics and sustainability

Tesco and Disney: attempting to enforce a snow white food policy

Disney is increasing its focus on healthy snacks with the introduction of a new co-branded line with UK supermarket Tesco. While helping present the company as a responsible business, the move could also be highly lucrative for Disney as it further exploits consumer interest in healthier foods. The deal will allow Disney cartoon characters to appear on selected fresh fruit lines at Tesco and it will expand to include yogurt and breakfast cereals. Disney is not merely forming these deals for altruistic reasons, but because it believes the healthy snack area will be highly lucrative in the long term. As long as the company remembers to keep its products fun-looking, it should succeed in appealing to children as well as parents. The advantages for Tesco are that Disney is well known in the children's market and could stimulate children to buy more fruit while at the same time it fits with Tesco's ethical policy of promoting good food to children.

Source: Adapted from Food MarketWatch, December 2007

Debate, discuss, disagree

Disney had a partnership with McDonald's Happy Meals for ten years and when it ended the deal cost the company approximately $100 million a year in royalties.

1   What would be the main purpose of Disney licensing its cartoon characters to Tesco?

2   Where do you draw the line at this kind of promotion directly aimed at children?

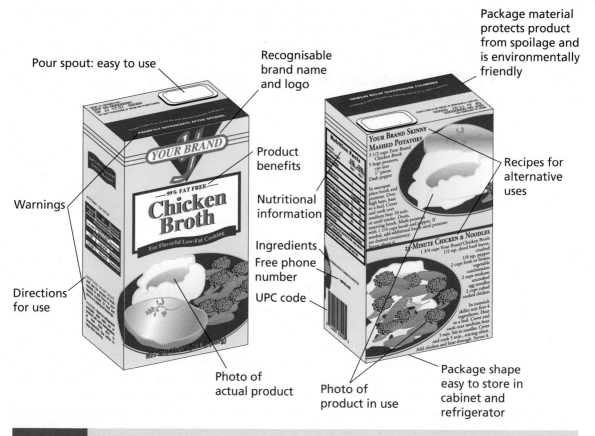

Figure 8.8	Functions of packaging
	Great packaging provides a covering for a product, and it also creates a competitive advantage for the brand

designs and pictures to provide brand and name identification for the product. Packaging is the silent salesperson sitting next to the competition on retail shelves. The product's packaging not only needs to get busy consumers' attention but also has to 'scream' BUY ME as they pass by. In addition, packaging provides specific information consumers want and need, such as information about the specific variety, flavour or fragrance, directions for use, suggestions for

Marketing ethics and sustainability

Sustainable packaging

Companies are increasingly incorporating environmentally friendly criteria into the design of their packaging, and for some this strategy is proving to be quite lucrative. Take Kenco's 'Eco-refill' instant coffee, advertised as '97% less packaging weight', it has entered 3 million UK households in only the first 12 months after its launch, while the glass-jar version remains on the shelves.

Debate, discuss disagree

1 If the benefits are obvious, why have companies not done this before?

other uses (for example, recipes), product warnings and product ingredients. Packaging may also include warranty information and a free phone number for customer service.

We've already talked about Häagen-Dazs; now let's see how rival Ben & Jerry's redesigned its ice-cream packaging in the late 1990s to make it more user friendly.[41] Because the top of the carton is the first thing customers see in a chest freezer, the company replaced the photo of Ben and Jerry that used to appear on the top lid with text identifying the flavour. Other changes included a more upmarket look with a black-on-gold colour scheme and enticing realistic watercolours of the product's ingredients. The result was increased ease of shopping for consumers.

A final communication element is the **Universal Product Code (UPC)**, which is the set of black bars or lines printed on the side or bottom of most items sold in grocery shops and other mass-merchandising outlets. The UPC is a national system of product identification. Each product has a unique ten-digit number assigned to it. These numbers supply specific information about the type of item (grocery item, meat, produce, medicines, or a discount voucher), the manufacturer (a five-digit code), and the specific product (another five-digit code). At checkout counters, electronic scanners read the UPC bars and automatically transmit data to a computer controlling the cash register, allowing retailers to track sales and control inventory.

Designing effective packaging

Should the package have a zip closing, feature an easy-to-pour spout, be compact for easy storage, be short and fat so it won't fall over, or be tall and skinny so it won't take up much shelf space? Designing effective packaging involves a multitude of decisions.

Planners must consider the packaging of other brands in the same product category. For example, milk usually comes in plastic bottles. Waitrose, the UK supermarket, offers milk in a bag, which uses 75 per cent less packaging. Not all customers are willing to accept a radical change in packaging, however, and other retailers may be reluctant to sell milk bags because they would need to adjust their shelf space to accommodate such packages. In addition to functional benefits, the choice of packaging material can make an aesthetic statement. Enclosing a fine liqueur in a velvet or silk bag may enhance its image. A fine perfume packaged in a beautifully designed glass bottle means consumers are buying not only the fragrance but an attractive dressing table accessory as well.

Firms seeking to act in a socially responsible manner must also consider the environmental damage caused by packaging. Shiny gold or silver packaging transmits an image of quality and opulence, but certain metallic inks are not biodegradable and are harmful to the environment. Some firms are developing innovative *green packaging* that is less harmful to the environment than other materials. Of course, there is no guarantee that consumers will accept such packaging. They didn't take to plastic pouch refills for certain

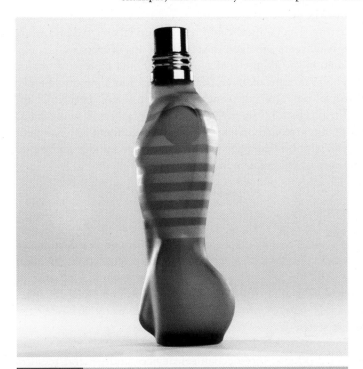

Photo 8.5 This is the good example of where the packaging itself can be advertising
Source: Alamy Images/Mary Germanou

Marketing misstakes

Tropicana – a case of mistaken identity

For consumer packaged goods, branding plays a vital role in the customer's experience. Brand image and recognition act as a shorthand for the desired product – consumers can cut through the noise and grab exactly the product they want. However, when Tropicana decided to change its brand image it created such a public outcry that it was forced to drop the new look and return to its image of old. The new design wasn't bad, the cartons per se were fine, but they lacked the distinctive personality of the orange-with-the-straw image, instead favouring a cool and generic aesthetic. The real issue was the carton 'in context'. The new cartons with their generic typography and more abstract imagery failed to make the brand stand out. Tropicana was so preoccupied with reinvigorating its brand, on establishing new emotional connections that it overlooked the actual supermarket experience.[42]

Why do you think this might be a marketing misstake?

spray bottle products even though the pouches may take up less space in landfills than the bottles do. They didn't like pouring the refill into their old spray bottles. Still, customers have accepted small packages of concentrated products such as laundry detergent, dishwashing liquid and fabric softener.

What about the shape: Square? Round? Triangular? Hourglass? How about an old-fashioned bottle that consumers can reuse as an attractive storage container? What colour should it be? White to communicate purity? Yellow because it reminds people of lemon freshness? Brown because the flavour is chocolate? Sometimes these decisions trace back to irrelevant personal factors. The familiar Campbell's Soup label is red and white because a company executive many years ago liked the sports kit at a university!

Finally, what graphic information should the package show? Should there be a picture of the product on the package? Should cans of green beans always show a picture of green beans? Should there be a picture of the results of using the product, such as beautiful hair? Should there be a picture of the product in use, perhaps a box of crackers showing crackers with delicious looking toppings arranged on a silver tray? Should there be a recipe or coupon on the back? Of course, all these decisions rest on a marketer's understanding of consumers, ingenuity and perhaps a little creative luck.

 ## Labelling regulations

The Trade Descriptions Act of 1968 prevents manufacturers, retailers or service industry providers in the UK from supplying misleading information to customers about their products. The law empowers courts to punish those companies that make false statements about their products or services. The EU introduced the Unfair Commercial Practices Directive, it gives consumers a high level of protection and it also aims to harmonise the fair trading laws of the member states.

In the UK the Customer Protection Act 1987 relates to liabilities a firm has to face if its defective pharmaceutical products, bio-mechanical devices and general medical equipment cause an injury. The General Product Safety Regulation 1994 amends the Customer Protection Act 1987 and extends it to all suppliers of all consumer goods and requires them to supply products that are safe in normal or reasonably foreseeable use.

Across the hall

Jamie Mitchell

CEO, Daylesord Organic Ltd
Teaching Fellow, London
Business School

A company that doesn't know or understand its values, or worse a company without a true set of values, is like a ship without a rudder. Being clear about your values, about who you are and why you exist, provides a backbone for any business, especially a growing and changing one. They not only help define the company's purpose, but they can and should form part of the criteria of strategic decision making, performance assessments and recruitment policies. This case shows a business that cares about its values, monitors and tracks them and has taken the positive and proactive step of challenging them. It is also the case of a company that has been carelessly allowing multiple additions and amendments to its value statements, such that, today, there is confusion and disagreement.

The right answer to this challenge is the clean-up proposed in Option 2. Values are not something to be dreamt up afresh ('reformulation'), and they do not exist for the sole purpose of marketing a business ('sub-branding'). They are a statement of who we are and what we believe in. And they are steeped in the history of the company and the people who work there.

Values, if well defined, can be applicable to many markets and across many different businesses, so Option 1 is self-defeating. They should be a description of what is important to the founders, owners and team members in the business. They should be kept simple and broad, but not shy away from conflict. Innocent, where I worked for many years, had values that in some instances found themselves in conflict: take 'being responsible' with 'being commercial'. This is good – it opens up debate; it provides richness to decision making.

The clean-up exercise at Kjaer should involve the entire company – values cannot be imposed on people. But the process should be tightly controlled. Values that are specific to customers or markets are not true values. Values that are obvious and universal don't help define us clearly. The rich history of the Kjaer group provides the starting point for a clean-up exercise. Try out the original values with the team (without the additions and alterations over the years) and I bet you find they provide a solid starting point for what makes the Kjaer group special today.

The Sale of Goods Act states that what your company sells in the UK must fit its description, be of satisfactory quality and be fit for its purpose. If not, then the supplier is obliged to sort out the problem.[43]

The Food Labelling Regulations 1998 and 1999 describe requirements that pre-packed food sold in the UK needs to contain on the label. The name of the food, date mark, weight and alcohol strength (if applicable) must be in the same field of vision. The producer also needs to list the place of origin, storage conditions and instructions for use

Marketing ethics and sustainability

I am what I eat – but who am I?

Society is becoming increasingly health conscious and companies are keen to capitalise on the market opportunities this growing trend is offering. Kellogg's advertised its Nutri-Grain Soft Oaties biscuits as 'Wholesome cookie goodness', referring to the fact they were a source of fibre, vitamins and iron, but the ad failed to mention that the product was also high in sugar and fat. Similarly, Coca-Cola's ads for its range of Vitaminwater soft drinks claimed they were nutritionally equivalent to vegetables and raised energy levels and resistance to illness, but could not provide adequate evidence to back up the claim.[45]

Debate, discuss, disagree

1   Where does one draw the line between promotional marketing and blatant product misrepresentation?

if it would be difficult to use the product without it, for example how to make a cake from cake mix. The list of ingredients must be indicated as well, in a descending order by weight, certain categories such as additives must be indentified by category name and by chemical name or serial number.[44]

Organising for effective product management

Of course, firms don't create great packaging, brands or products – people do. Like all elements of the marketing mix, the effectiveness of product strategies depends on marketing managers. In this section, we'll talk about how firms organise themselves to manage existing products and develop new products.

Management of existing products

In small firms, a single marketing manager usually handles the marketing function, being responsible for new product planning, advertising, working with the company's few sales representatives, marketing research and just about everything else. But in larger firms there are managers responsible for different brands, product categories or markets. Depending on the organisation, product management may include brand managers, product category managers and market managers. Let's take a look at how each operates.

Brand managers

Sometimes a firm sells different brands within a single product category. For example, Nestlé produces quite a few different brands of its Nescafé, including Gold Blend, Collection, Half Caff, Black Gold and Dolce Gusto. In such cases, each brand may have its own **brand manager** who is responsible for coordinating all marketing activities for a brand: positioning, identifying target markets, research, distribution, sales promotion, packaging and evaluating the success of these decisions.

While this assignment is still common, some big firms are changing the way they allocate responsibilities. For example, today Procter & Gamble's brand managers function more like internal consultants to cross-functional P&G teams located in the field that have responsibility for managing the complete business of key retail clients across all product lines. Brand managers are still responsible for positioning of brands and developing brand equity, but they also work closely with people from sales, finance, logistics and others to serve the needs of the major retailers that comprise the majority of P&G's business.

By its very nature, the brand management system is not without potential problems. Acting independently, and sometimes competitively against each other, brand managers may fight for increases in short-term sales for their own brand. They may push too hard with vouchers, 50 eurocents-off packages or other price incentives to a point at which customers will refuse to buy the product without them. Such behaviour can hurt long-term profitability and damage brand equity.

Product category managers

Some larger firms have such diverse product offerings that they need more extensive co-ordination. Take IBM, for example. Originally known as a computer manufacturer, IBM now generates much of its revenue from a wide range of consulting and related client services across the spectrum of IT applications (and the company doesn't even sell personal computers any more!). In cases such as IBM, organising for product management may include **product category managers**, who coordinate the mix of product lines within the more general product category, such as all products related to telephony solutions, and who consider the addition of new product lines based on client needs.

Market managers

Some firms have developed a **market manager** structure in which different managers focus on specific customer groups rather than on the products the company makes. This type of organisation can be useful when firms offer a variety of products that serve the needs of a wide range of customers. For example, Raytheon, a company that specialises in consumer electronics products, special mission aircraft and business aviation, sells some products directly to consumer markets, others to manufacturers and still others to the government. Their customers are best served by a differing focus on these very different markets.

Organising for new product development (NPD)

Because launching new products is so important, the management of this process is a serious matter. In some instances, one person handles new product development, but within larger organisations, new product development almost always needs many people. One person, however, may be assigned the role of *new product manager*. Often individuals who are assigned to manage new product development are especially creative people with entrepreneurial skills.

The challenge in large companies is to get specialists in different areas to work together in **NPD teams** or **venture teams**. These teams focus exclusively on the new product development effort. Sometimes the venture team is located away from traditional company offices, usually in a remote location called a 'skunk works'.

Now that you've learned about product management and branding, read 'Real people, real decisions' to see which strategy Mads Kjaer at Kjaer Group selected.

Real people, real decisions

How it worked out at the Kjaer Group

Mads Kjaer chose Option 3, to reformulate the corporate vision and mission. The company turned Maslow's triangle upside down, using the anthropological insight that even when people are acting primarily in order to survive, they do so with reference to the values that give meaning to their lives. You become who you are through your ties with the ones close to you: Your family, your friends, your colleagues and so on. This is why care is the basic value for a company like Kjaer and is the most fundamental reason for doing what Kjaer does. Human beings basically care and they self-actualise through caring. With help from the

researchers from Brand Base, Kjaer Group translated the upside down hierarchy of needs to central values of the company. The central values in Kjaer Group are: Care, Respect, Trust, Proactivity, Diversity and Win–win. These values were picked from the many existing values that Kjaer Group had developed over years. The rest were abandoned and the remaining five values were reorganised.

On the basis of mutual *care*, for each other and for customers, Kjaer aims at building relationships of *trust and respect*. This is true both inside and outside the organisation. Once there is this mutual respect and trust, it is actually not so difficult to go out there and dare, dare to care, dare to do business. This is what Kjaer means by *proactivity*. Proactivity has *diversification* as its logical consequence. The more you try, the more initiatives will actually persist and survive. Opening new markets, including new cultures, joining together people from all corners of the world with very different cultural backgrounds; such is the philosophy of Kjaer Group. The result is a *win–win* situation with customers, with suppliers, with employees and their families and everybody else with a stake in the company.

The advantages of Option 3 were that it represented a simplification of the corporate brand value universe without doing away with all the existing values of the company.

Secondly, it established a root metaphor, 'care', as the crux of the corporate values. As a result of the success of this process of transformation and clarification, Mads Kjaer, confident that the daily management of the business activities was now well framed, stepped down as CEO of Kjaer Group to became chairman of the board. He has now engaged in a new care project, MyC4 (www.MyC4.com), a microfinancing project for starting or developing businesses in third world countries.

This case was written by Soren Askegaard and Simon Torp of University of Southern Denmark

Chapter summary

Now that you have finished reading this chapter, you should be able to

1. **Explain the different product objectives and strategies a firm may choose.** Objectives for individual products may be related to introducing a new product, expanding the market of a regional product, or rejuvenating a mature product. For multiple products, firms may decide on a full or a limited line strategy. Often companies decide to extend their product range with an upward, downward or two-way stretch or with a filling out strategy, or they may decide to contract a product line. Firms that have several product lines may choose a wide product mix with many different lines or a narrow one with few. Product quality objectives refer to the durability, reliability, degree of precision, ease of use and repair, or degree of aesthetic pleasure.

2. **Explain how firms manage products throughout the product life cycle.** The product life cycle explains how products go through four stages from birth to death. During the introduction stage, marketers seek to get buyers to try the product and may use high prices to recover research and development costs or low prices to get it into the market. During the growth stage, characterised by rapidly increasing sales, marketers may introduce new product variations. In the maturity stage, sales peak and level off. Marketers respond by adding desirable new product features or with market development strategies. During the decline stage, firms must decide whether to phase a product out slowly, to drop it immediately, or, if there is residual demand, to keep the product without costly sales support but maybe some minimal advertising.

3. **Discuss how branding creates product identity and describe different types of branding strategies.** A brand is a name, term, symbol or other unique element of a product used to identify a firm's product. A brand should be selected that has a positive connotation and is recognisable and memorable. Brand names need to be easy to say,

spell, read and remember, and should fit the target market, the product's benefits, the customer's culture and legal requirements. To protect a brand legally, marketers obtain trademark protection. Brands are important because they help maintain customer loyalty and because brand equity or value means a firm is able to attract new customers. Firms may develop individual brand strategies or market many items with a family or umbrella brand strategy. National or manufacturer brands are owned and sold by producers, whereas private-label or shop brands carry the retail or chain store's trade name. Licensing means a firm sells another firm the right to use its brand name. In co-branding strategies, two brands form a partnership in marketing a new product.

4. **Explain the roles packaging and labelling play in developing effective product strategies.** Packaging is the covering or container for a product and serves to protect a product and to allow for easy use and storage of the product. The colours, words, shapes, designs, pictures and materials used in package design communicate a product's identity, benefits and other important product information. Package designers must consider cost, product protection and communication in creating a package that is functional, aesthetically pleasing and not harmful to the environment. Product labelling in the UK and EU are controlled by laws aimed at making package labels more helpful to consumers.

5. **Describe how organisations are structured for new and existing product management.** To successfully manage existing products, the marketing organisation may include brand managers, product category managers and market managers. Large firms, however, often give new product responsibilities to new product managers or to venture teams, groups of specialists from different areas who work together for a single new product.

Key terms

Brand 317

Brand equity 318

Brand extensions 321

Brand manager 330

Cannibalisation 307

Co-branding 324

Decline stage 316

Family brand 322

Generic branding 323

Growth stage 314

Ingredient branding 324

Introduction stage 313

ISO 14000 309

ISO 9000 308

Kansei engineering 307

Licensing 324

Market manager 331

Maturity stage 315

National or manufacturer brands 322

NPD teams 331

Own-label brands 322

Package 325

Private-label brands 322

Product category managers 331

Product life cycle 312

Product mix 307

Product range 304

Six Sigma 309

Total quality management (TQM) 307

Trademark 318

Universal Product Code (UPC) 327

Venture teams 331

Chapter review

Marketing concepts: testing your knowledge

1. Why might a company decide to expand a product range? What are some reasons for contracting a product range? Why do many firms have a product mix strategy?

2. Why is quality such an important product strategy objective? What are the dimensions of product quality? How has e-commerce affected the need for quality product objectives?

3. Explain the product life cycle concept. What are the stages of the product life cycle?

4. How are products managed during the different stages of the product life cycle?

5. What is a brand? What are the characteristics of a good brand name? How do firms protect their brands?

6. What is a national brand? A shop brand? Individual and family brands?

7. What does it mean to license a brand? What is co-branding?

8. What are the functions of packaging? What are some important elements of effective package design?

9. What should marketers know about package labelling?

10. Describe some of the different ways firms organise the marketing function to manage existing products. What are the ways firms organise for the development of new products?

Marketing concepts: discussing choices and ethical issues

1. Brand equity means that a brand enjoys customer loyalty, perceived quality and brand name awareness. What brands are you personally loyal to? What is it about the product that creates brand loyalty and thus brand equity?

2. Quality is an important product objective, but quality can mean different things for different products, such as durability, precision, aesthetic appeal and so on. What does quality mean for the following products?

    a. Car

    b. Pizza

    c. Trainers

    d. Hair dryer

    e. Deodorant

    f. University education.

3. Firms often take advantage of their popular, well-known brands by developing brand extensions because they know that the brand equity of the original or parent brand will be transferred to the new product. If a new product is of poor quality, it can damage the reputation of the parent brand while a new product that is of superior quality can enhance the parent brand's reputation. What are some examples of brand extensions

that have damaged and that have enhanced the parent brand equity?

4. Sometimes marketers seem to stick with the same packaging ideas year after year regardless of whether they are the best possible design. Following is a list of products. For each one, discuss what, if any, problems you have with the package of the brand you use. Then think of ways the package could be improved. Why do you think marketers don't change the old packaging? What would be the results if they adopted your package ideas?

   a. Breakfast cereal

   b. Washing-up liquid

   c. Orange juice

   d. Carton of milk

   e. Crisps

   f. Loaf of bread.

5. You learned in the chapter that it's hard to *legally* protect brand names across product categories – Quaker and Apple, for example, and also Delta, which is an airline and a tap. But what about the *ethics* of borrowing a name and applying it to some unrelated products? Think of some new business you might like to start up. Now consider some possible names for the business that are already in use as brands in other unrelated categories. Do you think it would be ethical to borrow one of those names? Why or why not?

 ## Marketing practice: applying what you've learned

1. The web allows consumers to interact directly through blogs and other means with other people so they can praise products they like and criticise those they don't. With several of your fellow students, conduct a brief survey of students and of older consumers. Find out if consumers complain to each other about poor product quality. Have they ever used a website to express their displeasure over product quality? Make a report to your class.

2. You may think of your college or university as an organisation that offers a range of different educational products. Assume that you have been hired as a marketing consultant by your university to examine and make recommendations for extending its product line. Develop alternatives that the university might consider:

   a. Upward line stretch

   b. Downward line stretch

   c. Two-way stretch

   d. Filling-out strategy.

   Describe how each might be accomplished. Evaluate each option.

3. Assume that you are the head of marketing for a firm that markets a large number of speciality food items (gourmet sauces, marinades, relishes and so on). Your firm is interested in improving its marketing management structure.

You are considering several alternatives: a brand manager structure, having product category managers or focusing on market managers. Outline the advantages and disadvantages of each type of organisation. What is your recommendation?

4. Assume that you are working in the marketing department of a major manufacturer of athletic shoes. Your firm is introducing a new product, a line of disposable sports clothing. You wonder if it would be better to market the line of clothing with a new brand name or use the family brand name that has already gained popularity with your existing products. Make a list of the advantages and disadvantages of each strategy. Develop your recommendation.

5. Assume that you have been recently hired by Kellogg, the cereal manufacturer. You have been asked to work on a plan for redesigning the packaging for Kellogg's cereals. In a role-playing situation, present the following report to your marketing superior:

   a. Discussion of the problems or complaints customers have with current packaging

   b. Several package options

   c. Your recommendations for changing packaging or for keeping the packaging the same.

 ## Marketing miniproject: learning by doing

In any supermarket in any town, you will surely find examples of all the different types of brands discussed in this chapter: individual brands, family brands, national brands, shop brands, and co-branded and licensed products. This miniproject is designed to give you a better understanding of branding as it exists in the marketplace.

1. Go to a typical supermarket in your community.

2. Select two product categories of interest to you: ice cream, cereal, laundry detergent, soup, paper products and so on.

3. Make a list of the brands available in each product category. Identify what type of brand each is. Count the number of shelf facings (the number of product items at the front of each shelf) for each brand.

4. Arrange to talk to the shop manager at a convenient time. Ask the manager to discuss the following:

   a. How the shop decides which brands to carry

   b. Whether the shop is more likely to carry a new brand that is an individual brand versus a family brand

   c. What causes a shop to drop a brand

d. The profitability of shop brands versus national brands

e. Other aspects of branding that the shop manager sees as important from a retail perspective.

5. Present a report to your class on what you learned about the brands in your two product categories.

Real people, real surfers

Exploring the web

As we discussed in this chapter and in Chapter 7, companies protect their products by obtaining patents and legal protection for their brands with trademarks. The UK Intellectual Property Office issues both of these forms of protection. Visit the Intellectual Property Office website at www.ipo.gov.uk. Use the website to answer the following questions.

1. What is a patent? What can be patented?
2. Who may apply for a patent? Can foreign individuals or companies obtain a UK patent? Explain.
3. What happens if someone infringes on a patent?
4. What does the term *patent pending* mean?
5. What is a trademark? What is a service mark?
6. Who may file a trademark application? Do firms have to register a trademark? Explain.
7. What do the symbols TM, SM and ® mean?
8. What are the benefits of trademark registration?
9. What are common-law rights regarding trademarks?
10. How long does a trademark registration last? How long does a patent last?
11. How would you evaluate the Patent and Trademark Office website? Was it easy to navigate? Was it useful? What recommendations do you have for improving the website?

Now, take a look at the website at www.pearsoned.co.uk/solomon to see some videos from YouTube relating to aspects of this chapter.

Marketing plan exercise

Irn-Bru is an interesting brand with a long history (the history is worth reading – go to www.irn-bru.co.uk, then click on 'History Timeline'). Suffice to say, it is one of the oldest soft drinks brands in the United Kingdom. Assume for a moment that A.G. Barr plc, the owner of Irn-Bru, is doing some marketing planning involving this brand.

1. What are some product line strategies you might suggest that Irn-Bru consider?

2. How important is TQM and product quality in general to a brand like Irn-Bru? How do these issues play into the company's marketing plan?

3. Take a look at the different Irn-Bru products portrayed on its website. Where does each fall on the product life cycle? What leads you to conclude this?

4. What realistic opportunities do you believe exist for brand extensions for Irn-Bru? Explain how the company might go about introducing each to the market.

5. Does Irn-Bru have high brand equity? What evidence do you have for your answer? What can Irn-Bru do to enhance its brand equity, given the 800-pound gorillas it competes against (Coke and Pepsi)?

Delve deeper into branding

Leslie de Chernatony

Professor of Brand Marketing Universita della Svizzera Italiana
and Aston Business School

Given the financial importance of brands, more attention is being paid to ensure that a coherent, pan-company approach is adopted, thereby increasing the likelihood of the brand being perceived as an integrated offering. In doing this the first challenge is that as brands are intangible assets, different managers have different views about their brand. The first paper clarifies on an evolutionary spectrum how managers may have different perceptions about their brand. The services sector dominates developed economies, yet a consideration of the most valuable brands does not show a dominance of services brands. The second paper uses research undertaken in the financial services sector and considers some of the factors that need taking into consideration to create and sustain successful services brands. One aspect of innovative thinking in branding comes about by not following market conventions and instead adopting a challenger perspective on brand management. The final paper explores how an organisation adopted a challenger perspective when it created and launched its new brand.

References

Leslie de Chernatony (2009) 'Towards the Holy Grail of Defining "Brand"', *Marketing Theory* 9, no.1, 101–5.

Leslie de Chernatony and Susan Cottam (2006) 'Internal Factors Driving Successful Financial Services Brands', *European Journal of Marketing* 40, no.5/6, 611–33.

Leslie de Chernatony and Susan Cottam (2009) 'Creating and Launching a Challenger Brand: A Case Study', *The Services Industries Journal* 29, no.1, 75–89.

Marketing in action case

Real decisions at Diageo

Formed in 1997 from the merger of Guinness and Grand Metropolitan, Diageo has enjoyed immense success in selling many alcoholic beverages. In particular, Diageo's spirits' success is seen by the company producing eight of the top 20 distilled spirits worldwide including the well-known Smirnoff vodka which has dominated the vodka market for a number of years.

However, Smirnoff's market share dipped from 50 per cent in 1990 to 32 per cent in 2003 as it has slowly started to lose sales to competitors including Absolut and Finlandia. Arch-rival Absolut may have the

edge as far as trend-setting is concerned, but Smirnoff has size on its side. It is sold in 130 countries worldwide, with an overall lead enhanced by the fact that, after the Second World War, it was virtually the only vodka available outside communist Russia for almost 30 years. More recently the brand enjoyed considerable success with ready-to-drink spin-off Smirnoff Ice. In America this so-called 'malternative' doesn't even contain vodka, allowing it to compete head-to-head with the local beer industry. Because a price war would ultimately hurt all the top competitors, most companies tend to compete with marketing-led campaigns and Diageo responded by pumping in £250 million to the marketing budget, but later increased this to a record-breaking £1.3 billion in 2008. This meant that Smirnoff received more advertising money than any of Diageo's other lines. Because Smirnoff's market stretches across the globe, grand-scale projects need to target a particular segment, namely the loyalty of generation Y.

In 2009, then, Smirnoff launched 'Be There', a campaign designed to attract millenials, which did not feature the vodka itself, but rather the experience of nightlife. A key part of this campaign was the Smirnoff Nightlife Exchange project. To connect with the world millenials, the Nightlife Exchange involved cities from different countries switching identities for one night by filling a crate with items and ideas that represent the local nightlife. It toured each nation for six weeks prior to the exchange to collect ideas from people from various regions. Then, on 27 November, the crates swapped cities and a massive Smirnoff-sponsored party was held simultaneously in each city in the spirit of the crate received. The 14 countries were: Great Britain, USA, Argentina, Australia, Brazil, Canada, Germany, India, Ireland, Lebanon, Poland, South Africa, Thailand and Venezuela. In Great Britain, for example, London and Miami swapped nights, where London's nightlife scene exploded onto the Wynwood Arts District for one night only. To make the project globally interactive, and knowing that the target market was tuned into technology, Diageo partnered with MTV for the event, granting the network exclusive television coverage and launched a Nightlife Exchange mobile channel, sending messages and enabling users to interact with the exchange at any time or place. This was supported by an online campaign utilising Smirnoff's Facebook page (www.facebook.com/Smirnoff?sk=info) which allowed users from all over the world to make suggestions for their countries' carts, vote on existing ideas and learn more about the opinion leaders, such as celebrity DJs and TV personalities who decided upon the final contents in their respective countries' crates.

In Great Britain the Miami nightlife exchange experience was an enormous success, which led Smirnoff to organise a small nationwide tour of the 'Miami Experience' to Edinburgh, Hatfield, Southampton and Swansea during March and May 2011. Smirnoff partnered with Sensation for another extraordinary nightlife experience, by bringing the world's leading dance event to Great Britain for the very first time. This event took place on 13 August 2011 at London's O2 arena, which was transformed into the world-famous Ocean of White show, with one-of-a-kind stage performances, acrobats, state-of-the-art lightshows, lasers, fireworks, the world's top DJs and of course Smirnoff cocktails, created by a team of professional mixologists. Smirnoff is dedicated to celebrating one-of-a-kind nightlife experiences – the type you look back on and say 'I Was There'. Through these communication methods Smirnoff tries to approach fans of nightlife and music to get involved with the world's leading vodka brand and share those extraordinary, unforgettable moments.

We acknowledge the assistance of Jina John, Anohkee Mepani and Anastasia Stathopoulou in the preparation of this case.

 ## Things to think about

1. Describe the three levels of the product for Smirnoff vodka

2. Where would you classify Smirnoff in the following categories and why?

   a. Durable vs non-durable product?

   b. Convenience, shopping, speciality or unsought product?

3. What factors are important in understanding the decision situation?

4. What are the alternatives?

5. What decision do you recommend?

Sources: Smirnoff Experience Berlin – 23 April Event Video: www.youtube.com/BeThereSmirnoff#p/u/8/LUoapxe4f7Y; www.adbrands.net/uk/smirnoff_uk.htm; www.soulofmiami.org/2010/11/14/smirnoff-nightlife-exchange-miami-meets-london-112710/; www.facebook.com/Smirnoff?sk=info; www.clash-music.com/news/smirnoff-miami-experience-returns; www.sensation.com/world/en/news/index/493/smirnoff-presents-sensation; www.facebook.com/smirnoffGB?sk=info

References

1. Joseph B. White, 'Lexus Tries to Redefine Hybrids', online.wsj .com/article_email/SB114242707250600173-1MyQjAxM-DE2NDlyMDUyMjA3Wj.html.

2. www.imdb.com/title/tt0317740/.

3. www.austin-rover.co.uk/index.htm?r50storyf.htm; www.mini2.com/2001/09/10/its-a-mini-adventure-across-the-uk/.

4. www.scottish-newcastle.com/.

5. www.haribo.com/planet/uk/info/frameset_verbraucherinfo.php?verbraucher=1.

6. www.uk.pg.com/products/products/ariel.html.

7. www.rolls-roycemotorcars.com.

8. www.hyundai.co.uk/.

9. Joann Muller and Robyn Meredity, 'Last Laugh', *Forbes*, 18 April 2005, 98.

10. Daniel Thomas, 'Relaunches: new Life or Last Gasps?', *Marketing Week*, 29 January 2004.

11. Lea Goldman, 'Big Gulp', *Forbes*, 10 January 2005, 68.

12. Material adapted from a presentation by Glenn H. Mazur, QFD Institute, 2002.

13. 'The Magical Demystifying Tour of ISO 9000 and ISO 14000', www.iso.ch/iso/en/iso9000-14000/understand/basics/general/basics_1.html.

14. 'The Sabre System of the Appliance Service Industry', *Appliance* (March 2004).

15. Mohanbir Sawhney, S. Balasubramanian and V. Krishnan. 'Creating Growth with Services', *MIT Sloan Management Review*, 34.no (Winter 2004), 34–43.

16. www.computerweekly.com/Articles/2007/02/20/221914/marks-spencer-extends-rfid-technology-to-120-stores.htm.

17. http://blogs.consumerreports.org/cars/toyota/.

18. Al Ries and Laura Ries, *The Origin of Brands* (New York: Collins, 2005).

19. Philip H. Francis, 'New Product Development, The Soul of the Enterprise', memagazine.org/contents/current/webonly/webex.html.

20. www.low-carb.org.uk/main.htm.

21. 'Today's Buzzword: Low-Carb', *Chain Drug Review*, 2 February 2004, 40.

22. http://search.ft.com/ftArticle?queryText=nokia+asia&aje=true&id=071212000271&ct=0.

23. 'P&G Joins Forces with MTV Asia to Attract Young Chinese', *European Cosmetic Markets* (March 2004), 84; 'Will P&G's Moisturinse Boost Personal Cleanser Sales?', *Household & Personal Products Industry* (April 2004), 125; www.pg.com/product_card/product_card_main_olay.shtml.

24. http://expendturereport.warc.com/Free Top LineData.aspx; www.telegraph.co.uk/finance/newsbysector/mediatechnologyandtelecoms/8232075/UK-Government-halves-advertising-spend.html.

25. Julian Hunt, 'Making Great Ideas Pay Off', *Grocer*, 27 March 2004, 2; Glen L. Urban, *Digital Marketing Strategies* (Englewood Cliffs, NJ: Prentice Hall, 2004).

26. http://snopes.com/horrors/food/kfc.asp.

27. Adapted from N. Bendle P. Farris Phillip. Pfeifer and D. Reibstein 'Metrics that Matter to Marketing Managers', *Marketing JRM* 1(2010), 18–23.

28. Apple wins logo lawsuit against Beatles, www.macnn.com/articles/06/05/08/apple.wins.logo.lawsuit/.

29. Susan Fournier, 'Consumers and Their Brands: Developing Relationship Theory in Consumer Research', *Journal of Consumer Research* 24 (March 1998), 343–73.

30. 'The Most Famous Name in Music', *Music Trades* (September 2003).

31. Kevin Lane Keller, 'The Brand Report Card', *Harvard Business Review* (January–February 2000) (Harvard Business School reprint R00104).

32. Based on '*The Substance of Style*, *The Economist*,17 March 2009, www.economist.com/node/14447276 (accessed 1 August 2011).

33. www.haagen-dazs.com.

34. Adapted from 'Innocent Hit by Dramatic Sales Slide' by Jemima Bokaie Marketing Magazine (2008), www.marketingmagazine.co.uk/news/847899/Innocent-hit-dramatic-sales-slide/ (accessed 1 August 2011).

35. P. Farris, N. Bendle, Phillip, Pfeifer, and D. Reibstein, Marketing Metrics: The Definitive Guide to Measuring Marketing Performance, 2nd ed. (New Jersey: FT Press, 2011).

36. www.competition-commission.org.uk/Inquiries/completed/2003/safeway/pdf/tescosummary.pdf.

37. Ron Ruggless, 'T.G.I. Friday's Beefs Up Menu with New Atkins Partnership', *Nation's Restaurant News*, 15 December 2003.

38. D.C. Denison, 'The Boston Globe Business Intelligence Column', *Boston Globe*, 26 May 2002.

39. 'Putting Zoom into Your Life', *Time International*, 8 March 2004, 54.

40. Stephanie Thompson, 'Brand Buddies', *Brandweek*, 23 February 1998, 26–30; Jean Halliday, 'L.L. Bean, Subaru Pair for Co-Branding', *Advertising Age*, 21 February 2000, 21.

41. Ed Brown, 'I Scream You Scream – Saaay, Nice Carton!', *Fortune*, 26 October 1998, 60.

42. Adapted from 'Tropicana's Marketing Folly, *Harvard Business Review*, 24 February 2009, http://blogs.hbr.org/merholz/2009/02/tropicanas-marketing-folly.html (accessed 1 july 2011).

43. www.businesslink.gov.uk/bdotg/action/layer?topicId=1074016261; www.accident999.eu/jurisdiction.html.

44. www.rbkc.gov.uk/EnvironmentalServices/foodhygieneandstandards/labelling.asp.

45. Adapted from ASA (2009) *Advertising Standards Authority Annual Report*; www.asa.org.uk/About-ASA/Annual-Report.aspx.

Chapter 9
Services marketing

Q & A with Karen Wosskow

First job out of school?
Hairdresser, claim to fame blow drying the hair of Twiggy and Phil Oakey (Human League – lead vocalist)

Career high?
Finding a band that nearly every major record label wanted to sign

Business books I am reading now
Marketing Real People, Real Decisions, First European Edition

My hero
My grandpa, he paid his way through medical school by driving a taxi to support himself and his family. He went on to become the doctor for Rotherham United Football Club and would run on the pitch with his brown medical bag every time a player was injured. I would sit on the terraces hoping someone would get hurt, just so I could watch him in action. He made me so proud

Don't do this when interviewing with me
Not maintain eye contact

My pet peeve
Smoking

Favourite UK Club and live music venue?
PLUG SHEFFIELD

Holiday resort
Not a resort but paradise, Ladakh in the Himalayas

Hobby/sport?
Travelling

Drink?
Fentimans ginger beer

Food?
Anything that's not English

Meet Karen Wosskow,
a decision maker at KBW Management

Karen Wosskow is the Founder and Owner of KBW Management. She has worked in the music industry for over 15 years, managing live music venues, promoting bands and running rehearsal studios. Having left school at the age of 16, Karen ventured overseas and taught English in a number of European countries, before returning to the UK to develop a career in the music industry. Whilst consulting in the music industry, Karen is also currently studying for a Master's degree in International Management & Marketing.

Following the failure of the National Centre for Popular Music, a national chain that manages and owns live music venues, called 'Barfly', took over the Centre and developed it into a live music venue. Due to Karen's reputation and knowledge of the industry, Barfly approached her to manage and promote the venue. After several successful years and experience in the sector she decided to establish her own music promotions company. The aim of the business was to develop new talent on the music scene, in terms of promoting and managing bands. A few of the artists that Karen promoted include Pete Doherty/The Libertines, Snow Patrol, Franz Ferdinand and the Kaiser Chiefs.

Karen lives with her son Emilio, daughter Gabriella and pet Giant Schnauzer Louie.

Real people, real decisions
Decisions at KBW Management

This case reports on a major decision facing Karen relating to the future of a local band. Karen had spotted a certain unique talent with a songwriter and a few musicians she had met when they were rehearsing in her studios. She soon realised their potential and firmly believed that given the right support they had the potential to make it big on the music scene. Karen made some suggestions to the band and virtually overnight the band was receiving a huge amount of attention from key players within the industry. These included major and independent record companies, alongside entrepreneurial producers, who were all eager to sign the band from Karen. It all happened so quickly for a band who literally had only been working in Karen's dark and dingy rehearsal rooms for just over a month. This band had never recorded a song, or even played together live on a stage. One evening after work, Karen met a friend (who was the manager of Mercury prize winning and internationally famous band Gomez), who was curious about what was going on, as he heard interesting music from the studios. Karen invited him into the studios to watch and listen. Then within two days she received a call from the Head of Artists and Repertoire at Virgin records, requesting to come and see the band play live.

That call was followed by the MD of PARLAPHONE EMI (home of the Beatles, Radiohead and Lily Allen), making the same request. By the end of that week Karen became inundated with requests from a number of record labels, publishers and producers who were all keen for a slice of the action. Over the subsequent few weeks, the band was rehearsing three times a day in front of a host of potential backers. They became overnight 'hot property' and the word-of-mouth buzz in London surrounding the band was rapidly spiralling. Following a very intense couple of months, the next stage involved the offer from various companies to visit London and be VIP pampered in the most luxurious of hotels with unprecedented wining and dining, all expenses trips abroad and promises of no compromised budgets for touring, promotions and recordings. The band had rapidly emerged from being unknown on one day, to becoming a sought-after band among the music industry the next. This was the type of lifestyle that most bands could only dream about. However, in the shadows of all this high flying celebrity status, Karen needed to see through all the glitter and decide on a sensible future to best promote the band. Having the potential to go all the way and perhaps become the next Beatles, Karen was faced with three options.

Photo 9.1	The National Centre for Popular Music

Source: Alamy Images/Eric Murphy

Option 1 Look to sign a lucrative deal with a major record company. This would involve the artists signing exclusively to the label on a long-term basis for a multi-album deal

This option was desirable and offered a large initial cheque (known in the industry as an advance). In return for the substantial advance, however, the record company would own all the recording rights made during the term of the agreement. The band would earn royalties on the sales of records and these royalties would be used to pay off the advance. Such a deal with a major label has certain advantages, as they have huge resources to exploit opportunities fully. They can fund expensive videos, substantial marketing campaigns and can often coordinate effective music campaigns on an international scale. Major companies are also able to fund expensive recordings with renowned producers and support extensive touring. They also have strong connections and clout with the media, giving them the ability to secure significant TV and radio exposure.

Major labels are behind the vast majority of music sold, downloaded, and, as such, benefit from huge economies of scale. They get the best production and ad deals and have strong purchasing power. However, as more and more recorded music is illegally downloaded and sales of traditional music like CDs have declined, record companies are now looking to alternative ways to recoup advances. The highly controversial multiple rights deal more commonly known as the 360 has been increasingly used over the last few years between lawyers and labels when negotiating a record contract. Managers are highly sceptical, as it means labels take a percentage of all concert revenue, merchandise sales, endorsement deals and ringtones.

Option 2 Establish a licensing deal with an independent record label

This option would provide greater flexibility to Karen and the band. However, the initial up-front cheque would not be as lucrative as with Option 1. This choice would allow for the band and Karen to have greater autonomy, more creative freedom and artistic control. Independents allow artists to decide on their choice of songs for future releases and select producers that they wish to work and record with. An independent company therefore tends to impose less control on artists, as there is far less investment in terms of up-front money and less spent on recording and touring etc. Independent companies do not require such long-term commitment from bands and tend not to tie them into such lengthy contracts. If the relationship between artist and label sours, the artist is free to negotiate a deal elsewhere. Another advantage of an independent label is that they limit their recording agreements to a few countries, thus allowing the artist to make separate agreements in the countries not covered by the initial deal. This allows artists to work with companies in other territories that may be of significant interest in the band's future.

Option 3 Sign a production agreement between the artist and a production company to make recordings which can then be licensed to a recording company

Production deals are becoming the mode of choice as major record labels are finding it increasingly difficult to sustain massive record deals. The production company will not pay any advances to the artist but will fund recording costs. Net profits are split between production company and artist, often with the artist taking a majority share of the cut. This strategy allows for total independence and the option to work with any record labels in any territories. The artist and manager have total creative freedom and once the production company has recouped all the money owed, the artist retains complete ownership of the songs

Now, put yourself in Karen's shoes. Which option looks the best and which one would you go for, and why?

Objectives

When you have finished reading this chapter, you will be able to:

1 Describe the four characteristics of services

2 Understand how services differ from goods

3 Explain marketing strategies for services

4 Explain how marketers create and measure service quality

5 Explain the marketing of people, places and ideas

Marketing what isn't there

Instead of something tangible like toothpaste or a new car, watching a band and listening to music at a live gig is a service experience. Karen Wosskow understands the challenges of marketing a service, i.e. a product that is intangible. Marketing a rock band is therefore quite distinct from marketing consumer goods like Coca-Cola. It's a challenge that Karen needed to manage daily, and not just with one band member, or band, but several different artists.

These challenges also apply to other types of services. For example, studying at university represents the consumption of a service, and so does going to support your favourite football team. Each represents a product (a service) that combines experiences with physical goods to create an event that the buyer consumes. You can't have a university without a library of textbooks, or sit and watch football without a seat. But these tangibles are secondary to the primary product, which is some act that in these cases can produce enjoyment, knowledge or excitement.

This chapter will consider some of the challenges and opportunities facing marketers such as Karen Wosskow, whose primary offerings are **intangibles**: services and other experience-based products that cannot be touched. The marketer whose job it is to build and sell a better football, car or iPod (all tangibles) must deal with different issues from someone who wants to sell tickets for a football match, arrange a taxi to the airport or sell seats at a music concert. In the first part of this chapter, we'll discuss services, a type of intangible that tends to be the fastest-growing sector in developed economies. As we'll see, all services are intangible, but not all intangibles are services. Then we'll move on to other types of intangibles.

Does marketing work for intangibles?

Does marketing work only for companies that sell washing detergent and cars, or does it apply to many types of 'products', including politicians, the arts and the places we live and visit? Yes, marketing does work for intangibles.

Even intangibles such as electricity or gas which we normally think of as commodities are now branded and marketed directly to consumers. Throughout the UK customers can select from a range of competing utility suppliers. Sound marketing concepts don't apply only to companies solely looking to make profit. Indeed, not-for-profit organisations, including charities, social welfare organisations, zoos, museums and religious congregations, increasingly are thinking about branding and image building. The not-for-profit sector plays a significant role in many leading economies, and with millions of volunteers the competition for both customers and donors is fierce. These organisations have to come up with innovative marketing strategies all the time.[1] Even the Salvation Army operates a state-of-the-art website complete with a chat room and online press kit.[2]

Still, some producers of intangibles have been slow to accept the idea that what they do *should* be marketed. Sometimes, people who work in healthcare, the legal profession or the arts resist the notion that the quality of what they produce and the demand for their services are affected by the same market forces driving the fortunes of paper producers, food suppliers or even power utilities. It is sometimes hard, for example, for nursing and administrative staff in hospitals to realise that they need to treat you as a customer and not just any old patient.

Let's take a quick look at how some basic marketing concepts would apply to an artistic product. Suppose a local theatre company wanted to increase attendance at its performances. Remembering the basics of developing a marketing plan, here are some marketing actions the organisation may consider to reach its goals:

iLove my Apple

I just wish it came in Green.

| Photo 9.2 | Many not-for-profit organisations, including charities, know that marketing is key to their success. This advert for Greenpeace uses the iconic visual style from the iPod advertising campaign to get attention *Source :* Greenpeace UK |

- The organisation could develop a *mission statement*, such as 'We seek to be the best provider of quality theatre in the region.'

- A *SWOT analysis* could include an assessment of the organisation's strengths and weaknesses and the environmental threats and opportunities. The arts marketer is, after all, competing for the consumer's disposable income against other theatre groups. The marketer is also up against other forms of entertainment. The consumer may choose instead to attend a pop concert at Wembley Stadium, go to the cinema to see a film or watch a football game.

- The theatre company should use information obtained in the SWOT analysis to develop measurable *objectives*, such as to 'increase the number of season ticket holders by 20 per cent over the next two years'.

- Next, the organisation must develop marketing strategies. For example, it must consider which *target markets* it wishes to attract. If audience levels for its plays have been stable for

Marketing metrics

M&S Mini Cash ISA

Marks & Spencer started selling financial services in the 1990s and by the year 2000 it was looking at ways of broadening its offer. It considered the highly competitive ISA tax-free savings market as a candidate, but wanted evidence that it could succeed. The company commissioned a conjoint research study with MORI to decide the product specification that would maximise returns. This used consumer research to determine the effects of interest rates, bonus, tiering, rate guarantees and withdrawal conditions on sales volumes, and used these to construct a 'what-if' financial model. Findings of this model were used by management to select the optimum product, which was launched successfully.

several years, it should consider new markets for its performances. This might lead to product modifications such as some opera companies have done by projecting English translations above the stage to draw new patrons who are unfamiliar with opera's international languages.

As you can see, by using the principles of effective marketing planning, just as with any tangible product, an organisation such as a theatre can reach its goals. More important, service organisations can be sure they are meeting the needs of their 'customers'. One way to develop an appropriate service offering is to undertake research to identify which attributes of service appeal to customers and can contribute effectively to bottom-line profits. This is exactly what Marks & Spencer did when diversifying from predominantly retail clothing into financial service retailing (see Marketing metrics box).

 ## What is a service?

www.pearsoned.co.uk/Solomon

Objective

1

Describe the four characteristics of services

As we've said, marketing can help sell all kinds of intangibles, from theatre performances to ideas about birth control. But first, let's take a look at services, an important type of intangible.

Services are acts, efforts or performances exchanged from producer to user without ownership rights. Like other intangibles, a service satisfies needs by providing pleasure, information or convenience. Nowadays in most developed economies the vast majority of employment is in services. If you pursue a marketing career, it's highly likely that you will work somewhere in the services sector of the economy.

Of course, the service industry includes many consumer-oriented services, ranging from dry cleaning to retail travel. But it also includes a vast number of services provided for organisations. Some of the more commonly used business services include vehicle leasing, computer technology services, insurance, security, legal advice, food services, consulting, cleaning and maintenance. In addition, businesses also purchase some of the same services as consumers, such as utilities, telecommunications and travel.

The market for business services has grown rapidly because it is often more cost effective for organisations to hire outside firms that specialise in these services than to try to hire a workforce and handle the service themselves. In other instances, firms buy business services because they do not have the expertise necessary to provide the service. Even the marketing function itself is not immune to being outsourced by organisations. It's not unusual for companies to hand over their advertising, public relations and other related functions to outside agencies.

Characteristics of services

Services come in many forms, from those performed for you, such as a massage or teeth cleaning, to those done to something you own, such as having your DVD player repaired or getting a respray on your classic 1965 Aston Martin. Regardless of whether they affect our bodies or our possessions, all services share four characteristics: intangibility, perishability, inseparability and variability. Table 9.1 shows how marketers can address the unique issues related to these characteristics of services that don't pop up when they deal with tangible goods.

Intangibility

Intangibility is the characteristic of a service that means customers can't see, touch or smell a service. Unlike the purchase of a tangible good, we can't inspect or handle services before we buy them. This makes many services much more difficult for consumers to evaluate. Although it may be easy to evaluate your new haircut, it is far less easy to determine whether the dental hygienist has done a great job cleaning your teeth.

Because they're buying something that isn't there, customers look for reassuring signs before purchasing, and marketers must ensure that these signs are readily available. That's why marketers try to overcome the problem of intangibility by providing physical cues to reassure the buyer. These cues might be the 'look' of the facility, its furnishings, logo, stationery, business cards, the appearance of its employees, and well-designed advertising and websites, just to name a few. Universities and business schools in Europe and beyond

Characteristic	Marketing Response
Intangibility	Provide tangibility through physical appearance of the facility
	Furnishings
	Employee uniforms
	Logo
	Websites
	Advertising
Perishability	Adjust pricing to influence demand
	Adjust services to match demand (capacity management)
Variability	Institute total quality management programmes
	Offer service guarantees
	Conduct gap analysis to identify gaps in quality
Inseparability	Train employees on successful service encounters
	Explore means for disintermediation

Table 9.1 Marketing strategies for different service characteristics

Photo 9.3	Financial services are highly intangible, so companies need to use vivid imagery to communicate their benefits *Source:* Getty Images/Mark Thompson

are now frequently trying to promote that their MBAs are accredited by AMBA (the Association of MBAs) or EQUIS (European Quality Improvement System) in an attempt to reassure students that what they are buying is a high quality programme.

Perishability

Perishability refers to the characteristic of a service that makes it impossible to store for later sale or consumption. It's a case of use it or lose it. When rooms go unoccupied at a ski resort, there is no way to make up for the lost opportunity to rent them for the weekend. Marketers try to avoid these problems by using the marketing mix to encourage demand for the service during slack times. One option is to reduce prices to increase demand for otherwise unsold services. Some chartered airlines do this by offering more lower-priced seats in the final weeks before a flight. TV channels also offer advertisers low-priced airtime at the last minute.

This relates to effective **capacity management** – representing the process by which organisations adjust their services in an attempt to match supply with demand. Capacity management may mean adjusting the product, or it may mean modifying the price. In the summer, for example, a winter ski resort could combat its perishability problem by opening its lifts to mountain bikers who tear down the sunny slopes. Rental car companies, for example, offer discounts on days of the week when business travel is light, and many hotels offer special weekend packages to increase their occupancy rates. Even cinemas are starting to catch on to the idea of encouraging greater usage of their facilities by offering incentives to pensioners and students during less busy periods.

Variability

Perhaps Wayne Rooney was on fire on Saturday when he netted his hat trick for Manchester United, however he may have a quiet game the next time out – there is no guarantee. **Variability** is the characteristic of a service which means that even the same service performed by the same individual for the same customer can vary. This means that there may be inevitable differences in a service provider's performances over time. It's rare when you get *exactly* the same cut from a hairstylist.

It is difficult to standardise services because service providers and customers vary. Think about your experiences in your university classes. A business school can standardise its offerings to some extent – course catalogues, content and classrooms. Lecturers, however, vary in their training, life experiences and personalities, so there is little hope of being able to make teaching uniform (not that this would necessarily be desirable anyway). Also, because students with different backgrounds and interests vary in their needs, the lecture that you find fascinating may put your friend to sleep. The same is true for customers of organisational services. Differences in the quality of individual security guards or cleaners mean variability in how these services get delivered.

In fact, we don't necessarily *want* standardisation when we purchase a service. Most of us want a hairstyle that fits our face and personality and a personal trainer who will address our unique physical training needs. Because of the nature of the tasks performed in services, customers often appreciate the firm that customises its service for each individual. One solution to the problem of variability is to implement total quality management (TQM) programmes for continuous improvement of service quality. As we learned earlier, TQM is a management effort to involve all employees from the assembly line onward in continuously working towards product quality improvement. This, briefly, is achieved through empowering staff at each level and providing them with the opportunity to have an input and make decisions. In addition to instituting TQM programmes, offering service guarantees assures consumers that if service quality fails, they will be compensated. We'll talk later in this chapter about how service marketers can provide greater quality and consistency in service delivery through gap analysis and employee empowerment.

Inseparability

Inseparability is the characteristic of a service, meaning that it is impossible to separate the production of a service from its consumption. Although a firm can manufacture goods prior to sale, a service can take place only at the time the service provider performs an act on either the customer or the customer's possession. It's hard to take notes on a lecture when the professor doesn't show up. In some cases, of course, the service can be sold before delivery, such as buying a ticket to see Celtic play Ajax in Amsterdam months before attending the event.

Still, the expertise, skill and personality of a provider or the quality of a firm's employees, facilities and equipment cannot be detached from the offering itself. The central role employees play in making or breaking a service underscores the importance of the **service encounter**, or the interaction between the customer and the service provider.[3] The most expertly cooked meal is not appreciated if an unpleasant or incompetent waiter brings it to the table. We'll talk more about the importance of service providers later in this chapter. To minimise the potentially negative effects of bad service encounters and to save on labour costs, some service businesses are experimenting with **disintermediation**, which means removing the 'middleman' and thus eliminating the need for customers to interact with people at all. Good examples include self-service petrol stations and hotels, which are becoming increasingly popular in places like France, and self-service checkouts at Tesco retail stores in the UK – you will soon be able fill up your digital trolley with groceries, which will be scanned upon entry and then flash your payment card on your way out and that will be sufficient. Even salad and dessert bars in hotel restaurants reduce reliance on waiter services. Although some consumers resist dealing with machines, or composing their own salad, most prefer the speed and efficiency that disintermediation provides.

The internet offers many opportunities for disintermediation, especially in the financial services area. Banking customers can access their accounts, transfer funds from one account to another and pay their bills with the click of a mouse. Many busy consumers can check on mortgage interest rates and even apply for a loan at their convenience. This is a much better option than taking an afternoon off work to sit in a branch and discuss your mortgage options. Online brokerage services are increasingly popular as many consumers seek to handle their investments themselves, thus eliminating the commission that a full-service brokerage firm would charge.

Classifying services

Objective

2

Understand how services differ from goods

By understanding the characteristics of different types of services and just which type of service they offer, marketers can develop strategies to improve customer satisfaction. As Figure 9.1 shows, we can classify services in terms of whether the service is performed directly on the customer or on something the customer owns and whether the service consists of tangible or intangible actions. Customers themselves receive tangible services to their bodies, a haircut or a heart transplant. The education you are receiving from your course is an intangible service directed at the consumer. A customer's possessions are the recipient of such tangible services, like having your car serviced or repaired by a mechanic. Intangible services directed at a consumer's possessions include insurance and even security, which is particularly valued for residents who live in blocks of flats, or own second homes in exclusive resorts overseas.

Services can be classified according to whether the customer or his or her possessions are the recipient of the service and as to whether the service itself consists of tangible or intangible elements.

	Tangible Services	*Intangible Services*
Customer	Haircut	University education
	Plastic surgery	A religious service
	Manicure	A TV programme
	Personal trainer	A flower-arranging course
		Marriage counselling
Possessions	Dry cleaning	Banking
	Car repair	Accounting services
	Housecleaning	Insurance
	Package delivery	Home security service

Figure 9.1   **Classification of services by inputs and tangibility**
Services can be classified according to whether the customer or his or her possessions are the recipient of the service and whether the service itself consists of tangible or intangible elements

The goods/services continuum

In reality, most products are a *combination* of goods and services. The purchase of a 'pure good' like a Mercedes-Benz still has service components, such as bringing it to the dealer for maintenance work. The purchase of a 'pure service' such as a makeover at a department store has product components, for example, make-up, eye shadow, lipsticks, etc. that the beautician uses.

The service continuum in Figure 9.2 shows that some products are dominated by either tangible or intangible elements. Where salt and teaching represent two extremes on the

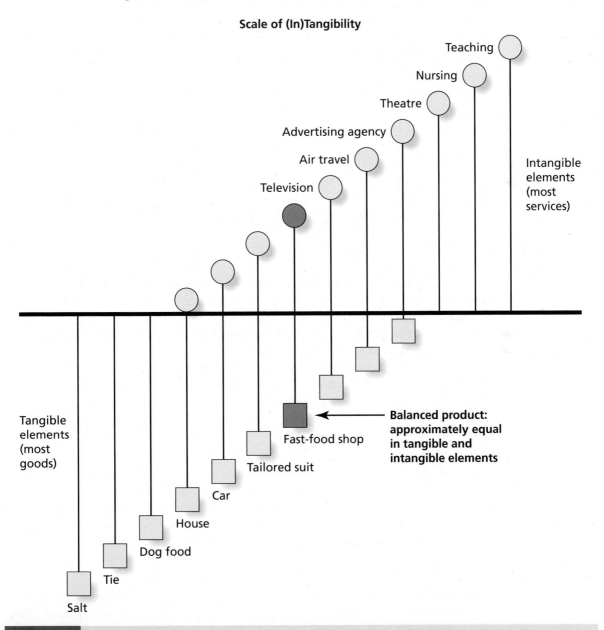

Scale of (In)Tangibility

Tangible elements (most goods)

Intangible elements (most services)

Salt · Tie · Dog food · House · Car · Tailored suit · Fast-food shop · Television · Air travel · Advertising agency · Theatre · Nursing · Teaching

Balanced product: approximately equal in tangible and intangible elements

Figure 9.2 **The service continuum**
Products vary in their level of tangibility. Salt is a tangible product, teaching is an intangible product, and the products offered by fast-food restaurants include both tangible and intangible elements

Source: Adapted from G. Lynn Shostack, 'How to Design a Service', *European Journal of Marketing* 16, no. 1 (1982), 52. © Emerald Group Publishing Limited, all rights reserved.

continuum, others tend to include a mixture of goods and services, such as a commercial airline flight. A product's placement on this continuum gives some guidance as to which marketing issues are most likely to be relevant. As the product approaches the tangible pole of this continuum, there is fairly little emphasis on service. The physical product itself is the focal point, and people will choose one option over others because of the product's function or image.

However, as the product gets near the intangible pole, the issues we've discussed such as intangibility and inseparability play a key role in shaping the service experience. In the middle of the continuum, both goods and services contribute substantially to the quality of the product because these products rely on people to satisfactorily operate equipment that will in turn deliver quality service. Let's consider each of these three positions as we move from products dominated by tangibles to those dominated by intangibles.

1. **Goods-dominated products.** Even if this only means that a company provides a free phone number for questions, or provides a 30-day warranty, companies that sell tangible products still must provide supporting services. Car manufacturers, home appliances and electronics firms can realise a major competitive advantage when they provide customers with this support better than their competitors. Services may be even more important for marketers of business-to-business tangibles. Business customers often will not even consider buying from manufacturers who don't provide services such as employee training and equipment maintenance. For example, hospitals that buy lifesaving patient care and monitoring equipment that costs hundreds of thousands of euros demand not only in-service training for their nursing and technical staff, but also require regular maintenance of the equipment (if needed) and a quick response to breakdowns.

2. **Equipment- or facility-based services.** As we see in Figure 9.2, some products include a mixture of tangible and intangible elements. While a restaurant is a balanced product because it includes the preparation and delivery of the food to your table plus the food itself, the tangible elements of the service are less evident for other products. Many hospitals and hotels fall in the middle of the continuum not because customers take a tangible good away from the service encounter, but because these organisations rely on expensive equipment or facilities to deliver a product. The Park Lane Hilton in London is just one example that relies on using expensive equipment and facilities to help portray a 'world class' image for its visitors. Facility-driven services, such as theme parks, amusement arcades, museums and health clubs, should be concerned with these factors.[4]

   - **Operational factors:** Clear signs and other guidelines must show customers how to use the service. In particular, firms need to minimise waiting times. Marketers have developed a number of tricks to give impatient customers the illusion that they aren't waiting too long. One hotel chain, responding to complaints about the long wait for lifts, installed mirrors in the lobby. People tended to look at their appearance until the lift arrived and, lo and behold, the number of complaints reduced.[5]

   - **Locational factors:** These are especially important for frequently purchased services, such as dry cleaning or retail banking, that we obtain from a fixed place. When you select a bank, a restaurant, an estate agent or a health club, its location often influences your decision. Marketers make sure their service sites are convenient and in places that are attractive to prospective customers.

   - **Environmental factors:** Service managers who manage a retail presence and require people to come to their location realise they must create an attractive environment to lure customers. One trend is for services to adopt a more retail-like philosophy, borrowing techniques from clothing shops or restaurants to create a pleasant environment as part of their marketing strategy. Banks, for example, are creating signature looks for their branches through the use of lighting, colour, art and music, and even local shops are now baking bread on their premises.

3. **People-based services.** At the intangible end of the continuum are pure people-based services. A roaming masseur, a mobile hair dresser, or car valeter are examples of people in professions that provide services for others. Because people have less and less time to get things done, the importance of people-based services is increasing. Self-improvement services such as wardrobe consultants and personal trainers are becoming increasingly popular, and in some places even professional dog walkers and mobile pet washing services do good business. Many of us hire someone to do our legal work, repair our cars and complete our end of year tax return.

Core and augmented services

When we buy a service, we may in fact be buying a *set* of services. The **core service** is a benefit that a customer gets from the service. For example, when your car breaks down, repairing the problem is a core service you seek from your car dealer or garage. In most cases though, the core service alone just isn't enough. To attract customers, a service firm often tries to offer **augmented services**, i.e. additional service offerings that differentiate the firm from the competition. When the car dealership provides the pick-up and delivery of your car, a free carwash, or a lounge with nice chairs, satellite TV and delicious coffee, these represent the kind of items that can help the provider to gain your loyalty as a customer.

Think about the core service you buy with an airline ticket, i.e. transportation. Yet airlines rarely stress the basic benefit of arriving safely at your destination. Instead, they emphasise augmented services such as frequent-flyer miles, speedy check-in and in-flight entertainment. In addition, augmented services may be necessary to deliver the core service. In the case of air travel, airports have added attractions to encourage travellers to fly to one site rather than another.[6] Here are some augmented services now available at airports around the world:

- London Gatwick: internet café, Planet Hollywood restaurant, personal shopper services.
- Amsterdam Schiphol: casino, airport television station, sauna, dry cleaner, grocery shop.
- Frankfurt International: supermarket, disco, sex shop.
- Singapore Changi: fitness centre, karaoke lounge, putting green.

And what about your university education? With increased competition and heightened course fees, universities are finding that their augmented products must offer a variety of amenities that provide added value, such as cafés and bars, sports and recreation facilities, etc.

Services on the web

From DVD rentals to fine restaurant cuisine, anything that can be delivered can be sold on the web. In some cities, website companies will arrange to have your dry cleaning picked up, your family photos developed, or your shoes repaired. Here are some of the newest and most popular web services:

- **Banking:** Customers can check their statements, pay bills, transfer money and balance their accounts 24 hours a day, seven days a week whether they're at home or travelling around the world. Some banks offer online customers better incentives, including higher interest rates on deposits and lower rates on loans.

- **Software:** Siebel Systems – market leaders in customer relationship management software, is spearheading an industry shift toward internet-accessed software sold or rented to user companies and paid for monthly.[7]

- **Travel:** Airline travel and tourism websites now command a large portion of the travel business for both business customers and individual consumers. Traditional travel agencies now tend to focus on specialised markets such as outsourcing a firm's business travel function or booking unique packaged travel deals for consumers.

- **Career-related sites:** Employment agencies and recruiting firms such as Monster.com provide important job services and a less expensive way for applicants and employers to advertise their availability.

To stay in the game, marketers of such services need to think seriously about developing an online presence as well. Effective websites not only allow customers to access the services online but also provide information on how to contact them for those customers who still want personal contact. Because customers seek access to internet-based services for convenience, marketers must make sure internet sites are fast, simple, continuously updated and easy to navigate.

Expansion of the Traditional Marketing Mix

As the provision of services is largely an intangible process, the traditional marketing mix, consisting of price, product, place and promotion has been expanded upon to incorporate the marketing of services. In addition to the four traditional Ps, three subsequent Ps consisting of People, Process and Physical Evidence have been added. We will now provide a short overview below relating to each of the extended marketing mix attributes before exploring these in much more depth throughout the rest of this chapter.

Marketing misstakes

Online service at a cost

Online shopping sounds like the perfect remedy; everything you need is just a mouse click away. You can find what you want, compare prices and go for the best deal. The benefits are obvious, it is quicker, more convenient and a lot cheaper, or is it? Apparently not at Domino's Pizza. Dominos offers an online service where you can order the takeaway pizza of your choice – a large 'deluxe' for instance is normally £17.99. All you have to do is put in your card details and it is ready for collection. But if you go to the store the same pizza could be bought for cheaper: 'Collection special. Any pizza, any size £10.99'. Had you ordered over the phone or passed by in person you would have been £7 better off. This is a reason why some Domino stores exclude online orders from this deal.

Why do you think this might be a marketing misstake?
Source: Based on www.bbc.co.uk/blogs/watchdog/2011/05/online_shopping_rant.html

- **People:** As we have seen earlier on the goods/services continuum, we realise that in services marketing, people often play a significant role in the customer experience. Think of travelling on your favourite airline. Think of eating in your favourite restaurant and think about your favourite lecturer at university. When you start to consider these services, you then begin to realise the importance of people in delivering the service. The management and motivation of people is therefore crucial in services marketing as this can help influence customer satisfaction and repeat custom, which in turn can leverage better financial performance for organisations.

- **Process:** This relates to the procedures, mechanisms and routines that are put in place by organisations in a bid to deliver value to the customer. In a services context, customers are often influenced by how they are treated in their entire service experience. If we take Disneyland Paris as an example, before even arriving at the theme park, processes are set in place to easily direct visitors to car parks so they can park safely and amicably. Upon arriving at the park entrance, visitors are kindly greeted by appropriate cast members and encouraged to enjoy their visit. Well-designed systems are also in place at Disneyland to manage lost property (each day hundreds of cameras are reclaimed), lost children (to reunite them with their families), parades, firework shows and even attraction down time. The Disney parks benefit from a tried and tested system, whereby procedures have been well developed and established for catering professionally to the mass public. Much of this stems from the company's ethos and its emphasis on employee training in order to maintain effective processes.

- **Physical evidence:** This relates to the environment where the service is delivered and can also include any tangible cues relating to the service on offer. When entering a bank, an aircraft or even a lecture theatre (particularly for the first time), we look around at the age and quality of the decor, the cleanliness of the surroundings, the layout and lighting etc. We may also gauge the service personnel by their attire, i.e. the uniform that they may wear or simply the cleanliness of their appearance. Other tangible cues relating to service may be a company's letterhead and logo, the design and quality of their business cards, their corporate brochure and nowadays even the quality of their website! Creating an appropriate environment is becoming increasingly significant and even business schools are attempting to look more like five-star hotels these days as they particularly look to impress high fee paying students (and their parents).

 ## The service encounter

www.pearsoned.co.uk/Solomon

Objective

3

Explain marketing strategies for services

Earlier we said that the service encounter occurs when the customer comes into contact with the organisation. This usually means interacting with one or more employees who represent that organisation. The service encounter has several dimensions of importance to marketers.[8] First, there is the social contact dimension, of one person interacting with another person. The physical dimension is also important, and customers often pay close attention to the environment where the service is delivered – where the consumer and the service provider interact. The interactive contact is also referred to as 'the moment of truth', and specifically the employee can often determine whether the customer will come away with a good or bad impression of the service. Our interactions with service providers can range from the most superficial, such as buying a cinema ticket, to telling a doctor our most intimate secrets. In each case, the quality of the service encounter can play a big role in determining how we feel about the service we receive.

Social elements of the service encounter: employees and customers

Because services are intimately tied to company employees who deliver the service, the quality of a service is only as good as its poorest employees. The employee represents the organisation. Actions, words, physical appearance, courtesy, and professionalism, or a lack of it reflect the values of the organisation. Customers entrust themselves and/or their possessions to the care of the employee, so it is important that employees look at the encounter from the customer's perspective.

The customer also plays a part in ensuring that a quality experience will result from a service encounter. When you visit a medical centre, the quality of the healthcare you receive depends not only on the doctor's competence but also on your ability to communicate accurately and clearly the problems you are experiencing and how well you comply with advice. The business customer must provide accurate information to his accounting firm. Even the best personal trainer is not going to make the desired improvements to a client's body if the client refuses to do the designated workout.

Physical elements of the service encounter: servicescapes and other tangibles

As we noted earlier in the chapter, because services are intangible, marketers focus attention on providing *physical evidence* of the service they deliver. An important part of this physical evidence is the **servicescape**; the environment in which the service is delivered and where the firm and the customer interact. Servicescapes include facility exteriors,

---

Real people, other voices

Advice for Karen Wosskow

Dr Angela Wright
Westminster Business School

Given the rapidity with which bands appear and disappear, and the fickle nature of the listening public, it is my opinion that the band should consider Option 1 – so as to 'hit the ground running'. Penetration of today's marketplace with a product/service which is faced with continuous, unpredictable and formidable competition requires the presence of a dedicated muscular organisation which the major labels are still capable of providing, in spite of a reversal in their fortunes in recent times. The help of an informed managerial and marketing assembly in this service environment is essential for the successful launch of such a musical group. The successful Italian tenor Luciano Pavarotti advised the importance of 'be heard, be seen' – get your music to as wide an audience as possible, i.e. maximise your 'reach' in the marketplace. With the ever-increasing 'noise and clutter' and media fragmentation in the world in which we live, the only hope and possibility for bands, I believe, is with the power of a major label behind them. A major label, supported generally by the magic of critical mass, has the influence to open doors, connecting and engaging with relevant decision makers, and, ultimately, they can raise the profile of the band quite quickly, at the very least. If the band makes it, and enjoy the success that the music business can provide, then they can argue about where the decimal point goes on the cheque with authority and with the leverage of the buying public behind them. The advantages posited in Options 2 and 3 of autonomy, self-determination and artistic control should be addressed in the fine print of a well written contract with a major label.

In the multifaceted, multichallenged, technological circus of the modern media world, a dedicated background team of experts is vital for the successful management of the complexities of marketing music in the realities of the current commercial milieu; therefore, I strongly recommend Option 1.

Internationalisation

Volvo brings classic drive-ins to the UK

The classic drive-in movies are making an interesting come-back, in markets that do not afford the space or time for expansive layouts and parking space. The UK joins the list, thanks to the efforts of Damian Barr, journalist and cultural entrepreneur, who, with the help of Volvo, has invented the Starlight Urban Drive-In. Based on the US drive-in movie concept, people can watch films while sat comfortably in one of a range of shiny new Volvos in East London. Reporting on this development, Ad Age says that movies like 'Grease' and 'Dirty Dancing' have been viewed by people at the drive-in with great enthusiasm. Cars at the drive-in are pre-parked, so the viewers don't need a drivers' licence. Just like real American drive-ins, there is plenty of food available to make a mess of those new Volvos.

Debate, discuss, disagree

1. Discuss the innovative idea behind the service concept offered.

2. Do you think the US drive-in cinema servicescape is likely to take off elsewhere in Europe?

www.nine.co.uk/news/article/volvo-starlite-urban-drive-in-brick-lane

www.network2media.com/index.php?option=com_content&view=article&id=2534:international-volvo-brings-alive-classic-drive-ins-in-uk-creates-new-branding-opportunities&catid=5:news&Itemid=3

elements such as the exterior design of the facility, the signs, parking and even the landscaping. They also include interior elements, such as the design of the office or shop, equipment, colours, air quality, temperature and smells. For hotels, restaurants, banks, airlines and business schools, the servicescape is quite elaborate. For other services, such as a dry cleaning service, the servicescape can be very simple.

Marketers know that carefully designed servicescapes can have a positive influence on customers' purchase decisions, their evaluations of service quality, and their ultimate satisfaction with the service. Thus, when London-based Arsenal Football Club considered moving to the Emirates Stadium, much planning needed to go into the design, not only the actual playing field, but also the exterior design of the stadium for its turnstyle entrances, landscaping, seating areas, toilets etc. Similarly, marketers pay close attention to the design of other tangibles that facilitate the performance of the service or provide communications. For visiting supporters, these include signs that direct fans to the ground, the game tickets themselves, the match day programmes, the kit design and colours, and hundreds of staff that help in the delivery of the service on match days. The servicescape may also provide a useful way for seeking a competitive advantage – see, for example, how some of the hoteliers in France are working from an ethical perspective to positively promote sustainability.

Nowadays, for many consumers the first tangible evidence of a business (service or otherwise) is its website. Websites that are unattractive or frustratingly dysfunctional provide a horrible first impression of the company and its service. Investments by service firms in user-friendly websites pay back through increased business as well as higher customer satisfaction and loyalty. Consider Lastminute.com as an example. Users can price their flight using various airlines, and consider a range of hotels. Users are therefore easily able to design a tailor-made package that suits their needs. This functionality not only makes customers happy, it also saves the company money by reducing the number of telephone enquiries.

Marketing ethics and sustainability

Hotels in France embrace the virtue of going green

Wood-burning stoves, in-room recycling, fine cuisine featuring local produce: from bed-and-breakfasts to five-star palaces, France's hotel industry is opening its eyes to the lucrative advantages of going green. 'Our business involves a lot of water, electricity and rubbish, so our goal is to limit our impact on the environment and considerably reduce our carbon emissions', said Bernard Granier, Director General of Concorde Hotels, which runs the opulent Le Crillon in Paris and the Hotel Martinez in Cannes. The chic Fouquet's Barriere, adjoining the eponymous bistro on the Champs-Elysees, wants to cut its CO_2 output by 20 per cent by 2020 and, in the same spirit, it offers guests the use of a hybrid car or an electric scooter. Olivier Petit of the global consulting firm Deloitte said sustainable development has become 'an element of positive discrimination' – something of an optional extra that makes a business look better. 'In five years, that will no longer be the case', he said. 'On the contrary, to not adhere [to sustainable development] will be a negative factor.'

Having recognised how going green can be good for business, the Gites de France network of bed-and-breakfasts has doubled to around 100 its number of certified 'eco-gites', with such features as solar heating. More than 200 more are in the pipeline, Gites de France says.

'The hotel industry has seen a real acceleration in this area over the past three years', said Philippe François, chairman of François Tourisme, a consultancy that specialises in sustainable development for hotels and tourism. But much remains to be done, as many hoteliers think that big investments are needed in order to come across as virtuous vis-à-vis the environment – no small consideration in hard economic times. 'In fact, 80 per cent of what needs to be done costs nothing, because they involve changes in conduct and attitudes which alone can be profitable in financial, environmental, social and image terms', François said.

Source: Agence France-Presse, 6 July 2010, Paris

Debate, discuss, disagree

1. What is the future for hotels that are currently not adopting 'green' strategies?

2. Are sales really affected by green issues in the services marketplace?

Providing quality service

Objective

4

Explain how marketers create and measure service quality

If a service experience isn't positive, it can turn into a *disservice* with nasty consequences. Quality service ensures that customers are satisfied with what they have paid for. However, satisfaction is relative because the service recipient compares the current experience to some prior set of expectations. That's what makes delivering quality service tricky. What may seem like excellent service to one customer may be mediocre to another person who has been 'spoiled' by earlier encounters with an exceptional service provider. So, marketers must identify customer expectations and then work hard to exceed them.

Of course, meeting or exceeding customer expectations is not always so easy. These expectations can be influenced by stories people hear from friends and acquaintances, and they are not always realistic in the first place.[9] Exaggerated customer expectations, such as level of personal service, may be impossible for a large company to accomplish, and account for about 75 per cent of the complaints reported by service businesses. However, providing customers with logical explanations for service failures and compensating them in some way can substantially reduce dissatisfaction.[10]

Service quality attributes

Because services are inseparable in that they are not produced until the time they are consumed, it is difficult to estimate how good a service will be until you buy it. Most service businesses cannot offer a free trial. Because services are variable, it is hard to predict the consistency of quality and there is little or no opportunity for comparison shopping. The selection process for services is somewhat different than for goods, especially for services that are highly intangible, such as those on the right end of the continuum. Service marketers have to come up with creative ways, such as developing 'search qualities', building on 'experience qualities' and utilising 'credence qualities' to illustrate the benefits their service will provide.

Search qualities are product attributes that the consumer can examine prior to purchase. These include colour, style, price, fit, smell and texture. Tangible goods, of course, are more likely to have these characteristics, so services need to build them in by paying attention to such details as the style of flight attendants' uniforms or the decor of a hotel room. The 'Service Experience Blueprint' in Figure 9.3 illustrates how one design firm tried to build in such cues for a retailer. The company planned an upgraded, freshly painted car park that included a special preferred parking space for expectant mothers (complete with a stork logo) to signal that the company cared.[11] Attention to detail makes a difference.

Experience qualities are product attributes that customers can determine during or after consumption. For example, we can't really predict how good a holiday we'll have until we experience it, so marketers need to reassure customers *before* the fact that they are

Figure 9.3	**Service experience blueprint**
	Firms often build in cues their customers can easily see because services quality is often difficult to determine. Grocery shops such as this one often use a variety of cues to convince consumers of superior quality
	Source: Lewis P. Carbone and Stephan H. Haeckel, 'Engineering Customer Experiences', *Marketing Management*, 8(3) (Winter 1994), reprint, Exhibit 4.

in for a good time. A travel agency may invest in developing a presentation complete with alluring images of a tropical resort and perhaps even supply enthusiastic recommendations from other clients who had a positive experience at the same location.

Credence qualities are product attributes we find difficult to evaluate even *after* we've experienced them. For example, most of us don't have the expertise to know if our doctor's diagnosis is correct.[12] Evaluations here are difficult, and to a great extent the client must trust the service provider. That is why tangible cues of professionalism, such as diplomas or an organised office, count toward purchase satisfaction, and is the reason, as mentioned earlier, why so many European business schools wish to acquire AMBA and EQUIS accreditation to support their MBAs.

Measuring service quality

Because the customer's experience of a service is crucial to determining future patronage, service marketers feel that measuring positive and negative service experiences is the 'Holy Grail' for the services industry. Marketers gather consumer responses in a variety of ways. For example, some companies hire 'mystery shoppers' to check on businesses and provide feedback. These shoppers usually work for a research firm, although some airlines reportedly recruit 'spies' from the ranks of their most frequent flyers.

The **SERVQUAL** scale is a popular instrument to measure consumers' expectations and perceptions of service quality. SERVQUAL identifies five dimensions or components of service quality:

- *Tangibles* – the physical facilities and equipment and the professional appearance of personnel.

- *Reliability* – the ability to provide dependably and accurately what was promised.

- *Responsiveness* – the willingness to help customers and provide prompt service.

- *Assurance* – the knowledge and courtesy of employees, and the ability to convey trust and confidence.

- *Empathy* – the degree of caring and individual attention provided to customers.[13]

The SERVQUAL scale developed by Parasuraman and his colleagues has been applied in thousands of service settings across the service continuum. It is most often administered in a survey format through a written, online or telephone questionnaire. Firms often track SERVQUAL scores over time to see how their service quality is (hopefully) improving. SERVQUAL can be used in the gap analysis approach we describe next.

Gap analysis is a measurement approach that gauges the difference between a customer's expectation of service quality and what actually occurred. By identifying specific places in the service system where there is a wide gap between what is expected and what is received, service marketers can get a handle on what needs improvement. Some major gaps include the following:[14]

- **Gap between consumer expectations and management perceptions:** A major quality gap can occur when the firm's managers don't understand what its customers' expectations are in the first place. Many service organisations have an operations orientation rather than a customer orientation. For example, banks often closed branches early in order to balance transactions because that was efficient for them, even though it was not convenient for customers who wanted to do their banking during their lunch hour or on their way home. Today more and more banks are open late, with several of those that are located in shopping high streets now choosing to open at weekends.

- **Gap between management's perception and quality standards that the firm sets:** Successful service firms develop written quality goals. If, for example, a company found that customers complained most about its responsiveness, accuracy and timeliness, it would be possible to develop action goals to correct such problems, and for example monitor how quickly employees answer phones in an effort to be more responsive. Management therefore ideally needs to focus on appropriate quality standards that will ultimately be valued among consumers.

- **Gap between established quality standards and service delivery:** One of the biggest threats to service quality is poor employee performance. When employees do not deliver the service at the level specified by the company, quality suffers. Teamwork is crucial to service success. Unfortunately, many companies don't clearly specify what they expect of employees.

- **Gap between service quality standards and consumer expectations:** Sometimes a firm makes exaggerated promises or does not accurately describe its service to customers. When the Holiday Inn hotel chain developed an advertising campaign based on the promise that guests would receive 'No Surprises', many operations personnel opposed the idea, saying that *no* service organisation, no matter how good, can anticipate every single thing that can go wrong. Sure enough, the campaign was unsuccessful. A service firm is better off communicating *exactly what the customer can expect* and what will happen if the company does not deliver on its promises.

- **Gap between expected service and perceived service:** Sometimes consumers misperceive the quality of the service. Thus, even when communications accurately describe what service quality is provided and what customers can expect, buyers are less than satisfied. It's therefore important that companies verify that all forms of communication do not mislead customers.

The **critical incident technique** is another way to measure service quality.[15] Using this approach, the company collects and closely analyses very specific customer complaints. It can then identify *critical incidents*, i.e. specific contacts between consumers and service providers that are most likely to result in dissatisfaction. An airline, for example, may analyse its customer complaints and discover that business customers are more likely to switch carriers if their planes fail to arrive on time. This then becomes 'critical' for the airline to rectify and the company would be wise to develop mechanisms to reduce the number of delayed take-offs that occur, and compensate business passengers accordingly.

Some critical incidents happen when the service organisation simply can't meet a customer's expectations. For example, it is impossible to satisfy a passenger who says to a flight attendant, 'Come sit with me, I don't like to fly alone'. In other cases, though, the firm is capable of meeting these expectations but fails to do so. For example, the customer might complain to a flight attendant, 'My seat won't recline'.[16] A potentially dissatisfied customer can be turned into a happy one if the problem is addressed or perhaps even if the customer is told why the problem can't be solved at this time. Customers tend to be fairly forgiving if they are given a reasonable explanation for the problem.

 ## Strategies for developing and managing services

We've seen that delivering quality should be the aim of every successful service organisation. What can the firm do to maximise the likelihood that a customer will choose its service and become a loyal customer? With services differing from goods in so many ways, decision makers struggle to market something that isn't there. An interesting example of marketing something that doesn't exist appears in the Marketing ethics and sustainability

Marketing in recession

Santander

Spanish bank Santander has performed well in the recession. Unlike many of its rivals in the international banking sector, Santander has been able to expand its business in both North and South America. Whilst the bank may be the largest lender in Spain, which has suffered one of its steepest housing down- turns in history, global revenue for Santander is showing no signs of slowing down. The bank has recently purchased Bank of America's Mexican business for US$2.5 billion and is now rapidly entering Brazil.

Discuss, debate, disagree

1. Why do you think Santander has been successful during the recession, whilst other banks have suffered?

2. What growth strategies are available for firms operating in an international services sector?

box. Here we see that the Co-operative Bank turns away significant business in return for promoting environmentally friendly issues. Attracting and retaining appropriate and like-minded ethical customers is more appealing to the bank. However, many of the same strategic issues apply. For example, Table 9.2 illustrates how three different types of service organisation can devise marketing strategies.

Table 9.2 Marketing strategies for service organisations

	Dry Cleaner	City Theatre Company	University
Marketing objective	Increase total revenues by 20 per cent within one year by increasing business of existing customers and obtaining new customers	Increase to 1000 the number of season memberships to theatre productions within two years	Increase applications to undergraduate and postgraduate programmes by 10 per cent for the coming academic year
Target markets	Young and middle-aged professionals living within an 8 km radius of the business	Clients who attend single performances but do not purchase season tickets	Primary market: prospective undergraduate and postgraduate students who live within the region
		Other local residents who enjoy theatre but do not normally attend local performances	Secondary market: prospective undergraduate and graduate students living in other regions and in foreign countries
Benefits offered	Excellent and safe cleaning of clothes in 24 hours or less	Experiencing professional quality theatre performances while helping ensure the future of the local theatre company	High-quality education in a student-centred campus environment
Strategy	Provide an incentive offer to existing customers such as one suit cleaned for free after ten suits cleaned at regular price	Write letters to former membership holders and patrons of single performances encouraging them to purchase new season tickets	Increase number of recruiting visits to local secondary schools. Arrange a special day of events for secondary school teachers and career advisers to visit campus
	Use newspaper advertising to communicate a limited time discount offer to all customers	Arrange for theatre company personnel and performers to be guests of local television and radio talk shows	Send letters to alumni encouraging them to recommend the university to prospective students they know

Marketing ethics and sustainability

Co-op Bank develops ethical financial products, but at a cost of £9 million

The Co-operative Bank turned away nearly £9 million of business in 2004–5 from companies it deemed to be unethical or environmentally unfriendly. Turning away business because of concerns over the prospective customer's approach to animal welfare lost the bank £1.2 million, declining business from companies with a poor record on human rights and labour practices

lost it close to £4 million. However, the Co-op's tough stand on ethical screening is also attracting customers in record numbers. More than a third of its profits come from people who decided to sign up to the bank because of its ethical values.

Source: The Independent (London), 25 July 2005

Debate, discuss, disagree

1. What are the main reasons why companies try to be involved in ethical/socially responsible activities?

Of course, sometimes service quality does fail. Some failures, such as when your dry cleaner places glaring red spots on your new white sweater, are easy to see at the time the service is performed. Other service failures, such as when the dry cleaner shrinks your sweater, may be less easy for you to recognise immediately. But no matter when or how the failure is discovered, the important thing is that the firm takes fast action to resolve the problem. Quick action means that the problem won't occur again (hopefully) and that the customer's complaint will be resolved. The key is speed: research suggests that customers whose complaints are resolved quickly are far more likely to buy from the same company again, than when complaints take longer to be resolved.[17]

To make sure that service failures are kept to a minimum and that recovery is fast, managers should first understand the service and the potential places where failures are most likely to occur and then make plans ahead of time to recover.[18] That's why the process of identifying critical incidents can be so important. In addition, employees should be trained to listen to complaints and be empowered to take appropriate actions immediately. As we look into the future, we recognise that the importance of service industries as part of the global economy will continue to grow. In fact, in recent years the accelerating importance of services as an integral part of any firm's value proposition has led to discussions of a new **dominant logic for marketing** that in part redefines service as the core deliverable and the actual physical products purveyed as somewhat incidental to the business proposition.[19]

Let's consider several important trends that will provide both opportunities and challenges for the marketers of services. In the future, we can expect services we can't even imagine yet. Of course, they will also provide many new and exciting job opportunities for future marketers.

- **Changing demographics:** As populations age, service industries that meet the needs of older consumers will see dramatic growth. Companies offering recreational opportunities, healthcare and living assistance for senior citizens will be in demand.

- **Globalisation:** The globalisation of business will increase the need for logistics and distribution services to move products around the world, and for accounting and legal services that facilitate these global exchanges. In addition, global deregulation will affect the delivery of services by banks, insurance and other financial service industries because globalisation means greater competition. For example, many patients now are going to countries like Thailand and India, where common surgical procedures may cost significantly less than half what they would be in Europe. In the hotel industry, demand for luxury properties is growing around the world. Hyatt International has expanded its five-star hotels in Tokyo, Hong Kong and Paris, and the company has an aggressive building campaign for luxury hotels in mainland China, where it expects to have as many as 24 properties by 2013.[20]

- **Technological advances:** Changing technology will provide opportunities for growth and innovation in global service industries such as telecommunications, healthcare, banking and online services. We can also expect technological advances to provide opportunities for services that we haven't even thought of yet but that will change and improve the lives of consumers.

- **Shift to flow of information:** In many ways, we have become an information society. Both organisations and individuals have experienced a dramatic increase in the importance of obtaining, manipulating, reporting and using information. The availability, flow and access of information are becoming increasingly critical to the success of organisations. These changes will provide greater opportunities for database services, artificial intelligence systems, communications systems and other services that facilitate the storage and transfer of knowledge.

Marketing people, places and ideas

By now, you understand that services are intangibles that marketers work hard to sell. But as we said earlier, services are not the only intangibles that organisations need to market. Intangibles such as people, places and ideas often need to be 'sold' by someone and 'bought' by someone else. Let's consider how marketing is relevant to each of these.

Across the hall

Advice for Karen Wosskow

Diane Earles
Chartered Institute of Marketing

What an exciting opportunity, three very appealing and viable options, each with their own merits. It's like going to a great restaurant with a vast menu and not being able to decide.

Option 1 is basically what has made the music industry the phenomenal success it is. Providing the band with security and pretty much guaranteed exposure, but at a high price of restricting the band's creative freedom because the 'big boys' will pander to popular demand and therefore the marketing opportunities will also be limited.

Option 3 goes to the other extreme, offering full creative amd marketing freedom but with no guaranteed exposure or income.

Option 2 is a mixture of 1 and 3, providing freedom and security. It was in this environment that Indie Music was born, Madchester – Stone Roses, Happy Mondays – who influenced bands such as Oasis, showing that independent labels can set the trend rather than be led by what was known to sell.

Without knowing the band's plans – i.e. are they in it to make money quickly and run (in which case I would recommend Option 1) or are they doing this as a hobby rather than career (in which case I would recommend Option 3) – I can only suggest a plan of action that allows them the best scope.

Option 2 will allow the band to grow and build a long-lasting career in the industry. It won't be the walk in the park suggested by Option 1 – hard work will be required – but given Karen's values and respect for hard work I think this will sit most comfortably for her too.

Marketing people

Objective

5

Explain the marketing of people, places and ideas

As we saw in Chapter 1, people are products too. If you don't believe that, you've never been for a job interview. Many of us find it distasteful to equate people with products. In reality, though, a sizeable number of people hire personal image consultants to devise a marketing strategy for them, and others undergo plastic surgery, physical conditioning or cosmetic makeovers to improve their 'market position' or 'sell' themselves to potential employers, friends or lovers.[21] Let's briefly touch on a few prominent categories of people marketing.

Politicians are created and marketed by sophisticated consultants who 'package' candidates and compete for 'market share' of votes. Actors, musicians, athletes, supermodels, the famous and near-famous are all competing for market position in popular culture. Agents carefully package celebrities by working to get their clients exposure on TV, star roles in films, recording contracts or product endorsements.[22] Like other products, celebrities even rename themselves to craft a 'brand identity', using the same strategies marketers use to ensure that their products make an impression on consumers.

In addition to these branding efforts, there are other strategies marketers use to 'sell' a celebrity, as Figure 9.4 shows.[23] These include (1) the *pure selling approach*, in which an agent presents a client's qualifications to potential 'buyers' until he finds one who is willing to act as an intermediary; (2) the *product improvement approach*, in which the agent works with the client to modify certain characteristics that will increase market value; and (3) the *market fulfilment approach*, in which the agent scans the market to identify unmet needs. After identifying a need, the agent then finds a person or a group that meets a set of minimum qualifications and develops a new 'product'.

Marketing Approach	*Implementation*
Pure Selling Approach	*Agent presents a client to* – Record companies – Film studios – TV production companies – Talk show hosts – Advertising agencies – Talent scouts
Product Improvement Approach	*Client is modified* – New name – New image – Voice lessons – Dancing lessons – Plastic surgery – New back-up band – New music genre
Market Fulfilment Approach	*Agent looks for market opening* – Identify unmet need – Develop a new product (band, singer) to the specifications of consumer wants

Figure 9.4 | **Strategies to sell a celebrity**
There is more than one approach to selling an intangible – even for selling a celebrity. Successful marketing has to determine the best approach to take for each product

Photo 9.4	Superstar Cheryl Cole is one of the latest celebrities to extend her `brand identity` by branching out to other areas. In addition to her singing career, she has been a panelist on television talent shows and is a spokeswoman for various products, including Elvive shampoo *Source:* Alamy Images/Jeff Morgan 02

Photo 9.5	Many cities, counties, and countries recognise that by using effective marketing strategies, they can increase vital tourism revenues and attract business investment needed for growth *Source:* Croatian National Tourist Board

There is more than one approach to selling an intangible – even for selling a celebrity. Successful marketing has to determine the best approach to take for each product.

Marketing places

Place marketing strategies regard a city, country or other location as a brand, and attempt to position it so that consumers select this over competing destinations when they plan their travel. Because of the huge amount of money associated with tourism, the competition to attract visitors is fierce. This probably explains the rivalry between Hong Kong, Singapore and Dubai as stopover destinations for passengers going to Australasia.

The marketing of ideas can be even more difficult than marketing goods and services. Consumers often do not perceive that the *value* they receive from recycling their household waste or reducing global warming is worth the *cost*, i.e. the extra effort necessary to realise these goals. Governments and other organisations use marketing strategies, often with only limited success, to sell ideas that will save the lives of millions of unwilling consumers or will help save our planet.

Now that you've learned about marketing intangibles, read 'Real people, real decisions' to see which strategy Karen Wosskow decided upon.

Real people, real decisions

How it worked out at KBW Management

Karen decided to go for Option 1, signing an exclusive worldwide recording agreement with PARLAPHONE records on the EMI label, as they are renowned for giving new artists time to develop. This was probably the last ever big deal to be offered to an emerging band, as record labels now realise they can't sustain such deals. With the professional help of top music lawyer John Stathem (Radiohead, Gorillaz etc.), Karen was able to negotiate a favourable deal allowing for an option to either leave the label after the release of two albums or stay on for a further two, on an extended contract. Karen therefore benefited from a substantial advance upon signature and further payments on commencement of recording and on delivery of the first album. Uniquely, the record company also agreed to pay all legal fees.

Directly after signing the contract, the band went into the recording studio with renowned producer, John Leckie (John Lennon, Stone Roses, Radiohead) and as a result, the band's first two singles secured massive amounts of mainstream radio exposure and both made the top 20 in the UK's music charts. Following such early success, unfortunately the music industry experienced turbulent times and EMI found themselves in financial crisis. Providing a glimmer of hope, Terra Firma, a private equity firm owned by entrepreneur Guy Hands then stepped in to try and revive the company. However, things soon hit rock bottom when Guy entered into a massive lawsuit with a leading international bank. This led to massive unrest and issues surrounding the future of EMI. All this brought the company and band to a standstill.

Despite the band being offered the opportunity to support on a 40-date worldwide tour playing to thousands each night, EMI was not in a position to commit and it was no surprise that the band and label went on to eventually part company. Because the label had broken the contractual agreement by not continuing with the release schedule, it was obliged to pay the band for both albums. The dissolution was no fault of any of the PARLAPHONE team that had worked incredibly hard and at all times had the band's best interests in mind in providing support; it was simply a case of the band being in the wrong place at the wrong time. It was a very unfortunate ending for a band that was destined for the top, but did not quite get the chance to progress.

Chapter summary

Now that you have finished reading this chapter, you should be able to answer any of the following potential examination questions:

1. **Describe the principal characteristics of services.** Services are products that are intangible and that are exchanged directly from producer to customer without ownership rights. Generally, services are acts that accomplish some goal and may be directed either towards people or towards an object. Both consumer services and business-to-business services are significant parts of the economy. Important service characteristics include (1) intangibility (they cannot be seen, touched or smelled), (2) perishability (they cannot be stored), (3) variability (they are never exactly the same from time to time) and (4) inseparability from the producer (most services are produced, sold and consumed at the same time).

2. **Explain how services differ from goods.** In reality, most products are a combination of goods and services. Some services are goods dominant (i.e., tangible products are marketed with supporting services). Some are equipment- or facility-based (i.e. elaborate equipment or facilities are required for creation of the service). Other services are people-based (i.e. people are actually a part of the service marketed). Like goods, services include both a core service or the basic benefit received and augmented services, including innovative features and convenience of service delivery.

3. **Explain how marketers create and measure service quality.** The customer's perception of service quality is related to expectations. Because services are intangible, evaluation of service quality is more difficult and customers often look for cues to help them decide whether they have received satisfactory service. Gap analysis measures the difference between customer expectations of service quality and what actually occurred. Using the critical incident technique, service firms can identify the specific contacts between customers and service providers that create dissatisfaction. The SERVQUAL instrument can be used to identify service quality gaps and look at remedies for improvement.

4. **Explain the marketing of people, places and ideas.** Managers follow the steps for marketing planning when marketing other intangibles as well. People, especially politicians and celebrities, are often packaged and promoted. Place marketing aims to create or change the market position of a particular location, whether a city, country, resort or institution. Idea marketing (gaining market share for a concept, philosophy, belief or issue) seeks to create or change a target market's attitude or behaviour. Marketing is used by religious organisations and to promote important causes. Marketing of ideas may be especially difficult, as consumers may not see that the value is worth the cost.

Key terms

Augmented services 351

Capacity management 346

Core service 351

Credence qualities 358

Critical incident technique 359

Disintermediation 347

Dominant logic for marketing 361

Experience qualities 357

Gap analysis 358

Inseparability 347

Intangibility 345

Intangibles 342

Perishability 346

Place marketing 364

Search qualities 357

Service encounter 347

Services 344

Servicescape 354

SERVQUAL 358

Variability 347

Chapter review

Marketing concepts: testing your knowledge

1. What are intangibles? How do basic marketing concepts apply to the marketing of intangibles?

2. What is a service? What are the important characteristics of services that make them different from goods?

3. What is the goods/services continuum? What are goods-dominated services, equipment- or facility-based services and people-based services?

4. What are core and augmented services? How do marketers increase market share with augmented services?

5. What are the physical and social elements of the service encounter?

6. Describe some popular means of marketing for services on the internet.

7. What dimensions do consumers and business customers use to evaluate service quality? How do marketers work to create service quality?

8. How do marketers measure service quality?

9. What are some ideas about the future of services?

10. What do we mean by marketing people? Marketing places? Marketing ideas?

Marketing concepts: discussing choices

1. Why are first impressions formed on the internet about a service so important? What can a service firm do to ensure a favourable first impression online?

2. Sometimes service quality may not meet customers' expectations. What problems have you experienced with quality in the delivery of the following services?
   a. A restaurant meal
   b. An airline flight

   c. Motor vehicle repairs
   d. Your university education.
   What do you think is the reason for the poor quality?

3. Many not-for-profit and religious organisations have found that they can be more successful by marketing their ideas. What are some ways that these organisations market themselves that are similar to and different from the marketing of for-profit businesses?

Marketing practice: applying what you've learned

1. Because of increased competition, you have been hired as a marketing consultant by a local bank. You know that the characteristics of services (intangibility, perishability, variability and inseparability) create unique marketing challenges. You also know that these challenges can be met with creative marketing strategies. Outline the challenges for marketing the bank created by each of the four characteristics of services. List your ideas for what might be done to meet each of these challenges.

2. Assume that you are a doctor. You are opening a new family practice clinic in your community. You feel that you have the best chance of being successful if you can create a product that is superior to that offered by competing businesses. Put together a list of ways in which you can augment the basic service offering to develop a better product. List the advantages and disadvantages of each.

3. You are currently a customer for a university, a very expensive service product. You know that a service organisation can create a competitive advantage by focusing on how the service is delivered after it has been purchased

i.e. making sure the service is efficiently and comfortably delivered to the customer. Develop a list of recommendations for your university for improving the delivery of its service. Consider both classroom and non-classroom aspects of the educational product.

4. Assume that you work for a marketing firm that has been asked to develop a marketing plan for a new up-and-coming pop band called Stalagmite, and their new CD 'Slow Drip'. Prepare an outline for your marketing plan. First, list the special problems and challenges associated with marketing people rather than a physical product. Then outline your ideas for product, price and promotion strategies.

5. Address the same issues in question 4 for a marketing plan for your own home town or city.

6. Assume that you have been recently hired by your city government to head up a programme to create 100 per cent compliance with recycling regulations. Develop a presentation for the local government in which you will outline the problems in 'selling' recycling. Develop an outline for the presentation. Be sure to focus on each of the four Ps.

Marketing miniproject: learning by doing

1. Select a service that you as a consumer will purchase in the next week or so.

2. As you experience the service, record the details of every aspect, including the following:
   a. People
   b. Physical facilities
   c. Location
   d. Waiting time
   e. Hours
   f. Transaction
   g. Other customers
   h. Tangible aspects
   i. Search qualities
   j. Credence qualities

3. Recommend improvements to the service encounter.

Further reading

Services Marketing: Global Edition, 7th Edition, Christopher Lovelock and Jochen Wirtz, Pearson, 2010

Part 1 of this book presents the Service Value Chain and its impact on the service firm's objectives, as proposed by the Service Profit Chain. Part 2 shows the customer interaction process and deals with the planning of the service encounters and reactions to service failures within these encounters, i.e. service recovery. Part 3 focuses on the Service Value Chain's secondary processes which aim at creating service value. The service product defines the service value, while service pricing determines price level and pricing schemes for the services purchased by consumers. Part 4 presents the three types of resources treated: service employees, service tangibles and service technology. Finally, in part 5 market strategies, international services marketing, service networks and service outsourcing are discussed as well as the internal environment, implementation and controlling issues are considered.

Real people, real surfers

Exploring the web

Theme and entertainment parks fall in the middle of the goods/services continuum – half goods and half services. To be successful in this highly competitive market, these parks must carefully develop targeting and positioning strategies. Through looking at the websites of two or three theme parks of your choice, investigate the following:

1. How is each website designed to appeal to each theme park organisation's target market?

2. How does each park position its product? How is this positioning communicated through the website?

3. What changes or improvements would you recommend for each website?

Now, take a look at the website at www.pearsoned.co.uk/solomon to see some videos from YouTube relating to aspects of this chapter.

Marketing plan exercise

Organisations that market services face special challenges because services are intangible. One way they address the challenges created by intangibility is by designing an effective servicescape. This represents the environment where the service is delivered and where the firm and the customer interact.

1. Select a service that you are familiar with, such as a bank, an airline, or even your university.

2. Describe the weaknesses there might be in a SWOT analysis for the business that occur because of the intangibility of the service.

3. Develop strategies for creating a servicescape that will be a positive influence on customers' purchase decisions, their evaluations of the service quality, and their ultimate satisfaction with the service.

Delve deeper into services marketing

Professor Ko de Ruyter

Professor of Interactive Marketing and International Services Research, Maastricht University, the Netherlands

A former mentor of mine expressed the well-known principle of selective perception as follows: 'he who has a hammer sees nails everywhere'. This certainly also holds for those who study services marketing and acknowledge its importance. Services are here, there and everywhere and after spending the better of 15 years studying services, I am certainly not going to argue with this. But it is not just personal and I invite you to look for clues in the three publications that are listed below. Probably one of the most, if not the most influential paper of the last two decades, written by Vargo and Lusch (2004), describes how marketing is moving towards a new dominant logic in which intangible resources, co-creation of value and relationship take central stage. In other words, services are replacing goods as the focal point of attention of economic exchange. The second article, by Homburg, Wieseke and Hoyer (2009), deals with one of services marketing's major challenges, how to link these intangible, touchy-feely concepts to the bottom line. In the paper, which has the Service Profit Chain as its basis, the authors introduce the idea that customer and employee identification are important elements in the chain of cause and effect that starts with employee behaviour and ends with hard cash. Finally, in the third article, written by Wiertz, Mathwick and myself (2008), we show that the evolution of the internet holds an exciting promise for companies as well as service researchers. We demonstrate how social capital within communities of customers contributes to after-sales support services and illustrate how technological as well as social developments form interesting challenges in our area. All three papers show that the focus is shifting toward services, information and knowledge and the return on interactive relationships, both online and offline. Services are everywhere. Please enjoy reading about them and put your knowledge to the test of experience.

References

Stephen Vargo, and Robert Lusch, (2004) 'Evolving to a New Dominant Logic for Marketing', *Journal of Marketing* 68, no. 1, 1–17.

Christian, Hombug, Jan Wieseke and Wayne D. Hoyer, (2009) 'Social Identity and the Service Profit Chain', *Journal of Marketing* 73, no. 3, 38–54.

Charla Mathwick, Caroline Wiertz and Ko de Ruyter (2008) 'Social Capital Production in a Virtual P3 Community', *Journal of Consumer Research* 34, no. 6, 832–49.

Professor Teck Yong Eng

Professor of Marketing, University of Essex

In my view, two major developments in the services marketing literature are worth noting: (1) a service-dominant logic and (2) network approach to strategy development. As suggested by Vargo and Lusch (2004), a product-based conceptualisation of services is limited and it needs to be reformulated into a service dominant logic that stresses value co-creation amongst participants in the marketplace such as the customer is always a co-producer of value. Service innovation is a consequence of service relationships and their interaction in the value chain (see Lusch et al. 2007). A service-dominant logic implicitly takes a network view of value creation, in that strategy development is evolving and emergence through the interaction with multiple actors and in relationships (Eng 2005). This network view highlights the importance of learning in networks as a dynamic approach to managing and developing service relationships, and hence value co-creation in services. I hope that these articles will stimulate your interest in service marketing and provoke debate on services marketing.

References

T.Y. Eng (2005) 'Conceptualisation of Strategy in Business Networks: An Assessment', *Journal of Marketing Channels* 13, no. 1, 79–92.

R.F. Lusch, S.L. Vargo and M. O'Brien, (2007) 'Competing through Service: Insights from Service-Dominant Logic', *Journal of Retailing* 83, no. 1, 5–18.

S.L. Vargo and R.F. Lusch (2004) 'Evolving to a New Dominant Logic for Marketing', *Journal of Marketing*, 68, no. 1, 1–17.

Marketing in action case

The music industry

For digital music, there is no longer a physical product to manufacture. Instead the product itself is information[1]

The ways we engage with music have been anything but constant. In its origins, music was mostly enjoyed as an ephemeral experience: it happened in a specific moment in time and space, one couldn't record it, music was to be appreciated then and there in what Walter Benjamin would describe as an 'auratic' experience.[2] However, thanks to technology, music, like many other human cultural activities, has had the opportunity to be recorded, stored, expressed, transformed, reproduced and distributed in a huge variety of ways. The invention of 'sheet music' (or written music) facilitated the sharing and performing of composed music, gramophones allowed for music to be physically recorded and distributed and radio allowed music to become for the first time a truly mass cultural experience.

Although the market for music originated with the sale of sheet music in the nineteenth century, its real take-off was witnessed in the twentieth century with the emergence of and demand for recorded music in the form of vinyl records, cassettes, CDs and now Mp3s [3] when music became a physical, tangible, reproducible artefact thanks to ground-breaking technologies such as Edison's phonograph in 1877 [4] and the first pieces of legislation that dealt with managing these reproductions such as the 1909 Copyright Act.[5]

The foundations that were laid then enabled music to become the commercial phenomenon that we experience today. Further development and refinement of recording technologies has given rise to institutions like the recording industry where music, now a physical product (vinyl, tape, CD), could be easily and clearly regulated, bought, sold and distributed with relative ease and control. Problems arose, however, once the product of music became digitalised and shifted over the internet alongside millions of bits of other information. It not only lost some of its physical qualities but furthermore become infinitely reproducible at no significant marginal cost or loss of quality. 'As consumption of music increasingly moves to the internet, music

as a product slides from the more tangible end of the scale towards the intangible end'.[6]

In recent times, new forms of technologies have revolutionised conventional sales structures and services for music (e.g. iTunes, Spotify, 7 Digital). The global piracy industry is now estimated to be worth over $4.8 billion, with 4.5 million fabricated CDs sold annually in the UK alone.[7] In addition, questionable actions and behaviours of consumers with regard to moral values and 'ethics' has become a key concern.[8] With the availability of free downloads, consumers prefer not to pay for music anymore, whether it is software piracy, peer-to-peer (P2P) file sharing, music piracy or digital piracy in general.[9]

Muncy and Vitell define consumer ethics as 'the moral principles and standards that guide behaviour of individuals or groups as they obtain, use, and dispose of goods and services'.[10] The entertainment industry is one most affected by the advent of piracy (Levin et al., 2004). Unethical consumer practices of downloading free music are cutting greatly into profits of record companies and making it difficult for the industry to survive.[11] However, with the availability of free music online (e.g. Limewire), piracy and copyrights are still crucial issues, weakening the very existence of this industry and threatening the strategic opportunities within it. This is supported by the fact that 95 per cent of all digital music comes from unlicensed sources.[12] Furthermore, piracy continues to be rampant, with more than 7 million illegal file-sharers operating in Britain alone.[13] These types of misbehaviour have resulted in a move away from sales-based models to one of 'monetising' access to music services. For example, music labels are persuading online retailers to raise wholesale prices for digital music downloads, in an attempt to capitalise on the burgeoning demand for legal online music.[14]

A number of key factors contribute to the current changes: unfaltering consumer demands; explosion of consumer choice; changing roles of key actors who typically include the artists, managers, producers, record label, distributors of music services, retailers, consumers etc. As specific players work in conjunction with one another to compete with piracy, different approaches for digital music business are being adopted. In 2008 the digital music business internationally saw a sixth year of expansion, growing by an estimated 25 per cent in trade value. The UK experienced the largest increase in digital sales in the first half of 2008, with sales up by 45 per cent.[15] The main problem for the recording industry has been to find a way to prevent digital music from being infinitely copied and finding a method of payment that consumers feel happy with.[16]

One such solution in the mid-1990s, marking another important development in technology and music, was 'streaming'. The creation of the compression technology that allowed streaming is mostly attributed to Rob Glaser and his company RealAudio.[17] Streaming allowed for audio (and later video) content to be passed from computer to computer 'instantly' in a similar fashion to 'live' television. There was no need to wait for the file to be completely downloaded before one could listen to/see it. The big difference between a download and a stream is that the media that is streamed isn't fully saved on the user's hard drive (it's just stored on the RAM), allowing for fast and vast media viewing without having to worry about storage. The concept is the basis upon which massively popular sites and applications like YouTube, the BBC iPlayer, digital Radio and Spotify is built on.

The online streaming service known as Spotify is one of the most recent and legally approved business structures of music distribution technologies to date. 'Out of all the start ups that have tried to reinvent the way we listen to music over the past decade, few have attracted as much attention as free streaming music service Spotify, which is deemed by some as the latest potential "iTunes killer"'.[18] Spotify, a company based partly in the UK and partly in Sweden, is not the first or the only streaming music service available online. There are other companies that provide a similar service, like We7, Last.

FM, Deezer, Napster (a reinvented legitimate version) and the USA-only service Pandora. However, it seems to be the service that has generated the most hype in current mainstream media, with much speculation over the possibilities of its business model becoming the dominant form of sustainable music consumption.

Some of the possible reasons for the Spotify hype may lie in the fact that the founders of the service, Daniel Ek and Andres Sehr, have made the audacious claim that Spotify is 'competing mainly with piracy' rather than other companies.[19] Another reason for the elevated media hype might be attributed to the fact that at the time of launch in 2008, Spotify was one of the first services of its kind to offer what can be described as an easy access 'content heavy' free version of the product, allowing a vast catalogue of music to be instantly available at no monetary cost and with no particular consumer discomfort other than having to listen to a few advertisements – this is a model known more commonly in the business world as 'freemium',[20] which is based on the notion of 'freeconomics'. Although to date moniteised packages for music streaming by Spotify has been introduced (Spotify Premium working like a subscription service) the interesting aspect about Spotify is its 'Free' model which offers, contrary to past subscription service models, a very good and complete quality service at the cost of listening to advertisements every 20 minutes or so.[21]

Critics and sceptics of the model in the form of economists and social commentators continue to question Spoitfy's viability as a business. This scepticism has most recently been represented by a possible licensing pull-out by Warner Music, one of the big four major record labels[22] and players in the music industry.[23] The ongoing tensions between the music industry and the technology industry are nothing new, but it is interesting how the music industry, in particular the recording industry, is attempting to find solutions for new sources of revenue in the digital era of music intangibility.

Things to think about

1. What key trends and driving forces have re-shaped the music industry?

2. Describe how music as a product has evolved on the service continuum?

3. Who are the key players involved in the creation, recording and selling of music as a service?

4. What are some of the implications of free online streaming services (i.e. Spotify) for the music industry?

Case study written by Dr Ronika Chakrabarti, Lancaster University Management School, and Gustavo Jacomelli, Service Event Manager, UK

References

1. J.C. Bockstedt, R.J. Kauffman and F. Riggins, 'The Move to Artist-Led Online Music Distribution: A Theory-Based Assessment and Prospects for Structural Changes in the Digital Music Market', *International Journal of Electronic Commerce* 10, no. 3 (2006), 3.

2. W. Benjamin, *Work of Art in the Age of Mechanical Reproduction* (1935), www.marxists.org/reference/subject/philosophy/works/ge/benjamin.htm.

3. C. Gillett, The *Sound of the City: The Rise of Rock & Roll,* 3rd ed. (London: Souvenir Press, 1996).

4. S. Lax, *Beyond the Horizon: Communication Technologies Past Present and Future* (Luton: University of Luton Press, 1997), 74.

5. G. Hull, *The Recording Industry*, 2nd ed. (New York: Routledge, 2004), 2.

6. M. Styven , 'The Intangibility of Music in the Internet Age', *Popular Music and Society* 30 , no. 1 (2007), 1.

7. D. Reece, 'An Industry Poleaxed by Power of the Net', *The Independent*, 31 March 2004, 40.

8. H.G. Gerson and G.E. Buerstatte, 'The E in Marketing: Ethics in the Age of Misbehaviour', *Journal of Healthcare Management* 48, no. 5 (2003), 292–4.

9. Aron M. Levin, Mary C. Dato-on and Kenneth Rhee, 'Money For Nothing And Hits For Free: The Ethics Of Downloading Music From Peer To-Peer Web Sites', *Journal of Marketing Theory and Practice* 12, no. 1, (2004), 48–60.

10. James A. Muncy and Scott J. Vitell, 'Consumer Ethics: An Investigation of the Ethical Beliefs of the Final Consumer' *Journal of Business Research* 24 (1992), 298.

11. Levin et al., 'Money For Nothing And Hits For Free'.

12. I. Youngs, 'Music Industry Scrambles for Cash', *BBC News*, 19 January 2009, http://news.bbc.co.uk/1/hi/entertainment/7837605.stm (accessed 9 March 2010).

13. Alexi Mostrous, 'Music Industry needs clear strategy and control over illegal downloads', *The Times*, 1 March 2010, http://business.timesonline.co.uk/tol/business/industry_sectors/retailing/article7044689.ece.

14. Scott Morrison and Tim Burt, 'Music Labels seek Higher Download Prices', *Financial Times*, 28 February 2005, www.msnbc.msn.com/id/7048053/.

15. IFPI, 'News Business Models For a Changing Environment', IFPI DIGITAL MUSIC REPORT, 2009.

16. D. Hesmondhalgh, *The Cultural Industries* (London: Sage, 2007), 253.

17. J. Alderman, *Sonic Boom: Napster, P2P and the future of Music* (London: Fourth Estate, 2002) (35).

18. P. Bonans, 'Spotify is the New Napster – But Which One?', *Gigaom*, 17 September 2009,http://gigaom.com/2009/09/17/spotify-is-the-new-napster-but-which-one/.

19. D. EK,'Newspeppernews: An evening with Daniel Ek CEO Spotify', Interviewed by Virginia Eastman at 'the Glasshouse', 17 september 2009, www.youtube.com/watch#!v=kQJ3xzYqlBY&feature=related.

20. R. Andrews, 'What Does Spotify's Funding Say About Freemium Music Fortunes' ,Guardian.co.uk, 5 August 2009.

21. D. EK, 'Daniel Ek, CEO, Spotify: Going Mobile, Saving the Music Business', interviewed by Robert Andrews, 9 March 2009, http://paidcontent.co.uk/article/419-interview-daniel-ek-ceo-spotify/.

22. In response to this crisis in the global music market, Sony and BMG merged in 2004. This was motivated by their will to have a stronger stance in the industry and to create the world's second largest record label after Universal Music. Thus, the big Five were reduced to the Big Four – and to the Big Three in 2011 when Universal acquired EMI.

23. R. Swash, 'Warner Music May Stop Licensing Songs to Free Online Streaming Sites', *The Guardian*, 10 February 2010, www.guardian.co.uk/business/2010/feb/10/warner-music-spotify-online-streaming: I. Youngs, 'Warner retreats Form free music Streaning', BBC News, 10 February 2010, http://news.bbc.co.uk/1/hi/8507885.stm', C. Finnamore, Warner Music to Pull Out of Spotify?', *Wired*, 12 February 2010, www,wired.co.uk/news/archive/2010-02/12/warner-music-to-pull-out-of-spotify. aspx.

References

1. *Giving and Volunteering in the United States: Key Findings,* www.independentsector.org/PDFs/GV01keyfind.pdf.

2. www.salvationist.org/intnews.nsf/vw_web_images_only?opeview&start=1&count=10.

3. John A. Czepiel, Michael R. Solomon and Carol F. Surprenant, eds., *The Service Encounter: Managing Employee/Customer Interaction in Service Businesses* (Lexington, MA: D.C. Heath and Company, 1985).

4. Lou W. Turley and Douglas L. Fugate, 'The Multidimensional Nature of Service Facilities: Viewpoints and Recommendations', *Journal of Services Marketing* 6 (Summer 1992), 37–45.

5. David H. Maister, 'The Psychology of Waiting Lines', in Czepiel et al., *The Service Encounter*, 113–24.

6. Jennifer Chao, 'Airports Open Their Gates to Profits', *Montgomery Advertiser*, 26 January 1997, 16A.

7. Jim Kerstetter and Jay Greene, 'Pay-As-You-Go Is Up and Running', *Business Week*, 12 January 2004, 69–70.

8. Cengiz Haksever, Barry Render, Roberta S. Russell and Robert G. Murdick, *Service Management and Operations* (Englewood Cliffs, NJ: Prentice Hall, 2000), 25–26.

9. Cynthia Webster, 'Influences upon Consumer Expectations of Services', *Journal of Services Marketing* 5 (Winter 1991), 5–17.

10. Mary Jo Bitner, 'Evaluating Service Encounters: The Effects of Physical Surroundings and Employee Responses', *Journal of Marketing* 54 (April 1990), 69–82.

11. Lewis P. Carbone and Stephan H. Haeckel, 'Engineering Customer Experiences', *Marketing Management* 3 (Winter 1994), reprint, exhibit 4.

12. Valarie A. Zeithaml, Mary Jo Bitner and Dwayne Gremler, *Services Marketing*, 4th ed. (Englewood Cliffs, NJ: Prentice Hall, 2005).

13. A. Parasuraman, Leonard L. Barry and Valarie A. Zeithaml, 'SERVQUAL: A Multiple-Item Scale for Measuring Consumer Perceptions of Service Quality', *Journal of Retailing* 64, no. 1 (1988), 12–40; A. Parasuraman, Leonard L. Barry and Valarie A. Zeithaml, 'Refinement and Reassessment of the SERVQUAL Scale', *Journal of Retailing* 67, no. 4 (1991), 420–50.

14. Valarie A. Zeithaml, Leonard L. Berry and A. Parasuraman, 'Communication and Control Processes in the Delivery of Service Quality', *Journal of Marketing* 52 (April 1988), 35–48.

15. Jody D. Nyquist, Mary F. Bitner and Bernard H. Booms, 'Identifying Communication Difficulties in the Service Encounter: A Critical Incident Approach', in Czepiel et al., *The Service Encounter*, 195–212.

16. Ibid.

17. Kristin Anderson and Ron Zemke, *Delivering Knock Your Socks Off Service* (New York: American Management Association, 1998).

18. Haksever et al., *Service Management and Operations*, 342–43.

19. Stephen L. Vargo and Robert F. Lusch, 'Evolving to a New Dominant Logic for Marketing', *Journal of Marketing* 68 (January 2004), 1–17.

20. Joe Sharkey, 'Hotels to Flaunt Brands and Add Amenities', New York Times, 1 December 2003, www.nyt.com.

21. Michael R. Solomon, 'The Wardrobe Consultant: Exploring the Role of a New Retailing Partner', *Journal of Retailing* 63 (Summer 1987), 110–28.

22. Michael R. Solomon, 'Celebritisation and Commodification in the Interpersonal Marketplace', unpublished manuscript, Rutgers University, 1991.

23. Adapted from a discussion in R. Rein et al., *High Visibility: Transforming Your Personal and Professional Brand* (New York; McGraw-Hill, 2006), p. 573.

Chapter 10
Pricing the product

Meet Mike Blundell,
a decision maker and
Senior Director at Blundells
Estate Agents

Q & A with Mike Blundell

First job out of school?
Learning the ropes as an estate agent with his father

Career high?
Establishing his own business 34 years ago and never looking back

Business book I'm reading now
Alan Sugar's Autobiography

My hero
Harry Robinson, former tutor from Dale Carnegie

Don't do this when interviewing with me
Interrupt and waffle on

My pet peeve
The usage of unnecessary long words

Favourite TV programme?
Master Chef

Holiday resort?
Barbados or Bournemouth

Hobby/Sport?
Golf to play, football to watch

Drink?
St. Emillion (red wine)

Food?
Traditional roast beef and Yorkshire pudding

ike Blundell is the proprietor of Blundells Estate Agents. He established the business over 34 years ago, and it now has 14 branches in operation and is associated with over 700 other offices throughout the UK. According to For Sale Sign Analysis Ltd, Blundells has more sold signs in the region than any other estate agent, so from a business and marketing perspective Mike must be doing something right in order for his company to be the region's market leader in terms of market share. Before starting his business, Mike left school at the age of 16 and went to work for his father's estate agency business, did some day-release courses and went on to study business and commerce. He is a qualified estate agent and is a Fellow of the National Association of Estate Agents.

Mike lives with long-term partner Kay. He has one son, Matthew, who is a Director of the company and currently manages the Chesterfield office, and a daughter, Hannah, who is a valuer and runs one of the company's other local branches.

Real people, real decisions
Decision time at Blundells

For most people, marketing and selling their home is likely to be the largest transaction that they will ever be involved with. Obtaining the highest possible price is therefore just as imperative for couples and families as they look to move up the property ladder as it is for those that are looking to downsize or retire with a significant amount that they have invested into their home over their working lives. Achieving the best possible price for his clients is something that Mike Blundell and his staff are highly committed to. However, he must also bear in mind that as an estate agent, his company will only receive significant revenue from clients if they manage to sell properties. The vast majority of the company's revenue comes from an agreed percentage of the house price sale. Therefore, the more a property sells for, the greater the return for both the client and Mike Blundell. All things being equal, then, why should Blundells simply not price properties at the highest price possible? That way, when they do sell, both client and company maximise their return.

Whilst economists or accountants may argue in favour of such practice, we know as marketers that other variables beyond simply supply and demand are likely to have an effect on the market. For example, the property market has always been a sexy market which attracts a great deal of competition. Some of this involves national players like Countrywide, Reeds Rains, Haybrook etc. and there are also a number of local entrepreneurial businessmen in the region (like Mike) that have a good track record and command a rightful share of the market. So what is the best way to compete?

There's more than one way to skin a cat!

Thinking about the situation and the highly competitive nature of the market, Mike had to make a decision relating to the strategy of his company and how he intended to compete in the marketplace. This would revolve around pricing. Rather than the normal notion of pricing which would directly relate to his product (in this case the estate agent's service) and what clients would pay, he had to think of a pricing strategy relating to his clients' properties, as this would be the key to success or failure. Three options came to mind when Mike was pitching for business:

Option 1 Marginally overvalue, so that the property 'for sale' figure would be 5–10 per cent more than what the market value was

This option is definitely feasible and Mike knew of at least one other agent that adopted this approach when valuing properties. The benefit of this strategy is that clients often perceive they will obtain this heightened value when the sale is made. In an ideal world, this option offers the best return for both the client and agent, who both receive greater revenue. However, by going in too high, Mike runs the risk that other agents pitching for the business will simply advise the client that the property is not likely to sell at this price and the client may then look to take the business to another agent. It could also backfire, if for example Mike obtained the business, but was later unable to sell the property at this price.

Option 2 Consider, the opposite angle and marginally undervalue, so that the property 'for sale' figure would be approximately 5 per cent less than the market value

Again this represents a feasible option and one that Mike seemed keen to experiment with. The problem with this approach being that clients may perceive that they are selling their property too cheaply, implying they will lose money. Other agents pitching for the business will be quick to point this out and are likely to advise accordingly. Such competitive agents may also make promises that they will be able to obtain a higher sale price for the property in question. However, due to the undervaluation in price more buyers may show interest which could result in multiple offers and quicker home sales.

Option 3 Price properties to reflect the market value

This option represents a halfway house between the two. Through opting for this approach, it is likely that clients will perceive Mike's valuation to be fair. One possible problem associated with this option is that many of the other agents are also likely to value properties similarly, thus making this option very competitive. On a positive note, being a local agent, Mike could stress his company's local reputation in order to support this strategy.

Now, put yourself in Mike's position. Which option looks best? Which one would you select, and why?

Objectives

When you finish reading this chapter, you will be able to:

1 Explain the importance of pricing and how prices can take both monetary and non-monetary forms

2 Understand the pricing objectives that marketers typically have in planning pricing strategies

3 Describe how marketers use costs, demands and revenue to make pricing decisions

4 Understand some of the environmental factors that affect pricing strategies

5 Understand pricing strategies

6 Explain pricing tactics for single and multiple products and for pricing on the internet

7 Understand the opportunities for online pricing strategies

8 Describe the psychological, legal and ethical aspects of pricing

Objective

1

Explain the importance of pricing and how prices can take both monetary and non-monetary forms

'Yes, but what does it cost?'

As Mike Blundell discovered, the question of establishing price is a central part of marketing decision making. In this chapter, we'll tackle the basic question, what is price? We'll also see how marketers begin to determine pricing strategies by developing pricing objectives and by looking at the role of demand, costs, revenues and the environment in the pricing decision process. Then we'll explore how the pricing decision process leads to specific pricing strategies and tactics. We've all heard that 'if you have to ask how much it is, you can't afford it', but how often do you buy something without asking the price? If price was not an issue, we'd all drive great cars, take trips to exotic places and live like royalty. In the real world, though, most of us need to consider a product's price before we buy it.

Price is the value that customers give up or exchange to obtain a desired product. Payment may be in the form of money, goods, services, favours, votes or anything else that has *value* to the other party. As explained in Chapter 1, marketing is the process that creates exchanges of things of value. We usually think of this exchange as people trading money for a good or a service. However, in some marketplace practices, price can mean the exchange of non-monetary value as well. Long before societies produced currency, people exchanged goods and services. This practice still occurs today. For example, someone who owns a home at a trendy ski resort may exchange a weekend stay for car repair or dental work. No money changes hands, but there is an exchange of value.

Other non-monetary costs are often important to marketers. What is the cost of wearing seat belts? What is it worth to people to camp out in a clean national park? It is also important to consider an *opportunity cost*, or the value of something that is given up to obtain something else. For example, the cost of going to university includes more than tuition and also includes the income that the student could have earned by working instead. How important are good pricing decisions? Even during the best of economic times, most consumers rank 'reasonable price,' i.e. a price that makes the product affordable and appears to be fair, as the most important consideration in a purchase and one that counts the most when they decide where to shop.[1]

Developing pricing objectives

As Figure 10.1 shows, there are six steps in price planning. The first crucial step is developing pricing objectives. Pricing objectives must support the broader objectives of the firm, such as maximising shareholder value, as well as its overall marketing objectives, such as increasing market share. Table 10.1 provides examples of different types of pricing objectives, which we'll discuss next.

1. Develop Pricing Objectives

2. Estimate Demand

3. Determine Costs

4. Evaluate the Pricing Environment

5. Choose a Pricing Strategy

6. Develop Pricing Tactics

Figure 10.1	Steps in price planning
	Successful price planning includes a series of orderly steps beginning with setting pricing objectives

Step 1: Develop sales or market share objectives

Objective

2

Understand the pricing objectives that marketers typically have in planning pricing strategies

Often the objective of a pricing strategy is to maximise monetary sales or to increase market share. Does setting a price that is intended to increase unit sales, market share or focus on sales objectives simply mean pricing the product lower than the competition? Sometimes this is the case. Providers of mobile phone services such as O$_2$, Orange or Vodafone relentlessly offer consumers better deals that include more minutes for a standard fee, free airtime minutes, rollover minutes and low-cost phones to keep them ahead in the mobile market. Service providers pay for numerous television and radio commercials to promote these changes, but lowering prices is not always necessary to increase market share. Table 10.1 illustrates that if a company's product has a competitive advantage, keeping the price at the same level as other firms may satisfy sales objectives.

 ## Profit objectives

As discussed earlier in the book, often a firm's overall objectives relate to a certain level of profit it hopes to realise. When pricing strategies are determined by profit objectives, the focus is on a target level of profit growth or a desired net profit margin. A profit objective is important to firms that believe profit is what motivates shareholders and bankers to invest in a company. Although profits are an important consideration in the pricing of all goods and services, they are critical when the product has a short market life. Fashion garments, for example, have a relatively short market life, making a profit is therefore essential to allow the firm to recover its investment in a short period of time. In such cases,

Table 10.1 Pricing objectives

Type of Objective	Example
Sales or market share	Institute pricing strategy changes to support a 5 per cent increase in sales
Profit	During the first six months, set a price to yield a target profit of €200,000 or set prices to allow for an 8 per cent profit margin on all goods sold
Competitive effect	Alter pricing strategy during first quarter of the year to increase sales during the competitor's introduction of a new product or maintain low end pricing policies to discourage new competitors from entering the market
Customer satisfaction	Simplify pricing structure to simplify decision process for customers or alter price levels to match customer expectations

the firm must achieve profits before customers lose interest and move on to the next fashion or fad.

Competitive effect objectives

Competitive effect objectives mean that the pricing plan is intended to have a certain effect on the competition's marketing efforts. Sometimes a firm may deliberately seek to pre-empt or reduce the effectiveness of one or more competitors. That's what happened when the likes of easyJet entered the European market with low-fare flights. In response, national and former national carriers began to reduce their fares in order to become more competitive on such routes.

Customer satisfaction objectives

Many quality-focused firms believe that profits result from making customer satisfaction the primary objective. These firms believe that by focusing solely on short-term profits a company loses sight of keeping customers for the long term. During the summer period in Dubai (July–August), traditionally a poor season for hotel occupancy due to the excessively hot climate, several of the leading hotel chains have managed to attract European visitors and retain business through providing greater value, and upgrading guests to full board and even club facilities.

Image enhancement objectives

Consumers often use price to make inferences about the quality of a product (see our Internationalisation vignette for an example). In fact, marketers know that price is often an important means of communicating not only quality but also image to prospective customers. The image enhancement function of pricing is particularly important with **prestige products** (or luxury products) that have a high price and appeal to status-conscious consumers. Most of us would agree that the high price tag on a Rolex watch, a Louis

STEP 2: ESTIMATE DEMAND **379**

Internationalisation

KFC and McDonald's in Sri Lanka

Multinational corporations such as the fast food chains KFC and McDonald's are focusing their primary objective on the pricing of their products in Sri Lanka. This is due to Sri Lankan consumers considering the issues surrounding price to be relatively more important than product quality when evaluating goods. As a result, these multinationals are amending their marketing strategies to suit local conditions by emphasising price in their ad campaigns and communication displays.

Discuss, debate, disagree

1 What price should KFC and McDonald's charge in emerging economies?

2 Are there any broader implications associated with such strategies?

Vitton handbag, or a Rolls-Royce car, although representing the higher costs of producing the product, is vital to shaping an image of an extraordinary product with ownership limited to wealthy consumers.

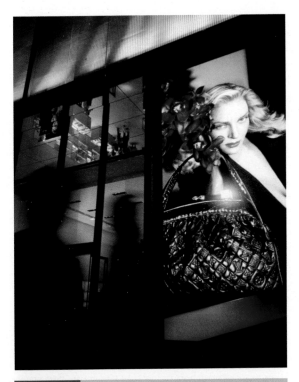

Photo 10.1	People are often willing to pay a premium price for a luxury product because they believe (rightly or wrongly) that it makes a statement about their own worth *Source:* Alamy Images/Lain Masterton

Objective

3

Describe how marketers use costs, demands and revenue to make pricing decisions

Step 2: Estimate demand

The second step in price planning is to estimate demand. *Demand* refers to customers' desires for a product: how much of a product are customers willing to buy as the price goes up or down? Obviously, marketers should know the answer to this question before setting prices. Therefore, one of the earliest steps that marketers take in price planning is to estimate demand for their products.

Demand curves

A graph using a *demand curve* nicely illustrates the effect of price on the quantity demanded of a product. The demand curve, which can be a curve or straight line, shows the quantity of a product that customers will buy in a market during a period of time at various prices if all other factors remain the same. Figure 10.2 shows demand curves for normal and prestige products. The vertical axis for the demand curve represents the different prices that a firm might charge for a product (P). The

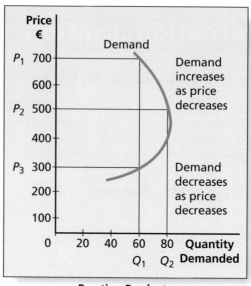

Figure 10.2	Demand curves for normal and prestige products

For normal products, there is an inverse relationship between price and demand. For prestige products, demand will increase – to a point – as price increases or will decrease as price decreases

horizontal axis shows the number of units or quantity (Q) of the product demanded. The demand curve for most goods (shown on the left side of Figure 10.2) slopes downward and to the right. As the price of the product goes up (P_1 to P_2), the number of units that customers are willing to buy goes down (Q_1 to Q_2). If prices decrease, customers will buy more. This is known as the *law of demand*. For example, if the price of bananas goes up, customers will probably buy fewer of them. If the price really goes so high, customers will simply switch to alternatives.

There are, however, exceptions to this typical price–quantity relationship. In fact, there are situations in which people desire a product more as it *increases* in price. For prestige products such as luxury cars or jewellery, an increase in price may actually result in an *increase* in the quantity demanded because consumers see these products as more valuable. In such cases, the demand curve slopes upward. If the price decreases, consumers perceive the product to be less desirable and demand may decrease. The right-hand side of Figure 10.2 shows the 'backward-bending' demand curve associated with prestige products. Still, the higher price/higher demand relationship has its limits. If the firm increases the price too much, making the product unaffordable for all but a few buyers, demand will begin to decrease, as shown by the backward direction taken by the top portion of the backward-bending curve.

 ## Shifts in demand

The demand curves shown assume that all factors other than price stay the same. But what if they don't? What if the product is improved? What happens when there is a trendy new advertising campaign that turns a product into a 'must-have' for a lot of people? What if a paparazzi photographer catches Hugh Grant using the product at home? Any of these things could cause an *upward shift* of the demand curve. An upward shift in the demand curve means that at any given price, demand is greater than before the shift occurs.

Figure 10.3	Shift in demand curve
	Changes in the environment or in company efforts can cause a shift in the demand curve. A great advertising campaign, for example, can shift the demand curve upwards

Figure 10.3 shows the upward shift of the demand curve as it moves from D_1 to D_2. At D_1, before the shift occurs, customers will be willing to purchase the quantity Q_1 (or 80 units in Figure 10.3) at the given price, P (or €60 in Figure 10.3). For example, customers at a particular shop may buy 80 barbecue grills at €60 a grill. Then the shop decides to run a huge advertising campaign, featuring celebrity chef Gordon Ramsay on his patio using the barbecue grill. The demand curve shifts from D_1 to D_2 (the shop keeps the price at €60). Take a look at how the quantity demanded has changed to Q_2. In our example, the shop is now selling 200 barbecue grills at €60 per grill. From a marketing standpoint, this shift is the best of both worlds. Without lowering prices, the company can sell more of its product. As a result, total revenues go up, and unless the new promotion costs as much as the increase in revenues it triggers, so do profits.

Changes in the environment or in company efforts can cause a shift in the demand curve. A great advertising campaign, for example, can shift the demand curve upward. Of course, demand curves may also shift downward. That's what has happened with the demand for first-class airline seats. As companies and families become more concerned about costs, fewer customers buy first-class seats. In response, airlines are offering some first-class tickets at 50 to 70 per cent off the standard rate.[2] In the real world, factors other than the price and marketing activities influence demand. If it rains heavily, the demand for umbrellas increases and the demand for playing golf or tennis declines. The development of new products may also influence demand for old ones. Even though some firms may still produce cassette tapes, the introduction of CDs and MP3s has greatly reduced the demand for vinyl records and turntables to play them on.

Estimating demand

Understanding and estimating demand is extremely important for marketers. First, a firm's production scheduling is based on anticipated demand that must be estimated well in advance of when products are brought to market. In addition, all marketing planning

Table 10.2
Estimating demand
for pizza

Number of families in market	180,000
Average number of pizzas per family per year	6
Total annual market demand	1,080,000
Company's predicted share of the total market	3 per cent
Estimated annual company demand	32,400 pizzas
Estimated monthly company demand	2,700
Estimated weekly company demand	675

and budgeting must be based on reasonably accurate estimates of potential sales. So how do marketers reasonably estimate potential sales? Marketers predict total demand first by identifying the number of buyers or potential buyers for their product and then multiply that estimate by the average amount each member of the target market is likely to purchase. Table 10.2 shows how a small business, such as a start-up pizza restaurant, estimates demand in markets. For example, a pizza entrepreneur may estimate that there are 180,000 consumer households in his market that would be willing to buy his pizza, and that each household will purchase an average of six pizzas a year. The total annual demand is over 1 million pizzas.

Once the marketer estimates total demand, the next step is to predict what the company's market share is likely to be. The company's estimated demand is then its share of the whole (estimated) pie. In our pizza example, the entrepreneur may feel that he can gain 3 per cent of this market, or about 2700 pizzas per month. Of course, such projections need to take into consideration other factors that might affect demand, such as new competitors entering the market, the state of the economy, and changing consumer tastes like a sudden demand for low-carbohydrate take-away food.

 ## The price elasticity of demand

In addition to understanding the relationship between price and demand, marketers also need to know how sensitive customers are to *changes* in price. In particular, it is critical to understand whether a change in price will have a large or a small impact on demand. How much can a firm increase or decrease its price before seeing a marked change in sales? If the price of a pizza goes up €1, will people switch to Chinese or Indian take-aways? What would happen if the pizza went up €2? Or even €5?

Price elasticity of demand is a measure of the sensitivity of customers to changes in price: if the price changes by 10 per cent, what will be the percentage change in demand for the product? The word *elasticity* indicates that changes in price usually cause demand to stretch or retract like a rubber band. Price elasticity of demand is calculated as follows:

$$\text{Price elasticity of demand} = \frac{\text{percentage change in quantity demanded}}{\text{percentage change in price}}$$

Sometimes customers are very sensitive to changes in prices, such a change may result in a substantial change in the quantity demanded. In these instances, we have a case of **elastic demand**. In other situations, such as **inelastic demand**, a change in price tends to have little or no effect on the quantity that consumers are willing to buy. For example, using the

Elastic demand

Price changes from €10 to €9

€10 – 9 = €1

1/10 = 10% change in price

Demand changes from 2,700 per month to 3,100 per month

$$
\begin{array}{r}
3,100 \\
-2,700 \\
\hline
400 \text{ pizzas}
\end{array}
$$

Increase

Percentage increase   400/2,700 = 0.148 ~ 15% change in demand

$$\text{Price elasticity of demand} = \frac{\text{percentage change in quantity demanded}}{\text{percentage change in price}}$$

$$\text{Price elasticity of demand} = \frac{15\%}{10\%} = 1.5$$

Inelastic demand

Price changes from €10 to €9

€10 – 9 = €1

1/10 = 10% change in price

Demand changes from 2,700 per month to 2,835 per month

$$
\begin{array}{r}
2,835 \\
-2,700 \\
\hline
135 \text{ pizzas}
\end{array}
$$

Increase

Percentage increase   135/2,700 = 0.05 ~ 5% change in demand

$$\text{Price elasticity of demand} = \frac{\text{percentage change in quantity demanded}}{\text{percentage change in price}}$$

$$\text{Price elasticity of demand} = \frac{5\%}{10\%} = 0.5$$

Figure 10.4   Price elasticity of demand

formula, suppose the pizza maker finds (from experience or from marketing research) that lowering the price of his pizza 10 per cent (from €10 per pizza to €9) will cause a 15 per cent increase in demand. He would calculate the price elasticity of demand as 15 divided by 10. The price elasticity of demand would be 1.5. If the price elasticity of demand is greater than one, demand is elastic; that is, consumers respond to the price decrease by demanding more. Or, if the price increases, consumers will demand less. Figure 10.4 shows these calculations.

As Figure 10.5 illustrates, when demand is elastic, changes in price and in total revenues (total sales) work in opposite directions. If the price is increased, revenues decrease. If the price is decreased, total revenues increase. With elastic demand, the demand curve shown in Figure 10.5 is more horizontal. With an elasticity of demand of 1.5, a decrease in price will increase the pizza maker's total sales. Price elasticity of demand represents how demand responds to changes in prices. If there is little change in demand, then demand is said to be price inelastic. If there is a large change in demand, demand is price elastic.

As we noted earlier, in some instances demand is *inelastic* so that a change in price results in little or no change in demand. For example, if the 10 per cent decrease in the price of a pizza resulted in only a 5 per cent increase in pizza sales, then the price elasticity

Figure 10.5	Price elastic and inelastic demand curves
	Price elasticity of demand represents how demand responds to changes in prices. If there is little change in demand, then demand is said to be price inelastic. If there is a large change in demand, demand is price elastic.

of demand calculated would be 5 divided by 10, which is 0.5 (less than 1), and our pizza maker faces inelastic demand. When demand is inelastic, price and revenue changes are in the same direction; that is, increases in price result in increases in total revenue, while decreases in price result in decreases in total revenue. With inelastic demand, the demand curve in Figure 10.5 becomes more vertical. Generally, the demand for necessities such as food and electricity is inelastic. Even large price increases do not cause us to buy less food or to give up our lights and hot water.

If demand is price inelastic, can marketers keep raising prices so that revenues and profits will grow larger and larger? What if demand is elastic? Does it mean that marketers can never raise prices? The answer to these questions is no. Elasticity of demand for a product often differs for different price levels and with different percentages of change. As a general rule, pizza makers and other companies can determine the *actual* price elasticity only after they have tested a pricing decision and calculated the resulting demand. Only then will they know whether a specific price change will increase or decrease revenues.

To estimate what demand is likely to be at different prices for new or existing products, marketers often do research. One approach is to conduct a study in which consumers tell marketers how much of a product they would be willing to buy at different prices. For example, researchers might ask participants if they would rent more DVD films if the price was reduced from €4 to €3, or how many bags of their favourite chocolates they would buy at €3, €4 or €5. At other times, researchers conduct *field studies* in which they vary the price of a product in different shops and measure how much is actually purchased at the different price levels.

Other factors can affect price elasticity and sales. Consider the availability of *substitute* goods or services. If a product has a close substitute, its demand will be elastic; that is, a change in price will result in a change in demand, as consumers move to buy the substitute product. For example, Coke and Pepsi may be considered close substitutes. If the price of Pepsi goes up, many people may buy Coke instead. Marketers of products with close substitutes are less likely to compete on price, recognising that doing so could result in less profit as consumers switch from one brand to another. Many consumers are finding that the cost of a mobile phone service is so reasonable that they are now giving up their landlines.

Changes in prices of other products also affect the demand for an item, a phenomenon called **cross-elasticity of demand**. When products are substitutes for each other, an increase in the price of one will increase the demand for the other. For example, if the price of bananas goes up, consumers may instead buy more strawberries, kiwis or apples. However, when products are complements – that is, when one product is essential to the use of a second – an increase in the price of one decreases the demand for the second. For example, if the price of petrol goes up, consumers may drive less or take public transport. As a result, the demand for car tyres will decrease.

Step 3: Determine costs

Estimating demand helps marketers develop possible prices to charge for a product. It tells them how much of the product they think they'll be able to sell at different prices. Knowing this brings them to the third step in determining a product's price: making sure the price will cover costs. Before marketers can determine price, they must understand the relationship of cost, demand and revenue for their product. In this next section, we'll talk about different types of costs that marketers must consider in pricing. Then we'll show two types of analyses that marketers use in making pricing decisions.

Types of cost

It's obvious that the cost of producing a product plays a big role when firms decide what to charge for it. If an item's selling price is lower than the cost to produce, it doesn't take a rocket scientist to figure out that the firm will lose money. Before looking at how costs influence pricing decisions, it is necessary to understand the different types of costs that firms incur.

Marketing misstakes

Outsourcing implications at Primark

The fashion chain Primark has enjoyed healthy sales figures and growth rates despite the recent downturns in the economy. The main reason is due to Primark's successful low pricing strategy. However, many observers question how the company manages to produce its products so cheaply. *Panorama* aired a well-researched and thoughtful documentary of Primark's supply chain, revealing issues on child labour, poor pay and ungoverned home-working. Nearly 20 per cent of the viewers, that is 4.2 million people, tuned in to watch the BBC documentary. As a member of the Ethical Trading Initiative and with a suppliers' charter and auditing programme, Primark appears to place great importance on preventing poor practice. However, it was clear from the documentary that these policies were nowhere near sufficient to prevent abuse. Primark responded by cutting off three offending suppliers immediately and is also liaising with an Indian charity to monitor for signs that its goods are made outside their suppliers' factory.

Why do you think this might be a marketing misstake?

Source: Adapted from www.drapersonline.com/comment/primark-pays-price-for-ethical-blunder/1675975.article

Variable Costs for Producing 100 Bookcases		Variable Costs for Producing 200 Bookcases		Variable Costs for Producing 500 Bookcases	
Wood	€13.25	Wood	€13.25	Wood	€9.40
Nails	0.25	Nails	0.25	Nails	0.20
Paint	0.50	Paint	0.50	Paint	0.40
Labour (3 hours × €12.00 per hr)	€36.00	Labour (3 hours × €12.00 per hr)	€36.00	Labour (2½ hours × €12.00 per hr)	€30.00
Cost per unit	€50.00	Cost per unit	€50.00	Cost per unit	€40.00
Multiply by number of units	100	Multiply by number of units	200	Multiply by number of units	500
Cost for 100 units:	€5,000	Cost for 200 units:	€10,000	Cost for 500 units:	€20,000

One bookcase = one unit.

Figure 10.6   Variable costs at different levels of production

Variable costs

First, a firm incurs **variable costs**; per-unit costs of production that will fluctuate depending on how many units or individual products a firm produces. For example, if it takes 25 cents' worth of nails (a variable cost) to build a single bookcase, it will take 50 cents' worth for two, 75 cents' worth for three and so on. For the production of bookcases, variable costs would also include the cost of timber and paint as well as the salaries factory workers would be paid. Figure 10.6 shows some examples of the variable cost per unit or average variable cost and the total variable costs at different levels of production (for producing 100, 200 and 500 bookcases). If the firm produces 100 bookcases, the average variable cost per unit is €50, and the total variable cost is €5,000 (€50 × 100). If production is doubled to 200 units, the total variable cost now is €10,000 (€50 × 200).

In reality, calculating variable costs is usually more complex than shown here. As the number of bookcases the factory produces increases or decreases, average variable costs may change. For example, if the company buys just enough wood for one bookcase, the timber yard will charge top price. If it buys enough for 100 bookcases, the company gets a better deal. If the company buys enough for thousands of bookcases, it may cut variable costs even more. Even the cost of labour goes down with increased production as manufacturers are likely to invest in labour-saving equipment that allows workers to produce bookcases faster. Figure 10.6 shows this to be the case. By purchasing wood, nails and paint at a lower price (because of volume discount) and by providing a means for workers to build bookcases more quickly, the cost per unit of producing 500 bookcases is reduced to €40 each. Of course, variable costs don't always go down with higher levels of production. Using the bookcase example, at some point the demand for the labour, timber or nails required to produce the bookcases may exceed the supply. The bookcase manufacturer may have to pay employees overtime to keep up with production. The manufacturer may have to buy additional wood from a distant supplier that will charge more to cover the costs of shipping. The cost per bookcase rises.

Fixed costs

Fixed costs are costs that do *not* vary with the number of units produced – the costs that remain the same whether the firm produces 1000 bookcases this month or only 10. Fixed

Marketing ethics and sustainability

Walker's crisps go green

There is a perception that cost of production will be increased if a manufacturer starts delivering a more sustainable product or package; hence, many companies pass on their increase in costs by raising consumer prices. In fact, it is not fair for those customers who are willing to pay a premier price for a more sustainable product or package, because researchers suggest that going green would not necessary increase the cost, particularly if it is implemented correctly.

Walker's crisps, the UK's largest crisps producer, has been representing those companies who receive benefits from both cost reduction and being environmental friendly, whilst keeping the production process sustainable. The question is

how to maintain more or less the same price for customers when the commodity cost has risen sharply at the same time? The answer is going green. The company has been putting a lot of effort into cost-effective production, which also has a positive impact on the environment. For example, it has been setting benchmarks for global crisp production in terms of water consumption, saving nearly 50 per cent of water and 17–18 per cent of other energy during production.

Source: Adapted from 'Walker's Crisps go green', www .themanufacturer.com/uk/detail.html?contents_id=7024

Discuss, debate, disagree

1 How does cost of production have an influence on pricing for Walker's crisps?

2 Is it a 'sustainable' strategy for Walker's to not pass on their costs to customers?

costs include rent or the cost of owning and maintaining the factory, utilities to heat or cool the factory, and the cost of equipment such as hammers, saws and paint sprayers used in the production of the product. While the cost of factory workers to build the bookcases is part of a firm's variable costs, the salaries of a firm's executives and marketing managers are fixed costs. All these costs are constant no matter how many items are manufactured.

Average fixed cost is the fixed cost per unit; the total fixed costs divided by the number of units (bookcases) produced. Although total fixed costs remain the same no matter how many units are produced, the average fixed cost will decrease as the number of units produced increases. Say, for example, that a firm's total fixed costs of production are €300,000. If the firm produces one unit, the total of €300,000 is applied to the one unit. If it produces two units, €150,000, or one-half of the fixed costs, is applied to each unit and so on. As we produce more and more units, average fixed costs go down, and so does the price we must charge to cover fixed costs. Of course, like variable costs, in the long term total fixed costs may change. The firm may find that it can sell more of a product than it has manufacturing capacity to produce, so it builds a new factory, its executives' salaries go up, and more money goes into manufacturing equipment.

Combining variable costs and fixed costs yields **total costs** for a given level of production. As a company produces more and more of a product, both average fixed costs and average variable costs may decrease. Average total costs may decrease, too, up to a point. As explained, as output continues to increase, average variable costs may start to increase. These variable costs ultimately rise faster than average fixed costs decline, resulting in an increase to average total costs. As total costs fluctuate with differing levels of production, the price that producers have to charge to cover those costs changes accordingly. Therefore, marketers need to calculate the minimum price necessary to cover all costs, i.e. the *break-even price*.

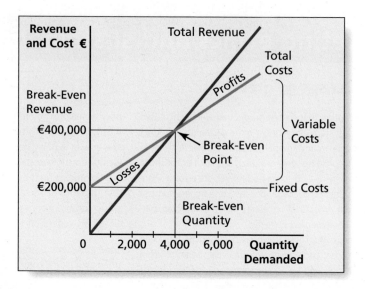

Figure 10.7	Break-even analysis
	Using break-even analysis, marketers can determine what sales volume to reach before the company makes a profit. This company needs to sell 4,000 bookcases at €100 each to break even

Break-even analysis

Break-even analysis is a technique marketers use to examine the relationship between cost and price, and to determine what sales volume must be reached at a given price before the company will completely cover its total costs, so will begin making a profit. Simply put, the **break-even point** is the point at which the company doesn't lose any money and doesn't make any profit. All costs are covered, but there isn't a penny extra. A break-even analysis allows marketers to identify how many units of a product they will have to sell at a given price to exceed the break-even point and be profitable.

Using break-even analysis, marketers can determine what sales volume to reach before the company makes a profit. Figure 10.7 uses our bookcase manufacturing example to demonstrate break-even analysis. The vertical axis represents the amount of costs and revenue in euros, and the horizontal axis shows the quantity of goods produced and sold. In this break-even model, we assume that there is a given total fixed cost and that variable costs do not change with the quantity produced. In this example, let's say that the total fixed costs (the costs for the factory, the equipment, and electricity) are €200,000 and that the average variable costs (for materials and labour) are constant. The figure shows the total costs (variable costs plus fixed costs) and total revenues if varying quantities are produced and sold. The point at which the total revenue and total cost lines intersect is the break-even point. If sales are above the break-even point, the company makes a profit. Below that point, the firm will suffer a loss.

To determine the break-even point, the firm first needs to calculate the **contribution per unit**, or the difference between the price the firm charges for a product (the revenue per unit) and the variable costs. This figure is the amount the firm has after paying for the wood, nails, paint and labour to contribute to meeting the fixed costs of production. For our example, we will assume that the firm sells its bookcases for €100 each. Using the variable costs of €50 per unit that we had before, contribution per unit is €100 − €50

$= €50$. Using the fixed cost for the bookcase manufacturing of €200,000, we can now calculate the firm's break-even point in units of the product:

$$\text{Break-even point (in units)} = \frac{\text{total fixed costs}}{\text{contribution per unit to fixed costs}}$$

$$\text{Break-even point (in units)} = \frac{€200,00}{€50} = 4000 \text{ units}$$

We see that the firm must sell 4000 bookcases at €100 each to meet its fixed costs and to break even. We can also calculate the break-even point in euros. This shows us that to break even the company must sell €400,000 worth of bookcases:

$$\text{Break-even point (in euros)} = \frac{\text{total fixed costs}}{1 - \dfrac{\text{variable cost per unit}}{\text{price}}}$$

$$\text{Break-even point (in euros)} = \frac{€200,00}{1 - \dfrac{€50}{€100}} = \frac{€200,000}{1 - 0.5} = \frac{€200,000}{0.5} = €400,000$$

After the firm's sales have met and passed the break-even point, it begins to make a profit. How much profit? If the firm sells 4001 bookcases, it will make a profit of €50. If it sells 5000 bookcases, we would calculate the profit as follows:

$$\text{Profit} = \text{quantity above break-even point} \times \text{contribution margin}$$
$$= €1000 \times 50$$
$$= €50,000$$

Often a firm will set a *profit goal*, which is the euro profit figure it desires to earn. The break-even point may be calculated with that euro goal included in the figures. In this case, it is not really a 'break-even' point we are calculating because we're seeking profits. It's more of a 'target amount'. If our bookcase manufacturer feels it is necessary to realise a profit of €50,000, the calculations would be as follows:

$$\begin{array}{l}\text{Break-even point (in units} \\ \text{with target profit included)}\end{array} = \frac{\text{total fixed costs} + \text{target profit}}{\text{contribution per unit to fixed costs}}$$

$$\text{Break-even point (in units)} = \frac{€200,000 + 50,000}{€50} = 5000 \text{ units}$$

Sometimes the target return or profit goal is expressed as a *percentage of sales*. For example, a firm may say that it wants to make a profit of at least 10 per cent on sales. In such cases, this profit is added to the variable cost in calculating the break-even point. In our example, the company would want to earn 10 per cent of the selling price of the bookcase, or 10 per cent $\times$ €100 = €10 per unit. We would simply add this €10 to the variable costs of €50 and calculate the new target amount as we calculated the break-even point before.

$$\text{Contribution per unit} = \text{selling price} - (\text{variable costs} + \text{target profit})$$
$$= €100 - (€50 + €10) = €40$$

$$\text{Break-even point (in units)} = \frac{\text{total fixed costs}}{\text{contribution per unit to fixed costs}}$$

$$\text{Break-even point (in units)} = \frac{€200,000}{€40} = 5000 \text{ units}$$

Break-even analysis does not provide an easy answer for pricing decisions. It provides answers about how many units the firm must sell to break even and to make a profit, but without knowing whether demand will equal that quantity at that price, companies can

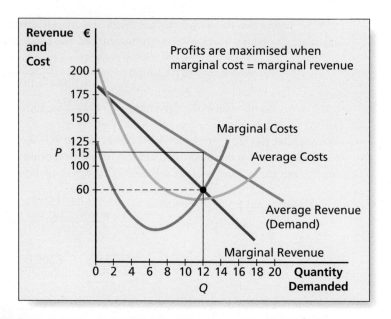

Figure 10.8	Marginal analysis
	Marginal analysis allows marketers to consider both costs and demand in calculating a price that maximises profits

make big mistakes. It is therefore useful for marketers to estimate the demand for their product and then perform a marginal analysis.

Marginal analysis

Marginal analysis provides a way for marketers to look at cost and demand at the same time and to identify the output and the price that will generate the maximum profit. Figure 10.8 shows the various cost and revenue elements considered in marginal analysis. Like Figure 10.7, the vertical axis in Figure 10.8 represents the cost and revenues in euros, and the horizontal axis shows the quantity produced and sold. Figure 10.8 shows the average revenue, average cost, marginal revenue and marginal cost curves. When doing a marginal analysis, marketers examine the relationship of **marginal cost** – the increase in total costs from producing one additional unit of a product – to **marginal revenue** – the increase in total income or revenue that results from selling one additional unit of a product. Average revenue is also the demand curve and thus represents that amount customers will buy at different prices – people buy more only if price and thus revenue decrease. Thus, both average revenue and marginal revenue decrease with each additional unit sold. Marginal analysis allows marketers to consider both costs and demand in calculating a price that maximises profits.

If the manufacturer produces only one bookcase, the average total cost per unit is the same as the marginal cost per unit. After the first unit, the cost of *producing each additional unit* (marginal cost) and the average cost at first decrease. Eventually, however, both marginal costs and average costs begin to increase since, as we discussed earlier, both average fixed costs and average variable costs may increase in the long term. Profit is maximised at the point at which marginal cost is *exactly* equal to marginal revenue. At that point, the cost of producing one unit is exactly equal to the revenue to be realised from selling that one unit. If, however, one additional unit is produced, the cost of producing that unit is *greater than* the revenue from the sale of the unit, and total profit actually begins to decrease. So it makes sense for firms to keep production and sales at the point of maximum profit.

One word of caution when using marginal analysis: although in theory the procedure is straightforward, in the real world things seldom are. Production costs may vary unexpectedly because of shortages, inclement weather, unexpected equipment repairs and so on. Revenues may also unexpectedly move up and down because of the economy, what the competition is doing or a number of other reasons. Predicting demand, an important factor in marginal analysis, is never an exact science. This makes marginal analysis a less than perfect way to determine the best price for a product. Indeed, it is theoretically sounder than break-even analysis, but most firms find the break-even approach more useful.

Step 4: Evaluate the pricing environment

Objective

4

Understand some of the environmental factors that affect pricing strategies

In addition to demand and costs, marketers look at factors in the firm's external environment when they make pricing decisions. Thus, the fourth step in developing pricing strategies is to examine and evaluate the pricing environment. Only then can marketers set a price that not only covers costs but also provides a competitive advantage, i.e. a price that meets the needs of customers better than the competition. This section will discuss some important external influences on pricing strategies, the economic environment, competition and consumer trends.

 ## The economy

Broad economic trends, like those we discussed earlier in the book, tend to direct pricing strategies. The business cycle, inflation, economic growth and consumer confidence all help

Marketing in recession

easyJet

As the recession hits, consumers are more price-conscious but still would like the luxury of going on holiday. Cheaper airlines such as easyJet are surviving the recession and hitting their profit targets. Former CEO Andy Harrison revealed the profits earned for the year 2009 came up to an amazing £43.7 million before tax, making easyJet amongst very few other airlines to record profit during these testing times. The formula of success, according to Andy, was their great value offering which includes great prices to the most convenient airports. easyJet has stuck to its core values, which allowed it to do well during the recession and, as business picks up in the country, it will see many further improvements which will lead to even greater profits.

In response to a question on fluctuating oil prices, he added that easyJet's hedging is a form of averaging, which means that fuel prices respond with a lag to movement in market prices. easyJet continues to grow steadily and passenger numbers grew by 3 to 4 per cent during the recessionary period. The company remains focused on short-haul flights, which are working as it seems to be in line with achieving healthy growth of 7 to 8 per cent annually. Passenger growth easily outstripped easyJet's capacity increase over the recessionary period of just 0.8 per cent, indicating that demand is still matching its growth strategy despite the European-wide recession. Gert Zonneveld, analyst at Panmure Gordon, said easyJet had weathered the recession so far but a lengthy downturn could dampen the airline's recovery. 'The company is performing well given the current economic environment, but a sustained downturn could clearly delay a profit recovery.'

Debate, discuss, disagree

1. Is price the main factor that affects easyJet's sales revenue?

2. What other strategies could easyJet adopt to increase sales?

www.guardian.co.uk/business/2009/may/06/easyjet-weathers-recession-but-losses-widen
www.centreforaviation.com/news/2009/11/19/easyjet-sees-large-profitability-decline-but-improvements-ahead/page1
www.quicklogodesign.com/blog/impact-of-recession-on-uk-low-cost-airline-industry

Photo 10.2 When the economy is weak, consumers are more interested in paying lower prices – and they're more sceptical about high-priced status symbols
Source: Alamy Images/geophoto

to determine whether one pricing strategy or another will succeed. The upswings and downturns in a national economy do not affect all product categories or all regions equally. Marketers need to understand how economic trends will affect their particular business. During *recession*, consumers become more price-sensitive. They switch brands to get a better price and seek discount stores and warehouse outlets. Even wealthy households, relatively unaffected by the recession, tend to cut back on conspicuous consumption. As a result, during periods of recession, many firms find it necessary to cut prices to levels at which costs are covered but the company doesn't make a profit to keep factories in operation.

There are also some economic trends that allow firms to increase prices, altering what consumers see as an acceptable or unacceptable price range for a product. Inflation may give marketers cause to either increase or decrease prices. First, inflation gets customers used to price increases. Customers may remain insensitive to price increases even when inflation goes away, allowing marketers to make real price increases, not just those that adjust for inflation. Of course, during periods of inflation consumers may grow fearful of the future and worry about whether they will have enough money to meet basic needs. In such a case, they may cut back on purchases. Then, as in periods of recession, inflation may cause marketers to lower prices and temporarily sacrifice profits to maintain sales levels.

 ## The competition

Marketers try to anticipate how the competition will respond to their pricing actions. They know that consumers' expectations of what constitutes a fair price largely depend on what the competition is charging. However, it's not always a good idea to fight the competition with lower and lower prices. Price wars such as those in the fast-food industry can change consumers' perceptions of what is a 'fair' price, leaving them unwilling to buy at previous price levels.

Most industries, such as airlines, restaurants and hotels, consist of a number of firms. These firms can belong to one of three industry structures – an oligopoly, monopolistic competition or pure competition. Which industry structure a firm belongs to will influence price decisions. Generally, firms like the airline KLM that do business in an oligopoly, in which the market has few sellers and many buyers, are more likely to adopt status quo pricing objectives in which the pricing of all competitors is similar. Such objectives are attractive to oligopolistic firms because avoiding price competition allows all players in the industry to remain profitable.

In a business like the restaurant industry that is characterised by monopolistic competition in which there are a lot of sellers, each offering a slightly different product, it is possible for firms to differentiate products and to focus on non-price competition. Each firm can therefore price its product on the basis of its cost without much concern for matching the exact price of competitors' products. Consumers don't necessarily have the time to shop and study the price of a burger at McDonald's versus Burger King before deciding which outlet to use. Providers of commodity goods like wheat farmers in a purely competitive market have little opportunity to raise or lower prices. Rather, the price of wheat, corn or fresh peaches is directly influenced by supply and demand. When bad weather decreases the supply of crops, prices go up and the price for almost any kind of fish has increased dramatically since health-conscious consumers began turning away from beef and other red meat.

Consumer trends

Another environmental influence on price is consumer trends. Culture and demographics determine how consumers think and behave and so have a great impact on all marketing decisions. Take, for example, the purchasing habits of women who opted for a career in their 20s, but now are hearing the ticking of their biological clocks as they enter their late 30s and 40s. Couples having babies later in their lives are often better off financially than younger parents, and on average they will have fewer children to spoil, so they are more willing to spend whatever it costs to give their babies the best. Another important trend is that even well-off people no longer consider it shameful to hunt for bargains – particularly in today's economic climate. As a marketing executive for a chain of shopping centres observed, 'Everybody loves to save money. It's a badge of honour today.' Luxury consumers are looking for prestigious brands at low prices, though they're still willing to splash out on some high-priced items. Industry analysts have called this new interest in hunting for sales 'strategic shopping'.[3]

Step 5: Choose a price strategy

Objective

5

Understand pricing strategies

An old Russian proverb says, 'There are two kinds of fools in any market. One doesn't charge enough. The other charges too much.'[4] In modern business, there is seldom any one-and-only, now-and-forever, best pricing strategy. Like playing a chess game, making pricing moves and countermoves requires thinking two and three moves ahead. The next step in price planning is to choose a price strategy. Some strategies work for certain products, with certain customer groups, in certain competitive markets. When is it best for the firm to undercut the competition and when is it best to just match the competition's prices? When is the best pricing strategy one that covers costs only and when is it best to use one based on demand?

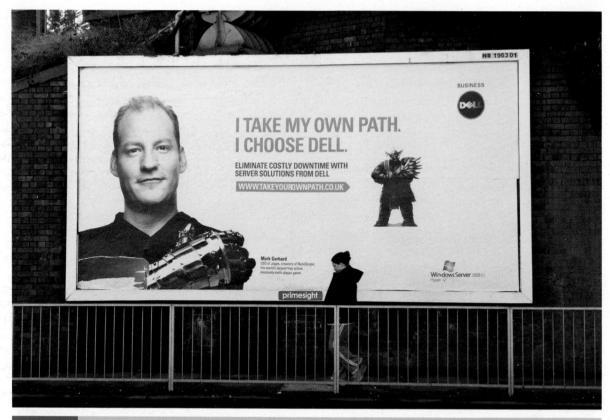

| Photo 10.3 | Dell competes on price by allowing its customers to customise their computer systems to match their budgets |

Source: Alamy Images/Jeff Morgan 10

 ## Pricing strategies based on cost

Marketing planners often choose cost-based strategies because they are simple to calculate and relatively risk free. They promise that the price will at least cover the costs the company incurs in producing and marketing the product. Cost-based pricing methods have drawbacks, however. For example, they do not consider such factors as the nature of the target market, demand, competition, the product life cycle and the product's image. Moreover, although the calculations for setting the price may be simple and straightforward, accurate cost estimating may prove difficult. Think about firms such as 3M, Nestlé and Heinz, all of which produce many products. How do financial analysts or accountants allocate the costs for the plant, research and development, equipment, design engineers, maintenance and marketing personnel so that the pricing plan accurately reflects the cost of producing any one product? For example, how do you allocate the salary of a marketing executive who oversees many different products? Should the cost be divided equally among all products? Should costs be based on the actual number of hours spent working on each product? Or should costs be assigned based on the revenues generated by each product? There is no one right answer. Even within these limitations, cost-based pricing strategies may often be a marketer's best choice.

The most common cost-based approach to pricing a product is **cost-plus pricing**, in which the marketer totals all the costs for the product and then adds an amount (or marks up the cost of the item) to arrive at the selling price. Many marketers, especially retailers and wholesalers, use cost-plus pricing because of its simplicity (users need only estimate the unit cost and add the mark-up). To calculate cost-plus pricing, marketers usually calculate either a mark-up on cost or a mark-up on selling price. With both methods, you calculate the price by adding a predetermined percentage to the cost, but as the names of the methods imply, for one the calculation uses a percentage of the costs and for the other a percentage of the selling price. Which of the two methods is used seems often to be little more than a matter of 'the way our company has always done it'.

Pricing strategies based on demand

Demand-based pricing means that the selling price is based on an estimate of volume or quantity that a firm can sell in different markets at different prices. To use any of the pricing strategies based on demand, firms must determine how much product they can sell in each market and at what price. As we noted earlier, marketers often use customer surveys where consumers indicate whether they would buy a certain product and how much of it they would buy at various prices. More accurate estimates may be obtained by some type of field experiment. For example, a firm might actually offer the product at different price levels in different test markets and gauge the reaction. Two specific demand-based pricing strategies are target costing and yield management pricing. Let's take a quick look at each approach.

Today, firms are finding that they can be more successful if they match price with demand using a process called **target costing**.[5] A firm first determines the price at which customers would be willing to buy the product and then works backward to design the product in such a way that it can produce and sell the product at a profit. With target costing, firms first use marketing research to identify the quality and functionality needed to satisfy attractive market segments and what price they are willing to pay *before the product is designed*. As Figure 10.9 shows, the next step is to determine what margins retailers and dealers require as well as the profit margin the company requires. On the basis of this information, managers can calculate the target cost, i.e. the maximum it will cost the firm to manufacture the product. If the firm

---

Step 1: Determine the price customers are willing to pay for the jeans
   €39.99

Step 2: Determine the markup required by the retailer
   40% (0.40)

Step 3: Calculate the maximum price the retailer will pay, the price customers are willing to pay minus the markup amount

   Formula: Price to the retailer = Selling price × (1.00 − markup percentage)
      Price to the retailer =   €39.99   × (1.00 − 0.40)
               =   €39.99   × 0.60 =   **€23.99**

Step 4: Determine the profit required by the firm
   15% (0.15)

Step 5: Calculate the target cost, the maximum cost of producing the jeans
      Formula: Target cost = Price to the retailer × (1.00 − profit percentage)
         Target cost = €23.99 × 0.85 =   **€20.39**

Figure 10.9	Target costing using a jeans example
	With target costing, a firm first determines the price at which customers would be willing to buy the product and then works backward to design the product in such a way that it can produce and sell the product at a profit

can meet customer quality and functionality requirements and control costs to meet the required price, it will manufacture the product. If not, it abandons the product.

Yield management pricing is another type of demand-based pricing strategy that hospitality companies like airlines, hotels and cruise lines use. These businesses charge different prices to different customers in order to manage capacity while maximising revenues. Many service firms practise yield management pricing because they recognise that different customers have different sensitivities to price. Some customers don't mind paying a standard price for an airline ticket, while others will travel only if there is a discount available. The goal of yield management pricing is to accurately predict the proportion of customers who fall into each category and allocate the percentages of the airline's or hotel's capacity accordingly so that no product goes unsold.

For example, an airline may charge two prices for the same seat: the full fare (€899) and the discount fare (€299). The airline must predict how many seats it can fill at full fare and how many can be sold only at the discounted fare. The airline begins months ahead of the date of the flight with a basic allocation of seats – perhaps it will place 25 per cent in the full-fare 'bucket' and 75 per cent in the discount-fare 'bucket'. While it can't sell the seats in the full-fare bucket at the discounted price, the airline may be able to sell the seats it allocated at the discounted price for the full fare if it's lucky. As the flight time gets closer, the airline might make a series of adjustments to the allocation of seats in the hope of selling every seat on the plane at the highest price possible. If the Barcelona football team needs to book the flight, the chances are some of the discount seats will be sold at full fare (the journalists will be happy to pay) – decreasing the number available at the discounted price. If, as the flight date nears, the number of full-fare ticket sales falls below the forecast, some of those seats may be moved to the discount bucket. This process continues until the day of the flight as the airline attempts to have every seat filled when the plane takes off. This is why you may be able to get a fantastic price on a late charter flight from say London Gatwick to Alicante or Malaga.

Pricing strategies based on the competition

Sometimes a firm's pricing strategy may be near to, at, above or below the competition. For many years, Esso for example operated a 'price watch' campaign on its petrol pump prices. It simply announced its prices and other players more or less fell into line. A **price leadership** strategy, which usually is the rule in an oligopolistic industry dominated by a few firms, may be in the best interest of all players because it minimises price competition. Price leadership strategies are popular because they provide an acceptable and legal way for firms to agree on prices without ever talking with each other.

Pricing strategies based on customers' needs

When firms develop pricing strategies that cater to customers, they are less concerned with short-term results than with keeping customers for the long term. New Era firms constantly assess customers' responses in developing pricing strategies. O₂, for example, negotiates with its business customers in an attempt to determine the best package of air time and features available. Firms that practise **value pricing** or **everyday low pricing (EDLP)**, develop a pricing strategy that promises ultimate value to consumers. What this really means is that, in the customers' eyes, the price is justified by what they receive.[6] Northern European retailer Netto views everyday low pricing as being a fundamental part of the company's success. The company seeks to buy branded goods at low prices, with the aim of passing on such savings to its customers.

When firms base price strategies solely or mainly on cost, they are operating under the old production orientation that we discussed in Chapter 1, rather than with a marketing orientation. Value-based pricing begins with customers, then considers the competition, and then determines the best pricing strategy. Changing pricing strategies at Procter & Gamble (P&G) in recent years illustrate value pricing in action. Until about a decade ago, P&G watched as sales volume dropped for its Charmin toilet tissue, Dawn dishwashing liquid, Pringles potato crisps and many other well-established brands. More and more shoppers were buying whatever brand was on sale or had a special promotion offer. To rebuild loyalty, P&G switched to an EDLP strategy. The company reduced everyday prices 12 to 24 per cent by cutting the amount it spent on trade promotions. P&G said, in effect, 'This really *is* our best price, and it's good value for the money. Buy now. There will be no sale next week. We won't do business that way.'

 ## New product pricing

As discussed earlier, new products are vital to the growth and profits of a firm, but they also present unique pricing challenges. When a product is new to the market or when there is no established industry price norm, marketers may use a skimming price strategy, a penetration pricing strategy or trial pricing when they first introduce the item to the market. Setting a **skimming price** means that the firm charges a high, premium price for its new product with the intention of reducing it in the future in response to market pressures. For example, when Top-Flite introduced its Strata golf balls with a dimple design and more solid core for better flight with metal clubs, the price was three times that of regular balls. Pro shops still couldn't keep them in stock.[7]

If a product is highly desirable and it offers unique benefits, demand is price inelastic during the introductory stage of the product life cycle, allowing a company to recover R&D and promotional costs. When rival products enter the market, the price is lowered in order for the firm to remain competitive. Firms focusing on profit objectives in developing their pricing strategies often set skimming prices for new products. A skimming price is more likely to succeed if the product provides some important benefits to the target market that make customers feel they must have it no matter what the cost. Handheld calculators were such a product when they were introduced in the late 1960s. To the total astonishment of consumers at that time, these magic little devices could add, subtract, multiply and divide with just the push of a button. It's equally hard for consumers today to believe that back then they sold for as much as €200 equivalent.

Second, for skimming pricing to be successful, there should be little chance that competitors can get into the market quickly. With highly complex, technical products, it may be quite a while before competitors can put a rival product into production. Finally, a skimming pricing strategy is most successful when the market consists of several customer segments with different levels of price sensitivity. There must be a substantial number of initial product customers who have very low price sensitivity. After a period of time, the price can go down, and a second segment of the market with a slightly higher level of price sensitivity will purchase and so on.

Penetration pricing is just the opposite of skimming. This strategy means that a new product is priced very low in order to sell more in a short period of time, thus gaining market share early on. One reason marketers use penetration pricing is to discourage competitors from entering the market. The firm first out with a new product has an important advantage. Experience shows that a pioneering brand is often able to maintain dominant market share for long periods of time. Penetration pricing may act as a *barrier to entry* for competitors if the prices the market will bear are so low that the company will not be able to recover development and manufacturing costs. Hoover (vacuum cleaners) is an example of a brand that was first to the market decades ago and still competes strongly today.

Real people, other voices

Tao Jiang

Senior Teaching Fellow, Marketing Division, Leeds University Business School

Personally, I would consider the following before making the final decision:

1. The industry: we need to acknowledge the fact that Blundells Estate Agents is a service provider, and by definition the best way for Mr Blundell to compete is to provide high quality services to his customers.

2. The competition: the case study mentioned that this is a 'sexy' market with many competitors, some of whom are national players that can easily match Mr Blundell's pricing strategies, especially where Option 1 and Option 2 are concerned. If that happened, Mr Blundell would find himself in a 'price war' against his competitors as a result of which end users (including both sellers and buyers) may well benefit while there could be a no-win situation for the service providers, i.e. the estate agents, including Mr Blundell.

3. Consumer perception: both Option 1 and Option 2 would risk a negative consumer perception towards Blundells Estate Agents which should be avoided at all costs for the obvious reason: it only takes one unhappy/unsatisfied customer to damage the reputation of a business, especially a well-known business with 34 years' history in the region.

4. The company: Blundells Estate Agents is a family-owned business which has the potential to minimise its internal operation costs faster than its competitors when necessary, e.g. Mr Blundells' daughter is a qualified valuer who can give credible valuation to properties and oversee the valuation process while incurring no extra costs to the company.

Taking the above into consideration, I personally would go for Option 3 because a realistic and fair valuation would create a positive image of Blundells Estate Agents, plus a well-established knowledgeable local agent would give consumers the confidence and trust they need from an estate agent.

Trial pricing means that a new product carries a low price for a limited period of time to generate a high level of customer interest. Unlike penetration pricing, in which the low price is maintained, the trial price is increased after the introductory period. The idea is to win customer acceptance first and make profits later, as when a new health club offers an introductory membership to start pulling people in. Marketers aim to lure customers to try the product at the lower price and then if they're impressed will consume at normal prices as well as persuade others to buy at the full price.

Step 6: Develop pricing tactics

www.pearsoned.co.uk/Solomon

Once marketers have developed pricing strategies, the last step in price planning is to implement them. The methods companies use to set their strategies in motion are their *pricing tactics*.

Pricing for individual products

Once marketers have settled on a product's price, the way they present it to the market can make a big difference. Here are two tactics with examples of each:

- *Two-part pricing* requires two separate types of payments to purchase the product. For example, golf and tennis clubs may charge yearly or monthly fees plus fees for each round of golf or game of tennis. Likewise, mobile phone service providers offer customers a set number of minutes for a monthly fee plus a per-minute rate for extra usage.

- *Payment pricing* makes the consumer think the price is 'do-able'[8] by breaking up the total price into smaller amounts payable over time. For example, many customers now opt to lease rather than buy a car. The monthly lease amount is an example of payment pricing, which tends to make people less sensitive to the total price of the car.[9]

Pricing for multiple products

A firm may sell several products that consumers typically buy at one time. A fast-food restaurant selling food for lunch usually invites the purchase of a soft drink and maybe a dessert as well. The sale of a paper-cup dispenser usually means a package of cups is not far behind. The two most common tactics for pricing multiple products are price bundling and captive pricing.

Price bundling means selling two or more goods or services as a single package for one price. A music follower can buy tickets to an entire concert series for a single price. A PC typically comes bundled with a monitor, a keyboard and software. Even an all you can eat special at the local Chinese restaurant is an example of price bundling. Phone service companies such as Talk-Talk Telecom offer customers unlimited national and European phone calls plus broadband for a flat monthly fee. From a marketing standpoint, price bundling makes sense. If products are priced separately, then it is likely that customers will buy some but not all the items. They might choose to put off some purchases until later, or they might buy from a competitor. Whatever revenue a seller loses from the reduced prices it makes up in increased total purchases.

Captive pricing is a pricing tactic a firm uses when it has two products that work only when used together. The firm sells one item at a very low price and then makes its profit on the second high-margin item. This tactic is commonly used to sell shaving products. The razor is relatively cheap, but the replacement blades are expensive. Similarly, some digital printers are marketed at almost giveaway prices – the aim being to entice you to purchase the manufacturer's refill cartridges.

Distribution-based pricing

Distribution-based pricing is a pricing tactic that establishes how firms handle the cost of shipping products to customers near, far and wide. Characteristics of the product, the customers and the competition figure in the decision to charge all customers the same price or to vary according to shipping cost. Often a price is given as FOB factory or FOB delivered. FOB stands for 'free on board', which means the supplier will pay to have the product loaded onto a truck or some other carrier. Also – and this is important – *title passes to the buyer* at the FOB location. FOB factory or **FOB origin pricing** means that the cost of transporting the product from the factory to the customer's location is the responsibility of the customer. **FOB delivered pricing** means that the seller pays both the cost of loading and the cost of transporting to the customer, which is included in the selling price. Delivery terms for pricing of products sold in international markets are especially important. Some of the more common terms used include the following:[10]

- *CIF* (cost, insurance, freight) is the term used for ocean shipments and means the seller quotes a price for the goods (including insurance), all transportation and miscellaneous charges to the point of debarkation from the vessel.

- *CFR* (cost and freight) means the quoted price covers the goods and the cost of transportation to the named point of debarkation but the buyer must pay the cost of insurance. The CFR term is typically used only for ocean shipments.

- *CIP* (carriage and insurance paid to) and *CPT* (carriage paid to) include the same provisions as CIF and CFR but are used for shipment by modes other than water.

Another distribution pricing tactic, **base-point pricing**, means marketers choose one or more locations to serve as base points. Customers pay shipping charges from these base points to their delivery destinations whether the goods are actually shipped from these points or not. For example, a customer in Lille (Northern France) may order a product from a company in Geneva (Switzerland). The product is shipped to Lille from the Brussels warehouse. However, if the designated base point is Paris, the customer pays transport charges from Paris to Lille – charges that were never incurred by the seller.

When a firm uses **uniform delivered pricing**, it adds an average shipping cost to the price, no matter what the distance from the manufacturer's plant – within reason. For example, when you order a CD from a music supplier, you may pay the cost of the CD plus €2.99 shipping and handling, no matter what the actual cost of the shipping to your particular location. Internet sales, catalogue sales, home television shopping and other types of non-store retail sales usually use uniform delivered pricing.

Freight absorption pricing means the seller takes on part or all of the cost of shipping. This policy works well for high-ticket items when the cost of shipping is a negligible part of the sales price and the profit margin. Marketers are most likely to use freight absorption pricing in highly competitive markets or when such pricing allows them to enter new markets.

 ## Discounting for channel members

So far we've talked about pricing tactics used to sell to end customers. Now we'll talk about tactics used for pricing to members of the channel of distribution. Whether a firm sells to businesses or directly to consumers, most pricing structures are built around list prices. A **list price**, also referred to as a *recommended retail price (RRP)*, is the price that the manufacturer sets as the appropriate price for the end consumer to pay. In pricing for members of the channel, marketers recognise that retailers and wholesalers have costs to cover and profit targets to reach as well. Thus, they often begin with the list price and then use a number of discounting tactics to implement pricing to members of the channel of distribution, i.e. wholesalers, distributors and retailers. Such tactics include the following:

- **Trade or functional discounts:** Because the channel members perform selling, credit, storage and transportation services that the manufacturer would otherwise have to provide, manufacturers often offer **trade or functional discounts**, usually set percentage discounts off list price for each channel level.

- **Quantity discounts:** To encourage larger purchases from distribution channel partners or from large organisational customers, marketers may use **quantity discounts**, or reduced prices for purchases of larger quantities. *Cumulative quantity discounts* are based on a total quantity bought within a specified time period, often a year, and encourage a buyer to stick with a single seller instead of moving from one supplier to another. Cumulative quantity discounts may be in the form of *rebates*, in which case the firm sends the buyer a rebate cheque at the end of the discount period or a credit against future orders. *Non-cumulative quantity discounts* are based only on the quantity purchased with each individual order and encourage larger single orders but do little to tie the buyer and the seller together.

- **Cash discounts:** Many firms try to entice their customers to pay their bills quickly by offering cash discounts. For example, a firm selling to a retailer may state that the terms of the sale are '2 percent 10 days, net 30 days', meaning that if the retailer pays the producer for the goods within 10 days, the amount due is cut by 2 per cent. The total amount is due within 30 days, and after 30 days the payment is late.

- **Seasonal discounts:** *Seasonal discounts* are price reductions offered only during certain times of the year. For seasonal products such as garden furniture or lawn mowers, marketers use seasonal discounts to entice retailers and wholesalers to buy off-season and either store the product at their locations until the right time of the year or pass the discount along to consumers with off-season sales programmes. Alternatively, discounts may be offered when products are in season to create a competitive advantage during periods of high demand.

Pricing and electronic commerce

Objective

7

Understand the opportunities for online pricing strategies

As we have seen, pricing for 'bricks-and-mortar' firms is a complex decision process. But our e-commerce world creates even more options. Because sellers are connected to buyers around the globe as never before through the internet, company networks and wireless setups, marketers can offer deals tailored to a single person at a single moment.[11] On the other hand, they're also a lot more vulnerable to smart consumers who can easily check out competing prices at the click of a mouse.

For firms that want to sell to other businesses (B2B firms), the web means that they can change prices rapidly to adapt to changing costs. For consumers who have lots of stuff in the attic they need to put in someone else's attic (C2C e-commerce), the internet means an opportunity for consumers to find ready buyers. Finally, for B2C firms, firms that sell to consumers, the internet offers other opportunities. In this section, we will discuss some of the more popular web online pricing strategies.

Dynamic pricing strategies

One of the most important opportunities the internet offers is **dynamic pricing**, where the seller can easily adjust the price to meet changes in the marketplace. If a retailer wants to change prices, employees/workers must place new price tags on items, create and display new display signage and media advertising, and input new prices into the retailer's computer system. For business-to-business marketers, employees/workers must print catalogues and price lists and distribute them to salespeople and customers. These activities can be very costly to a firm, so they don't want to change their prices too often. Because the cost of changing prices on the web is so low, firms are able to respond quickly, and if necessary frequently, to changes in costs, in supply and/or in demand. For example, Lastminute.com periodically adjusts the price of flights and hotels on the basis of supply and demand so that a five-star hotel in London might cost more or less depending on which day you log on to buy it.

Auctions

Hundreds of **online auctions** allow shoppers to bid on everything from golf clubs to health-and-fitness equipment to children's toys. Auctions provide a second internet pricing strategy. Perhaps the most popular auctions are the C2C auctions such as those on eBay. The eBay auction is an *open auction*, meaning that all the buyers know the highest price bid at any point in time. In many auction websites, the seller can set a *reserve price*, a price below which the item will not be sold.

Pricing advantages for online shoppers

The web also creates unique pricing challenges for marketers because consumers and business customers are gaining more control over the buying process. With the availability of search engines, they are no longer at the mercy of firms that dictate a price they must accept. The result is that customers have become more price sensitive. For example, on-line pharmacies have been stealing customers from traditional chemists by offering much lower prices. Detailed information about what products actually cost manufacturers, available from sites such as Consumerreports.org, can give consumers more negotiating power when shopping for new cars and other high price items. Finally, e-commerce potentially can lower consumers' costs because of the time and hassle associated with a trip to the shops or supermarket.

Psychological issues in pricing

Objective

8

Describe the psychological, legal and ethical aspects of pricing

Much of what we've said about pricing depends on economists' notions of a customer who evaluates price in a logical, rational manner. For example, the concept of demand is expressed by a smooth demand curve, which assumes that if a firm lowers a product's price from €10 to €9.50 and then from €9.50 to €9 and so on, then customers will simply buy more and more. In the real world, though, it doesn't always work that way. Let's look at some psychological factors that keep those economists up at night.

Buyers' pricing expectation

Often consumers base their perceptions of price on what they perceive to be the customary or *fair price*. For example, in the mid-1970s for many years a chocolate bar or a pack of chewing gum in the UK was priced at 5p. Consumers would have perceived any other price as too high or low. So when costs went up and inflation kicked in, some confectionary suppliers tried to reduce the size of the bar instead of changing the price. Eventually, inflation prevailed, consumers' salaries rose, and so did the price. When the price of a product is above or even sometimes when it's below what consumers expect, they are less willing to purchase the product. If the price is above their expectations, they may think of it as a rip-off. If it is below expectations, consumers may think quality is below par. By understanding the pricing expectations of their customers, marketers are able to develop better viable pricing strategies.

Internal reference prices

Sometimes consumers' perceptions of the customary price of a product depend on their **internal reference price**. That is, based on past experience, consumers have a set price or a price range in mind that they refer to in evaluating a product's cost. The reference price may be the last price paid, or it may be the average of all the prices they know of similar products. In the early 1990s, no matter which Parisian bakery you visited, the cost of a baguette would be 4 francs. In some hypermarkets it might have been 3.75FF, and in plush bakeries 4.25FF, but the average was 4FF. If consumers found a baguette priced much higher than this, say at 5FF, then they would feel it was overpriced and not buy. If they found it significantly lower, at say 2.50FF or 3FF, they might shy away from the purchase, wondering 'what is wrong' with the baguette.

In some cases, marketers try to influence consumers' expectations of what a product should cost by employing reference pricing strategies. For example, manufacturers may show their price compared with competitors' prices in advertising. Similarly, a retailer will display a product next to a higher priced version of the same or a different brand. The consumer must choose between the two products with different prices. Two results are likely. On the one hand, if the prices (and other characteristics) of the two products are fairly close, the consumer will probably feel the product quality is similar. This is called an *assimilation effect*. The customer might think, 'The price is about the same, they must be alike. I'll be smart and save a few euros' – so the customer chooses the item that is priced lower because the low price made it look attractive next to the higher priced alternative. This is why shop brands of deodorants, vitamins, pain relief tablets and shampoos sit beside national brands, often accompanied by a shelf display pointing out how much shoppers can save by purchasing the retailer's own label brand. On the other hand, if the prices of the two products are too far apart, a *contrast effect* may result, in which the customer equates it with a big difference in quality. 'This lower-priced one is probably not as good as the higher-priced one. I'll buy the more expensive one.' Using this strategy, an appliance store may place an advertised €300 refrigerator next to a €699 model to convince a customer the bottom-of-the-line model just won't do.

Price/quality inferences

Imagine that you are in a shoe shop looking for a pair of running shoes. You notice one pair that is priced at €89.99. On another aisle you see a second pair looking almost identical to the first pair but priced at only €24.95. Which pair do you want? Which pair do you think is the better quality? Many of us will pay the higher price because we believe the bargain-basement shoes aren't worth the risk at any price. Consumers make *price–quality inferences* about a product when they use price as a cue or an indicator of quality (an inference means we believe something to be true without any direct evidence). If consumers are unable to judge the quality of a product through examination or experience, they usually will assume that the higher priced product is the higher quality product.

Psychological pricing strategies

Setting a price is part science, part art. Psychological aspects of price are important for marketers to understand in making pricing decisions.

Odd–even pricing

In Europe, we usually see prices in euros and cents – €1.99, €5.98, €23.67 or even €599.95. We see prices in even euro amounts – €2, €10, or €600 – far less often. The reason? Marketers assume that there is a psychological response to odd prices that differs from the responses to even prices. Habit might also play a role here. Research on the difference in perceptions of odd versus even prices supports the argument that prices ending in 99 rather than 00 lead to increased sales.[12] At the same time, there are some instances in which even prices are the norm or perhaps necessary. Theatre and concert tickets, admission to sporting events, and lottery tickets tend to be priced in even amounts. Professional fees are normally expressed in even amounts too. If a dentist charged €39.99 for treatment, the patient might think the quality of medical care was less than satisfactory. Many luxury items such as jewellery, golf course green fees and resort accommodation use even figure prices to set them apart.

Price lining

Marketers often apply their understanding of the psychological aspects of pricing in a practice called **price lining**, where items in a product line sell at different prices, called *price points*. If you want to buy a new refrigerator, you will find that most manufacturers have one 'stripped-down' model for about €400. A better quality but still moderately priced model will be around €600. A better one will be about €800, and a large refrigerator with

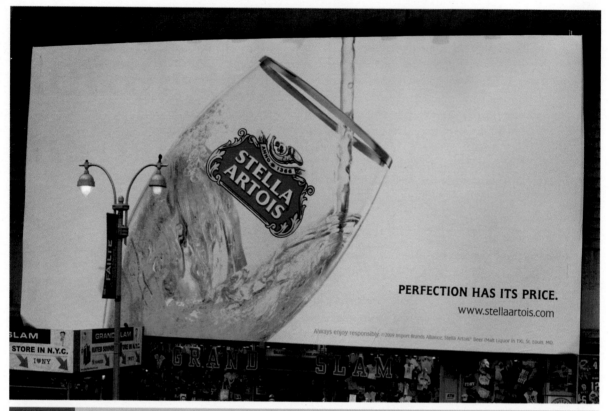

Photo 10.4 Consumers often associate higher prices with higher quality. This ad for Stella Artois builds on their former slogan 'reassuringly expensive'
Source: Getty Images/George Rose

lots of special features will be around €1,000. Recently, some appliance manufacturers have come out with new models, branded and marketed as special premium lines, with price tags of €3,000 or more. Price lining provides the different ranges necessary to satisfy each segment of the market.

Why is price lining a good practice? From the marketer's standpoint, price lining is a way to maximise profits. In theory, a firm would charge each individual customer the highest price that they were willing to pay. If the maximum one particular person would be willing to pay for a refrigerator is €550, then that would be the price. If another person would be willing to pay €900, that would be his price. Charging each consumer a different price is really not possible. Having a limited number of prices that generally fall at the top of the range customers find acceptable is a more workable alternative.

Legal and ethical considerations in pricing

The free enterprise system is founded on the idea that the marketplace will regulate itself. Prices will rise or fall according to demand. Firms and individuals will supply goods and services at fair prices if there is an adequate profit incentive. Unfortunately, the business world includes the greedy and the unscrupulous. National and local governments have found it necessary to enact legislation to protect consumers and to protect businesses from predatory rivals. For example, under current laws in Europe, car companies are allowed to charge wildly different prices for the same vehicle in different countries – prices can vary by as much as 30 per cent. New regulations are now being proposed to create a more level playing field among countries

Across the hall

John Flynn

Worshipful Company
of Marketors

Having recently sold a house in order to downsize to a city centre apartment, the following is based on experience. . . at times bitter experience. While all three options would be recognised by most estate agents, one in particular requires real marketing skills which, if correctly applied, will benefit both Mike and his client. There is, of course, a 'normal' or market price for any particular type of property at a given time in a specific area. Applying Option 1 and inflating the price is, as stated, to get hold of the business. Potential buyers are introduced but it will quickly become clear that the price is too high and so, if Mike can hang on to the client, it will eventually be sold at the market price. The downside for Mike is that his commission is a long time coming.

Business can be achieved by undervaluing the property as in Option 2, particularly if it is a buyers' market, either due to an economic crisis or a locally crowded market, in which case Mike will have plenty of examples to illustrate the need. The other reason for undervaluing is if the client needs to sell quickly. While this approach to pricing reduces Mike's commission it does offer him a faster return and less effort per sale.

The true market value, indicated in Option 3 could be defined as the average price for such a property in that area. However, my definition is 'the most you can get for the property'. Market research starts with defining what type of buyer it is likely to appeal to and what, emotionally, they are looking for. Then it is a matter of creating a property that looks and feels like their perfect home and then, and only then, create promotional material that sells rather than just shows. Mike needs to suggest to clients how they might create an environment that has the wow, or at least the ahh, factor; and also how the client should relate to potential buyers. It's a cross between window dressing and showbiz. Marketing is the key. I know; there were three other similar properties in my area and we sold fast and at premium price. None sold at our price and one is still on the market 18 months later.

---

belonging to the European Union – despite fierce opposition by some car manufacturers that want to retain control over their pricing decisions.[13] In this section, we'll talk about deceptive prices, unfair prices, discriminatory prices, price fixing, and some regulations to combat them. Please peruse the Marketing ethics and sustainability box to see how British Gas has attempted to use a form of 'predatory' pricing tactic to try and retain business.

Deceptive pricing practices

Unscrupulous businesses may advertise or promote prices in a deceptive way. One deceptive pricing practice that has been prevalent in North America and has been adapted in Europe is the **bait-and-switch** tactic, where a retailer will advertise an item at a very low price – the *bait* – to lure customers into the shop. However, it is almost impossible to buy the advertised item. Salespeople like to say (privately) that the item is 'nailed to the floor'. The salespeople do everything possible to get the unsuspecting customers to buy a different, more expensive, item – the *switch*. They might tell the customer 'confidentially' that 'the advertised item is really poor quality, lacking important features and full of problems'. Enforcing laws against bait-and-switch tactics is complicated because such practices are similar to the legal practice of 'trading up'. Simply encouraging consumers to purchase a higher priced item is an acceptable sales technique, but it is illegal to advertise a lower priced item when it's not a legitimate, *bona fide* offer that is available on demand.

Loss leaders

Not every advertised bargain is a bait-and-switch. Some retailers advertise items at very low prices or even below cost and are glad to sell them at that price because they know

Marketing ethics and sustainability

Pricing gas causes sparks

The energy regulator Ofgem has been urged by the UK's consumer watchdog Energywatch to investigate claims that British Gas has been undercutting rivals with predatory pricing when customers give notice to leave British Gas. There is an industry agreed code on customer switching. According to Energywatch Business Manager Paul Savage, British Gas's interpretation of it was 'unanimously opposed' by the rest of the industry. 'If this is consolidated into business practice, it will damage the vibrant competitive market Ofgem says it wants.'

Utility Week, 27, no. 16 (2011), 5

Debate, discuss, disagree

1   This seems to be a great deal for consumers, so why shouldn't British Gas be allowed to offer great deals to consumers in order to keep them?

that once in the shop, customers may buy other items at regular prices. This is called **loss leader pricing** and is aimed at building traffic and sales volume.

Price fixing

Price fixing occurs when two or more companies conspire to keep prices at a certain level. Oil companies have been accused of working a cartel in order to control supply and fix high prices. Such pricing can take two forms: horizontal and vertical.

Horizontal price fixing

In 2003, a number of top US fashion-modelling agencies were charged with conspiring to fix commissions they charged models. Such practices mean higher prices for customers, in this case the models who were buying the services of the agencies.[14] *Horizontal price fixing* occurs when competitors making the same product jointly determine what price each will charge. In industries in which there are few sellers, there may be no specific price-fixing agreement, but sellers will still charge the same price to 'meet the competition'. Such parallel pricing is not of itself considered price fixing. There must be an exchange of pricing information between sellers to indicate illegal price-fixing actions.

Vertical price fixing

Sometimes manufacturers or wholesalers attempt to force retailers to charge a certain price for their product. This is called *vertical price fixing*. If the retailer wants to carry the product, for example, it should charge the 'recommended' retail price.

Predatory pricing

Predatory pricing means that a company sets a very low price for the purpose of driving competitors out of business. Later, when they take over the supply and have a monopoly, they will increase prices.

Now that you've learned about product pricing read 'Real people, real decisions' to see which strategy Mike of Blundells Estate Agents selected.

Real people, real decisions

How it worked out at Blundells

Mike decided to go for Option 2 as he was not just keen to experiment with the market, but he strongly thought that this approach provided the best value for his clients to sell their homes. Whilst some degree of flexibility is used, particularly depending on the nature of the economy, Mike's pricing approach has been widely successful. He claims that although pricing slightly below the market rate sometimes worries vendors, buyers frequently rally for those properties that Blundells markets and they often end up paying prices that well exceed the market value. After making preliminary property visits, buyers fall in love with a particular house and don't want to lose the opportunity to purchase.

Therefore, whilst the pricing strategy may in hindsight offer the lowest value for the client and the smallest commission for Blundells, the actual sale price is often better than originally expected by the vendor, and as a result both the client and Mike are happy. One potential loser is the purchaser of the property; they often feel that because they have been in a bidding war, they have not obtained a bargain. However, Mike maintains that this approach to marketing properties is the best way for obtaining market value, as he firmly believes that the price for a product or service should only be ultimately judged by the amount the customer is willing to pay. Believe it or not, and even though they feel aggrieved, many buyers are also keen to use Blundells in the future when they come to market their homes.

Chapter summary

Now that you have finished reading this chapter, you should be able to answer any of the following potential examination questions:

1. **Explain the importance of pricing and how prices can take both monetary and non-monetary forms.**   Pricing is important to firms because it creates profits and influences customers to purchase or not. Prices may be monetary or non-monetary, when consumers or businesses exchange one product for another.

2. **Explain some of the pricing objectives that marketers typically have when planning pricing strategies.**   Effective pricing objectives are designed to support corporate and marketing objectives and are flexible. Pricing objectives often focus on sales (to maximise sales or to increase market share), on a desired level of profit growth or profit margin, on competing effectively to increase customer satisfaction or on communicating a certain image.

3. **Describe how marketers use costs, demands and revenue to make pricing decisions.**   In developing prices, marketers must estimate demand and determine costs. Marketers often use break-even analysis and marginal analysis to help in deciding on the price for a product. Break-even analysis uses fixed and variable costs to identify how many units must be sold at a certain price in order to begin making a profit. Marginal analysis uses both costs and estimates of product demand to identify the price that will maximise profits. In marginal analysis, profits are maximised at the point at which the revenue from selling one additional unit of a product equals the costs of producing the additional unit.

4. **Explain some of the environmental factors that affect pricing strategies.** Like other elements of the marketing mix, pricing is influenced by a variety of external environmental factors. These include economic trends such as inflation, recession, the firm's competitive environment – including the industry in which it operates, i.e. oligopoly, monopoly or a more competitive environment. Pricing may also be influenced by changing consumer trends.

5. **Illustrate some of the key pricing strategies used by firms.** Though easy to calculate and safe, frequently used cost-based strategies do not consider demand, competition, stage in the product life cycle, plant capacity or product image. The most common cost-based strategy is cost-plus pricing. Pricing strategies based on demand, such as target costing and yield management pricing, can require marketers to estimate demand at different prices in order to be certain the firm can sell what it produces. Strategies based on the competition may represent industry wisdom but can be tricky to apply. A price leadership strategy is often used in an oligopoly. Firms that focus on customer needs may consider everyday low price or value pricing strategies. New products may be priced using a high skimming price to recover research, development and promotional costs, or a penetration price to encourage more customers and discourage competitors from entering the market. Trial pricing means setting a low price for a limited time.

6. **Explain pricing tactics for single and multiple products.** To implement pricing strategies with individual products, marketers may use two-part pricing or payment pricing tactics. For multiple products, marketers may use price bundling, whereby two or more products are sold and priced as a single package. Captive pricing is often chosen when two items must be used together; one item is sold at a low price and the other at a high, profitable price. Distribution-based pricing tactics, including FOB, base-point and uniform delivered pricing address differences in how far products must be shipped. Similar pricing tactics are used for products sold internationally. Pricing for members of the channel may include trade or functional discounts, cumulative or non-cumulative quantity discounts to encourage larger purchases, cash discounts to encourage fast payment and seasonal discounts to spread purchases throughout the year or to increase off-season or in-season sales.

7. **To what extent is the internet having an impact on pricing strategies.** E-commerce may offer firms an opportunity to initiate dynamic pricing – meaning prices can be changed frequently

with little or no cost. Auctions offer opportunities for customers to bid on items in C2C, B2C and B2B e-commerce. The web allows buyers to compare products and prices, gives consumers more control over the price they pay for items and has made customers more price sensitive.

8. **Describe the psychologicl, legal and ethical aspects of pricing.** Consumers may express emotional or psychological responeses to prices. Customers may use an idea of a customary or fair price as an internal reference price in evaluating products. Sometimes marketers use reference pricing strategies by displaying products with different prices next to each other. A price–quality inference means that consumers use price as a cue for quality. Customers respond to odd prices differently than to even prices. Marketers can manipulate pricing with price lining strategies, a practice of setting a limited number of different price ranges for a product line. Most marketers try to avoid unethical or illegal pricing practices. One deceptive pricing practice is the bait-and-switch tactic.

Key terms

Average fixed cost 387

Bait-and-switch 405

Base-point pricing 400

Break-even analysis 388

Break-even point 388

Captive pricing 399

Contribution per unit 388

Cost-plus pricing 394

Cross-elasticity of demand 385

Demand-based pricing 395

Dynamic pricing 401

Elastic demand 382

Everyday low pricing (EDLP) 396

FOB delivered pricing 399

FOB origin pricing 399

Fixed costs 386

Freight absorption pricing 400

Inelastic demand 382

Internal reference price 402

List price 400

Loss leader pricing 406

Marginal analysis 390

Marginal cost 390

Marginal revenue 390

Online auctions 401

Penetration pricing 397

Prestige products 378

Price 376

Price bundling 399

Price elasticity of demand 382

Price fixing 406

Price leadership 396

Price lining 403

Quantity discounts 400

Skimming price 397

Target costing 395

Total costs 387

Trade or functional discounts 400

Trial pricing 398

Uniform delivered pricing 400

Value pricing 396

Variable costs 386

Yield management pricing 396

Chapter review

 ## Marketing concepts: testing your knowledge

1. What is price, and why is it important to a firm? What are some examples of monetary and non-monetary prices?

2. Describe and give examples of some of the following types of pricing objectives: market share, competitive effect, customer satisfaction and image enhancement.

3. Explain how the demand curves for normal products and for prestige products differ. What are demand shifts and why are they important to marketers? How do firms go about estimating demand? How can marketers estimate the elasticity of demand?

4. Explain variable costs, fixed costs, average variable costs, average fixed costs and average total costs.

5. What is break-even analysis? What is marginal analysis? What are the comparative advantages of break-even analysis and marginal analysis for marketers?

6. How does recession affect consumers' perceptions of prices? How does inflation influence perceptions of prices?

7. Explain cost-plus pricing, target costing and yield management pricing. Explain how a price leadership strategy works.

8. For new products, when is skimming more appropriate, and when is penetration pricing the best strategy? When would trial pricing be an effective pricing strategy?

9. Explain two-part payment pricing, price bundling, captive pricing and distribution-based pricing tactics. Give an example of when each would be a good pricing tactic for marketers to use.

10. Why do marketers use trade or functional discounts, quantity discounts cash discounts and seasonal discounts in pricing to members of the channel? What is dynamic pricing? Why does the internet encourage the use of dynamic pricing?

11. Explain these psychological aspects of pricing: price–quality inferences, odd–even pricing, internal reference price and price lining

12. Explain how unethical marketers might use bait-and-switch tactics, price fixing and predatory pricing.

Marketing concepts: discussing choices

1. Consumers often make price–quality inferences about products. What does this mean? What are some products for which you are likely to make price–quality inferences? Do such inferences make sense?

2. In pricing new products, marketers may choose a skimming or a penetration pricing strategy. While it's easy to see the benefits of these practices for the firm, what are the advantages or disadvantages of the practice for consumers and for industry as a whole?

Marketing practice: applying what you've learned

1. Assume that you are the director of marketing for a firm that manufactures confectionary goods. You feel the time is right for your company to increase the price of its products, but you are concerned that increasing the price may not be profitable. You feel you should examine the elasticity of demand. How would you go about doing this? What findings would lead you to increase the price? What findings would cause you to rethink the decision to increase prices?

2. Assume that you and your friend have decided to go into business together manufacturing your personally designed women's handbags. You know that your fixed costs (rent on a building, equipment and so on) will be €120,000 a year. You expect your variable costs to be €28 per handbag.

    a. If you plan on selling the handbags to shops for €35, how many must you sell to break even; that is, what is your break-even quantity?

    b. Assume that you and your partner feel that you must set a goal of achieving a €50,000 profit with your business this year. How many units would you have to sell to make that amount of profit?

    c. What if you feel that you will be able to sell no more than 10,000 handbags? What price will you have to charge to (i) break even and (ii) to make €50,000 in profit?

3. You are a marketing consultant, and your new client is the owner of a small chain of ice cream shops. The client has sold his ice cream at the same price since opening the shops seven years ago. Over time the costs of operating the shops has increased, cutting profits. The client feels he needs to increase his prices but is concerned that increasing prices may not be a good decision. Design a plan to measure price elasticity and thus determine if increasing prices will be good or bad for your client's profit. In a role-playing situation, explain to the client what you recommend.

4. Assume that you have been hired as the assistant manager of a local greengrocer. As you look over the shop, you notice that there are two different displays of tomatoes. In one display the tomatoes are priced at €1.39 per kilo, and in the other the tomatoes are priced at €0.89 per kilo. The tomatoes look very much alike. You notice that many people are buying the €1.39 tomatoes. Write a report explaining what is happening and give your recommendations for the shop's pricing strategy.

5. As the director of marketing for a firm that markets computer software, you must regularly develop pricing strategies for new software products. Your latest product is a software package that automatically translates any foreign language email messages to the user's preferred language. You are trying to decide on the pricing for this new product. Should you use a skimming price, a penetration price or something in between? With a classmate taking the role of another marketing professional with your firm, argue in front of your class the pros and cons for each option.

Marketing miniproject: learning by doing

The purpose of this miniproject is to help you become familiar with how consumers respond to different prices by conducting a series of pricing experiments. For this project, you should first select a product category that students such as yourself normally purchase. It should be a moderately expensive purchase such as trainers, a bookcase or a piece of luggage. You should next obtain two photographs of items in this product category or, if possible, two actual items. The two items should not appear to be substantially different in quality or in price.

Note: You will need to recruit separate research participants for each of the activities listed in the next section.

Experiment 1: Reference pricing

a. Place the two products together. Place a sign on one with a low price. Place a sign on the other with a high price (about 50 per cent higher will do). Ask your research participants to evaluate the quality of each of the items and to say which one they would probably purchase.

b. Reverse the signs and ask other research participants to evaluate the quality of each of the items and to suggest which one they would probably purchase.

c. Place the two products together again. This time, place a sign on one with a moderate price. Place a sign on the other that is only a little higher (less than 10 per cent higher). Again, ask research participants to evaluate the quality of each of the items and select which one they would probably purchase.

d. Reverse the signs and ask other research participants to evaluate the quality of each of the items and say which one they would probably purchase.

Experiment 2: Odd–even pricing

For this experiment, you will only need one of the items from experiment 1.

a. Place a sign on the item that ends in €.99 (for example, €59.99). Ask research participants to tell you if they think the price for the item is very low, slightly low, moderate, slightly high or very high. Also ask them to evaluate the quality of the item and to tell you how likely they would be to purchase the item.

b. This time place a sign on the item that ends in €.00 (for example, €60.00). Ask different research participants to tell you if they think the price for the item is very low, slightly low, moderate, slightly high or very high. Also ask them to evaluate the quality of the item and to tell you how likely they would be to purchase the item.

Develop a presentation for your class in which you discuss the results of your experiments and what they tell you about how consumers view prices.

Real people, real surfers

Exploring the web

Barter exchange is undertaken by organisations that facilitate barter or countertrade between each other. In the US, many such exchanges are members of the National Association of Trade Exchanges (NATE).

First, visit the NATE web page at www.nate.org. Using links on that page to NATE member exchanges or an internet search engine, locate and explore several barter exchange web pages. Based on your internet experience, answer the following questions:

1. What is NATE?

2. What are the benefits to a business of joining a barter exchange?

3. What types of products are bartered?

4. How does trade actually work with a barter exchange?

5. How does the exchange make its money? Who pays the exchange and how much is charged?

6. Assuming that the goal of barter exchange websites is to attract new members, evaluate the different websites you have recently visited. Which website do you think was best? What features of the site would make you want to join if you were the owner of a small business? What features of the other sites made them less appealing than this one?

Now, take a look at the website at www.pearsoned.co.uk/solomon to see some videos from YouTube relating to aspects of this chapter.

Marketing plan exercise

For many service organisations such as restaurants, hotels, airlines and resorts, pricing strategies are particularly important because of the perishability of services (i.e. services can't be stored). Pricing is a vital part of effective marketing strategies because it ensures that a maximum number of seats on the plane or rooms in the hotel are purchased – every day.

Think about a new seaside resort complex that offers holidaymakers luxury villas, available for rent for a few days, a week,

or longer. Consider possible pricing strategies such as cost-plus, yield management, everyday low pricing, skimming, penetration and trial pricing.

1. What pricing strategy do you recommend for the resort complex that would maximise their occupancy?
2. What recommendations for pricing tactics or for how to implement the strategy do you have?

Delve deeper into pricing

Dr Ben Lowe

Senior Lecturer in Marketing, University of Kent

Most managers agree that pricing is one of the most complex aspects of marketing, yet little time and resources are dedicated to pricing and decisions are often made on hunch or rule of thumb. Getting the price wrong can lead to costly implications for the bottom line. One consultant has estimated that a 1 per cent change in price can lead to a 10 per cent change in the bottom line! So contemporary research in pricing is focused on (1) determining what price to charge, and (2) examining the strategic function of price and how to respond to competition. Price is not just a number. It is also an aspect of the product that conveys information to people and helps them make decisions. As consumers rarely do, we correspond with models of economic man who is rational and has perfect information. So understanding the psychological side of pricing is critical to understanding how consumers react to a product. But there is much yet to be done! Interested readers can find out more with the following books and articles.

References

P. Ingenbleek, M. Debruyne, R.T. Frambach and T.M.M. Verhallen (2003) 'Successful New Product Pricing Practices: A Contingency Approach', *Marketing Letters* 14, no. 4, 289–305.

N. Kumar (2006) 'Strategies to Fight Low Cost Rivals' *Harvard Business Review* 84 (December), 104–12.

M.V. Marn, E.V. Roegner and C.C. Zawada (2003) 'Pricing New Products' *The McKinsey Quarterly* 3 (July), 40–49.

T. Mazumdar, S.P. Raj and I. Sinha (2005) 'Reference Price Research: Review and Propositions', *Journal of Marketing* 69 (October), 84–102.

K.B. Monroe (2003) *Pricing: Making Profitable Decisions*, 3rd ed. (New York: McGraw Hill).

T.T. Nagle, and J.E. Hogan (2006) *The Strategy and Tactics of Pricing: A Guide to Growing More Profitably*, 4th ed (Upper Saddle River, NJ: Prentice Hall).

Marketing in action case

Low cost, big profit, really low price? The case of low-cost airlines

The low-cost carrier (LCC) concept was originated by Southwest Airlines in the United States, following deregulation of the air transport sector in the late 1970s. The airline created a new business model to compete with coach operators. Since the early 1990s the model has been replicated in Europe, with the arrivals of budget airlines such as Ryanair, easyJet, Buzz, bmi baby, flybe and Jet2. Over the last two decades LCCs have been the main driver of growth of air travel within Europe. The industry as a whole has the low-cost sector to thank for some of the recovery in traffic since the 11 September 2001 tragedy. At the early stage, these LCCs seemed content to chip away at the traditional airlines' market share. However, now they are gearing up to take more significant share from their rivals. They have already become major operators on certain routes and over the next decade they may represent the most dominant force in European air travel. Even British Airways (BA) wanted to take part and launched its own low-cost carrier GO in 1997; however, after several unsuccessful years, GO was acquired by easyJet in 2003.

Though some air traffic business has shifted within the sector, nearly 60 per cent of this is from new customers who previously could not afford to fly. Air travel has therefore become a part of people's lifestyle. Low-cost air travel is also a more sensible option for the mass market when travelling within Europe. For example, on a 45-minute flight from London to Paris there is no need for a meal, to watch a film or have that much legroom. LCCs have made customers realise just how much extra they would have to pay for something they do not actually need. As a result, many customers are no longer willing to pay such premiums. There has also been more demand for family weekends away and short breaks, where price is often a critical element that influences decision making associated with travel. Passengers in general are happy to do without pre-assigned seats and complimentary drinks in order to save money, and this is particularly true in the current recessionary climate.

Low-cost travel seems to be a lucrative market that is growing, but as many as 40 per cent of start-up LCCs have failed and gone out of business for one reason or another over the past decade. These include Virgin Express, GO, AB Airlines, Duo, Now, Oasis.[1] To survive, LCCs must be genuinely low cost! A major source of their low-cost structure seems to be the efficiency of their operations which is operating on only a small, carefully selected number of routes. LCCs often fly from point-to-point and use secondary airports such as Stansted or Luton close to London, Beauvais near to Paris and Hahn near Frankfurt, rather than operating from congested airport hubs. This helps simplify scheduling and baggage handling and keeps turnaround time quick and landing fees as low as possible. For example, a typical aircraft owned by easyJet flies in the air for 11 hours a day on average compared to 8 hours by BA.[2] The use of uniform aircrafts, usually the Boeing 737, leads to lower maintenance and training costs, fuel efficiency and better crew utilisation.

LCCs typically have high seating density and load factors, which are over 80 per cent for both Ryanair and easyJet.[3] The system is almost ticketless, with the use of direct on-line internet bookings, rather than working through travel agents. The service offer is minimal, with 'no frills' i.e. no complimentary food, drinks, newspapers or even seat allocation. To extract maximum revenue from their potential customer base, LCCs utilise a yield management system, which involves drastic variation in fares according to time of departure, time of day, day of the week or season. The airline can be flexible to adjust the price band if demand is greater or lower than anticipated. Marginal revenue is significantly greater for LCCs due to low marginal costs. For instance, costs per available seat kilometre for easyJet are over 60 per cent lower than that of other scheduled airlines.

Many budget airlines are thriving whilst their relatively larger, more established counterparts are struggling. Since the millennium, the operating margin of

Ryanair has been approximately 23 per cent compared with British Airways 0.9 per cent, Air France 3.5 per cent, Luffthansa 5.7 per cent and KLM 1.5 per cent.[5] In 2009, easyJet had 18 per cent of the total market share in the UK (Ryanair 13 per cent) compared to BA at 14 per cent.[6] With a low-cost structure, budget airlines often enjoy big profits even though they use low pricing as the main feature of their marketing. Cheap fare offers are usually heavily publicised: for example London to Edinburgh at £9.99 or London to Barcelona at £12.99 single ticket by easyJet. Ryanair is a bit different with frequent 'free', 'half price' or even '99p' seat sales.

However, in reality most fares are higher than this, as Ryanair's average fare is about £40 per passenger, and easyJet around £60 excluding taxes and charges. Additional charges are not typically included in the advertised price, which is typically far from what customers eventually pay. Also, there can be little flexibility compared with full-price mainstream airline prices. Passengers might have to book up to five months in advance to get really low fares. Tickets might not be refundable and a charge might be made for changing tickets. Anything additional can be quite expensive, for example excess luggage or telephoning a customer helpline. Moreover, certain costs have been transferred to customers, such as printing their own tickets. Customers also have to make their own travel arrangements to such out-of-town airports, which are sometimes over an hour's drive from major city centres.

European LCCs, along with the industry in general, are presently facing challenges of higher fuel prices, falling consumer demand and rising airport fees. Some weaker LCCs across Europe have already cut back capacity or reduced their growth plans, whilst others are in a retrenchment mode. There will undoubtedly be further consolidation as smaller players either go bankrupt or become the target of acquisition strategies. Whilst the current economic climate is challenging, some major budget airlines have a positive outlook. For instance, the response of the market leader Ryanair has been to slash fares and yields to stimulate traffic in order to broaden its customer base even further through promoting new routes.

Things to think about

1. What are the factors influencing pricing decisions among low-cost carriers (LLCs)?

2. In this case, is there a relationship between price, cost and profit?

3. Do such airlines really compete on price?

4. How else could LCCs look to compete in the marketplace?

5. How can the lessons learnt from LCCs be applied to other sectors, if at all?

References

1 S. Smith *The Strategies and Effects of Low-Cost Airlines* (The International Consulting Economists' Association, 2005).

2 Ibid.

3 *Low-Cost Airlines International*, Mintel, November 2006.

4 *Low-Cost Airlines Europe*, Mintel, May 2008.

5 Smith, *The Strategies and Effects of Low-Cost Airlines*.

6 'Passenger Airlines – Western Europe: A Snapshot', *Mintel Global Market Navigator*, 2010.

Case study written by Dr Lien Le Monkhouse, University of Sheffield

References

1. Leslie Vreeland, 'How to Be a Smart Shopper', *Black Enterprise* (August 1993), 88.

2. Melanie Trottman, 'First Class at Coach Prices', 17 February 2004, http://online.wsj.com/article_email?article?pring/O,SB107 698413620331110-H0je4Nhl.

3. Quoted in Mercedes M. Cardonna, 'Affluent Shoppers Like Their Luxe Goods Cheap', *Advertising Age*, 1 December 2003, 6.

4. Steward Washburn, 'Pricing Basics: Establishing Strategy and Determining Costs in the Pricing Decision', *Business Marketing*, July 1985, reprinted in Valerie Kijewski, Bob Donath and David T. Wilson, eds., *The Best Readings from Business Marketing Magazine* (Boston: PWS-Kent Publishing, 1993), 257–69.

5. Robin Cooper and W. Bruce Chew, 'Control Tomorrow's Costs Through Today's Design', *Harvard Business Review* (January – February 1996), 88–97.

6. Nikki Swartz, 'Rate-Plan Wisdom', *Wireless Review*, 15 June 2001, http://industry click.com.

7. Jennifer Merritt, 'The Belle of the Golf Balls', *Business Week*, 29 July 1996, 6.

8. 'Numerical Nirvana', *Business Week*, 10 November 2003, 13.

9. Douglas Lavin, 'Goodbye to Haggling: Savvy Consumers Are Buying Their Cars Like Refrigerators', *Wall Street Journal*, 20 August 1993, B1, B3.

10. 'Pricing, Quotations, and Terms', *Advertising and Marketing Review*, www.ad-mkt-review.com/public_html/govdocs/bge/bgec10.html.

11. Amy E. Cortese and Marcia Stepanek, 'Good-Bye to Fixed Pricing?', *Business Week*, 4 May 1998, 71 –84.

12. Robert M. Schindler and Thomas M. Kibarian, 'Increased Consumer Sales Response through Use of 99-Ending Prices', *Journal of Retailing* 72 (1996), 187 –99.

13. Edmund L. Andrews, 'Europe to Seek Uniformity in Car Pricing', *New York Times*, 5 February 2002, www.nyt.com.

14. John R. Wilke, 'Top Modeling Agencies Face Federal Price-Fixing Inquiry', *Wall Street Journal*, 4 August 2003, www.wsj.com.

Chapter 11
Integrated marketing communications

Meet James Dalton,

Managing Director of
Fonemedia Ltd

Q & A with James Dalton

First job out of school?
Business Development Exec for MAN

Career high?
The day I opened the doors of Fonemedia

Business book I'm reading now?
Scoring Points: How Tesco Continues to Win Customer Loyalty by Hunt, Humby and Phillips

My hero?
My grandfather – an orphan, a soldier and an incredible man

Don't do this when interviewing with me?
Assume I'm your 'mate'

My pet peeve?
Lack of imagination

Favourite TV programme?
Ashes to Ashes

Holiday destination?
Nokomis, Florida with my family

Hobby/sport?
Brewing/golf

Drink?
Well brewed pint of bitter

Food?
Tuscan antipasti

James Dalton is Managing Director of Fonemedia Ltd, which he founded in 2008 having spent the previous ten years working within the recruitment advertising and education marketing industry. This experience, coupled with the knowledge capital from other members of the team in the mobile technology sector, has enabled the Fonemedia business to win key clients such as Sky, Virgin and the British Army. James was brought up in West Yorkshire and studied in Cardiff on a sponsorship from part of the MAN group of companies based in Augsburg, Germany. James lives with his wife Samantha and their two young children – Isabel and Alex – in the countryside of North Yorkshire. A keen golfer and a governor of a local primary school, James is also an equal shareholder in an up and coming micro brewery.

Real people, real decisions
Decision time at Fonemedia

Founded on the 8th day of the 8th month in 2008 (purely by chance), Fonemedia provides the knowledge and expertise to engage with target audiences through the mobile phone platform. Fonemedia works in partnership with its clients to understand how traditional media platforms work and how they complement mobile promotion since many of the most successful advertising campaigns in history have successfully combined a variety of media formats. Unlike many of the more traditional media streams such as radio and TV, mobile marketing utilises the information about each handset owner to provide it with a 'digital footprint' – allowing Fonemedia to be highly specific when it comes to identifying the correct target audience.

In 2011, a university business school was looking to develop its MBA intake from regions where it had previously delivered poor results in recruiting. While spending an estimated £100 million per annum in marketing and advertising to bring students to their doors, universities have adapted their marketing strategies over time. In the 1980s universities adopted more of a scatter-gun approach to their marketing with a reliance on the prospectus, reputation and the range of courses on offer. In the 1990s universities saw a massive shift in more local geographical catchment areas for their courses which resulted in the use of regional media formats such as press and radio. But with regionalisation came another problem. However, wanting to expand and faced with a decline in numbers of applications from the UK, universities began to look at catchment areas elsewhere in the world.

One particular post-graduate MBA course that had traditionally struggled to recruit people in the UK had its marketing team identify two key areas that could potentially deliver the number of students they were looking for to make the course a viable option and which would bring in a profitable revenue stream. They had seen that other similar courses had attracted students from both Nigeria and Kenya and had signed up to take part in two exhibitions in Lagos and Nairobi. The university approached Fonemedia to explore the potential routes to market. They considered their promotional options.

Option 1 Phone web advertising

This option would utilise optimised mobile web advertising on a cost per click basis. The advantage of this approach is that in countries such as Kenya and Nigeria where landline technology has only penetrated into the main cities and business areas, web-based access is far greater through the mobile handset than it is through PC-based web activity. In terms of targeting, the mobile handset gives us far more information about the user than many other media platforms. For example, the handset itself can give us some ideas of the demographics of the users themselves since used handsets that have a Migration Access Code (MAC) from a different country demonstrate that it's second-hand and will often be used by someone who is not in the top 2 per cent of the population in terms of wealth. Those handsets such as iPhone and Blackberry have a higher price tag and can be targeted solely for the purposes of advertising. The networks identify the handset make and model, location of the owner, media consumption habits of the owner as well as their approximate age and gender. By using these filters, it is possible to control which handset will actually view an advertisement. There are, however, disadvantages to this particular approach. The degree of control over the campaign is relatively limited – with large variances in the CTR (click through ratio), often ranging from 0.1 per cent to 1 per cent, the speed at which the campaign budgets are exhausted also varies greatly and with a higher CTR the potential to deliver brand recognition through this media also diminishes. It is also exposed to the 'unknown' variable – the element of creative appeal. Certain creative advertising using this format of media will have a greater appeal to the target audience than others – this is the one and only non-scientific element to the whole process.

Option 2 Web advertising through social media

Another option was PC-based web advertising through social networking and sponsored pay per click advertising. The advantages of this approach are that much of the web activity we engage in often leaves a digital footprint – enabling a certain degree of targeted advertising activity. By identifying the key demographics of the target audience, we can link these characteristics to the social networking opportunities available through relevant sites such as Facebook, Twitter and LinkedIn and execute a campaign that is targeted. For example, as part of a web campaign, we would make it clear that although it costs the equivalent of $40,000 for the course, which would automatically exclude some from clicking onto the advertisement (and therefore incurring cost to the campaign) as it's an unobtainable product to them. Web advertising through social media does however have its pitfalls. Because there are a large number of unknown variables in the web equation, targeting can be prone to inaccuracies and tends to become more of a scatter-gun approach, aimed more towards delivering higher numbers with less quality. The normal expectations of CTR would be in the region of 0.1–0.5 per cent at the very most. This is primarily due to the mixed digital footprint that tends to be left by PC-based web activity. With a large percentage of the population accessing the internet from their homes, work and public places such as libraries, it is impossible to give a particular PC a clear digital footprint of the user and, with out-of-home web activity becoming more frequent than that in the home, it is becoming increasingly difficult to target accurately.

Option 3 Use traditional media

The last option was to use the extensive national press newspaper titles of both Nigeria and Kenya to place advertisements for the university – informing them of the unique selling point (USP) of the course and the call to action – coming to visit the show in Lagos and Nairobi. Among the advantages of this approach is that opportunities to view using this format are higher than most other methods – with circulation in both countries being so high compared to other countries within the continent. In Nigeria, newspaper consumption rates are growing rapidly with 24 newspapers sold per 1000 population, a pattern echoed in Kenya where newspaper circulation is increasing by 5 per cent year on year. However, newspaper is a cheap commodity that is disposed of within one or two days; they are read by most members of society and therefore not targeted. Since only the top 2 per cent of the population have the financial wealth to afford an overseas education at this level, the main issue facing this media choice is the degree of wastage.

Now, put yourself in James's shoes. Which option should he pitch for and why?

Objectives

When you finish reading this chapter, you will be able to:

1 Understand the role of marketing communications

2 Understand the communications model

3 List and describe the traditional elements of the promotion mix

4 Explain how word-of-mouth marketing, buzz marketing, viral marketing and guerrilla marketing provide effective marketing communications

5 Describe integrated marketing communications and its characteristics

6 Explain the important role of database marketing in integrated marketing communications (IMC)

7 Explain the stages in developing an IMC plan

Tailoring marketing communications to customers

Objective

1

Understand the role of marketing communications

See how many of the following questions you can answer:

1. 'Have a break, have a _____'

2. Name one or more products for which Lewis Hamilton is a spokesperson.

3. Which bank is the world's local bank?

4. At Burger King, you can have it '_____', whereas at Hesburger from Finland the burgers are '_____' flame grilled.

5. Which brand makes you say 'Because I'm worth it'?

Did you get them all right? You owe your knowledge about these and 1000 other trivia questions to the efforts of people who specialise in marketing communications. As we said in Chapter 1, promotion is the coordination of marketing communications efforts to influence attitudes or behaviour. This function is one of the famous Seven Ps of the marketing mix and it plays a vital role – whether the goal is to sell hamburgers, insurance, ringtones or healthy diets. Of course, keep in mind that marketers use *all* the elements of the marketing mix to communicate with customers. The package in which the product comes, the price of the

Photo 11.1 | Some companies publicise their brands by buying space on hot air balloons. This promotional programme might be done independently of an ad campaign
Source: doughoughton

product and the type of retail outlet where the product is available are all part of effective marketing communications because they make statements about the nature of the product and the image it intends to convey.

Marketing communications can take many forms: quirky television commercials, sophisticated magazine ads, web banner ads boasting the latest Java-language applications, funky T-shirts and even do-it-yourself, customer-made advertising.

Marketing communications have different purposes; some can be to push specific products, whereas others try to create or reinforce a corporate image:

● Marketing communications *inform* consumers about new goods and services and where they can purchase them.[1]

● Marketing communications *remind* consumers to continue using certain products.

● Marketing communications *persuade* consumers to choose one product over others.

● Marketing communications *build* relationships with customers.

In today's competitive marketplace, the role of the successful marketer in communicating the value proposition means adopting an IMC perspective as this is the best way to get reinforcing messages. In this chapter, we'll first review the communication process of marketing. Next, we'll discuss both the traditional elements of the promotion mix and some of those new tricks marketers are using to communicate with us. Finally, we'll describe the characteristics of IMC and the communications planning process.

The communications model

Objective

2

Understand the communications model

A good way to understand what marketing communications is all about is to examine the **communications model** in Figure 11.1. In this model, a message is transmitted through some medium from a sender to a receiver who (we hope!) is listening and understands the message. *Any* way that marketers reach out to consumers, from a roadside hoarding to a customised message sent via email, is part of the basic communications process. The communications model specifies the elements necessary for communication to occur: a source, a message, a medium and a receiver. Regardless of how messages are sent – whether by a Jaguar mascot on luxury cars, a distinctive yellow and blue logo from IKEA or a televised fashion advert with supermodel Kate Moss promoting her clothing line for Topshop – they are designed to capture receivers' attention and relate to their needs. Now let's look at defining and explaining the terms in the communication model.

Encoding by the source (the marketer)

Encoding is the process of translating an idea into a form of communication that will convey the desired meaning. This involves deciding on what words and visuals will be used. The **source** is the organisation or individual sending the message. It's one thing for marketers

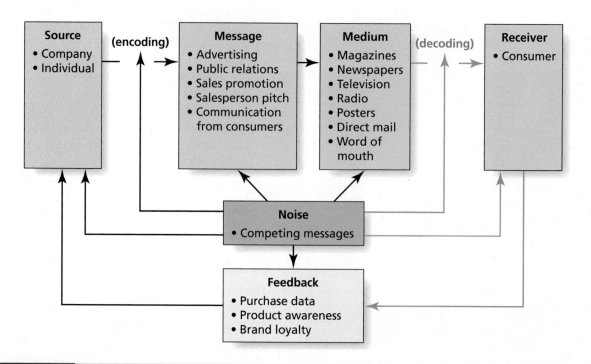

Figure 11.1	The communications model
	The communications model explains how ideas are translated into messages and transmitted from the marketer (the source) to the consumer (the receiver) who (we hope) understands what the marketer intended to say

to form an idea about a product in their own minds, but it's not quite as simple to express the idea so that other people get the same picture. To encode a message in the language of the intended audience, the National Health Service in the UK developed an anti-smoking campaign that featured patients talking about their smoking-related cancer. These testimonials can be a very convincing way of raising awareness and preventing people from smoking.[2] Danone presented ordinary people when it advertised its new healthy yoghurt drink 'Danone Bio Activia' on TV. The product users shown were all middle-aged women who talked about their positive experience after using Danone's drink. To make their messages more believable or more attractive to consumers, marketers sometimes choose a celebrity or expert to do the encoding (football player David Beckham for Motorola), hire an actor or a model (Keira Knightley for Chanel) or create a character (Tony the Tiger for Kellogg's Frosties) to represent the source. The toothpaste manufacturer Sensodyne uses similar techniques in promoting its products. Often, qualified dentists talk about Sensodyne toothpaste and try to convince the viewer of the good results the product brings with it.[3]

 ## The message

The **message** is the actual communication going from sender to receiver. It must include all the information necessary to persuade, inform, remind, or build a relationship. Messages may include both verbal and non-verbal elements, such as beautiful background scenery or unusual music. These elements must be carefully constructed so that they can connect with a wide variety of consumers or business customers. Think about a typical well crafted Guinness commercial. In contrast, the message a salesperson delivers can be carefully tailored for each individual customer, and the salesperson can respond to questions or objections.

Photo 11.2	Marketers often hire celebrities as spokespersons for their products, thus adding excitement to the 'source' of the message

Source: Getty Images/Chris Jackson

 ## The medium

No matter how the message is encoded, it must then be transmitted via a **medium**, a communications vehicle used to reach members of a target audience. This vehicle can be television, radio, a magazine, a company website, a blog, a personal contact, a poster or even a product logo printed on a coffee mug. Ideally, the attributes of the product should match those of the medium. For example, magazines with high prestige, such as *Vogue* , are more effective at communicating messages about overall product image and quality for Chanel or D&G, whereas specialised magazines, such as *What Car?* do a better job of conveying factual information.[4]

 ## Decoding by the receiver

Communication cannot occur unless a **receiver** is there to get the message. The receiver can be any individual or organisation that intercepts and interprets the message. Assuming that the customer is even paying attention (a big assumption in our overloaded, media-saturated society), he or she interprets the message in light of his or her unique experiences. **Decoding** is the process whereby a receiver assigns meaning to a message, that is, translates the message back into an idea. A good example of decoding is comedy. Sometimes you hear a joke and you don't understand it, but others around you are laughing. That's because they've decoded the message. Check out some funny international ads from YouTube on our website (www.pearsoned.co.uk/solomon) and type in 'Berlitz language ad' (www.youtube.com/watch?v=_1Vn9OwDjgQ) to see if you get the humour. It happens in the marketing communication process too. Marketers hope that the target consumer will decode the message the way they intended; that the idea in the mind of the receiver is identical to the idea the source sought to communicate.

Effective communication occurs only when the source and the receiver have a mutual frame of reference. They must share the same understanding about the world. For example, when in 2004 the Italian fashion producer Colours of Benetton published some advertisements with black children showing the word 'HIV' on their skin, not everyone who saw the commercial interpreted it quite the same way. Some saw it as a positive political statement showing the plight of millions of children who are born with HIV, others were furious that Benetton would use the suffering of young people to gain publicity for their brand. United Colours of Benetton's advertisements are famous for being provocative, showing for example a nun kissing a priest or a white infant being breast-fed by a black woman.[5] Indeed they do not want everyone to interpret it in the same way otherwise there would be no debate. The British HM Revenue and Customs advertisement from 2007 is another example of misunderstood commercials. It showed a self-employed plumber evading tax by hiding under the kitchen sink. The advertisement attracted complaints from a number of institutions who said that the ad implied self-employed people – plumbers in particular – were tax-evaders and was thus both misleading and offensive.[6]

 ## Noise

The communications model also acknowledges that **noise** – anything that interferes with effective communication – can block messages. As the many arrows between noise and the other elements of the communication model in Figure 11.2 indicate, noise can occur at any stage of communication. It can pop up at the encoding stage if the source uses words or symbols that the receiver will not understand. Or the receiver may be distracted from receiving the message by a nearby conversation. There may be a problem with transmission of the message through the medium – especially if it's drowned out by the chorus of other marketers clamouring for us to look at *their* messages instead. Gaining attention is one of the key challenges in today's crowded communication marketplace, which is why techniques like word-of-mouth (WOM) and guerrilla marketing techniques are being used which almost guarantee the consumers' attention. Marketers try to minimise noise by placing their messages where there are less likely to be distractions or competition for consumers' attention. Calvin Klein, for example, will often buy a block of advertising pages in a magazine so that the reader sees only pictures of its clothing.

High   Low

| Advertising | Sales promotion | Personal selling | Direct marketing | Public relations | Word of mouth |

Figure 11.2   **Control continuum**
The messages that consumers receive about companies and products differ in the amount of control the marketer has over the message delivered to the consumer

Feedback

To complete the communications loop, the source gets **feedback** from receivers (see section on copy testing and pre- and post-ad testing). Feedback is a reaction to the message that helps marketers gauge the effectiveness of the message so they can fine-tune it. Obtaining feedback reminds us of the importance of conducting marketing research (as we discussed in Chapter 3) to verify that a firm's strategies are working.

Marketing communications strategy and the promotion mix

Objective

3

List and describe the traditional elements of the promotion mix

Although **promotion** is one of the seven Ps, virtually *everything* an organisation says and does is a form of marketing communications. The ads it creates, the packages it designs, the uniforms its employees wear and even what other consumers say contribute to the impression people have of the company and its products. We can argue that *every element of the marketing mix is actually a form of communication*. After all, the price of a product, where it is sold and even the nature of the product itself contribute to the impression we form of it.

Within the marketing mix, we call the communication elements that the marketer controls the **promotion mix**. These elements include the following:

- Personal selling (e.g. Clinique make-up assistants).
- Advertising (Nicole Kidman and Daniel Craig wearing Omega watches).
- Sales promotions (a voucher in a student magazine for 2 for 1 meals at a local pub).
- Public relations (an Amnesty International press conference to highlight human rights issue in Burmah).

Just as a DJ combines songs or phrases to create an entertainment experience, the term mix implies that a company's promotion strategy is focused on more than one element, so the challenge is to integrate these different communication tools in an effective way.

Another challenge is to be sure that the promotion mix works in harmony with the overall marketing mix, which combines elements of promotion with place, price and product information to position the firm's offering in people's minds. For example, ads for luxury products such as Mont Blanc pens or Jaguar cars must be designed to communicate that same luxury character of the product and they should appear in places that reinforce that upmarket image such as *Monocle* magazine or in business class lounges in airports.

Marketers have a lot more control over some kinds of messages than they do others. As Figure 11.2 shows, mass-media advertising and sales promotion are at one end of the continuum, where the marketer has total control over what message is delivered. At the other end is WOM communication, where everyday people rather than the company run the show. Marketers know what consumers hear from one another is a vitally important component of the brand attitudes consumers form – and of their decisions about what to buy. Between the ends we find personal selling, where marketers have a lot but not total control over the message delivered, and public relations, where marketers have even less control because journalists and editors value their independence and will write what they think, not what the company wants them to write. Table 11.1 presents some of the pros and cons of each element of the promotion mix, which we discuss next.

Promotional Element	Pros	Cons
Advertising	• The marketer has control over what the message will say, when it will appear and who is likely to see it	• Often expensive to produce and distribute • May have low credibility and/or be ignored by audience
Sales promotion	• Provides incentives to retailers to support one's products • Builds excitement for retailers and consumers • Encourages immediate purchase and trial of new products • Price-oriented promotions cater to price-sensitive consumers	• Short-term emphasis on immediate sales rather than a focus on building brand loyalty • The number of competing promotions may make it hard to break through the promotional clutter
Public relations	• Relatively low cost • High credibility	• Lack of control over the message that is eventually transmitted and no guarantee that the message will ever reach the target • Hard to track the results of publicity efforts
Personal selling	• Direct contact with the customer gives the salesperson the opportunity to be flexible and modify the sales message to coincide with the customer's needs • The salesperson can get immediate feedback from the customer	• High cost per contact with customer • Difficult to ensure consistency of message when it is delivered by many different company representatives • The credibility of salespeople often depends on the quality of their company's image, which has been created by other promotional strategies
Direct marketing	• Can target specific groups of potential customers with different offers • Marketers can easily measure the results • Can provide extensive product information and multiple offers within a single appeal • Provides a means for collecting information for company marketing databases	• Consumers may have a negative opinion of some types of direct marketing • Costs more per contact than mass appeals

Table 11.1 A comparison of elements of the promotion mix

Personal appeals

The most immediate way for a marketer to make contact with customers is simply to tell them how wonderful the product is. This is part of the *personal selling* element of the promotion mix we mentioned previously. It is the direct interaction between a company representative and a customer that can occur in person, by phone or even over an interactive computer link. We'll learn more about this important process in Chapter 12. Salespeople are a valuable source of communications, because customers can ask questions and the salesperson can immediately address objections and describe product benefits.

Personal selling can be tremendously effective, especially for expensive and complicated consumer items such as computers or cars and for industrial products where the 'human touch' is essential. It can be so effective that some marketers, if given a choice, might neglect other forms of promotion. Unfortunately, for many products, especially consumer goods – a bottle of shampoo or a pair of running shoes – it's often too expensive to connect personally with each and every customer, so marketers need to use other forms of promotion as well.

Mass appeals

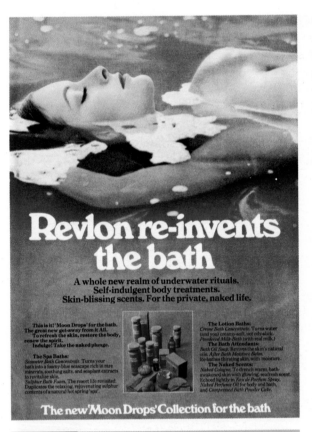

The other pieces of the promotion mix are those messages intended to reach many prospective customers at the same time which are impersonal and lack the 'human touch'. Whether a company posts an announcement to a few hundred local residents about a new restaurant opening or broadcasts a television commercial to millions, it is promoting itself to a mass audience. The following are the elements of the promotion mix that provide mass appeal opportunities:

- **Advertising:** Advertising is for many the most familiar and visible element of the promotion mix. It is non-personal communication from an identified sponsor using the mass media. Because it can convey rich and dynamic images, advertising can establish and reinforce a distinctive brand identity. Think about the ads for mobile phone companies which convey much more than just the talk plan. Advertising is also useful in communicating factual information about the product or reminding consumers to buy their favourite brand. Think about the ads that remind you of why you shop at Tesco. However, advertising sometimes suffers from a credibility problem because cynical consumers ignore messages they think are biased or are intended to sell them something they don't need. Advertising can also be very expensive, so firms must ensure their messages are effective. Reaching the university student market in the UK, Denmark, Holland, Sweden and Norway with their large discretionary spending power is a unique challenge for marketers since students are less likely to be influenced by advertising in traditional media. Instead, the university newspapers have proven effective for many companies.[7] For example, marketers like Google, Amazon and major film studios spend millions on university newspaper advertising.[8] In some countries an estimated 95 per cent of university students read the campus paper and newspaper ads can cost more than €1500 each.

- **Sales promotion:** Sales promotions are programmes such as contests, coupons or other incentives that marketers design to build interest in or encourage purchase of a product during a specified time period. Unlike other forms of promotion, sales promotions are intended to stimulate immediate action (often in the form of a purchase) rather than building long-term loyalty. More on this in Chapter 12.

- **Public relations:** Public relations relates to communications activities that seek to create and maintain a positive image of an organisation and its products among various audiences, including customers, government officials and shareholders. As we'll see in Chapter 12, public relations activities include writing press releases about product- and company-related issues, dealing with the news media and organising special events. Public relations also includes efforts to present bad company news in the best way, thus minimising harmful consequences. In contrast to sales promotions, public relations

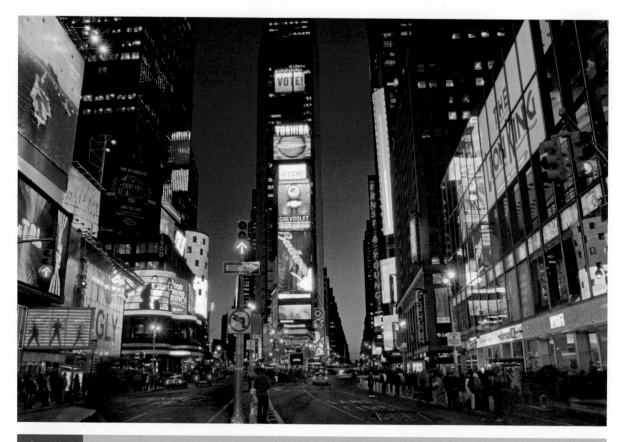

| Photo 11.4 | Marketers have a wide range of communications tools from which to choose, ranging from glitzy TV commercials to neon signs
Source: Alamy Images/Patrick Batchelder |

components of the promotion mix usually do not seek a short-term increase in sales. Instead, they try to influence feelings, opinions or beliefs for the long term. For example, car manufacturers might take motor journalists to Monaco to wine and dine them and let them test drive a new model.

Buzz appeals

Objective

4

Explain how word-of-mouth marketing, buzz marketing, viral marketing and guerrilla marketing provide effective marketing communications

In addition to these tried-and-tested methods, many marketers are starting to figure out that they must find alternatives to traditional advertising – partly because there is so much advertising it's hard to get noticed and partly because some consumers, especially young consumers, are very cynical about the efforts of big corporations to buy their allegiance. For these and other 'hard-to-get' consumers, marketers must find new 'out-of-the-box' tactics. These new tactics come under a variety of names, including word-of-mouth marketing, viral marketing and buzz and guerrilla marketing.

Buzz, word-of-mouth and viral marketing

Everywhere you turn in marketing today, it seems someone is talking about '**buzz**'. In fact, we hear so much about buzz and its counterparts viral marketing and word-of-mouth marketing that it's hard to know exactly what all the terms mean. The Word of Mouth Marketing Association (WOMMA), founded in 2004, has written the following definitions:[9]

Word-of-mouth: The act of consumers providing information to other consumers.

Word-of-mouth marketing: Giving people a reason to talk about your products and services, and making it easier for that conversation to take place.

Buzz marketing: Using high-profile entertainment or news to get people to talk about your brand.

Viral marketing: Creating entertaining or informative messages that are designed to be passed along in an exponential fashion, often electronically or by email.

In more general terms, marketers think of 'buzz' as people helping their marketing efforts by talking about a product or a company to their friends and neighbours.[10] As the examples in Table 11.2 illustrate, companies spend millions to create consumer buzz. Companies such as Dell even have word-of-mouth teleconferences where their named WOM marketing managers will share tactics and techniques covering this topic.[11] According to JWT Worldwide, the fourth-largest advertising agency in the world, over 85 per cent of the top 1000 marketing firms now use some form of word-of-mouth tactics.[12]

Company	Buzz Marketing Tactic
IKEA	To create attention for its mattresses, IKEA created a buzz having people sleeping on IKEA mattresses all over downtown Toronto in a one-day event[1]
Burger King	At www.Subservientchicken.com, consumers could have fun giving a man in a chicken suit orders to follow. The site attracted 418 million visitors who stayed on an average of 6 minutes.[2] Result: Burger King was seen as a more empathetic and relevant company for young people
Nike	Nike was supposedly the 'brains' behind a cool, illegal warehouse club in Berlin[3]
Hasbro	Consumers were encouraged to play Monopoly on the streets of London.[4] The fines and clean-up fees Hasbro was forced to pay to the city were far less than advertising costs
Puma	Encouraged consumers to stencil its cat logo all over Paris
Diesel (the retailer)	Lets dogs come in and gives them biscuits[5]
Audi	To introduce its A3 model, Audi staged a fake car theft at a New York Auto Show. Posters placed near the theft appealed to consumers for help and sent then to a website where they could participate in an alternate reality game (ARG) and find hidden clues to solve the mystery[6]
Kellogg's	Gave a video of never-before-seen ads for Pop-Tarts to 12,000 'tween' girl influencers[7]
Hard Rock Hotel	A blonde model in the Hard Rock Hotel dressing gown created buzz for the café by wandering around a park in Chicago, asking commuting businessmen if they knew the way back to the Hard Rock Hotel[8]
Procter & Gamble	P&G sent product and information to 250,000 teens who were not paid but were free to form their own opinions and talk about them[9]
Microsoft	When introducing its Halo 2 videogame, gave players identified as influencers bits of information about the game before its release so they could talk about the product with other avid gamers who, conveniently, were also heavy users of chat rooms and videogame message boards[10]
Nestlé	Nestlé created a buzz in London by hiring an agency which deliberately jackknifed a lorry in Covent Garden, spilling boxes and boxes of Nestle chocolate bars on the pavement. Roughly 70,000 passer-by were only too pleased to fill their pockets[11]

Table 11.2 How some marketers have created buzz

Company	Buzz Marketing Tactic
Scottish and Newcastle	The brewer Scottish and Newcastle achieved a buzz with its 250-strong team which visited 6000 pubs, chatted to customers about their boozing habits and then bought them a drink. Thousands of pints of Foster's, Kronenbourg 1664 and Strongow were handed out[12]

Notes:

[1] Bruce Philp, 'IKEA's buzz might wake consumers', *The Hamilton Spectator*, 22 September 2007 (Final Edition).
[2] 'Word-of-Mouth: Brands of the Unexpected', *Brand Strategy*, 5 December 2005, 24.
[3] Ibid.
[4] Ibid.
[5] Ibid.
[6] Ibid.
[7] Todd Wasserman, 'Blogs Cause Word of Mouth Business to Spread Quickly', *Brandweek*, 3 October 2005, 9.
[8] Jonny David, 'The Stealth Sell', *The Sunday Times* (London), 5 August 2007; Todd Wasserman, 'Word Games', *Brandweek*, 24 April 2006, 24.
[9] Suzanne Vranica, 'Getting Buzz Marketers to Fess Up', *The Wall Street Journal*, 9 February 2005, B9.
[10] Ibid.
[11] David, 'The Stealth Sell'.
[12] Ibid.

Table 11.2 How some marketers have created buzz (*continued*)

Of course buzz isn't *really* new. Many refer to the Mona Lisa as one of the first examples of buzz marketing. In 1911 the famous painting was stolen from the Louvre and became the topic of consumer talk around the globe, giving the previously little recognised painting fame that exists until today. When you think of the effect of consumers talking one-on-one nearly a century ago, imagine the exponential increase in influence of the individual consumer 'connectors' or 'e-fluentials' who use blogs and other computer-generated media to increase their reach.[13] Compared with traditional advertising and public relations activities, these endorsements are far more credible because they are generated by other consumers and thus more valuable to the brand.

Buzz works best when companies put unpaid consumers in charge of creating their own messages because the message is more credible and trusted. In the UK, Kellogg's is currently trying to make its first foray into buzz marketing with a campaign to promote FruitaBu, its range of bagged fruit snacks. Consumers can sign up to be sent product samples which in turn they will promote and recommend to friends. Kellogg's believes that this type of marketing offers an ideal way to introduce UK consumers to FruitaBu. The company gets help from buzz specialist agency BzzAgent, which established itself in the UK in 2007 and also assists clients such as Kraft, Procter & Gamble and Philips.[14] As Table 11.3 shows, WOMMA considers hiring actors to create buzz deceptive and unethical (more on this at the end of the chapter!). This is just what Sony Ericsson Mobile Communications did when it hired 60 actors to go to tourist attractions to act like tourists and get unsuspecting passers-by to take their photos using the new Sony Ericsson camera phone and then rave about the phone. WOMMA now has rules that state that anyone promoting products should identify for whom they work.[15] Some critics say buzz marketing should never be directed at children and teens as these consumers are more impressionable and easier to deceive than adults.[16] Companies must therefore be careful using buzz marketing because campaigns can backfire when the press get hold of them and publicise the way people are potentially being duped into believing the word of mouth is genuine.

Of course marketers don't have a hand in creating all the buzz around a product or service. WOMMA refers to buzz resulting from buzz marketing campaigns as 'amplified WOM' while it calls buzz that occurs naturally 'organic WOM'. Organic buzz allowed

Positive Word of Mouth Marketing Strategies	Unethical Word of Mouth Marketing Strategies
1. **Encouraging communication** Developing tools to make telling a friend easier Creating forums and feedback tools Working with social networks	1. **Stealth marketing** Any practice designed to deceive people about the involvement of marketers in a communication
2. **Giving people something to talk about** Information that can be shared or forwarded Advertising, stunts and other publicity that encourages conversation Working with product development to build WOM elements into products	2. **Shilling** Paying people to talk about (or promote) a product without disclosing that they are working for the company; impersonating a customer
3. **Creating communities and connecting people** Creating user groups and fan clubs Supporting independent groups that form around your product Hosting discussions and message boards about your products Enabling grassroots organisations such as local meetings and other real-world participation	3. **Infiltration** Using fake identities in an online discussion to promote a product; taking over a website, conversation, or live event against the wishes or rules set by the proprietor
4. **Working with influential communities** Finding people who are likely to respond to your message Identifying people who are able to influence your target customers Informing these individuals about what you do and encouraging them to spread the word Good-faith efforts to support issues and causes that are important to these individuals	4. **Comment spam** Using automated software 'bots' to post unrelated or inappropriate comments to blogs or other online communities
5. **Creating evangelist or advocate programmes** Providing recognition and tools to active advocates Recruiting new advocates, teaching them about the benefits of your products, and encouraging them to talk about them	5. **Defacement** Vandalising or damaging property to promote a product
6. **Researching and listening to customer feedback** Tracking online and offline conversations by supporters, detractors and neutrals Listening and responding to both positive and negative conversations	6. **Spam** Sending bulk or unsolicited email or other messages without clear, voluntary permission
7. **Engaging in transparent conversation** Encouraging two-way conversations with interested parties Creating blogs and other tools to share information Participating openly in blogs and discussions	7. **Falsification** Knowingly disseminating false or misleading information
8. **Co-creation and information sharing** Involving consumers in marketing and creating (feedback on creative campaigns, allowing them to create commercials, etc.) Letting customers 'behind the curtain' have first access to information and content	

Table 11.3 Positive and unethical word of mouth marketing strategies

Source: 'Word of Mouth 101: An Introduction to Word of Mouth Marketing' (accessed July 17, 2006, at www.woman.org/wom101.htm).

Procter & Gamble to discover that its Home Café coffee maker had a tendency to start fires after 3000 buzz agents complained.[17] Naturally occurring buzz also can create negative publicity, as when ex-journalist Jeff Jarvis detailed on a blog his problem getting a $1600 PC fixed due to poor service from Dell computers.[18] To create positive buzz, companies need to have a total customer focus, to empathise and care about their customers. With IMC, marketers like James Dalton of Fonemedia look at communication the way customers see it – as a flow of information from a single source.

Guerrilla marketing

When you see anyone dressed up as a light bulb, a cigarette or a sweet, the chances are it's an attempt at guerrilla marketing. A few years back, some companies with smaller advertising budgets developed innovative ways of getting consumers' attention. These activities – from putting advertising stickers on apples and heads of lettuce to placing product-related messages on the backs of theatre tickets and flags on a golf course – became known as **guerrilla marketing**. The term is not to be confused with Gorilla marketing which was used in a recent commercial for Cadbury's (www.youtube.com/watch?v=TnzFRV1LwIo). This strategy involves 'ambushing' consumers with promotional content in places where they are not expecting to encounter this kind of activity.[19]

Today, big companies are using guerrilla marketing strategies extensively. During the World Cup year 2006, the British company MindShare created 'Sure Fans United', a reality TV show sponsored entirely by Unilever for its Sure deodorant brand. The show portrayed extreme fans who even sold their mortgages to support local football teams. The reality TV show was shown on ITV1 and 'garnered an average of 490,000 viewers per episode, gaining a 9.9 per cent share'.[20] Burger King began a guerrilla marketing campaign to increase sales in its Asia-Pacific outlets by 25 per cent.[21] The company sent CDs with quirky marketing suggestions to local restaurant managers. These included putting 'I♥BK' on T-shirts and placing the shirts on Ronald McDonald, placing large footprints from McDonald's outlets to Burger King outlets, placing signs on empty benches saying 'gone

Marketing ethics and sustainability

Blogging or flogging: can you tell the difference?

As a marketing communications tool, 'blogs' have not caused much concern in the digital marketing environment to date. Technocrati.com, a leading technology website and commentator, estimates there are 35.5 million blogs in existence, as well as 75,000 created daily. As the prominence of blogs and their authors rise, blogs attract growing corporate attention as a digital word of mouth technique.

A number of businesses have fallen foul of the blogosphere community due to ethically questionable blogging practices. In 2007, reports emerged alleging that Microsoft delivered brand new high-spec laptops with new Vista software to influential tech bloggers before the Vista launch. However, perhaps the most infamous blogging misdemeanour was allegedly committed by Wal-Mart. In 2006, it was reported by the press that its communications agency, Edelman Public Relations Worldwide, 'masterminded the authorship of several pro-Wal-Mart blogs'.

It appears that the popularity and influence of blogs has led to a growing number of companies rewarding bloggers financially or in kind to report favourably on a company's product or service, otherwise known as 'flogging'.

Debate, discuss, disagree

1   Is the practice of flogging corporate deception or a legitimate form of advertising?

Marketing metrics

Social media and the new breed of marketing metrics

With millions of people around the world spending hours online, social media is promising news for advertisers looking to engage with potential customers. There is only one drawback: how do you measure such engagement? Take online video viewing; its dynamics have evolved dramatically in recent years and it has become an essential part of the digital consumer experience. This calls for the creation of new, media-specific metrics. Companies like ComScore offer the capability of filtering video viewing activity between advertising and editorial content, a ranking of video advertising networks by actual reach of ads delivered and additional metrics including average daily unique viewers, percentage of ads by time spent viewing video, ads per content video, and content minutes per ad minute. The service is now available in 16 countries, and the company plans to take it to more countries soon.[22]

to BK – Ronald' and placing large signs at BK locations that are near KFC locations that read 'It's why the chicken crossed the road.'

Companies can use guerrilla marketing to promote new drinks, cars or clothing styles. Nike, for example, mentions its website or celebrity tie-ins in chat rooms. This method has been hugely successful in attracting hundreds of thousands of visitors to its website. The website suits the young market, offering sport-focused video clips, email games or MP3 downloads.[23] Given the success of these campaigns, many of which operate on a shoestring budget, expect to see even more of this kind of tactic as other companies climb on the guerrilla bandwagon. Type in 'guerrilla marketing' to look for example videos on www.youtube.com.

Integrated marketing communications

www.pearsoned.co.uk/Solomon

Objective

5

Describe integrated marketing communications and its characteristics

The traditional forms of marketing communications are *advertising*, including mass media, direct mail, outdoor advertising and online advertising; *sales promotions* such as coupons, samples, rebates or contests; press releases and special events that *public relations* professionals organise; and *sales presentations*. Today's marketers have added newer types of communications tactics such as buzz, viral marketing and guerrilla marketing to their bag of tricks.

Many marketing experts now believe that integrating all forms of marketing communications is essential for successful marketing. **Integrated marketing communications (IMC)** is the process that marketers use to plan, develop, execute and evaluate coordinated, measurable, persuasive brand communication programmes over time to targeted audiences. The IMC approach argues that consumers see the variety of messages they receive from a firm – a TV commercial, a coupon, an opportunity to win a sweepstake and a display in a shop – as a whole, as a single company speaking to them but in different places and different ways. Take, for example, the Harry Potter books. The communications there are managed from the pre-release publicity events and online marketing to create buzz, through to event marketing and opening nights, to poster and newspaper advertising to remind people and finally the merchandising for all of the characters all communicate the same ideas.

That's a lot different from how traditional marketing communication programmes are created, where little effort is made to coordinate the varying messages consumers receive. An advertising campaign typically is run independently of a sweepstake, which in turn has no relation to a Formula One car racing sponsorship. These disjointed efforts can send conflicting messages that leave the consumer confused and unsure of the brand's identity. The customer is the focus for companies that adopt an IMC perspective. With IMC, marketers seek to understand what information consumers want as well as how, when and where they want it – and then to deliver the information about the product or service using the best combination of communications methods available to them. This should mean that communication becomes part of people's lives and not a distraction.

Marketers have been developing promotion strategies and using the elements of the promotion mix for many years, but the concept of integrated marketing communications is relatively new. While IMC has not been adopted by all firms, many marketing experts believe that IMC provides a competitive advantage to firms in the twenty-first century.

With IMC, marketers plan and then execute marketing communication programmes that create and maintain long-term relationships with customers by satisfying customer needs. This means that promotion tools are used in such a way as to build loyal relationships with customers or other stakeholders, rather than simply causing a one-time product purchase or short-term change in behaviour.[24] With IMC, marketers like James Dalton of Fonemedia look at communication the way customers see it – as a flow of information from a single source. Thus, marketers who understand the power of IMC seek to 'unify all marketing communication tools – from advertising to packaging – to send target audiences a consistent, persuasive message that promotes company goals'.[25]

So why is IMC so important today? A few years ago, marketers could communicate with consumers by placing a few ads on major television networks and perhaps in a few popular magazines. Today, with increased global competition, customers are bombarded with more and more marketing messages. And the sheer number of media outlets is also mushrooming. Marketers can choose from literally hundreds of cable and satellite stations, each of which can deliver its messages to a selected portion of the television viewing audience. All this means that consumers are less likely to be influenced by any single marketer-generated message. At the same time, widely available technology now enables even small firms to develop and effectively use customer databases, giving firms greater opportunities for understanding customers and for developing one-to-one communication programmes. And technology gives customers the ability to communicate among themselves about products and companies and even to view ads on the web at their leisure.[26]

 ## Characteristics of IMC

To fully understand what IMC is all about and before a firm can begin to implement an IMC programme, it is essential to understand some important characteristics of IMC.

IMC creates a single unified voice

Perhaps the most important characteristic of IMC is that it creates a single unified voice for a firm. If we examine the traditional communication programme of a typical consumer goods firm, say a manufacturer of frozen foods, we see that they often develop communication tactics in isolation. If marketers decide they need advertising, what do they do? They hire an ad agency to produce great advertising. Or they may even hire several different ad agencies to develop advertising aimed at different target markets. They may also realise they need public relations activities, so they hire a public relations firm. Then some other genius decides to sponsor a sweepstake and hires a sales promotion firm to do this. The sales department hires a different firm to develop trade show materials, and someone in the corporate communication department hires a sports-marketing firm to work on sponsoring a car race.

Each of these firms may well do a good job, but each may also be sending out a different message. The customer can't help but be confused. What is the product? What is the brand image? Whose needs will this product satisfy? IMC strategies present a unified selling proposition in the marketplace by eliminating duplication and conflicting communication. Because a company develops an IMC programme as a whole, there is a focus on *all* communications elements – advertising, public relations, sales promotion, and so forth – speaking with one voice, creating a single and powerful brand personality.

Having a single brand message, however, doesn't mean that marketers don't communicate to different segments of the market or different stakeholder groups with different tactics. The same brand message can be communicated to employees with a story in the company newsletter about how local workers have helped flood victims, to loyal customers via direct mail that explains how to make their home safe for toddlers, and to prospective customers through mass media and internet advertising.

The one-voice/one-message focus of IMC also considers other less obvious forms of communication. For example, a firm's communication with customers includes the letters sent to customers, the way company personnel talk on the phone with clients or customers, the uniforms delivery people or other employees wear, signage and other policies and procedures that may have an unintended effect on consumers' perceptions of the firm (even the stationery the company uses to correspond with vendors and customers).

IMC begins with the customer

The customer is the primary focus of the communication, *not* the goals of the company or the creative genius of the communication specialists whose creative ideals can become too abstract for the consumer to follow. First and foremost, the goal of IMC is to provide the information customers want when they want it where they want it and in the amount needed. Remember it's about becoming part of people's lives not a distraction from it! Sometimes that's as simple as letting consumers 'vote' on the shows or products they want to see, as when fans of the hit TV comedy *Friends* were allowed to choose their six favourite episodes at a website when the producers decided to end the series.[27]

IMC seeks to develop relationships with customers

As mass-marketing activities have become less effective, many marketers are finding that the road to success is through one-to-one or relationship marketing, where the focus is on building and maintaining a long-term relationship with each individual customer. To achieve this, marketers must continuously communicate with each customer or else risk losing them to the competition.

What we said earlier bears repeating – *it simply is easier and less expensive to keep an existing customer than to attract a new one* . Thus, IMC firms also measure their success by share of customer, not share of market, and on the lifetime value of a customer. This means prioritising customers so that greater resources go to communicating with high-value buyers or clients.

Because IMC is also much about building and maintaining relationships with customers, IMC strategies often incorporate databases and the CRM programmes and practices we talked about in Chapter 6. With these tools, marketers have the information they need to understand customers and to deliver unique messages to each consumer – messages that meet the needs of each consumer and that build relationships.

IMC involves two-way communication

Traditional communication programmes were built on one-way communication activities. Television, magazine, newspaper and outdoor advertising spouted clever messages at the consumer, but there was little if any way for the consumer to talk back. Today, we know

Real people, other voices

Marilyn Hunt
University of Worcester

I would use a *selective* combination of Option 3, followed and supported by Option 1. This will enable the university to effectively combine mass and personal appeals and deliver a coordinated, integerated and persuasive marketing communications campaign over time.

The university is new entrant into an existing and competitive market and is launching an expensive product. Deciding to study for an MBA and selecting the right course is an important, high-involvement purchase decision, which will entail extensive information search and evaluation of alternatives. The product will need to be very clearly explained to the target audience – current business professionals, mangers and exectives. In an established and competitive marketplace where the university is unknown, traditional media (newspapers) will help to establish a reputable brand and product image, awareness and understanding. The newspaper advertisements can also be used as a call to action to direct enquiries to the university and to attract potential students to exhibitions in both Lagos and Nairobi where the benefits of the course can be clearly explained by the university's 'sales' team. The university should select newspaper titles with the highest readership amongst businessmen and women in Lagos, Nairobi and other conurbations of economic and financial wealth.

Phone web advertising will complement the newspaper campaign in providing targeted and timely access/reminders to the appropriate audience profile. It will extend both the reach and impact of the newspaper campaign and similarly encourage attendance at the exhibitions. For example, it will be possible to target business managers who may not read the selected newspapers, or (if they do) may not see the campaign when it runs, perhaps because they are travelling for their work. Given that the mobile networks will reveral the media consumption habits of their users, there will also be an opportunity to link to the newspaper campaign where relevant.

The combination of a selective national newspaper campaign, together with targeted phone web advertising, will enable the universitiy to optimise and evaluate the impact of its expenditure by building a positive image for its (unknown) brand, reach its audience and support its exhibition activities.

Jenny P. Cotton
Morton's Marketing

The opening paragraph holds the key: combined media channels have delivered the best advertising outcomes. Can these options be cost-effectively combined? Similarly, advertising context as well as content is important; both can be pre-tested. MBA advertising has three timescales: before the exhibitionsin in Lagos and Nairobi, within the exhibition itself – which is typically in direct competition with others – and the postsexhibition follow-up and application encourgement. A national reach may be less important than a business sector coverage.

The exhibition follow-up is key to success. Budget must be retained for this vital stage. Every effort to develop all attendees and especially your own contacts is vital. Securing personal access detail before and during event is the first priority, which may help decide which direct contact channels will maximise post-event applications.

The event organisers should be a good associate, providing contacts in registrations and attendees afterwards. They often run group advertising offers. Broadsheet and business press often run advertorial special sections. Is this the case? What do your direct competitors do?

If the organisers are using traditional media – why? An MBA advertorial campaign based on informative and topical issues content should attract readers/listeners/viewers drawn by the exhibition budget. Are locally based alumni available to support a news item and social media campaign with a parallel buzz marketing of personal referral through social media? In this case advertising support can be extended as appropriate – all social media? Or selected media? Budgets should be focused.

This is presented as a pure channel-based decision; there is little target audience detail or costs. Should Fonemedia rely on the exhibition organisers to generate the attendees' interest and focus its own resources on the exhibition experience and the important follow-up? Options 1 and 2 are flexible, have higher support costs than traditional media but offer poor targeting.

Option 3, traditional media, is described as newspaper-based but may have radio or TV topical news options as well. Advertising may be supported by positive PR or may take the form of advertorial, additional content in editorial style to endorse the advertising messages.

that one-way, impersonal communication is highly ineffective at building long-term relationships with customers. Instead, marketers seek first to learn what information customers have and what additional information they want and then develop communication tactics that let them give information to their customers.

IMC focuses on stakeholders, not just customers

Stakeholders (not to be confused with shareholders) are any individuals or organisations that are important to the long-term health of an organisation. Some of these stakeholders include employees, suppliers, stockholders, the media, trade associations, regulators and even neighbours. One reason these other stakeholders are so important is that customers and prospective customers don't just learn about a company and its products from the firm. Their attitudes, positive or negative, are also heavily influenced by the mass media, government regulatory bodies, or even their neighbour who happens to work for the company. Thus, while the primary stakeholder is usually the customer, myriad other groups or individuals can significantly influence customers' attitudes and behaviours.

IMC generates a continuous stream of communication

A major characteristic of an IMC strategy is that tactics using many different elements of the communication programme – advertising, publicity, personal selling, sales promotion, customer testimonials and so on – are included in a single IMC plan. As a result, IMC strategies provide a continuous stream of communication. Instead of consumers being bombarded with messages from various sources for a week or two and then hearing nothing from the brand for months, IMC planning ensures that consumers receive information on a regular basis and in the right amount.

IMC measures results based upon actual feedback

Many IMC supporters suggest that the only adequate measure of effectiveness is to evaluate the return on investment. This means that if a firm spends €1 million on advertising, it should be able to determine what amount of revenue the firm receives as a result of that expenditure. While this type of relationship between promotion costs and revenues may be difficult to measure exactly because of such things as the long-term effects of advertising and other communication, most firms are seeking measures of accountability for their communication budgets and demand results. That's why we've made such a big deal out of *marketing metrics* in this book. (See Chapter 12 on how to measure advertising effectiveness.)

Marketing misstakes

Does a brand still require a website?

Once, TV ads used to end by directing viewers to the brand's website, most now feature an address of a Facebook page or Twitter account instead. French Connection is showing that even initiatives like online shopping are no longer restricted to its own webpage. Towards the end of 2010, the fashion retailer launched YouTique, an interactive shop that allows consumers to purchase products by clicking on the items on a YouTube video. Will Woodhams, the French Connection marketing director says 'We need to be ready for Generation Z' where they were 'born with a BlackBerry in their hands – even email is old fashioned to them. So we need to be in their spaces if we are to hold conversations with them.' For some brands, these developments are leaving them asking whether they need a website at all.[28]

Source: Adapted from Resurgent French Connection ditches blunt marketing tools, and thank FCUK, *The Guardian*, 13 March 2011 (Wood, Z.). Copyright Guardian News & Media Ltd 2011.

Why do you think not having a website might be a misstake?

Objective

6

Explain the important role of database marketing in integrated marketing communications (IMC)

IMC and database marketing

The effective use of databases is crucial for building relationships with consumers, a key characteristic of IMC. The development of a customer database allows an organisation to learn about the preferences of its customers, fine-tune its offerings, and build a relationship with its market. Tesco is a great example of database marketing: when you use your loyalty card, you tell Tesco what products you like buy buying from its shops. Your loyalty card also provides you with coupons and vouchers, and Tesco knows how effective it has been by how many you redeem.

Database marketing is the creation of a relationship with a set of customers with an identifiable interest in a product or service and whose responses to promotion efforts become part of the communications process.

Let's look at an example of how an IMC firm may make effective use of database marketing. What if you ordered a dozen roses to be delivered to a friend for his or her birthday last year? You (and your friend) have become a part of the florist's database. What are the possibilities for the florist? First, the database is a goldmine of information. By examining (or *mining* as it is often called) the records of thousands of customers, including you, the florist can find out which customers order flowers frequently (heavy users) and which order only occasionally (light users). They can identify customers who order flowers for themselves. They know which customers order flowers only for funerals, and which send flowers to their partners. And they can determine what type of customer accounts for their greatest sales and their greatest profits. This helps them to develop a better understanding of their target markets.

Of course, using the information in the database for understanding a firm's market is only the beginning. Even more important is how firms such as our florist *use* the database to create that one-to-one communication with their target markets. So you, our florist's customer, may get a call or an email next year reminding you of your friend's birthday and asking if you want the same dozen roses sent again this year. The customer who hosts dinner parties frequently may receive a brochure before the Christmas holiday season that shows various table arrangements. Heavy users might receive a special thank you for their business and an offer to receive a free arrangement after purchasing 12 arrangements. And by the way, what about your friend who received flowers but who has never purchased from our florist? Since we may assume that a consumer who likes to receive flowers will sooner or later want to purchase them as well, they become part of the florist's prospective customer database. As such, they may receive a catalogue of the most popular arrangements or perhaps a coupon for a discount on the first order.

The following list explains what database marketing can do:[29]

- **Database marketing is interactive:** Recall that interactive marketing requires a response from consumers, be it filling out an order form or calling an 0800 number for product information. For example, Jaguar.com wanted to rebuild its website to get the online brand in sync with the look of its ongoing traditional campaign. It hired a marketing agency which asked 200 Jaguar owners to rank their website preferences. As a result, the website was redesigned to show more information about security and the company's history.[30] This type of interactivity gives marketers more than one opportunity to develop a dialogue with the customer and possibly to create add-on sales by engaging the customer in a discussion about the product and related items or services in which they might be interested.

- **Database marketing builds relationships:** It's easier for the marketer to build promotion programmes that continue over time with database marketing because the marketer can best adapt them in light of consumers' responses. *The best predictor of who will buy a product is knowing who bought it in the past.* That's why *Reader's Digest's* 12 full-time statisticians sort its customers by likelihood of purchase and predict the probability that each will respond to a given offer.[31] Once sophisticated database marketers know who has already purchased, they can keep in touch with these consumers. They can reward loyal customers with money-saving coupons and keep them informed of upcoming prizes and promotions. As one executive whose company tracks high value customers explained, 'They are members of a club, but they don't know they are members.'[32]

- **Database marketing locates new customers:** In some cases, a marketer can create new customers by focusing communications on likely prospects with characteristics similar to current users. For example, after Tesco launched its Clubcard the company did not rest on its laurels. It soon introduced a Clubcard Plus which offered holders interest paid on their balances and therefore could be used like any other debit card. Within 12 months of being lauched, the Clubcard Plus became the most popular UK loyalty scheme.[33]

- **Database marketing stimulates cross-selling:** Database marketers can find it easy to offer related products to their customers. Interest in one product category boosts the odds that the customer is a good candidate for similar items. This explains why companies bombard consumers with mail offers for computer software, magazines or clothing after they purchase a similar product over the phone or through a catalogue. At British Gas, answering customer calls and solving their queries are not only important to achieve high customer satisfaction but are also crucial for a successful cross-selling strategy. Customer information is stored in a database and helps to sell appropriate products which are in line with customer's needs in the long term.[34] The European low-cost airline Germanwings uses its customer database to send out emails informing customers of cheap ticket deals for given periods. Some mailings have included questionnaires regarding specific interests of customers to help them decide on future product offerings.

- **Database marketing is measurable:** A common complaint of many marketers is the difficulty in pinpointing the impact a promotion had on the target market – what is a specific promotion's return on investment (ROI)? Who can say for sure that a single TV commercial motivated people to switch mobile phone? But the database marketers know exactly who received a specific message, so they are able to measure the effectiveness of each communication because they track each promotion and enter it into the database against your name.

- **Responses are trackable:** The marketer can assess the proportion of message recipients that responded, compare the effectiveness of different messages, and compile a history of which consumers are most likely to respond over time.[35]

Developing the IMC plan

Objective

7

Explain the stages in developing an IMC plan

Now that we've talked about the characteristics of an IMC strategy, we need to see how to make it happen. How do we develop an IMC plan that delivers just the right message to a number of different target audiences when and where they want it in the most effective and cost-efficient way? Just as with any other strategic decision-making process, the development of this plan includes several steps, as Figure 11.3 shows. Let's review each step.

Step 1: Identify the target audiences

An important part of overall marketing planning is to determine who the target market is. This is where a good customer database is most important. With a well-designed database, marketers can know who their target market is as well as the buying behaviour of different segments within the total market. This means they can develop targeted messages for each customer.

Figure 11.3 | Steps in developing the IMC plan

Step 2: Establish the communications objectives

The next step in communications planning is to establish communications objectives. The whole point of communicating with customers and prospective customers is to let them know that the organisation has a product to meet their needs in a timely and affordable way. It's bad enough when a product comes along that people don't want or need. But the bigger marketing sin is to have a product that they *do* want – but fail to let them know about it. Of course, seldom can we deliver a single message to consumers that magically transforms them into loyal customers. In most cases, it takes a series of messages that move consumers through several stages.

We can view this process as an uphill climb, such as the one Figure 11.4 depicts. The consumer is 'led' through a series of steps, often referred to as a **hierarchy of effects**, from initial awareness of a product to brand loyalty. The task of moving the consumer up the hierarchy becomes more difficult at each step. Many potential buyers may drop out along the way, leaving less of the target group inclined to go the distance and become loyal customers. Each part of this path entails different communication objectives to 'push' people to the next level.

To understand how this process works, consider how a firm would have to adjust its communication objectives as it tries to establish a presence in the market for a new men's cologne called Homme. Let's say that the primary target market for the cologne is single men aged 18–24 who care about their appearance and who are into health, fitness, working out and looking very fit. The company would want to focus more on some promotion methods (such as advertising) and less on others (such as personal selling). Here are some steps the company might take to promote Homme:

● **Create awareness:** The first step is to make members of the target market aware that there's a new brand of cologne on the market. Marketers would accomplish this through simple, repetitive advertising in magazines, on television and on the radio that push the brand name. The company might even consider creating a 'teaser' campaign where ads heighten interest because they don't reveal the exact nature of the product (for example, newspaper ads that simply proclaim, 'Homme is coming!'). The promotion objective

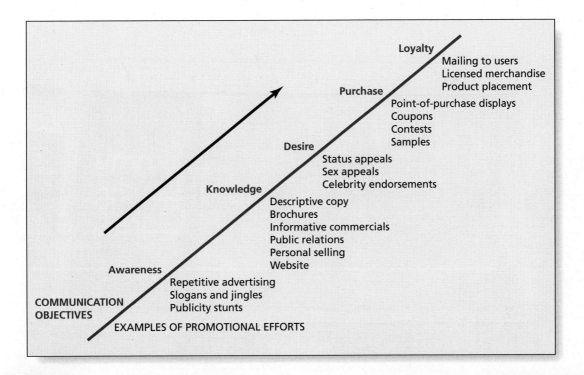

Loyalty
 Mailing to users
 Licensed merchandise
 Product placement

Purchase
 Point-of-purchase displays
 Coupons
 Contests
 Samples

Desire
 Status appeals
 Sex appeals
 Celebrity endorsements

Knowledge
 Descriptive copy
 Brochures
 Informative commercials
 Public relations
 Personal selling
 Website

Awareness
 Repetitive advertising
 Slogans and jingles
 Publicity stunts

COMMUNICATION
OBJECTIVES

EXAMPLES OF PROMOTIONAL EFFORTS

Figure 11.4	**The hierarchy of effects**
	Communication objectives seek to move consumers through the hierarchy of effects

might be to create an 80 per cent awareness of Homme cologne among 18–24-year-old men in the first two months.

- **Inform the market:** The next step would be to provide prospective users with knowledge about the benefits the new product has to offer, that is, how it is positioned relative to other fragrances (see Chapter 6). Perhaps the cologne has a light, slightly mentholated scent with a hint of a liniment smell to remind the wearer of how he feels after a good workout. Promotion would focus on communications that emphasise this position. The objective at this point might be to communicate the connection between Homme and muscle building so that 70 per cent of the target market develops some interest in the product.

- **Create desire:** The next task is to create favourable feelings and desires toward the product. The aim should be to convince men that Homme is preferable to other colognes. Communications at this stage might employ splashy advertising spreads in magazines, perhaps including an endorsement by a well-known celebrity such as a Pierce Brosnan. The specific objective might be to create positive attitudes towards Homme cologne among 50 per cent of the target market and brand preference among 30 per cent of the target market.

- **Encourage trial:** As the expression goes, 'How do you know you don't like it, until you've tried it?' The company now needs to get some of the men who have become interested in the cologne to try it. A promotion plan might encourage trial by mailing samples of Homme to members of the target market, inserting 'scratch-and-sniff' samples in bodybuilding magazines, placing elaborate displays in shops that dispense money-saving coupons, or even sponsoring a contest in which the winner gets to have a personal trainer for a day. The specific objective now might be to encourage trial of Homme among 25 per cent of 18–24-year-old men in the first two months.

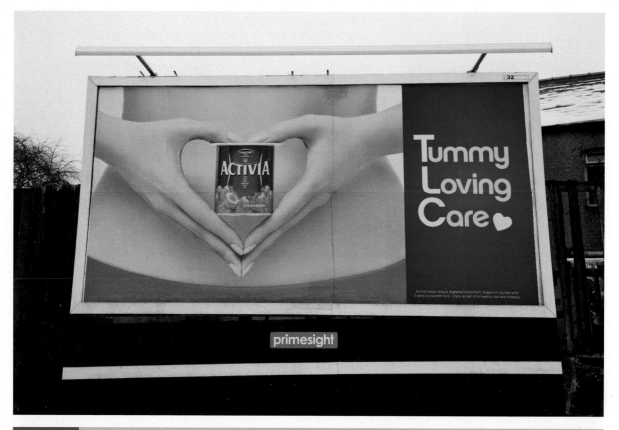

| Photo 11.5 | The second step in the hierarchy of effects is knowledge. Danone informs consumers about its new product
Source: Alamy Images/Jeff Morgan 16 |

- **Build loyalty:** Of course, the real test is loyalty: convincing customers to stay with Homme after they've gone through the first bottle. Promotion efforts must maintain communications with current users to reinforce the bond they feel with the product. As before, they will accomplish this with some mix of strategies, perhaps including direct mail advertising to current users, product placements in popular television programmes or films, and maybe even the development of a workout clothing line bearing a Homme logo. The objective might be to develop and maintain regular usage of Homme cologne among 10 per cent of men from 18 to 24 years old.

Step 3: Determine and allocate the marketing communications budget

While setting a budget for marketing communications might seem easy – you just calculate how much you need to accomplish your objectives – in reality it's not that simple. Determining and allocating communications budgets includes three distinct decisions:

- determining the total communications budget;
- deciding whether to use a push strategy or a pull strategy; and
- allocating how much to spend on specific promotion activities.

In the real world, firms often view communications costs as an expense rather than as an investment leading to greater profits. When sales are declining or the company is operating in a difficult economic environment, it is often tempting to cut costs by reducing spending on advertising, promotions and other 'soft' activities whose contributions to the bottom line are hard to quantify. When this is the case, marketers must work harder to justify these expenses.

Economic approaches to budgeting rely on marginal analysis (discussed in Chapter 10), in which the organisation spends money on promotion as long as the revenues realised by these efforts continue to exceed the costs of the promotions themselves, e.g, BOGOF offers, buy one get one free, often fall into this category. This perspective assumes that promotions are always intended solely to increase sales when in fact these activities may have other objectives, such as enhancing a firm's image.

Also, the effects of promotions often lag over time. For example, a firm may have to spend a lot on promotion when it first launches a product without seeing any immediate return. Because of these limitations, most firms rely on two budgeting techniques: top down and bottom up.

Top-down budgeting techniques require top management to establish the overall amount that the organisation allocates for promotion activities, and this amount is then divided among advertising, public relations and other promotion departments.

The most common top-down technique is the **percentage-of-sales method**, in which the promotion budget is based on last year's sales or on estimates for the present year's sales. The percentage may be an industry average provided by trade associations that collect objective information on behalf of member companies. The advantage of this method is that it ties spending on promotion to sales and profits.

Unfortunately, this method can imply that sales cause promotional outlays rather than viewing sales as the *outcome* of promotional efforts. As sales drop, firms might be reluctant to spend more on promotion even though the drop might be due to environmental changes, such as a change in economic conditions or a rival's recent introduction of a new product. If so, cutting promotion spending might not help the firm in the long run.

The **competitive-parity method** is another way of saying 'keep up with the Joneses'. In other words, match whatever competitors are spending. Some marketers think this approach simply mirrors the best thinking of others in the business. However, this method often sees each player maintaining the same market share year after year. This method also assumes that the same amount spent on promotion by two different firms will yield the same results, but spending a lot of money doesn't guarantee a successful promotion. Firms certainly need to monitor their competitors' promotion activities, but they must combine this information with their own objectives and capacities.

The problem with top-down techniques is that budget decisions are based more on established practices than on promotion objectives. Another approach is to begin at the beginning: identify promotion goals and allocate enough money to accomplish them. That is what **bottom-up budgeting techniques** attempt. For example, some marketers devise a budget that attempts to project the revenues and costs associated with a product over several years and then match promotion expenditures to a pattern – such as spending more on promotion in the first year to build awareness of the brand market share and then spending less once the product catches on.

This bottom-up logic is at the heart of the **objective-task method**, which is gaining in popularity. Using this approach, the firm first defines the specific communications goals it hopes to achieve, such as increasing by 20 per cent the number of consumers who are aware of the brand. It then tries to figure out what kind of promotional efforts it will take to meet that goal. Although this is the most rational approach, it is hard to implement because it obliges managers to specify their objectives and attach costs to them. This method requires careful analysis – and a bit of lucky 'guesstimating'.

One crucial issue in determining the promotion mix is whether the company is relying on a push strategy or a pull strategy. A **push strategy** means that the company wants to

Marketing metrics

Ford advertising models

Ford of Europe spends hundreds of millions of euros on advertising. Management wanted to optimise the allocation of spend across the main car brands and the countries in Europe. They used econometric modelling to assess the incremental sales value of advertising for different brand/country combinations, and also the saturation curves as advertising spend is increased. These 'elasticities' were then incorporated into an optimisation model that determined the allocation of advertising money that would produce the maximum financial returns. When management first ran the model it triggered vigorous debate, followed by refinement of the assumptions, and after an iterative process management agreed on a new allocation that significantly enhanced the financial results.

move its products by convincing members of the distribution channel such as wholesalers, agents or retailers to offer them and entice their customers to select these items. In this case, promotion efforts will 'push' the products from producers to consumer by focusing on personal selling, trade advertising and sales promotions, such as exhibits at trade shows.

In contrast, a company relying on a **pull strategy** is counting on consumers wanting its products and so convincing retailers to respond to this demand by stocking them. In this case, efforts will focus on media advertising and consumer sales promotion to stimulate interest among end consumers who will 'pull' the product onto shop shelves and then into their shopping baskets. So no supermarket would dare not to stock Heinz tomato ketchup because Heinz makes sure through lots of promotions that customers put it in their basket when they go shopping.

Once the organisation decides how much to spend on promotion and whether to use a push or a pull strategy, it must divide its budget among the elements in the promotion mix. Although advertising used to get most of the promotion budget, today sales promotions are playing a big role in marketing strategies. UK-based Dynamo Marketing Communications, for example, spurred its Christmas sales for three consecutive years by offering consumers personal and interactive promotions. In 2007, the company gave its customers a pot of earth, a miniature watering can and an amaryllis bulb. The customer had to nurture the plant and send a photo of the plant to the company. If successful, the customer won an Easter egg. If the customer produced a red flower, he or she could win a weekend away.[36] Procter & Gamble reduced consumer sales promotion spending in the early 1990s when adopting its 'value pricing' strategy. Since then, P&G has revamped its $2 billion-plus annual trade promotion budget to focus more on activities such as in-store merchandising, temporary price reductions and end-of-aisle displays.[37]

Whether we use a push or a pull strategy and how the promotion mix for a product is designed must vary over time because some elements work better at different points in the product life cycle than others. As an example, we might think about the state of electronic audio and video equipment in today's market and the relative positions in the product life cycle.

An example of an IMC strategy In the *introduction phase*, the objective is to build awareness of and encourage trial of the product among consumers, often by relying on a push strategy. That's the situation today with WiFi. Advertising is the primary promotion tool for creating awareness, and a publicity campaign to generate news reports about the new product may help as well. Business-to-business marketing that emphasises personal selling – that is, the marketing that a manufacturer does to retailers and other business customers – is important in this phase in order to get channel members to carry the product. For consumer goods sold through retailers, trade sales promotion may be necessary to encourage retailers to stock the product.

In the *growth phase* , promotions must now start stressing product benefits. For products such as MP3 players, advertising increases now, while sales promotions that encourage trial usually decline because people are more willing to try the product without being offered an incentive. Sales promotions (free samples and such, as when retailers like Starbucks or McDonald's set up free WiFi zones for customers) may be used to encourage trial.

The opposite pattern often occurs with products such as DVD players, now in their *maturity phase*, when many people have already tried the product. As sales stabilise, strategy now shifts to encouraging people to switch from competitors' brands. This can be tough if consumers don't see enough differences to bother. Usually, sales promotions, particularly coupons and special price deals, have greater chances of success than advertising because advertising is great at generating awareness but not great a creating action, i.e. buying. In some cases an industry revamps a widely used technology by introducing one or more new versions or formats that force consumers to convert (sometimes kicking and screaming), thus transforming a mature category back to a new one. That's what's happened in the 'DVD format wars', a high-stakes showdown between the Blu-ray disc that offered 50 gigabytes of storage and was backed by a large group of consumer electronics and computer companies and the HD DVD format, backed by Toshiba and favoured by a majority of film studios, which was more similar to the standard DVD.[38] In 2008, Toshiba blinked first and so became the decade's equivalent of the losing Betamax (versus the winning VHS format) in the earlier 'VCR format wars'.[39]

All bets are off for products such as VCR players, now in their *decline phase*. As sales plummet, the company dramatically reduces spending on all elements of the promotion mix. Sales will be driven by the continued loyalty of a small group of users who keep the product alive until it is sold to another company or discontinued.

Factors affecting the size of the IMC budget are:

- **Organisational factors:** Characteristics of the specific firm influence how it allocates its money. These characteristics include the complexity and formality of the company's decision-making process, preferences for advertising versus sales promotions or other elements in the promotion mix, past experiences with specific promotion vehicles and the 'comfort level' of the firm's advertising and promotion agencies with different approaches in marketing communications.

- **Market potential:** Some consumer groups are more likely to buy the product than others. For example, the marketers of Homme might find that men in blue-collar occupations would be more interested in the product than men in white-collar occupations. It makes sense for marketers to allocate more resources to areas with more sales potential.

- **Market size:** As a rule, larger markets are more expensive places in which to promote. The costs of buying media (such as local TV spots) are higher in major metropolitan areas, but high population density means it will be easier to reach more consumers at the same time. Advertising is good for mass-market products, while personal selling is good for expensive, specialised or highly technical products.

Step 4: Design the promotion mix

Designing the promotion mix is the most complicated step in marketing communication planning. It includes determining the specific communication tools that will be used, what message is to be communicated and the communication channel(s) to be employed.

Planners must ask how advertising, sales promotion, personal selling and public relations can be used most effectively to communicate with different target audiences. Each element of the promotion mix has benefits and shortcomings, all of which must be considered in making promotion decisions.

The message should focus on one of four objectives: it should get attention, hold interest, create desire, and produce action. These communications goals are known as the **AIDA model**. Here we'll review some different forms the message can take as well as how the information in the message might be structured. You could also use AIDA to help decide on the options for James at Fonemedia.

There are many ways to say the same thing, and marketers must take care in choosing what type of appeal, or message strategy, they will use when encoding the message. To illustrate, consider two strategies employed by rival car companies to promote similar cars. A few years ago, both Toyota and Nissan introduced a large luxury car that sold for more than €30,000. Toyota's advertising for its Lexus model used a rational appeal that focused on the technical advancements in the car's design. This approach is often effective for promoting products that are technically complex and require a substantial investment. Nissan, in contrast, focused on the spiritual fulfilment a driver might feel driving down the road in a fine machine. Much like Nissan, Volkswagen launched an international advertising campaign based on love poems linked to vehicles in an attempt to reach the strong emotions that underlie consumers' preferences for cars. In Germany, double-page newspaper and magazine ads featured a love poem with a paragraph explaining the feelings one of Volkswagen's cars represented.[40]

Across the hall

Advice for James Dalton

Florian Mayer
Senior Brand Manager
International Markets Carlsberg Group

I would recommend to James to pitch for option 1 as it provides for the highest possible accuracy in targeting potential new students. We know that a mere 2% of the population in Nigeria and Kenya have the financial means to afford an overseas MBA course. Therefore, option 3, the use of mass media which is primarily used to create brand awareness, is too wasteful as print media has wide reach which is not required here and becomes expensive when dialling up frequency which would be desirable for the task at hand. Option 2 seems more interesting at first sight since web access is likely to be high amongst our target group, however low click through rates and difficulties in targeting users accurately due to the fact that PCs are used by several people in several locations makes this option less attractive. Option 1 can deliver on the given objective of driving our affluent, young and urban target group to the two exhibitions in Lagos and Nairobi. Only owners of iPhones and

Blackberrys in and around these cities and within a certain age bracket (say 20 – 35) can be targeted with relevant messages. Also, mobile advertising offers the potential to extend the depth of the campaign as users can be provided with relevant, rich-media content which engages them far longer with the university's offering than print media, for example, would be able to deliver. Analysing the CTR and browsing behavior of users allows for different campaign messages and content to be tested live and optimised continuously. User data can also be collected to follow up with interested people that might not be able to attend the exhibitions or to target future campaigns

Furthermore, the CTR is higher than for web-based advertising and costs can be precisely controlled by limiting clicks to a certain amount that is pre-determined by the campaign budget. The only 'unknown' variable with this solution is the creative appeal which is the same for all other solutions on offer. Lastly, by using mobile advertising which is still a fairly novel way of interacting with your audience, the university can build its brand image as an innovative education provider. After all, students choose MBAs partly to learn about marketing and innovation. A campaign than can demonstrate that the university is cleverly using both is an important first step in recruiting new students.

Many marketing messages are similar to debates or trials in which someone presents arguments and tries to convince the receivers to shift their opinions. The way the argument is presented can be important. Most messages merely tout one or more positive attributes of the product or reasons to buy it. These are known as *supportive arguments* or *one-sided messages*. An alternative is to use a *two-sided message*, with both positive and negative information. Two-sided ads can be quite effective, but marketers seldom use them.[41]

A related issue is whether the argument should draw conclusions. Should the ad say only 'our brand is superior', or should it explicitly tell the consumer to buy it? The answer depends on the degree of a consumer's motivation to think about the ad and the complexity of the arguments. If the message is personally relevant, people will pay attention to it and draw their own conclusions. But if the arguments are hard to follow or the person's motivation to follow them is lacking, it is best to make these conclusions explicit.

Even the best message is wasted if it is not placed in communication channels that will reach the target audience effectively. See the marketing metrics insert for the latest way of measuring what media people are consuming. Communication channels include the mass media: newspapers, television, radio, magazines and direct mail. Other media include outdoor display signs and boards and electronic media, the most important of which is the internet. Sponsorships provide another channel for communications. Volvo heavily invests in tennis sponsorship. Its banners are displayed at tournaments, as are examples of its model range. As well as transporting celebrity tennis players in a Volvo car, the company also increases its TV advertisements during tournaments.[42] In Munich, golf players can play from tees sponsored by BMW for the International Open and the English football club Arsenal has a stadium which is called 'Emirates Stadium', which is related to the Saudi Arabian airline, reinforcing the message that these organisations are at the top of their game and compete at the highest levels.[43]

The internet provides a unique environment for promotional messages because it can include text, audio, video, hyperlinking and personalisation, not to mention opportunities for interaction with customers and other stakeholders. Websites can come alive with

Marketing metrics

IPA Touchpoints Survey

The UK's Institute of Practitioners and Advertisers' TouchPoints Survey questioned 5010 people through a substantial self-completion questionnaire and a PDA (personal digital assistant) time-based diary that collected data every half-hour for a week on how they were spending their time, their opinions and the role of media in their lives. It has been designed as a stand-alone survey and to be integrated with other media research. A snapshot of the research shows:

- The media hierarchy in hours for all adults between Monday and Friday is: 3.9 television, 1.3 radio and 0.8 internet. On Saturday and Sunday this changes to: 4.5 television, 1.5 radio and 1.0 internet.

- On a typical weekday a 15–24-year-old home internet user spends 2 hours surfing the web – this rises to 2.4 hours at the weekend and averages 14.8 hours for the week.

- The average individual receives 8.5 pieces of advertising mail each week, 4.9 (57 per cent) are personally addressed and 3.6 (43 per cent) are 'random' pieces of mail.

- Only 13 per cent of all written communication is now using pen and paper; 49 per cent is via email, 29 per cent via SMS text, 10 per cent via internet instant messaging.

Source: www.ipa.co.uk/content/touchpoints-site-home

the right mix of technical wizardry and good design. One advantage of the web is that companies can give customers a 'feel' for their products or services before they buy. Even nightclubs are going to the web to draw virtual crowds.[44] Sites like Thewomb.com feature real-time footage of what's happening in the clubs.

Step 5: Evaluate the effectiveness of the communications programme

The final step in managing marketing communications is to decide whether the plan is working. The marketer needs to determine whether the communication objectives are adequately translated into marketing communications that are reaching the right target market.

It would be nice if a marketing manager could simply report, 'The €3 million campaign for our revolutionary glow-in-the-dark surfboards brought in €15 million in new sales!' It's not so easy. There are many random factors in the marketing environment: a rival's manufacturing problem, a coincidental photograph of a movie star carrying one of the boards, or perhaps a surge of renewed interest in surfing sparked by a cult film hit like *Blue Crush*.

Still, there are ways to monitor and evaluate the company's communication efforts. The catch is that the effectiveness of some forms of communication is easier to determine than others. As a rule, sales promotions are the easiest to evaluate because they occur over a fixed, usually short period, making it easier to link to sales volume. Advertising researchers measure brand awareness, recall of product benefits communicated through advertising and even the image of the brand before and after an advertising campaign. The firm can analyse and compare the performance of salespeople in different territories, although again it is difficult to rule out other factors that make one salesperson more effective than another. For example, in 2007 the average Media Impact Unit for the Rugby World Cup 2007 was 14,983 United Business Media (UBM) in comparison to 32,900 during the Football World Cup in 2006. UBM represents a composite which integrates audiences from TV, press and radio who are likely to have received the information (age 15+). The score impact on the Rugby World Cup was much lower than the World Cup's in relation to the length of the total games, which lasted for one month and three weeks and one month respectively.[45]

Public relations activities are more difficult to assess because their objectives relate more often to image building than sales volume.

Now that you've read about IMC, and heard the advice for James at Fonemedia, read how it worked out for his promotional efforts.

Marketing metrics

Thomson Intermedia

Thomson Intermedia's advertising monitoring service captures pretty much every advertisement run in the UK in every medium – TV, press, direct mail, door drop, internet, outdoor, radio and cinema. It uses advanced technology to capture the images and these are matched with advertising expenditure data which are obtained from the fastest, most authoritative sources. The resulting data – creative and expenditure – is stored on its database and made available over the web 24 hours a day, 7 days a week, 365 days a year. Data goes back several years, and covers every advertiser in every industry. Clients can download individual ads, whole campaigns or information about the expenditure across entire industry sectors – for any period of time.

Real people, real decisions

How it worked out at Fonemedia

James and his colleagues went for Option 1, and encouraged the university to utilise the web through a mobile network instead of using traditional media or PC-based advertising. Because the university was looking for people who had the wealth to pay for their MBA courses, the mobile filtering route gave them the ability to limit the advertising purely to those handsets where it was likely that the owner and their family had an acceptable level of disposable income. The campaign also filtered out those age ranges that do not traditionally fit with the profile of student who undertakes an MBA course – therefore the under-21 age group was excluded, as was the over-45 age range. Filters were also applied to the types of mobile websites that the advert would be seen on. It was logical to include sites that were mainly delivered in English and with an international focus as these were an essential part of the target criteria, and to advertise at busy mobile web traffic times (such as Saturdays and Sundays during the times when the English Premiership is playing or when African football matches are taking place). Sport in general proved to be a key genre of mobile website for the campaign.

How far would an MBA from a world-class AMBA accredited programme take your career?

Figure 11.5   Sample of Fonemedia web ad campaign

Marketing metrics

Fonemedia

During the two – week campaign, the Fonemedia team delivered in excess of 6 million views of the advertisement – and over 23,000 clicks onto the specially created mobile website. The click-through rate was just short of 0.4 percent, which is almost twice as many as could be expected through a standalone PC web campaign. The end result was that the university was inundated with applications for its MBA course and delivered a return on investment over 1000 percent.

Chapter Summary

Now that you have finished reading this chapter, you should be able to:

1. **Understand the role of communications for successful marketing.** Firms use promotion and other forms of marketing communication to influence attitudes and behaviour. Through marketing communications, marketers inform consumers about new products, remind them of familiar products, persuade them to choose one alternative over another and build strong customer relationships. Today, firms believe that the integration of marketing communications, where firms look at the communication needs of customers, is essential for successful marketing communication programmes.

2. **Understand the communications model.** The traditional communications model includes a message source that creates an idea, encodes the idea into a message, and transmits the message through some medium. The message is delivered to the receiver, who decodes the message and may provide feedback to the source. Anything that interferes with the communication is called 'noise'.

3. **List and describe the traditional elements of the promotion mix.** The four major elements of marketing communications are known as the promotion mix. Personal selling provides direct contact between a company representative and a customer. Advertising is non-personal communication from an identified sponsor using mass media. Sales promotions stimulate immediate sales by providing incentives to the trade or to consumers. Public relations activities seek to influence the attitudes of various audiences.

4. **Explain how word-of-mouth marketing, buzz marketing, viral marketing and guerrilla marketing provide effective marketing communications.** Marketers have developed several new options to traditional marketing communications in order to reach 'hard-to-get' consumers. Viral marketing means firms create messages designed to be passed on in an exponential fashion, often electronically. With buzz marketing, marketers use entertainment or news to stimulate consumers to talk about a product or a company to friends and neighbours. These word-of-mouth (WOM) mar-

keting messages are more credible and thus more valuable, especially when unpaid consumers create their own messages. Guerrilla marketing includes promotional strategies that 'ambush' consumers in places they are not expecting it.

5. **Describe integrated marketing communications and its characteristics.** Integrated marketing communications (IMC) includes the planning, development, execution and evaluation of coordinated, measurable persuasive brand communications. IMC programmes mean a firm's marketing communication programmes include a single unified voice, begin with the customer, seek to develop relationships with customers, use targeted communications, use two-way communications, focus on all stakeholders rather than customers only, rely on the effective use of databases, generate a continuous stream of communications, and measure results based on actual feedback.

6. **Explain the important role of database marketing in integrated marketing communications (IMC).** The effective use of databases, key to an IMC strategy, allows organisations to learn about its customers, fine-tune its offerings and build a relationship with its market. Database marketing is interactive, i.e. it requires a response from consumers and it builds relationships allowing the marketer to adapt to consumers' needs. Database marketing provides a means to locate new customers and to stimulate cross-selling of related products. With database marketing, a company can measure the impact of its communication efforts and track which consumers responded.

7. **Explain the stages in developing an IMC plan.** An IMC plan begins with communication objectives, usually stated in terms of communications tasks such as creating awareness, knowledge, desire, product trial and brand loyalty. Which promotion mix elements will be used depends on the overall strategy (that is, a push versus a pull strategy, the type of product and the stage of the product life cycle).

Promotion budgets are often developed from such rules of thumb as the percentage-of-sales method, the competitive-parity method and the objective-task method. Monies from the total budget are then allocated to various elements of the promotion mix. Designing the promotion mix includes determining what communication tools will be used and the message that will be delivered.

Marketing messages use a variety of different appeals, including those that are rational and others that are emotional in nature. The message may provide one- or two-sided arguments and may or may not draw conclusions. Communication channels must be selected. The internet provides both challenges and opportunities for communication. Finally, marketers monitor and evaluate the promotion efforts to determine if the objectives are being reached.

Key terms

AIDA model 444
Bottom-up budgeting techniques 441
Buzz 426
Buzz marketing 427
Communications model 419
Competitive-parity method 441
Database marketing 436
Decoding 421
Encoding 419
Feedback 423

Guerrilla marketing 430
Hierarchy of effects 438
Integrated marketing communications (IMC) 431
Medium 421
Message 420
Noise 422
Objective-task method 441
Percentage-of-sales method 441
Promotion 423

Promotion mix 423
Pull strategy 442
Push strategy 441
Receiver 421
Source 419
Stakeholders 435
Top-down budgeting techniques 441
Viral marketing 427
Word-of-mouth 427
Word-of-mouth marketing 427

Chapter review

Marketing concepts: testing your knowledge

1. How is IMC different from traditional promotion strategies?
2. Describe the traditional communications model.
3. List the elements of the promotion mix and describe how they are used to deliver personal and mass appeals.
4. What are word-of-mouth marketing, buzz marketing and viral marketing? Why are such activities gaining in popularity?
5. Explain what guerrilla marketing means.
6. What is IMC? Explain the characteristics of IMC.
7. What is database marketing? How do marketers use databases to meet the needs of their customers?
8. List the stages in developing an IMC strategy.
9. Explain the hierarchy of effects and how it is used in communication objectives.
10. Describe the major ways in which firms develop marketing communications budgets.
11. How does the promotion mix vary with push versus pull strategies?
12. What are some different types of appeals marketers may use in their communications strategies?
13. How do marketers evaluate the effectiveness of their communications programmes?

Marketing concepts: discussing choices and ethical issues

1. Some people would argue that there is really nothing new about IMC. What do you think?
2. More and more companies are developing word-of-mouth or buzz marketing campaigns. Is buzz marketing just a craze that will fade in a year or two or is it here to stay? Do you think buzz is effective? Why do you feel that way?
3. With an IMC programme, firms need to coordinate all of the marketing communications activities. What do you see as the problems inherent in implementing this?

4. Consumers are becoming concerned that the proliferation of databases is an invasion of an individual's privacy. Do you feel this is a valid concern? How can marketers use databases effectively and, at the same time, protect the rights of individuals?

Marketing practice: applying what you've learned

1. As a marketing consultant, you are frequently asked by clients to develop recommendations for marketing communication strategies. The traditional elements used include advertising, sales promotion, public relations and personal selling. Which of these do you feel would be most effective for each of the following clients?

   a. A company that provides mobile phone services;

   b. A hotel;

   c. A university;

   d. A new soft drink.

2. Again, assume that you are a marketing consultant for one of the clients in question 1. You believe that the client would benefit from guerrilla marketing. Develop several ideas for guerrilla marketing tactics that you feel would be successful for the client.

3. As the director of marketing for a small firm that markets environmentally friendly household cleaning supplies, you are developing a marketing communication plan. With one or more of your classmates, provide suggestions for each of the following items. Then, in a role-playing situation, present your recommendations to the client:

   a. Marketing communication objectives;

   b. A method for determining the communication budget;

   c. The use of a push strategy or a pull strategy;

   d. Elements of the promotion mix you will use.

4. Assume that you are the word-of-mouth marketing manager for a sports shoe company such as Footlocker. Develop ideas on how to create buzz for your company's products.

5. As the marketing manager for a chain of bookshops, you are interested in developing a database marketing plan. Give your recommendations for the following:

   a. How to generate a customer database;

   b. How to use the database to better understand your customers;

   c. How to increase sales from your existing customers using your database;

   d. How to get new customers using your database.

6. As a member of the marketing department for a manufacturer of handheld power tools for home improvement, you have been directed to select a new agency to do the promotion for your firm. Of two agencies solicited, one recommends an IMC plan and the other has developed recommendations for a traditional advertising plan. Write a memo to your boss explaining each of the following:

   a. What is different about an IMC plan?

   b. Why is the IMC plan superior to conventional advertising?

Marketing miniproject: learning by doing

This miniproject is designed to help you understand how organisations use database marketing.

1. Visit your university alumni office and ask to discuss how it uses database marketing to enhance participation of alumni in the programmes of the university and in fundraising. Some of the questions you might ask include the following:

   a. How the office obtains names for an initial or expanded database;

   b. What information is included in the initial database;

   c. What information is added to the database;

   d. How the office uses the database for communicating with alumni.

2. Based on what you learn, consider other ways the school might use database marketing for enhancing its alumni programmes and its fundraising.

3. Make a presentation of your findings and recommendations to your class.

Further reading

Integrated Advertising, Promotion and Marketing Communications: Global Edition, 5th Edition, Kenneth Clow and Donald Baack, Pearson, 2011

Marketing products in the 21st century requires an integrated approach. With the rise of social media, new approaches such as interactive marketing, online advertising, social media, Twitter, blogs, consumer reviews, and search engine optimisation (SEO) must be incorporated into the overall communications approach. In some situations, more non-traditional approaches such as lifestyle marketing, guerrilla marketing, buzz marketing, experiential marketing, product placement and branded entertainment can be used. Choices range from traditional media such as television, magazines and outdoor to alternative channels such as video games, mobile phones and cinemas. Because of the complex nature of marketing communications, understanding advertising, promotions, and marketing communications is critical to successfully promoting products.

Real people, real surfers

Exploring the web

A vast majority of traditional media (television stations, newspapers, magazines and radio stations) are now using the web to build relationships with readers and viewers. For the media, the internet provides an excellent way to build a database and to communicate one on one with customers.

Although individual sites change frequently, some media sites that have provided opportunities for interactive communications with customers and for building a database are the following:

Business Week (www.businessweek.com)

Financial Times (www.ft.com)

Advertising Age (www.adage.com)

Brand Republic (www.brandrepublic.com)

Explore these or other sites that provide opportunities for consumers to register, answer questionnaires, or in some other way use the internet to build a database. After completing your exploration of each site, answer the following questions:

1. In what ways does each website facilitate interactive communications between the firm and customers?

2. How does each firm use the internet to gather information on customers? What information is gathered? Which site does a superior job of gathering information, and why?

3. How do you think the firm might use the information it gathers through the internet in database marketing activities? How can the information be used to build relationships with customers and prospective customers?

4. What recommendations do you have for each company to improve the interactive opportunities on its website?

Now, take a look at the website at www.pearsoned.co.uk/solomon to see some videos from YouTube relating to aspects of this chapter.

Delve deeper into branding

Professor Dr Suzanne C. Beckmann
Copenhagen Business School

Advertising and marketing communications in general are facing significant and fascinating challenges these years. Advertising has for many decades been synonymous with (one-way) mass communication. The past 10–15 years though have witnessed an ever-increasing interest in two-way communication, media convergence and interactivity, based on computer-mediated environments. Communication is becoming more and more individualised, digitalised and democratic. Communication takes place in a plethora of media and the virtual world especially 'never sleeps'. Every touchpoint, whether intended or unintended, between an organisation and its customers delivers communication content. Communication occurs internally and externally – and it continuously shapes the identity and image of the organisation. Business and public institutions must face the challenges presented by these developments to maintain and develop their position. One of the most striking developments can be found on Web 2.0, where consumers increasingly exchange consumption experiences and thereby help each other to make decisions.

(continued on the next page)

All this boosts the need for integrated marketing communications, which aims at combining, integrating and synergising all relevant elements of an organisation's communication mix. Strategic integration of the various communication functions is what makes IMC a new outside-in approach to reaching both consumers and other stakeholders alike. IMC is different from other customer-centric processes – such as the concept of market orientation – in that its foundation is communication, and as such it is a circular process rather than a linear (inside-out) one. Yet no matter what type of communication campaigns are developed and which media channels are chosen, measuring communication effectiveness remains another relevant challenge.

References

D.L. Hoffman and T.P. Novak (1996) 'Marketing in Hypermedia Computer-Mediated Environments: Conceptual Foundations', *Journal of Marketing* 60 no.3, 50–68.

K.L. Keller (2001) 'Mastering the Marketing Communications Mix: Micro and Macro Perspectives on Integrated Marketing Communication Programs', *Journal of Marketing Management* 17 no.7/8, 819-41.

A. Martensen, L. Grønholdt, L. Bendtsen and M.J. Jensen (2007) 'Application of a Model for the Effectiveness of Event Marketing', *Journal of Advertising Research*, 47 no. 3, 283–301.

Marketing in action case

Groupon keeps one buzz ahead

The lure of huge discounts on fun products, from a facial to sky-diving, has enabled local retailers to promote their products via a partnership with the viral marketing organisation Groupon and to access an entire new customer base at no risk. It has also enabled Groupon to become one of the fastest growing companies in US history. In just two and a half years since its launch in November 2008, Groupon has sold more than 46 million coupons, representing $1.9 billion of savings to more than 70 million subscribers worldwide.[1]

The business model is simple and based on online coupon distribution. Typically, Groupon subscribers are invited by email to purchase up front a 50–60 percent off coupon or discount to be redeemed in a local store up to several months later. Subscribers have 24 hours to make the purchase and, if a minimum (agreed with each retailer) number of buyers do so, the deal proceeds; if not the deal does not go ahead, and subscribers are not charged. Groupon simply takes a *c.* 50 percent share of the profit – so retailers cannot lose in that

they are assured of revenue in advance. A further key factor is that the offers can be targeted on a local basis.

David Diamond, President of strategic marketing firm David Diamond Associates, summarises the significance of Groupon for the promotion industry: 'Groupon brought promotion something it hasn't had in a long time: a truly new idea. It's not a coupon at all. Consumers must buy in advance, so redemption rates are more like 85% to 90% rather than the 1% or so typical for cents-off cereal coupons distributed in newspapers.'[2] Effectively, Groupon enabled small local retailers to use a marketing communications channel they would not normally be able to use effectively, and to find customers they would not easily be able to reach, and as Groupon's success and brand awareness grew, so did theirs.

Groupon also succeeded because it successfully captured the consumer psyche of the moment – the recession-induced inclination to look for bargains, the increasing engagement with the new social media tools and a desire for fun in trying times. There was, of course, a danger that a relationship founded on the fragile notion of a bargain would hardly engender loyalty amongst customers, so Groupon has understood the importance of finding regular and constantly innovative ways of engaging its customers and that group buying, powerful though it is, requires an interactive communications-driven strategy focused on repeat and loyal customers. For example, their Flickr stream enables customers to upload photos. According to Mark Desky, Groupon's vice president: 'We see photos from being on a whale watch to being on a trapeze to being at a wax museum. People are taking pictures at all these places, and I love to go and see how much happiness it's generating. We hear all the time, "If it wasn't for Groupon, I wouldn't have tried it".'[3]

Relationships with customers also drive Groupon's people-based customer service. Unlike other internet operators who typically use a technology-driven approach, Groupon focuses on 'service with a smile, phone calls and manpower'. For example, Groupon is determined that it will not jeopardise this culture in efficiency drives at its 1000-person plus Chicago call-centre by moving it abroad or to a third party.[4]

From an entry model whereby customers are engaged mostly via daily emails noted for their 'wry humor and occasional weirdness[5]', or visits to its website to buy coupons for redemption months in advance, Groupon is now exploiting mobile communications tools to attract and excite the a new type of 'cool' coupon customer who is typically younger, better educated and with a higher household income and discretionary spending power than the traditional print coupon customer.[6] Groupon has also understood the instant gratification needs of these customers and noted a trend for early redemption, with 10 per cent of coupons redeemed in the first ten days and 20 per cent in the first month, so Groupon is exploring new channels and purchase models. For example, a feature addition to its standard smartphone app called 'Groupon Now' enables users to indicate whether they are 'hungry' or 'bored'. A click routes them to a map of Groupon restaurant or entertainment/attraction deals to be bought and redeemed that day.[7] Groupon is also expanding beyond its present direct marketing model with a partnership with the price-comparison app ShopSavvy to include Groupon offers in its 'deals' tab.[8]

Groupon has developed a similar keen understanding of, and responsiveness to, the needs of its retail customers, for whom the venture into online retailing can pose challenges. It operates a large sales force to attract deals with large brands that will 'interest, surprise and delight readers'.[9] It also offers seminars to help retailers better cope with sudden surges in demand[10] and has developed a smartphone app for merchants to scan the coupons as they are redeemed so they can analyse how deals perform, including by demographics and purchase location. More recently Groupon has also begun exploring new B2B networking opportunities for its retailers with a new site called Bizy.[11]

As Groupon's phenomenal growth continues, it has begun to look beyond word-of-mouth social marketing techniques to more traditional offline tools in order to build credibility and front-of-mind recall. The wisdom of this approach was questioned by Sucharita Mulpuru, an e-commerce analyst at Forrester Research: 'The offline marketing will get them some new names, broaden their reach and make them a part of the daily lexicon and get a lot of PR', she said. 'But PR does not always translate into sales and that's important to keep in mind.'[12] Indeed, Groupon's attempt to use its wry/ weird humour in a TV commercial starring Timothy Hutton broadcast during the 2011 Super Bowl football game resulted in a perception that the company was trivialising the plight of Tibet.[13]

Nonetheless, Groupon appears committed to this next phase of its marketing communications strategy and has since launched a replacement ad on prime time TV. It appears to continue to be able to foresee, exploit and even initiate the next marcomms trends. For example, Groupon is now asking its consumers to propose products/services for Groupon deals.[14] According to Borrell Associates Online, while 'ad spending for small and medium-sized U.S. businesses will grow 20% over the next five years, local online promotions budgets (including couponing, loyalty programs and deals) is expected to explode from $566 million in 2010 to $8.2 billion in 2015'. 'Groupon is riding the trend', said Larry Shaw, VP-research for Borrell, one that's especially relevant for small business, which is Groupon's sweet spot.[15]

References

1. Brian Morrissey, 'The Space Between', *Brandweek*, 6 December 2010.

2. Jeff Nack, 'What Groupon Means for Grandma's Coupons', *Advertising Age* , 28 March 2011.

3. Jacqueline Renfrow, 'Groupon Goes Viral', *Response* 18(10) (July 2010.)

4. Kunur Patel, 'Groupon Primes Itself to Become Next Zappos', *Advertising Age* , 28 February 2011.

5. Brian Quinton, 'Can Groupon Grow Up?', *Chief Marketer*, (June/July 2011), 10–11.

6. Piet Levy, 'Ca$hing In on the Coupon Comeback', *Marketing News* , 30 April 2011.

7. Brian Quinton, 'The Rise of the Real-Time Deal', *Entrepreneur*, July 2011, Vol. 39 Issue 7.

8. Patel, 'Croupon Primer Itself'.

9. Quinton, 'Rise of the Real-Time Deal'.

10. Patel, 'Groupon Primer Itself'.

11. Levy, 'Cashing In'.

12. Rupal Parekh, 'Groupon Makes Big Bid on Traditional TV, Buys Super Bowl Pre-game', *Advertising Age* , 10 January 2011.

13. Rupal Parekh and Kunur Patel, 'Groupon CEO: We Shouldn't have Relied on the Agency', *Advertising Age* 21 March 2011.

14. Levy, 'Cashing In'.

15. Patel, 'Croupon Primer Itself'.

Things to think about

1. How is Groupon effectively combining personal and mass appeals as it grows?

2. In what ways is Groupon engaging in positive word-of-mouth strategies?

3. How is Groupon effectively integrating its marketing communications activities?

References

1. W. Leiss et al., *Social Communication in Advertising* , 3rd edn (New York: Taylor and Frances) George Stigler, 'The Economics of Information', *Journal of Political Economy* (1961), 69.

2. 'Anti-smoking ads to shock parents', *BBC News/Health,* 2004, http://news.bbc.co.uk/1/hi/health/4118857.stm.

3. Shane Coleman, 'PD Dentist Touches Raw Nerve with Broadcaster', *Sunday Tribune (Ireland)*, 28 January 2007.

4. Gert Assmus, 'An Empirical Investigation into the Perception of Vehicle Source Effects', *Journal of Advertising* 7 (Winter 1978), 4–10; for a more thorough discussion of the pros and cons of different media, see Stephen Baker, *Systematic Approach to Advertising Creativity* (New York: McGraw-Hill, 1979).

5. Sandra O'Loughlin and Steve Miller, 'Marketers Struggle With the "Dark" Side', *Brandweek.com*, 20 February 2007.

6. ASA Annual report, 2007, www.asa.org.uk/ASA_2004_Rebuild/ASAAppBase/AnnualReport2006/ASA_Top10.htm.

7. Sandra Yin, 'Degree of Challenge', *American Demographics* (May 2003), 20–22.

8. Nick Summers, 'College Papers Grow Up; They Have the Ads, the Readers – and Budgets to Match', *Newsweek* , 5 December 2005, 48.

9. Catharine P. Taylor, 'What's In a Word?', *Brandweek* , 24 October 2005, 30.

10. Lois Geller, 'Wow – What a Buzz', *Target Marketing,* June 2005, 21.

11. 'Word of Mouth Marketing Experts Launch New Training Series', *Market Wire* , 9 March 2006.

12. Todd Wasserman, 'Word Games', *Brandweek* , 24 April 2006, 24.

13. Todd Wasserman, 'Blogs Cause Word of Mouth Business to Spread Quickly', *Brandweek* , 3 October 2005, 9.

14. Gemma Charles, 'Buzz finds favour in the UK', *Marketing*, 27 February 2008, 2.

15. Suzanne Vranica, 'Getting Buzz Marketers to Fess Up', *The Wall Street Journal* , 9 February 2005, B9.

16. Wasserman, 'Word Games'.

17. Wasserman, 'Blogs Cause Word of Mouth Business to Spread Quickly'.

18. Ibid.

19. T.L. Stanley, 'Guerrilla Marketers of the Year', *Brandweek*, 27 March 2000, 28; Jeff Green, 'Down with the Dirt Devils', *Brandweek*, 27 March 2000, 41–4; Stephanie Thompson, 'Pepsi Favors Sampling Over Ads for Fruit Drink', *Advertising Age* , 24 January 2000, 8.

20. 'ENGAGEMENT: Trying to score with elusive male demo?', *Advertising Age* , 26 February 2007, S10

21. Jaimie Seaton, 'Burger King Guns for Rivals in Guerilla Push', *Media* , 9 September 2005, 6.

22. Based on T. Tarran 'ComScore upgrades UK online video measurement service' 2011 www.research-live.com/news/analytics/comscore-upgrades-uk-online-video-measurement-service/4004371.article (accessed 27 Jun 2011).

23. S. Dibb, L. Simkin, M. William and O.C. Ferrel, *Marketing, Concepts and Strategies*, 5th European ed. (Boston: Houghton Mifflin, 2006).

24. Tom Eppes, 'From Theory to Practice', Price/McNabb corporate presentation, 2002.

25. John Burnett and Sandra Moriarty, *Marketing Communications: An Integrated Approach* (Upper Saddle River, NJ: Prentice Hall, 1998).

26. Danny Kucharsky, 'Ads on Demand', *Marketing*, 15 May 2006, 9.

27. 'NBC to Hold Online Vote for Top "Friends" Episodes', *Wall Street Journal*, 7 January 2004, www.wsj.com.

28. Z. Wood 'French Connection pins hopes on baffling adverts', *The Guardian* (online), 13 March 2011, www.guardian.co.uk/business/2011/mar/13/french-connection-baffling-adverts. (accessed 1 August 2011).

29. Curt Barry, 'Building a Database', *Catalog Age* (August 1992), 65–68.

30. Adrienne Mand, 'IQ News: Jaguar.com Redesign on the Prowl for Luxury Car Buyers', *Adweek.com.* 6 July 1998.

31. Ian P. Murphy, 'Reader's Digest Links Profits Directly to Research', *Marketing News* , 31 March 1997, 7.

32. Elaine Santoro, 'NBO Markets with Style', *Direct Marketing* (February 1992), 28–31, quoted on p. 30.

33. David Benardy, 'Tesco Plays its Clubcard Right', *Marketing Week* , 3 November 1995, 30–1.

34. Claire Foss, 'Service with a Sale', *Marketing Direct,* 26 July 2007, Special Report, 5.

35. Martin Everett, 'This One's Just For You', *Sales and Marketing Management* , (June 1992), 119–126.

36. Paul Gander, 'Make it a Season to Remember', *Marketing Week* 30, no. 42, 18 October 2007, 35–38.

37. Jack Neff, 'P&G Trims Fat Off its $2B Trade-Promotion System', *Advertising Age* , 5 June 2006, 8.

38. John Borland, 'All Eyes on New DVD Format War', *CnetNews.com* , 11 July 2005.

39. Mariko Sanchanta and Paul Taylor, 'Toshiba Ready to Abandon DVD War', *Financial Times* (Asia edition), 18 February 2008, 1.

40. Bill Britt, 'Volkswagen Waxes Poetic to Stir Up Emotions and Sales', *Advertising Age* , 29 September 2003, 8.

41. Linda L. Golden and Mark I. Alpert, 'Comparative Analysis of the Relative Effectiveness of One- and Two-Sided Communication for Contrasting Products', *Journal of Advertising* 16 (1987): 18–25; Robert B. Settle and Linda L. Golden, 'Attribution Theory and Advertiser Credibility', *Journal of Marketing Research* 11 (May 1974), 181–85.

42. Dibb et al., *Marketing Concepts and Strategies* , 569.

43. 'Emirates Back as Official Airline of S'pore Masters', *The Straits Times (Singapore),* 7 March 2007.

44. Khanh T.L. Tran, 'Lifting the Velvet Rope: Nightclubs Draw Virtual Throngs with Webcasts', *Wall Street Journal* 30 August 1999, www.wsj.com.

45. 'Worldwide Event', *The Media Intelligence Journal* 20 (Fall 2007), www.tnsmi.co.uk/assets/issue20.pdf.

Chapter 12
Advertising and PR

Meet Anthony Levy
Chairman of the Fresh Produce Consortium

Anthony was appointed Chairman of the Fresh Produce Consortium board in 2006 to lead the fresh produce industry's initiative to grow the UK market. Although previously never having been involved with the produce industry he had worked with other trade associations and campaigns. Fortunately the rest of his very senior board has several lifetimes of experience of differing parts of the produce supply chain. Anthony spent the first part of his career working for Esso in a number of commercial and marketing roles, including running 1500 retail outlets and latterly responsible for Esso's entire UK Industrial & Speciality Fuels businesses. Since then he has combined a number of board positions in the private, public and not-for-profit sectors and been an adviser to several other business leaders. He was Chairman of Emo Oil, an Irish marketing and distribution company which has grown to become the largest fuels supplier in the UK and Ireland under the ownership of DCC Energy of which Anthony is now a non-executive director. He has also been on the board of three National Health Service organisations including Chairman of a hospital. The experience of listening to the public and dealing with many difficult issues in the health service has proved very valuable to Anthony in gaining a better understanding of people's needs and the ways that they express them. A Chartered Marketer with degrees from Oxford University, London Business School and the Open University, his approach has always been to integrate all the elements of a business to deliver for customers, staff and funders.

Real people, real decisions
Decision time at the Fresh Produce Consortium

The Fresh Produce Consortium is the trade body of growers, importers, distributors, wholesalers and retailers of fruit, vegetables and flowers in the UK. After Anthony was appointed, it decided on a strategic initiative to take more responsibility for the destiny of its markets, i.e. to become more proactive about increasing the overall demand for fresh produce in the UK. Encouraged by the UK government's 5 A-Day campaign, which is driven by the Department of Health and suggests we should all eat at least five portions of fruit and vegetables a day, they analysed what needed to be done. The 5 A-Day campaign had been very successful in raising awareness of the health benefits of eating more fruit and vegetables. The problem was that it hadn't translated into many consumers actually buying much more fresh produce, i.e. behaviour. As a trade body, they were more interested in behaviour change and sales. It was particularly noticeable some of the target groups of C2DE demographics ate less than one portion per day.

The Consortium decided to come together to fund a campaign called 'Eat in Colour' www.eatincolour.com, which the industry rather than the government would own and guide. The funding likely to be offered by the industry was not enough to buy much traditional advertising, so an inventive PR strategy was adopted. This was because normal advertising was unlikely to do more than the government's ad campaigns had achieved and PR is much better at getting into non-traditional media. Second, PR can be much more adaptable and the messages made more targeted and tailored to specific newspapers and magazines. It also needed to be more activating of behaviour and tackle some of the barriers to behaviour such as perceived difficulties in preparation, views that it can be very time-consuming and perceptions of expense. Third, PR is ideal for getting more interest than advertising as to get into newspapers, magazines and on TV, the message or story has to be much more interesting, engaging and involving than an ad campaign. This itself creates greater impact for the Eat in Colour campaign.

Anthony and his board appointed Bray Leino as their lead PR agency based on their creative approach and their enthusiasm for the campaign. With a close working relationship between client and agency it was decided to reinvent the language in which other campaigns talked about eating fruit and vegetables. The majority of the traditional government advertising was quite 'preachy and worthy', coming across as 'you should' eat more fruit and veg. The team wanted to change the tone of the message to a 'we' message, helping us all to make healthy eating a reality every day. As Anthony said, 'many of us know what we should do, but we actually tend to do what we *want* to do!' For example, they didn't say 'don't give your kids pizza to eat, make them a vegetable stew', but rather, 'if you are giving your kids pizza, why not give them half a pizza and a dollop of coleslaw?' The aim of the campaign was not to promote Eat in Colour as a brand, but to promote a better, quick, easy, fresh relationship between consumers and fruit and veg, reminding us of the pleasure and inspiring consumption. Anthony had to decide on which of the following PR campaigns might be most successful.

Option 1 Chocolate offsetting

Knowing that most of us would over-indulge in chocolate Easter eggs, the idea was to give consumers an easy way to offset their indulgence, i.e. how to balance their nutrition. They were encouraged to go to www.chocolateoffsetting.com and type in the amount of chocolate they had eaten. The site then makes suggestions as to how many extra pieces of fruit or veg are required to balance their diet and suggests exercises, such as an extra walk on Sunday or an extra hour ironing. The site has been designed using infotainment principles to make it both entertaining and informative. The advantages of this approach were that it also targeted a wealthier, more informed group who saw the humour of the analogy with carbon offsetting. It also allowed more chance for people to engage with the message as they could independently access the website any time and as many times as they wanted and even virally pass it onto friends, rather than just read the piece in the newspaper and maybe chat over coffee. The website was also useful for referring journalists interested in the story. Finally, the fact that there was a website which could offset your chocolate consumption was a piece of news in itself, let alone the good message it was encouraging. However, it was such a good idea, it would never have the same impact again, and it was largely time limited to Easter and maybe a Christmas re-run.

Option 2 £5 family challenge

This idea was to challenge families to move £5 of their weekly shopping spend from prepared foods and take-aways to fresh produce. This was to be a regional campaign targeting regional media. Local families in the core target demographic (C1C2D) from each area of the country were recruited to take the £5 challenge. The local newspaper then followed the family over a few weeks as they received tips from the Eat in Colour team on how to include more fruit and veg in their diets. This was a before and after story using the family and home as the main backdrop. The advantages were that once the regional media had run it, the national press saw the power of the story and ran it as well. If this worked, even on a small scale, it would be amazing because the average weekly spend on fresh fruit and veg per week in the UK is only £8. However, it might typecast the Eat in Colour campaign as being only for this low end target demographic and the families which emerged might put off some industry supporters who had a much more upmarket target customer market. It might also typecast the campaign in the eyes of some journalists.

Option 3 Soap opera survey

Inspired by watching many miserable people on the BBC's soap opera *Eastenders*, they decided that one reason everyone was miserable might be because of their diet. The agency then monitored the UKs three top soap operas (*Eastenders, Coronation Street* and *Emmerdale*) over a month to see what the characters ate. What they found were amazing differences and very few people eating in colour. So much so that the agency suggested to the BBC that *Eastenders* should perhaps be shot in black and white as they hardly ever ate any colourful fruit or veg.

The story had the advantages of being able to highlight, the north–south divide and city versus rural. Also, the newspapers could pick up on whichever soap their readers were most likely to watch. The research for it was low cost. It talked about fruit and veg in a humorous way using characters the public knew well and related to. Many of the target audience for soaps are the core target for encouraging them to eat more. However, being funny and irreverent might make people think the campaign is frivolous and superficial and the message may not be taken as seriously.

Now put yourself in Anthony's shoes, which option would you choose and why?

Objectives

When you finish reading this chapter, you will be able to:

1 Explain what advertising is and describe the main types of advertising

2 Explain the role of public relations

Objective

1

Explain what advertising is and describe the main types of advertising

Advertising: the image of marketing

Advertising is so much a part of marketing that many people think of the two as the same thing. As we saw in Chapter 11, that's not the case – there are many ways to get a message out to a target audience. Advertising is still very important – top global marketers spend millons per year, with Procter & Gamble, Unilever and L'Oréal being among the top spenders.[1] Still, in today's competitive environment, even the biggest companies such as Procter & Gamble and Unilever are rethinking how much they want to invest in pricey ad campaigns as they search for other ways to get their messages out there.

This is especially true as the number of media outlets mushrooms along with the number of TV viewers who use their trusty remote control or perhaps TiVo or Sky1 to skip over ads. 'Personal video recorders' that let viewers skip through commercials reached 30 per cent of UK households in 2010 and continue to rise, resulting in TV advertising being skipped by 86 per cent of viewers.[2] That's why product plugs in films, known as **product placement**, are turning up much more often (no, it's no accident that the logos are so visible!):[3]

- Audi cars are heavily featured in *I, Robot* with Will Smith.

- The movie *Fight Club* with Brad Pitt includes scenes where an Apple shop is broken into and the headlights of a Volkswagen Beetle are smashed.

- In *Desperate Housewives*, three characters drive Nissans.

- Nokia phones had played a very visible role in the first *Matrix* movie in 1999. They were visible as the entrance and exit points for the characters beaming themselves into the virtual reality mindset.

- Aston Martins are prominently featured in the James Bond film *A Quantum of Solace*.

Check out www.brandchannel.com for more recent examples in their 'brand cameo' section.

Meanwhile, other marketers are taking their messages to the streets as they rely on public relations events in addition to traditional advertising. For example, Coca-Cola opened lounges for teenagers at shopping centres, while BMW scored big points with its series of short films from famous directors that appeared on its website and included people like Madonna (www.bmw.com).[4] There are many ways to communicate with a mass audience. In this chapter, we'll learn about some of the major approaches, beginning with advertising.

Wherever we turn, advertising bombards us. Television commercials, radio spots, banner ads and huge hoardings scream, 'Buy me!' **Advertising** is non-personal communication paid for by an identified sponsor using mass media to persuade or inform an audience.[5] Advertising can be fun, glamorous, annoying, informative – and hopefully an effective way to let consumers know what they're selling and why people should run out and buy it *today*.

Advertising has been with us a long time. In ancient Greece and Rome, advertisements appeared on walls and were etched on stone tablets. Would the ancients have believed that today we get messages about products almost wherever we are, whether driving down the road or surfing the web? Some of us even get advertising messages on our mobile phones. It's hard to find a place where ads don't try to reach us.

Advertising is also a potent force that creates desire for products by transporting us to imaginary worlds where the people are happy, beautiful, rich or, annoyingly, all three! In this way, advertising allows the organisation to communicate its message in a favourable way and to repeat the message as often as it deems necessary to have an impact on receivers.

 ## Types of advertising

Although almost every business advertises, the types of media they choose to use for advertising can vary. In 2004, newspapers were the biggest advertisement medium in Europe, where companies and governments spent a total of €29 billion to advertise various products and services. €27 billion was spent on television and only €5 billion and €2.2 billion were spent on outdoor and internet respectively.[6] Because they spend so much on advertising, marketers must decide which type of ad will work best given their organisational and marketing goals. The advertisements an organisation runs can take many forms, so let's review the most common kinds.

Product advertising

When people give examples of advertising, they may recall the provocative poses in Agent Provocateur ads or a catchphrase such as 'Beanz Meanz Heinz' or the artwork from a Guinness poster. These are examples of **product advertising**, where the message focuses on a specific good or service. While not all advertising focuses on a product or a brand, most of the advertising we see and hear is indeed product advertising.

Institutional advertising

Rather than focusing on a specific brand, **institutional advertising** promotes the activities, personality or point of view of an organisation or company or can be used for recruitment purposes to attract potential employees to jobs. Some institutional messages state a firm's position on an issue to sway public opinion, a strategy called **advocacy advertising**.[7] For example, the Metropolitan Police launched its advocacy campaign against gun crime in London in November 2006. The police force worked closely with creative agencies and media planners and placed the gun-crime video on sites like Myspace.com and Youtube.com to raise awareness.[8] Other messages called **public service advertisements (PSAs)** are advertisements the media run free of charge. These messages promote not-for-profit organisations that serve society in some way, or they champion an issue such as increasing literacy or discouraging drunk driving. Advertising agencies often take on one or more public service campaigns on a pro bono (for free) basis. Public service advertising has included a campaign featuring the actress Emma Thompson aimed at promoting legislation to fight human trafficking. The campaign, in collaboration with The Body Shop and the Helen Bamber Foundation, shows Thomson from the view of her assailant as she is subjected to forcible, rough sex. Throughout the spot, she relates to two memories, those of Elena, a good girl full of hope and optimism and those of Maria, a prostitute, forced into many sex acts daily. As the spot finishes, Thompson shows that Elena and Maria are the same – a before and after picture of a life destroyed.[9]

Photo 12.1   This advert is designed to stimulate primary demand a generic category rather than a brand or organisation
Source: Alamy Images/Christian Ciureanu

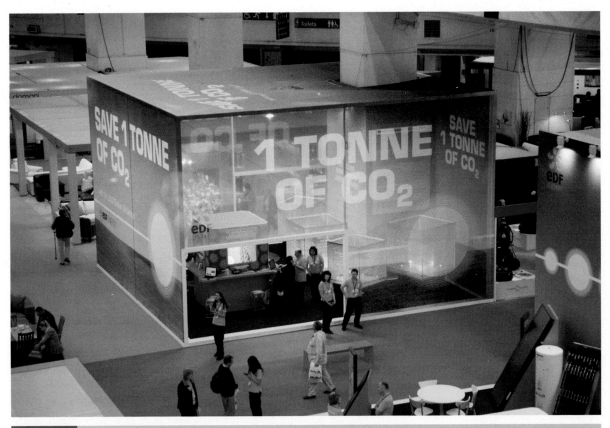

Photo 12.2	This advert conveys an institution's viewpoint on carbon footprints *Source:* Alamy Images/David Gee

Retail and local advertising

Both major retailers and small, local businesses advertise to encourage customers to shop at a specific shop or use a local service. Much local advertising informs us about shop hours, location and products that are available or on sale.

Consumer-generated advertising

Today, in what has been referred to as the 'Generation C' phenomenon, consumer-generated content such as that included in blogs is building on the web. To take advantage of this blog craze, some marketers are encouraging consumers to contribute to their next advertising campaign. In its Dove Cream Oil Body Wash contest, Unilever's Dove brand asked consumers to create their own 30-second commercial to support the launch of its Body Wash collection. The company worked closely with AOL to host the website which carried the contest rules, sample Dove ads, step-by-step tutorials and editing tools. The consumer-made ads were reviewed by an anonymous panel of judges and the winners received an all-expenses-paid trip to Los Angeles.[10] Other companies that have experimented with DIY advertising are L'Oréal ('You Make the Commercial'), JetBlue ('Travel Stories') and McDonald's ('Global Casting').[11] As we saw in Chapter 1, though, putting content in the hands of consumers is risky. During a commercial on the TV show 'The Apprentice' in the US, Chevrolet directed viewers to a website (www.chevyapprentice. com) to create their own ads for the Chevy Tahoe, a popular SUV. As Chevy expected, not all the submissions were complimentary (or suitable for airing on network TV!). In one video, a shiny SUV motors down a country road lined with sunflower fields, jaunty music playing in the background. But then, white lettering appears on the screen: '$70 to fill up the tank, which will last less than 400 miles. Chevy Tahoe'. Another submission asked: 'Like this snowy wilderness? Better get your fill of it now. Then say hello to global warming.' A spokeswoman for Chevrolet observed, 'We anticipated that there would be critical submissions. You do turn over your brand to the public, and we knew that we were going to get some bad with the good. But it's part of playing in this space.'[12]

Who creates advertising?

Although the trend towards DIY advertising illustrates how high-tech picture modifying software like Photoshop and Final Cut Pro can help almost anyone to become a director, most advertising is far more complicated. An **advertising campaign** is a coordinated, comprehensive plan that carries out promotion objectives and results in a series of advertisements placed in media over a period of time. Although a campaign may be based around a single ad, most employ multiple messages with all ads in the campaign having the same look and feel.

Creating and executing an advertising campaign often means many companies work together, and it requires a broad range of skilled people to do the job right. Some firms may do their own advertising. In many cases, though, the firm will retain outside *advertising agencies* to develop advertising messages on its behalf. A **limited-service agency** provides one or more specialised services, such as media buying or creative development. A **full-service agency** provides most or all of the services needed to mount a campaign, including research, creation of ad copy and art, media selection and production of the final messages. The five largest global agencies are the J. Walter Thompson Co., McCann-Erickson Worldwide, Leo Burnett Worldwide BBDO Worldwide and Ogilvy and Mather Worldwide.[13]

A campaign requires many different people to produce it. Big or small, an advertising agency hires a range of specialists to craft a message and make the communications concept a reality:

- **Account management:** The *account executive*, or account manager, is the 'soul' of the operation. This person develops the campaign's strategy for the client, supervises the day-to-day activities on the account, and is the primary liaison between the agency and the client. The account executive has to ensure that the client is happy while verifying that people within the agency are executing the desired strategy.

- **Creative services:** *Creatives* are the 'heart' of the communications effort. These are the people who actually dream up and produce the ads. They include the agency's creative director, copywriters and art director. Creatives are the artists who breathe life into marketing objectives and craft messages that (hopefully) will interest consumers.

- **Research and marketing services:** *Researchers* are the 'brains' of the campaign. They collect and analyse information that will help account executives develop a sensible strategy. They assist creatives in getting consumer reactions to different versions of ads or by providing copywriters with details on the target group.

- **Media planning:** The *media planner* is the 'legs' of the campaign. He or she helps to determine which communication vehicles are the most effective, and recommends the most efficient means for delivering the ad by deciding where, when and how often it will appear.

As we saw in Chapter 11, more and more agencies practise integrated marketing communications (IMC) in which advertising is only one element of a total communications plan. Because IMC includes more than just advertising, client teams composed of people from account services, creative services, media planning, research, public relations, sales promotion and direct marketing may work together to develop a plan that best meets the communications needs of each client.

Developing the advertising campaign

The advertising campaign is about much more than creating a cool ad and hoping people notice it. The campaign should be intimately related to the organisation's overall communications goals. That means the firm (and its outside agency if it uses one) must have a good idea of whom it wants to reach, what it will take to appeal to this market, and where and when the messages should be placed. Let's examine the steps required to do this (Figure 12.1).

Step 1: Identify the target audiences

The best way to communicate with an audience is to understand as much as possible about them and what turns them on and off. An ad that uses the latest slang may relate to teenagers but not to their parents – and

| Photo 12.3 | Advertisers often include imagery to capture the attention of their audiences
Source: Alamy Images/Caro |

Figure 12.1	Steps in developing an advertising campaign
	Developing an advertising campaign includes a series of steps that will ensure that the advertising meets communication objectives

this strategy may backfire if the ad copy reads like a 40-year-old trying to sound like a 20-year-old.

Most advertising is directed towards customers, whether the target audience includes college students or industry executives. As we discussed in Chapter 6, marketers/researchers often identify the target audience for an advertising campaign from research related to a segmentation strategy. Researchers try to get inside the customer's head to understand just how to create a message which he or she will understand and respond to. For example Toyota and Honda sent staff to live with families in order to test how they use their vehicles. This tactic led to the Honda's decision to add backseat room to the 1998 Accord.

 ## Step 2: Establish message and budget objectives

Advertising objectives should be consistent with the overall communications plan. That means that both the underlying message and its costs need to be related to what the marketer is trying to say about the product and what the marketer is willing or able to spend. Thus, advertising objectives generally will include objectives for both the message and the budget.

Setting message objectives

As we noted earlier, because advertising is the most visible part of marketing, many people assume that marketing *is* advertising. In truth, advertising alone is quite limited in what it can achieve. What advertising *can* do is to inform, persuade and remind. Accordingly, some advertisements are *informational*; they aim to make the customer knowledgeable about features of the product or how to use it. At other times, advertising seeks to *persuade* consumers to like a brand or to prefer one brand over the competition. But many ads are simply aimed at keeping the name of the brand in front of the consumer – *reminding* consumers that this brand is the one to choose when they go looking for a soft drink or a beefburger or a chocolate bar.

Setting budget objectives

Advertising is expensive. In 2006, Unilever, which led all European companies in advertising expenditures, spent €5.75 billion while second and third place ad spenders, l'Oréal and Nestlé, spent €3.875 billion and €2.63 billion respectively.[14]

Marketing metrics

Measuring value

More and more television viewers are bypassing commercials – whether by switching the channel, fast forwarding or just getting up to get a snack. Advertisers are demanding a more precise system that will let them know just which of their ads people are actually watching and how captivating their ads are. The firm PreTesting developed a system that 'records saccadic eye motion, the involuntary flicks and darts of the eye as consumers watch TV commercials and read billboards or print advertising'. This passive eye monitoring is a better and more accurate way of gauging a subject's response than focus groups or diaries. With the help of this new technology, the major pharmaceutical company Pfizer figured out that its latest TV ad for its Lipitor cholesterol medicine did not do very well among customers. The commercial featured Robert Jarvik, an American scientist and physician known for his role in developing the Jarvik-7 artificial heart medicine. During the ad, he was talking about the benefits of this new Lipitor cholesterol medicine. The saccadic tests revealed, however, that consumers had a 'blank stare' on Robert Jarvik's face instead of focusing on what he was saying. People were obviously trying to figure out who he was rather than listening to the commercial message.[15]

An objective of many firms is to allocate a percentage of their overall communications budget to advertising, depending on how much and what type of advertising the company can afford. Major corporations like Renault advertise heavily, using expensive media such as television to promote multiple products throughout the year. Other companies may be more selective, and smaller firms may want to put their advertising euros into cheaper media outlets, such as direct mail or trade publications.

The major approaches and techniques to setting overall promotional budgets, such as the percentage-of-sales and objective-task methods we discussed in Chapter 11, also set advertising budgets.

Step 3: Design the ads

Creative strategy is the process that turns a concept into an advertisement. It's one thing to know *what* a company wants to say about itself and its products, and another to figure out *how* to say it. Some marketers like to think of the creative process for an advertising campaign as the 'spark between objective and execution'

The goal of an advertising campaign is to present a series of messages and repeat it to a sufficient degree to meet the desired objectives. To do this, advertising creatives – art directors, copywriters, photographers and others – must develop a 'big idea', a concept that expresses aspects of the product, service or organisation in a tangible, attention-getting, memorable manner.

An **advertising appeal** is the central idea of the ad. Some advertisers use an emotional appeal complete with dramatic colour or powerful images, while others bombard the audience with facts. Some feature sexy people or stern-looking experts – even professors from time to time. Different appeals can work for the same product, from a bland 'talking head' to a montage of animated special effects. An attention-getting way to say something profound about cat food or laundry detergent is more art than science, but we can describe some common appeals:

- **Reasons why: A unique selling proposition (USP)** gives consumers a single, clear reason why one product is better at solving a problem. The format focuses on a need and points out how the product can satisfy it. For example, 'M&Ms melt in your mouth, not in your hands' is a USP. In general, a USP strategy is effective if there is some clear product advantage that consumers can readily identify and that is important to them.

- **Comparative advertising:** A comparative advertisement explicitly names one or more competitors. Comparative ads can be very effective, but there is a risk of turning off consumers who don't like the negative tone. While in many countries comparative advertising is illegal, it's a widely used tactic in the UK. Think about supermarkets such as Tesco and Sainsbury's which compare each other's prices in ads. Comparative advertising is best for brands that have a smaller share of the market, and for those firms that can focus on a specific feature which makes them superior to a major brand. When market leaders use comparative advertising, there is the risk consumers will feel that 'Goliath is picking on David!'

- **Demonstration:** The ad shows a product 'in action' to prove that it performs as claimed: 'It slices, it dices!' Demonstration advertising is most useful when consumers are unable to identify important benefits except by seeing the product in use. Who has not seen the numerous TV product advertisement shows where entire products like juice mixer, rasps or vacuum cleaners are seen in action under various conditions. The British firm Acdoco ran an ad for its laundry colour protector Glo Care Colour Catcher. The advertisements were set inside a washing machine and showed the product in action.[16]

- **Testimonial:** A celebrity, an expert, or a 'man in the street' states the product's effectiveness. Think about toothpaste ads that use dental practice managers, or make-up ads that use 'Hollywood make-up artists' to endorse products. The use of *celebrity endorsers* is a common, but expensive strategy, e.g. David Beckham and Motorola or Kate Moss and Rimmel. It is particularly effective for mature products that need to differentiate themselves from competitors, such as Coke and Pepsi that enlist celebrities to tout one cola over another.[17]

- **Slice of life:** A *slice-of-life* format presents a (dramatised) scene from everyday life. Slice-of-life advertising can be effective for everyday products such as washing powders and headache remedies that consumers may feel good about if they see 'real' people buying and using them. Washing powder commercials often feature typical dirty washing family scenarios or the 'Bisto family' sitting down to dinner each night.

- **Lifestyle:** A lifestyle format shows a person or persons attractive to the target market in an appealing setting. The advertised product is 'part of the scene', implying that the person who buys it will attain the lifestyle.

- **Fear appeals:** This tactic highlights the negative consequences of *not* using a product. Some fear appeal ads focus on physical harm, while others try to create concern for social harm or disapproval. Mouthwash, deodorant, dandruff shampoo makers and life insurance companies have successfully used fear appeals, as have ads aimed at changing behaviour, such as messages discouraging drug use or encouraging safe sex. Over-50s life insurance ads often start with 'what would happen to your loved ones if you were taken seriously ill or died?'

- **Sex appeals:** Some ads appear to be selling sex rather than products. In a Dolce & Gabbana advertisement for watches, various topless men and women lie next to each other while showing their watches. Ads such as these rely on sexuality to get consumers' attention. Sex appeal ads are more likely to be effective when there is a connection between the product and sex (or at least romance). For example, sex appeals will work well with a perfume but are less likely to be effective when selling a lawn mower.

- **Humorous appeals:** Humorous ads can be a way to break through advertising clutter. But humour can be tricky, because what is funny to one person may be offensive or stupid to another. Different cultures also have different senses of humour. A Reebok commercial in the US showed women at a basketball game checking out the all-male cheerleading squad – people from countries who don't have cheerleaders (you don't find too many pom-poms at football matches) might not 'get it'. Perhaps the benefit of humorous advertising is that it attracts consumers' attention and leaves them with a pleasant feeling. Of course, humour can backfire. In the UK, a Renault Megane 225 ad featuring people in everyday situations shaking uncontrollably as the car passed by was banned by the government's Office of Communications after viewers complained that the ad mocked people with illnesses such as Parkinson's disease.[18] Check out www.pearsoned.co.uk/solomon to see some of the funniest ads.

- **Slogans and jingles:** Slogans link the brand to a simple linguistic device that is memorable. Jingles do the same but set the slogan to music. We usually have no trouble reciting successful slogans (sometimes years after the campaign has ended); think of such die-hards as McDonald's 'I'm lovin' it', Sainsbury's 'Try Something New', Merrill Lynch's 'Be bullish', Thomas Cook's 'Don't just book it, Thomas Cook it', Nokia's 'Nokia has everyone talking', Orange's 'The future's bright, the future's Orange', IKEA's 'Make yourself at home' or P&G's 'Please don't squeeze the Charmin'.

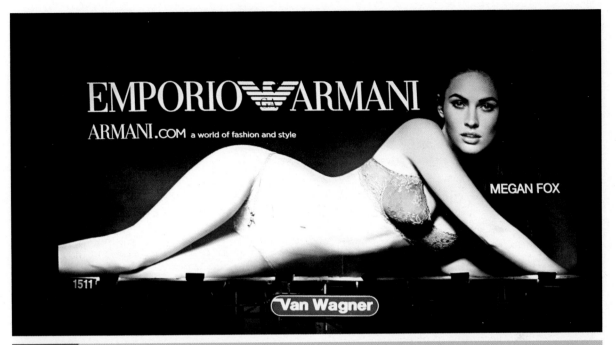

| Photo 12.4 | Companies often create eye-catching campaigns by using sex appeal to draw attention
Source: Getty Images/BuzzFoto/FilmMagic |

 ## Step 4: Pre-test what the ads will say

Now that the creatives have worked their magic, how does the agency know if the campaign ideas will work? Advertisers try to minimise mistakes by getting reactions to ad messages before they actually place them. Much of this **pre-testing**, the research that goes on in the early stages of a campaign, centres on gathering basic information that will help planners be sure they've accurately defined the products market, consumers and competitors. As we saw in Chapter 3, this information comes from quantitative sources, such as syndicated surveys, and qualitative sources, such as focus groups.

As the campaign takes shape, the players need to determine how well the advertising concepts will perform. **Copy testing** measures the effectiveness of ads. This process

Marketing misstakes

The ASA and alcohol

The UK advertising rules on alcohol are amongst the most stringent in the world because they specify content and placement restrictions on alcohol advertisements. 98.9 per cent of advertisements comply, some don't: for example, Magners cider ran into trouble with an advert which stated 'It's the perfect ice breaker' and 'Making sure the conversation flows'.

An advertisement for Wild Cape Liqueur featured a couple embracing, and scratch marks appeared next to the strapline 'Unleash your wild side'. An alcohol delivery service called Alcohol in Emergency, decided to use the abbreviation 'A in E' in its adverts to draw attention to the speedy nature of its service.

Why do you think these might be marketing misstakes?
Source: Based on Advertising Standards Authority Annual Report 2009

Marketing ethics and sustainability

Puffery

Often ads, although not illegal, create a biased impression of products with the use of **puffery** – claims of superiority that neither sponsors nor critics of the ads can prove are true or untrue. For example, Nivea bills itself as 'the world's number 1 name in skin care', Neutrogena claims that its cream cleanser produces 'the deepest feeling clean' and DuPont says that its Stainmaster Carpet is 'a creation so remarkable, it's practically a miracle'.

Debate, discuss, disagree

1 How harmful is a little exaggeration?

2 Don't consumers expect and adjust for it?

3 What are the dangers to the marketing discipline of puffery in advertising?

determines whether consumers are receiving, comprehending and responding to the ad according to plan.

Step 5: Choose the media type(s) and media schedule

Media planning is a problem-solving process for getting a message to a target audience in the most effective way. Planning decisions include audience selection and where, when and how frequent the exposure should be. Thus, the first task for a media planner is to find out when and where people in the target market are most likely to be exposed to the communication. This is called an **aperture**, the best 'window' to reach the target market. Many university students read the campus newspaper in the morning, so their aperture would include this medium at this time.

There is no such thing as one perfect medium for advertising. The choice depends on the specific target audience, the objective of the message, and, of course, the budget. For the advertising campaign to be effective, the media planner must match up the profile of the target market with specific media vehicles. For example, many young consumers are avid web users, so marketers wishing to reach this segment might allocate a relatively large share of their advertising budget to buying online advertising.

Choosing the right mix of media is no laughing matter, especially as new options including videos and DVDs, video games, personal computers, the internet, MP3 players, hundreds of new TV channels and even satellite radio now vie for our attention. Consider that by 2008, approximately 13 million British households had satellite and cable TV in their households, a 35 per cent increase from 2002. In the UK, the battle for dominance in the world of satellite and cable TV had boiled down to a fight between two main players: BSkyB and Virgin Media. In recent years, people are spending a lot more time watching cable and satellite channels, which explains the fierce fight for further market share by the two companies.[19] Figure 12.2 highlights some of these dramatic changes.

Where to say it: traditional media

What does a 52-inch plasma TV with Dolby Surround Sound have in common with a bus ticket? Each is a media vehicle that permits an advertiser to communicate with a potential customer. Depending on the intended message, each medium has its advantages and

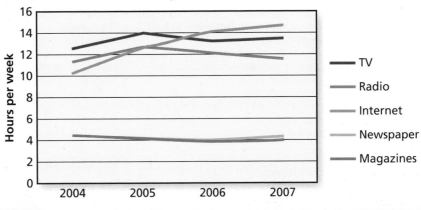

Hours spent using each media in a typical week 16–24-year-olds

Figure 12.2	Changes in media usage in the EU
	Source: www.eiaa.net/ftp/casestudiesppt/eiaa_mediascope_europe-pan-european_executive_summary. pdf (accessed 28 january 2009)

disadvantages. Let's take a look at the major categories of media (Table 12.1 summarises some of the pros and cons of each type).

● **Television:** Because of television's ability to reach so many people at once, it's the medium of choice for regional or national companies. Today there are literally hundreds of television choices available to advertisers. However, advertising on a television network can be very expensive. The cost to place a single 30-second ad on a popular prime-time TV show normally ranges between €300,000 and €750,000, depending on the size of the show's audience. Advertisers may prefer to buy cable, satellite or local television time rather than national network time because it's cheaper or because they want to reach a more targeted market, such as 'foodies' who are into cooking.

Marketing ethics and sustainability

Secrets and lies of beauty industry laid bare by advertising

The cosmetics market is thought to be worth more than £15 billion worldwide, but expensive beauty products are not doing what they say on the pack. They are promoted as products that will rejuvenate and bring bounce to your hair and a little brilliance to your demeanour. In a ruthlessly competitive market, pseudoscientific claims have become common. In a warning shot to an industry reliant on increasingly extreme claims, the Advertising Standards Authority upheld complaints about

'amino-acid replenishing' shampoo. Some claims attached to the product – Procter & Gamble UK's Pantene Pro-V shampoo – were found to be misleading and unsubstantiated, the watchdog ruled. A television advertisement for Pantene Pro-V, which promised to make hair 'up to ten times stronger' and would 'put back what life takes out', also misled viewers.

Source: Adapted from *The Times*, 11 May 2005

Debate, discuss, disagree

1   What is the main cause of misleading advertising?

2   Should companies be forced to run ads explaining how it was misleading and correcting the perception?

Vehicle	Pros	Cons
Television	• Extremely creative and flexible • National TV is the most cost-effective way to reach a mass audience • Cable and satellite TV allow the advertiser to reach a selected group at relatively low cost • A prestigious way to advertise • Can demonstrate product in use • Can provide entertainment and generate excitement • Messages have high impact because of the use of sight and sound	• The message is quickly forgotten unless it is repeated often • The audience is increasingly fragmented • Although the relative cost of reaching the audience is low, prices are still high on an absolute basis – often too high for smaller companies • Fewer people are viewing national television • People switch from station to station zapping commercials • Rising costs have led to more and shorter ads, causing more clutter
Radio	• Good for selectively targeting an audience • Is heard out of the home • Can reach customers on a personal and intimate level • Can use local personalities • Relatively low cost, both for producing a spot and for running it repeatedly • Because of short lead time, radio ads can be modified quickly to reflect changes in the marketplace • Use of sound effects and music allows listeners to use their imagination to create a vivid scene	• Listeners often don't pay full attention to what they hear • Difficulty in buying radio time, especially for national advertisers • Not appropriate for products that must be seen or demonstrated to be appreciated • The small audience of individual stations means ads must be placed with many different stations and must be repeated frequently
Newspapers	• Wide exposure provides extensive market coverage • Flexible format permits the use of colour, different size ads, and targeted editions • Ability to use detailed copy • Allows local retailers to tie in with national advertisers • People are in the right mental frame to process advertisements about new products, sales, etc. • Timeliness, i.e. short lead time between placing ad and having it run	• Most people dont spend much time reading the newspaper • Readership is especially low among teens and young adults • Short life span – people rarely look at a newspaper more than once • Very cluttered ad environment • The reproduction quality of images is relatively poor • Not effective in reaching specific audiences.
Magazines	• Audiences can be narrowly targeted by specialised magazines • High credibility and interest level provide a good environment for ads • Magazines have a long life and are often passed along to other readers. • Visual quality is excellent • Can provide detailed product information with a sense of authority	• Expensive: with the exception of direct mail, the highest cost per exposure • Long deadlines reduce flexibility • The advertiser must generally use several magazines to reach the majority of a target market • Clutter
Outdoor	• Most of the population can be reached at low cost • Good for supplementing other media • High frequency when signs are located in heavy traffic areas • Effective for reaching virtually all segments of the population • Geographic flexibility	• Hard to communicate complex messages because of short exposure time • Difficult to measure advertisements audience • Controversial and disliked in many communities • Cannot pinpoint specific market segments
Direct response	• Ads can target extremely narrow audiences • Messages can be timed by the advertiser at his or her convenience • Easy to measure the effectiveness of ads	• High cost per exposure • Target lists must be constantly updated • Ads lack credibility among many consumers

Table 12.1 Pros and cons of media vehicles

Sources: Based on Thomas J. Russell and Ron Lane, *Kleppner's Advertising Procedure*, 15th ed. (Upper Saddle River, NJ: Prentice Hall, 2002); Terence A. Shimp, *Advertising, Promtion and Supplemental Aspects of Integrated Marketing Communications*, 6th ed. (Australia: Thomson Southwestern, 2003); and William Wells, John Burnett, and Sandra Moriarty, *Advertising: Principles and Practice*, 6th ed. (Upper Saddle River, NJ: Prentice Hall, 2003).

Marketing metrics

Measuring magazine value

Marketing managers and media planners have a difficult time measuring a magazine's reach in time spans shorter than several months. Lately, magazines have been getting pressure to devise a system that provides readership measures more quickly and that also do a better job of tracking the total audience and the effectiveness of specific ads that run in an issue. More and more advertisement pricing in magazines is being linked to its effectiveness and return on investment – and on a short-term timescale. McPheters & Co. runs a website called Readership. com that is designed to do just this task: provide real-time information about a magazine's audience and distribution as well as audience engagement on an individual-issue basis.[21]

Nevertheless, 78 per cent of advertisers say TV advertising has become less effective as DVRs and video-on-demand grow in popularity.[20]

- **Radio:** Radio as an advertising medium goes back to 1922 in the US, when a New York City apartment manager went on the air to advertise properties for rent. One advantage of radio advertising is flexibility. Marketers can change commercials quickly, often on the spot by an announcer and a recording engineer.[22] Radio is attractive to advertisers seeking low cost and the ability to reach specific consumer segments.

- **Newspapers:** The newspaper is among the oldest types of media. Retailers in particular have relied on newspaper ads since the Victorian era to inform readers about sales and deliveries of new merchandise. Newspapers are an excellent medium for local advertising and for events (such as shop sales) that require a quick response. Today, most newspapers also offer online versions of their papers to expand their exposure.

- **Magazines:** Approximately 92 per cent of adults look through at least one magazine per month. New technologies such as *selective binding* allow publishers to personalise their editions, so that advertisements for local businesses can be included in issues distributed at specific locations only.

- **Directories:** Directory advertising is the most 'down-to-earth', information-focused advertising medium. In 1883, a printer in the US ran out of white paper while printing part of a telephone book, so he substituted yellow paper instead. Today, the Yellow Pages are still well-known throughout the world. The Yell Group is a leading international directories business covering markets such as the United Kingdom, United States, Spain and Latin America with products such as Yellow Pages, Business Pages, Yell.com and Yellow Book USA. Its Yellow Pages have been connecting buyers and sellers in the UK for over 40 years; 28.3 million copies were distributed in 2007 in the UK, having approximately 480,000 unique advertisers included. In 2007, the group had revenues of £2.075 billion.

- **Out-of-home media: Out-of-home media**, such as airships, transit ads and hoardings, reach people in public places. This medium works best when it tells a simple, straightforward story.[23] For example, to make sure it was not upstaged by Nike or other rivals, Adidas constructed a massive 3D advertisement at Munich airport for the 2006 World Cup. The billboard was stretched over the whole highway and received a lot of attention.[24] In the Netherlands, Hotels.nl, an online reservation company fitted 144 sheep with logo-emblazoned blankets. The advertising agency that created the 'sheep boards' plans to offer blankets for horses and cows in the future.[25]

- **Place-based media:** Marketers are constantly searching for new ways to get their messages out to busy people. The European low-cost airline Germanwings even transformed

Photo 12.5	Out-of-home media provide an excellent way to reach consumers on the go. Posters such as this one certainly grab our attention *Source:* Getty Images/Matthew Lloyd

the entire interior of its aeroplanes into advertising spaces. The inside of the airplane is painted in the firm's colours – lilac and yellow. Further ads can be seen on areas like the front wall or the luggage flap. **Place-based media** like 'The Airport Channel' transmit messages to 'captive audiences' in public places, such as doctors' offices and airports. At Luton Airport (London) easyJet shows videos on various screens before the check-in to educate people about the procedures that will take place (check-in, security check, boarding process). In one scene of the film, a woman goes through the security check and takes out her Apple laptop in order to let it be X-rayed. Throughout the whole video, you also see various easyJet ads of their products. Another example of place-based media is *in-store TV*. For example, the British supermarket chain Asda sells advertising space on its in-store TV channel 'Asda live'.[26] Tesco uses the outdoor media company JCDecaux, the bus stop poster people, to sell space for its Tesco TV network.

● And now some retailers can even follow you around the shop to deliver more intimate and personal messages: a new technology called *RFID* (radio frequency identification) tracks customers as they make their way through the aisles. So a shopper might receive a beep to remind her she just passed her family's favourite peanut butter.[27] You're not paranoid; they really *are* watching you!

Internet advertising

The web gives marketers the ability to reach customers in new and exciting ways. Online advertising has grown in the European Union to €6.8 billion in 2007, having substantially

Photo 12.6	West End theatre shows promote themselves on London buses to gain attention and interest
	Source: Alamy Images/Jinny Goodman

increased in the latter years. In the EU in 2005, the UK was the biggest spender on the internet with €2 billion, closely followed by France and Germany with €382 and €369 million respectively.[28] Online advertising offers several advantages. First, the internet provides new ways to finely target customers. Web user registrations and *cookies* allow sites to track user preferences and deliver ads based on previous internet behaviour. In addition, because the website can track how many times an ad is 'clicked', advertisers can measure how people are responding to online messages. Finally, online advertising can be interactive – it lets consumers participate in the advertising campaign. Guinness ran an interactive ad on Sky TV in the UK which aimed to educate viewers on how to pour the perfect pint of Guinness. The campaign consisted of video footage, a game to win a pint glass, a poll for the best Guinness ad and references to Guinness' association with the Premiership.[29] Vodafone Netherlands recently launched its KijkMij TV (Look at me) initiative, which involves not only customers uploading their (cameraphone) videos in different categories (funniest, sexiest, most informative) but also pays these 'minipreneurs' 10 per cent of revenues generated when other customers download their video. Vodafone works with PayPal's MassPay in order to pay out accrued earnings when accounts surpass €10 (which equals approximately 400 downloads).[30]

Specific forms of internet advertising include banners, buttons, pop-up ads, search engines and directories, and email:

- **Banners:** These rectangular graphics at the top or bottom of web pages were the first form of web advertising. Although the effectiveness of banners remains in question (banners now receive less than a 1 per cent click-through rate), they still remain the most popular form of web advertising.

- **Buttons:** These are small banner-type advertisements that a company can place anywhere on a page. Early in the life of the internet, buttons encouraging surfers to 'Download Netscape Now' became a standard on many websites and were responsible for much of Netscape's early success.

- **Search engine and directory listings:** Just as the Yellow Pages and other directories are advertising media, so too are search engines and online directory listings. Increasingly, firms are paying search engines for more visible or higher placement on results lists. Who have you Googled today?

- **Pop-up ads:** A pop-up ad is an advertisement that appears on the screen while a web page is being loaded or after it is loaded. Because pop-up ads take the centre of the screen while surfers are waiting for the desired page to load, they are difficult to ignore. Because many surfers find pop-ups a nuisance, most internet access software provides an option that blocks all pop-ups. A pop-up ad opens a separate browser window. Web advertisers are typically charged only if people actually click through to the ad.

- **Email:** For advertising, email is becoming as pervasive as radio and television. It is one of the easiest ways of communicating with consumers because marketers can send unsolicited email advertising messages to thousands of users by *spamming* – sending unsolicited email to five or more people not personally known to the sender. Many websites that offer email give surfers the opportunity to refuse unsolicited email via junk email blockers. This **permission marketing** gives the consumer the power to opt in or out. Spamming, however, is not always legal and can result in lawsuits if it is proven that practices have violated laws. In 2003, Microsoft claimed a victory in the fight against spamming when a man who called himself the 'Spam King' agreed to pay the company €8.05 million. The man's US-based company was alleged to have been one of the world's biggest spammers, sending out 38 billion emails a year.[31]

Media scheduling: when to say it

After choosing the advertising medium, the planner then creates a **media schedule** that specifies the exact media to use for the campaign as well as when and how often the message should appear. Figure 12.3 shows a hypothetical media schedule for the promotion of a new video game. Note that much of the advertising reaches its target audience in the months just before Christmas and that much of the expensive television budget is focused on advertising during specials at a time when people are buying presents. An extension

Marketing metrics

The web

When measuring the impact of the web, some of the metrics which can be used have been rated by marketing managers. Here are those metrics and what percentage of marketing managers found them 'very useful'. Visitors 37 per cent, Visits 36 per cent, Clickthrough Rate 35 per cent, Cost Per Customer Acquired 32 per cent, Cost Per Thousand Impressions (CPM) 27 per cent, Pageviews 28 per cent, Cost Per Click 27 per cent, Abandonment Rate 24 per cent and Cost Per Order 23 per cent.[32]

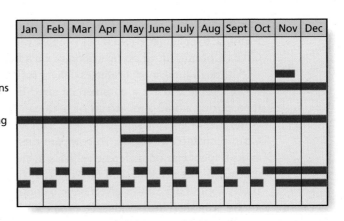

	Jan	Feb	Mar	Apr	May	June	July	Aug	Sept	Oct	Nov	Dec

Medium

Television
 Specials
 Saturday cartoons

Newspaper
 Co-op advertising

Direct mail

Magazines
 Mag 1
 Mag 2

Figure 12.3	Media schedule for a video game
	Media planning includes decisions on where, when and how much advertising will be done. A media schedule such as this one for a video game shows the plan visually

of this logic is the purchase frequency. For weekly purchases such as bread, a weekly ad schedule would be more appropriate than for cold remedies, which are highly seasonal.

The media schedule outlines the planner's best estimate of which media will be most effective in attaining the advertising objective(s) and which specific media vehicles will do the most effective job. The media planner considers such factors as the match between the demographic and psychographic profile of a target audience and the people reached by a media vehicle, the advertising patterns of competitors and the capability of a medium to convey the desired information adequately. The planner must also consider such factors as the compatibility of the product with editorial content. For example, viewers might not respond well to a lighthearted ad for a new snack food during a sombre documentary on world hunger.

When analysing media, the planner is interested in assessing **advertising exposure**; the degree to which the target market will see an advertising message in a specific medium. Media planners speak in terms of **impressions**; the number of people who will be exposed to a message placed in one or more media vehicles. For example, if 5 million people watch *MTV Total Request Live* on television, then each time an advertiser runs an ad during that programme it gets 5 million impressions. If the advertiser's spot runs four times during the programme, the impression count would be 20 million (even though some of these impressions would represent repeated exposure to the same viewers).

To calculate the exposure a message will have if placed in a certain medium, planners consider two factors: reach and frequency. **Reach** is the percentage of the target market that will be exposed to the media vehicle at least one time. This measure is particularly important for widely used products when the message needs to get to as many consumers as possible. **Frequency** is the average number of times that these members of the target market will be exposed to the message. This measure is important for products that are complex or those that are targeted to relatively small markets for which many exposures to the message are necessary to make an impact.

Say that a media planner wants to be sure her advertising for 18–30s holidays reaches university students. She learns that 25 per cent of the target market reads at least a few issues of *NME* music magazine each year (that's *reach*). She may also determine that these students on average are likely to see three of the 12 monthly ads that 18–30s holidays will run in *NME* during the year (that's *frequency*). Now, she calculates the magazine's **gross rating points (GRPs)** by multiplying reach by frequency, which in this case allows the media planner to compare the effectiveness of *NME* with other media. By using this same formula, the planner could then compare this GRP number to another magazine or to the GRP of placing an ad on television or on a bus or any other advertising medium.

Although some media vehicles deliver superior exposure, they may not be cost efficient. More people will see a commercial aired during the European Football Championship than during a 3.00 a.m. re-run of a Tarzan film. But the advertiser could run late-night commercials every night for a year for the cost of one 30-second European Football Championship Final spot. To compare the relative cost effectiveness of different media and of spots run on different vehicles in the same medium, media planners use a measure called **cost per thousand (CPT)**. This figure reflects the cost to deliver a message to 1000 people. CPT allows advertisers to compare the relative cost effectiveness of different media vehicles that have different exposure rates. CPM, the cost of a thousand impressions, is used for websites.

A medium's popularity with consumers determines how much advertisers must pay to put their message there. Television networks are concerned about the size of their audiences because their advertising rates are determined by how many viewers their programming attracts. Similarly, magazines and newspapers try to boost circulation (that explains all the freebies you get) so they can charge higher rates to their advertising clients.

Media scheduling: how often to say it

After deciding where and when to advertise, the planner must decide how often. What time of day? And what overall pattern will the advertising follow?

A *continuous schedule* maintains a steady stream of advertising throughout the year. This is most appropriate for products that we buy on a regular basis, such as shampoo or bread as well as unwanted goods such as household services like plumbers and electricians who often advertise continually in classified ads or directories. Some advertising industry trade groups maintain that continuous advertising sustains market leadership even if total industry sales fall.[33] On the downside, some messages can suffer from *advertising wear-out* because people ignore the same old ad messages.

A *pulsing schedule* varies the amount of advertising throughout the year based on when the product is likely to be in demand. A suntan lotion might advertise year-round but more heavily during the summer months. *Flighting* is an extreme form of pulsing in which advertising appears in short, intense bursts alternating with periods of little to no activity. It can produce as much brand awareness as a steady dose of advertising at a much lower cost if the messages from the previous flight were noticed.

 ## Step 6: Evaluate the advertising

A famous comment usually attributed to Lord Leverhulme goes: 'I am certain that half the money I spend on advertising is completely wasted. The trouble is, I don't know which half.'[34] Now that we've seen how advertising is created and executed, let's step back and see how we decide if it's working.

There's no doubt that a lot of advertising is ineffective. Ironically, as marketers try harder and harder to reach their customers, these efforts can backfire. Many consumers have a love–hate relationship with advertising. Over half the respondents in one survey said they 'avoid buying products that overwhelm them with advertising and marketing', and 60 per cent said their opinion of advertising 'is much more negative than just a few years ago'.[35] With so many messages competing for the attention of frazzled customers, it's especially important for firms to evaluate their efforts to increase the effect of their messages. How can they do that? Often advertisers do this by post-testing their advertising campaigns.

Post-testing means conducting research on consumers' responses to advertising messages they have seen or heard (as opposed to *pre-testing*, which as we've seen collects reactions to messages *before* they're actually placed in 'the real world'). Ironically, many creative ads that are quirky or even bizarre make an advertising agency look good within the industry (and on the CV of the art director), but are ultimately unsuccessful because they don't communicate what needs to be said about the product itself. On the other hand, nowadays to say less is to say more to consumers. The audience is bombarded with so much information that advertisers are left with little option but to try a different approach to reach people. If you think of brands such as Apple, O_2, easyJet, Tesco or Nike you will have an instant impression. These advertisers understand this concept. By saying less, they seem to tell the viewer more. Just think of the ad for the iPods from Apple. In the spot you see the black profile of dancing people and the only shiny object in the spot is the white iPod.[36]

Three ways to measure the impact of an advertisement are *unaided recall*, *aided recall* and *attitudinal measures*. **Unaided recall** tests by telephone survey or personal interview whether a person remembers seeing an ad during a specified period of time without giving the person the name of the brand. An **aided recall** test uses the name of the brand and sometimes other clues to prompt answers. For example, a researcher might show a group of consumers a list of brands and ask them to choose which items they have seen advertised within the past week. **Attitudinal measures** probe a bit more deeply by testing

Marketing metrics

Advertising

When measuring advertising, some of the metrics which can be used have been rated by marketing managers. Here are those metrics and what percentage of marketing managers found them 'very useful'. Effective Reach 42 per cent, Impressions 41 per cent, Effective Frequency 37 per cent, Share Of Voice 36 per cent, Net Reach 34 per cent, Average Frequency 31 per cent, and Gross Ratings 23 per cent.[37]

Marketing ethics and sustainability

Has America got it right?

Some deceptive ads make statements that can be proven false. For example, the US Federal Trade Commission (FTC) fined Volvo and its ad agency $150,000 each for an ad containing a 'rigged' demonstration. The Volvo 'Bear Food' ad campaign showed a monster truck running over a row of cars and crushing all but the Volvo station wagon. The Volvos, however, had been structurally reinforced, while the structural supports in some of the other cars had been cut. In addition to fining firms for deceptive advertising, the FTC also has the power to require firms to run corrective advertising, messages that clarify or qualify previous claims. For example, an FTC ruling required Novartis AG to spend $8 million to change packaging and advertising information about its Doan's Pills back medication saying 'Although Doan's is an effective pain reliever, there is no evidence that Doan's is more effective than other pain relievers for back pain'.[38]

Debate, discuss, disagree

1 What are the pros and cons of every country having an agency that can force companies to do corrective advertising?

consumer beliefs or feelings about a product before and after being exposed to messages about it. If, for example, Colgate's messages about '24 hour protection' make enough consumers believe that Colgate can protect their teeth for a whole day, marketers can consider the advertising campaign successful.

Public relations

Objective

2

Explain the role of public relations.

Public relations (PR) is the communications function that seeks to build good relationships with an organisation's *publics*; these include consumers, stockholders, legislators and other stakeholders in the organisation. Today marketers use PR activities to influence the attitudes and perceptions of various groups not only towards companies and brands but also towards politicians, celebrities and not-for-profit organisations.

The basic rule of good PR is: *Do something good, and then talk about it*. A company's efforts to get in the limelight – and stay there – can range from humanitarian acts to more lighthearted 'exposure'. Consider for example the British Flora Family Marathon that takes place every year in London. The marathon is used to raise awareness to control your weight and to help keep your heart and lungs healthy.[39]

The big advantage of this kind of communication is that when PR messages are placed successfully they are more credible than if the same information appeared in a paid advertisement. As one marketing executive observed, 'There's a big difference between hearing about a product from a salesman and from your trusted local newsreader.'[40] The value of publicity was clearly demonstrated by the huge success of Mel Gibson's controversial film *The Passion of the Christ*. Frequent news stories, TV appearances by Mr Gibson, radio debates and even a *Newsweek* cover that asked 'Who Really Killed Jesus?' built momentum. Even before the film opened, 81 per cent of cinemagoers were aware of it. This high level of interest didn't just 'happen' – a year before the film's release, Gibson toured churches with a rough cut of his movie, giving speeches and charming pastors. His film production company, Icon, signed up consultants to advise pastors on how best to use the film to promote the church and recruit new members.[41]

Public relations is crucial to an organisation's ability to establish and maintain a favourable image. Some types of PR activities, referred to as *proactive PR*, stem from the company's marketing objectives. For example, marketers create and manage **publicity**; unpaid communication about an organisation that gets media exposure. This strategy helps to create awareness about a product or an event, as when a local newspaper reporting on an forthcoming concert features an interview with the band's lead guitarist around the time that tickets go on sale. Although some publicity happens naturally, more typically a 'buzz' needs to be created by a firm's publicists. For example, take the drug Botox. Everyone has heard of it. But how? As Botox has 13 different clinical uses and can only be prescribed by doctors, it cannot be promoted directly to the public because the law prevents companies promoting prescription medicines to consumers. The answer is PR. The company uses the press to get Botox written about to create awareness and consumer interest.

The internet has expanded the capabilities of the traditional PR function.[42] Corporate websites post testimonials from customers, make new product announcements and respond quickly to important events. The internet can also be very effective in handling crises. Companies can respond to a crisis online in far less time than other forms of communication, such as press releases or conferences.[43] For example, as news regarding danger from Dell's batteries surfaced, Dell's digital media manager Lionel Menchaca used a corporate blog entry to announce that battery replacements would take 20 days to reach customers. Further, Dell reported that changes in lead times would be reported on the blog (www.direct2dell.com).[44]

Objectives of public relations

Companies that practise IMC know that PR strategies are best used in concert with advertising, sales promotions and personal selling to send a consistent message to customers and other stakeholders. As part of the total IMC plan, PR is often used to accomplish the following objectives:

- **Introducing new products to manufacturers:** When Weyerhaeuser Co. introduced Cellulon, a new biotechnology product, it distributed information kits that clearly explained the technical product and its applications in each of 12 markets to ensure that the trade press properly covered the introduction.[45]

- **Introducing new products to consumers:** When First Drinks Brands sponsored the launch of the premium vodka brand Russian Standard in the UK through TV, it hoped to gain a foothold in the growing expensively priced vodka market. The TV ad was boosted by sales promotion and public relations to get the vodka into magazine editorials in order to gain a good share in the almost £1.9 billion strong market.[46]

- **Influencing government legislation:** Airplane maker Boeing spent over a decade in public relations activities to persuade regulators that jetliners with two engines were as safe as those with three or four engines even for non-stop international flights, some as long as 16 hours. Boeing's rival Airbus argued that four-engine planes were necessary for the desired level of safety for such flights.[47]

- **Enhancing the image of an organisation:** Budget Rent-A-Car International, a car company operating in Europe, the Middle East and Africa and lying third in the European league table behind Hertz and Avis, used a variety of public relations and other promotions activities to generate business. The company wanted to secure a stronger presence in the international business traveller market and introduced the VIP Traveller card, which entitled the holder to unlimited mileage throughout Budget offices worldwide. Inflight magazines, such as *High Life* (British Airways), *Atlas* (Air France) or *Bordbuch* (Lufthansa) were used as a vehicle to promote this card offering coupons and information.[48]

- **Enhancing the image of a city, region or country:** Faced with international criticism about possible human rights abuses and restriction of trade, the Chinese government established an office in charge of 'overseas propaganda' to present a more favourable image of China to the rest of the world.[49]

- **Crisis management:** Whether it's product tampering or an accident at a company's facilities or some other company-related problem, such as British Airways' Terminal Five fiasco, a crisis can cause permanent damage to a company, the success of its products, and its stockholder equity. Public relations professionals know that when a firm handles crises well, it can minimise damage. Thus, a vitally important role of PR is to prepare a *crisis management plan*; a document that details what an organisation will do *if* a crisis occurs – who will be the spokesperson for the organisation, how the organisation will deal with the press and what sort of messages it will deliver to the press and the public. Public relations may be even more important when the company's image is at risk due to bad publicity, for example, product tampering.[50] The goal here is to manage the flow of information to address concerns so that consumers don't panic and distributors don't abandon the product. For example, in 2006 Dell and Sony suffered after bloggers posted images of 'exploding' laptops. This news resulted in Dell's largest recall in its 22-year history. The lithium laptop batteries made by Sony and used by Dell could overheat and catch fire. Dell responded quickly by providing essential information on its website, which registered 23 million visitors during that time.[51]

Marketing misstakes

Lost in translation? Nigaz name ignites racism debate

Russia's energy giant Gazprom's joint venture with Nigeria's oil company NNPC was called Nigaz. The event has caused a *virtual* uproar with one group on Facebook calling itself 'Nigerians No Nigaz' writing 'How more derogatory can it be . . . to set up a NEW company for the JV and name it NIGAZ . . . this is derogatory – surely not Nigerian-like'. Twitter users have equally expressed disdain at the decision, through hundreds of tweets. Surprisingly, however, the local Nigerian press was not as prompt in picking up the story. Some believe that faux pas like these are usually 'harmless' and while some people might take offence, it is rare that companies change their name because of it.[52]

Why do you think this was a marketing misstake?

The British firm Cadbury faced a salmonella scandal in 2006, when a rare Montevideo strain of salmonella was found in seven of its products. A major recall began and millions of products had to be destroyed. The product withdrawal cost Cadbury approximately £20 million. The negative PR was even worse because Cadbury faced huge criticism for its handling of the crisis and for the delay in coming clean and admitting its fault.[53]

● **Calling attention to a firm's involvement with the community:** In 2005, companies globally spent approximately £17.4 billion on sponsorship according to the European Sponsoring Association (ESA). For example, the US insurance company AIG signed a £56 million four-year deal to be the shirt sponsor for Manchester United. Norwich Union as another example announced a £50 million injection into UK Athletics as the dominant Olympic sport.[54] PR specialists work behind the scenes to ensure that sponsored events receive ample press coverage and exposure.

Planning a public relations campaign

A public relations campaign is a coordinated effort to communicate with one or more of the firm's audiences. This is a three-step process of developing objectives, executing and evaluating. Let's review each step.

Like an advertising campaign, the organisation must first develop clear objectives for the PR programme that define the message it wants people to hear. Next, the PR specialists must develop a campaign strategy that includes the following:

● A statement of objectives.

● A situation analysis.

● Specification of target audiences (publics), messages to be communicated and specific programme elements to be used.

● A timetable and budget.

● Discussion of how the programme will be evaluated.

For example, the International Apple Institute, a trade group devoted to increasing the consumption of apples, had to decide if a campaign should focus on getting consumers to cook more with apples, drink more apple juice, or simply to buy more fresh fruit. Because fresh apples brought a substantially higher price per pound to growers than apples used for apple sauce or apple juice, the group decided to push the fresh fruit angle. It used the theme 'An apple a day . . .' (sound familiar?) and mounted a focused campaign to encourage people to eat more apples by placing articles in consumer media extolling the fruit's health benefits.

Execution of the campaign means deciding precisely how the message should be communicated to the targeted public(s). An organisation can get out its positive messages in many ways: news conferences, sponsorship of charity events and other attention-getting promotions.

A barrier to greater reliance on PR campaigns is the difficulty of devising metrics to gauge their effectiveness. Who can say precisely what impact appearances by company executives on talk shows or sponsoring charity events has on sales? It is possible to tell if a PR campaign is getting media exposure, though compared with advertising it's much more difficult to assess bottom-line impact. Table 12.2 describes some common measurement techniques. Check out our PR case 'Eat in colour' at www.pearson.co.uk/solomon.

Public relations activities

Public relations professionals engage in a wide variety of activities. While some of these may seem more related to marketing and to marketing communications than others, they all lead to the same goal – creating and maintaining that positive image the organisation needs. Some of these efforts are as follows:

- **Press releases:** The most common way for PR specialists to communicate is a **press release**, which is a report of some event that an organisation writes itself and sends to the media in the hope that it will be published for free. A newer version of this idea

Table 12.2
Measuring the effectiveness of public relations (PR) efforts

Method	Description	Pros	Cons
In-house assessments conducted by a PR manager	Analyse media coverage in publications, looking for number and prominence of mentions	Relatively inexpensive because the major cost is the manager's time	Cannot guarantee objectivity in the analysis; crucial to specify up-front what the relevant indicators are
Awareness and preference studies	Assess company's standing in the minds of customers relative to competition	Good for broad-based strategy setting or to demonstrate the progress of a large programme	Difficult to connect results to specific PR events and to identify which actions had what level of impact on awareness; very expensive
Measurement of print and broadcast coverage generated by PR activities	The basic measurement tool in PR	Provides a quantifiable measure of press coverage; relatively inexpensive	Quantitative only; does not consider the content of the press coverage
Impression counts	Measure the size of the potential audience for a given article	Because a similar measure is used to assess advertising effectiveness, this method provides a common measure for comparison	Usually limited to the circulation of selected publications, so this method does not include pass-along readership; can be expensive

Source: Adapted from Deborah Holloway, 'How to Select a Measurement System That's Right for You', *Public Relations Quarterly* (Fall 1992), 15–17.

Across the hall

Advice for
Anthony Levy

Alan Giles
Chairman of Fat Face

To me there are three success criteria for this campaign; to secure good media coverage, to resonate with consumers, and finally to generate sustained behaviour change. Option 1 is fun, seasonally topical, cuts across all consumer groups, and I like the viral component. However, the idea is a bit complex, the lower socio-economic groups of greatest interest to Anthony may not get the analogy to carbon offsetting, and some of the resultant behaviour change will be to prompt more exercise rather than fruit and veg consumption – a good outcome for those consumers, but not in Eat in Colour's interest. It's also a two-stage mechanic, requiring the consumer to firstly access the website, and then make the offsetting behaviour.

Option 2 is a simple call-to-action, which if successful would directly meet Eat in Colour's objective. However, it's boring as hell, and I would be very sceptical about media interest (would you want to read about how someone else had changed the contents of their shopping trolley?). The £5 tag might also backfire, reinforcing concerns about the expense of fruit and veg. I therefore favour Option 3; the tabloid press can't get enough stories about the soaps and I would anticipate lots of coverage, and high levels of readership from the lower socio-economic groups of most interest to Anthony. Of course raising awareness of this issue might not change behaviour, but it's a start!

is a *video news release* (VNR) that tells the story in a film format instead. Some of the most common types of press releases include the following:

- *Timely topics* deal with topics in the news. For example, the British company WebitPR developed a way of sending press releases to news websites globally and then monitoring their impact. When the company started in 2001, it created a video news release to inform clients about its service. Nowadays you can look at the video on its website www.webitpr.com or on www.youtube.com.[55]

- *Research project stories* are published by universities highlighting breakthroughs by faculty researchers.

- *Consumer information releases* provide information to help consumers make product decisions, such as helpful tips from a gravy manufacturer about preparing dishes for Sunday lunch.

- **Internal PR:** These activities aimed at employees often include company newsletters and closed-circuit television. Internal releases help keep employees informed about company objectives, successes or even plans to 'downsize' the workforce. Often company newsletters also are distributed outside the firm to suppliers or other important publics.

- **Investor relations:** For publicly held companies, investors are a vitally important public as their financial support is critical to the future of the company. It is the responsibility of the PR department to develop and distribute annual and quarterly reports and to provide other essential communications with individual and corporate stockholders, with investment firms and with capital market organisations.

- **Lobbying:** Lobbying means talking to and providing information to government officials to persuade them to vote a certain way on pending legislation or even to initiate legislation that would benefit the organisation.

- **Speech writing:** An important job of a firm's PR department is to write speeches on a topic for a company executive to deliver. While some executives do actually write their own speeches, it is more common for a speechwriter on the PR staff to develop an initial draft of a speech after which the executive might add his or her own input.

- **Corporate identity:** PR specialists may provide input on corporate identity materials, such as logos, brochures, building design and even stationery that communicate a positive image for the firm.

- **Media relations:** One of the tasks of the PR professional is to work to develop and maintain positive relationships with the media. Of course, this is important if the company is going to receive the best media exposure possible for positive news, such as publicising the achievements of an employee who has done some notable charity work or for a product it developed that saved someone's life. For example, Tesco and Asda attracted favourable publicity following positive coverage of a trial involving radio frequencies to replace barcodes and a 'tough' stance on underage drinking and the cheapest supermarket petrol prices respectively.[56] And, as we've seen, good media relations can be even more important when things go wrong. News editors are simply less inclined to present a story of a crisis in its most negative way if they have a good relationship with PR people in the organisation.

- **Sponsorships:** These are PR activities through which companies provide financial support to help fund an event in return for publicised recognition of the company's contribution. Many companies today find that their promotion budgets are well spent to sponsor a golf tournament, a Formula One driver, a symphony concert or global events such as the London Olympics 2012 or World Cup football competition. These sponsorships are particularly effective because consumers often connect their enjoyment of the event with the sponsor, thus creating brand loyalty. McDonald's, a sponsor of the FIFA World Cup since 1994, has built on its sponsorship to create promotions in its restaurants around the world. McDonald's global Player Escort Programme sent 1408 children aged 6–10 to the World Cup in Germany, where they escorted players onto the field for all 64 FIFA matches. In Brazil, McDonald's restaurants offered customers sandwiches with flavours from countries competing in the World Cup. World Cup beverage cups were available for customers in some countries including China and the US and some locations in Europe offered consumers a World Cup burger which was 40 per cent larger than a Big Mac.[57]

- **Special events:** Another job of a PR department is the planning and implementation of special events. Whether it is the visit of a group of foreign investors to a firm's manufacturing facilities, a Bank Holiday picnic for company employees, or a hospitality booth set up during a motorcycle race where the company is a sponsor, the PR staff's job is to make sure the event happens without a glitch and people go home happy. For example, Skoda created a reception for the launch of the Fabia vRS model at the Tram

Marketing misstakes

Hidden messages

As part of a special promotional campaign during the 1994 World Cup, a famous North European brewer had the flags of all the qualifying countries imprinted under the bottle cap of one of its main beer brands. The featured countries included Saudi Arabia, whose flag portrays a verse from the Koran. The idea of the Holy Scripture being associated with an alcoholic beverage deeply offended Muslims worldwide. The brewer had no choice but to recall all the bottles and terminate its promotion.[58]

Why do you think this might be a marketing misstake?

Photo 12.7	Marketers often sponsor events or teams to gain publicity and exposures in their target markets *Source:* Getty Images/Sports Illustrated/ Simon Bruty

Studios in North London. This event was exclusively for 100 motoring and lifestyle journalists. Afterwards, the company invited 60 regional press delegates to participate in a ride and drive event to test the new model.[59]

● **Buzz-building:** Because people have increasingly criticised such traditional PR techniques as video news releases, many PR agencies are turning to word of mouth to build a positive buzz about an organisation. One PR firm even hires noted bloggers to help clients develop an expertise in blogging.[60]

● **Advice and consultancy:** When a firm fully understands and appreciates the importance of the PR function, top management recognises that PR professionals have much more to offer than just planning parties and writing news releases. Because of their expertise and understanding of the effects of communication on public opinion, PR professionals also play the role of consultants to top management. So when a firm needs to shut down a plant or to build a new one, to discontinue a product or add to the product line, to fire a director, or to give an award to an employee who spends hundreds of hours a year doing volunteer work in his community, it needs the advice of its PR staff. What is the best way to handle the situation? How should the announcement be made? Who should be told first? What is to be said and how?

Marketing ethics and sustainability

Crazy, insane PR?

A major teddy bear producer of hand-crafted teddy bears in the US has a mission to 'make the world a better place . . . one bear at a time'. One Valentine's Day it sold a bear called 'Crazy for You' which wore a straight jacket and had commitment papers that read: 'Can't Eat. Can't Sleep. My Heart's Racing. Diagnosis: Crazy for You'. Some mental health groups were annoyed by the company's lack of sensitivity toward mental illness suffers and complained, causing the company to stop manufacture of the bear, but to continue with the sale of bears already produced. Although, the company's CEO apologised, she apparently also said that she felt her company could not be told what to sell and what not to sell, which further inflamed some members of Vermont's Businesses for Social Responsibility Group. Nonetheless, the furore and media attention apparently increased sales by 33% from the previous year.

Debate, discuss, disagree

1 Do you agree the company acted in a socially irresponsible way?

2 How do you feel about the teddy bear company's PR response to the complaints?

3 What do you think the long-term consequences of the company's actions could be?

Having read the PR section, what do you think about Anthony's options to use PR for the fresh fruit and vegetable consortium? Now you've covered some of the key impersonal media such as advertising and PR, which are designed to create awareness, interest and even desire (remember AIDA?) in a product, the role of sales promotion, personal selling and direct marketing is to create action, the final stage of the AIDA communications model. In the next chapter we take a closer look at direct marketing.

Now that you've learned about the promotional mix, read 'Real people, real decisions' to see which strategy Anthony selected.

Real people, real decisions

How it worked out at Eat in Colour

Option 2 proved to be the winner. This idea is a more long-term PR strategy which can be replicated for other groups. It also created the behaviour change that was key to the campaign as well as creating ambassadors for the Eat in Colour campaign within the target communities. However, the main reason for the success was that one of the ways to create impact and change in people's lives is to show people like themselves changing and talking about fruit and veg in their own language so that people get the opinion that these people are not just like me, these people are me! It's the impact that real people with real voices make.

Whilst the other two options also proved very successful in gaining media coverage, including some extremely good media equivalent values per pound invested, they do not have the same direct impact and longevity. They did, however, reinforce some of the key messages of the £5 Family Challenge.

Marketing metrics

How Fresh Produce Consortium measures success

The Advertising Equivalent Value of the coverage generated during the campaign's first year January 2007–September 2007 was approximately £505,000. This was gained through 219 items of coverage reaching an audience of readers (print and online), listeners and viewers totalling 85 million. These articles included an average of 80 per cent of the key messages which the campaign seeks to proliferate. Key messages are:

Fruit and vegetables are quick and easy

Fruit and vegetables are a healthy option

Fruit and vegetables are a cost-effective healthy eating option

Eat in Colour campaign www.eatincolour.com

Inclusion of pictures/graphic images

In year one the campaign delivered a 4:1 (400 per cent) return on investment as measured by the budget spend compared to the media exposure.

Chapter summary

Now that you have finished reading this chapter, you should be able to answer any of the following potential examination questions:

1. **Explain what advertising is and describe the major types of advertising.** Advertising is non-personal communication from an identified sponsor using mass media to persuade or influence an audience. Advertising informs, reminds and creates consumer desire. Product advertising is used to persuade consumers to choose a specific product or brand. Institutional advertising is used to develop an image for an organisation or company, to express opinions (advocacy advertising), or to support a cause (public service advertising) and retail advertising informs customers about where to shop. Some advertisers are now encouraging consumers to participate in do-it-yourself advertising. Most companies rely on the services of advertising agencies to create successful advertising campaigns. Full-service agencies include account management, creative services, research and marketing services, and media planning, while limited service agencies provide only one or a few services.

2. **Describe the process of developing an advertising campaign.** Development of an advertising campaign begins with identifying the target audience and developing advertising message and budget objectives. Next, advertisers design the advertising, and select an effective type of advertising appeal. Pre-testing advertising before placing it in the media prevents costly mistakes. A media plan determines where and when advertising will appear. Media options include broadcast media (network and spot television and radio), print media (newspapers, magazines and directories), out-of-home media (outdoor advertising and place-based media), and internet advertising. A media schedule specifies when and how often the advertising will be seen or heard.

3. **Explain how marketers evaluate advertising.** Marketers evaluate advertising through post-testing. Post-testing research may include aided or unaided recall tests that examine whether the message had an influence on the target market.

4. **Explain the role of public relations.** The purpose of PR is to build good relationships between an organisation and its various publics and to establish and maintain a favourable image. Public relations is useful in introducing new products, influencing legislation, enhancing the image of a city, region or country, enhancing the image of an organisation and calling attention to a firm's community involvement.

5. **Describe the steps in developing a public relations campaign.** The steps in a PR campaign begin with setting objectives, creating and executing a campaign strategy, and planning how the PR programme will be evaluated. PR specialists often use print or video news releases to communicate timely topics, research stories and consumer information. Internal communications with employees include company newsletters and internal TV programmes. Other PR activities include lobbying, speechwriting, developing corporate identity materials, media relations, arranging sponsorships and special events, and providing advice for management.

Key terms

Chapter review

Marketing concepts: testing your knowledge

1. What is advertising, and what is its role in marketing?

2. What are the types of advertising that are most often used?

3. How do advertising agencies create campaigns for their clients? Describe the steps in developing an advertising campaign.

4. Describe some of the different advertising appeals used in campaigns.

5. What are the strengths and weaknesses of television, radio, newspapers, magazines, directories, out-of-home media, place-based media and the internet for advertising? What are the ways marketers advertise on the web?

6. Describe the media planning process. How do marketers pre-test their ads? How do they post-test ads?

7. What is the purpose of public relations? What is proactive PR? What is a crisis management plan?

8. What are the steps in planning a PR campaign?

9. Describe some of the activities that are a part of PR.

Marketing concepts: discussing choices

1. Some people are turned off by advertising because they say it is obnoxious, that it insults their intelligence, and that advertising claims are untrue. Others argue that advertising is beneficial and actually provides value for consumers. What are some arguments on each side? How do you feel?

2. Technology through television remotes, VCRs, computers and cable television is giving today's consumers more and more control over the advertising images they see. How has this affected the advertising industry so far, and do you think this will affect it in the future? What are some ways that advertising can respond to this?

3. Some people criticise PR specialists, calling them 'spin doctors' whose job is to hide the truth about a company's problems. What is the proper role of PR within an organisation? Should PR specialists try to put a good face on bad news?

Marketing practice: applying what you've learned

1. As an account executive for an advertising agency, you have been assigned to a new client, a new line of high quality, high price makeup. As you begin development of the creative strategy, you are considering different types of appeals:

a. USP

b. Comparative advertising

c. A fear appeal

d. A celebrity endorsement

e. A slice-of-life ad

f. Sex appeal

g. Humour

Outline the strengths and weaknesses of using each of these appeals for advertising the makeup.

2. Spend some time looking through magazines. Find an ad that fits each of the following categories:

   a.   USP strategy

   b.   Testimonial

   c.   Lifestyle format

   d.   Humour appeal

   Assess each ad. Explain who the target market appears to be. Describe how the appeal is executed. Discuss what is good and bad about the ad. Do you think the ad will be effective? Why or why not?

3. Assume that you are the head of PR for a regional fast-food chain that specialises in fried chicken and fish. A customer has claimed that he became sick when he ate a fried cockroach that was in his meal along with the chicken. As the director of PR, what recommendations do you have for how the firm might handle this crisis?

4. As a PR professional employed by your university, you have been asked to develop strategies for improving your school's PR programme. Write a memo to your university vice chancellor with your recommendations.

Marketing miniproject: learning by doing

The purpose of this miniproject is to give you an opportunity to experience the advertising creative process.

1. With one or more classmates, create (imagine) a new brand of an existing product (such as toothpaste, perfume, soft drink or the like).

2. Decide on an advertising appeal for your new product.

3. Create a series of at least three different magazine ads for your product, using the appeal you selected. Your ads should have a headline, a visual, and copy to explain your product and to persuade customers to purchase your brand.

4. Present your ads to your class. Discuss the advertising appeal you selected and explain your ad executions.

Real people, real surfers

Exploring the web

Much of the advertising you see every day on television and in magazines is created by a small number of large advertising agencies. To make their agency stand out from the others, the different agencies develop unique personalities or corporate philosophies. Visit the websites of several advertising agencies:

Leo Burnett Worldwide (www.leoburnett.com)

BBDO Worldwide (www.bbdo.com)

WPP (www.wpp.com)

Fallon (www.fallon.co.uk)

J. Walter Thompson (www.jwt.com)

Explore the websites to see how they differ. Then answer the following questions:

1. What is the mission of each agency? How does each agency attempt to position itself compared to other agencies?

2. Who are some of the major clients of the agency?

3. How does the site demonstrate the creative ability of the agency? Does the site do a good job of communicating the mission of the agency? Explain.

4. If available, tell a little about the history of the agency.

5. Of the agencies you visited, which would you most like to work for, and why?

6. As a client, based on your exploration of the websites, which agency would you choose for your business, and why?

Now, take a look at the website at www.pearsoned.co.uk/solomon to see some videos from YouTube relating to aspects of this chapter.

Marketing plan exercise

A. An advertising campaign consists of a series of advertisements placed in media over time. While ads may be placed in different media, all will have the same look, feel, and message. Think about one of the following products:
1. A new brand of toothpaste
2. Your home town or city
3. Your university

B. Assume that you are developing an advertising campaign. Outline how you would develop the campaign. Be sure to discuss the following:
1. The type of appeal you would use
2. The main message you will seek to communicate
3. The media you would use (be sure to include at least one print and one broadcast medium)
4. How you will develop the ads so that they have the same look and feel

Delve deeper into social media marketing

Professor Dr Thorsten Hennig-Thurau

Münster University and Cass Business School

Traditionally, marketing bore resemblance to bowling: marketing managers identified target customers or segments and 'hit' them with one-directional messages transmitted through advertising. With the rise of social media, this bowling analogy has to be substituted by a different one which refers to a much more dynamic activity: playing pinball. Today, managers serve up a 'marketing ball' (which might be a traditional advert or a YouTube clip) into a cacophonous environment. When hitting 'new media bumpers' and 'kickers' such as spoofs or mashups or other kinds of parodies created by consumers, the ball changes its direction in chaotic ways, with its speed often being dramatically accelerated. Think of Dove's famous 'Evolution' spot which serves as part of its 'Campaign for Real Beauty': consumer-generated parodies such as 'Slob Evolution' which satrise or criticise Dove's ambition have generated similar, if not more attention among consumers than the original ad. In the era of social media, marketing's role is no longer just to release information, but to guide the marketing ball's now increasingly non-linear and direction-changing course with agile use of the pinball machine's 'new media flippers'.

Media such as Facebook, YouTube and Twitter, but also eBay and Wikipedia are offering consumers a plethora of active roles in the marketplace, and consumers are accepting this offer thankfully and euphorically. An important implication of social media's consumer active paradigm is that pinball marketing requires marketers to engage in a 'conversation' about their brands whose images and associations are no longer shaped solely by marketing efforts, but also by the consumers who use them – or at least talk about them on the internet. Word of mouth has always been considered a major success factor, but now consumer statements about a brand are read by millions on their smart phones instantly and regardless of their location. United Airlines' claim 'Friendly skies' gets a different meaning for those 10.5 million consumers who have watched country musician Dave Carroll's song 'United Breaks Guitars' on YouTube, in which the local musician artfully and sarcastically summarises the improper treatment of his Tailor guitar by United personnel and the company's far from effective subsequent complaint handling efforts. Managing crises like this one will become an essential requirement of pinball marketers' jobs. But the pinball game also offers marketers substantial potential with regard to managing consumer-brand relationships interactively and on an individual level. The movie star Ashton Kutcher has established strong relationships with more than 6 million followers on Twitter by regularly sharing parts of his personal life with them at virtually no cost – a powerful lesson in how to generate strong brand attachment in the pinball marketing age.

References

Thorsten Hennig-Thurau, Edward C. Malthouse, Christian Friege, Sonja Gensler, Lara Lobschat, Arvind Rangaswamy and Bernd Skiera (2010) 'The Impact of New Media on Customer Relationships', *Journal of Service Research,* 13 no 3, 311–30.

John A.Deighton and Leora Kornfeld (2009) 'Interactivity's Unanticipated Consequences for Markets and Marketing', *Journal of Interactive Marketing*, 23, no.1 (Winter), 2–12.

Andreas. M. Kaplan and Michael Haenlein (2011) 'The Early Bird Catches the News: Nine Things You Should Know about Micro-blogging', *Business Horizons*, 54, no. 2 105–13.

Marketing in action case

Real decisions on viral marketing

Universal Orlando Resort is soon launching a new attraction called 'The Wizarding World of Harry Potter'. What would you do if you were head of marketing at the team park to announce the new attraction? Go out and spend millions of euros on TV and billboard adverts and on other traditional 'creative' advertising techniques? Probably yes, just as most companies would do. But that's not what the vice president of new media and marketing partnerships Cindy Gordon did. She knew that Harry Potter had a substantial fan base, thus she decided to organise a secret webcast, and initially only told this to seven rabid HP fans who were hand-selected by Gordon's team. After the event, which took place in 'Dumbledore's Office' set at Leavesden Studios, they blogged about it, which tens of thousands of people read; the media picked this up and eventually they wrote about the new attraction at the theme park in newspapers, talked about it on TV, radio and blogs. It was estimated that the news reached around 350 million people, just by telling about it to seven fans initially. And instead of spending millions of euros on the campaign, the theme park achieved the same, or even bigger publicity for a fraction of the cost.

The marketing problem

The problem is that although this form of marketing has a great potential and substantially lower costs associated with it than traditional marketing techniques, there is no guarantee that the viral content created will eventually go viral. It is best demonstrated by a bell curve. For a high percentage of viral campaigns, firms will just get their money back, or in a very few cases they will lose all their investment. So let's take a look at some success stories.

Examples of successful and unsuccessful campaigns

T-Mobile Dance

www.youtube.com/watch?v=VQ3d3KigPQM
According to viralvideochart.com, this advert already had 8.5 million online views on 7 March 2009, after being filmed only a few weeks earlier on 15 January. On 2 March, Universal Music released the music medley of the dance as a single, and also as an album featuring the eight songs. People talked about this video in thousands of blogs, and T-mobile used it on TV and the London tube as part of its marketing campaign. The success of the video greatly helped to raise brand awareness of the mobile operator.

David After Dentist

www.youtube.com/watch?v=txqiwrbYGrs
This home-made video of a kid after having his tooth removed generated over 16 million views within a month of going online. It was also featured on CNN's News to Me programme and has its own blog created on http://davidafterdentist.com/blog where further movies of David are available to watch.

Alliwantforxmasisapsp.com

www.youtube.com/watch?v=tX_3GEvF8RQ
During the Christmas holiday season in 2006 Sony launched a campaign which failed miserably. The company wanted to create a buzz about its PSP product. It posted a video on YouTube with a guy rapping about the PSP and also created a website where two friends were blogging about the product. Sony tried to create the impression that these were blogs from consumers, but after it was discovered that the firm itself hired a marketing agency to create these, it resulted in a very negative PR for Sony and became a good lesson for companies that should learn not to underestimate their consumers' intelligence.

Things to think about

1. What are the elements of a successful viral marketing strategy?
2. For each of the following videos, rate them on a scale of 1–10 on each of the following criteria:
    *   Creative and original
    *   Funny
    *   Relevant to the brand
    *   Engaging
    *   Authentic
    *   Suitable for viral marketing
    *   **Overall**

Will it Blend?

www.youtube.com/watch?v=qg1ckCkm8YI

*   Creative and original:
*   Funny:
*   Relevant to the brand:
*   Engaging:
*   Authentic:
*   Suitable for viral marketing:
*   *Overall:*

In this campaign, popular consumer items, such as iPhone, McDonald's extra value meal and a Chuck Norris figurine are used by the owner of Blendtec, to examine how well they blend. The marketers chose YouTube for their medium to transmit the message.

Miss South Carolina

www.viralvideochart.com/youtube/miss_teen_usa_2007__south_carolina_answers_a_ question?id=lj3iNxZ8Dww

*   Creative and original:
*   Funny:
*   Relevant to the brand: N/A
*   Engaging:
*   Authentic:
*   Suitable for viral marketing:
*   *Overall:*

Cadbury Eyebrows

www.viralvideochart.com/dailymotion/cadbury_eyebrows?id=x84djm

*   Creative and original:
*   Funny:
*   Relevant to the brand:
*   Engaging:
*   Authentic:
*   Suitable for viral marketing:
*   *Overall:*

Microsoft Origami

www.youtube.com/watch?v=lVLhvn4cvnQ

*   Creative and original:
*   Funny:
*   Relevant to the brand:
*   Engaging:
*   Authentic:
*   Suitable for viral marketing:
*   *Overall:*

Microsoft created a great buzz in 2006 about this product, as it only announced its code name before the release day and some even speculated that it would be an iPod killer.

Choose Your Surrogate

www.youtube.com/watch?v=I5FaoT5hLSQ
- Creative and original:
- Funny:
- Relevant to the brand:
- Engaging:
- Authentic:
- Suitable for viral marketing:
- *Overall:*

A viral website, called Choose Your Surrogate, was created a few months before the cinema release of the Surrogates.

Cravendale – Cats with Thumbs

www.youtube.com/watch?v=h6CcxJQq1x8
- Creative and original:
- Funny:
- Relevant to the brand:
- Engaging:
- Authentic:
- Suitable for viral marketing:
- *Overall:*

Blonde Girl Pregnancy Test

www.youtube.com/watch?v=IPlqhw8AoQI
- Creative and original:
- Funny:
- Relevant to the brand:
- Engaging:
- Authentic:
- Suitable for viral marketing:
- Overall:
- Discuss why they were or were not successful

Case study, written by Adam Szuts, Cass Business School

Sources: www.the7thchamber.com/pdf/The-Seventh-Chamber_Viral-Report.pdf; www.pocket-lint.com/news/news.phtml/22585/23609/t-mobile-adverts-music-available-download.phtml; www.viralvideochart.com; www.davidmeermanscott.com/documents/Viral_Marketing.pdf; www.businessweek.com/innovate/content/dec2006/id20061219_590177.htm?campaign_id=bier_innc.g3a.rssd1219o; www.wilsonweb.com/wmt5/viral-principles.htm; *International Journal of Business Science and Applied Management* 3, no. 1 (2008), http://medialoper.com/hot-topics/hardware/whatever-happened-to-the-origami/

References

1. '21st Annual Global Marketers', *Advertising Age*, http://adage.com/images/random/datacenter/2007/global-marketing2007.pdf.
2. www.guardian.co.uk/media/2010/aug/24/tv-advertising.
3. Stuart Elliott, 'On ABC, Sears Pays to Be Star of New Series', New york times 3 December 2003, www.nytimes.com; Brian Steinberg and Suzanne Vranica, 'Prime-Time TV's New Guest Stars: Products',*Wall Street Journal*, 12 January 2004 www.wsj.com.
4. Brian Steinberg and Suzanne Vranica, 'Five Key Issues Could Alter the Ad Industry', *wall street jounral* 4 January 2004.
5. William Wells, John Burnett and Sandra Moriarty, *Advertising: Principles and Practice,* 5th ed. (Englewood Cliffs, NJ: Prentice Hall, 2000).
6. *European Advertising and Media Forecast*, 19,1 no.(October 2004), 10–11.
7. Bob D. Cutler and Darrel D. Muehling, 'Another Look at Advocacy Advertising and the Boundaries of Commercial Speech', *Journal of Advertising* 20 (December 1991), 49–52.
8. W. Cooper, 'The Met Reaches out to Young People with Gun-crime Video', *New Media Age*, 16 November 2006, 5.

9. 'The Body Shop Takes on Human Trafficking', *Creativity* 15, 11 (November 2007), 50.

10. 'Dove Joins DIY Ad Creative Marketplace', *Brandweek.com*, 15 December 2006.

11. 'Customer-Made', www.trendwatching.com/briefing/; 'Generation C', www.trendwatching.com/trends/GENERATION_ C.htm.

12. Quoted in Stuart Elliott, 'Chevy Tries a Write-Your-Own-Ad Approach, and the Potshots Fly', *The New York Times Online*, 6 April 2006.

13. 'Top U.S. Agency Brands by Advertising Revenue', *Advertising Age*, 28 April 2006, www.adage.com/datacenter/article?article_id=108857.

14. 'Marketers', *Advertising Age* 78, no. 52, 31 December 2007.

15. G.E. Jordan, 'To Gauge Ads' Effectiveness, Watch Those Eyes', *Newhouse News Service*, August 2007.

16. 'Insider Information', *The Grocer*, 31 January 2004, 56.

17. Douglas C. McGill, 'Star Wars in Cola Advertising', *New York Times*, 22 March 1989, D1.

18. Jeremy Lee, 'Ofcom Bans Follow-Up Renault Megane Spot', *Campaign*, 6 August 2004, 10.

19. 'Satellite and Cable TV', *Mintel Reports,* October 2007.

20. 'TV Advertising is Less Effective: Survey' *PROMOMagazine*, www.promomagazine.com/news/tvadvertising_survey_032406/index/html.

21. N. Ives, 'Print Buyers Search for Real-time Ad Metrics', *Advertising Age* (February 2006), S2.

22. Phil Hall, 'Make Listeners Your Customers', *Nation's Business,* June 1994, 53R.

23. Lisa Marie Petersen, 'Outside Chance', *Mediaweek*, 15 June 1992, 20–23.

24. 'New Campaigns the World', *Asia's Media and Marketing Newspaper*, 16 June 2006.

25. Doreen Carvajal, 'Advertiser Counts on Sheep to Pull Eyes Over the Wool', *The New York Times*, 24 April 2006, www.nytimes.com.

26. J. Quilter, 'Asda Hunts Agency to Handle in-store TV Ad Sales', *Marketing*, 29 March 2006, 3.

27. Jeremy Wagstaff, 'Loose Wire', *Wall Street Journal* 31 July 2003, www.wsj.com (accessed 21 January 2004).

28. 'European Advertising and Marketing Forecast', 21 (April 2007), supplement, 9–127.

29. R. Britton, 'iTV data', *New Media Age*, 5 October 2007, 26.

30. www.springwise.com/telecom_mobile/user_generated_content_meets_p/.

31. J. Wilson and B. Johnson, 'He Sent 38 Billion Emails and Called Himself the Spam King. Then Bill Gates Went After Him: World's Biggest Spammer Faces $7m Bill after Legal Battle', *The Guardian*, 11 August 2005, 3.

32. Adapted from N. Bendle, P. Farris, Phillip Pfeifer and D. Reibstein 'Metrics that Matter to Marketing Managers', *Marketing JRM* 1 (2010), 18–23.

33. Bristol Voss, 'Measuring the Effectiveness of Advertising and PR', *Sales and Marketing Management* (October 1992), 123–24.

34. This remark has also been credited to British businessman Lord Leverhulme; see Charles Goodrum and Helen Dalrymple, *Advertising in America: The First 200 Years* (New York: Harry N. Abrams, 1990).

35. Stuart Elliott, 'New Survey on Ad Effectiveness', *New York Times*, 14 April 2004, www.nytimes.com.

36. S. Far, 'Only Visual Thought Can Beat Today's Information Overload', *Marketing Week* 29, no.13, 30 March 2006, 35.

37. Adapted from Bendle, et al., 'Metrics that Matter'.

38. 'Appeals Court Backs FTC Call for Changes to Doan's Pills Ads', *The Wall Street Journal*, 21 August 2000, 1.

39. www.florafamilymarathon.com/florahealthheartinitiatives/family-marathon.aspx.

40. K. Fitzgerald, 'Homemade Bikini Contest Hits Bars, Beach for 10th Year,' *advertising age* 69, no. 15, 13 April 1998, 18.

41. Melissa Marr, 'Publicity, PR and "Passion"', *Wall Street Journal,* 20 February 2004, www.wsj.com.

42. Steve Jarvis, 'How the Internet Is Changing Fundamentals of Publicity', *Marketing News*, 17 July 2000, 6–7.

43. Dana James, 'When Your Company Goes Code Blue', *Marketing News*, 6 November 2000, 1, 15.

44. 'Dell battery replacement to take 20 days', *Electronic News*, 21 August 2006, 49.

45. Judy A. Gordon, 'Print Campaign Generates Sales Leads for Biotechnology Product', *Public Relations Journal* (July 1991), 21.

46. 'Russian Vodka in UK launch drive', *Marketing,* 20 June 2007, 9.

47. Andy Pasztor, 'FAA Ruling on Long-Haul Routes Would Boost Boeing's Designs', *Wall Street Journal*, 5 June 2006, A3.

48. F. McEwan, 'Case history: Budget rent a car', *Financial Times (London)*, 24 April 1984, 10.

49. Ni Chen and Hugh M. Culbertson, 'Two Contrasting Approaches of Government Public Relations in Mainland China', *Public Relations Quarterly* (Fall 1992), 36–41.

50. Willie Vogt, 'Shaping Public Perception', *Agri Marketing* (June 1992), 72–75.

51. 'Dell's Exploding Battery Debacle', *Bulldog Reporter's Daily Dog*, 18 August 2006.

52. Based on BBC Online News – Have Your Say, http://news-forums.bbc.co.uk/nol/thread.jspa?forumID=6675&edition=1&ttl=20110628180803 (accessed 17 June 2011).

53. M. Carmichael, 'Cadbury', *The Grocer*, 23 September 2006, 43.

54. C. Turner, '*AIG* Banks on the Red army for Expansion in UK . . . and China?', *Marketing Week*, 20 April 2006, 9.

55. 'Expansion Enables Teenager to Become MD', *BBC*, 13 April 2002, www.bbc.co.uk/lincolnshire/asop/people/jonathan_dolby.shtml.

56. J. Lepper, 'M&S slumps as retailer rivals retain reign at top', *PR Week*, 1 October 2004, 4.

57. 'McDonald's Celebrates World Cup Fever with Global Campaign', *Promo Magazine*, www.promomagazine.com/eventmarketing/news/mcds_worldcup_camapign_060906/index.html.

58. Adapted from T. Dalgic, and R. Heijblom, 'Educator Insights: International Marketing Blunders Revisited' , *Journal of International Martketing* 4 no. 1 (1996), 81–91.

59. 'Mmm Secures Skoda Deal for PR Event Work', *Event*, September 2003, 5.

60. Brian Steinberg, 'PR Executive Turns to Bloggers to Spread Messages for Clients', *Wall Street Journal*, 17 May 2006, B3A.

61. Linda B. Shonesy et al. 'Vermont Teddy Bear Company', *Journal of the International Academy for Case Studies* 14, no. 7 (2008), 73–7.

Chapter 13
Sales promotions and sales management

Q & A with James McCaffrey

What do you do when not working?
Golf, travel and family

First job out of university?
Trainee insurance inspector

Career high?
Joining Towergate in 2003, a refreshingly different working environment to the corporate bureaucracy I had encountered in previous companies

Best business book you've read?
I don't read business books

Your hero?
Roger Hunt, boyhood hero ex-Liverpool striker and World Cup winner

Motto to live by?
Balance and harmony – a motto I picked up on holiday in Bali. I believe it is important to strike the balance between quality at work and quality at home

What drives me?
To deliver sales targets and gain respect from my peers as a leader

My management style is:
Man of the people, but results are all important, particularly in a sales environment.

My pet peeve:
Companies forgetting who their customer is

Don't do this when interviewing me:
Assume that there is some great worth to what I'm saying

Meet James McCaffrey
A decision maker at Towergate

James McCaffrey is Head of Sales and Marketing for the Underwriting Division. Towergate Underwriting is part of Towergate Partnership – one of the UK's leading providers of specialist insurance services. The company uses its underwriting expertise to provide a wide range of insurance policies, including cover for niche markets that are often difficult to obtain elsewhere. Before joining Towergate, James held a number of positions. He initially began his working career with Royal Insurance as a Graduate Trainee, and had a number of Sales Inspector roles in Chester and Southampton, before becoming a Sales and Marketing Manager. James then worked for Iron Trades Insurance Company as the Southern Development Manager for the UK, before going to work for Australian Mutual Provident (AMP) for three years in Wellington, New Zealand, undertaking a number of roles in the Financial Services Division. James returned to the UK with AMP Pearl in Peterborough, working as the General Insurance Development Manager for three years, before joining Towergate in 2003, where he held responsibility for the Sales function across Towergate. James lives in Westerham, Kent and is married with two daughters, aged 12 and 14.

Real people, real decisions
Decision time at Towergate

Towergate is one of the UK's most spectacular success stories. It was founded by Peter Cullum, Paul Dyer and Tony Proverbs in 1997, and in over 12 years it has become Europe's largest independent insurance intermediary with turnover in excess of £2.5 billion. Towergate is actually a UK insurance broker and underwriter (but not an insurer). That means it prices the risk of insuring things. For example, Towergate knows more about the risks of owning a caravan than those people who sell the caravan insurance, so Towergate gets the work price and administers such insurance products for the brokers who sell them. It has a specialist Underwriting Division which sells non-life insurance products to insurance brokers; some of these brokers are part of Towergate Group (50) but the majority (over 4000) are not.

The company has grown by a mixture of organic growth and 160 acquisitions. Providing sales support to the individual risk area specialisations within the group has always been a problem, as sales integration has been seen as a huge task and one that might not necessarily be productive. In 2007, a Broker Support Unit was established with telesales staff to support individual marketing campaigns for the underwriting businesses (e.g. home insurance), which acts as a 'road map' for brokers. This road map helps brokers to find someone inside Towergate who can help with a particular insurance product need since there are over 200 insurance products available within the group, e.g. caravan insurance, property owners' insurance.

After buying 20 underwriting businesses, many of them with their own sales force, research indicated that small provincial insurance brokers, that are part of the community and often have small high street branches from which they sell to their community, were struggling to make sense of Towergate's new group structure, and were finding the various means of accessing Towergate's products confusing. For example, under the heading of home insurance there are five separate business units inside Towergate which at face value could provide the same solution. Secondly, traditionally, insurance brokers had had the resource of large sales forces devoted to them by insurers and underwriting agents, but these had been reduced, and in many cases completely removed, in favour of IT solutions over the last 20 years. Much work had been carried out on e-communication within Towergate, as throughout the insurance market. Ordering online was the order of the day. Thirdly, Towergate was struggling to develop loyalty within the insurance brokers, who often saw the company as a competitor because of their ownership of other insurance brokers.

Option 1 Invest in online solutions

Towergate could commit to further considerable expenditure by further developing and extending online quote and buy facilities for brokers. Two years of development work had already gone into preparing quote online and buy facilities for ten products. This saved a lot of processing time and effort and was the industry trend. In the long term there could be huge processing cost savings. However, 190 products remained to be computerised, and many of them by their complex nature, were unsuitable for e-commerce solutions as computer systems reduced underwriting to a series of limited binary questions. Insurance brokers complained that the large proportion of their clients simply did not fit into a regular box devised from the binary questions. A fully online system for all products would require technical internal competence and resources which Towergate didn't have. Also, any computerised system solution reduces the risk specialisation which was one of Towergate's strength, i.e. underwriting non-standard risks.

Option 2 Recruit a new generalist sales force

In this option an entirely new sales force would come from the best elements of the existing sales forces and external candidates, which would be large enough to go out and visit brokers face to face and sell the complete range of 200 products. The human interface solution, either by phone or face to face, would need to have a lot of money invested in new recruitment and training to make specialist salespeople into generalists in order to sell any of the 200 Towergate products. This approach had been derided by most strategic thinkers in the industry, as being a retrograde step back to selling models of the 1970s. There would be internal resistance to existing specialist salespeople being retrained to sell many products. In addition, finding a significant number of new salespeople was going to be difficult as the industry had been moving away from personal selling for many years. The advantages were that research had indicated that the vast majority of insurance brokers in the UK had virtually no relationships of trust with underwriters. Thus Towergate could establish itself with a distinctive market position. With no personal relationships, there was very little proactive personal selling which this option would provide. In addition, brokers would need to have only one relationship with Towergate for all their needs and this would reduce their confusion.

Option 3 Extend the specialised sales force

Towergate could continue the development of its specialised sales forces in individual operating units. At face value this would enhance specialisation, and mean more brokers could be contacted and given specialist product advice and quotes on particular products such as owner house insurance or buy to let home insurance. Also, there is some credibility advantage in Towergate maintaining client relationships and providing specialist knowledge which each salesperson would have. This reinforces one of Towergate's main strengths of specialist underwriting. However, it would be expensive and time–consuming to train so many highly specialised sales staff. It was inevitable that individual insurance brokers would need to develop relationships and receive visits from a multitude of Towergate salespeople from different insurance areas of the group. This could further the confusion and lack of clarity as to who did what within Towergate. Another downside of this option is that the specialist sales force liked to operate their own individual relationships with brokers, which discouraged cross-selling of other services, as these were sold by a different sales team.

Now, put yourself in James's shoes: which option should he pitch for and why?

Objectives

When you finish reading this chapter, you will be able to:

1 Explain what sales promotion is and describe the different types of trade and consumer sales promotion activities

2 Understand the important role of personal selling

Objective

1

Explain what sales promotion is and describe the different types of trade and consumer sales promotion activities

Sales promotion

Sometimes taking a simple walk through your student union on campus puts you in contact with a parade of people eager for you to enter a contest, taste a new chocolate bar, or take home a free T-shirt with a local bank's name on it. These are examples of **sales promotion**; programmes that marketers design to build interest in or encourage purchase of a product or service during a specified time period.[1] Marketers have been placing an increasing amount of their total marketing communication budget into sales promotion for one simple reason, these strategies deliver short-term sales results.

Sales promotion sometimes can be elaborate and high profile. For example, Burger King launched a worldwide sales promotion for its Whopper hamburger to celebrate its 50th anniversary. The promotion centred around the website www.whopperat50.com, which feature facts about the Whopper.[2] Another example was McDonald's Tigger Happy Meal promotion that ran throughout Europe to coincide with the launch of Disney's *The Tigger Movie*. The UK, Finland, Sweden, Germany, Norway and Belgium all participated in this programme, which lasted about four weeks.[3]

How does sales promotion differ from advertising? Both are paid messages from identifiable sponsors intended to change consumer behaviour or attitudes. In some cases, the sales promotion itself is publicised using a traditional advertising medium. But while marketers craft many advertising campaigns to create long-term positive feelings about a brand, company or shop, sales promotion tends to focus on more short-term objectives, such as an immediate boost in sales or the introduction of a new product. Sales promotion is very useful if the firm has an *immediate* objective, such as quickly bolstering sales for a brand or encouraging consumers to try a new product. The objective of a sales promotion may be to generate enthusiasm among retailers to take a chance on a new product or provide more shelf space for an item they already carry. Thus, like advertising, sales promotion can target channel partners (the 'trade') or the selling firm's own employees, as well as end consumers.

Sales promotion is one part of a firm's integrated marketing communication programme and must therefore be coordinated with other promotional activities. For example, if a brand's marketing communication tries to position the product as an expensive, luxury item (think Porsche), a sales promotion activity that reduces the price or involves giving away free beefburgers and lemonade at the Porsche dealer served by a man dressed in a clown suit will undoubtedly send conflicting messages to the customer about the Porsche brand. In addition, sales promotions rarely, if ever are used alone as the sole form of marketing communications. By its nature, sales promotion is most often used to support a more extensive advertising, direct marketing, public relations and/or personal selling initiative. Table 13.1 summarises some of the key sales promotional techniques. Sales promotions are directed at two key groups: trade and consumers.

Sales promotion directed at the trade

Trade promotions focus on members of the trade, which includes distribution channel members, such as retail salespeople or wholesale distributors that a firm must work with to sell its products. (We'll discuss these and other distribution channel members in more detail in Chapter 14). Trade promotions take one of two forms: (1) discounts and deals and (2) increasing industry visibility. Discount promotions (deals) reduce the cost of the product to the retailer or help defray its advertising expenses. The promotions are designed to encourage shops to stock the item and be sure it's given a lot of attention. Trade promotions that focus on increasing awareness and sales (increasing industry visibility) do so by creating enthusiasm among salespeople and customers. Let's take a look at both types of trade promotions in more detail.

Discounts and deals

One form of trade promotion is a *price break*. A manufacturer can reduce a channel partner's costs through sales promotions that discount its products. For example, a manufacturer can offer a **merchandising allowance** that reimburses the retailer for in-store support of a product, such as when a shop features an off-shelf display for a brand. Another way in which a manufacturer can reduce a channel partner's cost is through a **case allowance**

Marketing metrics

Measuring value

Duracell invested heavily in promotion of its batteries but soon found out that proliferation of trade promotions, deals and product giveaways actually had a negative effect. Consumers felt bewildered and the retail partners were complaining about the complexity of pricing and promotional activity. As a result of this and being faced with tough competition, heavy promotional spending and product confusion in the marketplace, Duracell decided to lower its list prices for the top-selling AA and AAA batteries. The company further decided to eliminate inefficient promotions, lessen the overall depth and frequency of trade promotions and instead increase support for its new campaign called 'Trusted Everywhere'.[4]

Technique	Primary Target	Description	Example
Trade shows	Trade	Many manufacturers show their products to convention attendees	The Cebit in Hannover (Germany) is the world's biggest trade show for computer hardware and software
Incentive programmes	Trade	A prize is offered to employees who meet a pre-specified sales goal or who are top performers during a given period	The British company Carphone Warehouse flew 30 top retail staff out to the Primavera festival in Barcelona with a VIP access to the festival[1]
Point-of-purchase displays	Trade and consumers	In-store exhibits make retail environments more interesting and attract consumers' attention	As sombre music plays in the background, a huge plastic rat draped in a black shroud lies next to a tombstone to promote the Farnam Company's Just One Bite rat poison
Push money	Trade	Salespeople are given a bonus for selling a specific manufacturer's product	A retail salesperson at a cosmetics counter at a Nordstrom shop in the US gets $5 every time she sells a bottle of Glow by JLo
Promotional products	Trade and consumers	A company builds awareness and reinforces its image by giving out items with its name on them	Coors distributors provide bar owners with Coors Light neon signs promoting the beer
Cross promotion/ cooperative promotions	Trade and consumers	Companies team up to promote their products jointly	Burger King promotes its Spidey Sense game in conjunction with Columbia Pictures' Spider-Man 2
Coupons	Consumers	Certificates for money off on selected products, often with an expiry date, are used to encourage product trial	Tesco's wine club provides a magazine with coupons and exclusive offers[2]
Samples	Consumers	Retailers might get a demonstration product to help in sales presentations; consumers get a free trial size of the product	A free small bottle of Clairol Herbal Essences shampoo arrives in the post
Contests/ sweepstakes	Trade and consumers	A sales contest rewards wholesalers or retailers for performance; consumers participate in games to win prizes; builds awareness and reinforces image	Publisher's Clearing House announces its latest sweepstake
Special/bonus packs	Consumers	Additional product is given away with purchase; rewards users. Note that bonus packs usually mean the package must be altered in some way to accommodate the extra merchandise	Maxell provides 10 free blank CDs with purchase of a pack of 50
Gifts with purchase	Consumers	A consumer gets a free gift when a product is bought; reinforces product image and rewards users	The drink-maker Ribena offers a fridge jug as a giveaway; Andrex gives bathroom door hangers away with toilet tissue with messages encouraging good toilet behaviour from children[3]

Table 13.1   Sales promotion techniques: a sample

[1]Yasnub Razajm, 'Carphone Warehouse assigns incentives to fledging agency', *Conference and Incentive Travel*, 21 May 2007, 4.
[2]Carol Angrisani, 'The Grapevine', *Supermarket News*, 26 May 2008, 43.
[3]'Nothing comes for free' *Marketing*, 15 March 2006, 37.

that provides a discount to the retailer or wholesaler during a set period of time based on the sales volume of a product it orders from the manufacturer.

However, allowances and deals have a downside. As with all sales promotion activities, the manufacturer's expectation is that they will be of limited duration, after which the distribution channel partner will again pay full price for the items. Unfortunately, some channel members engage in a practice called *forward buying*, in which they purchase large quantities of the product during a discount period, store them, and don't buy them again until the manufacturer offers another discount. Some large retailers and wholesalers take this to an extreme by engaging in *diverting*, an ethically questionable practice. Here the retailer buys the product at the discounted promotional price, stores it and, after the promotion has expired, sells the inventory to other retailers at a price that is lower than the manufacturer's non-discounted price but high enough to turn a profit for the retailer. Both forward buying and diverting go against the manufacturer's intent in offering the sales promotion.

Increasing industry visibility

Other types of trade sales promotions increase the visibility of a manufacturer's products to channel partners within the industry. Whether an elaborate exhibit at a convention or a coffee mug with the firm's logo it gives away to channel partners, these efforts seek to keep the company's name topmost when distributors and retailers make decisions about which products to stock and push. These forms of sales promotions include the following:

- **Trade shows:** The thousands of industry **trade shows** held in Europe and around the world each year are major vehicles for manufacturers to show off their product lines to wholesalers and retailers. Usually, large trade shows are held in big convention centres, such as Earl's Court in London or NEC Birmingham, where many companies set up elaborate exhibits to show their products, give away samples, distribute product literature and trawl for new business contacts. One example of how technology is changing traditional marketing is the advent of online trade shows where potential customers can preview a manufacturer's wares remotely. This idea is growing in popularity, though many industry people are finding it a challenge to 'schmooze' in cyberspace (it's also a little harder to collect all the great freebies they give out at real life shows!). An important benefit of traditional trade shows is the opportunity to develop customer leads that the company then forwards to its sales force for follow-up. We'll talk more about the role of a sales force later in this chapter.

- **Promotional products:** We have all seen them: coffee mugs, visors, T-shirts, hats, key rings, refrigerator magnets and countless other items decorated with a company logo. They are examples of **promotional products**. Unlike licensed merchandise sold in shops, sponsors give away these goodies to build awareness of their organisation or specific brands. In many industries, companies vie for the most impressive promotional products and offer business customers and channel partners such upmarket items as watches, fleece jackets and expensive leather desk accessories – all showing a firm's logo so recipients never forget who gave them such gifts.

- **Incentive programmes:** The British supermarket chain Asda has an incentive programme that rewards employee teams for boosting product sales at their shop. The programme requires teams to choose a product that they think will be popular within their community. Regional winning teams receive a cash prize of £150 to spend in store, on gifts or on travel. From the winning teams, two are awarded the use of an Asda branded Mini S convertible over a three-week period.[5] These incentives, known as **push money**, may come in the form of cash bonuses, trips or other prizes.

Marketing ethics and sustainability

Guinness – is it time to pour your own drink?

Are you still queuing for ages in front of the bar, trying hard to attract bar tenders' attention and waiting for them to pour you a chilled drink? Now David Cameron's DIY society is being taken to new levels with the launch of the self-pour pint of Guinness and Amstel. Customers book tables in advance and are given a quick lesson on how to pour the perfect pint of Guinness when they try for the first time, then they are free to pour their own. Tables in the bar are reserved with a credit card deposit, while a digital display shows how many pints have been consumed and staff can control the system from behind the bar, via a panel that allows them to pause or stop the flow at any time. Volume sales of Guinness at the 220 Dublin venues in which the system was first introduced have seen an increase of 17 per cent.

Discuss, debate, disagree

1 Is the Guinness pour your own drink promotional strategy sustainable – or is it simply a gimmick?
2 Over the years, Guinness has been recognised for its innovative and entertaining advertising. How can the company best integrate such promotional strategies with its advertising in order to improve market performance?

Sales promotion directed at consumers

Some sales promotions directed at consumers create a buzz in the form of a contest or a special event. For example, Red Bull, the high-octane energy drink (and popular mixer), has become famous for this approach by making its auspicious Red Bull vans available at rave and hip-hop clubs to raise the party atmosphere profile for the venue. Red Bull's consistent efforts at consumer sales promotion became the signature aspect of its marketing communication to consumers, and for the early stages of Red Bull's product life cycle the company did very little traditional consumer advertising. The buzz created by these special events added to the mystique of the brand, fuelling popularity among its young target market much more effectively than would traditional advertising. Let's take a closer look at several popular forms of consumer-targeted sales promotion.

Marketing metrics

Typhoo tea sales promotions

Typhoo, a leading tea brand, wanted to understand whether it had allowed sales promotions to dilute its brand advertising too much. Under pressure from major retailers, its sales promotion expenditure had grown, but at the cost of advertising. It commissioned an econometric modelling study to find the answer. Analysts studied retail audit data from the main supermarket chains, identifying 19 types of sales promotions and the size of the promotional spike. For example, BOGOF (buy one get one free) promotions caused an uplift many tens of times above baseline sales. It also calculated the sales effect of advertising. These figures were incorporated into a simulation model that Typhoo management used to compare the effects of different combinations of advertising and promotions. As a consequence, the mix between promotions and advertising was changed, and financial performance improved.

Price-based consumer sales promotion

Many sales promotions target consumers' wallets. They emphasise short-term price reductions or rebates that encourage people to choose a brand – at least during the deal period. Price-based consumer promotion, however, has a downside similar to trade promotions that involve a price break. If used too frequently, consumers become conditioned to purchase the product at only the lower promotional price. Price-based consumer sales promotions include the following:

- **Coupons:** Try to pick up any Sunday newspaper without spilling some coupons. These certificates, redeemable for money off a purchase, are the most common price promotion. Indeed, they are the most popular form of sales promotion overall, with billions distributed annually. The company Tarantula Responsive Communications worked with Kimberly-Clark and launched a European campaign in order to promote its product Brevia. The promotion ran in the UK, Netherlands, France and Germany. The campaign itself was identical, just the mechanics varied from country to country. In France, for example, the company offered money-off coupons.[6] Even industries like pharmaceuticals that have never tried this approach before are turning to it in a big way. This industry sends out coupons that customers can redeem for free initial supplies of drugs. Coupons are also available through sites such as Viagra.com and Purplepill.com. Companies use the coupons to prompt patients to ask their doctor for the specific brand instead of a competing brand or a more economical generic version.[7]

  Today, many firms simply send consumers to their website for coupons. For example, Google uses a coupon service. This service lets advertisers embed their coupons in Google maps, offering savings from local businesses including pizza restaurants, local cleaners, supermarkets or pet shops. Google teamed up with the American direct marketing firm Valpak to offer the coupons to its clients, with new offers added on a daily basis. Currently, this service only exists in the US but Google is very keen to launch it in Europe as soon as possible.[8] In September 2006, the smoothie maker Innocent Drinks started its first e-couponing campaign. The company wanted to reward customers for their continued loyalty to the brand. Every individual who received the email was a recipient of the regular e-newsletter that Innocent sent out every week.[9]

Internationalisation

Dove's campaign for natural beauty

The Dove campaign for real beauty was a global effort launched in 2004, to serve as a starting point for societal change and act as catalyst for widening the definition and discussion of beauty. The campaign supports the Dove mission: to make more women feel beautiful every day by widening stereotypical views of beauty. The brand's commitment to the mission starts with using real women (not celebrities or professional models) of various ages, shapes and sizes to provoke discussion and debate about today's typecast beauty images. Employing various communication vehicles including advertising, website interaction, billboards, events, a Self-Esteem Fund and much more, the campaign invites women to join a discussion about beauty and share their views with women around the world.

Debate, discuss, disagree

1 In your eyes, has the promotion been successful?
2 What are the implications for Dove in international markets where ideal beauty and beautiful looks are considered to play a more significant role among women?

Marketing misstakes

Cadbury's buried treasure hunt

In February 2007, a sales promotion for soft drink Dr Pepper went disastrously wrong. A series of clues led treasure hunters seeking a significant prize to a graveyard in Boston containing the remains of historic American figures such as Samuel Adams. The managers of the graveyard – where Cadbury buried the winning gold coin – complained and a national outcry ensued. Cadbury admitted to 'poor judgement' but said none of the graves was damaged.

Why do you think this might be a marketing misstake?

- **Price deals, refunds, and rebates:** In addition to coupons, manufacturers often offer a temporary price reduction to stimulate sales. This *price deal* may be printed on the package itself, it may be a price-off flag or banner on the shop shelf or it may even be included in credit cards. Shell and Citigroup have launched a co-branded Mastercard in the UK, which gives customers a fuel rebate.[10]

- **Frequency (loyalty/continuity) programmes: Frequency programmes**, also referred to as *loyalty* or *continuity programmes* offer a consumer a discount or a free product for multiple purchases over time. The famous Miles & More frequent flyer programme of 12 European airlines was introduced by the German airline Lufthansa in 1993. The programme enables its 13 million members to earn and redeem frequent flyer miles on all of the fully integrated airlines as well as the Star Alliance members. All members are also able to build status, which gives them access to certain privileges, like upgrading seating options for example. Virgin Atlantic has gone one step further with its frequent flyer programme that allows Virgin Atlantic Flying Club members the chance to redeem miles for a trip to outer space – only 2 million miles required.[11] More 'down to earth' is Six Flags theme park's Carrothead Club that offers kids 6–10 who attend 'Brunch with Bugs' a club hat, a monthly newsletter and insider information about the park.[12]

- **Special/bonus packs:** Another form of price promotion involves giving the shopper more product instead of lowering the price.[13] How nice to go to Boots and find a 500ml bottle of Nivea lotion with 50ml free! A *special pack* also can be a separate product given away along with another product, such as a GoodNews! razor wrapped with a can of Gillette Foamy shaving cream.

Attention-getting consumer promotions

Attention-getting consumer promotions stimulate interest in and publicity for a company's products. Some typical types of attention getting promotions include the following:

- **Contests and sweepstakes:** According to their legal definitions, a contest is a test of skill, and a sweepstake is based on chance. Some examples of such programmes are:

  - Lynx ran a 'get-in-there' UK campaign, which aimed to help men to 'break the ice' with women and help them to take the first step. On its website people could send in their best videos on how to approach a woman. The winner received an iPod and other Lynx goodies. This campaign also got promoted on YouTube and the social networking site Bebo.[14]

  - As part of the kick-off for Disney's global marketing campaign themed 'Where Dreams Come True', Disney offered consumers an online sweepstake called Keys to the Magic Kingdom. The winning family received a trip to Walt Disney World Resort and a day at the Magic Kingdom.[15]

● Several wireless network operators in Europe offer contests among players in a mobile phonebased game called 'Mobile Millionaire', which resembles the famous TV show 'Who Wants to be a Millionaire'. The game is played with short message service (SMS) or wireless application protocol (WAP). Contestants are declared winners if they have the highest scores using the shortest time during a given period (e.g. a month). Prizes vary among countries, but the winner in the UK, for example, wins a weekend for two in Monte Carlo worth £10,000 whereas in Belgium the winner gets a weekend away including a helicopter flight, use of a sports car and luxury hotel.[16]

● **Premiums: Premiums** are items offered free for buying a product. The prize in the bottom of the box of cereal, i.e. the reason many university students open the box from the bottom, is an example of a premium. In the 1990s, prepaid phone cards were highly popular premiums. Companies jumping on the phone card bandwagon offered cards with pictures of sports heroes, products and rock bands. Phone cards made ideal premiums because they are compact, they can display brand logos or attractive graphics and they provide opportunities for repeat exposure. An important benefit for the marketer is the ability to build databases by tracking card usage.[17]

● **Sampling:** How many starving university students at one time or another have managed to scrape together an entire meal by scooping up free food samples at their local grocery shop? Some shops, such as wine merchants, actually promote Saturdays as sampling day in their advertising. **Sampling** encourages people to try a product by distributing trial-size versions in shops, in public places such as student unions, or through the post. Many marketers now distribute free samples through sites on the internet.[18] Companies like Procter & Gamble, Unilever, S.C. Johnson & Son and SmithKline Beecham are readily taking advantage of websites such as www.freesamples.com and www.startsampling.com that not only distribute the firms' samples but also follow up with consumer satisfaction surveys. Other free sample sites covering European countries such as the UK, Germany or Netherlands are www.free-stuff.co.uk, www.gratisproben.com or www.freetemplates.nl respectively.

● **Point-of-sale promotions (POS): POS** promotions attempt to influence consumers while they are in the shop by catching their attention with creative displays or signs.[19] Marketers are challenged to come up with new and innovative POS displays that will grab attention, such as the promotion Bausch & Lomb ran in Spain. The company wanted to encourage consumers with good vision to buy contact lenses that changed their eye colour. By letting shoppers upload their pictures to a computer in the shop and then digitally alter the photos, the promotion allowed people to see how they would look with five different eye colours without actually inserting the contacts.[20]

POS activities also include the use of *in-store media*, such as placards on shopping trolleys or TVs inside the shop to promote specific products. As the chief executive officer of one company that produces these in-store messages put it, 'Does it make any sense to spend millions of euros talking to people in their living rooms and cars and then let them wander around a supermarket with 30,000 product choices without something to remind them to buy your product?'[21] One very noticeable technique of this genre of POS promotion uses a motion detector box that flashes lights in the voucher dispenser as a shopper approaches a section of the shelf.

● **Product/brand placements:** As we've seen, *product placement* refers to getting your brand featured in film or television shows. When consumers see a popular celebrity using a brand when they watch a favourite film or TV programme, they might develop a more positive attitude towards the brand. Successful brand placements have included the Aston Martins driven by James Bond since the 1960s, the Nike shoes worn by Forrest Gump and the Dodge Grand Caravan and the Dodge Sprinter Cargo van in *Mr. & Mrs. Smith* driven by Brad Pitt and Angelina Jolie.[22] Master-Card combined its placement in the Jennifer Aniston and Vince Vaughn film *The Break Up* with special offers for free cinema tickets in its Priceless.com website, as well as a sweepstake in which consumers could win tickets to the film premier and free DVDs for consumers who used their MasterCard debit cards a certain number of times.[23]

Beyond movies and television shows, what better way to promote to the video generation than through brand placements in video games, an approach called **advergaming**. If you are a video game fanatic, watch for placements of real life brands such as Adidas, Burger King, Intel, Toyota and Sony embedded in the action of your game. Adidas approached the advergame by adapting an existing online title, Double Fusion's Powerchallenge – a virtual football game. It promoted their Predator and f50 boots and let gamers choose virtual 3D football team players wearing either pairs of the shoes. Each type had different qualities and in a survey 98 per cent of the game players thought that it was a good or excellent experience.[24]

● **Cross-promotion:** When marketers do a **cross-promotion (or cooperative promotion),** this means that two or more products or services join forces to create interest using a single promotional tool. In a way, this is similar to product/brand placement in that each promoted product appears on each other's turf. Cross-promoted products should share some logical connection, be compatible in image and put forth a message that helps both brands. The Burger King/*Spider-Man 2* sales promotion is an example of a cross-promotion that worked. In the cinema, moviegoers got a dose of the Burger King 'Spidey Sense' contest in the trailers that play before the feature. Then, when consumers went to their nearby Burger King, they saw *Spider-Man 2* cups and all sorts of Spidey decor throughout the restaurant.

Photo 13.1   A cross-promotion lets companies join forces to push their products using a single promotional tool. That's the plan behind DHL's partnerships, shown in this advert with Mercedes Benz
Source: DHL

Photo 13.2   Another DHL cross-promotion, this time with London Fashion Week
Source: DHL

Marketing metrics

Measuring product placements

Marketers' opportunities for product placement, where they embed their products into entertainment vehicles, are rapidly expanding. No longer are they limited to television and movies; iPods, mobile phones, TiVo or Skyplus, concerts, events and downloadable web-based films are providing numerous new platforms for marketers to showcase their brands. Unfortunately, as the opportunities become more and more complex it is more difficult to determine the relevance of a placement and measure its reach and effectiveness. There are now some companies that can measure this for you. Marketing Evolution offers a system to measure directly the impact, counting how many people recognise the product placement. Other programmes such as BuzzMetrics and Intelliseek look for more indirect measures such as word of mouth and perceptions of the product placement. TNS Media Intelligence provides the newest service with a technology measuring products and brand appearances (such as symbols or logos) on selected basic cable shows, all six broadcast networks' prime-time programming, and the three major late-night talk shows. TNS tracks such detailed information as any connection the plot or storyline in the programme has with the product placement as well as measures that relate to the impact of the product. iTVX is yet another company exploring the value of product placements, creating a measure called Q-Ratio that calculates and assigns a relative value of the traditional 30-second advertising spot to a product placement opportunity and will provide a starting rate for the cost of product placements.[25]

Personal selling

www.pearsoned.co.uk/Solomon

Objective

2

Understand the important role of personal selling

Personal selling occurs when a company representative interacts directly with a customer or prospective customer to communicate about a good or service. This form of promotion is a far more intimate way to talk to the market. Many organisations rely heavily on personal selling because at times the 'personal touch' can carry more weight than mass-media material. In a business-to-business market situation, such as at Lucore as earlier discussed in our Chapter 5 Real people case, personal selling is often needed to explain certain products and services, provide more of a personal touch and begin to develop crucial relationships with clients. Also, many industrial products and services are too complex or expensive to market effectively in impersonal ways (such as through mass advertising).

Marketing in recession

Time's up for phone giant's Boxes

Carphone Warehouse is considering options for its new loss-making consumer electronics arm. Best Buy UK, which operates ten Big Box stores, has reported an underlying loss of £62 million, compared with £21 million the previous year. The business, which launched its first store last year as part of a joint venture with US retailer Best Buy, has invested heavily in marketing and promotional activity in a bid to get the brand off the ground. Carphone's core business, including its European and US mobile phone retail chains, has continued to trade well and it reported a 67 per cent increase in underlying earnings to £63.3 million for the year to 31 March 2011. Carphone originally intended to open as many as 200 Big Box stores in Europe by 2013, but the goal was reduced to 100 and there is currently only one store in the pipeline.

Metro 15 June 2011,51

Debate, discuss, disagree

1 What options are available for Carphone Warehouse in the future?
2 Could the business be salvaged, if so, what course of action would you recommend?

Another advantage of personal selling is that salespeople are the firm's eyes and ears in the marketplace. They learn which competitors are talking to customers, what is being offered, what new rival products are on the way and all sorts of competitive intelligence. As such, salespeople perform a vital role in the success of a firm's customer relationship management system that we discussed in Chapter 6, i.e. providing a source of timely and accurate informational input about customers and the market. Personal selling has a special importance for students because many graduates with a marketing background will enter professional sales jobs. Jobs in selling and sales management often provide high upward mobility if you are successful, because firms value employees who understand customers and who can communicate well with them. The old business adage 'nothing happens until something is sold' translates into many firms placing quite a bit of emphasis on personal selling in their promotion mixes. Now let's take a closer look at how personal selling works and how professional sales people develop long-term relationships with customers.

The role of personal selling

When a man calls Dell Computer to place an order for a new PC configured with a DVD drive and gaming memory, he is dealing with a salesperson. When he sits in on a presentation by a computer technician presenting a new spreadsheet software package, he is dealing with a salesperson. Also, when that same man agrees over a business dinner at an expensive restaurant to buy a new computer network for his company, he also is dealing with a salesperson. For many firms, some element of personal selling is essential to land a commitment to purchase or a contract, making this type of marketing communication an important part of any marketing plan. To put the use of personal selling into perspective, Table 13.2 summarises some of the factors that make it a more or less important element in an organisation's promotional mix. Generally, a personal selling emphasis is more important when a firm engages in a *push strategy*, in which the goal is to 'push' the product through the channel of distribution so that it is available to consumers. As a vice-president at Hallmark Cards observed, 'We're not selling to the retailer, we're selling *through* the retailer. We look at the retailer as a pipeline to the hands of consumers.'[26]

Personal selling is also likely to be crucial in a business-to-business context when direct interaction with a client's management is required to clinch a big deal, and often when

Factors Increasing Emphasis on Personal Selling	Factors Limiting Emphasis on Personal Selling
• If a push strategy is used	• If the amount of individual orders will be small
• If the decision maker has higher status within the organisation	• If there are many small customers
• If the purchase is a 'new task' for the customer	• If the image of the salesperson is poor
• If the product is highly technical or complex	
• If the customer is very large	
• If the product is expensive	
• If the product is a custom good or personalised service	
• If there are trade-in products	
• If negotiation is required	

Table 13.2 Factors influencing a firm's emphasis on personal selling

intense negotiations about price and other factors will occur before the deal is signed. In a consumer context, inexperienced customers may need the hands-on assistance that a professional salesperson can provide. Firms selling products which consumers buy infrequently, such as houses, cars, computers, lawnmowers, even university education often rely heavily on personal selling. Likewise, firms whose products or services are complex or very expensive often need a salesperson to explain, justify and sell in both business and consumer markets.

If personal selling is so useful, why don't firms do away with their advertising and sales promotion budgets and hire more salespeople? Because there are some drawbacks that limit the role personal selling plays in the marketing communications mix. First, when the amount of individual purchases is low, it doesn't make sense to use personal selling. The cost per contact with each customer is very high compared with other forms of promotion. Analysts estimated that in 2007 the average total cost for a sales call with a consultative (or problem-solving) approach to selling was about €300, and this cost was increasing at a rate of 5 per cent per year. Of course this figure is an average, and depending on the industry some sales calls are much more expensive to make. In contrast, the per-contact cost of a national television commercial is miniscule by comparison. A 30-second, prime-time commercial may be €300,000 to €500,000 (or much much more during big events like the FIFA World Cup final), but with millions and millions of viewers, the cost per contact may be only €10 or €15 per 1000 viewers. For low-priced consumer goods like Coca-Cola, personal selling to end users doesn't make sense either.

Salespeople, even the *really* energetic types can make only so many calls a day. Thus, reliance on personal selling is effective only when the success ratio is at its highest. **Telemarketing**, sometimes called *teleselling*, involves person-to-person communication taking place via the phone. Because the cost of field salespeople is so high, telemarketing continues to grow in popularity and this is much to the dismay of many prospect customers who are interrupted during their evening meal to answer sales calls for double glazing, new kitchens or insurance. Ironically, consumer resistance to telemarketing has provided a powerful boost for a form of selling that has been around for a long time: *direct selling. Direct selling is not the same thing as direct marketing.* Direct sellers bypass channel intermediaries and sell directly from manufacturer to consumer through personal, one-to-one contact. Typically, independent sales representatives, or even members of the public, do the selling in person in a customer's home, a place of business or even in their own home. Well-known examples include Avon, Ann Summers and Tupperware. Many of these firms utilise a *party plan* approach to selling in which salespeople demonstrate products in front of groups of neighbours or friends. Direct selling is on the up, with domestic sales volume increasing significantly.[27]

Technology and personal selling

Personal selling is supposed to be 'personal'. By definition, a company uses personal selling for marketing communication in which one person (the salesperson) interacts directly with another person (the customer or prospective customer) to communicate about a good or service. All sorts of technologies are available to enhance the personal selling process. However, as anyone making sales calls knows, technology cannot and should not *replace* personal selling. As we'll discuss later in this chapter, nowadays a key role of personal selling is to manage customer *relationships* – and remember, relationships occur between people, not between computers.

However, without doubt, a number of technological advancements have made it easier for salespeople to do their jobs more effectively. One such technological advance is *customer relationship management (CRM) software*. For years now, salespeople have used and benefited from account management software such as ACT and GoldMine. Account management software is inexpensive, easy to use and allows salespeople to track all aspects of customer interaction. Currently, many firms are turning to 'on demand' online CRM applications, accessible online, which are more customisable and integrative than ACT or GoldMine, yet are less expensive than major company-wide CRM installations. Examples of widely used online CRM products include SalesForce.com and SalesNet, both of which are user-friendly for salespeople. A key benefit of online CRM systems is that the firm 'rents' them for a flat fee per month and avoids major capital outlay.[28] Recently, sales organisations have begun using a new generation system called *partner relationship management (PRM)* that links information between selling and buying firms. PRM differs from CRM in that at least some of the databases and systems of both supplier and buyer firms are shared in order to maximise the utility of the data for decision making purposes. When firms' information is shared, they are more likely to strive for win–win solutions.

Beyond CRM and PRM, numerous other technology applications are enhancing personal selling, including teleconferencing, videoconferencing and improved corporate websites that include FAQ pages that answer many customer queries. Many firms also use intranets and blogs to link internal and external communication.

Voice-over Internet Protocol (VoIP) – using a data network to carry voice calls – is beginning to get a lot of use in day-to-day correspondence between salespeople and customers. With VoIP, the salesperson on the road can just plug into a fast internet connection and then start making and receiving calls just as if he or she is in the office. Unlike using mobile phones, there are no bad reception areas, and unlike using hotel phones, there are no hidden charges. One popular VoIP product is Skype, whose tagline is 'The whole world can talk for free.'

According to its website, Skype 'is a little piece of software that allows you to make free calls to other Skype users and really cheap calls to ordinary phones'.

Of course, salespeople are using wireless technology in general more and more to provide seamless communication process with clients. BlackBerry has been around a while, but predictions are that as wireless becomes more and more predominant, the various devices salespeople use to communicate (mobile phone, laptop and so on) will become more and more integrated.

Types of sales jobs

As you might imagine, sales jobs vary considerably. The person who processes an IBM computer purchase over the phone is primarily an **order taker**, i.e. a salesperson who deals with transactions that the customer initiates. Many retail salespeople are order takers,

Real people, other voices

Advice for
James McCaffrey

Connie Nolan

Programme Director, MSc Marketing at Canterbury Christ Church University and Chartered Marketer, CiM

All options require resources: finance, time and training for staff so it is important not to become too preoccupied with costs. James should think through the costs of not implementing change. He says he wants to keep in contact with his customers but who are they? Are they the brokers, or the end customers? Towergate customers are the brokers so it is important to keep

and develop key relationship marketing strategies for them. This ties in well with the concept of developing loyalty – most acquisitions fail because the corporation does not implement new cohesive strategies to develop a unified sense. Why did Towergate acquire High Street brokers? was it opportunism or to develop a niche?

Adopting Option 2 would meet the relationship needs of the brokers. It may well be regarded as a retrograde step by organisations taking a more technological stance but it meets the needs of the brokers as identified in the research carried out. Further, relationship marketing has become a key strategy for most organisations and far from being retrograde Towergate will be in the vanguard which could consolidate their market competitiveness.

but often wholesalers dealers and distributors also employ salespeople to look after their business customers. Because little creative selling is involved in order taking, this type of sales job typically is the lowest paying sales position. In contrast, a **technical specialist** contributes expertise in the form of product demonstrations, recommendations for complex equipment and the setup of machinery. The technical specialist's job is to provide *sales support* rather than to actually close the sale. He or she promotes the firm and tries to stimulate demand for a product to make it easier for colleagues to actually achieve the sale.

Sometimes a person whose job it is to stimulate clients to buy is called a **missionary salesperson**. Like technical specialists, missionary salespeople promote the firm and work to stimulate demand for its products but don't actually take orders for products.[29] Pfizer's salespeople do missionary sales work when they call on doctors to influence them to prescribe the latest and greatest Pfizer medication over competing products. However, no 'sale' is made until doctors' prescriptions are passed to pharmacies, that in turn place orders for the drug through their wholesalers or distributors.

The **new-business salesperson** is responsible for finding new customers and calling on them to present the company's products or services. As you might imagine, gaining the business of a new customer usually means that the customer stops doing business with one of the firm's competitors. New-business selling requires a high degree of creativity and professionalism, so this type of salesperson is usually very well paid. Once a new-business salesperson establishes a relationship with a client, he or she often continues to service that client as the primary contact as long as the client continues to buy from the company. In that long-term relationship building role, this type of salesperson is an **order getter**. Order getters are usually the people most directly responsible for a particular client's business and may also have titles such as 'account manager'.[30]

More and more, firms are finding that the selling function is best handled by **team selling**. A selling team may consist of a salesperson, a technical specialist, someone from engineering and design, and other players who work together to develop products and programmes that satisfy the customer's needs. Inclusion of people from these various functional areas gives rise to the term *cross-functional team*.

Approaches to personal selling

Personal selling is one of the oldest forms of marketing communication. Unfortunately, its image was tarnished by smooth-talking sales representatives who would say anything to make a sale. The profession was not helped by Pulitzer Prize-winning playwright Arthur Miller's famous character Willie Loman in *Death of a Salesman*. Willie Loman is a pathetic, burned-out pedlar who leaves home for the road on Monday morning and returns late Friday evening, selling 'on a smile and a shoeshine'. His personal life is in shambles, with two dysfunctional sons and a disaffected wife who hardly know him. Fortunately, personal selling today is not as harsh as Arthur Miller's portrayal. Selling has moved from a transactional, hard-sell approach to an approach based on relationships with customers. Let's see how.

Transactional selling: putting on the hard sell

The *hard sell* practised by Willy Loman is a high-pressure process. We've all been exposed to the pushy electronics salesperson that puts down the competition by telling shoppers that if they buy elsewhere they will be stuck with an inferior product that will fall apart in six months. Or how about the crafty used-car salesman who plays good cop/bad cop games using the sales manager or finance manager at the dealership as a tactic? These type of hard-sell approaches reflect **transactional selling** – which focuses on making an immediate sale with no concern for developing a long-term relationship with the customer.

As customers, the hard sell makes us feel manipulated and resentful and thwarts customer satisfaction and loyalty. It is a very short-sighted approach to selling. As we said earlier in the book, constantly finding new customers is much more expensive than getting repeat business from the customers you already have. The behaviour promoted by transactional selling (that is, doing anything to get the order) also contributes to the poor image many of us have of salespeople, i.e. obnoxious and untrustworthy. Such salespeople engage in such behaviour because they don't care if they ever have the chance to sell to you again.

Relationship selling: building long-term customers

Today's professional salesperson is more likely to practise relationship selling than transactional selling. This means that the salesperson seeks to develop a mutually satisfying, win–win relationship with the customer. **Relationship selling** involves securing, developing and maintaining long-term relationships with profitable customers.[31] *Securing* a customer relationship means converting an interested prospect into someone who is convinced that the product or service holds value for him. *Developing* a customer relationship means ensuring that you and the customer find more ways to add value. *Maintaining* a customer relationship means building customer satisfaction and loyalty. Thus, the customer can be counted on to provide future business and won't switch to another source to purchase the products or services you sell. If doing business with the customer isn't *profitable* for you (unless you're a charitable organisation), you would probably like to see that customer go somewhere else.

The creative selling process

Many people find selling to be a great profession, partly because something different is always going on. Every customer, every sales call and every salesperson is unique. Some salespeople are successful primarily because they know so much about what they sell. Others are successful because they've built strong relationships with customers so that they're able to add value to both the customer and their own firm – a win–win approach to selling. Successful salespeople understand and engage in a series of activities to make the sales encounter mutually beneficial. Successful personal selling is probably more likely if the salesperson undergoes a systematic series of steps called the **creative selling process**. These steps require the salesperson to seek out potential customers, analyse their needs, determine how product attributes provide benefits and then decide how best to communicate this to the prospects. As Figure 13.1 shows, there are seven steps in the process. Let's take a look at each step.

Step 1: Prospecting and qualifying

Prospecting is the process of identifying and developing a list of potential customers, called *prospects* or *sales leads*. Leads can come from existing customer lists, telephone directories and commercially available databases. The local library usually contains directories of businesses (including those published by government agencies) and directories of association memberships. Sometimes companies generate sales leads through their advertising or sales promotion by letting customers request more information. As you learned earlier, trade shows are often an important source of sales leads, as are website visits by potential customers.

An emerging technology available to salespeople for prospecting is the development of online *social networks*. These are not 'friendship' social networks, but rather business networks. These sites enable salespeople to create profiles, upload their personal address books to the site and invite business colleagues to join the network. The site protocol then provides for contact, request for formal introductions and information exchange. Another way to generate leads is through *cold calling*, when the salesperson simply contacts prospects 'cold' without introduction or arrangement. It always helps to know the prospect, so salespeople might rely instead on *referrals*. Current clients who are satisfied with their purchase often give referrals and this is another reason for maintaining good

Figure 13.1	Steps in the creative selling process
	In the creative selling process, salespeople follow a series of steps to ensure successful long-term relationships with customers

customer relationships. However, the mere fact that someone is willing to talk to a salesperson doesn't guarantee a sale. Along with identifying potential customers, salespeople need to *qualify* prospects to determine how likely they are to become customers by asking questions such as the following: Are the prospects likely to be interested in what I'm selling? Are they likely to switch their allegiance from another supplier or product? Is the potential sales volume large enough to make a relationship profitable? Can they afford the purchase? If they must borrow money to buy the product, what is their credit history?

Step 2: Pre-approach

The **pre-approach** consists of compiling background information about prospective customers and planning the sales interview. Important purchases are not made lightly, and it's often difficult even to get an appointment to see a prospect. It's foolish for a salesperson to blindly call on a qualified prospect and risk losing the sale because of a lack of preparation. Salespeople try to learn as much as possible about qualified prospects early on. They may probe purchase history, look at current needs or, in some cases, find information about their interests. Salespeople can draw information about a prospect from a variety of sources. In the case of larger companies, salespeople can find financial data, names of top executives and other information about a business in publications like Dun & Bradstreet. They can also find a great deal of information for the pre-approach on customers' websites.

If the salesperson's firm has a CRM system, he or she can use it to see whether information on the prospect exists in the system's database. Say, for example, a salesperson at Michael's Bikes is planning a call on a buyer at Greg's Rentals. If Michael's Bikes has had a CRM system in place for some time, any contacts with customers and potential customers (prospects) will have been recorded in the CRM database. The salesperson can simply run an inquiry about Greg's Rentals and, with luck, the CRM database will have information on the company, purchases from Michael's Bikes, when and why they stopped buying from Michael's Bikes and even the preferences of the particular buyer (if he was with Greg's Rentals at the time the data were recorded). As useful as external databases and internal CRM systems are, the inside information relating to a prospect often comes from informal sources, such as non-competing salespeople who have dealt with the prospect before. This background information helps salespeople set their goals and plan their strategy for the sales call.

Step 3: Approach

After laying the groundwork with the pre-approach, it is time to **approach**, or contact, the prospect. During these important first minutes when the salesperson initiates contact with the prospective customer, several key events occur. The salesperson tries to learn even more about the prospect's needs, create a good impression and build rapport. If the salesperson made contact with the prospect through a referral, he or she will probably say so up-front: 'Rachel Gear from Pearson suggested I call you.' During the approach, the customer is deciding whether the salesperson has something to offer that is of potential value to him. Also, the old saying, 'You never get a second chance to make a good first impression', rings true here. A professional appearance tells the prospect that the salesperson means business and is competent to handle the sale. A good salesperson is well-groomed and wears appropriate business dress, doesn't chew gum, use poor grammar or inappropriate language, mispronounce the customer's name, or seem uninterested in the call.

Step 4: Sales presentation

Many sales calls involve a formal **sales presentation** that lays out the benefits of the product and its advantages over the competition. When possible and appropriate, salespeople should incorporate technology such as laptops and DVDs into their sales presentations to facilitate demonstrations. The focus of the sales presentation should always be on ways the salesperson, the products and the company can add value to the customer (and, in a business-to-business setting, to the customer's company). It is important for the salesperson to present this value proposition clearly, inviting involvement by the customer in the conversation. Let the customer ask questions, give feedback and discuss their needs. Pre-formulated approaches to sales presentations are a poor choice for salespeople attempting to build long-term relationships. In fact, sales managers rate *listening* skills, not talking skills, as the most important attribute they look for when hiring relationship salespeople.[32]

Step 5: Handling objections

It is rare when a prospect accepts everything the salesperson has to say without question. The effective salesperson anticipates *objections*, or reasons why the prospect is reluctant to make a commitment, and is prepared to respond with additional information or persuasive arguments. Actually, the salesperson should *welcome* objections because they show the prospect is at least interested enough to have considered the offer and seriously weighed up its pros and cons. Handling the objection successfully can move a prospect to the decision stage. For example, the salesperson might say, 'Ms Buonanno, you've said before that you don't have room to carry our new line of mountain bikes, although you mentioned that you might be losing some sales by carrying only one brand with very few different models. If we could come up with an estimate of how much business you're losing, I'd be willing to bet you'd consider making room for our line, wouldn't you?'

Step 6: Close the sales

The win–win nature of relationship selling should take some of the pressure off salespeople to make 'the dreaded close'. But there still comes a point in the sales call where one or the other party has to move towards gaining commitment to the objectives of the call, presumably a purchase. This is the decision stage, or **close**. Directly asking the customer for business doesn't need to be painful or awkward. If the salesperson has done a great job in the previous five steps in the creative selling process, closing the sale should be a natural progression of the dialogue between the buyer and seller.

There are a variety of approaches salespeople can use to close the sale. For example, a *last objection close* asks customers if they are ready to purchase, providing the salesperson can address any concerns they have about the product: 'Are you ready to order if we can prove our delivery time frames meet your expectations?' Using an *assumptive close*, the salesperson acts as if the purchase is inevitable, with only a small detail or two to be settled: 'What quantity would you like to order?' In some cases, the salesperson interjects urgency by using a *standing-room-only* or *buy-now close* that suggests the opportunity might be missed if the customer hesitates: 'This price is good until Saturday, so to save 20 per cent you should place the order now.' When making such closes, salespeople must be sure the basis they state for buying now is truthful. Relationship selling-minded salespeople don't stretch the truth for short-term gain, they know the customer's long-term loyalty to them, their company and its products is worth much more than booking one order today.

Step 7: Follow-up

The **follow-up** after the sale includes arranging for delivery, payment and purchase terms. It also means the salesperson makes sure the customer received delivery and is satisfied. Follow-up also allows the salesperson to *bridge* to the next purchase. Once a relationship develops, the selling process is only beginning. Even as one cycle of purchasing draws to a close, a good salesperson is already laying the foundation for the next one.

 ## Sales management

Few, if any, firms can succeed with just one star salesperson. Personal selling is a team effort that requires careful planning and salespeople available when and where customers need them. **Sales management** is the process of planning, implementing and controlling the personal selling function. Let's review some of the major decisions sales managers who oversee this function must make, as outlined in Figure 13.2.

 ## Setting sales force objectives

Sales force objectives state what the sales force is expected to accomplish and when. Sales managers develop such sales force performance objectives as 'acquire 100 new customers', 'generate 100 million in sales' or even 'reduce travel expenses by 5 per cent'. Firms engaged in relationship selling also state objectives related to customer satisfaction, loyalty and retention. Other common objectives are new customer development, new product suggestions, training, reporting on competitive activity and community involvement. Sales managers also work with their salespeople to develop *individual* objectives. We can identify two types of individual objectives. *Performance objectives* are readily measurable outcomes, such as total sales and total profits per salesperson. *Behavioural objectives* specify the actions salespeople must accomplish, such as the number of prospects to identify, the number of sales calls and the number of follow-up contacts they should make.

 ## Creating a sales force strategy

A sales force strategy establishes important specifics such as the structure and size of a firm's sales force. Each salesperson has the responsibility for a set group of customers – their **sales territory**. The territory structure allows salespeople to have an in-depth understanding of

Setting Sales Force Objectives
↓
Creating a Sales Force Strategy
↓
Recruiting, Training and Rewarding the Sales Force
↓
Evaluating the Sales Force

Figure 13.2 The sales force management process

Personal selling is a team effort that requires careful planning to place salespeople in the best locations at the best times

customers and their needs through frequent contact, both business and personal. The most common way to allocate territories is geographically, minimising travel and other field expenses. A *geographic sales force structure* usually is sized according to how many customers are in a given area. If the product line is diverse or technically complex, however, a better approach may be to structure sales territories based on different classes of products to enable the sales force to provide more focused product expertise to customers. Kraft Foods, for example, has separate sales teams for its major product areas, such as beverages, cheese and dairy, and grocery items.

Another structure is *industry specialisation*, in which salespeople focus on a single industry or a small number of industries. Firms can often refer to large clients as *key accounts* or *major accounts*. P & G uses cross-functional key account teams to focus on each of its major customers. The idea behind this is the old Pareto rule, i.e. 20 per cent of your customers account for 80 per cent of your sales (and profits). Those 20 per cent therefore deserve the bulk of your personal selling attention. Putting salespeople into the field is a very expensive proposition that greatly affects a company's profitability. Remember, cost per customer contact is far higher for personal selling than for any other form of promotion. Thus, determining the optimum number of salespeople is an important decision. A larger sales force may increase sales, but at what cost? A smaller sales force will keep costs down, but this could backfire if competitors move in with larger sales forces and are able to develop strong customer relationships because each of their salespeople doesn't have to call on as many customers.

A key contributor to the success of a sales force is keeping salespeople in front of customers as much of the time as possible, as opposed to spending their time travelling, in meetings, doing paperwork, or otherwise engaging in non-selling activities. Fortunately, the advent of *virtual meetings* (or *videoconferencing*) has cut down substantially on non-selling time for salespeople. Also, the ability to videoconference and have members of a geographically diverse sales team hold meetings from their home offices can cut non-customer related travel costs substantially. Along the same lines, more and more companies are allowing salespeople to work from virtual offices through *telecommuting*. This trend keeps salespeople from having to make trips back and forth from home to some office location, allowing them instead to use precious travel time visiting customers.[33]

Recruiting, training and rewarding the sales force

Because the quality of a sales force can make or break a firm, a top priority for sales managers is to recruit and hire the right set of people to do the job. These are people who have good listening skills, effective follow-up skills, the ability to adapt their sales style from situation to situation, tenacity (sticking with a task) and a high level of personal organisation,

Across the Hall

Nigel Tomlinson

is an experienced corporate and marketing strategist, having served at board level within multinational corporations and chambers of commerce

Although a great deal of time and resource has been invested in online solutions, Option 1 will not in itself deliver the solution that Towergate require. It may well alleviate some of the confusion that some brokers have encountered, but the product range does not readily lend itself to computerisation and it would do little if anything to develop loyalty to Towergate and its services from individual brokers. Furthermore, even though online service provision is a growing trend within the insurance industry Towergate specialise in niche markets which are often difficult to access and a more personalised service may give them the edge in a highly competitive market.

Options 2 and 3 present the choice of tactical deployment of a sales force in either a generalist or specialised approach. On paper a generalist approach is attractive in utilising the best elements of an existing sales function to promote the entire range of services whilst building much needed personal relationships but in reality such a move will be expensive both in training and deployment costs and is unlikely to promote the full service range. Extending the specialised sales force may be both expensive and time consuming to train but providing it is managed effectively it would provide Towergate with a credible advantage in specialised niche markets by forging durable client relationships whilst removing duplication of effort. Such a team would have to be highly trained and focussed if Towergate is to avoid further confusion and a lack of clarity in their client offer. Given the potential for sustainable growth of such a move I would choose Option 3.

among a variety of other well-documented key factors for salesperson success.[34] Companies evaluate potential salespeople for these skills, along with useful information about their interests and capabilities. Pencil-and-paper tests can determine quantitative skills and competencies in areas not easily assessed through interview.

Closely related to training, *development* (often called professional development) strives to prepare salespeople personally and professionally for new challenges, such as promotions and management responsibilities. It focuses on developing the salesperson more broadly than knowledge or skills training. Training and development should take place not just after the initial hire but throughout the salesperson's career. Many sales organisations turn to outside consultants to help them develop sales force training and development programmes. Sometimes a boost in creative thinking from the outside can do wonders for developing more productive salespeople. Today, with budgets tighter than ever, sales organisations are expecting identifiable returns on investments in training and outside firms can often deliver these quantifiable results.[35]

Of course, a way to motivate salespeople is to pay them well. This can mean tying compensation to performance. A *straight commission plan* is based solely on a percentage of sales the person closes. Under a *commission-with-draw plan*, earnings are based on commission plus a regular payment, or 'draw', that may be charged against future commissions if current sales are inadequate to cover the draw. With a *straight salary plan*, the salesperson is paid a set amount regardless of sales performance. Sometimes straight salary plans are augmented with a *quota-bonus plan*, in which salespeople are paid a salary *plus* a bonus for sales above an assigned quota or for selling certain products that may be new or more profitable. *Sales contests* provide prizes (cash or otherwise) for selling specific products during a specific time period and can provide a needed short-term boost to sales. However, sales contests can easily be over-used, motivating salespeople to simply wait to sell some products until the contest period, resulting in no real long-term sales increase. Popular prizes for contest winners include cruises, other types of travel and product selections from prize catalogues.

Although many salespeople like to work independently, supervision is essential for an effective sales force. Sales managers often require salespeople to develop monthly, weekly or daily *call reports*, a plan of action detailing which customers were called on and how the call went.

These call reports are likely to be generated electronically, often on laptop computers or even as a part of the firm's overall CRM initiative. They allow the sales manager to track what the salespeople are doing in the field, and they provide marketing managers with timely information about customers' responses, competitive activity and any changes in the firm's customer base.

 ## Evaluating the sales force

The job of sales management isn't complete until the total effort of the sales force is evaluated. First, it is important to determine if the sales force is meeting its objectives. If not, the sales manager must figure out the causes. Is it due to flaws in the design and/or implementation of the sales force strategy, or are there uncontrollable factors that have contributed? An overall downturn in the economy, such as recession, can make it impossible for the best of sales forces to meet their original sales objectives.

Managers normally measure individual salesperson performance against sales quotas for individual sales territories, even when compensation plans do not include bonuses or commissions based on the quotas. They may also use quantitative measures, such as number of sales calls and sales reports, in the evaluation. In addition to quantitative measures, many firms also evaluate their salespeople on qualitative indicators of performance, such as salesperson attitude, product knowledge and communication skills. Increasingly, as firms focus on relationship selling, the level of several important customer metrics such as customer satisfaction, loyalty and retention/turnover have become key measures of superior salesperson performance. Please read the Marketing metrics box to see how Northlight Sanitation worked on salesperson performance to improve the overall business performance of the company.

Finally, the company can consider the salesperson's expense account for travel and entertainment since the best sales record can mean little to a company's bottom line if the salesperson is bleeding the company dry with outrageous expenses. You think you're creative when spending money? Here are some expenses a few salespeople actually submitted according to *Sales and Marketing Management* magazine:[36]

- Chartering a private plane to make an appointment after missing a regularly scheduled flight.
- A round of golf for four people that cost about €2300.
- A set of china for a salesperson's wife to use for a client dinner party.
- A three-day houseboat rental with a crew and chef for the equivalent of €30,000.

Now that you've learned about sales management, read 'Real people, real decisions' to see which strategy James selected.

Marketing metrics

Northlight Sanitation

Northlight Sanitation manufactures and sells bathroom and kitchen fixtures and accessories. Its sales force had considerable autonomy negotiating prices, terms and conditions. However, after collecting and analysing data on salesperson performance and contributions, it discovered major differences between contributions, and in particular 'star performers' did not contribute much profit. After in-depth interviews it emerged that some salespeople were good at communicating the value proposition and held their ground in price negotiations, whereas others were bad at communicating value and conceded on price. As a consequence of this analysis the company retrained, reassigned or dismissed salespeople; it also adjusted the incentive system to focus on contribution more than volume. These steps boosted profits from 11.6 per cent to almost 14 per cent.

Real people, real decisions

How it worked out at Towergate...

James of Towergate chose Option 3, to retrain the best elements of its existing sales force and recruit new sales staff. This was difficult in the insurance industry, as so few were left. This new national sales force was allocated regionally to broker agents in the UK and act as front-line distributors of all Towergate services. Their role was to extend the work of the Telesales Unit by providing a 'road map' to the products on offer, solving individual problems and generally oiling the process of distribution. They were set targets to achieve the transfer of large portfolios of insurance broker business to Towergate. An elaborate performance reward structure was also put in place to further motivate them.

It became clear within the first two months of the early creation of the sales force that far from regarding salesmen calling at brokers' offices as unnecessary, old-fashioned and unwelcome, insurance brokers welcomed a friendly face to talk to with open arms. The common response from insurance brokers was they had not seen a personal representative of anyone from the insurance industry for some years, and desperately missed the social communication and trading, which had always been hallmarks of an insurance broker's life.

Moreover, insurance is a business of trust and this is mainly achieved on a person-to-person level. The national sales force gave brokers a trustable face and personal connection with Towegate. This helped improve the company's image and alleviate previous antagonistic relations that were associated with Towergate. The move fitted well with the company's mission of being a 'Trusted adviser' to businesses. Finally, these newly established relationships were not only for selling products, but also for potentially buying the small broker businesses – should they become available to acquire.

Towergate's marketing metrics used to assess success?

The results started to speak for themselves following the launch of the new sales force. At the end of 2008 Towergate Underwriting Division wrote £127 million worth of new business, a record, despite the most difficult economic conditions that the industry had faced in many years. New business from brokers not owned by Towergate was larger than new business emanating from Towergate's own brokers. This was a complete reversal of all previous 11 years of Towergate's existence. Many industry executives had doubted whether the old-fashioned human sales interface had any further life in it, but the reality proved to be quite different.

Although new business is a good metric, there was some evidence that Towergate's brand image had improved as the sales force represent the brand. Being personable, engaging, informed and action oriented were an excellent mechanism for enhancing the brand, given that Towergate does very little advertising or traditional marketing. Finally, there was a reduction in the brokers' time in finding products and the time saved in making the transaction, thus providing time to do more business.

Chapter summary

Now that you have finished reading this chapter, you should be able to answer any of the following potential examination questions:

1. **Explain what sales promotion is and describe some of the different types of trade and consumer sales promotion activities.** A sales promotion is a short-term programme designed to build interest in or encourage purchase of a product. Trade sales promotions include merchandising and case allowances, trade shows, incentive programmes, push money and promotional products, among others. Consumer sales promotions include coupons, price deals, refunds, rebates, frequency or loyalty programmes, bonus packs contests/sweepstakes, premiums, sampling, point-of-purchase promotions, product placements and cross-promotions among others.

2. **Explain the important role of personal selling in marketing.** Personal selling occurs when a company representative interacts directly with a prospect or customer to communicate about a good or service. Many organisations rely heavily on this approach because at times the 'personal touch' can carry more weight than mass-media material. Generally, a personal selling effort is more important when a firm engages in a 'push' strategy, in which the goal is to push

the product through the channel of distribution so that it is available to consumers. Today's salespeople are less likely to employ transactional selling (hard-sell tactics) in favour of relationship selling in which they pursue win–win relationships with customers.

3. **List the steps in the personal selling process.** The steps in the personal selling process include prospecting and qualifying, pre-approach, approach, sales presentation, handling objections, close and follow-up. These steps combine to form the basis for communicating the company's message to the customer. Learning the intricacies of each step can aid the salesperson in developing successful relationships with clients and in bringing in business for their companies.

4. **Explain the role of the sales manager.** Sales management includes planning, implementing and controlling the selling function. The responsibilities of a sales manager include the following: creating a sales force strategy, including the structure and size of the sales force; recruiting, training, compensating the sales force and evaluating the sales force.

Key terms

Advergaming 504
Approach 512
Case allowance 497
Close 512
Creative selling process 510
Cross-promotion (or cooperative promotion) 504
Follow-up 513
Frequency programmers 502
Merchandising allowance 497
Missionary salesperson 509

New-business salesperson 509
Order getter 509
Order taker 508
Personal selling 505
Point-of-sale (POS) 503
Premiums 503
Pre-approach 511
Promotional products 499
Prospecting 510
Push money 499
Relationship selling 510

Sales management 513
Sales presentation 512
Sales promotion 496
Sales territory 513
Sampling 503
Team selling 509
Technical specialist 509
Telemarketing 507
Trade promotions 497
Trade shows 499
Transactional selling 509

Chapter review

 ## Marketing concepts: testing your knowledge

1. What is sales promotion? Explain some of the different types of trade and consumer sales promotions frequently used by marketers.

2. What role does personal selling play within the marketing function?

3. What is relationship selling? How is it different from transactional selling?

4. What is prospecting? What does it mean to qualify the prospect? What is the pre-approach? Why are these steps in the creative selling process that occur before you ever even contact the buyer so important to the sale?

5. What are some different ways you might approach a customer? Would some work better in one situation or another?

6. What is the objective of the sales presentation? How might you overcome buyer objections?

7. Why is follow-up after the sale so important in relationship selling?

8. Describe the role of sales managers. What key functions do they perform?

Marketing concepts: discussing choices

1. Companies sometimes teach consumers a 'bad lesson' with the overuse of sales promotion. As a result, consumers expect the product always to be 'on offer' or have a rebate available. What are some examples of products where this has occurred? How do you think companies can prevent this?

2. In general, professional selling has evolved from hard-sell to relationship selling. Is the hard-sell style still used? If so, in what types of organisations? What do you think the future holds for these organisations? Will the hard-sell continue to succeed? Are there instances where transactional selling is still appropriate? If so, when?

3. What do you think about the quality of most retail salespeople you come into contact with? What are some ways retailers can improve the quality of their sales associates?

4. Would training and development needs of salespeople vary depending on how long they have been in the business? Why or why not? Would it be possible (and feasible) to have different training programmes for salespeople who are at different career stages?

5. What would be the best approach for a sales manager to take in determining the appropriate rewards programme to implement for his or her salespeople? What issues are important when determining the rewards to make available?

Marketing practice: applying what you've learned

1. Assume that you have just been hired as a field salesperson by a firm that markets university textbooks. As part of your training, your sales manager has asked you to develop an outline of what you will say in a typical sales presentation. Write that outline.

2. This chapter introduced you to several key success factors sales managers look for when hiring relationship salespeople. Are there other key success factors you can identify for relationship salespeople? Explain why each is important.

Marketing miniproject: learning by doing

The purpose of this miniproject is to help you understand the advantages of following the creative selling process.

1. With several of your classmates, create a new product in a category that most students buy regularly (for example, toothpaste, shampoo, pens, pencils, soft drinks . . . anything that interests you that might be sold through a supermarket). Make up a new brand name and some creative features and benefits of the new product you come up with.

2. Develop a plan for executing each of the steps in the creative selling process. Ensure that you cover all the bases of how you would go about selling your product to an organisational buyer at the supermarket for distribution to all their shops.

3. Report on your plan to your class and ask the other students for feedback on whether or not your approach will convince the buyer to purchase.

Further reading

Sales Management: Shaping Future Sales Leaders, John F. Tanner, Earl D. Honeycutt, Jr., and Robert C. Erffmeyer, Prentice Hall, 2008

Firms have changed the way they manage their selling functions tremendously in the past 20 years. The Internet has had a significant impact on sales management, but at the same time, so have customer contact centres, customer relationship management (CRM) technology, increased global competition, greater cultural and generational diversity, the importance of ethical responsibilities and a myriad of other factors. Developments such as these have greatly changed how sales teams are led. With this as a background managers must still be able to design and organise a sales force, recruit, select, train, develop, measure performance, compensate and motivate their sales team to achieve goals. Sales managers must combine these skills, while developing their own leadership style and ethical practices. A balance of theoretical and practical applications taken from the global sales environment provide the back drop one needs to know in order to lead top-performing sales teams.

Real people, real surfers

Exploring the web

A critical part of successful selling today is the effective use of technology and information by salespeople. Sometimes salespeople feel like they have information and technology 'overload' – just too much to cope with. A well-run CRM system can go a long way towards organising the important elements of selling.

Visit the websites www.crmguru.com and www.salesforce.com. Look at the content and then answer the following questions:

1. What do you gather are some of the most important issues surrounding successful use of CRM?

2. Pick any two experts featured on the sites and briefly summarise their key messages.

3. How do you suppose CRM can help link the marketing and sales functions in a firm? Hint: Consider the information needed by both groups, and how that information is collected, analysed and distributed for use.

4. Assume that you have been hired as a sales manager for a small firm with 20 outside salespeople. Would CRM be useful in such a setting? Why or why not?

Now, take a look at the website at www.pearsoned.co.uk/solomon to see some videos from YouTube relating to aspects of this chapter.

Finally, do our special online sales promotion exercise and you could throughout the year save enough to pay for this book.

Marketing plan exercise

Assume for a moment that you are James McCaffrey at Towergate. Consider the nature of the business and the services it offers to the marketplace. In developing a marketing plan, one must be very careful to use the elements of the marketing communication mix in an integrated way so that one communicates a consistent message that represents the best investment of promotional spend that will give the greatest returns.

1. Should personal selling be a high priority in the future? Why or why not?

2. What approach to personal selling would you recommend to be built into the plan? Why do you recommend this approach?

Delve deeper into sales promotion and sales management

Dr Sunil Sahadev

Senior Lecturer in Marketing, University of Sheffield

The personal selling function is very crucial for the success of any marketing strategy. Effective management of the sales force is without doubt the most important activity in managing the personal selling function. Managing the sales force is much different from managing the other employees of a firm as the sales force effectively acts as representatives of the company to its customers. A de-motivated or poorly managed sales force would present a poor image of the company to its customers thereby harming the long-term as well as the short-term image of the company.

Further, poor sales force management would lead to high turnover in the sales force which would make it impossible for the company to develop long-term relationships with customers. A poorly managed sales force could either be very aggressive and manipulative or extremely inefficient in going about their tasks. Sales force management could start with creating the right structure and systems. This by itself is however not enough as there is no substitute for effective and purposeful day-to-day management of individual salespeople. Managing the sales force involves managing the behaviour of the sales force as well as developing the correct attitude about the firm, the job and the customers among the sales force.

One important attitude that stands out is a salesperson's learning orientation. Learning orientation involves an overwhelming desire to learn from each interaction with the customers without particularly seeking to achieve short-term gains. Two classic articles that look into salespeoples' goal orientations are Sujan et al. (1994) and Kohli et al. (1998). Both the articles explain the concept of goal orientation in the context of personal selling and seek to understand how learning orientation can be fostered and the consequences of a high level of learning orientation among salespeople. An important issue often considered by sales managers is the linkage between happy/efficient sales personnel and satisfied customers. The paper by Homburg and Stock (2005) shows how satisfied sales personnel can make satisfied customers.

References

C. Homburg and R.M. Stock (2005) 'Exploring the Conditions Under which the Sales Person Work Satisfaction leads to Customer Satisfaction', *Psychology and Marketing* 22, no. 5, 393–420.

A.K. Kohli, T.A. Shervani and G.N. Challagalla 1998 'Learning and Performance Orientation of Salespeople: The Role of Supervisors', *Journal of Marketing Research*, 35, no. 2, 263–74.

H. Sujan, B.A. Weitz and N. Kumar (1994) 'Learning Orientation, Working Smart, and Effective Selling,' *Journal of Marketing* 58 (July), 39–52.

Marketing in action case

Promotions in energy at EDF

In the current economy, which is under constant flux and undergoing turbulence, more companies are realising that their most precious asset is their customer base. Companies are developing customer-focused strategies to satisfy the different and varied needs of their customers. Competition between the energy providers is strong and the market is saturated. The energy providers have to win back customers from their competitors and are constantly on the lookout for new ways to approach customers. In order to have a competitive edge and to satisfy the desires of all customers, EDF energy has been considering multiple options to reach out to its customers. For the purpose of this case, we consider a particular sales promotion whereby EDF energy has come together with Dixons Stores Group International (DSGI) to offer a money-back incentive for shoppers. DSGI is one of the largest electrical retailers in Europe, with revenue for the year 2008–09 around £8.3 billion. It currently operates 630 retail stores in the UK, trading under four brands: Curry's, PC World, Dixons and Pixmania.

This promotional campaign is designed to appeal to a distinct group of customers who are looking and willing to switch their energy provider. The promotion offers customers £100 cashback when they sign up to EDF Energy for both electricity and gas, or £50 cashback when they sign up solely for electricity. The company aimed to trial a new way of selling energy in these stores with the aim being to grow the customer base by 1 million accounts (from 5.1 million to 6.1 million product accounts) over five years. Specifically, in order to qualify for the sales promotion, when customers spend £100 or more in-store, they qualify and get £100 cash back if they switch to EDF Energy. This way, they can recoup some of the cost of the electrical appliance they have just purchased. This was a unique way of selling energy – requiring the customer to sign up online at home and removing the requirement and barriers of completing a contract there and then in store. The customer can also register for the promotion via a call centre if he/she prefers not to register online. Previous promotions included the use of an in-store sales representative, who needed to be on hand to run through the contract. This new approach moves responsibility from the in-store representative to the customer at home, so he or she can complete the documentation online, at a time which is convenient to them. The online sign-up potentially eliminates the complexity of the in-store sales process, which is often time-consuming and off-putting for customers. This offer provides a whole new approach to retailing energy in a non-intrusive, simple manner.

To maximise the sales opportunity, customers who are given the £100 cashback offer will have their details collected at the checkout (name, home address, postcode, phone number and email address), which will be used for future targeting should they not wish to sign up.

Things to think about

1.   What is the value proposition that EDF is offering?

2.   What kind of consumer-based sales promotions are EDF implementing and why?

3.   What are the implications associated with implementing the above sales promotion?

4.   Could competitors or service providers from other industries look to develop similar offers?

5.   Do you think the promotion can be sustained over a period of time?

Case edited from research by Jayaram Manda, Al Torkpour and Anastasia Stathopoulou, Cass Business School

References

1.   Howard Stumpf and John M. Kawula, 'Point of Purchase Advertising', in *Handbook of Sales Promotion*, ed. S. Ulanoff (New York: McGraw-Hill, 1985); Karen A. Berger, *The Rising Importance of Point-of-Purchase Advertising in the Marketing Mix* (Englewood Cliffs, NJ: Point-of-Purchase Advertising Institute).

2.   'The Whopper Waxes Nostalgic at 50', *Brandweek*, 12 October 2007.

3.   R. Miller, 'Promotions aim to cross borders', *Marketing*, 24 May 2001, 31.

4.   J. Malester, 'Duracell to Cut Prices', *TWICE: This Week in Consumer Electronics*, 20 January 2003, 39.

5.   'Asda Reviews Incentive Plans', *Employee Benefits* (September 2007), 9.

6.   Miller, 'Promotions Aim to Cross Borders'.

7.   Gardiner Harris, 'Drug Makers Offer Consumers Coupons for Free Prescriptions', *Wall Street Journal*, 13 March 2002, www.wsj.com.

8.   J. Whitehead, 'Redeeming Features', *New Media Age*, 14 September 2006, 25.

9.   O. Raeburn, 'Online Couponing', *Direct Response*, 5 September 2007, 12.

10.   'In Brief', *Marketing Week*, 20 September 2007, 5.

11.   'Virgin Atlantic Rolls Out Space Miles', *PROMO Magazine*, www.promomagazine.com/incentives.virgin_atlantic_miles_011106/index.html.

12.   'Six Flags Launches Kids Loyalty Club', *PROMO Magazine*, www.promomagazine.com/entertainmentmarketing/news/sixflagskids/iondex.html.

13.   This section based on material presented in Don E. Schultz, William A. Robinson and Lisa A. Petrison, *Sales Promotion Essentials*, 2nd ed. (Lincolnwood, IL: NTC Business Books, 1993).

14.   www.lynxeffect.com/.

15.   'Lengthy Research Leads Disney to Global "Dreams" Theme', *Promo Magazine*, www.Promomagazine.com/research/Disney_research_061206/index.html.

16.   D. Liu, X. Geng and A. Whinston, 'Optimal Design for Consumer Contests', *Journal of Marketing* 71, no. 4 (October 2007), 140–156.

17.   Kerry J. Smith, 'It's for You', *PROMO: The International Magazine for Promotion Marketing* 41, no. 4 (August 1994); Sharon Moshavi, 'Please Deposit No Cents', *Forbes*, 16 August 1993, 102.

18.   Amanda Beeler, 'Package-Goods Marketers Tune in Free-Sampling Sites', *Advertising Age*, 12 June 2000, 58.

19. *The Point-of-Purchase Advertising Industry Fact Book* (Englewood Cliffs, NJ: Point-of-Purchase Advertising Institute, 1992).

20. 'Bausch & Lomb Makes Eyes with Consumers in Spain', *PROMO: The International Magazine for Promotion Marketing* (October 1994), 93.

21. Patricia Sellers, 'Winning Over the New Consumer', *Fortune*, 29 July 1991, 113.

22. J. Stein, 'Automakers go Hollywood', *Automotive News*, 22 March 2004, 42–43.

23. 'Mastercard and Bud Tie Unique Concepts to *Break Up*', *PROMO Magazine*, www.promomagazine,com/entertainment-marketing/news/mastercard-breakup_060806/index.html.

24. R. Gray, 'Play the Brand', *Marketing,* 25 July 2007, 33.

25. K.J. Bannan, 'No End to Placement Data Services', *Advertising Age* (February 2006), S3.

26. Quoted in Jaclyn Fierman, 'The Death and Rebirth of the Salesman', *Fortune*, 25 July 1994, 88.

27. Direct Selling Association, www.dsa.org; Scott Reeves, '"Do Not Call" Revives Door-to-Door Sales', *Marketing News*, 8 December 2003, 13; Maria Puente, 'Direct Selling Brings It All Home', *USA Today*, 28 October 2003, 5D.

28. www.salesforce.com; Daniel Tynan, 'CRM Software: Who Needs It?', *Sales and Marketing Management* (July 2003), 30; Daniel Tynan, 'CRM: Buy or Rent?', *Sales and Marketing Management* (March 2004), 41–5.

29. Dan C. Weilbaker, 'The Identification of Selling Abilities Needed for Missionary Type Sales', *Journal of Personal Selling and Sales Management* 10 (Summer 1990), 45–58.

30. Derek A. Newton, *Sales Force Performance and Turnover* (Cambridge, MA: Marketing Science Institute, 1973), 3.

31. Mark W. Johnston and Greg W. Marshall, *Relationship Selling and Sales Management*, 2nd ed. (Boston, MA: McGraw-Hill, 2008).

32. Greg W. Marshall, Daniel J. Goebel and William C. Moncrief, 'Hiring for Success at the Buyer – Seller Interface', *Journal of Business Research*, 56 (April 2003), 247–55.

33. Andy Cohen, 'Selling from Home Base', *Sales and Marketing Management* (November 2003), 12.

34. Marshall et al., 'Hiring for Success at the Buyer-Seller Interface'.

35. Julia Chang, 'Making the Grade', *Sales and Marketing Management* (March 2004), 24–9.

36. Adapted from Erin Strout, 'The Top 10 Most Outrageous T&E Expenses', *Sales and Marketing Management* (February 2001), 60.

Chapter 14
Retail and distribution

Meet Julia Gash
A decision maker
at Bag It Don't Bin It

Julia Gash is the Founder and Company Director of Bag It Don't Bin It. She has 20 years of business experience, achieved predominantly in directing print-led fashion and retail. Her retail business 'Gash' was voted the 34th best shop in the country by *Elle* magazine in 2004. Her aim at the time was to create a stylish ambience to purchase lingerie products. Famously, the retail store provided many other value propositions to clients, including teaching men how to 'powerflirt' and women how to dance 'erotically'.

The lingerie retail business achieved international accolades for its creativity and vision, which even inspired the legendary brand 'Durex' to appoint Julia as a consultant to their business. The brand was stocked in the most prestigious of stores around the world and the company won a National Export Award and an invitation to the Queen's residence – Buckingham Palace. The company's huge success brought about other publicity and Julia is widely regarded as a key national spokesperson on business, environmental and European issues, having contributed to many flagship TV and radio current affairs programmes.

Following an amazing six years with Gash, Julia decided it was time to take on another challenge and work on other personal ambitions that she had. In response she handed the Gash franchise to a business acquaintance and decided to build on her print background by establishing Bag It Don't Bin It. The company aims to help the world to get rid of plastic bags that harm the environment by producing alternative eco-friendly, fairly traded branded cloth bags. The business was established in 2007 and in 2010 Julia was awarded the Sheffield Entrepreneur of the Year Award for her achievements with the company.

Real people real decisions
Retailing decisions at Bag It Don't Bin It

Faced with a new challenge in 2007, Julia set out to revolutionise the carrier bag industry by providing environmentally friendly cloth bags at affordable prices. In attempting to take care of the environment, Julia decided to work with Fairtrade companies that supplied her with the cotton bags from India. Through working with Sedex-audited Fairtrade companies she believed this provided an opportunity for her company to help those in most need. Julia was also ethically sensitive to the local community and decided to open her print works in a deprived area of Sheffield (Burngreave), where unemployment is amongst the highest per capita in this region of the United Kingdom. Her ambition was to recruit unemployed individuals and provide them with appropriate training to print professionally. Julia prides her company as being a 'green collar' business and even the paints that she purchases for printing are eco-friendly.

From a standing start in 2007, the company has had amazing success and this is despite operating in one of the worst recessions in history. The Bag It Don't Bin It cotton bag has therefore become iconic as a fashionable, lifestyle garment. Julia likes to describe the bag as not a 'new bag', but the 'it bag'. As a result the company has worked with and supplied a number of clients including Harvey Nichols, Liberty of London, Jimmy Choo, River Island, WWF, Waterstone's and the British Museum. The company is obviously doing something right to perform extraordinarily well during the recession. One reason may be related to the fact that 40 per cent of the company's revenue is repeat business. Faced with growth opportunities, Julia was determined to make a continued success of this business by providing employment opportunities for locals and growing her business, despite the recession. Therefore, following a few good years of trading she was faced with three options:

Jula considers her options . . .

Option 1: Look to strengthen the company's current position, by working with the leading grocery retailers to supply them with bespoke cotton bags that could be sold at point-of-sale checkouts

This option was feasible, particularly as during the recession grocery retailers have made huge profits and prices for groceries have increased beyond inflation. At the same time, some retailers are also trying to promote environmentally friendly goods and provide support for less well off regions of the world, which the Fairtrade brand sets out to achieve. This represented a reasonable pathway for Julia and her company to go down, one advantage being that Julia had the business experience to make a success of this through establishing a close relationship with key buyers in Europe's retail grocery sector.

Option 2: Open a small boutique in London (Spittalfields)

This would provide a further feasible option, as Julia would therefore be able to build on her previous retailing expertise to make this a major success. Having a London presence would make a mark with international tourists and would also provide an appropriate vehicle to further promote the brand to other key retailers. Remember that Julia had a range of designer retail brands that were all regularly purchasing bespoke bags. This option would therefore strengthen her presence and also provide an opportunity to further develop the market by appealing to tourists in London.

Option 3: Diversify the operations and move into e-tailing

This again represented a safe and possible option, as the company could simply invest more to develop online services. This would of course mean that Julia and her team would move from operating in business-to-business markets with huge supply and demand, to operate more at the consumer level, with potentially a greater number of transactions that would need servicing through developing an interactive web page facility.

Now, put yourself in Julia's position. Which option looks most feasible? Which one would you go for, and why?

Objectives

When you finish reading this chapter, you will be able to:

1 Understand what a distribution channel is and what functions distribution channels perform

2 Describe the types of distribution channel and the steps in planning distribution channel strategies

3 Define retailing and understand how retailing evolves

4 Describe B2C e-commerce and its benefits, limitations and future promise

5 Understand the importance of shop image to a retail positioning strategy and explain how a retailer can create a desirable image in the marketplace

Objective

1

Understand what a distribution channel is and what functions distribution channels perform

Place: the final frontier

Distribution may be the 'final frontier' for marketing success. After years of hype, many consumers no longer believe that 'new and improved' products really *are* new and improved. Nearly everyone, even upmarket manufacturers and retailers, tries to gain market share through aggressive pricing strategies. Advertising and other forms of promotion are so commonplace they have lost some of their impact. Marketers know that *place* may be the only one of the Four Ps to offer an opportunity for competitive advantage, especially since many consumers have come to expect 'instant gratification' by getting just what they want when the urge strikes.

This chapter is about the science and art of getting goods and services to customers. A large part of the marketer's role in delivering the value proposition deals with understanding and developing effective distribution strategies. In this chapter, we will begin with a broad view of the company through the lens of the value chain concept. You'll recall from earlier on that the *value chain* is a broad concept that spans all the activities involved in designing, producing, marketing, delivering and supporting any product. Then we focus on the supply chain, which spans activities across many firms. The *supply chain* includes all the activities necessary to turn raw materials into a good or service and put it into the hands of the consumer or business customer. Often, of course firms outside your own company accomplish these activities, firms with which your company has probably developed some form of partnership or cooperative business arrangement.

Next, we talk about distribution channels, which are a subset of the supply chain. Distribution channels are important because a large part of the marketer's role in delivering the value proposition deals with understanding and developing effective distribution strategies. We look at logistics management, which is the process of actually moving goods through the supply chain. Finally, the chapter will explore the world of retailing, which is the final stop on the distribution path, the process by which goods and services are sold to consumers for their personal use. We will define each of these terms in greater detail in subsequent sections of this chapter, but for now let's look at the broader activities of the value chain.

 ## The value chain

Delivering value to the customer is of primary importance. As we saw way back in the book, the value chain concept is a way of looking at how firms deliver benefits to consumers. They do this by coordinating a range of activities that result in providing a product or service to the customer. As we can see in Figure 14.1, the value chain consists of five primary activities (inbound logistics, operations, outbound logistics, marketing and sales, and service) and four support activities (procurement, technology development, human resource management and firm infrastructure).

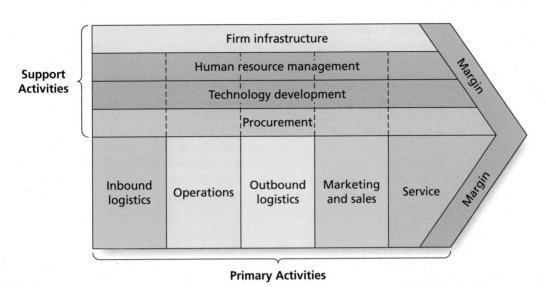

Figure 14.1	The generic value chain
	The value chain (a concept first proposed by Professor Michael Porter) encompasses all the activities a firm does to create goods and services that in turn create value for the consumer and make a profit for the company
	Source: Reprinted with the permission of Free Press, a Division of Simon & Schuster, Inc. from *Competitive Advantage: Creating and Sustaining Superior Performance* by Michael E. Porter. Copyright© 1985, 1998 by Michael E. Porter. All right reserved.

Specifically, during the stage of *inbound logistics* activity the company receives materials it needs to manufacture its products. This activity includes receiving the input materials, warehousing and stock control. In *operations*, activities transform the materials into a final product form by machining, packaging and assembly. *Outbound logistics* involve shipping the product out to customers, while *marketing and sales* handle advertising, promotion, channel selection and pricing. *Service* activities enhance or maintain the value of the product, via offering installation or repair. The process is called a value chain because each of these activities adds value to the product or service the customer eventually buys.

Links in the supply chain

Whereas the value chain is an overarching concept of how firms create value, the **supply chain** also encompasses components external to the firm itself, including all activities that are necessary to convert raw materials into a good or service and put it in the hands of the consumer or business customer. Thus, **supply chain management** is the coordination of flows among the firms in a supply chain to maximise total profitability. These 'flows' include not only the physical movement of goods but also the sharing of information about the goods. That is, supply chain partners must synchronise their activities with one another. For example, they need to communicate information about which goods they want to purchase (the procurement function), about which marketing campaigns they plan to execute (so that the supply chain partners can ensure there will be enough product to supply the increased demand from the promotion), and about logistics (such as sending advance shipping notices informing their partners that products are on their way). Through these information flows, a company can effectively manage all the links in its supply chain, from sourcing to retailing.

One interesting development in supply chain management is that some companies traditionally known for other things are remaking themselves as specialists which take over the coordination of clients' supply chains for them. UPS is perhaps the best example of a former messenger delivery service that today is much, much more because it specialises in **insourcing**; a term used when companies contract with a specialist who services their supply chains. Unlike outsourcing, where a company delegates non-essential tasks to sub-contractors, insourcing implies that an external company is brought into the client company to run its essential operations. While we tend to associate UPS with transportation and the delivery of boxes, etc., the company also provides several other functions for its customers. For example, if your Toshiba laptop needs to be repaired, you can drop it off at a UPS shop and it's shipped to a UPS unit where UPS employees (not Toshiba) actually get your machine back on track. If you order a pair of trainers at Nike.com, it could be a UPS employee who fills the order, bags it, labels it and delivers.[1]

The difference between a supply chain and a *channel of distribution* is the number of members and their function. A supply chain is broader; it consists of those firms that supply the raw materials, component parts and supplies necessary for a firm to produce a good or service, plus the firms that facilitate the movement of that product to the ultimate users of the product. This last part, the firms that get the product to the ultimate users – is the **channel of distribution**.

Hewlett-Packard uses hundreds of suppliers in manufacturing its notebooks and it sells those items through hundreds of online and offline retailers worldwide. It is noteworthy that the role of individual firms within the supply chain will depend on your perspective. If we are looking at Hewlett-Packard's supply chain, Intel is a supplier and PC World is a member of its channel of distribution. From Intel's perspective, Hewlett-Packard is a customer. From the perspective of PC World, Hewlett-Packard is a supplier. Intel takes raw materials such as silicon and adds value by turning them into Pentium chips. Intel ships these chips to Hewlett-Packard, which combines them with the other components of a computer, again adding value. PC World takes the finished product and adds value by providing display, sales support, financing and so forth for the customer. Now that you understand the basics of the value chain and the supply chain, let's go deeper into the importance of distribution.

The importance of distribution: you can't sell what isn't there!

So you've created your product, priced it and you've done the research to understand your target market and created a marketing message. It does not finish there! You now need to deliver what you make to the marketplace. As we noted earlier, a channel of distribution is a series of firms or individuals that facilitate the movement of a product from the producer to the final customer. In many cases, these channels include an organised network of producers (also called manufacturers), wholesalers and retailers that develop relationships and work together to make products conveniently available to keen buyers.

Distribution channels come in different shapes and sizes. The bakery around the corner where you buy nice cakes is a member of a channel, as is the baked goods section at the local supermarket, and the café bistro on the high street that sells biscotti to go with your cappuccino.

A channel of distribution consists of at a minimum, a producer – the individual or firm that manufactures or produces a good or service – and the customer. This is a *direct channel*. For example, when you buy a kilo of strawberries at a farm where they're grown, that's a direct channel relationship. Firms that sell their own products through catalogues, use freephone numbers and factory outlet shops use direct channels.

But life and marketing usually isn't that simple: channels often are *indirect* because they include one or more **channel intermediaries**; firms or individuals such as wholesalers, agents, brokers and retailers who in some way help move the product to the consumer or business user. For example, a baker may choose to sell his buns to a wholesaler that will in turn sell boxes of buns to supermarkets and restaurants that in turn sell them to consumers.

Functions of distribution channels

Distribution channels perform a number of functions that make possible the flow of goods from the producer to the customer. These functions must be handled by someone, be it the producer or a channel intermediary. Sometimes the activities are delegated to the customer, like the person who picks up a new chair from the warehouse instead of having it delivered to his home. Channels that include one or more organisations or intermediaries often can accomplish certain distribution functions more effectively and efficiently than can a single organisation. This is especially true in international distribution channels where differences in countries' customs, beliefs and infrastructures can make global marketing a nightmare. Even small companies can be successful in global markets by relying on distributors that know local customs and laws.

Overall, channels provide the time, place and ownership utility we described earlier in the book. They make desired products available when, where and in the sizes and quantities that customers desire. Suppose for example, you want to buy that perfect bouquet of flowers for someone special. You *could* grow them yourself? Fortunately, however, you can probably just accomplish this task with a simple phone call or a few mouse clicks, and 'like magic' the flowers are delivered to your fiancée's door. Just think about what happened behind the scenes to make this possible. These days large growers harvest and electronically sort acres of flowers, then auction them to buyers at a huge wholesale flower market in Amsterdam. From there they are shipped by air to importers in other European locations who inspect them for insects and disease, and who in turn transport them to various wholesalers within the EU, who finally distribute the cut flowers to local florists who combine them into bouquets for their customers. The channel members consist of the growers, the auction house, the importers, the wholesalers and the local florists, who all work together to create just the gifts for admirers – and save you lots of time and hassle.

Distribution channels provide a number of logistics or physical distribution functions that increase the efficiency of the flow of goods from producer to customer. How would we buy groceries without our modern system of supermarkets and hypermarkets?

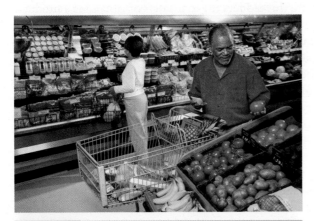

Supermarkets like this one are channel intermediaries. They buy fresh fruits and vegetables from farmers and make them available to consumers on a daily basis
Source: Shutterstock/iofoto

We'd have to get our milk from a dairy, our bread from a bakery, our tomatoes from a local farmer and so on. The companies that make these items would then have to handle literally hundreds of transactions to sell to every individual who wanted to buy. Distribution channels create *efficiencies* by reducing the number of transactions necessary for goods to flow from many different manufacturers to large numbers of customers. This occurs in two ways. The first is called **breaking bulk**. Wholesalers and retailers purchase large quantities (usually cases) of goods from manufacturers but sell only one or a few at a time to many different customers. Second, channel intermediaries reduce the number of transactions by creating **assortments**, i.e. providing a variety of products in one location so that customers can conveniently buy many different items from one seller at one time.

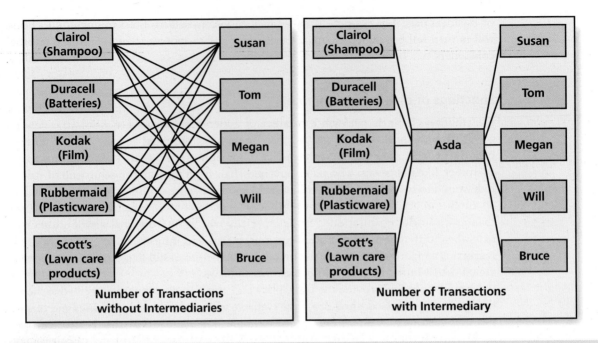

One of the functions of distribution channels is to provide an assortment of products. Because the customers can buy a number of different products at the same location, this reduces the total costs of obtaining a product

Figure 14.2 provides a simple example of how distribution channels work. This simplified illustration includes five producers and five customers. If each producer sold its product to each individual customer, 25 different transactions would have to occur, which is not an efficient way to distribute products. But with a single intermediary which buys from all five manufacturers and sells to all five customers, the number of transactions is cut to ten. If there were ten manufacturers and ten customers, an intermediary would reduce the number of transactions from 100 to just 20. One of the functions of distribution channels is to provide an assortment of products. Because the customers can buy a number of different products at the same location, this reduces the total costs of obtaining a product.

The transportation and storage of goods is another type of physical distribution function. Retailers and other channel members move the goods from the production point to other locations where they can be held until they are wanted by consumers. Channel intermediaries also perform a number of *facilitating functions* that make the purchase process easier for customers and manufacturers. For example, intermediaries often provide customer services such as offering credit to buyers. Many of us like to shop in department stores because if we are not happy with the product, we can take it back to the shop, where cheerful customer service personnel may be happy to give us a refund. These same customer services are even more important in business-to-business markets where customers purchase larger quantities of higher priced products.

Some wholesalers and retailers assist the manufacturer by providing repair and maintenance service for products they handle. An appliance, television, hi-fi or computer dealer may serve as an authorised repair centre, provide maintenance contracts and sell essential supplies to customers. Channel members also perform a risk-taking function. For example, a retailer buys a product from a manufacturer and it just sits on the shelf because no customers want it, they are stuck with the item and must take a loss. Perishable items present an even greater risk of spoilage.

Finally, intermediaries perform a variety of communication and transaction functions. Wholesalers buy products to make them available for retailers and sell products to other channel members. Retailers handle transactions with final consumers. Channel members can provide two-way communication for manufacturers. They may supply the sales force, advertising and other types of marketing communication necessary to inform consumers and persuade them that a product will meet their needs. The channel members can also be invaluable sources of information regarding consumer complaints, changing tastes and new competitors in the market.

The internet in the distribution channel

The internet has become an important place for consumers to shop for everything from Amsterdam tulip bulbs to exotic holidays. By using the internet, even small firms with limited resources enjoy the same market opportunities as their largest competitors in making their products available to customers around the globe. E-commerce has resulted in radical changes in distribution strategies. Manufacturing firms like Dell and Apple in the personal computer sector rely heavily on internet-driven direct-to-end user distribution strategies, although both have also begun to expand outside this channel. In most cases, though, end users still don't obtain products directly from manufacturers. Rather, goods flow from manufacturers to intermediaries and then on to the final customers. With the web, this need for intermediaries and much of what we assume about the need and benefits of channels is changing. As more and more consumers have access to faster broadband internet service, downloadable DVDs may replace firms such as Blockbuster as the favoured means of gaining access to films for home viewing.

In the future, channel intermediaries that physically handle the product may become obsolete. Already, many traditional intermediaries are being eliminated as companies question the value added by layers in the distribution channel – a process called **disintermediation**. For marketers, disintermediation reduces costs in many ways: fewer employees, no need to buy or lease expensive retail property in high-traffic locations, and no need to furnish a shop with fancy fixtures and decor. You can also see this process at work when you withdraw cash from an ATM, or when you eat out at self-service restaurants. This reduces or even eliminates the need for an intermediary, in this case the server.

Some companies are using the internet to make coordination among members of a supply chain more effective, and in ways that consumers never see. Such firms are developing better ways to implement **knowledge management**, which refers to a comprehensive approach to collecting, organising, storing and retrieving a firm's information assets. These assets include both databases and company documents and the practical knowledge of employees whose past experience may be relevant to solving a new problem. If a firm tries to share this knowledge with other supply chain members, this can result in a win–win situation for all the partners.

For example, the supply chain in the textile and clothing industry begins with a raw material extraction or production stage (that is, harvesting cotton or developing new synthetic fibres) which supplies the second stage of primary manufacturing. The second stage usually produces a standardised output of commodity material (fibres and fabrics) used to produce commodity products. Progressing downstream, commodity products from the previous stage are used by manufacturers, who apply product development technologies, patents and proprietary features to further add value. The next stage includes marketers of consumer products, followed by distributors and, finally, the retailers who sell to the final consumer.

As technology continues to evolve, some companies are capitalising on the ability of the internet to link partners in the supply chain quickly and easily. The textile and apparel division of DuPont (now a separate company known as Invista) manufactures such products as Lycra that usually goes into active-wear clothing. Invista works closely with companies like Nike and Levi Strauss to develop fibres and fabrics that meet the needs of consumers. Invista's Lycra Assured programme helps to differentiate Invista's 'stretch and recover' Lycra fibre from low-cost competitors that sell the generic version (called Spandex) by providing manufacturers with extensive information they can access online about the performance characteristics of their products.[2] So far, we've learned what a distribution channel is and about some of the functions it performs. Now let's find out about different types of channel intermediaries and channel structures.

Channel composition: types of wholesaling intermediaries

How can you get your hands on a new Arctic Monkeys T-shirt? You could pick one up at your local music shop, maybe at a trendy clothing shop, or directly over the internet. You might buy an 'official concert T-shirt' from sellers during a live concert. Alternatively, you might acquire an unauthorised copy of the same shirt being sold from a suitcase by a shady character standing *outside* the concert venue. Perhaps you shop online if the group has a website. It might even be possible to catch a deal for one on QVC. Each of these distribution alternatives traces a different path from producer to consumer. Let's look at the different types of wholesaling intermediaries and the different channel structures. We'll hold off focusing on retailers, which are usually the last link in the chain, until later on in this chapter.

Wholesaling intermediaries are firms that handle the flow of products from the manufacturer to the retailer or business user. There are many different types of consumer and business-to-business wholesaling intermediaries. Some of these are independent, but manufacturers and retailers can own them, too. Table 14.1 summarises the important characteristics of each.

Independent intermediaries Such companies do business with many different manufacturers and many different customers. Because they are not owned or controlled by any manufacturer, they make it possible for many manufacturers to serve customers throughout the world while keeping prices low. **Wholesalers** are independent intermediaries that buy goods from manufacturers and sell to retailers and other business-to-business customers. Because wholesalers take title to the goods (that is, they legally own them), they assume certain risks and can suffer losses if products get damaged, become outdated or obsolete, are stolen, or just don't sell. On the other hand, because they own the products, they are free to develop their own marketing strategies, including setting the prices they charge their customers.

- *Full-service merchant wholesalers* provide a wide range of services for their customers, including delivery, credit, product-use assistance, repairs, advertising and other promotional support – even market research. Full-service wholesalers often have their own sales force to call on businesses and organisational customers. Some general merchandise wholesalers carry a large variety of different items, whereas speciality wholesalers carry an extensive assortment of a single product line. For example, a confectionery wholesaler would carry pure confectionery goods but stock enough different varieties to give your dentist nightmares for a year.

- In contrast, *limited-service merchant wholesalers* provide fewer services for their customers. Like full-service wholesalers, limited-service wholesalers *take title* to merchandise but are less likely to provide such services as delivery, credit or marketing assistance to retailers. Specific types of limited-service wholesalers include the following:

- *Cash-and-carry wholesalers* which provide low-cost merchandise for retailers and industrial customers that are too small for other wholesalers' sales representatives to call on.

Intermediary Type	Description	Advantages
INDEPENDENT INTERMEDIARIES	Do business with many different manufacturers and many different customers	Used by most small- to medium-sized firms
Cash-and-carry wholesalers	Provide products for small-business customers who purchase at wholesaler's location	Distribute low-cost merchandise for small retailers and other business customers
Mail-order wholesalers	Sell through catalogues, telephone, or mail order	Provide reasonable price selling options to small organisational customers
Agents and brokers	Provide services in exchange for commissions	Maintain legal ownership of product by the seller
Manufacturers' agents	Utilise independent salespeople; carry several lines of non-competing products	Supply sales function for small and new firms
Selling agents, including export/import agents	Handle entire output of one or more products	Handle all marketing functions for small manufacturers
Commission merchants	Receive commission on sales price of product	Provide efficiency primarily in agricultural products
Brokers	Identify likely buyers and bring buyers and sellers together	Enhance efficiency in markets where there are lots of small buyers and sellers
MANUFACTURER-OWNED INTERMEDIARIES	Limit operations to one manufacturer	Create efficiencies for large firms
Sales branches	Maintain some inventory in different geographic areas (similar to wholesalers)	Provide service to customers in different geographic areas
Sales offices	Carry no stock; availability in different geographic areas	Reduce selling costs and provide better customer service
Manufacturers' showrooms	Display products attractively for customers to visit	Facilitate examination of merchandise by customers at a central location

Table 14.1 Types of intermediary

Customers pay cash for products and provide their own delivery. Some popular cash-and-carry product categories include groceries, office supplies, and building materials.

- *Mail-order wholesalers* sell products to small retailers and other industrial customers, often located in remote areas, through catalogues rather than a sales force. They usually carry a stock of products and require payment in cash or by credit card before shipment. Mail-order wholesalers supply such products as cosmetics, hardware and sporting goods.

Agents or brokers are a second major type of independent intermediary. Agents and brokers provide services in exchange for commissions. They may or may not take possession of the product, but they never take title – that is, they do not accept legal ownership of the product. Agents normally represent buyers or sellers on an ongoing basis, whereas brokers are employed by clients for a short period of time.

- *Manufacturers' agents*, also referred to as *manufacturers' reps*, are independent salespeople who carry several lines of non-competing products. They have contractual arrangements with manufacturers that outline territories, selling prices and other specific aspects of the relationship. These agents have little if any supervision and are compensated with commissions based on a percentage of what they sell. Manufacturers' agents often develop strong customer relationships and provide an important sales function for small and new companies.

- *Selling agents*, including export/import agents, market a whole product line or one manufacturer's total output. They are often seen as independent marketing departments because they perform the same functions as full-service wholesalers but do not take title to products. Unlike manufacturers' agents, selling agents often have unlimited territories and control the pricing, promotion and distribution of their products. Selling agents are found in such industries as furniture, clothing and textiles.

- *Commission merchants* are sales agents who receive goods, primarily agricultural products such as grain or livestock, on *consignment*. That is, they take possession of products without taking title. Although sellers may state a minimum price they are willing to take for their products, commission merchants are free to sell the product for the highest price they can get. Commission merchants receive a commission on the sales price of the product.

- *Merchandise brokers*, including export/import brokers, are intermediaries that facilitate transactions in markets such as real estate, food and used equipment in which there are lots of small buyers and sellers. Brokers identify likely buyers and sellers and bring the two together in return for a fee received when the transaction is completed.

Manufacturer-owned intermediaries

Sometimes manufacturers set up their own channel intermediaries. In this way, they are able to have separate business units that perform all the functions of independent intermediaries while at the same time maintaining complete control over the channel.

- *Sales branches* are manufacturer-owned facilities that, like independent wholesalers, carry inventory and provide sales and service to customers in a specific geographic area. Sales branches are found in such industries as petroleum products, industrial machinery and equipment, and motor vehicles.

- *Sales offices* are manufacturer-owned facilities that, like agents, do not carry inventory but provide selling functions for the manufacturer in a specific geographic area. Because they allow members of the sales force to be located close to customers, they reduce selling costs and provide better customer service.

- *Manufacturers' showrooms* are manufacturer-owned or leased facilities in which products are permanently displayed for customers to visit. Retailers and the public can visit to see the manufacturer's merchandise and make business-to-business purchases.

Objective

2

Describe the types of distribution channels and the steps in planning distribution channel strategies

Types of distribution channel

Firms face many choices when structuring distribution channels. Should they sell directly to consumers and business users? Would they benefit by including wholesalers, retailers or both in the channel? Would it make sense to sell directly to some customers but use retailers to sell to other customers? Of course, there is no single best channel for all products. The marketing manager must select a channel structure that creates a competitive advantage for the firm and its products based on the size and needs of the target market. Let's consider some of the factors these managers need to think about.

When developing place or distribution strategies, marketers first consider different **channel levels**, or the number of distinct categories of intermediaries that make up a channel of distribution. Many different factors have an impact on this decision. What channel members are available? How large is the market, how frequently do consumers purchase the product, and what services do they require? The producer and the customer are always members, so the shortest channel possible has two levels. Using a retailer adds a third level, a wholesaler adds a fourth level, and so on. Different channel structures exist for both consumer and business-to-business markets.

What is the role of service? As we saw earlier, services are intangible so there is no need to worry about storage, transportation and the other functions of physical distribution. In most cases, the service travels directly from the producer to the customer. However, distribution of some services can be enhanced through the use of an intermediary, often called an *agent*, who helps the parties complete the transaction. Examples include insurance agents, stockbrokers and travel agents.

 ## Consumer channels

As we noted earlier, the simplest channel is a direct channel. Why do some producers sell directly to customers? One reason is that a direct channel may allow the producer to serve its customers better and at a lower price than is possible through using a retailer. By using a direct channel, a strawberry farmer makes sure his customers have fresher strawberries than if he sells them through a local supermarket. Furthermore, if the farmer sells them through a supermarket, the price will be higher because of the supermarket's costs of doing business and required profit. In fact, sometimes this is the *only* way to sell the product, because using channel intermediaries may boost the price above what consumers are willing to pay.

Another reason to use a direct channel is control. When the producer handles distribution, it maintains control of pricing, service and delivery, i.e. all the elements of the transaction. Because distributors and dealers carry many products, it can be difficult to get their sales forces to focus on selling one product. In a direct channel, a producer works directly with customers, gaining insights into trends, customer needs and complaints and the effectiveness of its marketing strategies. Why do producers choose to use indirect channels to reach consumers? A reason in many cases is that customers are familiar with certain retailers or other intermediaries. It's where they always go to look for what they need. Getting customers to change their normal buying behaviour, for example convincing consumers to buy their washing powder or frozen pizza from a catalogue or over the internet instead of from the supermarket may prove difficult.

In addition, intermediaries help producers in all the ways described earlier. By creating utility and transaction efficiencies, channel members make producers' lives easier and enhance their ability to reach customers. The *producer–retailer–consumer channel* portrays the shortest indirect channel. Heinz uses this channel when it sells its products through large retailers such as Carrefour or Wal-Mart. Because the retailers buy in large volume, they can buy at a low price which may be passed along to shoppers. The size of these retail giants also means they can provide the physical distribution functions such as transportation and storage that wholesalers handle for smaller retail outlets.

The *producer–wholesaler–retailer–consumer channel* is a common distribution channel in consumer marketing. Take ice cream, for example. A single ice-cream factory supplies, say, four or five regional wholesalers. These wholesalers then sell to 400 or more retailers such as grocery shops. The retailers in turn each sell the ice cream to thousands of customers. In this channel, the regional wholesalers combine many manufacturers' products to supply to grocery shops. Because the grocery shops do business with many wholesalers, this arrangement results in a broad selection of products.

Business-to-business channels

Business-to-business distribution channels, as the name suggests, facilitate the flow of goods from a producer to an organisational or business customer. Generally, business-to-business channels parallel consumer channels in that they may be direct or indirect. For example, the simplest indirect channel in industrial markets occurs when the single intermediary – a merchant wholesaler referred to as an industrial distributor rather than a retailer buys products from a manufacturer and sells them to business customers. Direct channels are more common in business-to-business markets than business-to-consumer markets. This is because business-to-business marketing often means selling high-priced, high-profit items (a single piece of industrial equipment may cost hundreds of thousands of euros) to a market made up of only a few customers. In such markets, it makes sense financially for a company to develop its own sales force and sell directly to customers. The investment in an in-house sales force may well pay off.

Dual distribution systems

Marketing is not so simple and producers, dealers, wholesalers, retailers and customers alike may actually interact with more than one type of channel. We call these *dual* or *multiple distribution systems*. The pharmaceutical industry provides a good example of multiple-channel usage. Pharmaceutical companies distribute their products in at least three types of channels. First, they sell to hospitals, clinics and other organisational customers directly. These customers buy in quantity, purchasing a wide variety of products. Because in hospitals and clinics pills are dispensed one at a time rather than in bottles of 50, hospitals and clinics require different product packaging than when the products are sold to other types of customers. Pharmaceuticals suppliers' second channel is an indirect consumer channel in which the manufacturer sells to large chemist groups that distribute the medicines to their shops across a country. Alternatively, some of us would rather purchase our prescriptions in a more personal manner from the local independent chemist where we can browse the shelves while we wait. In this version of the indirect consumer channel, the manufacturer sells to wholesalers that in turn supply these independents. Finally, third-party payers such as insurance companies are a third type of channel that pharmaceutical companies may sell to directly.

Hybrid marketing systems

Instead of serving a target market with a single channel, some companies have added new channels – direct sales, distributors, retail sales and direct mail. As they add channels and communications methods, they create a **hybrid marketing system**.[3] For example, at one time you could only buy a Xerox photocopier directly through a Xerox salesperson. Today, unless you are a very large business customer, you will probably purchase a Xerox machine from a local Xerox authorised dealer, or possibly through Xerox On-line. Xerox turned to an enhanced dealer network for distribution because such hybrid marketing systems offer companies certain competitive advantages, including increased coverage of the market, lower marketing costs and a greater potential for customisation of service for local markets.

Now we know what distribution channels and channel intermediaries are and the role of channel members in the distribution of goods and services. We also know that not all channels are alike. Some are direct while others are indirect, and indirect channels can be quite complex. The next section is about how marketers plan channel strategies to meet customer needs better than the competition, that is, seeking the all-important competitive advantage.

 ## Planning a channel strategy

Do customers want products in large or small quantities? Do they insist on buying them locally, or will they purchase from a distant supplier? How long are they willing to wait to get the product? As marketers we need to know! Distribution planning is best accomplished when marketers follow the steps in Figure 14.3. In this section, we will first look at how manufacturers decide on distribution objectives and then examine what influences distribution decisions. Finally, we'll talk about how firms select different distribution strategies and tactics. Firms that operate within a channel of distribution, i.e. manufacturers, wholesalers and retailers, perform *distribution planning*. In this section, our perspective focuses on distribution planning by producers and manufacturers rather than intermediaries because they, more often than intermediaries, take a leadership role in creating a successful distribution channel.

Figure 14.3 Steps in distribution planning
Distribution planning begins with setting channel objectives and includes developing channel strategies and tactics

Step 1: Develop distribution objectives

The first step in deciding on a distribution plan is to develop objectives that support the organisation's overall marketing goals. How can distribution work with the other elements of the marketing mix to increase profits? To increase market share? To increase sales volume? In general, the overall objective of any distribution plan is to make a firm's product available when, where and in the quantities customers want at the minimum cost. More specific distribution objectives, however, depend on the characteristics of the product and the market.

For example, if the product is bulky, a primary distribution objective may be to minimise shipping costs. If the product is fragile, a goal may be to develop a channel that minimises handling. In introducing a new product to a mass market, a channel objective may be to provide maximum product exposure or to make the product available close to where customers live and work. Sometimes marketers make their product available where similar products are sold so that consumers can compare prices.

Step 2: Evaluate internal and external environmental influences

After setting the distribution objectives, marketers must consider their internal and external environments to develop the best channel structure. Should the channel be long or short? Is intensive, selective or exclusive distribution best? Short, often direct, channels may be better suited for business-to-business marketers where customers are geographically concentrated and require high levels of technical know-how and service. Expensive or complex products are frequently sold directly to final customers. Short channels with selective distribution also make more sense with perishable products, since getting the product to the final user quickly is a priority. However, longer channels with more intensive distribution are generally best for inexpensive, standardised consumer goods that need to be distributed broadly and where little technical expertise is required.

The organisation must also examine such issues as its own ability to handle distribution functions, what channel intermediaries are available, the ability of customers to access these intermediaries, and how the competition distributes its products. Should a firm use the same retailers as its competitors? It depends. Sometimes, to ensure customers' undivided attention, a firm sells its products in outlets that don't carry its competitors' products. In other cases, a firm uses the same intermediaries as its competitors because customers expect to find the product there. Finally, by studying competitors' distribution strategies, marketers can learn from their successes and failures and avoid repeating them. If the biggest complaint of competitors' customers is delivery speed, developing a system that allows same-day delivery can make the competition pale in comparison.

Step 3: Choose a distribution strategy

Planning distribution strategies means making at least three decisions. First, distribution planning includes decisions about the number of levels in the distribution channel. The options here were discussed earlier in the section on consumer and business-to-business channels. Beyond the number of levels, distribution strategies also involve decisions about channel relationships, such as whether a conventional system or a highly integrated system will work best, and the distribution intensity or the number of intermediaries at each level of the channel.

Conventional, vertical, or horizontal marketing system?   Participants in any distribution channel form an interrelated system. In general, these systems take one of three forms: conventional, vertical and horizontal marketing systems. A **conventional marketing system** is a multi-level distribution channel in which members work independently of one another. Their relationships are limited to simply buying and selling from one another. Each firm seeks to benefit with little concern for other channel members. Even though channel members work independently, most conventional channels are highly successful. For one thing, all members of the channel are working toward the same goals – to build demand, reduce costs and improve customer satisfaction. Each channel member also knows that it's in everyone's best interest to treat other channel members fairly.[4]

A **vertical marketing system (VMS)** is a channel in which there is formal cooperation among channel members at two or more different levels: manufacturing, wholesaling and retailing. Vertical marketing systems were developed as a way to meet customer needs better by reducing costs incurred in channel activities. Often a vertical marketing system can provide a level of cooperation and efficiency not possible with a conventional channel, maximising the effectiveness of the channel while also maximising efficiency and keeping costs low. Members share information and provide services to other members, recognising that such coordination makes everyone more successful in reaching a desired target market. There are three types of vertical marketing systems: administered, corporate and contractual.

- In an *administered* VMS, channel members remain independent but voluntarily work together because of the power of a single channel member. Strong brands are able to manage an administered VMS because resellers are eager to work with the manufacturer to carry the product.

- In a *corporate* VMS, a single firm owns manufacturing, wholesaling and retailing operations. Thus, the firm has complete control over all channel operations.

- In a *contractual* VMS, cooperation is enforced by contracts (legal agreements) that spell out each member's rights and responsibilities and how they will cooperate. This arrangement means that the channel members can have more impact as a group than they could alone.

In a wholesaler-sponsored VMS, wholesalers get retailers to work together under their leadership in a voluntary chain. Retail members of the chain use a common name, cooperate in advertising and other promotion, and even develop their own private-label products. In other cases, retailers themselves organise a cooperative marketing channel system. A *retailer cooperative* is a group of retailers that has established a wholesaling operation to help them compete more effectively with the large chains. Each retailer owns shares in the wholesaler operation and is obligated to purchase a certain percentage of stock from the cooperative operation.

Franchise organisations are a third type of contractual VMS. In these organisations, channel cooperation is explicitly defined and strictly enforced through contractual arrangements in which a franchiser (a manufacturer or a service provider) allows an entrepreneur (the franchisee) to use the franchise name and marketing plan for a fee. In most franchise agreements, the franchiser provides a variety of services for the franchisee, such as helping to train employees, giving access to lower prices for needed materials and selecting a good location. In return, the franchiser receives a percentage of revenue from the franchisee. Usually the franchisees are obliged to follow the franchiser's business format very closely in order to maintain the franchise. From the manufacturer's perspective, franchising a business is a way to develop widespread product distribution with minimal financial risk, while at the same time maintaining control over product quality. From the entrepreneur's perspective, franchises are a popular way to start off in business.

In a **horizontal marketing system**, two or more firms at the same channel level agree to work together to get their product to the customer. Sometimes these agreements are between unrelated businesses. For example, many supermarkets now have formed a horizontal marketing system with banks that maintain a manned branch in the shop. For example in the UK, HSBC branches are sometimes located in Morrisons retail stores and customers like it because they can do their food shopping and their banking simultaneously. Most airlines today are members of a horizontal alliance that allows them to cooperate in providing passenger air service. For example, Ireland carrier Aer Lingus is a member of the 'one world' alliance, which also includes American Airlines, British Airways, Cathay Pacific Airways, Finnair, Iberia and Qantas Airways. These alliances increase passenger volume for all airlines because travel agents that book passengers on one of the airline's flights will be more likely to book a connecting flight on the other airline. To increase customer benefits, they also share frequent-flyer programmes and airport lounges.[5]

Intensive, exclusive or selective distribution?   How many wholesalers and retailers will carry the product within a given market? This may seem like an easy decision: distribute the product through as many intermediaries as possible, but guess again. If the product goes to too many outlets, there may be inefficiency and duplication of efforts. For example, if there are too many Honda dealerships in a particular city, there will be a lot of unsold Hondas sitting on dealer forecourts, and no single dealer will be successful. Alternatively, if there are not enough wholesalers or retailers carrying a product, total sales of the manufacturer's products (and profits) will not be maximised. If customers have to drive hundreds of miles to find a Honda dealer, they may settle for a Ford. Thus, a distribution objective may be to either increase or decrease the level of distribution in the market. The three basic choices are intensive, exclusive and selective distribution. Table 14.2 summarises five decision factors: company, customers, channels, constraints and competition – exploring how they help marketers determine the best fit between distribution system and marketing goals.

Intensive distribution aims to maximise market coverage by selling a product through as many wholesalers or retailers that will stock and sell the product as possible. Marketers use intensive distribution for products such as soft drinks, milk and bread that are quickly consumed and must be frequently replaced. Intensive distribution is necessary for these products because availability is more important than any other consideration in customers' purchase decisions. In contrast to intensive distribution, **exclusive distribution** means limiting distribution to a single outlet in a particular region. Marketers often sell pianos, up-market cars, executive training programmes and other products with high price tags through exclusive distribution arrangements. They typically use these strategies with products that are high priced, that have considerable service requirements and when there are a limited number of buyers in any single geographic area. Exclusive distribution

Decision Factor	Intensive Distribution	Exclusive Distribution
Company	Oriented towards mass markets	Oriented towards specialised markets
Customers	High customer density	Low customer density
	Price and convenience are priorities	Service and cooperation are priorities
Channels	Overlapping market coverage	Non-overlapping market coverage
Constraints	Cost of serving individual customers is low	Cost of serving individual customers is high
Competition	Based on a strong market presence, often through advertising and promotion	Based on individualised attention to customers, often through relationship marketing

Table 14.2   Characteristics that favour intensive over exclusive distribution

enables wholesalers and retailers to better recoup the costs associated with long selling processes for each customer and in some cases extensive after-sales service.

Of course, not every situation neatly fits a category in Table 14.2. Market coverage that is less than intensive distribution but more than exclusive distribution is called **selective distribution**. Selective distribution fits when demand is so large that exclusive distribution is inadequate, but selling costs, service requirements or other factors make intensive distribution a poor fit. Selective distribution strategies are suitable for so-called *shopping products* such as household appliances and electronic equipment for which consumers are willing to spend time visiting different retail outlets to compare alternatives. For producers, selective distribution means freedom to choose only those wholesalers and retailers that have a good credit rating, provide good market coverage, serve customers well and cooperate effectively. Wholesalers and retailers like selective distribution because it results in higher profits than are possible with intensive distribution where sellers often have to compete on price.

Step 4: Develop distribution tactics

As with planning for the other marketing Ps, the final step in distribution planning is to develop the distribution tactics necessary to implement the distribution strategy. These decisions are usually about the type of distribution system to use, such as a direct or indirect channel or a conventional or an integrated channel. Distribution tactics relate to the implementation of these strategies, such as selecting individual channel members and managing the channel. These decisions are important because they often have a direct impact on customer satisfaction.

Selecting channel partners   When firms agree to work together in a channel relationship, they become partners in what is normally a long-term commitment. Like a marriage, it is important to both manufacturers and intermediaries to select channel partners wisely, or they'll regret the match-up later. In evaluating intermediaries, manufacturers try to answer questions such as these: Will the channel member contribute substantially to our profitability? Does the channel member have the ability to provide the services customers want? What impact will a potential intermediary have on channel control?

For example, which small-to medium-sized firm wouldn't jump at the chance to have its products distributed by European retail giant Carrefour? With Carrefour as a channel partner, a small firm could double, triple or quadruple its business. Actually, some firms, recognising that size means power in the channel, have decided against selling to Carrefour because they are not willing to relinquish control of their marketing decision making. There is also a downside to choosing one retailer and selling only through that one retailer. If that retailer stops carrying the product, for example, the company will lose all its customers and it will be back to square one. See the Marketing ethics and sustainability box to consider some of the issues surrounding product placement, as suppliers to retail stores grapple to obtain prominent shelf space.

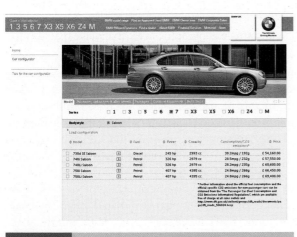

Another consideration in selecting channel members is by analysing a competitors' channel partners. Because people spend time comparing different brands when purchasing a shopping product, firms need to make sure their products are displayed near

Photo 14.3   BMW's new streamlined distribution strategy lets buyers customise the car online resulting in faster delivery
Source: BMW

Marketing ethics and sustainability

Making the product available ethically

Because their size gives them great bargaining power when negotiating with manufacturers, many large retail chains force manufacturers to pay a slotting allowance – a fee paid in exchange for agreeing to place the manufacturer's products on the retailer's valuable shelf space. Although the retailers claim that such fees pay the cost of adding products to their inventory, many manufacturers feel that slotting fees are more akin to highway robbery. Certainly, the practice prevents smaller manufacturers that cannot afford the slotting allowances from getting their products into the hands of consumers.

Debate, discuss, disagree

1 Do you think this is ethical?

2 How might you realistically resolve this issue satisfactorily?

similar competitors' products. If most competitors distribute their electric drills through mass retailers, a manufacturer has to make sure its brand is there also. A firm's dedication to social responsibility may also be an important determining factor in the selection of channel partners. Many firms have developed extensive programmes to recruit minority-owned channel members. Starbucks' organisation-wide commitment to good corporate citizenship translates in one way into its supplier diversity programme that works to help minority-owned businesses thrive.[6]

Managing the channel Once a manufacturer develops a channel strategy and aligns channel members, the day-to-day job of managing the channel begins. The **channel leader**, sometimes called a *channel captain*, is the dominant firm that controls the channel. A firm becomes the channel leader because it has power relative to other channel members. This power comes from different sources:

- A firm has *economic power* when it has the ability to control resources.
- A firm such as a franchiser has *legitimate power* if it has legal authority.

A producer firm has *reward or coercive power* if it engages in exclusive distribution and has the ability to give profitable products and to take them away from the channel intermediaries. In the past, producers traditionally held the role of channel captain. Anglo-Dutch giant Unilever, for example, developed customer-oriented marketing programmes, tracked market trends and advised retailers on the mix of products most likely to build sales. As large retail chains evolved, the key retailers have begun to assume a leadership role because of the sheer size of their operations. Today it is much more common for such big retailers to dictate their needs to producers instead of producers controlling what product is available to retailers.

Because producers, wholesalers and retailers depend on one another for success, channel cooperation helps everyone. Channel cooperation is also stimulated when the channel leader takes actions that help make its partners more successful. High intermediary profit margins, training programmes, cooperative advertising and expert marketing advice are invisible to end customers but are motivating factors in the eyes of wholesalers and retailers.[7] By improving the speed and accuracy of re-orders, retailers are able to maintain inventory levels necessary to satisfy customers while avoiding ordering errors.

Of course, relations among members in a channel are not always so sweet, particularly as each firm has its own objectives, channel conflict may therefore threaten a manufacturer's distribution strategy. Such conflict most often occurs between firms at different levels of the same distribution channel. Incompatible goals, poor communication and disagreement over roles, responsibilities and functions cause conflict. For example, a producer is likely to feel the firm would enjoy greater success and profitability if intermediaries carry only its brands, but many intermediaries believe they will do better if they carry a variety of brands.

Distribution channels and the marketing mix

How are decisions regarding place related to the other three Ps? For one thing, place decisions affect pricing. Marketers that distribute products through low-priced retailers such as Aldi and Lidl will have different pricing objectives and strategies than will those that sell to speciality retailers. Distribution decisions can sometimes give a product a distinct position in its market. For example, Enterprise Rent-a-Car avoids being overly dependent on the cut-throat airport rental car market by seeking primary locations in residential areas and local business centres. This strategy takes advantage of the preferences of those customers who are not flying and who want short-term use of a rental vehicle, such as when their primary vehicle is in the repair shop. Enterprise built up such a successful following around this business model that loyal customers began to request more Enterprise counters at airports. Now it is a rising competitive threat for traditional airport car rental agencies such as Hertz and Avis.

Of course, the choice of retailers and other intermediaries is also strongly tied to the product itself. Manufacturers select mass retailers to sell mid-price-range products while they distribute top-of-the-line products such as expensive jewellery through high-end department and speciality outlets. In this section, we've been concerned with the distribution channels firms use to get their products to customers. In the following section, we'll look at the area of logistics, i.e. physically moving products through the supply chain.

 # Logistics: implementing the supply chain

Some marketing textbooks tend to depict the practice of marketing as 90 per cent planning and 10 per cent implementation. In the 'real world', many managers would argue that this ratio should be reversed. Marketing success is very much the art of getting the timing right and delivering on promises – *implementation*. That's why marketers place so much emphasis on efficient **logistics**, the process of designing, managing and improving the movement of products through the supply chain. Logistics covers purchasing, manufacturing, storage and transport. From a company's viewpoint, logistics take place both *inbound* (raw materials, parts, components and supplies) and *outbound* (work-in-progress and finished goods). Logistics is also a relevant consideration regarding product returns, recycling and material re-use, and waste disposal – *reverse logistics*.[8] As we saw in earlier chapters, such issues are becoming even more important as firms start to consider *sustainability* as a competitive advantage and put more effort into maximising the efficiency of recycling and disposal to save money and the environment at the same time. So you can see logistics is an important issue across all elements of the supply chain. Let's examine logistics more closely.

Understanding logistics

Logistics was originally a military term used to describe everything needed to deliver soldiers and equipment to the right place, at the right time and in the right condition. In business, logistics is similar in that its objective is to deliver exactly what the customer wants at the right time, in the right place and at the right price. The application of logistics is essential to the efficient management of the supply chain. Just as it's said 'an army marches on its stomach' (meaning it can't function without adequate supplies, such as food), a business relies on efficient logistics to be sure it has the resources it needs to successfully compete in the marketplace.

The delivery of goods to customers involves **physical distribution**, which refers to the activities used to move finished goods from manufacturers to final customers. Physical distribution activities include order processing, warehousing, materials handling, transportation and inventory control. This process affects how marketers physically get products where they need to be, when they need to be there and at the lowest possible cost. Effective physical distribution is at the core of successful logistics. When doing logistics planning, however, the focus is also on the customer. When managers thought of logistics as physical distribution only, the objective was to deliver the product at the lowest cost. Today, firms consider the needs of the customer first. The customer's goals become the logistics provider's goals, and this means that with most logistics decisions, firms must decide on the best trade-off between low costs and high customer service. The appropriate goal is not just to deliver what is needed at the lowest cost, but rather to provide the product at the lowest cost possible *so long as the firm meets* delivery requirements. Although it would be nice to transport all goods quickly by air, that is certainly not practical. Sometimes, however, air transport may be necessary to meet the needs of the customer, no matter what the cost.

Logistics functions

When developing logistics strategies, marketers must make decisions related to the five functions of logistics: order processing, warehousing, materials handling, transportation and stock control. For each decision, managers must consider how to minimise costs while maintaining the service customers want.

Order processing includes the series of activities that occurs between the time an order comes into the organisation and the time a product goes out the door. After an order is received, it is typically sent electronically to an office for record keeping and then on to the warehouse to be filled. When the order reaches the warehouse, personnel there check to see if the item is in stock. If it is not, the order is placed on back-order status. That information is sent to the office and then to the customer. If the item is available, it is located in the warehouse, packaged for shipment and scheduled for pick-up by either in-house or external shippers. Fortunately, many firms have automated this process through **enterprise resource planning (ERP) systems**. An ERP system is a software solution that integrates information from across the entire company, including finance, order fulfilment, manufacturing and transportation. Data only need to be entered into the system once, and then the data are automatically shared throughout the organisation and linked to other information. For example, information on the stock of products is tied to sales information so that a sales representative can immediately tell a customer whether the product is available.

Warehousing – storing goods in anticipation of sale or transfer to another member of the channel of distribution – enables marketers to provide time utility to consumers by holding on to products until consumers need them. Whether we speak of fresh-cut flowers, tinned fruit or computer chips, at some point these goods (unlike services) must be stored. Storing goods allows marketers to match supply with demand. For example, toys and other gift items are big sellers at Christmas, but toy factories operate for 12 months of the year. Part of developing effective logistics means deciding how many warehouses a firm needs and where and what type of warehouse each should be. A firm determines the location of its warehouse(s) by the location of customers and access to major motorways, airports or rail transportation. The number of warehouses often depends on the level of service customers require. If customers generally require fast delivery (today or tomorrow at the latest), then it may be necessary to store products in a number of different locations where they can be delivered to the customer quickly.

Firms use private and public warehouses to store goods. Those that use *private warehouses* have a high initial investment, but they also lose less stock due to damage. *Public warehouses* are an alternative, allowing firms to pay for a portion of warehouse space rather than having to own an entire storage facility. Most countries offer public warehouses in all large cities and many smaller cities to support domestic and international trade. A *distribution centre* is a warehouse that stores goods for short periods of time and that provides other functions, such as breaking bulk.

Materials handling is the moving of products into, within and out of warehouses. When goods come into the warehouse, they must be physically identified, checked for damage, sorted and labelled. Next they are taken to a location for storage. Finally, they are recovered from the storage area for packaging and shipment. All in all, the goods may be handled over a dozen separate times. Procedures that limit the number of times a product must be handled decrease the likelihood of damage and reduce the cost of materials handling.

Logistics decisions take into consideration options for **transportation**, the mode by which products move among channel members. Again, making transportation decisions entails a compromise between minimising cost and providing the service customers want. As Table 14.3 shows, modes of transportation, including railroads, water transportation, trucks, airlines, pipelines and the internet, differ in the following ways:

- **Dependability:** The ability of the carrier to deliver goods safely and on time.
- **Cost:** The total transportation costs for moving a product from one location to another, including any charges for loading, unloading and in-transit storage.
- **Speed of delivery:** The total time for moving a product from one location to another, including loading and unloading.
- **Accessibility:** The number of different locations the carrier serves.
- **Capability:** The ability of the carrier to handle a variety of different products such as large or small, fragile or bulky.
- **Traceability:** The ability of the carrier to locate goods in shipment.

Each mode of transportation has strengths and weaknesses that make it a good choice for different transportation needs. Table 14.3 summarises the pros and cons of each mode.

- **Rail:** Rail is best for carrying heavy or bulky items, such as coal and other mining products, over long distances. Rail is about average in cost and provides moderate speed of delivery. Although rail transportation provides dependable, low-cost service to many locations, trains cannot carry goods to every community.
- **Water:** Ships and barges carry large, bulky goods and are very important in international trade. Water transportation is relatively low in cost but can be slow.
- **Trucks:** Trucks or motor carriers are the most important transportation mode for consumer goods, especially over shorter distances. Such transport allows flexibility because trucks can travel to locations missed by boats, trains and planes. Trucks are also able to carry a wide variety of products, including perishable items. Although costs are fairly high for longer distance shipping, they are economical for shorter deliveries.

Transportation Mode	Dependability	Cost	Speed of Delivery	Accessibility	Capability	Traceability	Most Suitable Products
Railroads	Average	Average	Moderate	High	High	Low	Heavy or bulky goods, such as coal and steel
Water	Low	Low	Slow	Low	Moderate	Low	Bulky, non-perishable goods, such as durable components and heavy machine tools
Trucks	High	High for long distances; low for short distances	Fast	High	High	High	A wide variety of products, including those that need refrigeration
Air	High	High	Very fast	Low	Moderate	High	High-value items, such as light electronic goods and fresh flowers
Pipeline	High	Low	Slow	Low	Low	Moderate	Petroleum products and other chemicals
Internet	High	Low	Very fast	Potentially very high	Low	High	Services such as banking, information and entertainment

Table 14.3   A comparison of transportation modes

Marketing metrics

Supply chain example

Companies can track a wide range of metrics within the supply chain area. Some of the most common ones are the following:

- On-time delivery
- Forecast accuracy
- Value-added productivity per employee
- Returns processing cost as a percentage of product revenue
- Customer order actual cycle time
- Perfect order measurement.

Let's take a look at the last measure in more detail. The perfect order measure calculates the error-free rate of each stage of a purchase order.[9] This measure helps managers track the steps involved in getting a product from a manufacturer to a customer so that they can pinpoint processes in need of improvement. For example, a company can calculate its error rate at each stage and then combine these rates to create an overall metric of order quality. Suppose the company identifies the following error rates:

- Order entry accuracy: 99.95 per cent correct (five errors per 10,000 order lines)
- Warehouse pick accuracy: 99.2 per cent
- Delivered on time: 96 per cent
- Shipped without damage: 99 per cent
- Invoiced correctly: 99.8 per cent

The company can then combine these individual rates into an overall pe rfect order measure by multiplying them together: 99.95% × 99.2% × 96% × 99% × 99.8% = 94.04%.

Because trucks provide door-to-door service, product handling is minimal, reducing the chance of product damage.

- **Air:** Air transportation is the fastest and most expensive transportation mode. It is ideal to move high-value items such as certain mail, fresh-cut flowers and live lobsters. Passenger airlines, air-freight carriers and express delivery firms provide such air transportation. Ships remain the major mover of international cargo, but air transportation networks are becoming more important in the development of international markets.

- **Pipeline:** Pipelines are used to carry petroleum products such as oil and natural gas and a few other chemicals. Pipelines flow primarily from oil or gas fields to refineries. They are very low in cost, require little energy and are not subject to disruption by weather.

- **The internet:** As we discussed earlier in this chapter, marketers of services such as banking, news and entertainment are taking advantage of distribution opportunities provided by the internet.

Inventory control: JIT and fast fashion   Another component of logistics is **stock control**, which means developing and implementing a process to ensure that the firm always has sufficient quantities of goods available to meet customers' demands, no more or no less. That explains why firms work so hard to track merchandise so they know where their products are and where they are needed in case a low stock situation appears imminent. Some companies are even phasing in a sophisticated technology known as **radio frequency identification (RFID)**. RFID lets firms tag clothes, pharmaceuticals or virtually any kind of product with tiny chips containing information about the item's content, origin and destination. This new technology has the potential to revolutionise stock control and help marketers ensure that their products are on the shelves when people want to buy them. Great for manufacturers and retailers, but some consumer groups are fighting against RFID, which they refer to as 'spy chips'. Through blogs, boycotts and other anti-company initiatives, these groups proclaim RFID is invading human privacy.

Firms store goods (that is, create stock) for many reasons. For manufacturers, the pace of production may not match seasonal demand, and it may be more economical to produce skis all year round than to produce them only during the winter season. For channel members that purchase goods from manufacturers or other channel intermediaries, it may be economical to order a product in quantities that don't exactly parallel demand. For example, delivery costs make it prohibitive for a petrol station to place daily orders for just the amount of fuel people will use that day. Instead, stations usually order tanker loads and hold fuel in underground tanks. The consequences of running out of fuel may be very bad. Hospitals must keep adequate supplies of blood, certain fluids, drugs and other supplies on hand to meet emergencies, even if some items go to waste.

Stock control has a major impact on the overall costs of a firm's logistics initiatives. If supplies of products are too low to meet fluctuations in customer demand, a firm may have to make expensive emergency deliveries or lose customers to competitors. If stock is above demand, unnecessary storage expenses and the possibility of damage or deterioration occur. To balance these two opposing needs, manufacturers are turning to **just in time (JIT)** stock techniques with their suppliers. JIT sets up the delivery of goods just as they are needed on the production floor, thus minimising the cost of holding stock while ensuring it will be there when it is needed. A supplier's ability to make on-time deliveries is the critical factor in the selection process for firms that have adopted this kind of system. JIT systems reduce stock to very low levels or even zero and ensure consistency by timing deliveries so that they arrive only when a customer needs them. The advantage of JIT systems is the reduced cost of warehousing. For both manufacturers and re-sellers that use JIT systems, the choice of supplier may come down to one whose location is nearest. To win a large customer, a supplier may even have to be willing to set up production facilities close to the customer to guarantee JIT delivery.[10]

Most JIT systems are largely invisible to you as an end consumer. However, if you're a dedicated follower of fashion, you may have encountered this cutting-edge supply chain approach. Several clothing chains such as H&M and Zara have experienced great success recently because they consistently offer up-to-date styles at affordable prices. Their secret? A concept the industry calls **fast fashion** – which is really another way to say JIT. Zara (from Spain) offers customers a constant supply of new products but only a limited supply of each garment. This means that the shop has to constantly send small batches of new styles through its supply chain. Zara's system depends upon a constant exchange of information among supply chain members so that the company can keep track of which specific styles and colours are selling at which shops in order to replenish stock very quickly. The retailer's fast fashion system has to follow about 300,000 new *stock-keeping units (SKUs)* every year to be sure that its customers continue to get their new fashion fix no matter how many times they visit a shop.[11]

Retailing: special delivery

Objective
3

Define retailing and understand how retailing evolves

Shop 'til you drop! For many people, obtaining the product is only half the fun. Others, of course, would rather walk over hot coals than spend time shopping. Marketers need to find ways to deliver products and services that please both types of consumers. **Retailing** is the final stop on the distribution path, the process by which goods and services are sold to consumers for their personal use. A retail outlet is more than a place to buy something. The retailer adds or subtracts value from the offering with its image, stock, service quality, location and pricing policy. In many cases, the shopping experience *is* what we buy as well as the products we take home.

This section will explore the many different types of retailers, keeping one question in mind: how does a retailer, whether store or non-store (selling via television, phone or computer) manage to entice the consumer? Answering this question isn't getting any easier, as the competition for customers continues to intensify and is fuelled by the explosion of websites selling branded merchandise (or auctioning it like eBay). This, combined with developers continuing to build elaborate shopping centres along with improvements in communications and distribution make it more and more possible for retailers from around the world to enter local markets.

Retailing: a mixed (shopping) bag

Although we tend to associate huge shops such as Tesco and Carrefour with retailing activity, in reality most retailers are small businesses.[12] Certain retailers are also wholesalers, because they provide goods and services to businesses as well as to end consumers. As explained earlier, retailers belong to a channel of distribution and as such provide time, place and ownership utility to customers. Some retailers save people time or money by providing an assortment of merchandise under one roof. Others search the world for the most exotic delicacies, allowing shoppers access to goods they would otherwise never see. Still others, such as Borders bookshops with cafés, provide us with interesting environments in which to spend our leisure time and money.

The evolution of retailing

Retailing has taken many forms over time, including the pedlar who sold his wares from a horse-drawn cart, a majestic urban department store, an intimate boutique and a huge 'hyperstore' that sells everything from snacks to mountain bike tyres. As the economic, social and cultural times change, different types of retailers emerge, often replacing older, outmoded types. How can marketers know what the dominant types of retailing will be tomorrow or ten years from now?

The wheel of retailing

One of the oldest and simplest explanations for these changes is the **wheel of retailing** hypothesis. This hypothesis states that new types of retailers find it easiest to enter the market by offering goods at lower prices than competitors.[13] After they gain a foothold, they gradually trade up, improving their facilities, increasing the quality and assortment of merchandise and offering amenities such as parking and gift wrapping. This trend results in greater investment and operating costs, so the shop must raise its prices to remain profitable, which then makes it vulnerable to still newer entrants that can afford to charge lower prices, and therefore the wheel turns. The wheel of retailing helps us explain the development of some but not all forms of retailing. For example, some retailers never trade up; they simply continue to occupy a niche as discounters. Others, such as upmarket speciality shops, start out at the high end. Of course, some retailers move down after experiencing success at the high end. Sometimes they open sister divisions that sell lower priced products, or they develop outlets that sell lower priced versions of their own products.

The retail life cycle

Of course, retailers sell products, but in a way retailers also *are* products because they provide benefits such as convenience or status to consumers and they must offer a competitive advantage over other retailers to survive. Sometimes where a product is purchased either adds to or takes away from its allure. From the value chain perspective, a manufacturer's

Photo 14.4	Waterstone's provides a relaxing environment in which you can visit an in-store coffee shop in between browsing the books and magazines *Source:* Alamy Images/Howard Harrison

selection of a retail location adds value in two ways: by the utility the retailer provides and by the extent to which the shop enhances the product's image. When a manufacturer makes its product available at Tesco, the value added is primarily the time, place and ownership utility it provides. When a product is available at say Marks & Spencer, the value of the product is also increased because the high-end image of the retailer transfers to the product.

Another way to understand how retailers evolve is the **retail life cycle**. Like the product life cycle, this perspective recognises that (like people, soft-drink brands and vacation destinations) retailers are born, they grow and mature, and eventually they die or become obsolete. The life cycle approach allows us to categorise retail stores by the conditions they face at different points in the cycle.[14] In the *introduction* stage, the new retailer often is an aggressive entrepreneur who takes a unique approach to doing business. This may mean competing on the basis of low price, as the wheel of retailing suggests. However, this newcomer may also enter the market by offering a distinctive assortment or a different way to distribute items, such as through the internet, as Lastminute.com did. In the introduction stage, profits are low because of high development costs. As the business enters the *growth* stage, the retailer hopefully catches on with shoppers, therefore sales and profits rise. A new idea, however, doesn't stay new for long. Others start to copy and competition increases, so the shop needs to expand what it offers. Often the retailer responds by opening more outlets and develops systems to distribute goods to these new shops, which may in turn cut profits as the firm invests in new buildings and fixtures.

By the time the business reaches the *maturity* stage, many other individual retailers have copied the unique idea of the original entrepreneur to form an entire industry. The industry has over-expanded, and intense competition makes it difficult to maintain customer loyalty. Profits decline as competitors resort to price cutting to keep their customers. We can observe this pattern with fast-food chains like McDonald's. During the maturity stage, firms seek to increase their share of the market or to attract new customers. McDonald's, having found that many of its customers frequently bought beverages from convenience stores, service stations and other retailers, carried out experiments by adding convenience store-style coolers to its traditional drink dispensers.[15] This would mean McDonald's customers would no longer be limited to a couple of beverages, usually Coke and Sprite, but would have additional beverage choices such as Lucozade, Dr. Pepper and Redbull.

In the *decline* stage, retail businesses, like the general store, become obsolete as newer ways of doing business emerge. Of course, the outdated retailer does not have to fold its tent at this stage. Marketers who anticipate these shifts can avert decline by changing to meet the times. Some retailers such as Starbucks have found growth opportunities in foreign markets. Starbucks now operates over 11,000 coffee shops in America, Latin America, Europe, the Middle East and Pacific Rim. Petrol filling stations had difficulty competing with self-service discount outlets. Many responded by adding variety stores to their retail mix to let drivers buy convenience goods while filling up. Or, what about a shop that plans to close even as it opens? That's just what happened in Berlin with the launch of a new concept called the Comme des Garçons Guerrilla Store. The shop closed in a year – deliberately! Instead of spending millions to build or renovate a building, Comme des Garçons spent just €2500 to fix up a former bookshop. This 'here today, gone tomorrow' strategy (that insiders call **pop-up retailing**) acknowledges consumers' desires to have different shopping experiences all the time in a unique way.[16]

The evolution continues: what's 'in store' for the future?

As our world continues to change rapidly, retailers are scrambling to keep up. Three factors motivate and inspire merchants to reinvent the way they do business: demographics, technology and globalisation.

Demographics   As we noted earlier in the book, keeping up with changes in population characteristics is at the heart of many marketing efforts. Retailers can no longer afford to stand by and assume that their customer base is the same as it has always been. They must come up with new ways to sell their products to diverse groups. For example, although many retailers chase after the same set of affluent customers, others are carving out markets by targeting lower income households. Shops like Poundland in the UK have been successful by selling everything in their shops for £1 (about €1.20). By aiming to focus on this particular market segment, this retailer has been quite successful. Here are some of the ways changing demographics are altering the face of retailing:

- **Convenience for working consumers:** Some retailers are expanding their operating hours because consumers no longer have time to shop during the day. Other retailers, including dry cleaners and pharmacies, are adding drive-up windows. In areas from financial services to interior decorating, enterprising individuals have turned time shortage into a business opportunity by becoming shopping consultants for busy consumers. Many major department stores now offer in-house consultants. Walk-in GP clinics located close to retail stores provide not only convenience but save patients time and money.[17]

- **Recognising cultural diversity:** Although members of different cultural groups can usually find local retailers that cater to their specific needs, larger companies must tailor their strategies to the cultural makeup of specific areas. For example, at Disneyland Paris the overwhelming majority of employees are able to communicate with 'les guests' in at least two different languages.

Technology   In addition to demographics, technology is revolutionising retailing. As we all know, the internet has brought us the age of e-tailing. Whether it's a retailer that purely sells on the web or a traditional UK retailer like Tesco that *also* sells on the web (its motto is 'you shop, we drop'), we can see that retailing is steadily evolving from bricks to clicks. Our personal computers have turned our homes into virtual shopping centres. There are other technological advances that have little to do with the internet that are also helping to change our shopping experiences.

Some of the most profound changes are not even visible to shoppers, such as advanced electronic **point-of-sale (POS) systems**, which contain computer chips that collect sales data and are connected directly into the shop's inventory control system. While no longer new, in the 1990s Benetton led in the use of technology with its point-of-sale system. Every day, data was sent from Benetton shops to its corporate headquarters. From there, computer programmes analysed patterns of demand for different products and automatically planned to match supply with demand. Such systems make shops efficient. If shoppers in an area are buying a lot of wide-legged jeans, for example, the retailer can make sure there are plenty available.

What about skipping the checkout altogether? At the Extra Future Store in Rheinberg, Germany, shoppers are given a small touch-screen computer with a built-in barcode scanner when they enter. The trolley-top computer also allows shoppers to scan their purchases for payment as they move through the shop. For items like produce that require weighing, the shop has installed scales equipped with digital cameras that use image-recognition software to work out and then price the object they are weighing.[18] Central to the concept are the quarter-size radio-frequency identification (RIFD) tags we discussed earlier. These tags are attached to individual products, tracking their movement from storeroom to shelves to shopping trolley. While only a relatively few products now carry these tags, retailers say eventually they will appear on all items – replacing bar codes.

Photo 14.5   Starbucks is now a household name in Japan
Source: Alamy Images/Jochen Tack

Globalisation   As we also saw earlier in this book, the world is becoming a much smaller place. Retailers are busy expanding to other countries and bringing with them innovations and new management philosophies. McDonald's, Carrefour and Starbucks are among the global retail success stories. Starbucks has become a household name in Japan (where it's pronounced *STAH-buks-zu*). The coffee shops feature comfortable sofas, hip-hop music and generous servings. These are relatively new concepts in Japan, where café patrons had been accustomed to sitting in dimly lit shops and sipping tea from thimble-size cups.[19] Of course, understanding global retailing means recognising that the way things are sold differs

Internationalisation

£23 million profit birthday gift for Mulberry

Luxury handbag maker Mulberry has celebrated its 40th anniversary by more than quadrupling its annual profits. The group posted pre-tax profits of £23.3 million in the year to 31 March 2012, compared with £5.1 million in the previous 12 months. Mulberry, which has 86 stores worldwide, including 44 in Britain, reported a high demand for its goods – including its Alexa handbag, which costs £3750 when made in oak ostrich.

The company said sales were up 69 per cent in the year, to £121.6 million, and it reported continued like-for-like growth in the ten weeks to 4 June of 42 per cent. International revenues more than doubled in the period to £40.5 million, while online sales were up 64 per cent to £9.2 million. It has doubled the production of women's handbags and is expanding capacity at its Somerset factory by 30 per cent, creating about 50 manufacturing jobs.

John Cummins, analyst at Altium Securities, said it could still be 'just the beginning of the Mulberry store'. He said: 'Mulberry remains under-represented in most of the largest luxury goods markets globally, with only two stores in the US, one in China and limited exposure in Japan.' Mulberry opened nine stores in the year, including in China, Malaysia and Qatar, as well as a flagship shop in New Bond Street, London. Further openings are planned for New York, Amsterdam, Germany and Korea.

Debate, discuss, disagree

1   To what extent do you feel the growth at Mulberrry is down to the company's international retail strategy?

2   Should Mulberry now venture into other territories? If so, where else would you recommend and why?

Source: Jane Atherton, '£23 m profit Birthday Gift for Mulberry', *Metro*, 17 June 2011

---

from country to country. In many developing countries, the retailing industry is made up of small individual retailers who sell cigarettes, soft drinks, snacks, cassette tapes, batteries and just about anything else you can think of.

Family shops to hypermarkets: classifying retail stores

We've seen that exciting things are happening in the world of retailing. But the field of retailing covers a lot of ground, from elegant department stores and roadside sellers to websites and trendy café bars. Retail marketers need to understand all the possible ways that they might offer their products in the market and they also need a way to benchmark their performance to other similar retailers.

Classifying retailers by what they sell

One of the most important strategic decisions a retailer makes is *what* to sell, i.e. its **merchandise mix**. This choice is similar to settling on a market segment (as discussed earlier): if a shop's merchandise mix is too limited, it may not have enough potential customers, whereas if it is too broad, the retailer runs the risk of being a 'jack of all trades, master of none'. Because what the retailer sells is central to its identity, we will describe some retail types by merchandise mix. While we learned earlier that a manufacturer's product line consists of product offerings that satisfy a single need, in retailing, a *product line* is a set of related products offered by a retailer, such as kitchen appliances or leather goods. However, a word of caution: as retailers experiment with different merchandise mixes, these direct comparisons are getting harder to make. For example, even though marketers like to distinguish between food and non-food retailers, in reality these lines are blurring. Supermarkets are adding hardware product lines, and some department stores offer gourmet food. In Japan, for example, the major department stores have one floor, which like free-standing supermarkets sells meats, vegetables and other fresh food items, while another entire floor offers store customers a wide range of prepared foods ready for the modern Japanese working woman (or man) to carry home for dinner.

Classifying retailers by level of service

Retailers differ in the amount of service they provide for consumers. Firms recognise that there is a trade-off between service and low prices, so they tailor their strategies to the level of service they offer. Customers who demand higher levels of service must be willing to pay for that service, and those who want lower prices must be willing to give up services. Unfortunately, some consumers don't understand this trade-off and still insist on top-level service while paying low prices! Retailers like Lidl and Aldi which offer low prices are often resourced very efficiently and tend not to provide so much in-store service. When customers shop there, they make their product selection without any assistance and must bring their own bags (or buy them) to transport their goods home. Based on our Marketing in recession vignette, there may be evidence to suggest that such low price retailers can buck the trend during economic downturns.

In contrasting that experience to visiting a *full-service retailer*, many of us prefer the likes of Marks & Spencer as it provides supporting services such as gift wrapping and offers trained retail assistants who can help us select that perfect gift. Other specialised services may be available in such shops. Full-service clothing retailers, for instance, normally

Marketing in recession

Cash-strapped Britons flock to discount stores

It was the shopping trend that defied the recession – a mass exodus from supermarket giants such as Tesco and Asda to more obscure German rivals Aldi and Lidl in a quest to save money. While the so-called 'Aldi effect' had appeared to be short-lived, the discounters are once again on the march as hard-up Britons try to beat the biggest squeeze on household spending since the 1920s by trading down to cheaper stores.

Surprising industry data for 2010/11 showed Aldi and Lidl romping ahead in the three months leading into January with sales growth of close to 10 per cent, more than twice that of their larger rivals. The figures also suggest that the top end of the market was buoyant, with Waitrose and Sainsbury's performing well. Analyst Edward Garner said the food market was polarising. 'This shows us that not everybody is the same and that both Waitrose and Aldi can grow at the same time', he said. 'Some people could have had a good old bash at Christmas and are now looking for ways to save money, whereas others still feel better off because their mortgage payments have gone down.'

Although the UK may have come out of recession, retailers are seeing dramatic changes in spending patterns as the aftershocks persist. Households are faced with a toxic combination of soaring food and fuel prices at a time when pay freezes or anaemic rises are the order of the day.

Discuss, debate, disagree

1 How is the economic climate affecting consumer spending?

2 What are the supermarket giants doing in response to the 'Aldi-effect'?

Source: Adapted from Z. Wood 'Cash-strapped Britons Flock to Discount Stores Aldi and Lidl', *The Guardian*, 1 February 2011 www.guardian.co.uk/business/2011/feb/01/retail-industry-discount-stores (accessed 16 May 2011) © Copyright Guardian News & Media 2011.

provide an alteration service. Bridal consultants may also be useful for helping to plan with the wedding gift process. Falling in between self-service and full-service retailers are *limited-service retailers*. Stores like Asda/Wal-Mart and Carrefour offer credit and goods return services, but little else. Customers select merchandise without much assistance, preferring to pay a bit less rather than be waited on a bit more.

Classifying retailers by merchandise selection

Another way to classify retailers is in terms of the selection they offer. A retailer's **merchandise assortment**, or selection of products it sells, has two dimensions: breadth and depth. **Merchandise breadth** (or variety) is the number of different product lines available. A *narrow assortment*, such as that found in convenience stores, means that shoppers will find only a limited selection of product lines. A *broad assortment*, such as that in a warehouse store, means there is a wide range of items available. **Merchandise depth** is the variety of choices available for each specific product. A *shallow assortment* means that the selection within a product category is limited, so a factory outlet shop may sell men's shirts (all made by the same manufacturer) and only in standard sizes. In contrast, a men's speciality shop may feature a *deep assortment* of shirts in varying shades and in hard-to-find sizes. Now that we've seen how retailers differ in the breadth and depth of their assortments, let's review some of the major forms these retailers take.

Convenience stores   Such shops carry a limited number of frequently purchased items, including basic food products, newspapers etc. They cater for consumers willing to pay a premium for the ease of buying staple items close to home. In other words, convenience stores meet the needs of those who are pressed for time, who buy items in smaller quantities or who shop at irregular hours. But these shops are starting to change, especially in urban areas where many time-pressed shoppers prefer to visit these outlets even for speciality items.

Supermarkets   These are food shops that carry a wide selection of edible and non-edible products. Although large supermarkets and hypermarkets appear as a fixture in some European countries, they have not caught on everywhere. Some Europeans still prefer to walk or cycle to small shops near their homes. In such places, relatively smaller food purchases are made per trip and there is a tendency to shop more frequently. Although wide variety is less important than quality and local ambiance for some Europeans, shopping habits are starting to change as hypermarkets are becoming more popular.

Speciality shops   Such shops have a relatively narrow and deep stock of goods. They do not sell a lot of product lines, but they offer a good selection of brands within the lines they sell. For many women with less than perfect figures, shopping at a shop that sells only swimsuits means there will be an adequate selection to find a suit that really fits. The same is true for larger, taller men who can't find suits that fit in regular shops but have lots of choices in shops that cater for the big and tall. Speciality shops can tailor their assortment to the specific needs of a targeted consumer, and they often offer a high level of knowledgeable service.

The **factory outlet** is another type of discount retailer. A manufacturer owns these shops. Some factory outlets enable the manufacturer to sell off defective merchandise or excess stock, while others carry items not available at full-price retail outlets and are designed to provide an additional distribution channel for the manufacturer. Although the assortment is not wide because a shop carries only products made by one manufacturer, most factory outlet shops are located on estates where other similar shops are.

Department stores   These sell a broad range of items and offer a deep selection organised into different sections of the shop. Grand department stores dominated urban centres in the late Victorian era and much of the twentieth century. In many countries, department stores are thriving and remain consumers' primary place to shop. In Japan, department stores are always crowded with shoppers buying everything from a takeaway sushi dinner to a string of fine pearls. In Spain, a single department store chain, El Corte Engles, dominates retailing. Its branch stores include shop-size departments for electronics, books, music and gourmet foods, and each has a vast supermarket covering one or two floors of the store. Because of increased competition and other retailing options, over recent times department stores have experienced some difficulties. In response, some retail shops have pruned their assortments to concentrate more on *soft goods*, such as clothing and home furnishings, and less on *hard goods*, such as appliances.

Hypermarkets   Such places combine the characteristics of warehouse shops and supermarkets. Originally introduced in Europe, these are huge establishments that are several times larger than other shops. A supermarket might be 10,000 to 20,000 square metres, whereas a hypermarket takes up 50,000 to 80,000 square metres, or four football pitches. They offer one-stop shopping, often for over 50,000 items, and feature restaurants, beauty salons and children's play areas. Hypermarkets, such as those run by the French firm Carrefour, are popular in Europe, the Middle East and Latin America, where big shops are somewhat of a novelty. More recently, Carrefour has expanded to developing countries such as Egypt, where a burgeoning population and a lack of large retailers provide hyper-opportunities.

 ## Non-shop retailing

Many products are readily available in places other than shops. Think of the familiar Avon beauty products that are sold to millions of women around the world. Avon allows customers to place orders by phone, online, catalogue or through a representative. Avon's success at giving customers alternatives to traditional shop outlets illustrates the increasing importance of **non-shop retailing**, which is any method a firm uses to complete an exchange that does not require a customer visit to a shop. Indeed, many conventional retailers from upmarket fashion retailers like Next, to supermarket chain Tesco offer options such as catalogues or websites for customers interested in buying their merchandise.

 # B2C e-commerce

Objective

4

Describe B2C e-commerce and its benefits, limitations and future promise

Business-to-consumer (B2C) e-commerce is the online exchange between companies and individual consumers. As more people shop, more retailers will enter the web marketplace, making more types of products available. At the same time, enhanced technology and improvements in delivery and security entice even more consumers to shop online. Electronic commerce in retailing has enormous potential. The continued success of this non-shop format will depend on the ability of retailers to offer sites that are entertaining and informative and that are worth surfing, even after the novelty wears off.

 ## Benefits of B2C e-commerce

For both consumers and marketers, B2C e-commerce provides a host of benefits and some limitations. Table 14.4 lists some of these. E-commerce allows consumers and marketers to easily find and make exchanges in a global marketplace. Consumers can choose

Benefits	Limitations
For the consumer:	**For the consumer:**
Shop 24 hours a day	Lack of security
Less travelling	Fraud
Can receive relevant information in seconds from any location	Can't touch items
More product choices	Exact colours may not reproduce on computer screens
More products available to less-developed countries	Expensive to order and then return
Greater price information	Potential breakdown of human relationships
Lower prices, so less affluent can purchase	**For the marketer:**
Participate in online auctions	Lack of security
Fast delivery	Must maintain website to reap benefits
Electronic communities	Fierce price competition
For the marketer:	Conflicts with shops
The world is your marketplace	Legal issues not resolved
Lower cost of doing business	
Very specialised businesses can be successful	
Real-time pricing	

Table 14.4 Benefits and limitations of e-commerce

from hundreds of thousands of sellers worldwide; while marketers can tap into consumer and business markets with virtually no geographic limitations. From the consumer's perspective, electronic marketing has increased convenience by breaking down many of the time barriers and location issues. You can shop 24 hours a day without leaving home. In less developed countries, the internet lets consumers purchase products that may not be available at all in local markets. Thus, the internet can improve the quality of life without the necessity of developing costly infrastructure, such as opening retail stores in remote locations.

Understanding just what online shoppers really desire and why they are shopping online makes marketers more successful. For some consumers, online shopping provides an additional benefit by fulfilling their experiential needs, that is their need to shop for fun. Consumers who are collectors or who enjoy hobbies are most likely to be **experiential shoppers**. Most online consumers engage in goal-directed behaviour, i.e. they wish to satisfy their shopping goal as quickly as possible; however between 20 and 30 per cent of online consumers shop online because they enjoy the thrill as much or more than the actual acquisition of the item. Experiential shoppers linger at sites longer and are motivated by a desire to be entertained. Consequently, marketers who wish to attract these customers must design websites that offer surprise, uniqueness and excitement. How well a site satisfies experiential needs might determine how much money consumers will choose to spend at that site.

Marketing misstakes

Blockbuster goes bust

Blockbuster built its success by offering more new releases than its competitors, a marketing strategy that allowed it to achieve around 50 per cent of the US market share.

But then came the dotcom boom and with it in 1999, a new rental firm was launched – Netflix. This new start-up offered a subscription service whereby customers could order DVDs over the phone or internet and have them delivered to their homes. The service would later include internet video streaming of movies at no additional cost. Senior management at Blockbuster were dismissive of the Netflix threat and regarded Netflix's customers as more 'spur-of-the-moment renters who did not necessarily plan their movie watching in advance'. According to its research, of the $8 billion that US customers spent on renting movies in 2002, less than $200 million came from online rentals. Online movie rentals were therefore seen as a 'limited business opportunity'. Seven years later, Netflix is the market leader with a 36 per cent share of the $6 billion US rental market compared with Blockbuster's rapidly declining 22 per cent. In September 2010, Blockbuster, the Texas-based movie rental company, filed for Chapter 11 bankruptcy protection in a US court. Changing competitive forces had resulted in $900 million in debts and a freefall in market share.

Why do you think this might be a marketing misstake?

Source: Adapted from R. Ritson, 'This blockbuster is one you mustn't miss' *Marketing Week*, 30 September 2010

Marketers realise equally important benefits from e-commerce. Because marketers can reach such a large number of consumers with electronic commerce, it is possible to develop very specialised businesses that could not be profitable if limited by geographic constraints. As discussed earlier, one of the biggest advantages of e-commerce is that it's easy to get price information. Want to buy a new mountain bike, the latest mobile phone or just about anything else you can think of? Instead of going from shop to shop in order to compare prices, many web surfers use search engines that compile and compare prices from suppliers. With readily available pricing information, shoppers can browse brands, features, reviews and information on where to buy a particular product. The benefit is that consumers can find all of this information in one central location, making it easy to spend their money more efficiently. E-commerce also allows businesses to reduce costs. Compared with bricks-and-mortar retailers, e-tailers' costs are minimal. No expensive retail sites to maintain and no sales assistants to pay. For some products, such as computer software and digitised music, e-commerce provides fast, almost instantaneous delivery.

 ## Limitations of B2C e-commerce

All is not perfect in the virtual world. E-commerce does have its limitations. One drawback relative to shopping in a shop is that customers still must wait a few days to receive most products, which are often sent via private delivery services. So shoppers can't achieve instant gratification by walking out of a shop clutching their latest 'finds'. Many e-commerce sites still suffer from poor design that people find confusing or irritating. One study found that 65 per cent of online shoppers empty their trolleys before they complete their purchase because they find the process hard to follow and there are no real life customer service people available to answer questions. To make matters worse, 30 per cent of

Marketing metrics

E-commerce conversion rates

E-commerce marketers often want to measure a metric they call the *conversion rate*, which is the percentage of visitors to an online shop who purchase from it. This is a useful metric, but if this rate is low it doesn't help the retailer understand the possible factors affecting the website's performance. So, in addition to knowing the conversion rate, researchers at IBM compute other metrics called *microconversion rates* that enable them to pinpoint more precisely what may need to be improved in the online shopping process.[20] This technique breaks down the shopping experience into the stages that are involved between visiting a site and actually making a transaction:

- **Product impression:** Viewing a hyperlink to a web page presenting a product.
- **Click-through:** Clicking on the hyperlink and viewing the product's web page.
- **Basket placement:** Placing the item in the 'shopping basket'.
- **Purchase:** Actually buying the item.

These researchers calculate microconversion rates for each adjacent pair of measures to come up with additional metrics that can pinpoint specific problems in the shopping process:

- **Look-to-click rate:** How many product impressions are converted to click-throughs? This can help the e-tailer determine if the products featured on the website are the ones that customers want to see.
- **Click-to-basket rate:** How many click-throughs result in a product being placed in the shopping basket? This metric helps to determine if the detailed information provided about the product is appropriate.
- **Basket-to-buy rate:** How many basket placements are converted to purchases? This metric can tell the e-tailer which kinds of products are more likely to be abandoned in the shopping basket instead of being bought. It can also pinpoint problems with the checkout process, such as forcing the shopper to answer too many questions or making them wait too long for their credit card to be approved.

online shoppers who have problems with a website say they won't shop there again, and 10 per cent say they won't shop online at all any more.[21]

Security is a concern to both consumers and marketers. We hear horror stories of consumers whose credit cards and other identity information have been stolen. Although an individual's financial liability in most theft cases is limited, because credit card companies usually absorb most or all of the loss, the damage to one's credit rating can last for years. Consumers also are concerned about internet fraud. Although most of us feel competent to judge a local bricks-and-mortar business by its physical presence, by how long it's been around and from the reports of friends and neighbours who shop there, we have little or no information on the millions of internet sites offering their products for sale, even though sites like eBay try to address these concerns by posting extensive information about the reliability of individual vendors. Another problem is that people need 'touch-and-feel' information before buying many products. Although it may be satisfactory to buy a computer or a book on the internet, buying clothing and other items where touching the item or trying it on is essential may be less attractive. As with catalogues, even though most online companies have liberal return policies, consumers can still get stuck with large delivery and return shipping charges for items that don't fit or simply aren't the right colour.

Traditional bricks-and-mortar companies are actually *more* likely to be successful in cyberspace than are internet-only start-ups because they already have established brand names and a base of loyal customers. Traditional retailers are going online, many combining their web retailing with existing shops. Catalogue companies have had the easiest time making the transition to the web since they have the most experience delivering goods directly to consumers. That explains why almost three-quarters of these firms have profitable e-commerce sites, whereas less than 40 per cent of other web retailers are in the black so far.[22] We're also seeing movement in the opposite direction. Online travel companies like Expedia.com are adding offline operations and buying traditional travel agencies. These businesses recognise that many shoppers use the web to research their travel options but then actually purchase their tickets offline because of concerns about security and privacy.

Developing countries with primarily cash economies pose yet another obstacle to the success of B2C e-commerce. In these countries, few people use credit cards, so they can't easily pay for items they purchase over the internet. An alternative for payments that may gain popularity in the future is *digital cash*. Currently, digital cash is available on prepaid cards and smart cards such as a prepaid phone card. Another alternative is e-cash, developed by Digicash of Amsterdam. E-cash provides secure payments between computers using email or the internet. You can use e-cash to buy a pizza or to get money from home. To do so, you need e-cash client software and a *digital bank account*, a web-based account that allows you to make payments to internet retailers directly from the account while online. You withdraw money from your bank account, store it on your computer and spend it when you need to. As major marketers aim to have a greater presence on the web, they worry that their sales online may *cannibalise* their actual retail store sales.

B2C's effect on the future of retailing

Does the growth of B2C e-commerce mean the death of bricks-and-mortar shops as we know them? Don't plan any funerals for your local shops prematurely. Although some argue that virtual distribution channels will completely replace traditional ones because of their cost advantages, this is unlikely. For example, although a bank saves 80 per cent of its costs when customers do business online from their home computers, not all customers wish to use PC-based banking services. At least in the short term, too many people are accustomed to obtaining goods and services from shops, and of course shopping provides a social outlet that (for now) can't be replaced by solitary surfing. At least in the near future, clicks will have to coexist with bricks. Shops as we know them will have to continue to evolve to entice shoppers away from their computer screens. In the future, the trend will be *destination retail*. That is, consumers will visit retailers not so much to buy a product but for the entertainment provided by the total experience. Many retailers are already developing ways to make the shopping in bricks-and-mortar shops an experience rather than just a place to pick up stuff.

Marketing metrics

Abacus

A company called Abacus helps catalogue retailers to measure the shopping habits of their customers. While Abacus relies heavily on the traditional metric of past purchases to determine what people will buy in the future, this database marketer also tracks purchases across countless categories in combination with demographic factors to help retailers, for example, target a single 30-year-old male who likes to surf. Additionally, Abacus keeps track of 'trigger events' such as when a person in its database is getting ready to move, so it can alert a retailer that a consumer may be ready to purchase household items like kitchenware.[23]

Developing a shop positioning strategy: retailing as theatre

Objective

5

Understand the importance of shop image to a retail positioning strategy and explain how a retailer can create a desirable image in the marketplace

A 'destination retail' strategy reminds us that shopping often is part buying, part entertainment and part social outlet. So far we've seen that shops can be distinguished in several ways, including the types of products they carry and the breadth and depth of their assortments. But recall that a shop is itself a product that adds to or subtracts from the goods the shopper came to buy there. When we are deciding which shop to buy at, many of us are less likely to say 'I'll go there because their assortment is broad', or say 'That place is so cool. I really like socialising there.' Shops can entertain us, bore us, make us angry, or even make us sad. In today's competitive marketplace, retailers have to do more than offer good inventory at reasonable prices. They need to position their shops so that they offer a competitive advantage over other shops also fighting for the shopper's attention – not to mention catalogues, websites and shopping channels that may offer the same or similar merchandise without having to leave the home.

Earlier we discovered that staging a service is much like putting on a play. Similarly, many retailers recognise that much of what they do is theatre. At a time when it is possible to pick up a phone or log on to a computer to buy many items, a customer must have a reason to make a trip to a shop. Shoppers are an audience to entertain. The 'play' can cleverly employ stage sets (shop design) and actors (retail assistants) that together create a 'scene'. For example, think about buying a pair of trainers. Retailers which sell these type of goods are far different from the old days, when a tired shop owner waded through box after box of shoes as children ran around the dingy floors. Now retail assistants (actors) are dressed in costumes such as black-striped referee outfits. Shops like Foot Locker are ablaze with neon, with the shoes displayed in clear acrylic walls so that they appear to be floating.[24] All these special effects make the buying occasion less about buying and more about having an experience. As one marketing strategist commented, 'The line between retail and entertainment is blurring.' Even traditional banks are coming on board and re-vamping their buildings to look more like coffee shops and retail boutiques. Some branch banks now offer customers such amenities as comfortable settees, WiFi internet access and movie screens.[25] In this section, we'll review some of the tools available to the retailing playwright.

Shop image

When people think of a shop, they often have no trouble portraying it in the same terms they might use in describing a person. They might use words such as *exciting, depressed, old-fashioned, tacky* or *elegant*. **Shop image** is how the target market perceives the shop (its market position relative to the competition). Check out the Marketing ethics and sustainability box to discover how UK retailer Sainsbury's would like to be perceived by the public. Even shops operated by the same parent company can be quite different from one another. But images don't just happen. Just as brand managers do for products, shop managers work hard to create a distinctive and appealing personality.

To appreciate this idea, consider the dramatic makeover at Selfridges – a well-known British department store chain. At the flagship store in London, shoppers can wander over to a body-piercing salon staffed by teenagers in dreadlocks. In the children's department, giant white plastic blobs hold racks of shocking-pink playsuits. If you need a break from browsing, go to one of the store's 14 restaurants, which often share a theme with the adjacent selling floor. Base Bar, a stripped-down cafeteria full of gleaming aluminium, is next to computers; Lab Cafe is minimalist, next to young designers' clothes. The shop's makeover was publicised by periodic events that screamed cutting edge, including one called 'Body Craze', where thousands of shoppers flocked to see 650 naked people ride the escalators. Do not attempt this at home.[26]

Marketing ethics and sustainability

Sainsbury's and the environment

Many people may find it annoying when they receive a long receipt after shopping in supermarkets, even when they have only bought a bottle of juice. After all, you are highly likely to throw away the receipt immediately after the transaction. It is not hard to discover that nowadays, the cashier at Sainsbury's will ask if you would like a print-out of your receipt. If you decline, you are helping the environment and if you accept, you are still helping the environment since the retailer now prints them double-sided. The supermarket giant won a special award at the Environmental Leadership Awards ceremony in London 2011 in recognition of successfully reducing its use of paper by almost half (or 186 tonnes).

Source: Based on www.eweekeurope.co.uk/news/news-it-infrastructure/sainsburys-wins-with-two-sided-receipts-at-environmental-awards-1296

Not every shop can or wants to have naked people running around, but even more modest strategies to enliven the atmosphere make a big difference. In developing a desirable shop image, the resourceful retailer has a number of choices. Ideally, all these elements should work together to create a clear, coherent picture that meets consumers' expectations of what that particular shopping experience should be. **Atmospherics** is the use of colour, lighting, scents, furnishings, sounds and other design elements to create a desired setting. Marketers manipulate these elements to create a certain 'feeling' about the retail environment.[27]

Shop design: setting the stage The elements of shop design should correspond to management's desired image. A bank lobby needs to convey respectability and security because people need to be reassured about the safety of their money. In contrast, a used bookshop might create a disorderly look so that shoppers think treasures lie buried beneath piles of tattered novels. Here are some other design factors that retailers consider:

- **Shop layout:** This is the arrangement of merchandise in the shop. The placement of fixtures such as shelves, racks and cash registers is important because shop layout determines **traffic flow**; how shoppers will move through the shop and what areas they will pass or avoid. A *grid layout*, usually found in supermarkets, consists of rows of neatly spaced shelves that are at right-angles or parallel to one another. This configuration is useful when management wants to systematically move shoppers down each aisle, being sure that they pass through such high-margin sections as deli and meat.

  A typical strategy is to place staple goods in more remote areas. The designers know that traffic will move to these areas because these are frequently purchased items. They try to place impulse goods in spots shoppers will pass on their way elsewhere. Then they place eye-catching displays to pull people in. In contrast, department and speciality shops typically use a *free-flow layout* because it is more conducive to browsing. A retailer might arrange merchandise in circles, arches or perhaps in separate areas, each with its own distinct image and merchandise mix.

- **Fixture type and merchandise density:** Just as we may form impressions of people from their home decor, our feelings about shops are affected by furnishings, fixtures (shelves and racks that display merchandise) and even how much 'stuff' is packed into the sales area. Generally, clutter conveys a shop with lower priced merchandise. Up-market shops allocate space for sitting areas, dressing rooms and elaborate displays of merchandise.

- **The sound of music:** An elegant restaurant softly playing Mozart in the background is worlds apart from music venues like the Hard Rock Café, where loud rock-and-roll forms part of the atmosphere. The music playing in a shop has become so central to its personality that many retailers, including Ralph Lauren and Starbucks, have even sold the soundtracks specially designed for them.[28]

- **Colour and lighting:** Marketers use colour and lighting to set a mood. Red, yellow and orange are warm colours. Fast-food chains use a lot of orange to stimulate hunger, whereas blue, green and violet signify elegance and cleanliness. Light colours make one feel more serene, whereas bright colours convey excitement. Fashion designer Norma Kamali replaced fluorescent lights with pink ones after management found that pink lighting was more flattering and made female customers more willing to try on bathing suits.[29]

Shop personnel   Shop staff (the actors) should complement the image. Each employee has a part to play, complete with props and costumes. Many shops provide employees with scripts to use when they present products to customers.

Although the presence of knowledgeable sales personnel is important to shoppers, they generally rate the quality of service they receive from retail personnel as low, often because shops don't hire enough people to wait on their customers. Retailers are working hard to upgrade service quality, though they often find that the rapid turnover of salespeople makes this a difficult goal to achieve. Perhaps they can learn from Japanese retailers. A visitor to a Japanese shop is greeted by an enthusiastic, cheerful, polite and immaculately dressed employee who, no matter how busy he or she is, tells each new customer they are welcome and bows to them.

Pricing policy: how much for a ticket to the show?   When consumers form an image of a shop in their minds, the *price points* or price ranges of its merchandise often play a role. Discount shops and general merchandisers are likely to compete on a price basis by

---

Across the Hall

Philippe Gardiner

Vice-President, Hilton Hotels

If I were in Julia's position I would first reject the option I believe least in. This would be Option 2: Setting up a bricks-and-mortar shop represents a significant investment in terms of rent and manning. Furthermore, even though Spitalfields is an up and coming destination in London it is probably not quite there yet in terms of a central London location drawing significant numbers of international tourists. More importantly, the volumes you are likely to sell in one shop are probably going to be very limited.

The next option to rule out would be Option 1. Granted, working with the major supermarket chains in the UK is likely to generate significant volumes, but this would soon be at the expense of the brand that Julia has successfully built so far. Julia has already done the right thing by associating the bag with brands such as Harvey Nichols, but if the bag is the 'it' thing, then it would lose brand equity by being associated with supermarket chains such as Tesco or ASDA. At a time when the leading grocery retailers are under scrutiny for topics such as food miles or purchasing practices, Julia could see her commitment to Fairtrade and Community support questioned by association.

This leaves Option 3. The investment would focus on a robust web and payment platform. The website could build on the growing strength of the brand. Logistically Julia could use the existing infrastructure and then gradually invest in Search Engine Marketing to maximise sales opportunities.

An additional benefit of this option is that as web sales grow, Julia will gather more insights on her final customers, which a pure B2B distribution would not allow. In turn understanding her customers' expectations will ensure that the appropriate and innovative products are developed in the future.

offering brand names for less. In recent years, department stores have been hurt by consumers' desires for bargains. The response of many department stores was to run frequent sales, a strategy that often backfired because many consumers would buy *only* when the shop held a sale. Some shops have instead reduced the number of sales they run in favour of lowering prices across the board. As we saw earlier, some shops offer an everyday low pricing (EDLP) strategy; they set prices that are between the list price suggested by the manufacturer and the deeply discounted price offered by shops that compete on price only.

Building the theatre: shop location   Any estate agent will tell you the three most important factors in buying a home are 'location, location and location'. The same is true in retailing and much success is due to not only what type of shop, but also *where* it is. When choosing a site, planners consider such factors as proximity to motorways and major routes. By carefully selecting 'undiscovered' areas, a company may be able to acquire land in towns with expanding populations. In this section we'll review some important aspects of retail locations.

Types of shop location   There are several basic types of retail location. A shop can be found in a busy city or shopping centre, as a freestanding entity, or in a non-traditional location:

- **Business districts:** A **central business district (CBD)** is the traditional business area found in a town or city centre. Many people are drawn to the area to shop or work and public transportation is usually available. CBDs have suffered in recent years because of concerns about security, a lack of parking, and the lack of customer traffic at evenings and weekends. To combat these problems, many cities provide incentives such as tax breaks to encourage the opening of shops and entertainment areas.

- **Shopping centres:** A **shopping centre** is a group of commercial establishments owned and managed as a single property. They offer variety and the ability to combine shopping with entertainment. Rents tend to be high in shopping centres, making it difficult for many shops to be profitable. In addition, small speciality shops may find it hard to compete with a shopping centre's key stores as such major department stores typically draw many shoppers.

- **Freestanding retailers:** Some shops, usually larger ones such as IKEA or PC World, are freestanding and are located by themselves in a separate building. These retailers benefit from lower rents and fewer parking problems. However, the shop must be attractive enough on its own to be a destination point for shoppers because it can't rely on spillover from consumers visiting other shops at the same place.

- **Non-traditional shop locations:** Innovative retailers find new ways to reach consumers. Many entrepreneurs use *carts*, which are small, movable shops that can be set up in many locations including inside shopping centres, in airports or in other public facilities; or *kiosks*, which are slightly larger and offer shop-like facilities including telephone points and electricity. Carts and kiosks are relatively inexpensive and a good way for new businesses to get started.

Site selection: choosing where to build   Long-term population patterns, the location of competitors and the demographic makeup of an area enter into retailers' decisions. The choice of where to open a new shop should reflect the company's overall

| Photos 14.6–14.8 | Different types of shop locations are best for different types of retailers. Retailers choose from among central business districts, shopping centres, freestanding shops and non-traditional locations
Sources: Pearson Education Ltd(t,c), Paris Franz (b) |

growth strategy. It should be consistent with long-term goals and be in a place that allows the company to best support the outlet. Location planners look at many factors when selecting a site. They want to find a place that is convenient to customers in the shop's **trade area**, i.e. the geographic zone that accounts for the majority of its sales and customers.[30] A *site evaluation* considers such specific factors as traffic flow; number of parking spaces available; ease of delivery access; visibility from the street; local planning laws that determine the types of buildings, parking, and signage allowed; and such cost factors as the length of the lease and the amount of local taxes.

Planners also consider such population characteristics as age profile and demographic characteristics, as well as mobility, i.e. how often people are moving in and out of the area? This type of information is available from a variety of private as well as public sources. Planners also have to consider the degree of competition they will encounter by locating in one place rather than another. One strategy followed by fast-food outlets is to locate in a *saturated trade area*. This is a site where a sufficient number of shops already exist so that high customer traffic is present, but where the retailer believes it can compete successfully by going head to head with the competition. The task, however, is getting harder and harder because at this point many of the good sites are already taken. Another strategy is to find an *understored trade area*, where too few shops exist to satisfy the needs of the population. The retailer can therefore establish itself as a dominant presence in the community. Over time, these areas may become *overstored* so that too many shops exist to sell the same goods. Those that can't compete are forced to move or close, as has happened to many small family-run shops that can't beat the supermarkets at their sophisticated retailing games.

A shop's targeted consumer segment also determines where it locates. For example, a new, growing community would be appealing for hardware retailers that can supply hammers and saws to homeowners, while upmarket dress shops and travel agencies might find better locations in more established areas because people living there have the income to spend on fashion items and holidays. Now that you've learned more about retail and distribution, read 'Real people, real decisions' to see which strategy Julia Gash decided upon.

Real people, real decisions

How it worked out at Bag It Don't Bin It

Julia decided to go for Option 3 and invested in e-tailing. The interactive website cost around €15,000 to build and has now generated in excess of €375,000 as a result. In order to make this a great success Julia devoted most of her marketing budget to developing the website and pays around €2,000 per month in website search optimisation fees. This ensures that the company appears on the first page when search engines are used to locate such bag suppliers. Today approximately 40 per cent of the company's total revenue comes from the website. A further 40 per cent, as previously explained, comes from repeat business and the remainder is from new business that is non-website generated – which is generated from exhibiting at trade shows and through word-of-mouth referrals. In addition to the website, with a cost of approximately €60 per month, Julia supplies an e-newsletter to existing customers. This is used to foster regular communication and provides information about new product development and sales promotions. The e-newsletter further helps to direct customers to the webpage and encourage direct orders, thus facilitating new business in an integrated fashion.

Chapter summary

Now that you have finished reading this chapter, you should be able to answer any of the following potential examination questions:

1. **Explain the concept of the value chain and the key elements in a supply chain.** The value chain consists of five primary activities (inbound logistics, operations, outbound logistics, marketing and sales, and service) and four support activities (procurement, technology development, human resource management and firm infrastructure). The process is called a value chain because each of these activities adds value to the product or service the customer eventually buys. Whereas the value chain is an overarching concept of how firms create value, the supply chain also encompasses components external to the firm itself, including all activities that are necessary to convert raw materials into a good or service and put it in the hands of the consumer or business customer.

2. **Explain what a distribution channel is and what functions distribution channels perform.** A distribution channel is a series of firms or individuals that facilitates the movement of a product from the producer to the final customer. Channels provide time, place and ownership utility for customers and reduce the number of transactions necessary for goods to flow from many manufacturers to large numbers of customers by breaking bulk and creating assortments. Channel members make the purchasing process easier by providing important customer services. Today the internet is becoming an important player in distribution channels.

3. **Describe the types of wholesaling intermediaries found in distribution channels.** Wholesaling intermediaries are firms that handle the flow of products from the manufacturer to the retailer or business user. Wholesalers are independent intermediaries that take title to a product. Agents and brokers are independent intermediaries that do not take title to products. Manufacturer-owned channel members can include sales branches, sales offices and manufacturers' showrooms.

4. **Describe the types of distribution channels and the steps in planning distribution channel strategies.** Distribution channels vary in length

from the simplest two-level channel to longer channels with three or more channel levels. Distribution channels include direct distribution, in which the producer sells directly to consumers, and indirect channels, which may include a retailer, wholesaler or other intermediary. Marketers begin channel planning by developing channel objectives and considering important environmental factors. The next step is to decide a distribution strategy, which involves determining the type of distribution channel that is best. Distribution tactics include the selection of individual channel members and management of the channel.

5. **Explain how logistics is used in the supply chain.** The supply chain includes all the firms that engage in activities that are necessary to turn raw materials into a good or service for a consumer or business customer, including those in the marketing channel of distribution. Every firm occupies a position in a value chain. Companies add value to inputs received from firms upstream. Logistics is the process of designing, managing and improving supply chains, including all those activities that are required to move products through the supply chain. Logistics activities include order processing, warehousing, materials handling, transportation and inventory control.

6. **Define retailing and explain how retailing has evolved.** Retailing is the process by which goods and services are sold to consumers for their personal use. The wheel of retailing hypothesis suggests that new retailers compete on price and over time become more upmarket, leaving room for other new, low-price entrants. The retail life cycle theory suggests retailing institutions are introduced, grow, reach maturity and then decline. Three factors that motivate retailers to evolve are changing demographics, technology and globalisation.

7. **Describe how retailers are classified.** Retailers can be classified by the level of service offered (self-service, full-service and limited-service retailers) and

by the merchandise assortment offered. Merchandise assortment is described in terms of breadth and depth, which refer to the number of product lines sold and the amount of variety available for each. Shops can be classified as supermarkets, speciality shops, department stores and hypermarkets.

8. **Describe B2C e-commerce and its benefits, limitations, and future promise.** B2C e-commerce and online exchanges between companies and consumers are growing rapidly. B2C benefits include greater convenience and greater product variety for consumers and opportunities for specialised businesses, lower business costs and instantaneous delivery of some products for marketers. For consumers, the downside of B2C e-commerce includes having to wait to receive products, security issues, and the inability to touch and feel products. For internet-only marketers, success may be difficult to achieve, whereas cannibalisation may be a problem with traditional retailers' online operations.

9. **Explain the importance of shop image to a retail positioning strategy and how a retailer can create an image in the marketplace.** Shop image is how the target market perceives the store relative to the competition. It incorporates the results from many different elements working together to create the most desirable shopping experience, and to ensure that shoppers view a shop favourably relative to the competition. Colour, lighting, scents, furnishings and other design elements called atmospherics are used to create a 'feel' for a shop environment. Use of atmospherics includes decisions on (1) layout, which determines traffic flow and influences customer behaviour in the shop; (2) the use of fixtures and open space; (3) the use of sound to attract (or repel) certain types of customers; and (4) the use of colour and lighting that can influence customers' moods. The number and type of shop personnel, pricing of products sold in the shop and store location contribute to a shop's image. Major types of retail locations include shopping centres, freestanding retailers and non-traditional locations.

Key terms

Chapter review

Marketing concepts: testing your knowledge

1. What is a value chain?

2. What is a supply chain, and how is it different from a channel of distribution?

3. What is a channel of distribution? What are channel intermediaries?

4. Explain the functions of distribution channels.

5. What factors are important in determining whether a manufacturer should choose a direct or indirect channel? Why do some firms use hybrid marketing systems?

6. What are conventional, vertical and horizontal marketing systems?

7. Explain intensive, exclusive and selective forms of distribution.

8. Explain the steps in distribution planning.

9. What is logistics? Explain the functions of logistics.

10. Define retailing. What is the role of retailing in today's world?

11. How do the wheel of retailing and retail life cycle theories explain the evolution of retailing? How do demographics, technology and globalisation affect the future of retailing?

12. How are shops classified? Describe the differences in merchandise assortments for supermarkets, speciality shops, discount stores, department stores and hypermarkets.

13. What is B2C e-commerce? What are some benefits of B2C e-commerce for consumers and for marketers? What are the limitations of B2C e-commerce?

14. What are some possible effects of B2C e-commerce on traditional retailing?

15. How is shop positioning strategy like theatre?

16. What is shop image? Why is it important?

17. What is meant by atmospherics? How can the elements of atmospherics be used to increase a shop's success? How are shop personnel a part of shop image?

18. What are some of the different types of locations? What are their advantages and disadvantages?

Marketing concepts: discussing choices

1. The supply chain concept looks at both the inputs of a firm and the means of firms that move the product from the manufacturer to the consumer. Do you think *marketers* should be concerned with the total supply chain concept? Why or why not?

2. You have probably heard someone say, 'The reason products cost so much is because of all the intermediaries'. Do intermediaries increase the cost of products? Would consumers be better off or worse off without intermediaries?

3. Many entrepreneurs choose to start a franchise business rather than 'go it alone'. Do you think franchises offer the typical business person good opportunities? What are some positive and negative aspects of purchasing a franchise?

4. As universities are looking for better ways to satisfy their customers, an area of increasing interest is the distribution of their service, i.e. education. Describe the characteristics of your business school's channel(s) of distribution. What types of innovative distribution might make sense for your school to try?

5. The wheel of retailing theory suggests that the normal path for a retailer is to enter the marketplace with lower priced goods and then to increase quality, services and prices. Why do you think this happens? Is it the right path for all retailers? Why or why not?

6. Department stores in the UK appear to be declining in popularity but remain consumers' primary place to shop in other countries such as Japan. Why do you think this is so? Are there ways that department stores can turn this trend around?

Marketing practice: applying what you've learned

1. Assume that you have recently been hired by a firm that manufactures furniture. You feel that marketing should have an input into supplier selection for the firm's products, but the purchasing department says that should not be a concern for marketing. You need to explain to them the importance of the value chain perspective. In a role-playing exercise, explain to the purchasing manager the value chain concept, why it is of concern to marketing and why the two of you should work together.

2. Assume that you are the director of marketing for a firm that manufactures cleaning chemicals. You have traditionally sold these products through manufacturer's reps and are now considering adding a direct internet channel to your distribution strategy, but you aren't sure whether this will create channel conflict. Make a list of the pros and cons of this move. What do you think is the best decision?

3. As a one-person marketing department for a confectionery manufacturer (your firm makes high-quality, hand-dipped chocolates using only natural ingredients), you are considering making changes in your distribution strategy. Your products have previously been sold through a network of food brokers that call on speciality food and gift shops. However, you think that perhaps it would be good for your firm to develop a corporate vertical marketing system (that is, vertical integration). In such a plan, a number of company-owned shops would be opened across the country. The chief executive of your company has asked that you present your ideas to the company executives. In a role-playing situation with one of your fellow students, present your ideas to your boss, including the advantages and disadvantages of the new plan compared to the current distribution method.

4. Assume that you have recently been given a new marketing assignment by your firm. You are to head up development of a distribution plan for a new product line – a series of do-it-yourself instruction DVDs for home gardeners. These DVDs would show consumers how to plant trees, shrubbery and bulbs; how to care for their plants; how to prune; and so on. You know that in developing a distribution plan, it is essential that you understand and consider a number of internal and external environmental factors. Make a list of the information you will need before you can begin developing the distribution plan. How will you adapt your plan based on each of these factors?

5. Assume you are a business consultant for a chain of traditional department stores. In recent years, the stores have seen declining revenues as speciality shops and hypermarkets have begun to squeeze the department stores out. The chain has asked you for suggestions on how to increase its business. Develop an outline of your recommendations and present your plan to your class.

6. As a university graduate, you and a friend think the career you really would enjoy means being your own boss – you want to start your own business. You feel the future of e-commerce is the place for you to make your fortune. You and your friend are considering two options: (1) a business that sells custom-made jeans based on customers' measurements online and (2) a business that sells gourmet foods from around the world online. In a role-playing exercise, debate with your friend the pros and cons of each of these two online retail businesses and make a decision on which is the best option.

7. All your life you've wanted to be an entrepreneur and to own your own business. Now you're ready to graduate from university, you've decided to open a combination coffee shop and bookshop in a location near your university. You know that to attract both the college student market and other customers from the local community, it will be necessary to design the shop's image carefully. Develop a detailed plan that specifies how you will use atmospherics to create the image you desire.

8. In your job with a marketing consulting firm, you are often asked to make recommendations for shop location. Your current client is a local caterer that is planning to open a new retail outlet for selling take-away gourmet dinners. You are examining the possible types of locations: a shopping centre, a freestanding entity or some non-traditional location. Outline the advantages and disadvantages of each type of location. Present your recommendations to your client.

9. Assume that you are the director of marketing for a national chain of convenience stores. Your firm has about 200 stores across Europe. The stores are fairly traditional both in design and in the merchandise they carry. Because you want to be proactive in your marketing planning, you are concerned that your firm may need to consider making significant changes because of the current demographic, technological and global trends in the marketplace. You think it is important to discuss these things with the other executives at your firm. Develop a presentation that includes the following:

   a. A discussion of the demographic changes that will affect your stores.

   b. A discussion of the technological changes that will affect your stores.

   c. A discussion of how global changes may provide problems and opportunities for your organisation.

   d. Your recommendations for how your firm might meet the challenges faced in each of these areas.

Marketing mini project: learning by doing

(A) In Europe the distribution of most products is fairly easy. There are lots of independent intermediaries (wholesalers, dealers, distributors and retailers) that are willing to cooperate to get the product to the final customer. State of the art motorway networks often combine with rail, air and water transportation to provide excellent means for moving goods from one part of Europe to another. In many other countries, the means for distribution of products are far less efficient and effective. For this miniproject, you and one or more of your classmates should first select a consumer product, probably one you normally purchase. Then use either library sources or other people or both (retailers, manufacturers, dealers, classmates and so on) to gather information to do the following:

1. Describe the path the product takes to get from the producer to you. Draw a model to show each of the

steps the product takes. Include as much as you can about transportation, warehousing, materials handling, order processing, stock control and so on.

2. Select another country in which the same or a similar product is sold. Describe the path the product takes to get from the producer to the customer in that country.

3. Determine if the differences between the two countries cause differences in price, availability or quality of the product.

4. Make a presentation to your class on your findings.

(B) This project is designed to help you understand how atmospherics play a role in consumers' perceptions of a shop.

1. First, select two retail outlets where students at your university are likely to shop. It will be good if you can select two outlets that you feel are quite different in terms of shop image but that sell the same types of products. You might consider two speciality women's clothing shops, two jewellery shops, two department stores or two coffee shops.

2. Visit each of the shops and write down a detailed description of the atmosphere, i.e. colours, materials used, types of displays, lighting fixtures, product displays, shop personnel and so on.

3. Survey some of the students in your university. Develop a brief questionnaire asking about the perceptions of the two shops you are studying. You may want to ask about such things as the quality of merchandise, prices, competence and friendliness of the shop personnel, the attitude of management towards customer service and so on. What is the 'personality' of each shop?

4. Develop a report of your findings. Compare the description of the shops with the results of the survey. Attempt to explain how the different elements of the shop atmosphere create each shop's unique image.

Real people, real surfers

Exploring the web (A)

Visit the website for UPS (www.ups.com). UPS has positioned itself as a full service provider of logistics solutions. After reviewing its website, answer the following questions:

1. What logistics services does UPS offer its customers?

2. What does UPS say to convince prospective customers that its services are better than those of the competition?

Exploring the web (B)

Many traditional retailers now have websites. Other online retailers do not have actual shops but practise only direct selling. Visit the sites of one or two popular retailers of your choice, then visit the site of a direct-only retailer.

1. Describe each retailer's website. What information is available on each site? How easy was each to navigate? What information did you find interesting and useful on each site? What did you find that you didn't expect to find at a retailer site? What did you find lacking at each site?

2. What differences are there for sites that have traditional bricks-and-mortar shops from those that do not? Does the site encourage consumers to visit the physical shop or just to remain an online shopper?

3. How do the retailers' websites communicate the image or personality of their shops? How are they alike? How are they different? If you had no information except that available on the web, would you know what types of products are sold; whether the products sold are expensive, prestige products or low-priced products; and what types of consumers each retailer is attempting to attract to its shops? How does each site use graphics or other design elements to represent the 'setting' as retailers do in their shops? How do they communicate the type of consumer they consider their primary market?

4. What recommendations would you make to each retailer to improve its website?

Now, take a look at the website at www.pearsoned.co.uk/solomon to see some videos from YouTube relating to aspects of this chapter.

Marketing plan exercise

A. Dell is a company that has traditionally used one fairly simple supply chain system – direct sales over the internet or by phone to both business and consumer users. In planning for the future, Dell has been exploring potentially making use of other distribution channels and outlets. They are already using kiosks at major airports to demonstrate and sell products. Yet in considering expanding their channels they certainly don't want to damage the backbone of their supply chain process – the direct channel.

1. If you were a marketing executive at Dell, what supply chain options would you suggest in designing a marketing plan beyond the company's traditional distribution model?

2. Can Dell successfully coexist in retail store distribution and in distribution through their traditional direct means? Justify your answer.

3. Assume that your plan recommends Dell become more aggressive in pursuing distribution through shops and other means beyond their traditional direct channel. What intermediaries do you recommend become part of their supply chain? Why?

B. The wheel of retailing suggests that new retailers enter the marketplace by offering goods at lower prices than competitors and that after they gain a foothold they 'trade up', improving their facilities and their merchandise assortment. Think about a new retail venture, a speciality shop that sells time pieces, such as men's and ladies' watches and clocks.

1. What retailing strategies do you recommend for the new retailer for their first two years in business – what merchandise, what shop image and what location(s)?

2. What long-term retailing strategies do you recommend?

Delve deeper into retailing and distribution

Now that you have obtained an overview relating retailing and distribution, you may wish to explore the subject in greater depth. We have therefore called on the expertise of Professor Leigh Sparks (Professor of Retail Studies, Institute for Retail Studies University of Stirling) to discuss the area further and recommend some key readings.

Professor Leigh Sparks

Institute for Retail Studies, University of Stirling

All of us think we know about retailing. Many of us feel that we might know something about supply chains, or how products get into consumers' hands. This chapter shows that distribution channels are inherently variable and are socially and economically constructed. Retailers have gained power in the channel and have become ever more important in meeting consumer needs. The ways retailers structure channels, organise manufacturers, replace wholesalers and organise product distribution are ever more critical in consumer and business-to-business marketing. Doing this sustainably given pressures on supply chains is becoming a massive contemporary issue.

The two papers I have selected cover aspects of this retail transformation and its impacts. Dawson (2000) reviews the state of retailing at 2000 and points to the challenges facing retail executives and researchers. He identifies key issues including scale, brands, overcapacity of retail space, consumer change, the remit and scope of retailing and the impact of e-retail. Levy et al. (2005), writing a few years later, likewise identify challenges for retailers in the structure and evolution of retailing and note five key 'levers': merchandise, technology, supply chain management, price optimisation and store name/image. Whilst there are similarities in the two frameworks for discussion, a close reading of both will provide an understanding of changing retail but also perhaps a greater awareness of the different European and American perspectives. Enjoy!

References

J. A. Dawson (2000) 'Retailing at Century End: Some Challenges for Management and Research', *International Review of Retail, Distribution and Consumer Research* 10, 119–48.

M. Levy, D. Grewal, R. A. Paterson and B. Connolly (2005) 'The Concept of the "Big Middle"', *Journal of Retailing* 81, 83–8.

Marketing in action case

Real decisions, Wal-Mart in Germany

Wal-Mart was approaching the start of the twenty-first century as one of the most successful and globally known retail chains in the world. The strategy of low pricing and huge inventory had proven to be a massive hit in the North American market, and the company had recently expanded into the Southern American countries of Argentina and Brazil. As the turn of the century approached the organisation was looking to expand its business further into the highly lucrative European Union.

As the largest country in Europe, with the largest consumer population and strongest performing economy, Germany seemed like the perfect pre-made market for Wal-Mart to launch its European invasion. A highly developed economy as well as a democratic, western culture provided Wal-Mart with what it believed to be the perfect opportunity for a fast market entry and quick market share growth. However, ten years after market entry the world expressed its shock as Wal-Mart announced its retreat after making huge losses. What had gone wrong for Wal-Mart?

Wal-Mart entered the German market in 1998 on the back of huge success in the US and as the world's largest international retailer. Wal-Mart considered Germany as an ideal market. The large population, demographics, strong economy and already established infrastructure would allow the retailer to simply purchase an existing chain and begin operating in a quick, convenient market entry strategy. Suitable German retail chains were therefore identified as acquisition targets (Wertkauf and Interspar), and Wal-Mart were ready to begin trading. As Germany was considered a western European culture, there was no forethought that the United States-engineered business styles or consumer and employee practices would enjoy anything other than the success seen in the US.

However, after losing an estimated $200 million a year until it finally withdrew in 2006, at a further estimate of $1 billion, management of Wal-Mart were left considering how they had got it so wrong. How could a firm with such strong business structures, a proven recipe for success in competitive markets face such a disastrous failure in what was the third biggest retail market in the world?

Wal-Mart envisaged no issues with its entry strategy, and did not consider how the differences in the German market could impact on the success of its existing competitive strategies. However, the firm was faced with a far more complex and competitive environment than it had been expecting. The simple entry strategy of adopting the established US practices to a foreign market alienated an extremely different German consumer market. As Wal-Mart spokesperson Beth Keck put it, 'We literally bought the two chains and said, Hey, we are in Germany, isn't this great?'

The mistake that Wal-Mart made was to oversimplify the international management landscape by ignoring cultural management, with catastrophic consequences. When Wal-Mart entered Germany it decided not to adapt to the German market by adopting any cultural or business norms, but rather to impose its own successful culture from the US into the German market. The cultural clash began with the appointment of an American who could not speak German as the mastermind of Wal-Mart's move. The appointment outlined from an early stage that Wal-Mart was going to keep its American culture and principles of business activities in the German market. It also demonstrated that the organisation missed opportunities to involve locals from the German market who would have been able to advise the company on how to avoid some of the mistakes, through their home-market knowledge and understanding.

The chain quickly became infamous in German press for a 'Bizarre' company culture that left both employees and customers feeling awkward and uncomfortable. The Americanised rituals, including a morning 'Wal-Mart chant' that was forced upon employees, were seen as ridiculous by employees, and word quickly got out to the public. Customers were also subjected to Americanised customs through 'Welcomers' who greeted shoppers at the door and bag packers. These were used despite being seen as very unusual in

German retailing. Wal-Mart also failed due to a lack of market research, not only into the culture of the target market, but also into purchasing habits and the competitive environment. Wal-Mart failed to properly research the chains that it had bought and ended up buying stores that were in undesirable locations. Whilst a higher percentage of US consumers are willing to drive to remote stores, out-of-town locations in Germany are far less desirable for German consumers.

Wal-Mart's failure in the German market can be marked down in part to a hubristic approach to business. After its success in the US, Wal-Mart believed it could simply incorporate its values and strategy in any consumer market and be successful. The company was not guilty of misunderstanding the complicated cultural differences of the German consumer market, it simply did not recognise it until it was too late. However, it has shown in its expansion activities since the German failure that it is far more willing to adapt to the local environment, even operating under different localised names such as Asda in the UK, Seiyu in Japan and Bompreço in Brazil.

Things to think about

1. What decisions was Wal-Mart faced with after entering the German market?

2. What aspects of culture need to be considered when moving to international markets?

3. What changes could Wal-Mart have made when entering the German retail market to ensure success and why?

4. What role does market research play when moving a business internationally?

5. If you were responsible for establishing a retail outlet overseas, which factors would you consider to be the most important?

Case study written by Richard Hodgins, University of Sheffield.

Further information relating to Wal-Mart has also been provided by Richard. www.youtube.com/watch?v=_KA9LqsHSfY www.youtube.com/watch?v=Cur173EbQLU www.youtube.com/user/WalmartCorporate#p/c/1D8F048F9BC92179/19/NySa2ps1OVU

References

1. Thomas L. Friedman, *The World is Flat: A Brief History of the Twenty-First Century* (New York: Farrar, Straus and Giroux, 2006).

2. Paula D. Harveston, Basil G. Englis, Michael R. Solomon and Marla Goldsmith, 'Knowledge Management as Competitive Advantage: Lessons from the Textile and Apparel Value Chain', *Journal of Knowledge Management* 9, no. 2 (2005), 91–102.

3. Rowland T. Moriarty and Ursula Moran, 'Managing Hybrid Marketing Systems', *Harvard Business Review* (November–December 1990), 2–11.

4. Nirmalya Kumar, 'Living with Channel Conflict', *CMO: The Resource for Marketing Executives*, www.cmomagazine.com/read/100104/channel_conflict.html.

5. www.oneworld.com/home.cfm.

6. www.starbucks.com/aboutus/sup_div.asp.

7. Kumar, 'Living with Channel Conflict'.

8. Toby B. Gooley, 'The Who, What, and Where of Reverse Logistics', *Logistics Management* 42 (February 2003), 38–44; James R. Stock, *Development and Implementation of Reverse Logistics Programs*, Council of Logistics Management (1998), 20.

9. www.supplychainmetric.com/perfect.htm.

10. Faye W. Gilbert, Joyce A. Young and Charles R. O'Neal, 'Buyer–Seller Relationships in Just-in-Time Purchasing Environments', *Journal of Organizational Research* 29 (February 1994), 111–20.

11. Kasra Ferdows, Michael A. Lewis and Jose A.D. Machuca, 'Zara's Secret for Fast Fashion', *Harvard Business Review*, 21 February 2005, http://199.94.20.134/item.jhtml?id=4652&t=operations.

12. Michael Levy and Barton A. Weitz, *Retailing Management*, 3rd ed. (Boston, MA: Irwin/McGraw-Hill, 1998).

13. Stanley C. Hollander, 'The Wheel of Retailing', *Journal of Retailing* (July 1960), 41.

14. William R. Davidson, Albert D. Bates and Stephen J. Bass, 'The Retail Life Cycle', *Harvard Business Review* (November–December 1976), 89.

15. Lauren Foster and Andrew Ward, 'McDonald's Drinks Menu May Grow', *Food and Beverage*, 19 June 2006, 28.

16. Cathy Horyn, 'A Store Made for Right Now: You Shop until It's Dropped', *New York Times*, 17 February 2004, www.nytimes.com.

17. Thomas M. Anderson, 'Checkups on the Run', *Kiplinger Personal Finance* (May 2006), 96.

18. Ian Austen, 'In Germany, Customers Scan as They Shop', *New York Times*, 12 May 2003, www.nytimes.com; Annick Moes, 'Technology Rules "Future Store" by Tracking Shoppers and Sales', *Wall Street Journal*, 19 June 2003, www.wsj.com.

19. Ken Belson, 'As Starbucks Grows, Japan, Too, Is Awash', *New York Times*, 21 October 2001, http://query.nytimes.com/search/abstract?res= F50F14FF3B50C728EDDA90994D9404482

20. Juhnyoung Lee, Robert Hoch, Mark Podlaseck, Edith Schonberg and Stephen Gomory, 'Analysis and Visualization of Metrics for online Merchandising', www.research.ibm.com/iac/papers/lncs.pdf.

21. Joan Raymond, 'Nomore Shoppus Interruptus', *American Demographics* (May 2001), 39.

22. Rebecca Quick, 'Hope Springs A new for web Retailers: Study Shows Many are Making Money', *Wall Street Journal* 18 April 2000, www.wsj.com; Randy Myers, 'E-Tailers & Space Invaders', e-CFO 47(7) (April 2000).

23. Helen Coster, 'Consumer Spy: Do You Have Quirky Tastes in Mail-Order Shopping? Chances are Abacus Knows All About You', *Forbes* (January 2006), 91.

24. 'A Wide World of Sports Shoes: Fixtures Enhance Appeal of World Foot Locker', *Chain Store Age Executive* (January 1993), 176–81.

25. Jane J. Kim, 'A Latte with Your Loan?', *The Wall Street Journal*, 17 May 2006, D1.

26. Tracie Rozhon, 'High Fashion, from Front Door to the Top Floor', *New York Times*, 31 July 2003, www.nytimes.com.

27. L.W. Turley and Ronald E. Milliman, 'Atmospheric Effects on Shopping Behavior: A Review of the Experimental Evidence', *Journal of Business Research* 49 (2000), 193–211.

28. Julie Flaherty, 'Ambient Music Has Moved to Record Store Shelves', *New York Times*, 4 July 2001, www.nytimes.com.

29. Deborah Blumenthal, 'Scenic Design for In-Store Try-Ons', *New York Times*, April 1988. 'Service: Retail's No. 1 Problem', *Chain Store Age*, 19 January 1987.

30. Michael Levy and Barton A. Weitz, *Retailing Management*, 3rd ed. (Boston: Irwin/McGraw-Hill, 1998).

Appendix A
Sample marketing plan
The B & V Smoothie Company

Executive summary

Situation analysis

B & V Smoothie Company is an entrepreneurial organisation that produces fruit-and-yogurt-based beverages with superior flavour and nutritional content and unique packaging. Within Europe, B & V has targeted a consumer market of younger, health-conscious, upmarket consumers who regularly exercise at gyms and health clubs, and two broad re-seller markets: (1) gyms and health clubs and (2) small upmarket food markets. B & V distributes its products through agents in the EU and via the internet. An analysis of the internal and external environments suggests the firm enjoys important strengths in its product, its employees and its reputation, while weaknesses are seen in its limited size, financial resources and product capabilities. B & V faces a supportive external environment, highlighted by a growing interest in healthy living, and limited threats, primarily from potential competitive growth.

Marketing objectives

The B & V marketing objectives are to increase awareness, gross sales (50 per cent) and distribution, and to introduce two new product lines over the next three years:

- a line of low-carbohydrate smoothies
- a line of gourmet flavoured smoothies

Marketing strategies

To accomplish its growth goals, B & V will direct its marketing activites toward the following strategies:

1. *Target Market Strategy:* B & V will continue to target its existing consumer markets while expanding its business-to-business markets to include hotels and resorts, golf and tennis clubs, and university campuses.

2. *Positioning Strategy:* B & V will continue to position its products as the first-choice smoothie beverage for the serious health-conscious consumer, including those who are seeking to lower their carbohydrate intake.

3. *Product Strategy:* B & V will introduce two new product lines, each identifiable through unique packaging/labelling:

    a. **B & V Smoothie Gold:** a product similar to the original B & V Smoothie beverages but in six unique flavours.

    b. **Low-Carbohydrate B & V Smoothie:** a product with 50 per cent fewer grammes of carbohydrates.

4. *Pricing Strategy:* B & V will maintain the current pricing strategy for existing and new products.

5. *Promotion Strategy:* B & V will augment current personal selling efforts with television and magazine advertising, with sponsorships of key sporting events in major cities and with a sampling programme.

6. *Supply Chain Strategy:* B & V will expand its distribution network to include the business-to-business markets targeted. In addition, to encourage a high level of inventory in larger health clubs, B & V Smoothie will offer free refrigerated display units.

Implementation and control

The Action Plan details how the marketing strategies will be implemented including the individual(s) responsible, the timing of each activity, and the budget necessary. The measurement and control strategies provide a means of measurement of the success of the plan.

Situation analysis

The B & V Smoothie Company[1] was founded in September 1998 in London with the goal of creating and marketing healthy 'smoothie' beverages for sale to health-conscious consumers. B & V Smoothie expects to take advantage of an increasing desire for healthy foods in Europe – and to ride the wave of consumer interest in low-carbohydrate alternatives. While there are other companies, both large and small, competing in this market, B & V Smoothie feels it has the expertise to create and market superior products that will appeal to its target market.

Internal environment

Mission statement

The strategic direction and actions of the B & V Smoothie Company are driven by its mission:

> B & V Smoothie seeks to meet the needs of discriminating, health-conscious consumers for high-quality, superior-tasting smoothie beverages and other similar products.

Organisational structure

As an entrepreneurial company, B & V Smoothie does not have a very sophisticated organisational structure. Key personnel include the following:

- Patrick Bradley, founder and co-director. Bradley is responsible for the creation, design, packaging, and production management of all B & V Smoothie products.
- William Vince, founder and co-director. Vince is responsible for international and domestic distribution and marketing.
- Gayle Humphries, head of finance. Humphries develops the financial strategy and keeps the company's books.
- Alex Johnson, national sales manager. Johnson is responsible for maintaining the sales force of independent sales reps. He also advises on product development.
- Rob LeMay, Pam Sartens and Paul Sartens, shareholders. Next to Patrick Bradley and William Vince, Rob, Pam and Paul own the largest number of shares. They consult and sit on the company's board of directors. Rob is a lawyer and also provides legal services.

Corporate culture

B & V Smoothie is an entrepreneurial organisation. Thus, a key element of the internal environment is a culture that encourages innovation, risk taking and individual creativity. The company's beginning was based on a desire to provide a unique, superior product, and company decisions have consistently emphasised this mission.

Products

The original B & V Smoothie, introduced in mid-1999, was a fruit-and-yogurt-based beverage that contained only natural ingredients (no additives) and was high in essential nutrients. Table A.1 provides nutritional information for the 340g size B & V Smoothie beverage. Because of the company's patented manufacturing process, B & V Smoothie beverages do not have to be refrigerated and have a shelf life of over a year. Therefore, the product can be shipped and delivered via non-refrigerated carriers. B & V Smoothie currently sells its beverages exclusively through gyms, health clubs and small upmarket food markets.

At present, the single product line is the B & V Smoothie fruit-and-yogurt beverage. This healthy beverage product has a flavour and nutritional content that makes it superior to competing products. The present product comes in five flavours: strawberry, blueberry, banana, peach and cherry. B & V offers each in a 340g and a 565g size. B & V packages the product in a uniquely shaped, frosted glass bottle with a screw-off cap. The bottle design makes the product easy to hold, even with sweaty hands after workouts. The frosted glass allows the colour of the beverage to be seen but at the same time communicates an upmarket image. The labelling and lid visually denote the flavour with an appropriate colour. Labelling includes complete nutritional information. In the future, B & V Smoothie plans to expand its line of products to increase its market share of the health drink market.

Pricing of B & V Smoothie beverages is as follows:

	340g	565g
Suggested retail price	€4.00	€6.00
Price to retail outlets (health clubs, etc.)	€2.00	€3.00
Price to distributor/discount to sales agent	€1.00	€1.50

Thus, B & V Smoothie receives €1.00 in revenue for each 340g bottle and €1.50 in revenue for each 565g bottle it sells.

Table A.1
Nutritional information: B & V Smoothie beverage

Serving Size: 340g	Amount per Serving	% Daily Value
Calories-	140	
Calories from fat	6	
Total fat	0.5 g	1
Saturated fat	0.5 g	2
Cholesterol	6 mg	2
Sodium	70 mg	3
Potassium	100 mg	3
Total carbohydrates	10 g	3
Dietary fibre	5 g	20
Sugar	1 g	
Protein	25 g	50
Vitamin A		50
Vitamin C		50
Calcium		20
Iron		30
Vitamin D		40
Vitamin E		50
Thiamin		50
Riboflavin		50
Niacin		50
Vitamin B_6		50
Vitamin B_{12}		50
Biotin		50
Pantothenic acid		50
Phosphorus		10
Iodine		50
Chromium		50
Zinc		50
Folic acid		50

At present, B & V Smoothie outsources actual production of the product. Still, the company takes care to oversee the entire production process to ensure consistent quality of its unique product. With this method of production, variable costs for the 340g B & V Smoothie beverages are €0.63, and variable costs for the 565g are €0.71. Current annual fixed costs for B & V Smoothie office space, management salaries and professional services are as follows:

Salaries and employee benefits	€275,000
Office rental, equipment, and supplies	€24,600
Expenses related to sales (travel, etc.)	€32,000
Advertising and other marketing communications	€50,000
Total fixed costs	**€381,600**

Sales of the two sizes of the product are approximately equal; that is, half of sales are for the 340g size and half are for the 565g size. Thus, there is an average contribution margin of €0.58 per bottle. Based on this, to achieve breakeven, B & V Smoothie must sell

$$€381,600/.58 = 657,931 \text{ units}$$

Again, assuming equal sales of the two size products, the break-even point in euros is €822,413.

Previous sales

Sales of B & V Smoothie products have continued to grow since their introduction to the market in 1999. Actual sales figures for 2004 through to 2011 are shown in Table A.2.

Markets

The consumer market for B & V Smoothie products is made up of anyone who is interested in healthy food and a healthy lifestyle. Although according to published research, nearly 70 per cent of European consumers say they are interested in living a healthy lifestyle, the number of those who actually work to achieve that goal is much smaller. It is estimated that approximately 40 million Europeans actually engage in exercise and/or follow nutritional plans that would be described as healthy. As experts expect the trend

Table A.2
Company sales performance

Year	Gross Sales
2004	€87,000
2005	€238,000
2006	€311,000
2007	€436,000
2008	€618,000
2009	€650,000
2010	€710,000
2011	€765,000

toward healthier living to grow globally, the European and international markets for B & V Smoothie products are expected to expand for some time.

Within the European consumer market, B & V Smoothie targets upmarket consumers who regularly work out at gyms and health clubs. While these consumers are primarily younger, there is also a growing older segment that seeks to be physically fit and that also uses health clubs.

Channels

In order to reach its target market, B & V Smoothie places primary emphasis on health clubs and other physical fitness facilities and small, upmarket speciality food markets. The company began developing channel relationships with these outlets through individual contacts by company personnel. As sales developed, the company solicited the services of agents and speciality food distributors. Agents are individuals who sell products for a number of different non-competing manufacturers. By contracting with these agents in various geographic regions, the company can expand its product distribution in a significant number of countries throughout Europe.

The company handles various large accounts for national gym chains. While total sales to these chains are fairly substantial, when considering the large number of facilities within each chain the sales are very small, with much room for growth. The internet is a secondary channel for B & V Smoothie. Online retail outlets currently account for only 5 per cent of B & V Smoothie sales. While this channel is useful for individuals who wish to purchase B & V Smoothie products in larger quantities, B & V does not expect that online sales will become a significant part of the business in the near future.

 # External environment

Competitive environment

B & V Smoothie faces several different levels of competition. Direct competitors are companies that also market smoothie-type beverages and include the following:

1. Franchise smoothie retail operations.

2. Online-only smoothie outlets.

3. Other smaller manufacturers.

4. Larger companies such as Nestlé that produce similar products.

Indirect competition comes from the following:

1. Homemade smoothie drinks made from powders sold in retail outlets and over the internet.

2. Homemade smoothie drinks made using a multitude of available recipes.

3. Other healthy beverages, such as juices.

Economic environment

B & V Smoothie first introduced its products during a period of relative prosperity. Economic growth in Europe has remained somewhat stable during recent years and sales have increased. Analysts estimate that total gross domestic product (GDP) will increase a little over 2 per cent annually over the next few years in Europe.

Technological environment

Because B & V Smoothie produces a simple food product, technological advances have minimum impact on the firm's operations. Nevertheless, the use of current technology enables and enhances many of the company's operations. For example, B & V Smoothie uses the internet to enhance its operations in two ways. First, the internet provides an additional outlet for sales. In addition, agents and channel members can keep in contact with the company, allowing for fewer problems with deliveries, orders, and so on.

Political and legal environment

Because they are advertised as nutritional products, all B & V Smoothie products must be approved by the appropriate food regulatory body in each European country where the goods are destined. Labelling must also conform to similar regulations. In Europe, there are numerous regulations that are country-specific which the company must constantly remain aware of.

Sociocultural environment

The social and cultural environment continues to provide an important opportunity for B & V Smoothie. The trend toward healthy foods and a healthier lifestyle has grown dramatically for the past decade or longer. In response to this, the number of health clubs across Europe and the number of independent tourist resorts and spas have also grown. In addition, many travellers demand that hotels offer health club facilities.

During the past three years, consumers around the world have become more aware of the advantages of a low-carbohydrate diet. Analysts project that the target age group of 15- to 44-year-olds will remain stable in the foreseeable future, with an increase of less than 8 per cent projected to 2025. Similarly, their income should neither decrease nor increase significantly in the near future.

SWOT analysis

The SWOT analysis provides a summary of the strengths, weaknesses, opportunities and threats identified by B & V Smoothie through the analysis of their internal and external environments.

Strengths

The following are the strengths identified by B & V Smoothie:

- A creative and skilled employee team.
- A high-quality product recipe that provides exceptional flavour with high levels of nutrition.
- Because of its entrepreneurial spirit, the ability to remain flexible and to adapt quickly to environmental changes.
- A strong network of European agents and distributors.
- The growth of a reputation of a high-quality product among health clubs, other retail outlets and targeted consumer groups.

Weaknesses

The following are the weaknesses identified by B & V Smoothie:

- Limited financial resources for growth and for advertising and other marketing communications.
- Little flexibility in terms of personnel due to size of the firm.
- Reliance on external production to maintain quality standards and to meet any unanticipated surges in demand for the product.

Opportunities

The following are the opportunities identified by B & V Smoothie:

- A strong and growing interest in healthy living, both among young, upmarket consumers and among older consumers.
- Continuing consumer interest in low-carb alternatives that offer opportunities for additional product lines.

Threats

The following are the threats identified by B & V Smoothie:

- The potential for competitors, especially those with large financial resources who can invest more in promotion, to develop products that consumers may find superior.
- Economic downturn that might affect potential sales.
- Movement away from low-carbohydrate diets, particularly if other forms of dieting gain in popularity.

Marketing objectives

The following are the marketing objectives set by B & V Smoothie:

- To increase the awareness of B & V Smoothie products among the target market.
- To increase gross sales by 50 per cent over the next two years.
- To introduce two new product lines over the next three years: a line of low-carbohydrate smoothies and a line of gourmet flavoured smoothies.
- To increase distribution of B & V Smoothie products in more countries throughout the EU.

Marketing strategies

Target markets

Consumer markets

B & V Smoothies will continue to target its existing consumer markets. The primary consumer target market for B & V Smoothie beverages can be described as follows:

Demographics

- Male and female teens and young adults, ages 15–39
- Household income: €50,000 and above
- Education of head of household: university degree or above
- Primarily located in mid-sized to large European major cities

Psychographics

- Health-conscious, interested in living a healthy lifestyle
- Spend much time and money taking care of their bodies
- Enjoy holidays that include physical activities
- Live very busy lives and need to use time wisely to enjoy all they want to do
- Enjoy spending time with friends

Media habits

- The target market is more likely to get their news from television or the internet than from newspapers. They are likely to view not only the news channels but also the financial news networks.
- They prefer watching satellite to traditional TV channels.

Business-to-business markets

In the past, B & V Smoothie has targeted two categories of re-seller markets: (1) health clubs and gyms and (2) small upmarket speciality food markets. To increase distribution and sales of its products, B & V Smoothie will target the following in the future:

1. Hotels and resorts.

2. Golf and tennis clubs.

3. University campuses.

Upmarket young professionals frequently visit hotels and resorts, and they demand that business travel includes quality accommodation and first-rate health club facilities. The membership of golf and tennis clubs, while including many older consumers, is also an excellent means of providing products conveniently for the targeted groups. University students, probably more than any other consumer group, are interested in health and in their bodies. In fact, many universities have built large, fairly elaborate health and recreational facilities as a means of attracting students. Thus, providing B & V Smoothie beverages on university campuses is an excellent means of meeting the health beverage needs of this group.

 # Positioning the product

B & V Smoothie seeks to position its products as the first-choice smoothie beverage for the serious health-conscious consumer, including those who are seeking to lower their carbohydrate intake. The justification for this positioning is as follows. Many smoothie beverages are available. The B & V Smoothie formula provides superior flavour and nutrition in a shelf-stable form. B & V Smoothie has developed its product, packaging, pricing and promotion to communicate a superior, prestige image. This positioning is thus supported by all its marketing strategies.

 # Product strategies

To increase its leverage in the market and to meet its sales objectives, B & V Smoothie needs additional products. Two new product lines are planned:

1. *B & V Smoothie Gold:* This product will be similar to the original B & V Smoothie beverages but will come in six unique flavours:

   a. Piña colada

   b. Chocolate banana

   c. Apricot nectarine

   d. Pineapple berry crush

   e. Tropical cherry

   f. Peach delight

   To set the product apart from the original-flavour Smoothie beverages – the labels will include the name of the beverage and the logo in gold lettering, and the bottle cap will be black.

2. *Low-carbohydrate B & V Smoothie:* The low-carbohydrate B & V Smoothie beverage will have approximately 50 per cent fewer grammes of carbohydrates than the original Smoothie beverage or the B & V Smoothie Gold. The low-carbohydrate B & V Smoothie will come in the following four flavours:

   a. Strawberry

   b. Blueberry

   c. Banana

   d. Peach

Packaging for the low-carbohydrate B & V Smoothie will be similar to other B & V Smoothie beverages but will include the term 'Low Carbohydrate' in large type. The label will state that the beverage has 50 per cent fewer carbohydrates than regular smoothies.

Pricing strategies

The current pricing strategy will be maintained for the existing and new products. This pricing is appropriate for communicating a high-quality product image for all B & V Smoothie products. The company feels that creating different pricing for the new beverages would be confusing and could create negative attitudes among consumers. Thus, there is no justification for increasing the price of the new products.

Promotion strategies

In the past, B & V Smoothie has used mainly personal selling to promote its products to the trade channel. To support this effort, signage has been provided for the re-sellers to promote the product at the point of purchase. Posters and stand-alone table cards show appealing photographs of the product in the different flavours and communicate the brand name and the healthy benefits of the product. Similar signage will be developed for use by re-sellers who choose to stock the B & V Smoothie Gold and the Low-Carb Smoothies.

Selling has previously been handled by a team of over 75 agents who sell to re-sellers. In addition, in some markets, an independent distributor does the selling. To support this personal selling approach, B & V Smoothie plans for additional promotional activities to introduce its new products and meet its other marketing objectives. These include the following:

1. *Television advertising*: B & V Smoothie will purchase a limited amount of relatively inexpensive and targeted satellite channel advertising. A small number of commercials will be shown during prime-time programmes with high viewer ratings by the target market. Television advertising can be an important means of not only creating awareness of the product but also enhancing the image of the product. Indeed, consumers are prone to feel that if a product is advertised on prime-time TV, it must be a good product.

2. *Magazine advertising*: Because consumers in the target market are not avid magazine readers, magazine advertising will be limited and will supplement other promotion activities. During next year, B & V Smoothie will experiment with limited advertising in appropriate sporting magazines. The company will also investigate the potential of advertising in university newspapers.

3. *Sponsorships*: B & V Smoothie will attempt to sponsor several key sporting events in major cities. The advantage of sponsorship is it provides visibility for the product while at the same time showing that the company supports activities of interest to the target market.

4. *Sampling*: Sampling of B & V Smoothie beverages at select venues will provide an opportunity for prospective customers to become aware of the product and to taste the flavours. Sampling will include only the two new products being introduced. Venues for sampling will include the following:

   a. marathons

   b. Tour de France (cycling)

   c. gymnastic meetings

   d. student unions on selected campuses

Supply chain strategies

As noted earlier, B & V Smoothie distributes its beverages primarily through health clubs and gyms and small upmarket speciality food stores. B & V Smoothie plans to expand its target re-seller market to include the following:

- hotels and resorts
- golf and tennis clubs
- university campuses

To increase leverage in larger health clubs, B & V Smoothie will offer free refrigerated display units. This will encourage the facility to maintain a high level of stock of B & V Smoothie beverages which are ready to consume.

Implementation

The Action Plan details the activities necessary to implement all marketing strategies. In addition, the Action Plan includes the timing for each item, the individual(s) responsible and the budgetary requirements. Table A.3 shows an example of one objective (to increase distribution venues) and the action items B & V Smoothie will use to accomplish it.[2]

Table A.3
Action items for accomplishing marketing objective regarding supply chain: objective – increase distribution venues

Action Items	Beginning Date	Ending Date	Responsible Party	Cost	Remarks
1. Identify key hotels, resorts, golf clubs and tennis clubs where B & V Smoothies might be sold	1 July	1 September	Wm Vince (consulting firm will be engaged to assist in this effort)	€25,000	Key to this strategy is to selectively choose re-sellers so that maximum results are obtained from sales activities. Because health club use is greater during the months of January to May, effort will be timed to have product in stock no later than 10 January
2. Identify 25 key universities where B & V Smoothies might be sold	1 July	1 August	Wm Vince	0	Information about universities and their health club facilities should be available on the university web pages
3. Make initial contact with larger hotel and resort chains	1 September	1 November	Wm Vince	€10,000	
4. Make initial contact with larger individual (non-chain) facilities	1 September	1 November	Wm Vince	€5,000	
5. Make initial contact with universities	15 August	15 September	Agents	0	Agents will be assigned to the 25 universities and required to make an initial contact and report back to Wm Vince on promising prospects
6. Follow up initial contacts with all potential re-sellers and obtain contracts for the coming 6 months	15 September	On-going	Wm Vince and agents	€10,000	Although €10,000 is budgeted for this item, actual expenditures will be on an as-needed basis, as follow-up travel cannot be pre-planned

Measurement and control strategies

A variety of activities will ensure effective measurement of the success of the marketing plan and allow the firm to make adjustments as necessary. These include market research and trend analysis.

Research

Firms need continuous market research to understand brand awareness and brand attitudes among their target markets. B & V Smoothie will therefore commission exploratory research and descriptive benchmark studies of its target consumer and re-seller markets.

 ## Trend analysis

B & V Smoothie will carry out a monthly trend analysis to examine sales by re-seller type, country, chain, agent and distributor. This analysis will allow B & V Smoothie to take corrective action when necessary.

Notes

[1]B & V Smoothie Company is a fictitious company created to illustrate a sample marketing plan. The market data and statistics are also fictitious to provide a practical scenario for students to follow.
[2]Note that the final marketing plan should include objectives, action items, timing information and budget information necessary to accomplish all marketing strategies. We have only one objective in this sample marketing plan.

Appendix B
Marketing maths

To demonstrate the value of marketing, marketers must be detectives, tracking evidence about the marketing value chain. This requires the collection of financial and non-financial data and the application of some basic mathematics.

| Marketing Cost Utilisation | → | Customer Response | → | Profitable Revenues |

Environment → Customer Response

Figure B.1   The marketing value chain

We examine this first by looking at a simple example.

Mail-order firm

This example is a simplified illustration of the analysis carried out by mail-order businesses. It has been chosen for its simplicity in order to reveal the key pieces of evidence and their relevance to evaluating marketing's contribution.

Demonstrating value – the four steps

1. **Marketing cost allocation** The marketing department spends money sending direct mail to acquire new customers at a cost of 50p per letter. It can vary the volume of its acquisition mailing and in recent years has annually mailed between 1 million and 3 million letters.

2. **Customer response** Historical analysis of its mailing discloses a response rate of 2 per cent for annual mail volumes up to 2 million items and then response drops to 1 per cent for volumes above 2 million.

3. **Profitable revenues** Customer spending activity generates a profit contribution of £15 per customer per annum.

4. **Environment** After joining, members can continue buying from the wine club for many years. However, most do not continue but become inactive, and the number of active customers remaining from year to year is 70 per cent of the previous year's numbers.

Prediction

On the basis of the evidence in items 1–4 a predictive model (Table B.1) can be constructed to test alternative marketing expenditure decisions. The top section of the model contains

Marketing expenditure decision						
Marketing costs – printing, postage and lists	£/year	£ 1,500,000				
Linking expenditure to activity						
Production and postage	£/item	£0.50				
Mail volume = 2m	Mail items	2,000,000				
Mail volume > 2m	Mail items	1,000,000				
Linking our marketing to customer activity						
Response rate at volume = 2m	%	2				
Response rate at volume > 2m	%	1				
New customers	Customers/year	50,000				
Linking other factors to customer activity						
Retention rate	%	70	70	70	70	70
Customers – opening balance	Customers	50,000	35,000	24,500	17,150	12,005
Customers – closing balance	Customers	35,000	24,500	17,150	12,005	8,404
Linking customer activity to financial results						
Margin per customer	£/customer	£15	£15	£15	£15	£15
Margin from total customers	£/year	£750,000	£525,000	£367,500	£257,250	£180,075
Contribution after marketing	£/year	(£750,000)	£525,000	£367,500	£257,250	£180,075
Discount Rate (WACC)	%	10	10	10	10	10
Discounted cash flow (Years 1–5)		(£750,000)	£472,500	£297,675	£187,535	£118,147
Financial result (NPV 1–5)		£325,857				

Table B.1 Predictive model of mail-order wine club

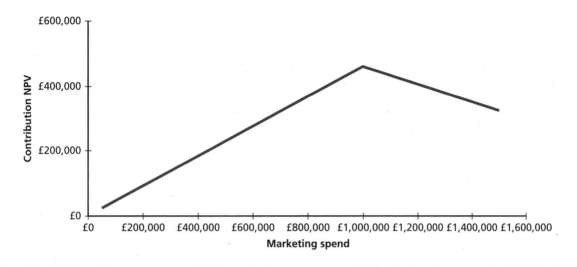

Figure B.2   Investigation of alternative levels of marketing expenditure

a cell for entering the financial expenditure decision to be evaluated. In this example an expenditure of £1.5 million is being evaluated.

The model next follows the links from expenditure to activity, arriving at a mailing volume of 3 million items. These have been split at the 2 million level, because in the next stage of the calculation responses will be calculated. The response to the first 2 million mailing at 2 per cent is 40,000 new customers and to the remaining 1 million mailing at 1 per cent is 10,000 new customers, making 50,000 in total. The model then looks at the effect of retention on customer numbers and shows them declining from 50,000 at the start of Year 1 to 8404 at the end of Year 5. Next the model links customer activity to financial results over Years 1–5. The accounting profit is negative in Year 1, as the marketing cost has been attributed to Year 1, but in Years 2, 3, 4 and 5 there are positive contributions. Finally on a Discounted Cash Flow basis, applying the Weighted Average Cost of Capital (WACC) of 10 per cent for the business, the Net Present Value (NPV) of this option is £325,857. Having constructed the model it can be used to investigate alternatives.

Ideas to increase value

The model can now be used to investigate alternative levels of marketing expenditure. The results of this investigation are shown in Figure B.2. The analysis finds a maximum financial value of £460,686 to be delivered at an expenditure level of £1 million.

The important lesson from this example is that there is no one magic metric that proves that marketing is doing the best possible job. What this example shows is there is a systematic process that can be followed, involving four kinds of evidence, that can reveal whether marketing resources are being applied with the maximum effectiveness.

Four elements of the marketing value chain

1. Marketing cost allocation

The following questions are important for you to answer.

1.1 Can we accurately assign costs to marketing activity?

1.2 Do we maintain effective records of marketing activity attributes?

1.3 Do we investigate cost-efficiency and drive down waste, scrap and re-work?

1.4 Do we source cost ingredients using effective procurement disciplines?

1.1 Cost accounting
Can we accurately assign costs to all marketing activity?

Marketing has been described as a mixer of ingredients. For example, direct marketing's ingredients are print, postage and address lists; TV advertising's ingredients are TV media spots and film footage. Each activity will have a different mix of ingredients and although these ingredients may be accurately accounted for under cost categories such as print and postage, the cost accounting system may not assign these costs to specific activities. For example, assigning costs to a TV campaign may require digging out information on media spot costs at a greater level of detail than held on the cost accounting system. Gathering this data provides valuable detail that will be needed as evidence.

1.2 Marketing activity attributes
Do we maintain effective records of marketing activity attributes?

Marketing activity can be described in many ways and it is important to record details of the activity at or around the time it occurs. Attributes are coding schemes associated with each marketing activity that facilitate evaluation of the value it adds. Three especially important attributes are: audience, offer and creative. Audience attributes are coding schemes for the people who were exposed to the marketing activity. Offer attributes are coding schemes for the product and price including any special deals, discounts etc. Creative attributes are coding schemes for the actual information and imagery to which the audience is exposed (in addition to offer information).

Audience attributes are usually threefold: audience profile, reach and frequency. The audience profile may be defined in terms of demographics (age, sex, income etc.), geographics (country, region, town etc.), psychographics (attitudes, interests) and in the case of B2B industry sector (retail, banking, etc.). The reach is the number of individuals exposed to a marketing activity within a given period of time and the frequency is the number of times they were exposed. There is no universal terminology, it is media specific, and related terms in specific media include coverage, penetration, exposure, footfalls, hits, insertions, circulation, readership, opportunities to see and ratings points. These attributes are generally obtained via the media owner and tend to be based on market and audience research. This research data is usually maintained by the media agency but often it is not passed to clients unless specifically requested.

Offer attributes are coding schemes for product and price. Marketing activities may make specific offers and in these cases it is very important to record the specifics of each offer. In other cases, for example corporate image campaigns, no explicit offer is made, and it is important to include codes for these situations too.

Creative attributes define the information and imagery. Sometimes there may be only a few creative executions, for example there may be five variants of a TV advertisement, in which case each one can have its own unique code. For direct marketing too, codifying the envelope, the letter and the enclosure (for example, the brochure) may suffice. For telesales, the script or call guide should be recorded. For pharmaceutical sales, the 'detail' is a scripted discussion of a particular medication.

Note that in other areas of business – such as logistics, back and front office and manufacturing – activity attributes are recorded as a matter of course. Gathering this data in marketing is simply bringing them up to the level of the rest of the business, and will provide detail needed as evidence.

1.3 Waste, scrap and re-work
Do we investigate cost-efficiency and drive down waste, scrap and re-work?

The process of supplying marketing activity (sometimes called the marketing supply chain) is like other manufacturing processes except that the levels of waste, scrap and re-work can be much higher. The chain begins with idea generation and finishes with placement of the finished executed ideas in the channels – this process is iterative, backstepping from time to time, scrapping ideas and material, re-working and polishing material until it achieves sign-off by the client. Studies of the marketing supply chain show it to be unusually inefficient and in need of streamlining. Gathering information of the process efficiency is another important item of evidence.

1.4 Marketing procurement
Do we source cost ingredients using effective procurement disciplines?

Finally, the raw ingredients that are bought to drive marketing activity should be sourced as cost-effectively as all other materials that the firm buys, and it is important therefore that effective procurement disciplines are applied to the marketing supply chain. In particular, where agencies buy materials on behalf of clients, it is important that the costs passed on to clients should be competitive and reasonable. At the same time, the aim is to not to source the cheapest resources and where procurement is involved their role needs to be kept under review to ensure they do an effective job.

2. Customer response

The following questions are important:

2.1 Are we collecting data from customers that provides evidence of marketing's value?

2.2 Are we using good practice analysis methods to link marketing activity to customer activity?

2.3 Does our response analysis provide evidence of 'special effects'?

2.1 Customer activity data
Are we collecting data from customers that provides evidence of marketing's value?

Customer data is routinely collected by many businesses, but does its existence necessarily add to the evidence about the value added by marketing? The answer is that only limited parts of the data will provide evidence on this question and the remainder is used for other purposes.

The relevant part of the data needed as evidence concerns customer activity relating to sales revenues. For example, in the specimen evaluation, the relevant data concerned customer membership applications (successful ones). This was linked to revenues in Year 1, but also to Years 2, 3, 4 and beyond.

Much of the customer data collected by your business will not be directly relevant. For example, customer satisfaction data and brand tracking research may not contain evidence directly relevant to estimating the financial value of marketing. We will consider this in more detail later in this paper.

So, it's important to review thoroughly the sources of data and select carefully the ones you need to analyse. Sometimes the data needed may not exist, and in that case it will need to be collected in order to analyse marketing's value.

2.2 Response analysis methods
Are we using good practice analysis methods to link marketing activity to customer activity?

Having gathered data on marketing activity and customer activity it is time to investigate the link between them. It is good practice to apply some method of statistical analysis to the data, as these methods enable the analyst to assess their confidence in the model and the variables in it.

In the vast field of data analysis there are many analytical techniques and their applicability is governed by the number of variables involved which may range from one to many. For example, in the specimen evaluation the analyst found a 'response equation':

New customers = 2% of mailing volume (up to 2m mailing items)

This is known as a *univariate* relationship, as only one variable is needed. For many situations, more than one variable is important, and so *multivariate* methods will be needed. For example, for a consumer product the response equation may have the form:

Sales = function (advertising, price, promotional offer, environmental factors)

Having collected the data, you should plot a graph, and look for patterns that link sales to factors such as advertising, price, promotion, etc. Spreadsheets are the tool of choice for this, and most novices can plot graphs. Even with limited data, there are some patterns that you may notice:

● **Trends** which rise (or fall) steadily over the time period you are examining.

● **Seasonal patterns** which repeat, more or less the same, every 12 months.

● **Short-term peaks** that are the effects of events such as price promotions or important sporting fixtures.

These features are illustrated in Figure B.3.

| Figure B.3 | Patterns in time-series data |

Source: R. Shaw and D. Merrick, *Marketing Payback*, FT Prentice Hall, 2005. © with permission from Pearson Education Ltd.

The analyst would assess their confidence in this model. For example, 90 per cent of the variation in the data might be explained by the model, and also the significance of all the variables is greater than 95 per cent.

2.3 Special effects
Does our response analysis provide evidence of 'special effects'

Marketing activity has several important effects that are not obvious at first sight and therefore the analyst should be vigilant in investigating them. The most important of these are:

- Persistence of response after marketing activity is finished.
- Synergies between marketing activities.
- Halo effects across products and brands.
- Unintended consequences, such as diminishing returns, stockpiling, cannibalisation and substitution.

Persistence in our specimen evaluation was easily observable: after customers became members of the wine club, they persisted in buying from the club for several years. In the case of TV advertising there are short-term persistence effects (sometimes called 'adstock') which last for a few weeks after the activity, and longer term brand building effects that last several years.

Synergies between marketing activities can occur. For instance, there is published case evidence of synergy between price changes and advertising: when both occur together the effect is larger than the separate effects. Synergies are used as justification for multichannel or integrated campaigns.

Halo effects are where the marketing of one thing shines on another. For example, where Product A is advertised then Product B's sales increase. Halo effects are often cited by agencies to help justify their work.

Unintended consequences of marketing are also common and should be investigated. The commonest ones are: diminishing returns, stockpiling, cannibalisation and substitution. Diminishing returns occur when returns decrease as an activity increases. Stockpiling occurs in the case of sales promotions, discounts and offers. Sales peaks can be the visible response, but very often it represents existing customers buying and stockpiling the product, and so a dip in sales may be observed following the peak. Cannibalisation occurs when the peak in sales of one product causes a dip in sales of another. This is often caused by substitution, where customers choose to buy the promoted product by substituting it for a different product that they habitually buy.

3. Environment – uncontrollable factors that affect results

The key question here is:

3.1 Other factors
Have we gathered evidence of how other factors have impacted our results?

Our results will be affected by other factors than your own marketing. Three such other factors should be investigated:

- Environmental factors such as temperature, the economy, the seasons, day of week.
- Competitor activity.
- Market trends.

Environmental data can usually be found from governmental sources and other agencies. It can be a rich source of insights for the analyst. For example, the model of consumer products cited in section 2.2 (p. 596) might be improved by including average daily temperature in the model. The reason for this is that the extra variable improves confidence in the overall model without significantly reducing confidence in the individual variables. Note that the parameters in the equation have changed as a result of temperature being included in the equation.

Competitors are frequently cited as causing problems with business results, and are often cited in the financial press. These comments may be based on detailed analysis but may also be based on anecdote and hearsay. To strengthen the evidence it's important to gather key competitor data, and market research firms can often provide the data required. Key competitor data elements to collect can include:

- price changes
- discounts and sales promotions
- distribution changes
- advertising and direct marketing activity

These should be included as factors for the analyst to evaluate and some, but not all, will be significant variables.

Market trends can provide useful evidence for disentangling the effects of our marketing from other factors. Ratio analysis can help differentiate between the behaviour of our firm and the market as a whole:

- Market share refers to the ratio between our revenue and the total for the market.
- Penetration refers to the ratio of our customers to the total in the market.
- Share of wallet is used in the context of individual customers and refers to the percentage of their spending that goes to our company.

These may also be included as factors for the analyst to evaluate.

4. Profitable revenues

4.1 Do we have good practice financial models linking customer activity to sales and profit figures?

The final step of historical analysis is to link customer activity to financial results and in particular profits. For example, in the specimen evaluation the analyst found that the profit contribution is £15 per customer per year. This example is simple, but in some situations the financial model may be more complex. In particular, not all customer activity will be equally profitable, for example due to:

- product profitability differences
- customer profitability differences

Product profitability differences will be important if different marketing activities drive different product mixes. Some activities may drive high-margin product sales, whereas other activities drive low-margin product sales. For instance, building societies need to ensure their marketing drives the right mix of mortgages and savings. Customer profitability differences need to be taken into account in the same way – for example, high-margin and low-margin customers may need to be distinguished in the analysis.[1]

Notes

[1] For more detail on these and other techniques, the reader is referred to R. Shaw and D. Merrick, *Marketing Payback* (Harlow: FT Prentice Hall, 2005).

Appendix C
Marketing case

Marketing in a downturn

Many of the world economies are in or near a recession. The credit crunch and the ensuing banking crisis have transformed the business environment to such an extent that most businesses are operating under conditions not seen for a generation, if ever at all. Overall, the consensus view of the UK economy is that GDP will fall and then stage a weak recovery thereafter.

Three things happen in a downturn: 1. there is reduced demand leading to lower sales, less cash flow, tighter credit; 2. pressure to cut discretionary spending especially R&D and marketing budgets; 3. delay of new product launches, and all these lead to a vicious downward cycle. Consequently, all company expenditure is subject to re-evaluation.

What should businesses do differently in a recession than in the grand inflationary years? The obvious answer is to cut costs! In broad terms this advice is undoubtedly sound. But which costs need to be cut most? Cutting needs to be selective, and closely related to maintaining shareholder value, otherwise the long-term value of the enterprise will be compromised.

Marketing is a good example. Many marketers, with enthusiastic support from their marketing agencies, will be eager to make the case for maintaining marketing spend in a recession. They will be emphasising the importance of the brand and that marketing is an investment and not a cost. Meanwhile, the financiers will be arguing for draconian cuts in marketing spend as a quick win in cutting 'soft' discretionary budgets.

Questions

1. How do customers react during a downturn?

2. Which sectors might do better or worse in a downturn?

3. Discuss the reasons you think marketers should spend more, spend the same or spend less in the downturn on marketing.

4. What are some of the upward and downward pressures on the marketing budget during a downturn?

5. Using the diagram below, give advice for a company in each of the four quadrants on why they should increase or decrease their marketing spend.

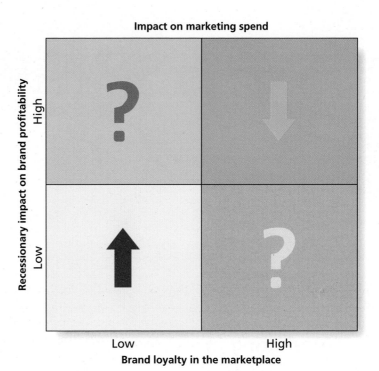

Written by David Merrick and Bryan Finn, Business Economics Ltd and Vince Mitchell

Glossary

80/20 rule A marketing rule of thumb that 20 per cent of purchasers account for 80 per cent of a product's sales.

A

Action plans Individual support plans included in a marketing plan that provide the guidance for implementation and control of the various marketing strategies within the plan. Action plans are sometimes referred to as marketing programmes.

Advertising Non-personal communication paid for by an identified sponsor using mass media to persuade or inform.

Advertising appeal The central idea or theme of an advertising message.

Advertising campaign A coordinated, comprehensive plan that carries out promotion objectives and results in a series of advertisements placed in media over a period of time.

Advertising exposure The degree to which the target market will see an advertising message placed in a specific vehicle.

Advocacy advertising A type of public service advertising provided by an organisation that is seeking to influence public opinion on an issue because it has some stake in the outcome.

Agents or brokers Channel intermediaries that provide services in exchange for commissions but never take title to the product.

AIDA model The communications goals of attention, interest, desire and action.

Aided recall A research technique that uses clues to prompt answers from people about advertisements they might have seen.

Aperture The best place and time to reach a person in the target market group.

Approach The first step of the actual sales presentation in which the salesperson tries to learn more about the customer's needs, creates a good impression and builds rapport.

Atmospherics The use of colour, lighting, scents, furnishings and other design elements to create a desired shop image.

Attitude A learned predisposition to respond favourably or unfavourably to stimuli on the basis of relatively enduring evaluations of people, objects and issues.

Attitudinal measures A research technique that probes a consumer's beliefs or feelings about a product before and after being exposed to messages about it.

Augmented services The core service plus additional services provided to enhance value.

Average fixed cost The fixed cost per unit produced.

B

Baby boomers The segment of people born between 1946 and 1964.

Back-translation The process of translating material into a foreign language and then back into the original language.

Bait-and-switch An unethical marketing practice in which an advertised special price is used as bait to get customers into the shop with the intention of switching them to a higher-priced item.

Banners Internet advertising in the form of rectangular graphics at the top or bottom of web pages.

Base-point pricing A pricing tactic where customers pay shipping charges from set base point locations whether the goods are actually shipped from these points or not.

BCG growth–market share matrix A portfolio analysis model developed by the Boston Consulting Group that assesses the potential of successful products to generate cash that a firm can then use to invest in new products.

Behavioural learning theories Theories of learning that focus on how consumer behaviour is changed by external events or stimuli.

Behavioural segmentation A technique that divides consumers into segments on the basis of how they act toward, feel about or use a good or service.

Benefit The outcome sought by a customer that motivates buying behaviour – that satisfies a **need or want**.

Born-global firms Companies that try to sell their products in multiple countries from the moment they're created.

Bottom-up budgeting techniques Allocation of the promotion budget based on identifying promotion goals and allocating enough money to accomplish them.

Brand A name, a term, a symbol, or any other unique element of a product that identifies one firm's product(s) and sets them apart from the competition.

Brand competition When firms offering similar goods or services compete on the basis of their brand's reputation or perceived benefits.

Brand equity The value of a brand to an organisation.

Brand extensions A new product sold with the same brand name as a strong existing brand.

Brand loyalty A pattern of repeat product purchases, accompanied by an underlying positive attitude toward the brand, that is based on the belief that the brand makes products superior to its competition.

Brand manager An individual who is responsible for developing and implementing the marketing plan for a single brand.

Brand personality A distinctive image that captures a good's or service's character and benefits.

Break-even analysis A method for determining the number of units that a firm must produce and sell at a given price to cover all its costs.

Break-even point The point at which the total revenue and total costs are equal and beyond which the company makes a profit; below that point, the firm will suffer a loss.

Breaking bulk Dividing larger quantities of goods into smaller lots in order to meet the needs of buyers.

Business analysis The step in the product development process in which marketers assess a product's commercial viability.

Business cycle The overall patterns of change in the economy – including periods of prosperity, recession, depression, and recovery – that affect consumer and business purchasing power.

Business plan A plan that includes the decisions that guide the entire organisation.

Business planning An ongoing process of making decisions that guide the firm both in the short term and for the long haul.

Business portfolio The group of different products or brands owned by an organisation and characterised by different income-generating and growth capabilities.

Business-to-business (B2B) e-commerce Internet exchanges between two or more businesses or organisations.

Business-to-business marketing The marketing of those goods and services that business and organisational customers need to produce other goods and services, for resale or to support their operations.

Business-to-business markets The group of customers that include manufacturers, wholesalers, retailers and other organisations.

Business-to-consumer (B2C) e-commerce Online exchanges between companies and individual consumers.

Buttons Small banner-type advertisements that can be placed anywhere on a web page.

Buy class One of three classifications of business buying situations that characterises the degree of time and effort required to make a decision.

Buying centre The group of people in an organisation who participate in a purchasing decision.

Buzz Word-of-mouth communication that is viewed as authentic and generated by customers.

Buzz marketing Using high-profile entertainment or news to get people to talk about your brand.

C

Cannibalisation The loss of sales of an existing brand when a new item in a product line or product family is introduced.

Capacity management The process by which organisations adjust their offerings in an attempt to match demand.

Captive pricing A pricing tactic for two items that must be used together; one item is priced low, and the firm makes its profit on the other, high-margin item essential to the operation of the first item.

Case allowance A discount to the retailer or wholesaler based on the volume of product ordered.

Case study A comprehensive examination of a particular firm or organisation.

Catalogue A collection of products offered for sale in book form, usually consisting of product descriptions accompanied by photos of the items.

Causal research A technique that attempts to understand cause-and-effect relationships.

Channel intermediaries Firms or individuals such as wholesalers, agents, brokers or retailers who help move a product from the producer to the consumer or business user.

Channel leader A firm at one level of distribution that takes a leadership role, establishing operating norms and processes based on its power relative to other channel members.

Channel levels The number of distinct categories of intermediaries that populate a channel of distribution.

Channel of distribution The series of firms or individuals that facilitates the movement of a product from the producer to the final customer.

Classical conditioning The learning that occurs when a stimulus eliciting a response is paired with another stimulus that initially does not elicit a response on its own but will cause a similar response over time because of its association with the first stimulus.

Close The stage of the selling process in which the salesperson actually asks the customer to buy the product.

Cobranding An agreement between two brands to work together in marketing a new product.

Cognitive learning theory Theory of learning that stresses the importance of internal mental processes and that views people as problem solvers who actively use information from the world around them to master their environment.

Collectivist cultures Cultures in which people subordinate their personal goals to those of a stable community.

Commercialisation The final step in the product development process in which a new product is launched into the market.

Communications model The process whereby meaning is transferred from a source to a receiver.

Competitive advantage The ability of a firm to outperform the competition, thereby providing customers with a benefit the competition can't.

Competitive intelligence The process of gathering and analysing publicly available information about rivals.

Competitive-parity method A promotion budgeting method in which an organisation matches whatever competitors are spending.

Component parts Manufactured goods or subassemblies of finished items that organisations need to complete their own products.

Concentrated targeting strategy Focusing a firm's efforts on offering one or more products to a single segment.

Conformity A change in beliefs or actions as a reaction to real or imagined group pressure.

Consumer The ultimate user of a good or service.

Consumer behaviour The process involved when individuals or groups select, purchase, use, and dispose of goods, services, ideas or experiences to satisfy their needs and desires.

Consumer goods The goods purchased by individual consumers for personal or family use.

Consumer interview One-on-one discussion between a consumer and a researcher.

Consumer orientation A management philosophy that focuses on ways to satisfy customers' needs and wants.

Consumer satisfaction/dissatisfaction The overall feelings or attitude a person has about a product after purchasing it.

Consumer-to-consumer (C2C) e-commerce Communications and purchases that occur among individuals without directly involving the manufacturer or retailer.

Continuous innovation A modification of an existing product that sets one brand apart from its competitors.

Contribution per unit The difference between the price the firm charges for a product and the variable costs.

Control A process that entails measuring actual performance, comparing this performance to the established marketing objectives, and then making adjustments to the strategies or objectives on the basis of this analysis.

Convenience product A consumer good or service that is usually low priced, widely available and purchased frequently with a minimum of comparison and effort.

Convenience stores Retailers that carry a limited number of frequently purchased items and cater to consumers willing to pay a premium for the ease of buying close to home.

Conventional marketing system A multiple-level distribution channel in which channel members work independently of one another.

Conventions Norms regarding the conduct of everyday life.

Convergence The coming together of two or more technologies to create a new system with greater benefits than its parts.

Cookie Text file inserted by a web site sponsor into a web surfer's hard drive that allows the site to track the surfer's moves.

Copy testing A marketing research method that seeks to measure the effectiveness of ads by determining whether consumers are receiving, comprehending, and responding to the ad according to plan.

Core service The basic benefit of having a service performed.

Corporate culture The set of values, norms and beliefs that influence the behaviour of everyone in the organisation.

Cost per thousand (CPM) A measure used to compare the relative cost-effectiveness of different media vehicles that have different exposure rates; the cost to deliver a message to 1000 people or homes.

Cost-plus pricing A method of setting prices in which the seller totals all the costs for the product and then adds an amount to arrive at the selling price.

Counter trade A type of trade in which goods are paid for with other items instead of cash.

Creating assortments Providing a variety of products in one location to meet the needs of buyers.

Creative selling process The process of seeking out potential customers, analysing needs, determining how product attributes might provide benefits for the customer, and then communicating that information.

Creative strategy The process that turns a concept into an advertisement.

Credence qualities Product characteristics that are difficult to evaluate even after they have been experienced.

Critical incident technique A method for measuring service quality in which marketers use customer complaints to identify critical incidents – specific face-to-face contacts between consumer and service providers that cause problems and lead to dissatisfaction.

Cross-elasticity of demand When changes in the price of one product affect the demand for another item.

Cross-promotion (cooperative promotion) Two or more products or services combine forces to create interest using a single promotional tool.

Cross-sectional design A type of descriptive technique that involves the systematic collection of quantitative information.

Cultural diversity A management practice that actively seeks to include people of different sexes, races, ethnic groups and religions in an organisation's employees, customers, suppliers and distribution channel partners.

Cultural values A society's deeply held beliefs about right and wrong ways to live.

Culture The values, beliefs, customs, and tastes valued by a group of people.

Custom A norm handed down from the past that controls basic behaviours.

Custom marketing strategy An approach that tailors specific products and the messages about them to individual customers.

Custom research Research conducted for a single firm to provide specific information its managers need.

Customer equity The financial value of a customer relationship throughout the life-time of the relationship.

Customer relationship management (CRM) A philosophy that sees marketing as a process of building long-term relationships with customers to keep them satisfied and to keep them coming back. A concept that involves systematically tracking consumers' preferences and behaviours over time in order to tailor the value proposition as closely as possible to each individual's unique wants and needs.

D

Data mining Sophisticated analysis techniques to take advantage of the massive amount of transaction information now available.

Database marketing The creation of an ongoing relationship with a set of customers who have an identifiable interest in a product or service and whose responses to promotional efforts become part of future communications attempts.

Decline stage The final stage in the product life-cycle in which sales decrease as customer needs change.

Decoding The process by which a receiver assigns meaning to the message.

Demand Customers' desire for products coupled with the resources to obtain them.

Demand-based pricing A price-setting method based on estimates of demand at different prices.

Demographics Statistics that measure observable aspects of a population, including size, age, gender, ethnic group, income, education, occupation and family structure.

Department stores Retailers that sell a broad range of items and offer a good selection within each product line.

Derived demand Demand for business or organisational products derived from demand for consumer goods or services.

Descriptive research A tool that probes more systematically into the problem and bases its conclusions on large numbers of observations.

Developed country A country that boasts sophisticated marketing systems, strong private enterprise, and plenty of market potential for many goods and services.

Developing countries Countries in which the economy is shifting its emphasis from agriculture to industry.

Differential benefit Properties of products that set them apart from competitors' products by providing unique customer benefits.

Differentiated targeting strategy Developing one or more products for each of several distinct customer groups and making sure these offerings are kept separate in the marketplace.

Diffusion The process by which the use of a product spreads throughout a population.

Direct mail A brochure or pamphlet offering a specific product or service at one point in time.

Direct marketing Any direct communication to a consumer or business recipient that is designed to generate a response in the form of an order, a request for further information, and/or a visit to a shop or other place of business for purchase of a product.

Direct-response advertising A direct marketing approach that allows the consumer to respond to a message by immediately contacting the provider to ask questions or order the product

Direct-response TV (DRTV) Advertising on TV that seeks a direct response, including short commercials of less than two minutes, 30-minute or longer infomercials, and home shopping networks.

Discontinuous innovation A totally new product that creates major changes in the way we live.

Disintermediation Eliminating the interaction between customers and salespeople so as to minimise negative service encounters.

Disintermediation (of the channel of distribution) The elimination of some layers of the channel of distribution in order to cut costs and improve the efficiency of the channel.

Disposable income The portion of income people have left over after paying for necessities such as housing, utilities, food and clothing.

Distinctive competency A superior capability of a firm in comparison to its direct competitors.

Diversification strategies Growth strategies that emphasise both new products and new markets.

Dumping A company tries to get a toehold in a foreign market by pricing its products lower than they are offered at home.

Durable goods Consumer products that provide benefits over a long period of time, such as cars, furniture and appliances.

Dynamic pricing A pricing strategy in which the price can easily be adjusted to meet changes in the market place.

Dynamically continuous innovation A change in an existing product that requires a moderate amount of learning or behaviour change.

E

Early adopters Those who adopt an innovation early in the diffusion process but after the innovators.

Early majority Those whose adoption of a new product signals a general acceptance of the innovation.

e-Commerce The buying or selling of goods and services electronically, usually over the Internet.

Economic communities Groups of countries that band together to promote trade among themselves and to make it easier for member nations to compete elsewhere.

Economic infrastructure The quality of a country's distribution, financial, and communications systems.

Economic sanctions Trade prohibitions imposed by one country against another.

Elastic demand Demand in which changes in price have large effects on the amount demanded.

e-Marketers Marketers who use e-commerce in their strategies.

Embargo A quota completely prohibiting specified goods from entering or leaving a country.

Encoding The process of translating an idea into a form of communication that will convey meaning.

Enterprise resource planning (ERP) systems A software system that integrates information from across the entire company. Data need to be entered into the system only once, at one point, and then the data are automatically shared throughout the organisation.

Equipment Expensive goods that an organisation uses in its daily operations that last for a long time.

Ethnocentrism The tendency to prefer products or people of one's own culture.

Ethnographic study A detailed report based on observations of people in their own homes or communities.

European Union (EU) An economic community that now includes most of Europe.

Evaluative criteria The dimensions used by consumers to compare competing product alternatives.

Everyday low pricing (EDLP) See **Value pricing**.

Exchange The process by which some transfer of value occurs between a buyer and a seller.

Exclusive distribution Selling a product only through a single outlet in a particular region.

Experience qualities Product characteristics that customers can determine during or after consumption.

Experiential shoppers Consumers who engage in online shopping because of the experiential benefits they receive.

Experiment Technique that tests prespecified relationships among variables in a controlled environment.

Exploratory research A technique that marketers use to generate insights for future, more rigorous studies.

Export merchants Intermediaries used by a firm to represent them in other countries.

Expropriation A domestic government's seizure of a foreign company's assets without any compensation.

External environment The uncontrollable elements outside an organisation that may affect its performance either positively or negatively.

Extranet A private, corporate computer network that links company departments, employees, and databases to suppliers, customers, and others outside the organisation.

F

Facilitating functions Functions of channel intermediaries that make the purchase process easier for customers and manufacturers.

Family brand A brand that a group of individual products or individual brands share.

Family life cycle A means of characterising consumers within a family structure on the basis of different stages through which people pass as they grow older.

Feedback Receivers' reactions to the message.

Fixed costs Costs of production that do not change with the number of units produced.

FOB delivered pricing A pricing tactic in which the cost of loading and transporting the product to the customer is included in the selling price and is paid by the manufacturer.

FOB origin pricing A pricing tactic in which the cost of transporting the product from the factory to the customer's location is the responsibility of the customer.

Focus group A product-oriented discussion among a small group of consumers led by a trained moderator.

Follow-up Activities after the sale that provide important services to customers.

Franchising A form of licensing involving the right to adapt an entire system of doing business.

Freight absorption pricing A pricing tactic in which the seller absorbs the total cost of transportation.

Frequency The number of times a person in the target group will be exposed to the message.

Frequency programmes Consumer sales promotion programmes that offer a discount or free product for multiple purchases over time; also referred to as loyalty or continuity programmes.

Full-service agency An agency that provides most or all of the services needed to mount a campaign, including research, creation of ad copy and art, media selection and production of the final messages.

Functional planning A decision process that concentrates on developing detailed plans for strategies and tactics for the short term that support an organisation's long-term strategic plan.

G

Gap analysis A marketing research methodology that measures the difference between a customer's expectation of a service quality and what actually occurred.

General Agreement on Tariffs and Trade (GATT) International treaty to reduce import tax levels and trade restrictions.

Generation X The group of consumers born between 1965 and 1976.

Generation Y The group of consumers born between 1977 and 1994.

Geodemography A segmentation technique that combines geography with demographics.

Good A tangible product that we can see, touch, smell, hear or taste.

Government markets The various governmental levels that buy goods and services to carry out public objectives and to support their operations.

Grey market goods Items manufactured outside a country and then imported without the consent of the trademark holder.

Gross domestic product (GDP) The total value of goods and services produced by a nation within its borders in a year.

Gross national product (GNP) The value of all goods and services produced by a country's citizens or organisations, whether located within the country's borders or not.

Gross rating points (GRPs) A measure used for comparing the effectiveness of different media vehicles: average reach × frequency.

Growth stage The second stage in the product life cycle during which the product is accepted and sales rapidly increase.

Guerrilla marketing Marketing activity in which a firm 'ambushes' consumers with promotional content in places they are not expecting to encounter this kind of activity.

H

Heuristics A mental rule of thumb that leads to a speedy decision by simplifying the process.

Hierarchy of effects A series of steps prospective customers move through, from initial awareness of a product to brand loyalty.

Hierarchy of needs An approach that categorises motives according to five levels of importance, the more basic needs being on the bottom of the hierarchy and the higher needs at the top.

Horizontal marketing system An arrangement within a channel of distribution in which two or more firms at the same channel level work together for a common purpose.

Hybrid marketing system A marketing system that uses a number of different channels and communication methods to serve a target market.

Hypermarkets Retailers that are several times larger than supermarkets and offer virtually everything from grocery items to electronics.

I

Idea generation The first step of product development in which marketers brainstorm for products that provide customer benefits and are compatible with the company mission.

Idea marketing Marketing activities that seek to gain market share for a concept, philosophy, belief, or issue by using elements of the marketing mix to create or change a target market's attitude or behaviour.

Import quotas Limitations set by a government on the amount of a product allowed to enter or leave a country.

Impressions The number of people who will be exposed to a message placed in one or more media vehicles.

Impulse purchase A purchase made without any planning or search effort.

Independent intermediaries Channel intermediaries that are not controlled by any manufacturer but instead do business with many different manufacturers and many different customers.

Individualist cultures Cultures in which people tend to attach more importance to personal goals than to those of the larger community.

Industrial goods Goods bought by individuals or organisations for further processing or for use in doing business.

Inelastic demand Demand in which changes in price have little or no effect on the amount demanded.

Information search The process whereby a consumer searches for appropriate information to make a reasonable decision.

Ingredient branding A form of co-branding in which branded materials are used as ingredients or component parts of other branded products.

Innovation A product that consumers perceive to be new and different from existing products.

Innovators The first segment (roughly 2.5 per cent) of a population to adopt a new product.

Inseparability The characteristic of a service that means that it is impossible to separate the production of a service from the consumption of that service.

Institutional advertising An advertising message that promotes the activities, personality, or point of view of an organisation or company.

Intangibility The characteristic of a service that means customers can't see, touch or smell good service.

Intangibles Experience-based products that cannot be touched.

Integrated marketing communications (IMC) A strategic business process that marketers use to plan, develop, execute, and evaluate coordinated, measurable, persuasive brand communication programmes over time to targeted audiences.

Intensive distribution Selling a product through all suitable wholesalers or retailers that are willing to stock and sell the product.

Interactive marketing A promotion practice in which customised marketing communications elicit a measurable response from individual receivers.

Internal environment The controllable elements inside an organisation, including its people, its facilities, and how it does things that influence the operations of the organisation.

Internal reference price A set price or a price range in consumers' minds that they refer to in evaluating a product's price.

Intranet An internal corporate communication network that uses Internet technology to link company departments, employees and databases.

Introduction stage The first stage of the product lifecycle in which slow growth follows the introduction of a new product in the marketplace.

Involvement The relative importance of perceived consequences of the purchase to a consumer.

ISO 14000 Standards of the International Organization for Standardization concerned with 'environmental management' aimed at minimising harmful effects on the environment.

ISO 9000 Criteria developed by the International Organization for Standardization to regulate product quality in Europe.

J

Joint demand Demand for two or more goods that are used together to create a product.

Joint venture A strategic alliance in which a new entity owned by two or more firms is created to allow the partners to pool their resources for common goals.

Just in time (JIT) Stock management and purchasing processes that manufacturers and resellers use to reduce stock to very low levels and ensure that deliveries from suppliers arrive only when needed.

K

Kansei engineering A Japanese philosophy that translates customers' feelings into design elements.

Knock-off A new product that copies with slight modification the design of an original product.

Knowledge management A comprehensive approach to collecting, organising, storing and retrieving a firm's information assets.

L

Laggards The last consumers to adopt an innovation.

Late majority The adopters who are willing to try new products when there is little or no risk associated with the purchase, when the purchase becomes an economic necessity, or when there is social pressure to purchase.

Learning A relatively permanent change in behaviour caused by acquired information or experience.

Less developed country (LDC) A country at the lowest stage of economic development.

Licensing An agreement in which one firm sells another firm the right to use a brand name for a specific purpose and for a specific period of time.

Licensing (in foreign markets) An agreement in which one firm gives another firm the right to produce and market its product in a specific country or region in return for royalties.

Lifestyle The pattern of living that determines how people choose to spend their time, money and energy and that reflects their values, tastes and preferences.

Lifetime value of a customer How much profit companies expect to make from a particular customer, including each and every purchase she will make from them now and in the future. To calculate lifetime value, companies estimate the amount the person will spend and then subtract what it will cost the company to maintain this relationship.

Limited-service agency An agency that provides one or more specialised services, such as media buying or creative development.

List price The price the end customer is expected to pay as determined by the manufacturer; also referred to as the suggested retail price or retailers' recommended price (RRP).

Local content rules A form of protectionism stipulating that a certain proportion of a product must consist of components supplied by industries in the host country.

Logistics The process of designing, managing and improving the movement of products through the supply chain. Logistics includes purchasing, manufacturing, storage and transport.

Longitudinal design A technique that tracks the responses of the same sample of respondents over time.

Loss leader pricing The pricing policy of setting prices very low or even below cost to attract customers into a shop.

M

Maintenance, repair, and operating (MRO) products Goods that a business customer consumes in a relatively short time.

Marginal analysis A method that uses cost and demand to identify the price that will maximise profits.

Marginal cost The increase in total cost that results from producing one additional unit of a product.

Marginal revenue The increase in total income or revenue that results from selling one additional unit of a product.

Market All the customers and potential customers who share a common need that can be satisfied by a specific product, who have the resources to exchange for it, who are willing to make the exchange and who have the authority to make the exchange.

Market development strategies Growth strategies that introduce existing products to new markets.

Market fragmentation The creation of many consumer groups due to a diversity of distinct needs and wants in modern society.

Market manager An individual who is responsible for developing and implementing the marketing plans for products sold to a particular customer group.

Market penetration strategies Growth strategies designed to increase sales of existing products to current customers, non-users, and users of competitive brands in served markets.

Market position The way in which the target market perceives the product in comparison to competitors' brands.

Market segment A distinct group of customers within a larger market who are similar to one another in some way and whose needs differ from other customers in the larger market.

Marketing An organisational function and a set of processes for creating, communicating and delivering value to customers and for managing customer relationships in ways that benefit the organisation and its stakeholders.

Marketing concept A management orientation that focuses on identifying and satisfying consumer needs to ensure the organisation's long-term profitability.

Marketing decision support system (MDSS) The data, analysis software and interactive software that allow managers to conduct analyses and find the information they need.

Marketing information system (MkIS) A process that first determines what information marketing managers need and then gathers, sorts, analyses, stores, and distributes relevant and timely marketing information to system users.

Marketing intelligence system A method by which marketers get information about everyday happenings in the marketing environment.

Marketing mix A combination of the product itself, the price of the product, the place where it is made available, and the activities that introduce it to consumers that creates a desired response among a set of predefined consumers.

Marketing plan A document that describes the marketing environment, outlines the marketing objectives and strategy, and identifies who will be responsible for carrying out each part of the marketing strategy.

Marketing research The process of collecting, analysing, and interpreting data about customers, competitors and the business environment in order to improve marketing effectiveness.

Marketplace Any location or medium used to conduct an exchange.

Mass customisation An approach that modifies a basic good or service to meet the needs of an individual.

Mass market All possible customers in a market, regardless of the differences in their specific needs and wants.

Materials handling The moving of products into, within, and out of warehouses.

Maturity stage The third and longest stage in the product life cycle in which sales peak and profit margins narrow.

m-Commerce Promotional and other e-commerce activities transmitted over mobile phones and other mobile devices, such as personal digital assistants (PDAs).

Media planning The process of developing media objectives, strategies and tactics for use in an advertising campaign.

Media schedule The plan that specifies the exact media to use and when.

Medium A communications vehicle through which a message is transmitted to a target audience.

Merchandise assortment The range of products sold.

Merchandise breadth The number of different product lines available.

Merchandise depth The variety of choices available for each specific product line.

Merchandise mix The total set of all products offered for sale by a retailer, including all product lines sold to all consumer groups.

Merchandising allowance Reimburses the retailer for in-store support of the product.

Message The communication in physical form that goes from a sender to a receiver.

Metrosexual A man who is heterosexual, sensitive, educated, and an urban dweller who is in touch with his feminine side.

Mission statement A formal statement in an organisation's strategic plan that describes the overall purpose of the organisation and what it intends to achieve in terms of its customers, products, and resources.

Missionary sales person A sales person who promotes the firm and tries to stimulate demand for a product but does not actually complete a sale.

Modified re-buy A buying situation classification used by business buyers to categorise a previously made purchase that involves some change and requires limited decision making.

Monopolistic competition A market structure in which many firms, each having slightly different products, offer unique consumer benefits.

Monopoly A market situation in which one firm, the only supplier of a particular product, is able to control the price, quality, and supply of that product.

Mores Customs with a strong moral overtone.

Motivation An internal state that drives us to satisfy needs by activating goal-oriented behaviour.

Multiple sourcing The business practice of buying a particular product from many suppliers.

Myths Stories containing symbolic elements that express the shared emotions and ideals of a culture.

N

National or manufacturer brands Brands that the manufacturer of the product owns.

Nationalisation A domestic government's takeover of a foreign company for its assets with some reimbursement, though often not for the full value.

Need The recognition of any difference between a consumer's actual state and some ideal or desired state.

New Era orientation A management philosophy in which marketing means a devotion to excellence in designing and producing products that benefit the customer plus the firm's employees, shareholders and communities.

New-business sales person The person responsible for finding new customers and calling on them to present the company's products or services.

New-task buy A new business-to-business purchase that is complex or risky and requires extensive decision making.

Noise Anything that interferes with effective communication.

Non-durable goods Consumer products that provide benefits for a short time because they are consumed (such as food) or are no longer useful (such as newspapers).

Non-probability sample A sample in which personal judgement is used in selecting respondents.

Non-shop retailing Any method used to complete an exchange with a product end-user that does not require a customer visit to a store.

Norms Specific rules dictating what is right or wrong, acceptable or unacceptable.

North American Free Trade Agreement (NAFTA) An economic community composed of the United States, Canada and Mexico.

Not-for-profit institutions Organisations with charitable, educational, community and other public service goals that buy goods and services to support their functions and to attract and serve their members.

O

Objective-task method A promotion budgeting method in which an organisation first defines the specific communications goals it hopes to achieve and then tries to calculate what kind of promotional efforts it will take to meet these goals.

Oligopoly A market structure in which a relatively small number of sellers, each holding a substantial share of the market, compete in a market with many buyers.

Online auctions e-Commerce that allows shoppers to purchase products through online bidding.

Operant conditioning Learning that occurs as the result of rewards or punishments.

Operational planning A decision process that focuses on developing detailed plans for day-to-day activities that carry out an organisation's functional plans.

Operational plans Plans that focus on the day-to-day execution of the marketing plan. Operational plans include detailed directions for the specific activities to be carried out, who will be responsible for them, and timelines for accomplishing the tasks.

Opinion leader A person who is frequently able to influence others' attitudes or behaviours by virtue of his or her active interest and expertise in one or more product categories.

Order getter A sales person who works to develop long-term relationships with particular customers or to generate new sales.

Order processing The series of activities that occurs between the time an order comes into the organisation and the time a product goes out the door.

Order taker A sales person whose primary function is to facilitate transactions that the customer initiates.

Organisational markets Another name for business-to-business markets.

Out-of-home media A communication medium that reaches people in public places.

Outsourcing The business buying process of obtaining outside vendors to provide goods or services that otherwise might be supplied in-house.

P

Package The covering or container for a product that provides product protection, facilitates product use and storage, and supplies important marketing communication.

Patent Legal documentation granting an individual or firm exclusive rights to produce and sell a particular invention.

Penetration pricing A pricing strategy in which a firm introduces a new product at a very low price to encourage more customers to purchase it.

Perceived risk The belief that choice of a product has potentially negative consequences – financial, physical, or social.

Percentage-of-sales method A method for promotion budgeting that is based on a certain percentage of either last year's sales or on estimates for the present year's sales.

Perception The process by which people select, organise, and interpret information from the outside world.

Perceptual map A vivid way to construct a picture of where products or brands are 'located' in consumers' minds.

Perfect competition A market structure in which many small sellers, all of whom offer similar products, are unable to have an impact on the quality, price or supply of a product.

Perishability The characteristic of a service that makes it impossible to store for later sale or consumption.

Permission marketing Email advertising where online consumers have the opportunity to accept or refuse the unsolicited email.

Personal selling Marketing communication by which a company representative interacts directly with a customer or prospective customer to communicate about a good or service.

Personality The psychological characteristics that consistently influence the way a person responds to situations in his or her environment.

Physical distribution The activities used to move finished goods from manufacturers to final customers, including order processing, warehousing, materials handling, transportation and stock control.

Place The availability of the product to the customer at the desired time and location.

Place marketing Marketing activities that seek to attract new businesses, residents or visitors to a town, country or some other site.

Place-based media Advertising media that transmit messages in public places, such as doctors' offices and airports, where certain types of people congregate.

Product mix The total set of all products a firm offers for sale.

Point-of-purchase (POP) promotion In-store displays or signs.

Point-of-sale (POS) systems Retail computer systems that collect sales data and are hooked directly into the shop's inventory control system.

Portfolio analysis A management tool for evaluating a firm's business mix and assessing the potential of an organisation's strategic business units.

Positioning Developing a marketing strategy aimed at influencing how a particular market segment perceives a good or service in comparison to the competition.

Post-testing Research conducted on consumers' responses to actual advertising messages they have seen or heard.

Pre-approach A part of the selling process that includes developing information about prospective customers and planning the sales interview.

Premiums Items offered free to people who have purchased a product.

Press release Information that an organisation distributes to the media, intended to win publicity.

Prestige products Products that have a high price and that appeal to status-conscious consumers.

Pre-testing A research method that seeks to minimise mistakes by getting consumer reactions to ad messages before they appear in the media.

Price The assignment of value, or the amount the consumer must exchange to receive the offering.

Price bundling Selling two or more goods or services as a single package for one price.

Price elasticity of demand The percentage change in unit sales that results from a percentage change in price.

Price fixing The collaboration of two or more firms in setting prices, usually to keep prices high.

Price leadership A pricing strategy in which one firm first sets its price and other firms in the industry follow with the same or very similar prices.

Price lining The practice of setting a limited number of different specific prices, called price points, for items in a product line.

Primary data Data from research conducted to help in making a specific decision.

Private exchanges Systems that link an invited group of suppliers and partners over the web.

Private-label brands Brands that are owned and sold by a certain retailer or distributor.

Probability sample A sample in which each member of the population has some known chance of being included.

Problem recognition The process that occurs whenever the consumer sees a significant difference between his or her current state of affairs and some desired or ideal state; this recognition initiates the decision-making process.

Processed materials Products created when firms transform raw materials from their original state.

Producers The individuals or organisations that purchase products for use in the production of other goods and services.

Product A tangible good, service, idea, or some combination of these that satisfies consumer or business customer needs through the exchange process; a bundle of attributes including features, functions, benefits and uses.

Product adoption The process by which a consumer or business customer begins to buy and use a new good, service or idea.

Product advertising An advertising message that focuses on a specific good or service.

Product category managers Individuals who are responsible for developing and implementing the marketing plan for all the brands and products within a product category.

Product competition When firms offering different products compete to satisfy the same consumer needs and wants.

Product concept development and screening The second step of product development in which marketers test product ideas for technical and commercial success.

Product development strategies Growth strategies that focus on selling new products in served markets.

Product lifecycle A concept that explains how products go through four distinct stages from birth to death: introduction, growth, maturity and decline.

Product line A firm's total product offering designed to satisfy a single need or desire of target customers.

Product specifications A written description of the quality, size, weight, and so forth required of a product purchase.

Production orientation A management philosophy that emphasises the most efficient ways to produce and distribute products.

Projective technique Test that marketers use to explore people's underlying feelings about a product, especially appropriate when consumers are unable or unwilling to express their true reactions.

Promotion The coordination of a marketer's marketing communications efforts to influence attitudes or behaviour; the coordination of efforts by a marketer to inform or persuade consumers or organisations about goods, services or ideas.

Promotion mix The major elements of marketer-controlled communications, including advertising, sales promotions, public relations and personal selling.

Promotional products Goodies such as coffee mugs, T-shirts and magnets given away to build awareness for a sponsor. Some freebies are distributed directly to consumers and business customers; others are intended for channel partners such as retailers and vendors.

Prospecting A part of the selling process that includes identifying and developing a list of potential or prospective customers.

Protectionism A policy adopted by a government to give domestic companies an advantage.

Prototypes Test versions of a proposed product.

Psychographics The use of psychological, sociological and anthropological factors to construct market segments.

Public relations (PR) Communication function that seeks to build good relationships with an organisation's publics, including consumers, stockholders and legislators.

Public service advertisements (PSAs) Advertising run by the media without charge for not-for-profit organisations or to champion a particular cause.

Publicity Unpaid communication about an organisation appearing in the mass media.

Pull strategy The company tries to move its products through the channel by building desire for the products among consumers, thus convincing retailers to respond to this demand by stocking these items.

Push money A bonus paid by a manufacturer to a sales person, customer, or distributor for selling its product.

Q

Quantity discounts A pricing tactic of charging reduced prices for purchases of larger quantities of a product.

R

Radio frequency identification (RFID) Product tags with tiny chips containing information about the item's content, origin and destination.

Raw materials Products of the fishing, lumber, agricultural and mining industries that organisational customers purchase to use in their finished products.

Reach The percentage of the target market that will be exposed to the media vehicle.

Rebates Sales promotions that allow the customer to recover part of the product's cost from the manufacturer.

Receiver The organisation or individual that intercepts and interprets the message.

Reciprocity A trading partnership in which two firms agree to buy from one another.

Reference group An actual or imaginary individual or group that has a significant effect on an individual's evaluations, aspirations, or behaviour.

Relationship selling A form of personal selling that involves securing, developing, and maintaining long-term relationships with profitable customers.

Reliability The extent to which research measurement techniques are free of errors.

Re-positioning Re-doing a product's position to respond to market place changes.

Representativeness The extent to which consumers in a study are similar to a larger group in which the organisation has an interest.

Research design A plan that specifies what information marketers will collect and what type of study they will do.

Resellers The individuals or organisations that buy finished goods for the purpose of reselling, renting, or leasing to others to make a profit and to maintain their business operations.

Retail lifecycle A theory that focuses on the various stages that retailers pass through from introduction to decline.

Retailing The final stop in the distribution channel by which goods and services are sold to consumers for their personal use.

Return on investment (ROI) The direct financial impact of a firm's expenditure of a resource such as time or money.

Return on marketing investment (ROMI) Quantifying just how an investment in marketing impacts the firm's success, financially and otherwise.

Reverse marketing A business practice in which a buyer firm attempts to identify suppliers who will produce products according to the buyer firm's specifications.

S

Sales management The process of planning, implementing and controlling the personal selling function of an organisation.

Sales presentation The part of the selling process in which the sales person directly communicates the value proposition to the customer, inviting two-way communication.

Sales promotion Programmes designed to build interest in or encourage purchase of a product during a specified time period.

Sales territory A set of customers often defined by geographic boundaries for whom a particular sales person is responsible.

Sampling (1) Distributing free trial-size versions of a product to consumers.

Sampling (2) The process of selecting respondents who statistically represent a larger population of interest.

Scenario Possible future situation that futurists use to assess the likely impact of alternative marketing strategies.

Scrambled merchandising A merchandising strategy that offers consumers a mixture of merchandise items that are not directly related to each other.

Search qualities Product characteristics that the consumer can examine prior to purchase.

Secondary data Data that have been collected for some purpose other than the problem at hand.

Segment profile A description of the 'typical' customer in a segment.

Segmentation The process of dividing a larger market into smaller pieces based on one or more meaningful, shared characteristics.

Segmentation variables Dimensions that divide the total market into fairly homogeneous groups, each with different needs and preferences.

Selective distribution Distribution using fewer outlets than in intensive distribution but more than in exclusive distribution.

Self-concept An individual's self-image that is composed of a mixture of beliefs, observations and feelings about personal attributes.

Selling orientation A managerial view of marketing as a sales function, or a way to move products out of warehouses to reduce inventory.

Service encounter The actual interaction between the customer and the service provider.

Services Intangible products that are exchanged directly from the producer to the customer.

Servicescape The actual physical facility where the service is performed, delivered, and consumed.

SERVQUAL A multiple-item scale used to measure service quality across dimensions of tangibles, reliability, responsiveness, assurance and empathy.

Sex roles Society's expectations regarding the appropriate attitudes, behaviours and appearance for men and women.

Share of customer The percentage of an individual customer's purchase of a product that is a single brand.

Shopping centre A group of commercial establishments owned and managed as a single property.

Shopping product A good or service for which consumers spend considerable time and effort gathering information and comparing alternatives before making a purchase.

Single sourcing The business practice of buying a particular product from only one supplier.

Skimming A very high, premium price that a firm charges for its new, highly desirable product.

Slotting fees Fees a retailer may charge a manufacturer for setting up a new product in inventory and providing it with shelf space.

Social class The overall rank or social standing of groups of people within a society according to the value assigned to such factors as family background, education, occupation and income.

Source An organisation or individual that sends a message.

Specialised services Services purchased from outside suppliers that are essential to the operation of an organisation but are not part of the production of a product.

Specialty product A good or service that has unique characteristics and is important to the buyer and for which the buyer will devote significant effort to acquire.

Specialty shops Retailers that carry only a few product lines but offer good selection within the lines that they sell.

Sponsorships PR activities through which companies provide financial support to help fund an event in return for publicised recognition of the company's contribution.

Stakeholders Buyers, sellers and investors in a company; community residents, and even citizens of the nations where goods and services are made or sold – in other words, any person or organisation that has a 'stake' in the outcomes.

Standard Industrial Classification (SIC) system The numerical coding system commonly used to classify firms into detailed categories according to their business activities.

Standard of living An indicator of the average quality and quantity of goods and services consumed in a country.

Stimulus generalisation Behaviour caused by a reaction to one stimulus occurs in the presence of other, similar stimuli.

Store image The way a retailer is perceived in the marketplace relative to the competition.

Straight re-buy A buying situation in which business buyers make routine purchases that require minimal decision making.

Strategic alliance Relationship developed between a firm seeking a deeper commitment to a foreign market and a domestic firm in the target country.

Strategic business units (SBU) Individual units within the firm that operate like separate businesses, with each having its own mission, business objectives, resources, managers and competitors.

Strategic planning A managerial decision process that matches an organisation's resources and capabilities to its market opportunities for long-term growth and survival.

Subculture A group within a society whose members share a distinctive set of beliefs, characteristics or common experiences.

Supermarkets Food shops that carry a wide selection of edibles and related products.

Supply chain All the firms that engage in activities necessary to turn raw materials into a good or service and put it in the hands of the consumer or business customer.

Supply chain management The management of flows among firms in the supply chain to maximise total profitability.

SWOT analysis An analysis of an organisation's strengths and weaknesses and the opportunities and threats in its external environment.

Syndicated research Research by firms that collect data on a regular basis and sell the reports to multiple firms.

T

Take title To accept legal ownership of a product and the accompanying rights and responsibilities of ownership.

Target costing A process in which firms identify the quality and functionality needed to satisfy customers and what price they are willing to pay before the product is designed. The product is manufactured only if the firm can control costs to meet the required price.

Target market The market segments on which an organisation focuses its marketing plan and toward which it directs its marketing efforts.

Target marketing strategy Dividing the total market into different segments on the basis of customer characteristics, selecting one or more segments, and developing products to meet the needs of those specific segments.

Tariffs Taxes on imported goods.

Team selling The sales function when handled by a team that may consist of a sales person, a technical specialist, and others.

Technical development The step in the product development process in which a new product is refined and perfected by company engineers and the like.

Technical specialist A sales support person with a high level of technical expertise who assists in product demonstrations.

Telemarketing The use of the telephone to sell directly to consumers and business customers.

Test marketing Testing the complete marketing plan in a small geographic area that is similar to the larger market the firm hopes to enter.

Top-down budgeting techniques Allocation of the promotion budget based on the total amount to be devoted to marketing communications.

Total costs The total fixed costs and the variable costs for a set number of units produced.

Total quality management (TQM) A management philosophy that focuses on satisfying customers through empowering employees, from the assembly line onward, to be an active part of continuous quality improvement.

Trade or functional discounts Discounts off list price of products to members of the channel of distribution that perform various marketing functions.

Trade promotions Promotions that focus on members of the 'trade', which include distribution channel members, such as retail sales people or wholesale distributors, that a firm must work with in order to sell its products.

Trade shows Events at which many companies set up elaborate exhibits to show their products, give away samples, distribute product literature, and identify new business contacts.

Trademark The legal term for a brand name, brand mark, or trade character; trademarks legally registered by a government obtain protection for exclusive use in that country.

Traffic flow The direction in which shoppers will move through the shop and what areas they will pass or avoid.

Transactional data An ongoing record of individuals or organisations that buy a product.

Transactional selling A form of personal selling that focuses on making an immediate sale with little or no attempt to develop a relationship with the customer.

Transportation The mode by which products move among channel members.

Trial pricing Pricing a new product low for a limited period of time in order to lower the risk for a customer.

U

Unaided recall A research technique conducted by telephone survey or personal interview that asks whether a person remembers seeing an ad during a specified period of time.

Undifferentiated targeting strategy Appealing to a broad spectrum of people.

Uniform delivered pricing A pricing tactic in which a firm adds a standard shipping charge to the price for all customers regardless of location.

Unique selling proposition (USP) An advertising appeal that focuses on one clear reason why a particular product is superior.

Universal Product Code (UPC) The set of black bars or lines printed on the side or bottom of most items sold in grocery shops and other mass-merchandising outlets. The UPC, readable by scanners, creates a national system of product identification.

Unsought products Goods or services for which a consumer has little awareness or interest until the product or a need for the product is brought to his or her attention.

Usage occasions An indicator used in one type of market segmentation based on when consumers use a product most.

Utility The usefulness or benefit consumers receive from a product.

V

Validity The extent to which research actually measures what it was intended to measure.

Value The benefits a customer receives from buying a product or service.

Value chain Encompasses all the activities in a firm (designing, producing, marketing, delivery and supporting) which create products and services that in turn create value for the consumer and make a profit for the company. Each link in the chain has the potential to either add or remove value from the product the customer eventually buys.

Value pricing A pricing strategy in which a firm sets prices that provide ultimate value to customers.

Value proposition A marketplace offering that fairly and accurately sums up the value that will be realised if the product or service is purchased.

Variability The characteristic of a service that means that even the same service performed by the same individual for the same customer can vary.

Variable costs The costs of production (raw and processed materials, parts and labour) that are tied to and vary depending on the number of units produced.

Venture teams Groups of people within an organisation who work together focusing exclusively on the development of a new product.

Vertical marketing system (VMS) A channel of distribution in which there is formal cooperation among members at the manufacturing, wholesaling and retailing levels.

Viral marketing Creating entertaining or informative messages that are designed to be passed along in an exponential fashion, often electronically or by e-mail.

W

Want The desire to satisfy needs in specific ways that are culturally and socially influenced.

Warehousing Storing goods in anticipation of sale or transfer to another member of the channel of distribution.

Wheel-of-retailing hypothesis A theory that explains how retail firms change, becoming more upscale as they go through their life cycle.

Wholesalers Intermediaries that buy goods from manufacturers (take title to them) and sell to retailers and other business-to-business customers.

Wholesaling intermediaries Firms that handle the flow of products from the manufacturer to the retailer or business user.

Word-of-mouth The act of consumers providing information to other consumers.

Word-of-mouth marketing Giving people a reason to talk about your products and services, and making it easier for that conversation to take place.

World trade The flow of goods and services among different countries – the value of all the exports and imports of the world's nations.

World Trade Organization (WTO) An organisation that replaced GATT, the WTO sets trade rules for its member nations and mediates disputes between nations.

Y

Yield management pricing A practice of charging different prices to different customers in order to manage capacity while maximising revenues.

Index